THE CAMBRIDGE COMPANION TO
PLATO

The first edition of *The Cambridge Companion to Plato* (1992), edited by Richard Kraut, shaped scholarly research and guided new students for thirty years. This second edition introduces students to fresh approaches to Plato's dialogues while advancing the next generation of research. Of its seventeen chapters, nine are entirely new, written by some of today's leading scholars. Six others have been thoroughly revised and updated by their original authors. The volume covers the full range of Plato's interests, including ethics, political philosophy, epistemology, metaphysics, aesthetics, religion, mathematics, and psychology. Plato's dialogues are approached as unified works and considered within their intellectual context, and the revised introduction suggests a way of reading the dialogues that attends to the differences between them while also tracing their interrelations. The result is a rich and wide-ranging volume which will be valuable for all students and scholars of Plato.

DAVID EBREY is Researcher at Humboldt-Universität zu Berlin

RICHARD KRAUT is Charles and Emma Morrison Professor in the Humanities at Northwestern University

T0371206

Continued at the back of the book

The Cambridge Companion to
PLATO

SECOND EDITION

Edited by
David Ebrey
Humboldt-Universität zu Berlin

Richard Kraut
Northwestern University, Illinois

CAMBRIDGE
UNIVERSITY PRESS

University Printing House, Cambridge CB2 8BS, United Kingdom

One Liberty Plaza, 20th Floor, New York, NY 10006, USA

477 Williamstown Road, Port Melbourne, VIC 3207, Australia

314–321, 3rd Floor, Plot 3, Splendor Forum, Jasola District Centre,
New Delhi – 110025, India

103 Penang Road, # 05–06/07, Visioncrest Commercial, Singapore 238467

Cambridge University Press is part of the University of Cambridge.

It furthers the University's mission by disseminating knowledge in the pursuit of
education, learning, and research at the highest international levels of excellence.

www.cambridge.org
Information on this title: www.cambridge.org/9781108471190
DOI: 10.1017/9781108557795

First edition © Richard Kraut 1992

Second edition © David Ebrey and Richard Kraut 2022

This publication is in copyright. Subject to statutory exception
and to the provisions of relevant collective licensing agreements,
no reproduction of any part may take place without the written
permission of Cambridge University Press.

First published 1992

22nd printing 2010

Second edition 2022

A catalogue record for this publication is available from the British Library.

Library of Congress Cataloging-in-Publication Data
Names: Ebrey, David, 1978– editor. | Kraut, Richard, 1944– editor.
Title: The Cambridge companion to Plato / edited by David Ebrey, Humboldt-
Universität zu Berlin, Richard Kraut, Northwestern University, Illinois.
Description: Second edition. | Cambridge, United Kingdom ; New York, NY, USA :
Cambridge University Press, 2022. | Series: Cambridge companions to philosophy |
Includes bibliographical references and index.
Identifiers: LCCN 2021025369 (print) | LCCN 2021025370 (ebook) | ISBN
9781108471190 (hardback) | ISBN 9781108457262 (paperback) | ISBN
9781108557795 (ebook)
Subjects: LCSH: Plato.
Classification: LCC B395 .C28 2122 (print) | LCC B395 (ebook) | DDC 184–dc23
LC record available at https://lccn.loc.gov/2021025369
LC ebook record available at https://lccn.loc.gov/2021025370

ISBN 978-1-108-47119-0 Hardback
ISBN 978-1-108-45726-2 Paperback

Cambridge University Press has no responsibility for the persistence or accuracy of
URLs for external or third-party internet websites referred to in this publication
and does not guarantee that any content on such websites is, or will remain,
accurate or appropriate.

Contents

Contributors

Elizabeth Asmis is Professor of Classics at the University of Chicago. She is author of *Epicurus' Scientific Method* (1984) and of diverse articles on ancient philosophy and aesthetics. Her current research is on Epicurean ideas of sociability, including justice, pity, and parental love.

Gábor Betegh is Laurence Professor of Ancient Philosophy at the University of Cambridge, and Fellow of Christ's College Cambridge. He is the author of *The Derveni Papyrus: Cosmology Theology and Interpretation* (Cambridge, 2004) and co-editor of *Cicero's* De Finibus*: Philosophical Approaches* (with J. Annas) (Cambridge, 2015).

Leonard Brandwood was Lecturer in the Department of Greek and Latin at Manchester University. He is the author of *A Word Index to Plato* (1976) and *The Chronology of Plato's Dialogues* (Cambridge, 1990).

Eric Brown is Associate Professor of Philosophy at Washington University in St. Louis. He is the author of *Stoic Cosmopolitanism* (Cambridge, forthcoming), and articles on ethical and psychological topics in many ancient authors.

Agnes Callard is Associate Professor of Philosophy at the University of Chicago. She is the author of *Aspiration: The Agency of Becoming* (2018).

David Ebrey is Researcher at Humboldt-Universität zu Berlin. He is author of *Plato's* Phaedo*: Forms, Death, and the Philosophical Life* (forthcoming), editor of *Theory and Practice in Aristotle's Natural*

Science (Cambridge, 2015), and author of articles on a variety of topics in Plato and Aristotle.

Gail Fine is Professor of Philosophy Emerita at Cornell University and Senior Research Fellow Emerita at Merton College, Oxford. She is the author of *On Ideas: Aristotle's Criticism of Plato's Theory of Forms* (1993), *Plato on Knowledge and Forms: Selected Essays* (2003), *The Possibility of Inquiry: Meno's Paradox from Socrates to Sextus* (2014), and *Essays in Ancient Epistemology* (2021); she is also the editor of *Plato 1* and *2* in the Oxford Readings in Philosophy series (1999) and of the *Oxford Handbook of Plato* (2nd ed. 2019).

Emily Fletcher is Associate Professor Vilas Distinguished Achievement Professorship, and Mellon Chair of Ancient Greek Philosophy at University of Wisconsin-Madison. Her research focuses on Plato's ethics and psychology, especially in the *Philebus* and *Timaeus*.

Michael Frede was Professor Emeritus of the History of Philosophy at University of Oxford and Emeritus Fellow of Keble College. His books included *Prädikation und Existenzaussage* (1967), *Die Stoische Logik* (1974), *Essays in Ancient Philosophy* (1987), a translation and commentary on Aristotle's *Metaphysics* Zeta (with Günther Patzig, 1988), *Free Will: origins of the notion in ancient thought* (2011), and *The Pseudo-Platonic Seventh Letter* (with Myles Burnyeat, 2015).

Verity Harte is George A. Saden Professor of Philosophy and Classics at Yale University. She is the author of *Plato on Parts and Wholes: the Metaphysics of Structure* (2002) and co-editor of *Aristotle and the Stoics Reading Plato* (with M.M. McCabe, R.W. Sharples & Anne Sheppard, 2011), *Politeia in Greek and Roman Philosophy* (with Melissa Lane, Cambridge, 2013), and *Rereading Ancient Philosophy: Old Chestnuts and Sacred Cows* (with Raphael Woolf, Cambridge, 2018).

T. H. Irwin is Emeritus Professor of Ancient Philosophy at the University of Oxford and Emeritus Susan Linn Sage Professor of

Philosophy at Cornell University. He is the author of *Aristotle's First Principles* (1988), *Classical Thought* (1988), *Plato's Ethics* (1995), *The Development of Ethics* (in three volumes, 2007–9), *Aristotle: Nicomachean Ethics* (trans. with notes, 3rd ed., 2019), and *Ethics Through History* (2020). His books have been translated into Italian, Chinese, Japanese, Greek, and Spanish.

Rachana Kamtekar is Professor of Philosophy and Classics at Cornell University. She is author of *Plato's Moral Psychology: Intellectualism, the Divided Soul, and the Desire for Good* (2017) and many articles in ancient philosophy, contemporary moral psychology, and virtue ethics.

Richard Kraut is the Charles E. and Emma H. Morrison Professor in the Humanities, Northwestern University. His more recent books are *Aristotle: Political Philosophy* (2002), *What is Good and Why* (2007), *Against Absolute Goodness* (2011), and *The Quality of Life* (2018).

Constance C. Meinwald is Professor of Philosophy Emerita at the University of Illinois at Chicago. She is the author of *Plato's Parmenides* (1991) and *Plato* (2016).

Henry Mendell is Professor Emeritus at California State University, Los Angeles. He has published articles on Plato and Aristotle, ancient Greek mathematics, and ancient astronomy.

Suzanne Obdrzalek is Associate Professor of Philosophy at Claremont McKenna College. She is the author of numerous articles on Plato's ethics and moral psychology, as well as on Hellenistic epistemology.

Rachel Singpurwalla is Associate Professor at the University of Maryland. She has written numerous articles on Plato's ethics, politics, and moral psychology.

Acknowledgments

We would like to thank Malcolm Todd for his meticulous copy editing and Andrew Hull for producing the indices. We are also grateful to Hilary Gaskin for proposing and patiently supporting the second edition of this Companion. Finally, David would like to thank Conni Pätz for her support through this lengthy process.

Chronology

All dates are BCE.

Chapter 2 situates Plato's dialogues in relation to many of these people and events.

People*	Events
Hesiod: flourished (fl.) 700	Composition of Homer's *Iliad* and *Odyssey*: second half of eighth century
Pythagoras: ±570–490	
Xenophanes ± 570–>478	
Heraclitus: fl. 500	Solon's political reforms in Athens: 594
Aeschylus: ± 525–456/5	
Parmenides: born ± 515	Cleisthenes' political reforms in Athens: 508
Anaxagoras: ± 499/8–428/7	
Sophocles: ± 497–405	Second Persian invasion: 480–79
Empedocles: ± 492–432	
Protagoras: ± 490–420	Athens' so-called "Golden Age": 478–431
Gorgias: ± 485– ±380	
Herodotus: ± 485–420	Pericles' and Ephialtes' democratic reforms: 462
Euripides: ±485–407/6	
Hippias: ± 470s–>399	Peloponnesian War: 431–404
Democritus: fl. 425	
Socrates: 469–399	
Thucydides: ± 455–400	Aristophanes' *Clouds* produced: 423
Cratylus: b. 450s–440s	
Isocrates: ±436–338	

(*cont.*)

People*	Events
Hippocrates of Chios (mathematician): fl. end of fifth century	Socrates' execution: 399
Xenophon: ±425–≥355	Plato's alleged first voyage to Sicily**: 383
Plato: 424/3–348/7	
Theaetetus: ± 415–391	Plato's Academy begins: 380s
Aristotle: 384–322	Aristotle arrives at the Academy: 367
Euclid: fl. 300	
	Plato's alleged second voyage to Sicily**: 366
	Plato's alleged third voyage to Sicily**: 361/60

* All dates from Nails 2002, when possible. Note that when these people lived and flourished is often difficult to determine and so a matter of conjecture.

** Dates from Nails 2002. Plato's journey to Sicily is described in the *Seventh Letter*, whose authenticity has recently been substantially questioned (see esp. Burnyeat and Frede 2015). These journeys are described by later authors, but it is unclear how much of their evidence was truly independent of the *Seventh Letter*.

Abbreviations

I ANCIENT AUTHORS

ARISTOPHANES

| Acharn. | Acharnians |

ARISTOTLE

Ath. Pol.	Constitution of the Athenians
Cat.	Categories
De An.	De Anima
GC	On Generation and Corruption
Met.	Metaphysics
N.E.	Nicomachean Ethics
Phys.	Physics
Poet.	Poetics
Post. An.	Posterior Analytics
Pr. An.	Prior Analytics
Rh.	Rhetoric
Soph. El.	Sophistici Elenchi
Top.	Topics

ISOCRATES

| Antid. | Antidosis |
| Panath. | Panathenaicus |

OLYMPIODORUS

Prol. Anonymous Prolegomena to the Philosophy of Plato

PLATO

Alc.	*Alcibiades*
Ap.	*Apology*
Chrm.	*Charmides*
Cleit.	*Cleitophon*
Cra.	*Cratylus*
Cri.	*Crito*
Criti.	*Critias*
Epin.	*Epinomis*
Epist.	*Epistles (Letters)*
Euphr.	*Euthyphro*
Euthd.	*Euthydemus*
Grg.	*Gorgias*
H. Ma.	*Hippias Major*
H. Mi.	*Hippias Minor*
La.	*Laches*
Lys.	*Lysis*
Menex.	*Menexenus*
Phd.	*Phaedo*
Phdr.	*Phaedrus*
Phil.	*Philebus*
Pol.	*Politicus (Statesman)*
Prm.	*Parmenides*
Prt.	*Protagoras*
Rep.	*Republic*
Smp.	*Symposium*
Sph.	*Sophist*
Theag.	*Theages*
Tht.	*Theaetetus*
Ti.	*Timaeus*

SEXTUS EMPIRICUS

A.M.   *Adversus Mathematicos*
P.H.   *Pyrrhoniae Hypotyposes*

OTHER WORKS

D.L.   Diogenes Laertius, *Lives of Eminent Philosophers*
OF   Orphic Fragment

II MODERN TEXTS

CPD   L. Brandwood, *The Chronology of Plato's Dialogues*, 1990
DK   H. Diels and W. Kranz, *Die Fragmente Der Vorsokratiker*,
        7th edition, 1954
OCT   Oxford Classical Texts

I Introduction to the Study of Plato

David Ebrey and Richard Kraut

I APPROACHING PLATO'S DIALOGUES

Plato (424/3–348/7 BCE)[1] stands at the head of the Western philosophical tradition, the first to write on a wide range of topics still discussed by philosophers today under such headings as metaphysics, epistemology, ethics, political theory, and the philosophies of art, love, language, mathematics, science, and religion. He may in this sense be said to have invented philosophy as a distinct subject, for although all of these topics were discussed by his intellectual predecessors and contemporaries, he was the first to give them a unified treatment. He conceives of philosophy as a subject with a distinctive intellectual method, and he makes radical claims for its position in human life and the political community. Because philosophy scrutinizes assumptions that other studies merely take for granted, it alone can provide genuine understanding; since it discovers things inaccessible to the senses and yields an organized system of truths that go far beyond and frequently undermine common sense, it should transform the way we live our lives and arrange our political affairs. It is an autonomous subject and not the instrument of any other subject, power, or creed; on the contrary, because it alone can grasp what is most important in human life, all other human endeavors should be subordinate to it.[2]

We are most grateful to Terence Irwin, Constance Meinwald, and Ian Mueller for their helpful comments on drafts of the first edition of this chapter, and Jonathan Beere, Emily Fletcher, and Suzanne Obdrzalek for comments on drafts of the second edition.

1

This conception of philosophy and the theories that support it were controversial from the very start; although there have been long periods during which some form of Platonism flourished,[3] there have always been at the same time various forms of opposition to Plato's astonishingly ambitious claims. For this reason he can be considered not only the originator of philosophy but the most controversial figure in its historical development. For one cannot argue that philosophy must limit its ambitions without understanding the almost limitless hopes that gave birth to the subject and explaining why these – all of them or some – are misguided or unachievable. If we are forced to retreat from his ideal of a comprehensive and unitary understanding that transforms our lives and society, we must decide what alternative intellectual goal to put in its place. Thus, Plato is an invaluable standard of comparison: our conception of what philosophy should be (and whether there should be any such thing) should be developed in agreement with or opposition to alternatives provided by the history of the subject, and so inevitably we must ask whether the ambitions of the subject's inventor are worthy and capable of fulfillment.

Many of Plato's works are masterful works of literature. They are also an invaluable source for historians interested in many aspects of ancient Athens. But they are first and foremost philosophical works, and for most readers their greatest interest lies here. Of course, they were not created in a vacuum, and so to understand how he arrived at his views we must take account of the intellectual currents of his time. His attitudes toward political developments in Athens and Sparta and his reaction to the intellectual issues raised by the science, speculation, and poetry of the fifth and fourth centuries decisively shaped his philosophical development. The Sophistic movement, Pythagorean and Orphic religious practices, contemporary mathematics, the theory of flux advocated by Heraclitus and Cratylus, the unchanging and unitary being argued for by Parmenides – each of these played an important role in his thinking. But the intellectual influence that was paramount was Socrates, a man who wrote nothing but whose personality and ideas were so powerful that no one who came into contact with him could react with indifference. For Socrates, to philosophize was to reason together with someone about how best to live; because the ideas he expressed and the questions he raised were seen as threatening – and perhaps because he associated with some of those who became Athens' thirty tyrants – he was tried, convicted, and put to death on the charges of refusing to recognize the gods of the city, introducing new divinities, and corrupting the youth.[4] While Socrates was alive, Plato was one of many young people who admired him, and so great was his influence that Plato made him the central figure in most of his works, which were likely composed after Socrates' death in 399 BCE, when Plato was between twenty-five and thirty years old (depending on how one understands the conflicting reports about his dates).[5] Plato's writings are almost without exception in dialogue form.[6] He did not write a part for himself in these dialogues; rather, when they put forward philosophical ideas and arguments, it is typically the character named "Socrates" who advances them. And so newcomers to Plato's dialogues naturally ask how to understand the relationship between the character, Socrates, and the author, Plato.

As we will see, this is a complicated question and in general one need not answer it to engage fruitfully with Plato's works. The greatest philosophical interest of Plato's dialogues lies in working through their ideas and arguments, regardless of to whom we should attribute them. Nonetheless, it is important to think about the character Socrates that Plato makes the lead figure in most of his dialogues. Authors other than Plato offer reports about Socrates (including Plato's pupil, Aristotle) and many others wrote dialogues with Socrates as the main character (but only Xenophon's survive intact).[7] Aristophanes wrote a satirical play, the *Clouds*, whose main character is Socrates. The evidence from these other accounts is often difficult to assess, but the consensus among scholars is that the historical

Socrates' interests were primarily ethical, rather than epistemological, methodological, cosmological, or metaphysical.[8] Scholars also agree that Plato is not offering a verbatim account of what the historical Socrates said, but is rather shaping his own character, Socrates, who is nonetheless based on the historical figure who deeply inspired him.

Most of Plato's dialogues are conversations between Socrates and a broad array of his contemporaries, including elite young men, major intellectuals of his time, and his close companions. In general, each dialogue is a self-contained philosophical conversation, prompted by a question or offhand comment, in which the interlocutors make progress, but leave many questions unanswered and puzzles unsolved. It is important to examine the ideas and arguments in a given dialogue first and foremost within the context of that dialogue. Plato's dialogues are not a contrived puzzle that must be decoded to reveal his unified theory; instead, they show how Socrates (and other characters), when speaking to specific people and asked specific questions, responds with relevant questions, puzzles, arguments, and theories. Many difficult interpretive questions that arise in a dialogue can be answered by attending to its details and overall structure – how its conversation develops, what arguments come earlier and later in the dialogue, and how the different characters respond to the evolving discussion. Moreover, Plato seems to portray Socrates differently in different dialogues; this raises difficult questions about how to understand the relationship between the dialogues. Half of the articles in this collection focus on just one dialogue, thereby illustrating the fruitfulness of examining a work on its own. At the same time, Plato puts clear cross-references in some of the dialogues, and given the overlapping ideas, arguments, and topics in them, it is natural and inevitable to ask how they relate to one another. Our suggestion is that this should be done after one has carefully thought through each dialogue on its own terms, and that one should continue to keep the unity of each dialogue in mind when thinking through how the ideas and arguments from one dialogue relate to those in another.

When beginning to study Plato, it is useful to have an overview of his large corpus. Our first step is to divide the dialogues into three groups.

The "Socratic dialogues," as they are often called, correspond more closely to Socrates' account of himself in Plato's *Apology*. In this work, Socrates says that although his whole life has been devoted to the discussion of virtue, he has not been able to acquire knowledge of this – instead, his merely human wisdom consists in realizing that he has no knowledge of such things. In this group of dialogues, Socrates typically converses with people who claim to have such knowledge but who, Socrates shows, do not. At the end of these dialogues, Socrates reiterates his ignorance, but insists that progress has been made by bringing his interlocutor's ignorance to light. These dialogues are generally shorter than the others.

Let us for now skip over the second group of dialogues to the third, which are widely viewed as having been written late in Plato's life. The main reason they are viewed as a single group are the studies of Plato's style of composition, called "stylometry," that have been undertaken since the nineteenth century (described by Brandwood in chapter 3 of this volume).[9] This is the only group to include dialogues that do not feature Socrates as a main speaker.[10] In fact, only in one of the works that stylometry indicates is late – the *Philebus* – is Socrates a main speaker, and this dialogue does not thematize his profession of ignorance. The late dialogues cover a wide variety of topics, some that fit with the historical Socrates' interests in ethics and politics, but others that do not.

Finally, there is a group of dialogues that are more or less the remainder: not Socratic dialogues and not stylometrically categorized as late. The discussions here cover ethical and political matters, but also a wide range of other subjects, including psychology, epistemology, methodology, natural philosophy, and metaphysics. In them, Socrates typically argues that examining his ethical interests requires discussing these other, non-ethical topics. The *Republic* is a classic example of such a work. As in the Socratic dialogues, here too

Socrates denies that he has knowledge, but he devotes much more time to developing his own theories than to showing others that they lack knowledge. Many scholars think that Socrates presents views in these dialogues that are incompatible with those in the Socratic dialogues, although this is a controversial issue.

These works are typically called "middle period dialogues," although that terminology itself is contentious. This name comes from the hypothesis, accepted perhaps by most but certainly not by all scholars, that Plato wrote these dialogues in the middle of his career, after the Socratic dialogues (sometimes called "early dialogues") and before the late dialogues. Those who accept this hypothesis typically think that Plato began by writing dialogues whose protagonist, Socrates, was closely modeled on the historical Socrates. However, having written such dialogues for several years, Plato wanted to present more of his own positive ideas; because he viewed these as continuous with the questions and interests of the historical Socrates, he presented Socrates as holding these views. It is important to note that stylometry does not provide any significant evidence in favor of (or against) seeing the middle dialogues as coming after the Socratic dialogues. However, some important evidence in favor of this developmental hypothesis is that Aristotle, who spent twenty years in Plato's academy, regularly refers to views found in the Socratic dialogues as belonging to Socrates, whereas those in the middle period dialogues – although expressed by the character "Socrates" – he attributes to Plato or to "Socrates in" a specified dialogue, for example "Socrates in the *Phaedo*."[11] So as not to take a stand on chronology, we will refer to these as "middle dialogues."

Before the development in the nineteenth century of the practice of dividing Plato's dialogues into early, middle, and late, they were often organized by their pedagogical function, rather than by a perceived shift in their author's views. According to this way of grouping them, their differences are explained by whether they are more appropriate for beginners or advanced readers and what one can learn by working through specific dialogues. Perhaps Plato wanted his audience to work through the Socratic dialogues first, as a necessary preliminary step toward understanding certain issues. Differences between early and middle dialogues can, on this hypothesis, be understood as reflecting what Plato thought should be taught to a beginning student as opposed to a more advanced one.[12]

A third option is to understand the differences between dialogues in terms internal to the composition of the dialogues themselves. In the Socratic dialogues, Socrates rarely speaks to close companions or sympathetic intellectuals; instead, he generally speaks to a young member of the educated elite, or someone with a claim to expertise (a military general or a sophist, for example). By contrast, in the middle dialogues, he typically speaks to sympathetic intellectuals who already acknowledge their ignorance and are eager to learn from him. Speaking to a rhapsode like Ion or a general like Laches would not have led to a conversation like the one in the *Republic*. In fact, the *Republic* nicely illustrates how Socrates' interlocutors influence the conversation. Most of the first book of the *Republic* is a conversation between Socrates and the sophist Thrasymachus. This heated discussion ends with Thrasymachus deeply disagreeing with Socrates but refusing to discuss the topic any further; however, once Plato's two brothers take over the conversation, it continues for another nine books, leading Socrates to develop many positive theories.

Note that these three explanations are compatible with one another. Plato could have started writing the Socratic dialogues, thinking they would be a good way to introduce someone to philosophy, and then as his ideas developed he wrote dialogues for advanced readers that explore new ideas. He may have thought it appropriate in these dialogues for Socrates to speak to different sorts of interlocutors, given the topics discussed. Of course, one can also accept some of these explanations without others. Some scholars think that the dialogues do not show any development in Plato's views, but they can still group them according to their pedagogical function, or according to the sort of interlocutors involved in the conversation.

While the most significant differences are between dialogues from one group and those from another, it would be a mistake to assume that the views within each group are clearly consistent with one another. Here it is especially worth considering the possibility that Plato himself was not firmly committed to the views that he presents Socrates (and the other main speakers) as defending. As we will argue at the end of this chapter, it is likely that Plato shared the same basic commitments that he ascribes to Socrates. For example, throughout the dialogues Socrates is committed to the value of discovering the truth; surely Plato is too. But such broad commitments are compatible with Plato thinking that some ideas are worth thinking through and considering – they may well be right – without being firmly committed to them. For example, in the *Phaedo* Socrates says that so long as he is embodied he cannot acquire the wisdom that he seeks, but that a philosopher, suitably prepared, has reason to hope that he can acquire such wisdom in the afterlife. In the *Republic* he says that in a truly just city – which currently does not exist and may never exist, but is at least in some sense possible – a properly trained philosopher could acquire the greatest wisdom. These two views are incompatible: either it is possible to acquire the greatest wisdom while embodied or not. But note that these views share the same broad commitments that genuine wisdom is extraordinarily difficult to achieve and requires rigorous philosophical preparation. One possibility is that Plato changed his mind. Another is that he thought each account deserves serious consideration, and so explored each in separate dialogues.

These complications about how to understand the relationship between dialogues provide further reasons to study Plato's works first as individual whole compositions, aiming to understand the ideas in a given dialogue, at least initially, on their own terms. A further advantage to doing so is that it allows one to appreciate the literary unity of the work, and the way that its literary aspects are carefully connected to its philosophical discussion. In the last twenty-five years, there has been a growing reluctance among scholars to use the developmental hypothesis to explain apparent discrepancies between the dialogues. Some scholars hold that there are no major developments in Plato's thinking, but more often the idea seems to be that a fuller, subtler, and more satisfying account of the differences is available using the resources internal to each dialogue. Once internal considerations are taken into account, the different views in different dialogues become more nuanced and frequently turn out to be compatible with each other.[13]

Part of what makes it difficult to decide when to read one dialogue in the light of another is that although there are hazards in doing so, they do present a broadly consistent and mutually reinforcing set of views. In thinking through a view one finds in a dialogue, it is often productive to ask how well it fits with what is said in other dialogues – not in the first instance to see if Plato changed his mind or was inconsistent, but to explore the consequences and details of the views themselves. Questions that are set aside in one dialogue are sometimes taken up in another; bringing these together carefully can reveal a larger, interconnected set of ideas and arguments. And, of course, drawing on other works may help settle interpretive questions, once the resources of a given dialogue are exhausted. So, while it is good to begin by approaching each dialogue on its own terms, it would be a mistake, when thinking through a dialogue, never to draw on others. Furthermore, it is natural to wonder what views emerge from considering a number of Plato's works taken together. Does he have basic commitments that underlie many dialogues? Do these commitments change in different groups of dialogues?

Most of the remainder of this chapter provides an overview of Plato's corpus, focusing on those dialogues that are normally read first. This introduces some of the main ideas in Plato's dialogues, situates the individual dialogues within the overall corpus, and hopefully will help those beginning to read Plato to decide which dialogues they would like to read. The next three sections discuss the three groups of dialogues we have identified (Socratic, middle, late) in turn. After this, we consider evidence about Plato's views that come from outside his dialogues and

his reservations about writing. Lastly, we return to the question of
which views in the dialogues, if any, can be attributed to Plato himself.

II   THE SOCRATIC DIALOGUES

The Socratic dialogues include the *Apology, Charmides, Crito,
Euthyphro, Gorgias, Hippias Minor, Ion, Laches, Lysis, Menexenus,*
and *Protagoras.*[14] Of these, the *Apology* is the most important for
understanding Plato's portrayal of Socrates. It is Plato's account of
Socrates' speech against the charges of impiety and corrupting the
youth – for which Socrates was put to death. In a way, almost all of
Plato's Socratic and middle dialogues further defend him against
these charges or help clarify why he faced them, and so the *Apology*
is an important subtext to most other dialogues. Moreover, it provides
a basic portrait of Socrates. He is deeply religious, but rather than
simply accepting traditional religious accounts, he carefully scrutinizes them. He views it as his religious mission to persuade everyone to
care about virtue and the state of their soul, and to recognize that they
lack knowledge of virtue – knowledge they would need to make good
choices about how to live. He has humiliated many of his fellow
citizens by questioning them about these matters, revealing that
they do not have the knowledge they assume they have. Socrates
himself recognizes that he lacks such knowledge, and so devotes
himself to the search for it.

In most of the Socratic dialogues listed above, Socrates is presented as questioning people about some ethical question, and, when
they reveal that they do not have the knowledge that they suppose
that they have, trying to get them to recognize this. Three of these
dialogues, the *Euthyphro, Laches,* and *Charmides,* focus on answering a "what is it?" question about one of the virtues. Socrates' interlocutors typically think it is obvious what this virtue is, but Socrates
argues against several of their proposed accounts. This is presented
throughout Plato's dialogues as a typical Socratic conversation, and
several other dialogues refer to this practice of searching for an answer
to the "what is it?" question. The *Meno* and *Republic* begin with such

a search for an answer to a "what is it?" question, but this then leads into a very different sort of conversation. Plato's *Theaetetus*, a middle dialogue, is also devoted to a "what is it?" question, in this case, "what is knowledge?" Although the *Theaetetus* has many elements of the middle dialogues, it also builds on the standard features of the Socratic dialogues. Socrates takes a leading role in asking questions and raising difficulties, but he says that he is like a barren midwife who can only help others give birth by testing their ideas to see whether they are viable; he cannot produce wisdom of his own.

In Socratic dialogues not devoted to answering "what is it?" questions, Socrates typically explores more specific ethical questions, or interrelated sets of questions. For example, the *Protagoras* is structured around the question of whether virtue is teachable, the *Hippias Minor* around whether we can do wrong willingly, and the *Gorgias* around a set of interrelated questions having to do with rhetoric, power, desire, and the doing and suffering of wrongs. Moreover, every Socratic dialogue one way or another addresses questions about expertise. In questioning whether his interlocutor has an expertise, Socrates frequently raises questions about what this expertise is, how one can tell if someone is an expert, and what expertise allows one to do. For example, Socrates argues in the *Ion* that Ion, a professional reciter of poetry, must do what he does from divine inspiration, rather than from any sort of expertise.

In some of the Socratic dialogues, Socrates speaks to a promising teenager (*Charmides* and *Lysis*), in others to an adult who has a distinct claim to expertise (*Euthyphro, Ion, Laches*). A special type of conversation with a proclaimed expert occurs when Socrates speaks to a leading sophist of his day – one of the itinerant intellectuals who traveled through the Greek world offering lessons for a fee (*Gorgias, Hippias Minor*, and *Protagoras*). Only the *Crito* offers a conversation between Socrates and one of his close companions; however, Crito is not presented as one of Socrates' more intellectual companions, and their conversation focuses on the very practical question of whether Socrates should escape from jail to avoid execution. Differences between

Socratic dialogues can often be traced back to a difference in the interlocutors. For example, Charmides does not claim that he has knowledge – making the *Charmides* unlike the other dialogues that examine a "what is it?" question. But this is what one would expect from a teenager like Charmides, as opposed to a general like Laches or a professed religious expert like Euthyphro. Similarly, while most Socratic dialogues are short, the *Protagoras* and *Gorgias* are longer (the *Gorgias* is the third-longest Platonic dialogue), and these are where Socrates engages with leading sophists and their followers. The dialogues not only show how Socrates argues with different sorts of people, but also how he carefully responds to their emotions and other reactions as he tries to lead them to the sort of conversation he thinks they should have. While he clearly takes his task quite seriously, there is at the same time a lightness and joviality underlying the Socratic dialogues, which are often full of playful banter.

Because Socrates himself denies having any knowledge of ethical matters, he typically draws on his interlocutors' claims to argue against their proposals. He offers suggestions of his own, but thinks it important that they agree to them before proceeding. Although these works portray Socrates as someone who raises questions to which neither he nor his interlocutors find answers, it would be a mistake to see him as a purely negative thinker with no convictions of his own. On the contrary, he defends theses – often arguing from his interlocutors' own views – that are radically at odds with the common sense of his time (and ours). For example, he holds in the *Apology* that the worse person cannot harm the better person (30 c–d) and that the unexamined life is not worth living (38a). Both in the *Apology* and in other Socratic dialogues he argues: that human well-being requires putting virtue above wealth, power, and fame (*Ap.* 29d–e); and that to possess the virtues requires intellectual mastery over a distinct subject matter (*La.* 199c–e). In Socratic dialogues other than the *Apology*, he argues that everyone desires the good (*Grg.* 467e–468b) and that all of the virtues are identical, and are a form of wisdom (*Prt.*). Since Socrates is, in these dialogues, engaging with ordinary members of the public or antagonistic intellectuals, he often starts from claims that seem acceptable to most readers. This is part of what makes a pedagogical reading of Plato's dialogues natural – and why courses on Plato typically start with them, whether or not the teacher accepts the developmental hypothesis.

One unusual feature of the *Protagoras* and *Gorgias* – especially surprising to those who come to Plato from traditional modes of philosophical argumentation – is the prominent role given to myths.[15] These play an important role in many of Plato's dialogues, Socratic, middle, and late. They are typically either creation myths or describe the soul's journey after death. While they seem to have different functions in different places, one common feature is that they allow the speaker to provide a detailed account that fits with his overall philosophical views without needing evidence that these details are correct. In this way, they allow us to see how a view could be fleshed out, even if we are not in a position to be certain of the details. For example, the myth in the *Protagoras* offers an account of the creation of human beings that explains Protagoras' thesis that nearly everyone can teach virtue. Without needing to take Protagoras' myth literally, it suggests one way in which human nature could be complex and how there could be a fundamental difference between virtue and ordinary craft knowledge. The myths at the end of the *Gorgias*, *Phaedo*, and *Republic* offer different accounts of a view that Socrates is committed to throughout many dialogues: that the souls of good people will fare better after death than those of the bad. In Plato's late *Timaeus*, Timaeus says that his overall account of the cosmos – which takes up most of the dialogue – is a type of myth, despite being extremely detailed natural philosophy that aims to explain the cosmos as we observe it. What he means by this is a matter of considerable debate.[16]

III   THE MIDDLE DIALOGUES

The middle dialogues include the *Cratylus*, *Symposium*, *Phaedo*, *Republic*, *Phaedrus*, *Parmenides*, and *Theaetetus* (the last three of which are often considered "late middle period dialogues").[17] Socrates presents views in them that seem incompatible with those of the Socratic dialogues. For example, in the *Protagoras* he seems to hold that one will always act in accordance with what one believes to be good, whereas the *Republic* seems to allow that one could rationally believe that something is good, but have a stronger non-rational motivation that leads one to act contrary to this belief.[18]

Although the Socratic dialogues apparently present some views that are incompatible with those in the middle dialogues, the greatest contrast between these groups of dialogues lies in their different emphases and scope of topics. While Socrates maintains his profession of ignorance in the middle dialogues, he spends much more time developing positive theories than showing others that they lack knowledge. Further, the Socratic dialogues focus almost exclusively on questions of ethics and politics, whereas in the middle dialogues Socrates repeatedly argues that addressing his ethical interests requires sustained treatment of a broad range of topics covering epistemological, metaphysical, psychological, and methodological issues. Again, these differences can be explained by the developmental hypothesis, the pedagogical hypothesis, or in terms of the characters and internal aims of the discussions. In the middle dialogues, Socrates' main interlocutors typically are sympathetic intellectuals who acknowledge that they lack ethical knowledge. This leaves him free to propose new accounts, since he need not do the preliminary work of getting his interlocutors to admit their ignorance.

The *Meno* is often considered a "transitional" dialogue – between Socratic and middle – in part because it nicely illustrates features characteristic of each group.[19] The first third is similar to the *Euthyphro*, *Laches*, or *Charmides*, beginning with a typical Socratic question – what is virtue? – and revealing that Meno, like Socrates, does not have an adequate answer. However, Meno then raises a pair of questions (80d) – traditionally called "Meno's Paradox" – that challenge our ability to acquire knowledge through inquiry. This turn in the dialogue illustrates how Socrates' search for ethical knowledge requires grappling with general epistemological questions. Socrates responds to Meno's challenge by proposing a radical theory of learning according to which the soul is born with the ability to recollect what it learned before birth (81a–e). He defends this theory by showing that someone who has not been taught geometry, a slave from Meno's household, can make significant progress toward understanding how to solve a specific geometrical problem, if asked the right questions (82a–86a). It is widely believed that the historical Socrates did not develop any such account of learning as recollection – an account that arises again, in somewhat different forms, in the *Phaedo* and *Phaedrus*. The geometrical problem of the *Meno* reflects Plato's deep interest in mathematics, which is evident in several middle and late works, but nearly absent from the Socratic dialogues.[20] The extent to which the Socratic dialogues reflect the historical Socrates – his ideas, interests, and way of engaging with people – is disputed. But views found only in the middle or late works are likely to be Platonic inventions, ones which draw on a variety of intellectual influences and are inspired by some of Socrates' questions and concerns.

Although the *Phaedo* portrays the last conversation and death of Socrates – and therefore forms a dramatic unity with the *Euthyphro* (Socrates on his way to court), *Apology* (on trial), and *Crito* (refusing to escape from prison) – it is in many ways quite different from those Socratic dialogues. Like the *Meno*, the main conversation is prompted by a typical Socratic ethical concern: how a philosopher should approach death. But Socrates argues that defending his view requires considering a wide range of topics outside of ethics. Unlike the *Meno* or any of the Socratic dialogues, it is a prolonged conversation between Socrates and some of his closest intellectual companions, who agree with Socrates on many basic points that many other interlocutors would not accept. The *Phaedo* covers a significantly wider range of topics than does the *Meno*, not only epistemological and methodological topics, but also about the nature of the soul, the afterlife, causation, and natural science, as well as Plato's famous commitments about the "forms." "Form" is Socrates' term for what one is searching for when one asks a "what is it?" question. He argues in the *Phaedo* that the forms are utterly different from the things we perceive: they are changeless,[21] revealed to us by thought rather than sensation, and eternal (65d–66a, 78d–79d).[22] Socrates argues that the form of equality, which he sometimes calls "the equal itself," cannot be identical to equal sticks or any other observably equal objects (74b–d). The equal sticks are in some way inferior to the form of equality, though when Socrates makes this claim (74d–e) he does not say explicitly what it is about them that is defective, and why equality does not share this deficiency. The defectively equal sticks "participate in" the form of equality and are "called after" that form, but they are not equality itself.[23]

Across the dialogues, including the Socratic *Euthyphro* and the "transitional" *Meno*, Socrates uses the Greek terms "*eidos*" and "*idea*," conventionally translated "form," to designate what one is searching for when one asks the "what is it?" question about something like justice or virtue.[24] So, when one asks, "what is holiness?" one is searching for the form of holiness; this is what a correct account would refer to. The Greek word "*idea*" gave rise to our word "idea," though Plato does not view these entities as thoughts or any other creations of a mind, and their existence is not dependent on being known or thought. While the Socratic dialogues focus on such questions as "what is temperance?" – and, according to Aristotle, Socrates was the first to engage in this sort of inquiry[25] – those dialogues show no interest in a further series of second-order questions raised in middle dialogues like the *Phaedo*: these things we are searching for when we ask "what is it?" – the forms – can they be detected by means of the senses? Can they change or perish? How is it possible for us to learn about them? How are they related to each other? Do they exist independently of human beings?

Plato's views about forms in his middle dialogues are often called his "theory of forms," but this name is misleading, since it suggests that he developed a dogmatic system that gave definitive answers to important questions that can be asked about the forms.[26]

On the contrary, Socrates is presented as developing and perhaps revising his views in different dialogues in ways appropriate to the demands of the specific conversations. In general, the claims he makes about the forms in any given passage are the ones needed for the argument in that passage, rather than a statement of a complete theory. For example, in the *Phaedo* he appeals to the forms to explain why philosophers do not use their senses to investigate (65d–66a), and why the soul exists before birth and after death (73b–77d, 78b–80d, and 99c–107b). One reason to focus on the differences between forms and perceptible things in this dialogue is that these differences are needed for the dialogue's arguments. By contrast, the primary questions of the *Cratylus* are whether names reveal the nature of things, and what we can learn from names' etymologies. Cratylus argues that names reveal the truth of a Heraclitean view of the world, which holds that all is in flux. Near the end of the dialogue (439b–440d), Socrates brings in the forms to argue against this Heraclitean view. Here the stability of forms, rather than their being non-sensible, is what is relevant for his arguments. In the *Symposium*, as in the *Cratylus*, forms are not discussed as frequently as they are in the *Phaedo*, but again they arise at a key point. Socrates endorses a view he attributes to Diotima: that the form of the beautiful is the true object of love – rather than beautiful bodies, beautiful souls, beautiful laws, or any such thing (210e–212a). Here, the description of the form of the beautiful provides what is needed by Diotima's theory: it reveals how different the ultimate, true object of love is from its lower objects.

We turn now to the *Republic*, which in many ways represents the height of Plato's ambition for philosophy. We noted at the beginning of this chapter a number of topics that Plato included within philosophy and that still fall under it today. All of these are discussed in the *Republic*: metaphysics, epistemology, ethics, political theory, and the philosophies of language, art, love, mathematics, science, and religion. We will discuss this dialogue at length here, not because it is significantly more important than the others, but because it is frequently read early in one's study of Plato and it brings together so many different strands in his thought. This wide-ranging, complex work again emerges from the typical Socratic failure to find a satisfactory answer to an ethical question – in this case, "what is justice?" But this failure takes up only the first of ten books of the *Republic;* the remainder are structured by one of the interlocutors, Glaucon, challenging Socrates to show that justice is beneficial in its own right, independently of any instrumental benefit it may provide. This challenge requires Socrates to develop his own account of justice, which he does using the full range of philosophical topics mentioned above. What follows is a unified metaphysical, epistemological, ethical, political, and psychological theory that goes far beyond the views of the Socratic dialogues. At the same time, its range of topics is still determined by what is needed to respond to Glaucon's challenge. For example, the afterlife is discussed only briefly and at the end of the dialogue (608c–end), after Socrates has completed the main argument of the dialogue, since responding to Glaucon requires explaining the value of justice in its own right, not in terms of any future reward after death.

Socrates provides his account of what justice is and why it benefits an individual by first examining justice in a city and then arguing that justice in the soul is analogous. His argumentative strategy requires an account of the structure of a just city, and the parallel structure within our soul, which he presents in Book IV. In developing this account, he presents a sophisticated political theory alongside a sophisticated moral psychology. He famously argues that a just city would have to be guided by those who know what is good and just, and that only philosophers can have such knowledge; hence, the noble city (*kallipolis*) would have to be run by philosopher rulers. He also argues that the stories told by poets must be heavily censored, because otherwise children will be raised internalizing bad ethical views. This censorship is part of an overall educational program in the *kallipolis* that stems from the idea that merely having rational beliefs about the good does not ensure that one will act well; the non-rational parts of the soul must be developed as well.

In Book VII of the *Republic* we find Plato's well-known and powerful image of the human condition: people that are untouched by philosophical education are likened to prisoners in a cave who are forced to gaze on shadows created by artificial light and cast by artifacts paraded by unseen manipulators (514a–521c). Their conception of what exists and of what is worth having is so severely distorted and the deception by which they are victimized is so systematic that they cannot even recognize that they are confined, and would not regard an interruption in their routine ways of thought as a liberation. Here Plato is of course thinking of the psychological resistance Socrates encountered to his questioning (517a); but he is also making a far more audacious claim, downgrading the reality of the ordinary world of sensible objects.

Let us first consider a feature of Plato's political philosophy highlighted by the cave: that those who lack genuine knowledge are limited in their conception of what is worthwhile, are not the best judges of their own interests, and can be expected to resist initial efforts to improve their lives. A political system requires the consent of the governed, but this alone does not make it good, for if false values are prevalent people may willingly accept only those political systems that perpetuate their confinement. A good political community, Plato thinks, must promote the well-being of the citizens as a whole; and if the citizens fail to understand where their own good lies, then polit-ical leaders should educate them. Although Plato is therefore in favor of giving extraordinary powers to rulers who themselves have a philosophical understanding of the human good, he is concerned with the possibility that such power might be misused or arouse resentment, undermining broad agreement about who should rule, which is crucial for having a good city. It is partly to avoid such misuse of power that private wealth and the family are abolished in the ruling class: these powerful sources of political corruption and favoritism are eliminated (416d–417b, 457c–d), providing some assurance to those who are ruled that they are not being exploited by those who are more powerful. This helps to insure one of the key features of the ideal city, according to Plato: in such a society there must be a deep feeling of community among all the citizens, in spite of the fact that they cannot all share an equal understanding of the human good. The ideal city is not designed for the maximal happiness of the philosophers or any other group; instead, institutions must be designed so that there is a fair pattern of benefits for all (419a–421a). Although there is much in the political philosophy of the *Republic* that we rightly reject, there are also good reasons to accept elements of it. It offers an attractive vision of a community in which no one is favored by traditional privileges of wealth, birth, or gender; one in which no one's well-being is ignored and no one is allowed to be indifferent to others; one in which every member of the community leads a life that is objectively worthwhile.

Let us turn to the metaphysical aspects of the cave. Just as the shadows cast on the wall of the cave are less real than the objects of which they are images (515a–e), so, when the prisoners make progress, leave the cave, and come to understand the forms, they recognize the existence of objects that are more real than the things that made the shadows in the cave (516c–517c). Similarly, in Book X of the *Republic*, Socrates distinguishes three types of thing to which the word "bed" can be given – a painting of a bed, a bed created by a carpenter, and the form – and he holds that they constitute a series of increasing reality. The painter does not make a real bed, but only an image of a bed, and similarly the product of the carpenter is not completely real either. It is only the form that is "really real" (596e–597a). It would be a mistake to think that Socrates is here trying to cast doubt on the *existence* of things in the sensible world. After all, in saying that the painter's image of a bed is not a true bed, he is not expressing doubts about the existence of the painting. Instead, one thing he seems to be doing is pointing out that the painter's image is in some way derivative from or dependent on the object he is representing. It is this same relationship of dependency that he thinks exists between the visible bed of the carpenter and the form: beds depend on there being something that it is to be a bed. The forms provide the standard by which we judge a perceptible thing to be a bed, to be beautiful, or any other ordinary features, despite the fact that the perceptible thing is radically different from the forms. Philosopher rulers must grasp this objective standard provided by the forms in order to properly rule their cities.

Merely being dependent on the forms does not seem like it would be enough to downgrade the reality of perceptible things; after all, each of us is dependent on our parents, and in a different way on breathable air, and yet neither of these are thereby more real than us. Another factor in Socrates' downgrading of the reality of perceptible things seems to be that in the *Republic*, as well as in other dialogues like the *Phaedo*, *Cratylus*, and *Symposium*, he holds that perceptible things manifest what scholars call "the compresence of opposites": they are both large and small, hot and cold, moving and at rest, etc. They manifest this for a variety of reasons. In some cases, it is because something is large in relation to one thing, small in relation to another. In other cases, it is that something has a feature at one time, the opposite feature at another time. Socrates does not think that the same thing can have opposite features at the same time, in relation to the same thing, in the same respect (*Rep.* 436b). Instead, he thinks that the fact that perceptible things can have opposite features at different times, or in relation to different things, or in different respects, shows that perceptible things are by nature very different from the forms, which cannot have such opposite features.[27] The form of equality is never unequal, whereas sensible equal things are both equal and unequal (*Phaedo* 74b–c, 78c–e) and every sensible double is also half (*Rep.* 479b). This compresence of opposites seems to be part of why Socrates holds in the *Phaedo* that perceptible things are inferior to forms, and why he holds in the *Republic* that forms are more real than perceptible things.[28]

In the *Republic* Socrates hints at a few different ways that the forms do not exist isolated from one another, but rather are somehow interrelated, forming an ordered *kosmos* (500c). The very thing we must strive for both in our souls and as members of a political order – the unification of diverse elements into a harmonious whole – is something that the forms possess by their very nature. Socrates does not provide much clarification in the *Republic* about the structure possessed by the forms, perhaps because he says that he lacks knowledge of them. One tantalizing suggestion that he makes has to do with the central role of the form of the good. After emphasizing his ignorance about the good and saying that he cannot give even the sort of account of it that he has given of justice (506c–e), he says in the sun analogy that the form of the good is responsible for the being and knowability of all the other forms (508d–509b).

Questions about the relationships among the forms are taken up in a number of other dialogues. In the *Phaedrus* Socrates assigns to the dialectician the tasks of finding unity in a diversity of forms and diversity in a unity, and uses his conception of love as one kind of divine madness to illustrate such a structure (265d–266b). The *Parmenides* offers a complex treatment of the relationship between unity, on the one hand, and sameness and difference, motion and rest, limited and unlimited, on the other. If Plato equates goodness and unity – and there are some reasons to believe that he does[29] – then the elaborate treatment of unity found in the *Parmenides* could be read as a continuation of Plato's preoccupation with the good. And in the *Timaeus* the entire sensible world is viewed as the product of a divine craftsman who looks to the forms and shapes the recalcitrant and disorderly stuff at his disposal into a good (29a–30b), though far from perfect (46d–e), cosmos. The exploration of such relationships plays an especially important role in several of Plato's stylistically late dialogues: the *Statesman*, *Sophist*, and *Philebus*. Hence, the ideas briefly suggested in the *Republic* – that the forms constitute a structured whole, that the good is foremost among them, that the goodness of a complex group of objects is connected to their unification – continue to guide Plato's thoughts in his late works.

The *Republic* is in one sense the centerpiece of Plato's corpus, since no other single work brings together so many different strands of his interests; but at the same time it provides an incomplete treatment of many of his ideas, because nearly all of the dialogue's central topics are discussed at greater length, in response to different questions and concerns, in other dialogues. Love is discussed at greater length in the *Symposium* and *Phaedrus*, language in the *Cratylus* and *Sophist*, the existence of the soul after death in the *Phaedo*. Abstract metaphysical topics are explored at greater length in the *Parmenides* and *Sophist*; epistemological puzzles in the *Theaetetus*; pleasure, knowledge, and the good life in the *Philebus*; feasible institutions for a good political community are most fully described in the *Laws*; and his thoughts about moral psychology are developed in different ways in the *Phaedrus*, *Philebus*, and *Laws*. Rather than seeing the *Republic* as the statement of Plato's overall views, it is better seen as the fullest example of how Plato regards these topics, questions, and concerns as systematically and tightly interconnected.

An account of the forms strongly reminiscent of Socrates' in the *Symposium*, *Phaedo*, and *Republic* is challenged in the first part of the *Parmenides* (126a–135d). There, Socrates as a young man puts forward an account of the forms that Parmenides criticizes in several ways that the young Socrates is unable to answer. In fact, these objections receive no explicit answers in this or any other dialogue. Aristotle thought that one of them, the so-called "third man objection," was fatal to one of the basic ways for arguing for the existence of Platonic forms, and sought to avoid a similar problem for his own conception of forms as immanent universals.[30] Did Plato modify his views of the forms in the light of the challenges recorded in the *Parmenides*? Although many scholars think that the *Parmenides* was written after the *Phaedo* and *Republic*, it is not late by stylometric measures. In the late *Timaeus* Plato presents a view of the forms that seems very similar to the one in the *Phaedo* and *Republic*. Moreover, the *Parmenides* is a conversation between Parmenides and a very young Socrates. Together these suggest that Plato did not view these puzzles about the forms as being as problematic as Aristotle did, but rather as puzzles that could be solved, and that we too should work through before accepting the forms' existence.[31]

IV THE LATE DIALOGUES

Studies of Plato's style, initiated in the nineteenth century and continuing to the present, begin with the point, about which there is universal consensus, that the *Laws* is a late work.[32] A good deal of cumulative evidence has pointed to the conclusion that there are five other works that are closely related to the *Laws* as measured by a variety of stylistic features. These are (to list them alphabetically) the *Critias, Philebus, Sophist, Statesman,* and *Timaeus*.[33] Within this group, it is clear that the *Statesman* was written after the *Sophist*, since it refers back to it several times,[34] and that the *Timaeus* precedes the *Critias*, since the latter's depiction of the lost island of Atlantis is obviously a sequel to the account of Atlantis in the Timaeus. Any further attempt to order their composition is more conjectural. Plato's *Phaedrus, Parmenides,* and *Theaetetus* are often thought of as "late middle period" works, although the evidence for this on the basis of stylometry is weaker. This view mostly rests on the fact that they seem to develop ideas found in the late dialogues and respond to material found in some of the other middle dialogues.

The late dialogues treat many of the questions that Plato raises in the early and middle works, but they are also marked by an apparently new set of interests. The process of collection and division – a means of coming to answer the "what is it?" question – is thoroughly explored in the *Sophist, Statesman,* and *Philebus*. While examples of division seem to occur in the Socratic dialogues (e.g., *Euthyphro* 11e–12e), and a version of it is described in the *Phaedrus* (265d–266c), it is explored in much greater depth in the late dialogues. Like the middle dialogues, the late dialogues continue to show how apparently distinct topics and questions are connected; however, each tends to focus on a smaller number of topics: sophistry, being, non-being, and falsehood in the *Sophist*; pleasure, knowledge, and the good life in the *Philebus*; the expertise needed to govern in the *Statesman*; the constitution and legal code of a good society in the

Laws. Although the *Timaeus* covers a wide range of seemingly disparate topics, from the nature of time to moral psychology, these all contribute to its main topic: a general account of the origin and structure of the cosmos and the place of human beings within it.

As noted earlier, the *Philebus* is the only late dialogue in which Socrates is the main speaker. In the others, he plays either a minor role (the *Timaeus, Critias, Sophist,* and *Statesman*) or is completely absent (the *Laws*). It is clear why Plato chose a different main speaker in the *Timaeus*: in the *Apology* Socrates says that he does not discuss topics of natural philosophy, and so it makes sense for someone else to present Plato's great work on that subject. Similarly, it makes sense that Socrates is the main interlocutor in the *Philebus*, since it is devoted to a central Socratic topic: the place of pleasure and knowledge in the best human life. It is less clear why Socrates is not the main speaker in the other late dialogues. While there are differences in the views defended, there are certainly many continuities between these late dialogues and the Socratic and middle dialogues. For example, in the *Laws* the main speaker, the Athenian stranger, maintains the Socratic thesis, proposed in several Socratic dialogues, that no one does wrong willingly (731c, 860d–e).

One possible explanation for Socrates not being the main speaker relates to the kind of conversation they dramatize, as opposed to the views defended. In the *Statesman* and *Sophist* the main interlocutor is the Eleatic stranger, who tries to coax answers out of his young interlocutors, but who is also very willing to act as a teacher. He explicitly asks to converse with someone who is easy to handle and not a troublemaker (*Sph.* 217d). Unlike Socrates, he makes no profession of ignorance. Similarly, the Athenian stranger in the *Laws* simply puts forward a legal code without a Socratic profession of ignorance. The respondents in the late dialogues are not hostile – unlike the sophists whom Socrates speaks to in the Socratic dialogues and *Republic* I – nor are they sympathetic intellectuals who develop significant objections and concerns of their own, as one often finds in the middle dialogues. The *Philebus* begins after a truly hostile interlocutor, Philebus, has left, replaced by someone who can defend, in a good-willed and earnest way, Philebus' position that pleasure is the good. The other late dialogues are much closer to being the promulgation of theories (*Timaeus* and *Laws* V–XII) or a joint inquiry led by someone with developed views (*Sophist* and *Statesman*, *Laws* I–IV) than to a debate. The respondents are good-willed, but have not thought deeply about the issues, and, in comparison with the Socratic and middle period dialogues, the conversations are driven far less by the personalities of the characters and contain far less banter.

The *Timaeus* is the only late dialogue in which Plato continues to emphasize several central claims about the forms that play an important role in the middle dialogues. He maintains there that they are changeless, and contrasts their invulnerability to alteration with the constant fluctuation of perceptible things; because of these radical differences, the forms are capable of being known, whereas objects of perception are not.[35] Furthermore, the forms are described in the *Timaeus* as paradigms[36] – objects to which the divine craftsman looks in creating the sensible world, and to which we must look in order to acquire knowledge – and this too is a central view in the Socratic and middle dialogues.[37] However, there is no emphasis on these features of the forms in the *Sophist*, *Statesman*, and *Philebus*. They do not play a crucial role at climactic points in these dialogues, as they do in the *Cratylus*, *Symposium*, *Phaedo*, and *Republic*. Does this reflect a shift in Plato's thinking, or is this simply not relevant to the projects of those dialogues? In the *Sophist*, the Eleatic stranger attempts to find middle ground between the "friends of the forms" (as they are called there) and those who think that the only things that are real are what they can touch and see (246a–249d). Perhaps, then, Plato did not change his mind about the importance of the forms, but rather turned his attention to finding a common argumentative ground with those who do not accept them. This is not to say that he stops investigating the forms altogether. His explorations of them continue, and may reflect his changing his mind about their features. For example, several late dialogues contain arguments that the compresence of opposites found in the sensible world also applies to the forms (e.g., *Philebus* 14d–15c). This is elaborated in greatest detail in the *Sophist*, where the Eleatic stranger discusses the interweaving of the "greatest kinds" (categories that contain everything) with one another.

It is remarkable that, after giving in the *Republic* an elaborate blueprint for an ideal society, Plato took up a similar project near the end of his life and devoted his longest work – the *Laws* – to the development of a complex political system and legal code. Some of the main doctrines of the *Republic* are preserved intact here: Moral education is the principal business of the political community, and there is no toleration for those who put forward doctrines that would undermine the virtue of the citizens. But there are also striking differences between the ideal community of the *Republic* and the more easily realized ideal depicted in the *Laws*: No specialized training in mathematics or dialectic is prescribed for an elite group of citizens, and instead of assigning total responsibility and power to one small group of decision makers, the functions of government are widely distributed, with an elaborate system of safeguards against the abuse of power. Although power is unevenly divided, no citizen is completely deprived of a legislative or judicial role. Does this mean that in his later period Plato came to be less opposed to democratic ideas than he once had been? It may be that in the *Laws* he accepts limited democratic features and envisages a smaller role for philosophers because in this work he is merely describing a second-best political community (739a–740a); if that is the proper explanation, then he might have continued to believe that ideally philosophers would have absolute control over political matters.

V ARISTOTLE'S TESTIMONY AND THE LIMITATIONS OF WRITING

We are remarkably fortunate to have so much from Plato's own hand; in fact, we seem to possess every philosophical work he ever composed, in the form of copies made during the medieval period, which derive ultimately from the rolls of papyrus on which Plato's works were originally circulated. (By contrast, the vast majority of Greek tragedy and comedy, as well as almost all earlier Greek and later Hellenistic philosophy, are entirely lost to us. While we have many of Aristotle's works, many others are lost, including all of the works he wrote for the wider public.) Are there any other sources of information relevant for the study of Plato? The last potential sources to consider are the reports from Aristotle and later philosophers about Plato's teaching in the Academy. The value of these reports for our understanding of Plato is, however, considerably less clear.

Before turning to these reports, we should take note of Plato's recognition, at *Phaedrus* 274b–278b, of the limitations of the written word and his insistence upon the superiority of speech as an instrument of teaching and learning. For some scholars have thought that, in view of Plato's low opinion of writing, it is a matter of urgency that we try to interpret the reports we have about his oral teaching.[38] Socrates points out in the *Phaedrus* that when one discusses philosophy with another person, one has an opportunity to respond to questions and defend one's assertions. In addition, what one says to one person may be different from what one says to another, and to some one should say nothing at all – presumably because some listeners will be less sympathetic or prepared than others, and will therefore raise different challenges or obstacles. Written philosophy lacks this flexibility; it says the same thing to everyone, and leaves the questions of its audience unanswered (275c–276a). Furthermore, the existence of philosophical books can lead to a deterioration of memory, if they are used as a substitute for understanding; and they entice students into thinking that reading by itself creates wisdom (275a–b). They are no substitute for the give-and-take of dialogue, for this alone, and not the mere spouting of doctrine, can give rise to understanding and wisdom.

Of course, these assertions of the supremacy of speech and reservations about the value of philosophical writing do not lead Plato to reject the written word completely. As we have seen, he did a great deal of writing after the (middle dialogue) *Phaedrus*, and so we cannot take this dialogue as a farewell to the written word or a repudiation of the value of writing philosophy. Plato does say in the *Phaedrus* that writing, when properly used, can come to the aid of a memory weakening with age, and can be helpful to the students with whom one discusses philosophy (276d). Moreover, his dialogues, taken together, are very useful in modeling how one engages in philosophical conversations, illustrating how these conversations differ depending on who the interlocutors are. The point is that written works can serve a purpose, but only so long as they lead to philosophical examination, rather than substituting for it. It is no mystery, then, that Plato wrote voluminously. The *Phaedrus* gives us no good reason to doubt that Plato put into writing views that he himself took seriously; nor does it provide evidence that he deliberately refrained from putting some of his convictions into writing.

Some of Plato's letters express stronger misgivings about writing, but there are significant doubts about their authenticity. The misgivings in the letters about writing are expressed briefly in the second letter (314b–c) and more fully in the seventh (341b–345a); the former is widely agreed not to be authentic and there are many reasons to doubt the latter's authenticity.[39] In the *Seventh Letter*, the author writes that he (supposedly Plato) is greatly annoyed because he has heard that Dionysius, the tyrant of Syracuse, recently composed a work based on philosophical discussions they had had. Plato is eager to dissociate himself from anything Dionysius may have written, and to do so he says that the matters he discussed with Dionysius are ones he never has and never will commit to writing (341c). Why not? Several of the reasons coincide with those found in the *Phaedrus*. The *Seventh Letter* adds that the few who are capable of understanding his views will be able to discover the truth without relying on a written exposition (341d–e) and seems to suggest that certain thoughts are not to be expressed either orally or in written form, because words themselves are matters of convention and this makes them ill-suited instruments for grasping true being (341c, 342e–343c).

If this were Plato's view, it would mean that any reports of his oral teaching would also not help us understand what he saw as the deepest truths. Hence, even if authentic, the *Seventh Letter* would not give us reasons to expect to understand Plato's fundamental ideas from his oral teachings.

Aristotle frequently looks to Plato's dialogues for his information about what Plato thought; he never suggests that because of Plato's views about the defects of writing he communicated his deepest philosophical thoughts only in speech. He refers at one point to Plato's "so-called unwritten opinions" (*Phys.* IV.2 209b14–15) but when he refers to them, he says that they provide the same views as in the *Timaeus*, only expressed differently. Elsewhere, Aristotle attributes to Plato views without assigning them to any particular dialogue, but also without saying explicitly that these opinions were unwritten. For example, in the *Metaphysics* he says that according to Plato there are, between perceptible objects and forms, mathematical objects which differ from sensible objects in that they are eternal and unchangeable and from forms in that they are many and alike (Alpha 6 987b14–18).[40] In addition, he attributes to Plato the doctrine that the two elements of the forms are (1) the great and the small – which Aristotle describes in his terminology as constituting the matter – and (2) unity – which is its substance (987b18–21). This latter passage is especially significant, for according to it, the forms are not the most basic entities for Plato, but are in some way derived from something else.

But on what basis does Aristotle attribute this view to Plato? And is this a view that Plato held onto for a long period of his life? Aristotle does not say. The report is only valuable for understanding Plato if it was one of Plato's central views that he did not commit to a dialogue, but we have no way of knowing whether it was. Furthermore, it is not clear that such a view would help us better understand any of Plato's dialogues. Again, the dialogues are not mere window dressing for presenting a theory, but rather are coherent discussions spurred by some specific questions. Of course, if we can make sense of some otherwise obscure part of a dialogue using these later reports, then they will have proven to be of great worth. At present, it is fair to say that very few scholars have found them useful in this way.[41]

VI THE DIALOGUE FORM

We have maintained that the greatest interest of Plato's dialogues is to be found in working through the ideas and arguments put forward in them, regardless of whether Plato accepted these views. But, returning to the opening question of this chapter, it is natural to wonder whether he did accept the arguments he has Socrates and others put forward. When we read a play of Sophocles or Euripides, we recognize that what the characters say need not represent the beliefs of the author. And so why should we make a different assumption when we read a Platonic dialogue? Why think that some figures in these works present views that reflect Plato's own thinking? Some scholars, using this analogy between a dramatic work and a Platonic dialogue, hold that Plato's thought is no more contained in the words of any one interlocutor than the beliefs of dramatists are revealed by the words of any of their characters.[42]

But the comparison between Plato's dialogues and dramatic works is misleading in a number of ways, in spite of the fact that in each genre there is dialogue among two or more characters. Plato is not assigning lines to speakers in order to compose a work that will be considered best by official judges or an immense audience at civic religious festivals, as were the plays of the Greek tragedians and comedians. If it suits the playwright's purpose to have his main characters express views that differ from his own, he will do so. But Plato's dialogues seem like they were meant, at least at first, to help people remember or come to understand Socrates, a person who was deeply committed to working with others to discover the truth and to improve their souls. It is difficult to believe that Plato would devote his dialogues to preserving and developing this legacy if he did not himself share those ideals. The parts of the dialogues that seem most likely to help with these aims are Socrates' arguments – or the arguments of the other primary interlocutors – and so it is at least a good working hypothesis that he wanted us to take them seriously.

Of course, just because Plato shares Socrates' commitment to truth and to the value of philosophy does not mean that every argument that he has Socrates present is one that Plato himself was convinced by. It is clear from the discussion of writing in the *Phaedrus*, and from the composition of the dialogues themselves, that Socrates presents different sorts of arguments to different sorts of interlocutors. Thus, the reasons that Socrates provides in a dialogue for a given conclusion may not be the reasons that Plato himself accepted this same conclusion, or the reasons that Plato thinks a true philosopher should ultimately accept this conclusion. Moreover, as mentioned earlier, Plato's serious commitment to truth is compatible with his exploring different theories that he thinks are serious possibilities, or options that are well worth exploring to find the truth. If Plato himself thought he lacked genuine knowledge of the important matters – as he presents Socrates as believing – then it seems all the more likely that the dialogues are serious explorations that work within some settled convictions. When the dialogues are read in their entirety, there is development and perhaps there are reversals, but there is at the same time the kind of sincerity and continuity that, in our view, strongly suggests that Plato takes these views to be ones that we should take seriously as well. And regardless of what Plato thought or what he may have wanted us to think, more than a hundred generations of readers have found them valuable when approached in just this way.

But why, then, did he not simply write philosophical treatises? First note that Plato is arguably the first to develop the subject of philosophy as we understand it. While philosophical prose and poems had been written before Plato, he clearly saw himself as doing something new, and the dialogue format may have seemed perfect for this new subject. At the same time, Socratic dialogues were a new genre, to which many other authors contributed.[43] Plato likely began writing dialogues to give expression to the philosophy and way of life of Socrates. He clearly regarded Socrates as a model of wisdom and insight, and wanted others to have an enduring portrait of this remarkable man. Since Socrates is above all someone who engages in dialogue with others, the dialogue form is the most appropriate medium for this portrait.

The misgivings expressed in the *Phaedrus* about writing may have added to Plato's reasons for retaining the dialogue form. Oral exchange is the essential tool of philosophy, yet reading books can entice one into thinking that arguments are not tailored to particular people, or that the written word is by itself sufficient for wisdom. So it is appropriate for Plato to put into his writing something that reminds the reader that insight comes through discussion with others and not through mere reading. Moreover, this form provides a natural way to air challenges some reader might make to the theories under discussion; assigning an objection to a speaker is a vivid way of clarifying and defending the views being presented. Finally, the dialogues give Plato an opportunity to use his considerable literary talent to support his philosophical ends.

Forty years ago, scholars focused on Plato's arguments often did not give much attention to the distinctive characters, setting, and other literary features of the dialogues. On the other hand, those who focused on these literary features often used them as a way to try to undercut the claims that Socrates and other interlocutors put forward in the dialogue.[44] Today, in our estimation, the situation is much better. It is much more common for scholars to pay close attention to both, seeing Plato as carefully choosing the literary aspects and the ideas and arguments to complement one another. Each are worth studying and each should be understood in light of the other.

So we are led back to a recommendation near the outset of this chapter: focus first and foremost on understanding the dialogues in their own right, situating their characters, ideas, and arguments within their larger intellectual contexts. Begin by taking each dialogue on its own, to understand how its parts form an organic whole, and then carefully draw the dialogues together. This is not an a priori view about how Plato must be read, but rather a successful working hypothesis confirmed by its fruitfulness. The dialogues are the material that we have, and it is deeply rewarding to work through them carefully, thinking through the questions, ideas, and arguments that they contain, as well as the approach to philosophy that they dramatize. Reading Plato in this way allows us to make use of whatever material is in the dialogues – along with their cultural and intellectual context – to contribute to our understanding of them.

There is a special joy in reading Plato. One is reading philosophy by a masterful writer, one whose considerable literary talents are used to complement the philosophical goals of the dialogues. The dialogues exhibit a stunning attention to detail even as they grapple with some of the most fundamental questions ever posed about who we are, how we should live, the nature of the world around us, and how we can come to know it. It is easy to become absorbed in the details and the way they are systematically connected to each other; happily, this attention to detail often is rewarded, clarifying the fundamental questions, ideas, and arguments that draw one to Plato in the first place. We hope that this collection will be a guide to exploring the dialogues and will foster or further nourish a love of these fascinating works.

NOTES

1 The ancient sources conflict on the dates for Plato's life. We provide here the dates defended by Nails 2002: 243–7. The more traditional view is 427/ 8–347/8.

2 Plato's name for the subject described in this paragraph is *dialektikē* ("dialectic"); Socrates argues in the *Republic* that the philosopher will study or master this subject (509d–11d, 531d–4e).

3 The school Plato founded (c. 384 BCE), called the Academy after a park located on the outskirts of Athens and sacred to the hero Academus, was in continuous existence until 86 BCE, but the members of the

Academy typically disagreed with Plato on significant matters. In the early first century BCE the rise of "Middle Platonism" and then, with Plotinus (204/5–70CE), "Neoplatonism," marked a long period in which many philosophers thought that Plato was fundamentally right.

4 For two excellent accounts of the trial of Socrates, see Brickhouse and Smith 1989 and Reeve 1989.

5 See note 1.

6 The possible exceptions are the *Apology* and the *Letters*. The former is a speech that includes a short dialogue. As for the latter, modern scholars generally think that the seventh letter is most likely to be authentic, but recently a sustained set of serious doubts have been raised about it by Burnyeat and Frede 2015.

7 For the existence of a genre of Socratic dialogues, see Aristotle's *Poet.* 1447b11; c.f. *Rh.* 1417a20; *On Poets* fr. 72. For translations of fragments from other Socratics, see Boys-Stones and Rowe 2013.

8 This is not to say that Socrates had no interests in these topics. Xenophon, in particular, attributes to Socrates a type of creationist argument from design. For a defense of attributing this to the historical Socrates, see Sedley 2007a: ch. 3.

9 For an account complementary to Brandwood's, but with a different emphasis, see Kahn 2003.

10 The possible exceptions are the *Symposium* and *Parmenides*. In the *Symposium* there is no primary speaker, but rather a series of speeches; nonetheless, Socrates' speech seems marked as the most important of them. In the *Parmenides* a young Socrates is questioned by Parmenides. Socrates speaks at some length, offering an account of the forms, but the primary speaker is Parmenides.

11 For "Socrates in the *Phaedo*" see *GC* II.9 (335b10). However, in *Politics* II.6, after Aristotle says that the *Laws* is a late work of Plato's, he ascribes its views to Socrates, who does not appear in the dialogue. Evidently, he was not always careful in his attributions. For a discussion of the evidence from Aristotle about Socrates, see Smith 2018.

12 Kahn 1996 offers a modern defense of such a reading.

13 In the last twenty-five years there has been less discussion of methodology among Plato scholars, although there have been significant shifts in the way many approach Plato. We see one of the original contributions of this introduction as articulating, and to some degree defending, an approach

that fits with these trends. For another contemporary approach, see Kamtekar 2017: ch. 1.

14 The *Euthydemus* is often studied by those interested in the ethics of the Socratic dialogues, although it includes ideas that are widely acknowledged as characteristic of the middle dialogues, and many would put it after the *Republic*, although this goes against the stylometric considerations mentioned in note 17.

15 For a general discussion of myths in Plato, see Partenie 2009. Socrates denies in the *Gorgias* that what he is offering is a myth (523a).

16 The recent debate was initiated by Burnyeat 2005 (reprinted in Partenie 2009). See also Johansen 2004: ch. 3, Broadie 2012: 31–8.

17 See note 14 on the *Euthydemus*. For the *Meno*, see this section, below. There are stylometric reasons for treating the *Republic, Phaedrus, Parmenides*, and *Theaetetus* as later than the other Socratic and middle dialogues. While not as strong as the reasons for grouping the late dialogues together, they are still significant. For a discussion of this, see Brandwood's chapter in this volume.

18 In *Magna Moralia* 1182a15–28 the author (either Aristotle or one of his followers) says that Socrates neglects the irrational part of the soul, and that Plato corrects this error. Here, in line with the developmental hypothesis, the *Republic* and *Phaedrus* are taken to present the thought of Plato and the *Protagoras* that of Socrates.

19 For a recent discussion, see Scott 2006: 6–7 and 200–8. Scott notes that developmentalist views have sometimes had the unfortunate result that scholars have not treated the *Meno* as a unified whole.

20 For this contrast, see Vlastos 1991: ch. 4. He discusses mathematical texts in Socratic dialogues on pp. 271–3.

21 It is a frequent refrain of Plato's dialogues that, by contrast with the forms, perceptible things are always becoming and never remain the same. See *Phd.* 78e; *Rep.* 508d–510a; *Ti.* 27d–28a, 37e–38b, 49d–50d, 52a, cf. *Smp.* 211a–b; *Rep.* 479a–e.

22 For the idea that the forms are eternal in a way that is prior to time, and perhaps outside of it, see *Ti.* 37c–d.

23 See *Phd.* 100c, 101c, 102b; *Smp.* 211b; *Rep.* 476c–d; *Prm.* 130b, 130e–131a.

24 Plato frequently uses these terms also to refer to other things, for example the "form" – i.e., appearance – of a young man (e.g., *Lys.* 204e, *Cha.* 154d). Another example is that he uses "*eidos*" sometimes simply to refer to

a class of things; for example, in the *Phaedo* he says that the visible things and the unseen things are each an *eidos* (79a).

25 See *Met.* A6 987b2–4, M4 1078b17–19, M9 1086b2–5. Cf. *Parts of Animals* I.1 642a25–31.

26 For an opposing interpretation to the one provided here, see Shorey 1903. For a recent general account of the theory of forms, aimed for a general audience, see Sedley 2016.

27 As we discuss in the next section, in the late dialogues forms too are described as manifesting compresence of opposites.

28 For further discussion of degrees of reality in Plato, see Vlastos 1981: chs. 2 and 3. For further discussion of the verb "to be," see Brown 1999, Kahn 2004.

29 The closest he comes to such an identification is at *Philebus* 65a, where Socrates says that even if the good cannot be captured by means of one characteristic, it can be understood in terms of beauty, measure, and truth. The first two members of this triad are tied by Plato to some notion of unity. Beauty and measure result when a limit is placed on what is unlimited and excessive (*Phil.* 24a–26b), and so goodness (insofar as it involves beauty and measure) is conceptually connected with unity (insofar as what is limited is thereby unified).

30 See *De Sophisticis Elenchis* 179a3, *Met.* A9 990b17, Z13 1039a2. Aristotle says that Plato, unlike Socrates, separated universals and thereby went astray (*Met.* A6 987b1–10, M4 1078b30, M9 1086b2–7), but it is controversial what Aristotle means by "separation." In general, Plato does not speak in terms of "universals" or "separation." The exception is at *Prm.* 130b ff., where Socrates agrees that the forms exist separately, and although this separate existence is not treated as one of their problematic features, neither is it explained. Whether separation is implicit in the term *auto kath auto* is a matter of some dispute. See Vlastos 1991: 256–62.

31 This is the approach defended by Prior (1985: 2) and Meinwald (1991, e.g., 171).

32 Some of the evidence for the lateness of the *Laws*: Aristotle says in the *Politics* (1264b26) that it was written after the *Republic*; Plutarch (*De Is.* 37ff.) says that Plato wrote it when he was an old man; a battle referred to at *Laws* 638b is often identified as one that took place in 356 BCE (nine years before Plato died). Diogenes Laertius (III 37) suggests that work on the *Laws* was not entirely finished when Plato died, but in the same paragraph he reports a story that the *Phaedrus* was Plato's first dialogue, so

his chronological information does not inspire confidence. For further references, see Guthrie 1978: 322.

33 For a summary of this evidence, see Brandwood in this volume. Owen (1953) famously argued against *Timaeus* being a late dialogue, but this view is rarely defended by modern scholars. Cherniss (1957) is an influential reply to Owen. Both are reprinted in Allen (1965).

34 *Pol.* 257a, 258b, 266d, 284b, and 286b.

35 *Ti.* 27d–28a, 51e–52b, cf. 37e–38b, 49b–50d.

36 *Ti.* 29b, 48e–49a, 50d, 52a.

37 E.g., *Euphr.* 6e, *Rep.* 500c–d, 540a–b; *Prm.* 132d.

38 This view, associated with the "Tübingen School," has become much less common. For an introduction to the problem and a guide to some of the literature, see Guthrie 1978: ch. 8.

39 See note 6 above. Even if it is not settled that the seventh letter is inauthentic, it is now incumbent upon anyone who wishes to rely on its authenticity to address the serious doubts that have been raised about it.

40 Aristotle's *Metaphysics* Mu and Nu describe differing opinions about mathematical objects that seem to come from Plato's Academy. Plato's first and second successors as head of the Academy, Speusippus and Xenocrates, departed from Plato's views in significant ways. For an account of their views, see Dillon 2003.

41 Gerson (2013) is a rare modern author who thinks Aristotle's reports are important for our understanding of Plato's views. Note that he does not think that the dialogue format undermines our ability to know Plato's own views.

42 For a sympathetic treatment of this idea, see Blondell 2002.

43 See note 7 above.

44 This way of reading Plato is suggested by Strauss (1952: 22–37), and followed by many Straussians since. For criticism of Strauss's methodology, see Burnyeat 1985; later issues of the *New York Review of Books* contain replies by Strauss.

2 Plato in his Context

T. H. Irwin

I INFLUENCES ON PLATO

Plato's philosophical thinking begins from views and assumptions that he presupposes in his readers or in himself, whether or not he states them explicitly.[1] From them we may learn something about why some questions and not others appeared urgent to him, and about what views he thought it worthwhile to consider, endorse, or oppose.[2]

According to Aristotle, Plato was first influenced by Cratylus the Heraclitean, and later by Socrates (*Met.* 987a32–b10).[3] The claim about Socrates does not surprise a reader of the Platonic dialogues, but the claim about Cratylus is more surprising. Aristotle implies that Plato was influenced by the "Presocratic" tradition of the "naturalists" (*phusiologoi*; cf. *De Caelo* 289b25–9) whom Aristotle has just been discussing in *Metaphysics* I.[4] Cratylus was a minor member of this tradition, being an extreme follower of Heraclitus' doctrine of change. Since Plato's references to Cratylus do not suggest that Plato had adhered to his views, it is unlikely that Aristotle derived his claim about Cratylus from reading Plato;[5] he probably had some independent source.

Plato's philosophical predecessors had engaged in natural philosophy, but – according to Aristotle – in Socrates' time people turned to the study of moral and political questions (*PA* 642a25–31).[6] Greek philosophy began with the application of rational, critical, argumentative, non-mythical thinking to cosmology and to nature as a whole.

For helpful comments on at least one version of this chapter I am grateful to Richard Kraut, David Ebrey, Susan Sauvé Meyer, and Gail Fine.

39

In the lifetime of Socrates reflection on morality and human society becomes another area for critical thinking.[7] Plato unites the more recent Socratic pursuit of moral philosophy with the older naturalist preoccupations.

Aristotle is right to suggest that Plato engages with the naturalistic tradition. The dialogues mention Pythagorean mathematical speculation,[8] Heraclitus,[9] Anaxagoras,[10] Zeno and Parmenides,[11] and Empedocles.[12] Plato never mentions Democritus by name, but probably he refers to him.[13] He also refers to the medical theories that are often closely related to Presocratic speculations.[14]

We should not consider only these philosophical influences that Aristotle mentions. Both natural and moral philosophy draw on literary sources that help to determine the distinctive shape of Plato's philosophy. While systematic philosophical inquiry into morality begins with Socrates, he did not create it from nothing, but drew on a longer tradition of reflection and argument about moral questions. In the Greek tradition natural philosophy arises before moral philosophy, but reflection on moral questions precedes philosophical reflection on the universe, and indeed influences the outlook of some natural philosophers.

II   HOMER

Plato devotes a short dialogue, the *Ion*,[15] to a conversation between Socrates and Ion the "rhapsode," whose profession was the public recitation of the Homeric poems. Socrates expects Ion not merely to have memorized the poems, but to understand them, and to be able to expound them.[16] This was a recognized occupation in Athens and elsewhere because Homer was often recited, quoted, and used as an authority. From at least the mid sixth century onward, Homer was recited at the festival of the goddess Athena (the Panathenaia).[17] Educated Greeks were expected to know Homer well enough to recognize quotations and to remember relevant passages. The familiar characters and incidents in the poems provided influential patterns for the actions and attitudes of many Greeks.[18]

The leading character of the *Iliad* is Achilles, who is well-born, rich, powerful, fiercely jealous of his own honor, concerned to display his power and status, and comparatively indifferent to the interests of other members of his community.[19] Throughout Greek history the self-absorbed, jealous hero remains an object of fear, resentment, suspicion, and admiration all at the same time. This pattern is easy to recognize in the attitude and behavior of Alcibiades, as he is presented by Thucydides, Aristophanes, and Plato.[20] It is equally recognizable in Alexander the Great, who modelled himself on Achilles.[21]

III   POLITICAL DEVELOPMENTS AND MORAL QUESTIONS

Plato's mother Perictione traced her descent back to Solon the Athenian lawgiver. Solon's legislation introduced the first Athenian constitution that gave some protection to the interests and rights of the governed. Solon was given this task as a result of prolonged conflict between different groups of aristocrats, and the effects of this conflict on the poorer classes, especially on those who lost their land and were enslaved because of their debts.

Political instability is not surprising in a society that was governed by aristocrats who shared Homeric attitudes. As the example of Achilles suggests, a Homeric attitude to political power and social status does not easily accept rules or laws or constitutional provisions that require a well-off and powerful individual to give up the pursuit of his own honor and status for the benefit of his community.

None the less, Solon's reforms began a tendency that continued during the next century in Athens. Solon's constitution prescribed equal treatment for rich and poor under written laws, and gave the lower classes some voice in elections, legislation, and the administration of justice. To this extent it tended to remove politics and law from the whims of aristocratic families. The growth of attitudes that favored "equal law" (*isonomia*) – both equality under the laws and the wider political participation that safeguards this equality – influenced the political reforms of Cleisthenes in Athens (508–6).

Herodotus observes that different societies encourage different outlooks, and different patterns of education and upbringing (e.g., Hdt. II 35.2; VII 102.1).[22] Herodotus has Athens especially in mind; for he remarks on how the introduction of equal law and greater democracy in Athens increased the Athenians' enthusiasm for their city (V 78).

Athens was remarkably successful in making its better-off citizens loyal to a democratic constitution in circumstances where (one might have thought) they had more to gain from an oligarchic constitution in which they could compete, as Homeric heroes do, against each other for power, wealth, and honor.[23] Between the end of the Persian Wars in 478 and the outbreak of the Peloponnesian War in 431, Athens reached the peak of its power and prosperity in the Greek world. It kept a stable democratic constitution (without interruption from 506 to 411), and established an empire among Greek states (in the Aegean islands and in Asia Minor) that had been its allies against the Persians.

Democracy, however, did not require completely uncompensated sacrifice from the upper classes.[24] Athens was governed by an assembly in which all citizens (adult, male, free) were eligible to attend, speak, and vote; but the richer and nobler families still tended to take a leading role as speakers, as generals (elected officials with both military and political roles), and as governors of the dependent states in the Empire. Contributions from the dependent states were used not only for their original purpose of defense against the Persians, but also to build temples in Athens, and to pay Athenians for sitting on juries (large courts, chosen by lot from the citizens). Aristocrats such as Cimon, Aristeides, and Pericles could compete for leadership in a great city with extensive military and political responsibilities overseas; and less preeminent members of the upper classes could hope to govern a subject city in the Empire.

This period in the political and social history of Athens might be summed up, therefore, as a partly successful struggle against Homeric attitudes. It results from an attempt to impose order, law, and justice on the unstable society that conformed to Homeric patterns.

IV   NATURAL PHILOSOPHY AND RELIGION

In these ways Greek political thought tries to impose law and order on conflict and disorder. Greek reflection on the universe tries to do something similar. The Homeric gods are similar to human individuals in being competitive and quarrelsome, out for their own honor, and unwilling to submit to law and authority. Their disorderly behavior makes the universe disorderly as well. Gods interfere with the normal course of nature when they fight one another, or when they want to help one of the human beings they favor.

The early naturalist philosopher and poet Xenophanes attacks Homer and Hesiod for their immoral conception of the gods. According to Xenophanes, we ought not to attribute human follies (as Xenophanes, though not Homer, conceives them) to the gods. Indeed we ought not to think of the gods simply as more powerful human beings. We ought to recognize a single non-anthropomorphic god who guides the universe with impartial wisdom, to produce cosmic law and order. Xenophanes rejects the disorderly universe that results from the struggles among the different gods who manipulate natural processes.

Naturalists agree with Xenophanes' rejection of the disorderly Homeric universe. In their view, the belief that natural processes are irregular and unpredictable results from our ignorant and superficial view of the world. If I simply observe what goes on, I notice that sometimes it rains on my birthday, but sometimes a hailstorm destroys the crops of my enemy and leaves mine alone. I may be inclined to infer that sometimes things happen as they do for no particular reason, but sometimes the gods favor one person and show their hostility to another by destroying his crops. According to the naturalists, however, deeper knowledge will show that natural processes do not vary for these sorts of reasons, but follow unvarying laws from which we could predict what will happen if we knew enough.

Anaximander says that the opposing forces of the universe compensate each other in accordance with a just order (DK 12 A 9).[25] Since this order is not visible to naive observation, Heraclitus says that the hidden order is stronger than the apparent (DK 22 B 54). The appeal to natural order leaves no room for the Homeric view that natural processes are basically irregular and unpredictable, and that gods can interfere with them or manipulate them as they please.[26]

Since the naturalists reject the irregular Homeric universe, they deny that we sometimes incur divine punishment by failing to sacrifice the right number of oxen or by fighting on an ill-omened day, and that we can sometimes placate the gods by offering the right sacrifices. Traditional and civic religion – from a farmer's sacrifices to the local nymphs and heroes to the Panathenaic civic procession bringing a new robe to Athena in the Parthenon[27] – sought to secure a god's favor by offering gifts. People regularly assumed that a natural disaster or a defeat in a war resulted from some ritual offense.

Naturalist objections to the outlook of traditional religion do not imply atheism. Anaximander, Xenophanes, and Heraclitus (among others) regard the world-order as a manifestation of divine justice. In their view, the mark of divine action is regular and orderly sequence, contrary to the Homeric view that the gods engage in capricious disruption of the usual order of the world. Socrates and Plato follow the naturalists in affirming the reality of a just god.

Some naturalist arguments, however, might reasonably be taken to allow or to imply atheism. The Atomism of Leucippus and Democritus tends to eliminate any role for a designing or controlling intelligence. Given the motions of the atoms in the void for infinite past time, and given the laws of their combination, nothing else is needed (in the Atomist view) to explain the existence, maintenance, and eventual dissolution of the world-order.[28]

V   NATURALIST EPISTEMOLOGY

Naturalists attack traditional religion because they believe it is unreasonable. They give arguments (*logoi*), in contrast to the traditional

stories (*muthoi*) told about the gods by the poets (Ar. *Met.* 1000a9–20).
Instead of appealing simply to authority and tradition, they claim to
explain natural processes by some rationally convincing principle or
argument.

It is not obvious to immediate inspection that natural processes
are as regular as the naturalists claim they are. Naturalists admit this,
but they claim to describe some reality that underlies and explains the
appearances. They can do this only if they have some cognitive access
to this reality, through reason, argument, and theory, beyond what is
immediately accessible to the senses. As Parmenides says, we must
not let the senses mislead us, but we must follow the argument to its
necessary conclusions (DK 28 B 7.1–8.1). If we rely on reason against
the senses, we discover the non-apparent facts underlying the
apparent.

According to the naturalists, these non-apparent facts belong to
the real nature (*phusis*) in contrast to the mere "convention" (*nomos*)
that most people accept.[29] "Convention" consists of the beliefs that
are widely shared because they rely on the obvious and superficial
view of things that is easily accessible to everyone. Once we discover
that superficial appearances are misleading, we recognize that convention is mere convention, because it has no basis in the reality
discovered by reason. According to Democritus, all the properties
recognized by the senses are mere matters of convention, and have
no basis in reality: "By convention there is sweet, bitter, hot, cold,
color, but in reality atoms and void" (Sextus, *A.M.* VII 135).

VI   FROM NATURALISM TO SKEPTICISM

While naturalists agree in drawing these connected contrasts between
reason and appearance and between nature and convention, they do
not agree about the character of the reality that reason discovers, or
about how reason discovers it. Plato explores some of the questions
raised by two accounts of reality: Heraclitus' claim that there is far
more change and instability than the senses reveal to us, and
Parmenides' claim that there is no change at all.

Aristotle mentions Plato's early interest in Cratylus' extreme version of a Heraclitean doctrine of flux. According to Plato, "Heraclitus says somewhere that everything passes away and nothing remains, and in likening beings to the flow of a river says that you could not step into the same river twice" (*Cra.* 402a). Elsewhere he ascribes to Heraclitus the view that everything "is always being drawn together in being drawn apart" (*Sph.* 242e2–3). Plato implies that the doctrine of flux includes two claims:[30]

1) The first claim is about succession of properties in the same subject over time. Heraclitus argues that there is more change over time than we suppose there is. The river has been replaced by a different one when we step into "it" for the second time; for, since it has different waters, it violates the assumption that x is the same from time t1 to time t2 if and only if x has the same components at t2 that x had at t1. The same assumption implies that trees, rocks, and other apparently stable things go out of existence during the time when we suppose they are stable (since everything is always having some of its matter replaced).

2) The second claim about flux is about coexistence of opposite properties in the same subject at the same time. We suppose that things have stable, fixed, and unqualified properties; for we suppose that some things are straight and other things are crooked, some good and others bad, some just and others unjust. In fact, however, things lack this sort of stability; they are both "drawn together" and "drawn apart" at the same time (not just at different times, as in the first kind of flux). One and the same letter at the same time (e.g., the letter r) is both straight (if it has a straight stroke) and crooked (if it has a crooked stroke), sea water is good (for fish) and bad (for human beings), and striking a blow is just (if done by an official exacting a punishment) and unjust (if done by an individual in a private feud). The stability in the universe does not consist in the absence of change, but in regularity and constancy of change and opposition.

Heraclitean claims provoke an extreme reaction in Parmenides, who rejects the possibility of change altogether (DK 28 B 5.7–9). Parmenides affirms that we cannot speak of, think of, or know, what is not; but any true cosmology that requires the existence of change requires us to be able to speak and think of what is not (since change requires something to become what it previously was not); hence no cosmology is true.[31]

Parmenides draws these startling conclusions from premises that seem self-evident, even trivial. He argues:

1) We cannot think (say, know) and think nothing (since thinking nothing is not thinking at all)
2) But what is not (or "not being") is nothing.
3) Hence we cannot think (etc.) what is not.

Parmenides assumes that thinking, saying, and knowing are analogous to other activities referred to by transitive verbs. For to kick or grasp what is not is to kick or grasp nothing, and so is not to kick or grasp at all; similarly, it seems obvious that to think or say what is not is to think or say nothing, and so not to think or say at all; and to know what is not would be to know what is false, and so not to know anything at all. To Parmenides' naturalist successors, his argument seemed largely convincing. They tried to show that their cosmological principles did not require the sort of reference to "what is not" that Parmenides had challenged.[32]

Parmenides goes further than Heraclitus, since he rejects the evidence of the senses altogether. The senses seem to present a changing world, but belief in change is simply a result of human convention (DK 28 B 8.38–9). Cosmology, therefore is mere "belief" or "seeming" (*doxa*) that tells us how things appear, even though the appearance corresponds to no reality.

Democritus follows Heraclitus and Parmenides in relying on reason against the senses. He formulates a skeptical argument, from conflicting and equipollent sensory appearances. If the same water appears cold to you and warm to me, there is no reason (Democritus claims) to prefer either your appearance or mine (the two appearances are equipollent); but they cannot both be true (since they are contradictory), and so they must both be false (Ar. *Met.* 1009a38–b12; cf. Plato, *Tht.* 152bc). Since the same form of argument applies to all colors, sounds, smells, tastes, and temperatures. things really have none of these properties.

In contrast to ordinary sensible things, the atoms that constitute reality have, in Democritus' view, only weight, shape, size, and motion, which explain the appearances of sensible things. Democritus assumes that something analogous happens at the atomic level to what we observe at the sensory level; for instance, just as strands of Velcro stick together, so atoms with a similar structure stick together. If, however, our senses are unreliable, we have no reason to believe that strands of Velcro really stick together; why, then should we suppose that sensory appearances and the real structure of atoms are analogous? As Democritus makes the senses say to reason, "Wretched mind, do you take your proofs from us and then overthrow us? Our overthrow is your downfall" (DK 68 B 125; cf. Ar. *Met.* 1009b11–12).

VII   SOPHISTIC AND RHETORIC

In order to understand the next steps in the treatment of the skeptical questions that arise from naturalist inquiries, we need to consider the sophists and orators of the later fifth century. These professional teachers were not naturalists, but some of them were familiar with naturalist views and the resulting epistemological questions.

Once democracy was firmly established in Athens, the popular assembly became used to exercising its power to make the vital decisions and to scrutinize the conduct of political leaders. A successful politician had to be a good speaker who could present a convincing case to a critical audience.[33] Since the Athenians had no mass media, they relied on political speakers for information and for advice. Gradually the role of "politician" (*politeuomenos*) became more professional, and the trained and well-informed speakers tended to dominate debate in the assembly.[34] Instruction that would help in these areas would be useful to the aspiring political leader. This instruction was provided by sophists.

"Sophist" (*sophistēs*, derived from *sophos*, "wise") in fifth-century Greek is sometimes a non-pejorative term applied to experts in different areas.[35] In the second half of the century the term was applied especially to teachers offering higher education for fees. The education varied in content from sophist to sophist, but its main goal was to equip someone to take an active part in public life (*Prt.* 318d–319a). The leading sophists traveled from city to city, and gained an international reputation as "stars" in Greek cultural life. The *Protagoras* (309a–314e) describes the excitement aroused in upper-class Athenian circles by the visit of the eminent sophist Protagoras, and the sense of anticipation among his potential students.

Sophistic aroused suspicion, especially among people who thought that someone's birth, family, and gentlemanly upbringing gave him a right to be listened to. From this conservative point of view, sophistic training might seem to make people too clever by half, and the sophists might be accused of teaching unscrupulous people the skills they needed to achieve undeserved success. This is what Anytus thinks about sophists in Plato's *Meno* (91a–92e). Such attitudes explain why Socrates at his trial suggests that his accusers want to arouse prejudice against him by accusing him of being a sophist (*Ap.* 19de).

Sophistic was closely connected with another development in higher education – the growth of rhetorical theory and teaching.[36] Rhetoricians concerned themselves primarily with techniques of persuasion, and not with the general moral and political education promised by the sophists (Plato, *Grg.* 464b–465c). This does not mean that they were wholly concerned with rhetorical "form" rather than "content"; they advised their students that this opinion rather than that one was likely to be well received. But they did not engage professionally in the concerns of the sophist and the philosopher.

VIII SKEPTICISM, SUBJECTIVISM, CONVENTIONALISM

Now that we have introduced the sophists and orators, we can turn to their discussion of the epistemological questions that arise from naturalist inquiries.

The sophist Protagoras reacts to Democritus' skeptical argument not by supposing (as Democritus does) that there is some objective, mind-independent world that we cannot claim to know, but by rejecting the contrast between reality and appearance. He claims that "a man is the measure of all things, of those that are, of how they are, and of those that are not, of how they are not," and that "as things appear to each of us, so they are" (Plato, *Tht.* 152a). If the wind appears warm to you and cold to me, we should not (according to Protagoras) draw Democritus' conclusion that at least one of us must be wrong; instead we should conclude that the wind is both warm and cold, and that there is no objective, mind-independent wind. Contrary to Democritus, there is no objective "nature" that can be contrasted with "convention." Different people's appearances seem to conflict, since to you the wind appears cold, and to me the same wind appears warm. But this is not a genuine contradiction in our beliefs. Protagoras, therefore, rejects skepticism. In his view, the only reality that concerns us is the way things appear to us, and we need not worry about any unknown non-apparent reality.

Protagoras' contribution to the discussion of knowledge and skepticism may be compared with the contribution of Gorgias the rhetorical theorist. While the naturalists wrote works on nature, because they treated nature as the underlying reality, one of Gorgias' essays is entitled *On Nature or What Is Not* (DK 82 B 3), because it argues that there is no such thing as nature, as the naturalists conceived it. Parmenides argues that only what is can be spoken of or thought or known, but Gorgias argues that there is no such thing as being, and, if there were, it could not be spoken of, or thought, or known. If the only possible object of knowledge is a being that altogether excludes any not-being, but no being can altogether exclude not-being (since any being must also not be various things), then nothing can be known. We cannot do better than the plausible appearances and persuasive arguments that rhetoric offers us.

Gorgias' speech in defense of Helen (DK 82 B 11) considers arguments to show that Helen is responsible and blameworthy for running off with Paris. Gorgias rejects all these arguments. He suggests that no sound argument can be given for holding anyone responsible for anything. If we object to a skillful advocate's ability to secure the acquittal of a client who is obviously guilty, we should think again, since it can be plausibly argued that no one is ever really guilty. Orators were sometimes accused of "making the weaker argument stronger" – that is to say, of making the objectively weaker argument prevail in a particular dispute. This accusation is warranted only if there is an objectively weaker and stronger argument; but Gorgias casts doubt on whether there is any such thing.

IX   POLITICAL AND INTELLECTUAL TENSIONS

To understand some of the impact of these intellectual developments, we should now consider the history of Athens in the lifetime of Socrates and Plato. We noticed earlier that Solon tried to reconstruct Athenian political institutions on a rational basis that would bring order into the destructive struggles for power and honor among aristocrats. In the same way critical thought applied to religion and to the study of nature tried to bring rational order into the disorderly Homeric universe. Inquiry into nature resulted in disagreement, which encouraged the doubts of some sophists and orators about whether there are any objective facts about nature to be discovered. Gorgias' *Helen* extends these doubts to questions about responsibility and punishment. Apparently they might be extended to moral and political questions more generally.

In 431 a war (which the Athenians called the "Peloponnesian War") broke out between Athens and Sparta. It lasted for twenty-seven years (with interruptions), including the first twenty-four years of Plato's life.[37] Athens was eventually defeated, partly because of treachery by a fifth column, who formed the oligarchic regime of the Thirty, and abolished the democratic assembly and jury-courts. The regime of the Thirty came to power (with Spartan help) after the end of the war in 404, and was defeated by the supporters of democracy (with Spartan help, after a change of kings in Sparta) in 403.[38] The Thirty included two of Plato's relatives, Critias and Charmides, who appear in the *Charmides*.[39] Their association with Socrates probably helps to explain why he was tried and convicted, under the restored democracy, of not recognizing the gods of the city and of corrupting the young men.[40]

According to Thucydides, the Peloponnesian War revealed the conflicts that result from antagonisms between the perceived interests of different classes and groups in a state. He suggests that a relatively stable state is the product of some force strong enough to keep the peace and to assure some protection for the different groups; but when one or another group sees a chance to take the dominant place, it takes the chance (III 82.2; V 89, 105.2). Since war involves an external power willing to support a revolution, it tends to increase political instability within a state. Thucydides describes the civil conflict in Corcyra (III 82–5) that resulted from Athenian support for the democrats and Spartan support for the oligarchs. The same pattern was followed by civil wars all over the Greek world. In these circumstances, according to Thucydides, the basic impulses in human nature – toward security for oneself and domination over others – came to the surface.

Democritus argues unconvincingly that the requirements of justice and the demands of nature, as understood by Atomism, can be expected to coincide.[41] Protagoras applies his arguments against objective mind-independent reality to morality. It seems obvious that some provisions of law and other moral and social norms are matters of convention; for they are established by human enactment, differ from one society to another, and can be changed by new legislation. Protagoras infers that morality has no standing in any independent reality. In his view, moral beliefs may be true and well grounded, for those who hold them, but correspond to no further reality. Admittedly they are matters of convention, but so are all other beliefs about the world. This line of argument removes any ground for preferring nature over convention, but at the same time seems to remove any rational ground for preferring one convention over another. One might infer that if the requirements of other-regarding morality conflict with the demands of self-interest, we have no reason to pay attention to other-regarding morality. Self-interest might appear to be non-conventional, determined by human nature, and therefore entitled to override the purely conventional demands of morality.

In Protagoras' view, however, acceptance of his argument against moral objectivity does not require rejection of the demand for self-sacrifice in the common interest. Protagoras (as Plato presents him) argues that questions about justice are (as John Rawls puts it) "political, not metaphysical."[42] In his view, everyone will prefer on reflection to be part of a human society rather than an outcast. Membership in such a society requires law, justice, and a disposition to conform to them (this disposition is "shame," *aidōs*); therefore we will prefer to cultivate such a disposition rather than reject law and justice. It may not seem to matter, then, whether anything is really just apart from how things appear to the Athenians; for acceptance of how things appear to them is necessary for the preferable condition of membership in Athens.

This argument for observance of law and justice in the common interest did not persuade all of Plato's contemporaries. Perhaps we prefer belonging to a society to being outcasts, but we may not prefer the present condition of Athens to other conditions that we might be able to bring about. An opportunity for radical change arose in Athens toward the end of the Peloponnesian War. The war created in Athens the sorts of tensions that Thucydides describes in other cities. Obligations to the community required greater sacrifice than in peacetime, and presented a clearer conflict with the self-seeking "Homeric" pursuit of increased status and power for oneself. In political terms, people had to decide whether or not to plot against the democracy to bring off an oligarchic coup. In moral terms they had to decide whether or not to ignore the rights and interests of their fellow-citizens, in favor of their own honor, status, and power.

If earlier Athenian social and political history is a series of attempts to impose law, order, and justice on the competitive and disorderly social world of Homeric individuals, the Peloponnesian War and its aftermath show that such attempts did not always succeed. The arguments of natural philosophers and sophists did not persuade everyone that they had a good reason to prefer justice and equal rights to the pursuit of their own power and honor.

Doubts about other-regarding morality and justice are raised in some passages in Thucydides (III 82.5–6, 84.2; VI 38.5–39.2), in Antiphon the sophist (DK 87 B 44), and in Plato's characters Callicles (*Grg.* 482e–484c) and Thrasymachus (*Rep.* 344a–c). They are presented in a comically exaggerated form by the "Unjust Argument" in Aristophanes' *Clouds* (1075–82).[43] Plato might reasonably conclude that none of the philosophical outlooks of his naturalist contemporaries and predecessors offered any convincing defense of other-regarding morality.

X   PAST AND PRESENT IN THE DIALOGUES

These tensions in fifth-century Athens provide the dramatic setting of many of the dialogues, and they give us some idea of the questions that Plato thought he needed to discuss. But he wrote the dialogues during the rather different circumstances of the fourth century. The democratic regime that was restored in 403 lasted through the rest of Plato's lifetime, past his death in 347, and even beyond the conquest of Greece by Alexander (who died in 323). In the fourth century the essential institutions of democracy remained, even without an empire to pay for them.[44]

Plato is hostile, but not wholly hostile, to Athenian democracy.[45] In the *Laws* he praises the constitution of his ancestor Solon, who introduced equal rights under the law and wider political participation. Plato agrees with Herodotus that the Athenian constitution explains

Athenian unity and freedom from internal conflict at the time of the
Persian invasion in 480 (*Laws* 698a–700a).[46] In his view, the later
constitutional developments in Athens undermined the supremacy of
the laws and gave excessive power to the preferences and whims of the
lower classes. Plato's attitude to Athenian political history rests on his
questionable division between the period from Solon to 480 and the
period after 480. None the less his appreciation of some elements of
Athenian democracy is worth remembering when we try to understand
the *Republic*, *Politicus*, and *Laws*.

Plato does not offer proposals for the reform of democracy;[47] nor
does he advocate a violent anti-democratic revolution of the sort that
some of his relatives attempted at the end of the Peloponnesian War.
However much he objects to democracy, he assumes that, practically
speaking, the Athenian democracy is stable, and that no feasible
alternative is likely to be superior.

The main rival to democratic Athens, with its relatively free,
unregulated, tolerant, and open-minded social and cultural
atmosphere,[48] was the rigidly controlled, militaristic, and (in certain
respects) oligarchic society that developed in Sparta.[49] Plato certainly admires some aspects of Sparta, including its rigorous system
of state-supervised upbringing, education, and indoctrination that
regulated every aspect of life for the ruling class; but this admiration
does not lead him to admire the moral and political outlook that
underlay the Spartan way of life, or to suppose that it would be better
to replace the Athenian democracy with a constitution modeled on
Sparta. While he argues that the "timocratic" type of constitution
found in Sparta (*Rep.* 547b–548d) is, as such, superior to democracy
as such, this does not lead him to advocate an attempt to imitate
Sparta.[50] The disastrous experiment of pro-Spartan oligarchy in
Athens showed that oligarchy did not arouse broad enough support
in Athens to be maintained without force, intimidation, and foreign
military aid.

Plato's doubts about the prospects of gradual reform or
a purely political revolution rest partly on his views about the

sources of political conflict. For existing cities he agrees with part of Thucydides' analysis. In his view, every city contains the sources of the instability that sometimes breaks out in open struggle; for each of them is really not just one city, but two – the city of the rich and the city of the poor (*Rep.* 421d–422a, 422e–423b). Plato recognizes the conflict of perceived interests that results in class conflict and, in the appropriate circumstances, in civil war and revolution. He even agrees with Thucydides' view that people's interests, as they conceive them, will conflict as long as the dominant class consists of either the rich or the poor. He argues, however, that class conflict is not inevitable. To avoid it, the ruling class must be freed from the conflicts that result from the possession of private property, and must educate the other citizens in a true conception of their interest.[51] Whatever we think of Plato's attempted resolutions of class conflict, his diagnosis of the conditions that need to be removed is defensible in the light of Greek, and especially Athenian, historical experience.

These political questions lead Plato back to ethical questions. The apparent conflict between justice and self-interest for the individual, and the apparent conflicts between the interests of different groups and classes within a state, result from a particular conception of the interests of individuals and groups. Plato argues that this conception is mistaken. In his view, we do not need to find arguments to persuade people to sacrifice their own interests to the common good, because the belief that the common good requires a sacrifice of one's own good is false. On this point he seeks a philosophical defense of Socrates' conviction.

Socrates and Plato could not take it for granted that moral and political questions were appropriately treated by philosophers – by those who recognized some allegiance to the forms of inquiry begun by the naturalists. They had to define the subject-matter and methods of philosophy in contrast to the claims of other outlooks and approaches. The two main rival approaches that Plato confronts are those of the sophist and the rhetorician.

XI SOCRATES, PLATO, AND NATURALISM

We have some reason to believe that both Socrates and Plato studied natural philosophy before they pursued systematic moral philosophy. Plato's early interest in this area is attested by Aristotle's reference to Cratylus. In the *Clouds* Aristophanes presents Socrates in midlife (in the 420s) as a student of nature who believes in non-personal cosmic forces, as opposed to the gods who support morality.[52]

Other sources besides Aristophanes attribute a serious interest in natural philosophy to Socrates. In the *Apology* Socrates recalls the *Clouds*, in order to explain how he had acquired a reputation for rejecting the gods of the city. Socrates tells the jury that they have never heard him discussing natural philosophy. He implies that natural philosophy was not a topic of his discussions with other people. He does not say, however, that he was never interested in it. According to the *Phaedo*, he was interested in naturalism, and especially in Anaxagoras, early in his life (*Phaedo* 96a–99d).

Some sources say that Archelaus the naturalist was a teacher of Socrates, and that he and Socrates visited Melissus in Samos. Some of the theories discussed in the *Clouds* resemble the views of Archelaus. The evidence about Archelaus as Socrates' teacher may support the partial accuracy of Aristophanes' presentation of Socrates. Alternatively, some later reader may have recognized Archelaus in the *Clouds* and inferred that he must have been Socrates' teacher. Aristophanes probably used Archelaus as a basis for his presentation of Socrates, simply because Archelaus' theories could be used to make fun of Socrates.[53]

According to Plato, Socrates was disappointed in his study of natural philosophy because naturalists did not try to explain how the natural order is ordered for the best by an intelligent designer.[54] Plato also criticizes naturalists for treating the natural order as merely the product of "chance" and "necessity" without any design or purpose (*Laws* 889a–890a; cf. *Phil.* 28c–30e). In the cosmology of the *Timaeus* he recognizes two causes – intelligent design aiming at the best, and the non-teleological necessity of the "wandering" cause (47e–48e).[55] The wandering cause marks Plato's agreement with non-theistic naturalism, since he allows that some tendencies in the material world are simply brute facts, with no explanation showing why it is best for them to be as they are. But in recognizing intelligence as the cause partly controlling the material world, Plato affirms a theistic view.

He agrees with the aspect of naturalism that denies (as Xenophanes does) anger, jealousy, spite, and lust to the gods (Ti. 29e). In his view, the gods are entirely just and good. They lack the desires, aims, and caprices that might well seem to be essential to the gods who are the traditional objects of propitiatory cult and sacrifice.[56] Plato recognizes that he disagrees with tradition; for in his ideal state he advocates a thorough censorship of the Homeric poems and other sources of the traditional views (Rep. 377b–392a).

Plato's view has some precedent in the traditions derived from Homer. The Homeric Zeus leads a double life among the gods. Sometimes he has ordinary passions and caprices, but happens to be more powerful than the other gods, and imposes his will on them by force and threats. But sometimes he is the controller of the universe, and his designs are above the normal anthropomorphic level of the Homeric gods.[57] Greeks were familiar with the view that the gods demand justice and punish injustice (in later generations or in an afterlife); but they did not wholly reconcile this view with the presuppositions of propitiatory sacrifice, which sought to placate the gods by material transactions that were independent of the moral character of the one who sacrifices.[58]

Some of the tensions between different elements of the traditional views appear in Euthyphro, a self-styled expert in piety. In prosecuting his father for causing the death of a slave, he violates a traditional bond of filial loyalty (whose influence is strong in, e.g., the Aeschylean Orestes).[59] If, however, he had done nothing, he might have been accused of indifference to the pollution caused by unpunished homicide. In Euthyphro's view, if an injustice has been committed, the gods demand punishment for it (Euphr. 4b7–c3, 5d8–6a5,

7b7–9). At first, he claims that the approval of the gods by itself determines what is pious (9e1–3). He is shown that this claim makes the gods' moral outlook, and therefore the requirements of piety, the mere product of their arbitrary will; and then he agrees that the gods demand piety and justice because of the nature of these virtues themselves, not simply because the gods happen to approve of justice and piety (10d–11b). Euthyphro is by no means a thoughtless or unenlightened representative of traditional views; and Socrates' interrogation of him shows how the moral component of traditional theism conflicts with other elements of traditional views.

Opponents were wrong, therefore, to suppose that Socrates and Plato were abandoning belief in the gods of Athens and the gods of the Greeks, and thereby shattering people's conception of what it meant to be Athenians and Greeks.[60] Plato's most elaborate answer to such a charge is given in the *Laws*, which presents detailed provisions for the cult of the gods of the city, in accordance with Greek tradition. But he does not revert to the traditional conception of these gods. The civic cult rests partly on assumptions about the gods that Plato rejects. On this point the *Laws* reaffirms his earlier view about the errors of traditional religion.

XII PLATO'S VIEW OF HIS PHILOSOPHICAL TASK

Though Plato is influenced by the naturalist tradition, he does not simply continue it. His attitude is transformed by his reflections on Socrates. Aristotle distinguishes the naturalist tradition from Socrates' preoccupation with moral and political questions. He recognizes that Plato's philosophy covers both areas, in the sense that it includes the metaphysical and epistemological questions that (as we have seen) arise from naturalist inquiries. Plato concerns himself with both areas of inquiry because, in his view, the moral and political inquiries that concern Socrates raise questions in metaphysics and epistemology that make a difference to our view about morality. He believes that naturalists and sophists have not found the right basis for knowledge of the world and morality. Democritus' naturalism reaches a skeptical conclusion. Sophists have not shown that skepticism makes no difference to moral and political thought.

The primary error of the sophists, according to Plato, is not that their moral and political views are false. Some modern readers have falsely supposed that Plato blames the sophists as a group for defending a specific theoretical position that he takes to be responsible for some decay in moral standards that he sets out to correct.[61] In particular, it is sometimes supposed that the rejection of conventional morality by such speakers as Callicles in the *Gorgias* and Thrasymachus in *Republic* I is a typical result of sophistic teaching. This view of the sophists, and of Plato's attitude to them, is baseless. Admittedly, some sophists, including Antiphon, hold views similar to those of Callicles and Thrasymachus. Other sophists, however, held quite a different position. Protagoras defends conventional justice and morality and does not try to turn people against them. In the *Meno* Socrates rejects Anytus' indiscriminate hostility to the sophists (91a–92d). In the *Protagoras* Plato's portrait of leading sophists is sometimes satirical, but not hostile (*Prt.* 315cd; cf. *HMa* 281a–283b). Both in the *Protagoras* and in the *Theaetetus* he takes Protagoras seriously; indeed he defends Protagoras against Socratic objections that might satisfy us too easily (*Prt.* 350c–351b, *Tht.* 165e–168c). Plato criticizes sophists not primarily for their conclusions (though he rejects many of them), but for the arguments they rely on.

Moreover, he denies that the sophists are the main influence on moral and political attitudes. In his view, the prejudices of the masses determine the range of acceptable views, and the sophists simply repeat these prejudices (*Rep.* 493a). This description most obviously fits Protagoras, whose epistemological position implies that the views that appear true to the many are true for them (cf. *Tht.* 167c). But Plato thinks it also fits sophists in general; they do not attempt to found their views on any rational basis that goes beyond the unexamined beliefs and prejudices of the majority. This is why he connects sophistic with "appearances" and "images" (*Rep.* 515a5–6; *Sph.* 232a–236d). Since conventional views are all that sophists offer, they have no answer to critics who ask why they should take conventional views seriously.

Similarly, Plato distrusts rhetoric not primarily because he thinks rhetoricians hold false moral beliefs, but because they can give no good reason for them. Plato's contemporary Isocrates was both a well-known public speaker and a teacher and defender of rhetoric. His speeches often attack Plato and Plato's conception of philosophy. Isocrates regards training in rhetoric as "philosophy" in the truest sense (*Antid.* 50, 270, 285). Unlike the studies practiced by naturalists, mathematicians, and eristics, it is practically relevant and applicable, in contrast to Plato's foolish paradoxes about morality (*Helen* 1). In general, "plausible belief about useful things is far superior to exact knowledge about useless things" (*Helen* 5). It is pointless, in Isocrates' view, to examine the foundations of moral and political theory. The proper role of the theorist is not to question the recognized virtues (*Antid.* 84–5) or to find some philosophical basis for them, but to present the recognized virtues in a persuasive and attractive form. According to Plato, Isocrates is something between a philosopher and a politician, since he is intellectually promising, but he cannot distinguish genuine "dialectic" from "eristic" (competitive argument, *Euthyd.* 305b–306c).[62]

The political role of rhetoric arouses Plato's suspicion and criticism. He asks why the Athenian democracy regards rhetorical ability as a sufficient qualification for giving political advice. If, as Isocrates admits, the orator does not try to reach independent rational convictions of his own on moral and political questions, he will simply repeat popular prejudices. If he simply follows the ignorant and prejudiced moral and political assumptions of the majority, his advice will not promote the common good. The method of democratic government undermines its stated goal – to govern in the interest of all the citizens. Moreover, if the orator persuades people, not because he convinces them that the course of action he advises will really benefit them, but because he arouses their feelings and prejudices, even against their better judgment, what he persuades people to do is not even what they want to do. Government by rhetorical persuasion does not even execute the will of the majority.

Plato's criticisms do not show that there could be no legitimate use for rhetoric, or that everyone who practices it is morally misguided.[63] But they raise some questions about the social, educational, and political role of rhetoric in contemporary Athens. Since ancient Athens is not the only society that has allowed skill in non-rational manipulation to be a dominant influence in democratic debate, the force of Plato's criticisms is not confined to his own historical situation.

XIII   SOCRATIC INQUIRY

Many of Plato's works are dialogues that depict Socrates' characteristic method of inquiry. Socrates relies on the sort of systematic questioning and refutation that Zeno had begun.[64] In the dialogues he cross-examines one or more interlocutors, in order to expose conflicts in their views. He begins from commonsense beliefs, and seems to rely on them at each stage of his argument.

The mere use of cross-examination and refutation does not distinguish Socrates from the sophists. Though Protagoras is represented as being unfamiliar with Socratic conversation (*Prt.* 334c–335c), he was familiar with techniques of destructive argument.[65] The *Euthydemus* exhibits the techniques of eristic argument, a technique practiced by some sophists.[66] Techniques of cross-examination and refutation are obviously useful in debate and argument; and the young men who learned them from Socrates enjoyed practicing them on others.[67] Socrates' interlocutors sometimes accuse him of using eristic techniques;[68] and we have seen that Isocrates describes Plato as an eristic.[69]

Socrates, however, claims that his arguments are not eristic, but dialectical. He does not simply try to refute his interlocutors. Each interlocutor is expected to state his own view (instead of maintaining something for the sake of argument to avoid refutation; *Prt.* 331c). Socrates claims to offer constructive arguments for true conclusions that support his paradoxically uncompromising defense of the moral virtues (*Grg.* 508a–c). Some of his arguments aim to give an account of the virtues that will explain the features that are reasonably attributed to them. Some dialogues end without endorsing a definite answer, but none the less make progress. Plato claims to show by Socratic cross-examination that weakness of will is impossible (*Protagoras*), that Socrates ought not to disobey the law by trying to escape from prison (*Crito*), and that virtue is sufficient for happiness (*Gorgias*).

If Plato maintains these controversial philosophical views, should we be surprised that he regards Socratic conversations as the right way to argue for them? If he intends to offer more than eristic argument, why does he write dialogues? Since Plato was a pioneer in writing moral philosophy (as opposed to including some remarks on morality within a treatise on natural philosophy), he had to find a suitable literary form.[70] Among the earlier Presocratics, Parmenides and Empedocles wrote in epic verse, while Heraclitus apparently expressed his views (at least sometimes) in aphorisms, maxims, riddles, and paradoxes. The Presocratics, therefore, offered a wide choice of literary forms.[71]

Many of the naturalists wrote continuous expositions of their views. So did the medical writers. Why does Plato not follow these precedents, and why does he decide that conversations are a better way to present his views?

XIV ARGUMENT THROUGH DIALOGUE

The most obvious precedent for systematic cross-examination through dialogue is argument in the Athenian assembly of citizens and in the law courts.[72] Advocates before a jury did not simply make speeches; they also examined witnesses, in order to represent them as reliable or unreliable. A jury who listened to speeches and interrogations on each side of the case were expected to make up their mind about the truth or falsity of a charge. In this respect the use of the adversarial method to discover the facts was familiar to Socrates' and

Plato's intended audience. Though Socrates in the *Apology* says he is unaccustomed to speaking in a court, he skillfully weaves some Socratic cross-examinations into his defense. The jury expect to hear a cross-examination, and Socrates provides it, but in his own way.

The histories of Herodotus and Thucydides use fictitious speeches and debates to explore moral and political questions. Herodotus presents a debate on different Greek political systems during an episode in Persian history (Hdt. III 80–2); and Thucydides presents an elaborate dialogue between Athenians and Melians about whether the Athenians ought to massacre all the Melians for their support of Sparta (Thuc. V 84–113).

While these debates are inserted into the narrative structure of the histories, debates have a more central place in Athenian tragic and comic drama. Plato criticizes drama for its dangerous moral influence, but he also learns from it. His attacks on tragedy treat it as a form of rhetoric (*Grg.* 502b, *Rep.* 602c–606d). His objections are easier to understand if we remember that the Athenian dramatic festivals took the place of some of the mass media familiar to us.[73] In Plato's view, Euripides (for instance) arouses our sympathy for Medea not because he can rationally convince us to see on reflection that Medea deserves our sympathy, but because he presents some features of her situation in ways that appeal to our prejudices. Many tragedies use debates to present moral and political questions.[74] Especially in the plays of Euripides and the later plays of Sophocles,[75] the debates are elaborate and theoretical. Plato's readers were used to dialogue as a medium for exploring moral questions.

Many Platonic dialogues are similar to Athenian tragedies insofar as the participants are not mere speakers, but distinct characters and personalities. Most Athenian tragedies, however, are about heroic figures from the distant and legendary past.[76] The participants in most Platonic dialogues are Socrates and his contemporaries. They include well-known philosophers, playwrights, sophists, rhetoricians, politicians, and generals. In contrast to them, Socrates is in many ways an ordinary (even exaggeratedly ordinary) plain-spoken person.

Characters such as Socrates are familiar not from tragedy, but from the comedies of Aristophanes.[77] A comic hero in Aristophanes (such as Dikaiopolis in the *Acharnians*) is usually un-heroic, outside the circle of Athenians who distinguished themselves by their wealth, ancestry, and military and political careers. Though he appears to be an ignorant and vulgar peasant, Dikaiopolis understands why the Peloponnesian War broke out, while his "betters" do not; and he stands alone against them in concluding his own peace treaty with the Peloponnesians. The "establishment" figures mentioned in the play – including the "Olympian" Pericles who started a war for the sake of a few prostitutes, and the boastful, empty-headed general Lamachus – are shown to be pretentious and foolish. Dikaiopolis outwits his "betters" by his clever tongue and his understanding of the situation.

After he makes his private peace with the Peloponnesians, Dikaiopolis begins his own idyllic peacetime existence, fulfilling the dreams of Athenians who were suffering from the rigors of war. This fantastic element is developed further in the utopian "Cloudcuckooland" of the *Birds*. This use of utopia and fantasy to make a serious moral and political point may have helped to suggest to Plato that the description of a utopia (not without some humorous elements; cf. *Rep.* 372c–d) would be an effective way to present some of his own moral and political views.[78]

Athenians who had laughed at the foolishness of Aristophanes' Athenian generals and cheered for Dikaiopolis or Lysistrata would be able to appreciate the comic aspects of Socrates and the other characters in the dialogues. Many of the interlocutors are Socrates' social superiors – the aristocrats in the *Laches* and *Charmides*, the leading intellectuals and experts in the *Protagoras*, *Gorgias*, *Ion*, and *Hippias Minor* and *Major*. Often they begin with a rather complacent, even patronizing, attitude to Socrates, but they find that he understands more than they do. Socrates says that while he cannot claim to know that his views are true, he has found anyone who rejects them has turned out to be "laughable" (*Grg.* 509a; cf. *Prt.* 355a6). When Socrates thinks it would be impolite to argue too aggressively, he attributes his arguments to a rude and aggressive critic who is like some speakers in comedies (*Prt.* 355c–e; *H. Ma.* 286c–291b). Plato shows us an unlikely hero deflating the pretensions of people whose reputation exceeds their understanding.

A particular type of comic situation provides one of the most important elements – comic and serious at the same time – of the dialogues.[79] Aristophanes' comedies include a "contest" (*agōn*), in which two contestants argue over some question until one wins. Often, but not always, the hero of the comedy is the winner in the contest of arguments. In the *Clouds*, however, two personified abstractions, the Just Argument and the Unjust Argument, are the contestants, and the Unjust Argument wins, with bad results for Strepsiades, his son Pheidippides, and the Socratic school.[80] In the *Frogs* Aeschylus and Euripides engage in a contest of wisdom (*agōn sophias*, *Frogs* 882) to see who can give the best advice to the city.[81] Plato's dialogues place Socrates in the comic as well as the tragic tradition of adversarial argument.

Perhaps the *Symposium* shows us that Plato recognizes the dramatic sources of Socratic argument. The last three speakers before Socrates are the physician Eryximachus, the comic poet Aristophanes, and the tragic poet Agathon, all friends of Socrates. Eryximachus' speech recalls some of the natural philosophy that Socrates is supposed to have studied. Aristophanes begins by making fun of this natural philosophy (as the *Clouds* does), and then offers an entertaining story about the ridiculous origins of love between human beings, which turns out to contain a grain of truth. Agathon offers an elaborate rhetorical eulogy on love. Socrates subjects Agathon, not Aristophanes, to cross-examination that exposes the limits of Agathon's understanding.[82] In one respect, therefore, he takes Agathon to need more criticism than Aristophanes needs. In another respect, however, he implies that the tragedian's views are worth taking seriously and examining in detail. Comedy makes a further appearance with the arrival of Alcibiades at the end of the dialogue.

XV   PLATO'S ATTITUDE TO SOCRATIC DIALOGUE

Most Platonic dialogues are not simply records of arguments on different questions.[83] They are encounters between individuals with distinct personalities and outlooks who are willing to examine a question seriously on the basis of their considered views, and are willing to recognize the implications of these views. These features separate Socrates' interlocutors from eristics, sophists, and rhetoricians. In these respects Socratic adversarial arguments are more similar to the debates in tragedy and comedy in which the participants recognize that something important needs to be discussed, and assume that they will act on the arguments that seem best after serious debate.

In the light of these precedents, Plato chose the dialogue form because he thought it stuck most closely to the essential features of Socratic argument. Socrates claims that the systematic, rule-governed form of interrogation that he practices allows him to secure his interlocutors' agreement to moral positions that they would have firmly, often indignantly, rejected before they faced Socrates' questions. The fact that the conclusion is reached through this sort of interrogation of this sort of interlocutor is part of the reason Socrates offers us for believing his conclusion. He claims that his arguments are those that actually convince an interlocutor who approaches the questions in the right way.[84] The interlocutor (Socrates claims) is not dazzled by rhetoric, or bullied by eristic, or overawed by elaborate disquisitions on natural philosophy; he is rationally convinced. A Platonic dialogue is meant to show how such conviction is possible.

If Socrates makes these claims about the epistemological role of inquiry through dialogue, and if Plato agrees with Socrates about them, he might reasonably find it difficult to present the essential elements of Socratic philosophy in any other form than the one he chooses. He might have been able to explain in his own voice what Socrates was trying to do and why Socrates thought he could do it; and such an explanation would have been useful to us. But it would scarcely have been an effective or economical method for capturing our attention and forcing us to take Socrates seriously. Since Plato takes Socratic philosophy seriously, he writes Socratic dialogues. We have no reason to suppose that the dialogues are, or were taken to be, transcripts of actual conversations; but they are intended to communicate a central element in Socrates' defense of his moral position.

The epistemological claims implied in Socrates' use of the dialogue are controversial. Once Plato reflects on these claims, he decides that they need to be modified. Modifications in the epistemological claims also require modification in the sort of dialogue that Plato regards as the best medium for his philosophical views; and so he writes different sorts of dialogues, following different rules, to achieve different ends. The conversational and adversarial character of some Socratic dialogues is drastically modified; the *Timaeus* and *Laws*, for instance, contain long stretches of continuous exposition. But Plato does not simply drop the Socratic dialogue characteristic of his early period. The *Theaetetus* and *Philebus* are later dialogues that share many important characteristics with the dramatic and conversational early dialogues. Plato's choice of the dialogue form, and of a particular variety of dialogue, is determined by his philosophical aims.

XVI   RETURN TO THE PRESOCRATICS

The changing form of the Platonic dialogues partly results from changes in Plato's views about Socratic philosophy. Plato's early association with Cratylus suggests to him that he must go beyond Socrates and take up the wider philosophical questions that Socrates had set aside in order to concentrate on ethics. Socrates' efforts to define the virtues assume that objectively correct answers can be found, and that they must correspond to some objective realities independent of our beliefs and inquiries. But what sorts of objective realities could correspond to our moral beliefs? And even if we can conceive what the relevant realities might be like, how can we reasonably suppose that we know anything about them?

These questions take Plato back to some of the metaphysical and epistemological preoccupations of the Presocratics. The interlocutors who can deal with these questions are different from those who appear in the earlier dialogues. Instead of Socrates' friends and associates, including generals, politicians, and young men aspiring to political careers, the interlocutors are philosophers (Parmenides and Zeno) or serious students of mathematics and philosophy (Theodorus and Theaetetus). In some dialogues (*Parmenides*, *Sophist*, *Politicus*, *Timaeus*, *Laws*) Socrates is not even the main speaker. In the *Sophist* and *Politicus* the main speaker is an "Eleatic Visitor," whose origin indicates his interest in the questions raised by Parmenides and Zeno. The dialogues are on the whole more expository and less adversarial than many of the earlier dialogues.

In the *Meno*, *Phaedo*, and *Cratylus*, Plato argues that Socratic inquiry relies on epistemological and metaphysical principles that the naturalists have overlooked, and that the success of Socratic inquiry provides an argument for the truth of these principles. In particular, the Socratic search for accounts of the virtues and other moral properties succeeds to the extent that it grasps the characteristics of "forms" (*eidē*),[85] such as the just, the fine, and the good, that are objective, stable, and knowable.

Socrates' search for definitions draws Plato's attention to the second type of Heraclitean flux, involving the compresence of opposites (the writing that is straight and crooked, the water that is good and bad, and so on).[86] Plato points out that ordinary observation of the properties that mark different types of just or good actions or people suggests that these properties suffer compresence of opposites; bright color, for instance, is both beautiful (in some contexts) and ugly (in others), and giving back what you have borrowed is both just (in normal circumstances) and unjust (if a suicidal person asks you to return his sword).[87] Such examples induce Heraclitus to infer that justice is both paying your debts and not paying them.

Plato replies that Heraclitus offers the wrong sort of account of justice. Observable types of just actions are in flux from just to unjust, but justice itself is exempt from the compresence of opposites. An adequate definition of the Forms (of justice, bravery etc.) that Socrates was trying to define must, in Plato's view, show that the Forms display Parmenidean stability rather than Heraclitean flux. At the end of the *Cratylus* (named after this extreme Heraclitean), Socrates argues that, even if all particular just, fine, etc. things are unstable, the just and the fine themselves must be stable. He does not endorse the antecedent of this conditional.

In the *Theaetetus*, he discusses a more radical thesis. One might take Heraclitus to claim that we cannot step into the same river twice because it undergoes some change, and nothing that undergoes any change remains in being. The extreme Heraclitean doctrine of flux (which Aristotle attributes to Cratylus) asserts that every subject of change changes all the time in every respect. Plato argues that if the doctrine of total flux is accepted without qualification, so that we deny the existence of persisting subjects altogether, it actually refutes itself; for we cannot say what is in flux, and since we cannot speak of flux without saying that something is in flux, the extreme doctrine of flux cannot be true unless it is false.[88] In this case also, Heraclitus' doctrine of flux leads us to the correct non-Heraclitean conclusion.

The end of the *Cratylus* agrees with Parmenides, to the extent that it asserts that some things (the forms) are wholly stable. But Plato rejects Parmenides' reason for believing in wholly stable objects. Parmenides' rejection of change rests on his more general claim that we cannot speak or think of what is not, because what is not is nothing, and to speak or think of nothing is not to speak or think at all. We can use words as we can use gestures to point out and identify something; and just as I cannot pick out something that is not there, I apparently cannot name what is not there. And so if we look at certain aspects of thinking and speaking, we may incline to

Parmenides' assumption that they consist in a direct causal inter-
action with some external object, and therefore require an existing
object. In the *Theaetetus* Plato considers these apparent analogies
between seeing and thinking, and shows how they lead to the
unacceptable conclusions that we cannot have false beliefs (because
they would be beliefs about what is not) and we cannot have beliefs
about the nonexistent (because they would be beliefs about nothing)
(*Tht.* 188a–189b).

In *Republic* V Plato agrees, in one respect, with Parmenides'
claim that we cannot know what is not, but he disagrees, in one
respect, with his claim that we cannot speak or think of what is not.
His disagreement with Parmenides rests on an implicit distinction
between different ways in which Parmenides speaks of "what is
not." Parmenides is right to claim that we can know only what is
and we cannot know what is not; but we should take this claim to
mean that we can know only what is the case (i.e., what is true).
Since belief, in contrast to knowledge, does not imply truth, we can
believe what is not (i.e., what is not the case, what is false), but
believing what is not does not imply believing nothing, since what
is not (i.e., what is false) is not nothing. This discussion of knowledge and belief relies on distinguishing the use of "is" and "is not"
for truth and falsity from their use for existence and nonexistence.
Though Plato draws these distinctions implicitly, he does not make
them explicit.[89]

In the *Sophist* he offers a more explicit treatment of some of the
relevant questions. He argues that we must be able, in one sense, to
speak of what is not, and tries to explain how this is possible. The
Eleatic Visitor alludes to Parmenides' arguments about being; he
observes that the question of how things can appear, but not be, and
how one can speak of something but speak falsely "has always been
full of puzzlement, in previous times and up to the present"; and then
he introduces Parmenides' rejection of not-being (*Sph.* 236e–237a).
The rest of the dialogue seeks to explain how, and in what sense, it is
possible to speak and think of what is not. Though the visitor is from

Elea, as Parmenides was, his inquiry into not-being results in the rejection of Parmenides' conclusion.

These few examples show that Plato finds philosophical significance in the paradoxical conclusions that seem to result from some naturalist inquiries. The Heraclitean and the Parmenidean conclusions are both unacceptable, but the arguments that lead to them are not to be dismissed. Examination of the apparently reasonable premises that lead to the unacceptable conclusions show which premises need to be rejected and where the arguments need to be challenged. Plato takes the same view about the arguments that lead some Presocratics to a skeptical conclusion. The challenge of skepticism is important for Plato because, following Socrates, he affirms that we can achieve knowledge, which the skeptic does not affirm. It is equally important for him to reject Protagoras' solution to the questions raised by skepticism. For Plato believes in the existence of a knowable mind-independent reality, whereas Protagoras believes that we can refute skepticism only if we agree with the skeptic that there is no knowable mind-independent reality. In developing his Theory of Forms, Plato makes it clear that he rejects both skepticism and Protagoras' solution. But in the dialogues where he discusses the Forms, he assumes the falsity of Protagoras' position, and discusses it only briefly.[90]

In the *Theaetetus*, however, Plato discusses both Protagoras and Heraclitus at some length, and combines epistemological and metaphysical argument. He argues that Protagorean epistemology is plausible only if it relies on an indefensible metaphysics; for it leads into the self-refuting extreme Heraclitean doctrine about change. To this extent his attitude to Protagoras is similar to his attitude to Heraclitus and Parmenides; Plato realizes fairly late in his philosophical life that the questions raised by his predecessors require a direct and fundamental examination.

The dialogues, therefore, bear out Aristotle's claim that reflection on Socratic inquiry about ethics leads Plato back to the study of questions derived from the naturalists. Throughout his philosophical life Plato remains a careful and appreciative critic of his predecessors. But while he faces some of the same questions, Plato thinks he can avoid the skeptical conclusions that seem to threaten the foundations of Presocratic naturalism. For he thinks we have enough firm and reliable convictions about some questions to justify us in arguing from these convictions to the conditions that are presupposed by their truth.

NOTES

1 On the general topic of this chapter see Field 1930, reviewed in Cherniss 1933; Irwin 1989: chs. 2–4; Rutherford 1995; Meinwald 2016.

2 On the life of Plato see Schofield 2019: 41–68. Evidence on Plato's life is unreliable. (Plato names himself in the dialogues only at *Ap.* 34a2, 38b6, *Phd.* 59b10.) The best of the ancient lives is D.L. III 1–47. But we cannot trust D.L. even when he cites an early and well-informed source; for he cites Plato's own nephew Speusippus, who succeeded Plato as head of the Academy, as a source for the story (which Speusippus is not said to endorse) that Plato was the son of Apollo (III 2).

The Platonic Corpus includes letters that are probably spurious. The seventh of them includes some ostensibly autobiographical remarks. On this letter see Burnyeat and Frede 2015 (see esp. Scott's "Editor's guide," at 85–97); Irwin 2009: 7–40. The authenticity of some of the letters, including this one, is defended by Morrow (1962).

3 See the Chronology in this volume for the dates of many of the people and events mentioned in this chapter. I assume without argument: (1) The historical claims by Aristotle that I mention are correct; (2) Plato's earlier dialogues express the views of the historical Socrates, which Plato accepts at the time of writing; (3) His later dialogues express Plato's views, but not Socrates' views. These questions are discussed elsewhere in this volume. I have said something about them in Irwin 1995a and 2019.

4 Evidence on the Presocratics and sophists (see this chapter, section VII) is collected in Kirk, Raven, and Schofield 1983, and (more fully) in Graham 2010, and in Laks and Most 2016. I have cited passages from Diels and Kranz

1954, cited as "DK." The other collections use the numbering of DK. An informative short chapter is Schofield (2003).

   Despite the labels "Presocratics" and "Early Greek Philosophy," the later "Presocratics" were contemporaries of Socrates and Plato. Democritus is reported to have lived to the age of 109 (and so to have died around 350, only a few years before Plato), D.L. IX 43.

5 Since the *Cratylus* presents Cratylus as a "noodle" (Crombie 1963: 476), it is an unlikely source for Aristotle's belief that he influenced Plato. On Cratylus in the dialogue see Sedley 2003: 16–23; Ademollo 2011: 14–18.

6 Aristotle's generalizations need to be qualified: (1) As we saw, the later "Presocratics" are not pre-Socratic at all. (2) Xenophanes, Heraclitus, Empedocles, Democritus, and Archelaus have something to say on moral questions.

7 Hume comments on this interval between the development of natural philosophy and the development of moral philosophy, in the Introduction to the *Treatise*.

8 On Pythagorean mathematics and metaphysics see Kahn 2001: chs. 1–2. On the importance of mathematics see *Grg.* 507e6–508a8;. *Rep.* 522c–525c; Vlastos 1991: ch. 4. On astronomy and cosmology see especially Vlastos 1975.

9 See *HMa* 289a; *Cra.* 402d, 440c; *Phd.* 78de; *Smp.* 187a–b, 207d; *Rep.* 485b; *Tht.* 152e, 179d–e; *Sph.* 242e.

10 See *Ap.* 26d6–e4; *Cra.* 400a9, 409a7; *Phd.* 72c, 97b–98c.

11 See *Smp.* 178b–c; *Parm.* 127a–128e; *Tht.* 183e; *Sph.* 217c.

12 See *Meno* 76c; *Tht.* 152e; *Sph.* 242d–e. On the *Timaeus* see Cornford 1937: 334; Taylor 1928, on 73d7, 77c6, 78e, and 650–4.

13 Democritus called his atoms *ideai* ("shapes"), using the word that Plato uses for his "Forms" or "Ideas"; see DK 68 A 57, B 141. Plato's failure to name Democritus is not surprising if Democritus was still alive at the time these dialogues were written (see n. 4 above). Plato characteristically refrains from discussing the views of his contemporaries by name. He normally uses descriptions; see e.g., *Sph.* 251b6; *Phil.* 44b–c.

14 See *Ch.* 156d–e; *Smp.* 186b–e; *Phdr.* 270c–e; *Laws* 719e–720e.

15 The ancient subtitle of the *Ion* is "On the *Iliad*."

16 On the abilities and accomplishments expected of a rhapsode see Rijksbaron 2007: 124–8. On Plato's attitude to Homer see Murray 1996: 19–24.

17 The evidence on Homer and mid-sixth-century Athens is discussed by Kirk (1962: 306–10).

18 Ethical questions arising from Homer: Adkins 1960; Irwin 1989: ch. 2; Long 1970: 121–39; Creed 1973: 213–31; Dover 1974; Adkins 1978: 143–58; Taylor 1990: ch. 27.

19 The hero's indifference to other people is only comparative; he is expected to fulfil certain obligations to others and is criticized for failing in them, as Achilles is criticized. Still, when there is a sharp conflict between these obligations to others and the hero's own power and status, he is expected to choose for himself and against others, as both Achilles and Hector do.

20 Different attitudes to Alcibiades are expressed by Euripides and Aeschylus in Aristophanes, *Frogs* 1422–32. The old-fashioned Aeschylus is more sympathetic to Alcibiades.

21 On Alexander see Hornblower 2011: 197–8.

22 For possible references in Plato to Herodotus see *Rep.* 566c, *Ti.* 25c, *Laws* 609a–d, 692e (cf. Hdt. VII 139), 805a (cf. IV 116–17), 947a6 (cf. II 37). See Morrow 1960: 91, 330, 417; Shorey 1933: 8, 447.

23 Here and later, I give a one-sided picture of Athenian political history. For more detail see Murray 1993; Hornblower 2011.

24 On democracy and the upper classes in Athens see Ober 1989: chs. 5–6.

25 The wording of Anaximander's remark on cosmic justice varies in different sources. They are displayed in Kirk, Raven, and Schofield 1983: 106–8.

26 Natural law: Vlastos 1975: ch. 1.

27 This is the subject of the "Elgin Marbles," the sculptures taken from the Parthenon to the British Museum. The Panathenaic festival is mentioned as evidence of traditional beliefs at *Euphr.* 6b7–c4. It included the recitation of Homer; see this chapter, section II. On Athenian festivals see Parker 1996: ch. 6; 2005: ch. 8.

28 Some texts on Democritus' denial of providence are collected by Taylor (1999: 93). On Democritus' view of the gods see Guthrie 1969, 2: 478–83.

29 "Nomos" may be translated by "convention," "custom," "law," "rule," "norm" on different occasions.

30 The claim that Heraclitus' doctrine of flux covers both types of instability is supported by Plutarch, *De E.* 392bc (= DK 22 B 91); Plutarch introduces compresence in his explanation of the river fragment. See Irwin 1995a: 161–2.

31 Parmenides states his main thesis in DK 28 B 2.7–8; 3.1; 6.1–2, and he
     develops its consequences for time and change in B 8. On the
     interpretation of his main thesis see Owen 1986: ch.1 ("Eleatic
     questions"); Furth 1974: ch. 11; Sedley 1999b: ch. 6.

32 Replies to Parmenides: Barnes 1979: ch. 6.

33 On the sophistication of Athenian audiences see Thuc. III 38.7. Cleon
     denounces the use of sophisticated techniques in debate; his denunciation
     of them is itself a standard rhetorical ploy.

34 On *hoi politeuomenoi* see Demosthenes 3.30–1; cf. Plato, *Grg.* 473e6. On
     political speakers see Ober 1989: ch. 3.

35 On the use of "sophist" see Kerferd 1981: 24; Isocrates, *Antid.* 235, 268;
     Aeschylus (?), *Prometheus Vinctus* 62, 944.

36 Pericles is supposed to have spoken in public from a written text instead
     of improvising (Souda s.v. Pericles; see Jebb 1893, 1: cxxviii); and the
     popular leader Cleon is supposed to have begun the use of ostentatious
     techniques of intonation and gesture ([Aristotle], *Ath. Pol.* 28.3).

37 The major source for the history of the Peloponnesian War is the history of
     Thucydides. Hornblower 2011: chs. 13–14 is a useful short account of the
     war and its effects.

38 On the Thirty see Xenophon, *Hellenica* II 3.11 – end; Lysias 12–13;
     [Aristotle], *Ath Pol.* 5.

39 Both Socrates and Plato, however, also had friends and connections on the
     democratic side (Chaerephon the disciple of Socrates; Pyrilampes the
     great-uncle and stepfather of Plato). See Nails: 2002: 86–7, 257–9. It should
     not be assumed that Plato's aristocratic background must have turned him
     against democracy.

40 I have discussed some questions about Socrates' trial and its background
     in Irwin 2005. The Seventh Letter purports to describe Plato's attitude to
     the democracy, the Thirty, and the trial of Socrates (324c–325c). But if the
     letter is spurious, the author's political aims may well have colored the
     views he attributes to Plato, and it is unwise to treat them (as most
     accounts of Plato's life do) as historical.

41 On Democritus' ethics see Vlastos 1995: ch. 16 ("Ethics and Physics in
     Democritus"); Taylor 1967; 1999: 222–34. The writer known as
     "Anonymus Iamblichi" (in DK 89 #6) presents a defense of conventional
     morality. On this writer and Democritus see Hussey 1985. An intriguing

point about Democritus' familiarity with some features of political life in his native Abdera is made in Lewis (1990).

42 This phrase is borrowed from Rawls (1999). I do not mean to imply that the similarity between the views of Protagoras and of Rawls is deep or significant.

43 The Unjust and Just Arguments are characters in the school ("reflectory") of Socrates, who does not take responsibility for what either of them says. The stupidity of the Just Argument, ostensibly representing conventional morality, suggests that Aristophanes may not have been an unqualified supporter of conventional morality. See Dover 1968: lvii–lxvi.

44 On fourth-century history see Hornblower 2011: chs. 14–19.

45 Schofield (2006: chs. 2–3) discusses Plato and democracy.

46 Plato ignores the fact that the reforms of Cleisthenes made the constitution far more democratic than it had been under Solon. On Plato's attitude to the Athenian constitution see Morrow 1960: 77–86.

47 This claim needs to be qualified, but not abandoned, in the light of the *Laws*.

48 See Thucydides VII 69.2; Plato, *Grg.* 461e1–3, *Rep.* 557b–c. On Athenian democracy see Jones 1957: chs. 3, 5; Ober 1989.

49 It is over-simplified, but not too misleading, to describe the Spartan constitution as oligarchical, in comparison with Athens.

50 On Sparta see, e.g., *Cri.* 52e5, *Smp.* 209d, *Rep.* 544c, 545a, 547d–e, *Laws* 631a, Morrow 1960: ch. 2.

51 This is the solution offered in the *Republic*. In the *Laws* Plato does not advocate the abolition of private property as a practical proposal; but he advocates other measures for the distribution and restriction of property with the same aim of preventing the sorts of inequalities between rulers and ruled that provoke civil war.

52 See *Clouds* 367–81, 423–4. A naturalistic explanation of traditionally-recognized divine signs is provided at 368–411.

53 The relation of Archelaus to Socrates and Aristophanes is discussed in Betegh 2013: 87–106. Some features of the *Clouds* have also been traced to Diogenes of Apollonia and the Pythagoreans. See Rashed 2009: 107–36.

54 Socrates and Plato on intelligent design are discussed in Sedley 2007a: chs. 3–4.

55 On the importance of the contrast between teleological reason and non-teleological necessity in Plato see Vlastos 1981: ch. 7; Morrow 1954: 7–9.

56 In the *Apology* (26a4–5) Socrates mentions the charge against him of not believing in the gods of the city, but in "other newfangled supernatural beings" (*hetera de daimonia kaina*). We do not know whether Socrates' accusers knew anything about his religious views or (as Socrates suggests, 19c) they were simply trying to exploit the religious charges made in Aristophanes' *Clouds*.

57 For a protest against the view that gods are to be blamed for causing harm to human beings see Zeus's remarks in *Odyssey* I 32–43. Cf. Aeschylus, *Agamemnon* 1481–8. Protests against stories of immorality among the gods appear in Xenophanes, DK 21 B 11; Euripides, *Hercules Furens* 1340–6. Bond (1981, *ad loc.*) suggests that Xenophanes influenced Euripides. Other passages in tragedy that may be influenced by naturalists are collected by Laks and Most (2016), vol. 9.

58 Contrast Aeschylus, *Agamemnon* 67–71 with the commonsense attitude expressed by Cephalus at *Republic* 330d–e. Plato comments on Cephalus' attitude at *Laws* 905d–907b.

59 See Aeschylus, *Choephori* 924–5. On the religious and legal issues raised by Euthyphro's action see Parker 1983: 366–8. For related issues about pollution see Parker 1983: ch. 4, and 196–8. See also Heidel 1902, on 4b; Kidd 1990.

60 The Greeks' sense of their identity as a people depended partly on their shared cults and shrines of the Greek gods, according to Herodotus VIII 144. On the role of religion and kinship (themselves closely connected) in Greek "national" consciousness see Walbank 1985: ch. 1, esp. 10–13; Cartledge 1993: 154–6.

61 The sophists and Plato's attitude to them: Cope 1854: 145–88; Grote 1888: ch. 67; Sidgwick 1905, "The Sophists"; Guthrie 1969, vol. 3: chs. 1, 3; Kerferd 1981: ch. 2; Irwin 1995b.

62 The *Phaedrus* probably alludes to Isocrates without naming him. See Thompson 1868: 170–83; Gifford 1905: 17–20. Isocrates and Plato: Nightingale 1995: ch. 1. The *Gorgias*: Guthrie 1969, 4: 308–11. On the *Phaedrus* see Howland 1937.

63 Plato takes a different view of rhetoric in the *Phaedrus* from the one he takes in the *Gorgias* (partly because of differences in his moral psychology).

64 Aristotle's remarks about the early history of dialectical reasoning seem to suggest some role for Zeno, but insist that Socrates marks a new development; cf. *Met.* 1078b23–30 with *Sophist* fr. 1 (see Ross 1955: 15).

65 On Protagoras see DK 80 A 1 (= D.L. IX 55), B 1 (where "Destructive Arguments" is an alternative title for his work "On Truth"), 6.

66 The rules of the eristic game require the interlocutor to answer Yes or No; he is not allowed to qualify his reply or to point out that he did not mean it in this sense (e.g., *Euthd.* 287c–d, 295b–c, 296a–b). See also *Meno* 75c–d; Thompson 1901: 272–85; Taylor 1911: 91–8; Kerferd 1981: 62–6.

67 See *Ap.* 23c–d; *Rep.* 537d–539a; Xenophon, *Mem.* I 2.39–46.

68 See *Grg.* 482d, 489b–c, *Rep.* 338d. Plato rejects this charge against Socratic method.

69 See Isocrates, *Panath.* 26; *Antid.* 265–6 (cf. Plato, *Grg.* 484c).

70 There are some references to "Socratic discourses"; see Aristotle, *Poet.* 1447a28–b20, *De Poetis* fr. 4 [Ross], Field 1930: ch. 11. But we do not know their historical relation to Plato's dialogues.

71 The fragmentary character of our surviving evidence on Anaxagoras and Democritus, for instance, makes the exact literary form of their works obscure, though some of their works must presumably have been continuous treatises. One fragment of Democritus presents a conversation between the intellect and the senses (B 125, quoted in this chapter, section VI), but we do not know how often he used this form.

72 Since many Athenian juries were large (Socrates' trial had 501 jurors), the skills needed for forensic and for political speeches were not very different.

73 The place of tragedy in Athenian society: Pelling 1997; Cartledge 1997: ch. 1; Griffin 1999.

74 The story that Plato wrote tragedies, but burned his compositions after hearing Socrates (D.L. III 5) might have been invented by someone who was struck by the dramatic qualities of the dialogues and their criticism of tragedy.

75 These features are especially clear in (e.g.) the *Hecuba* and *Troades* of Euripides and in the *Philoctetes* and *Oedipus Coloneus* of Sophocles. See further Solmsen 1975: ch. 2.

76 One exception to this rule is the *Persians* of Aeschylus.

77 Among the significant exceptions to this generalization about tragedy are the Nurse in Aeschylus' *Choephori* (who may be compared with the Porter in *Macbeth*) and Electra's husband in Euripides' *Electra*. Some criticized Euripides for bringing too many ordinary people into his plays.

78 It has sometimes been suggested that there is some connection between the views on marriage and property in the *Republic* and the views parodied in Aristophanes' *Ecclesiazusae*; but there is insufficient reason to believe that the similarities between the two works indicate any knowledge by either writer of the work of the other. See Adam 1902, 1: 345–55.

79 Plato and comedy: Greene 1920; Dover 1980: 104, 113; Clay 1983: 198; Brock 1990; Nightingale 1995: ch. 5.

80 The *Crito* uses a personified abstraction, the Laws of Athens, as an imagined speaker.

81 This contest is discussed in Dover 1993: 10–37.

82 On the speeches of Aristophanes and Agathon see Hunter 2004: 53–77. On the contribution of the early speeches to the main themes of the dialogue see Sheffield 2006: ch. 1.

83 The dialogues are therefore to be distinguished from collections of arguments such as the *Dissoi Logoi* (DK 90). Some parts of Aristotle's *Topics* have a similar function. Part 2 of the *Parmenides* is the closest that Plato comes to this sort of collection.

84 The interlocutors: Coventry 1990: 174–84. A longer study is Beversluis 2000.

85 I use "forms" for Socratic forms and "Forms" for Platonic forms in accordance with the division mentioned in Irwin 1995a: 374 n. 1.

86 See section VI in this chapter.

87 See *H. Ma.* 293a–b, *Phd.* 74a–c, 78c–e, *Smp.* 211a–b, *Rep.* 331c–332a, 479a–c, 485b, 495a–b.

88 Plato introduces Heracliteanism (embracing both types of flux, *Theat.* 152d2–3) to explain the consequences that he takes to follow from the acceptance of a Protagorean position. There is no basis for supposing that he agrees with Heraclitus about the extent of flux (of the first type) in the sensible world. See Fine 1988; Burnyeat 1990: 7–10.

89 On the argument of *Rep.* 475–9 see Fine 1990: ch. 5. Different interpretations of "knowledge is of what is" result in different views about what Plato accepts and rejects from Parmenides. See, e.g., Vlastos 1981: ch. 3 ("Degrees of reality in Plato"); Annas 1981: ch. 8; Sedley 2007b.

Questions about how to distinguish senses of "to be" are discussed in
Brown 1994.

90 *Prt.* 356d4 may allude to Protagoras' characteristic doctrine, which,
however, is not the focus of discussion in this dialogue. *Cra.* 384c–391c
contains a discussion of Protagoras' position, and 439b–440e contains
a discussion of Heraclitean flux. In these ways the *Cratylus* (which I take
to be a middle dialogue, earlier than the *Phaedo*) anticipates the
Theaetetus, and shows that the *Theaetetus* indicates Plato's return to
questions that had occupied him earlier (just as the *Sophist* returns to
some questions raised in the *Euthydemus*, which I take to be an early
dialogue).

3   Stylometry and Chronology

Leonard Brandwood

For a correct understanding of Plato, account needs to be taken of the fact that his philosophical activity spanned some fifty years, during which time certain doctrines underwent considerable changes. To trace this development and so be able to identify the final expression of his thought, it is essential to know in what order the dialogues were written, but there is little help in this quest either from external sources or from the dialogues themselves.[1] Regarding the former, the only information likely to be reliable is Aristotle's statement that the *Laws* was written after the *Republic*.[2] This is repeated by Diogenes Laertius (III 37) and Olympiodorus (*Prol.* VI 24), who add that the *Laws* was still in an unrevised state on wax tablets when Plato died and was published posthumously by one of his students, Philip of Opus. As for internal evidence, cross-references in the *Sophist* (217a) and *Politicus* (257a, 258b) indicate the prior composition of the former, while the *Timaeus* (27a) mentions the *Critias* as its sequel. Rather less definite are the apparent reference in the *Timaeus* (17b–19b) to the *Republic*, in the *Sophist* to the *Parmenides* (217c)[3] and *Theaetetus* (216a), and in the *Theaetetus* to the *Parmenides* (183e). There is one other important piece of evidence: In the introduction to the *Theaetetus* (143c), Plato renounces the reported dialogue form with a clear indication that the use of introductory formulae, such as καί ἐγώ εἶπον ("I myself said"), and of interlocutors' replies, was becoming a nuisance. It seems unlikely, therefore, that any of his works written in this form are later than the *Theaetetus*.

In the eighteenth century and the first half of the nineteenth attempts to establish the chronological sequence were based on an assessment of each dialogue's argument, followed by the formulation of a line of development for the philosopher's ideas. Not surprisingly the subjective nature of this approach led to a considerable discrepancy among the conclusions of the various scholars,[4] so that by the 1860s hope was beginning to fade, and G. Grote, for example, was to be found declaring that the problem was incapable of solutions.[5]

Two years later, however, hope was revived with the introduction of the stylistic method by L. Campbell.[6] Observing an increased use of technical terminology in what were then taken to be Plato's latest works, the *Timaeus*, *Critias*, and *Laws*, he calculated from Ast's *Lexicon* the number of words that each of twenty-four dialogues[7] had in common exclusively with these three. Then dividing this figure by the number of pages in each dialogue, he arrived at the average occurrence per page and arranged the dialogues in a series according to their relative degree of affinity to the three latest works in respect of vocabulary. The series was headed by the *Politicus*, *Phaedrus*, and *Sophist*, each showing an average occurrence of more than one word per page. Mindful of the influence of subject matter on the choice of words, Campbell did not follow his figures slavishly in drawing conclusions about chronological order, but remarked that, combined with some further observations on rhythm and word order,[8] they did at least support his view of the close temporal affinity of the *Sophist* and *Politicus* to the *Timaeus*, *Critias*, and *Laws*.

The usefulness of this method for determining the chronological order of works was discovered independently by W. Dittenberger,[9] who investigated two aspects of Plato's vocabulary, the first being the use of μήν ("indeed") with certain other particles. The distribution of three of these (see Table 3.1) enabled him to divide the dialogues into two groups according to their occurrence or nonoccurrence,[10] the later group being indicated by the presence in it of the *Laws*. The fact that all three expressions were found together in each work except for the *Symposium* and *Lysis* led him to conclude that these two works were the earliest of the second group. Since the date of the *Symposium*'s composition was fixed as shortly after 385 BCE by what is clearly a topical allusion in it to the dispersal of

Mantinea, which took place in that year,[11] he believed that τί μήν was a conversational idiom of the Dorians in Sicily, which Plato had visited a few years before. In support of this view he noted that the expression was not to be found either in earlier Attic prose or in Aristophanes, though significantly the equivalent Doric σά μάν did occur in the latter.[12]

Counting two instances of γε μήν in the *Republic* in contrast to twenty-four in the *Laws*, and recalling Aristotle's testimony about their relative dates, Dittenberger concluded that the works of group IIa (see Table 1, next page), where the occurrence of this expression is sparse, were earlier than those of IIb.

As the subject of his second investigation he took two pairs of synonyms, ὥσπερ–καθάπερ ("like") and ἕως(περ)–μέχριπερ ("until"), together with the pleonastic combination τάχα ἴσως ("maybe perhaps"). Although these criteria did not distinguish works of the first group from those of the second, they did reinforce the evidence of γε μήν for a division of the second group, since all the IIb dialogues with the exception of the *Parmenides* show a preference for καθάπερ over ὥσπερ and the exclusive (apart from a solitary instance in the *Apology*) use of μέχριπερ and τάχα ἴσως. As for the *Parmenides*, he was so puzzled by its inconsistencies that he was inclined to doubt its authenticity.

Dittenberger, like Campbell, considered his main achievement to be the demonstration of the lateness of the *Sophist* and *Politicus*, works that previously had been thought to be much earlier. He had also provided evidence for a later dating of the *Philebus*, *Phaedrus*, and *Theaetetus*, the former after the *Republic*, the latter two close to it, the position for the *Phaedrus* being especially significant in that it had frequently been regarded in the past as one of Plato's earliest compositions.

The next worthwhile contribution came from M. Schanz,[13] whose research resembled Dittenberger's second investigation in that it compared pairs of synonyms, in this case three in number, all denoting "in reality" or "in truth" (Table 3.2). On the basis of his figures he too divided the dialogues into three chronological groups.

Table 3.1 *Frequency of occurrence of certain expressions in the dialogues, used by Dittenberger as a means of ordering them chronologically*

	Pages (Didot)	τί μήν;	ἀλλά ... μήν;	γε μήν	ὥσπερ	καθάπερ	ἕως (περ)	μέχριπερ	τάχα ἴσως
I									
Ap.	19.7				31		3		(1)
Cri.	9.5				8				
Euphr.	11.7				7				
Prt.	39.5				68		6		
Chrm.	18.1				9		3		
La.	17.8				12	1	2		
H. Mi.	10.1				8				
Euthd.	27.9				30	1	2		
Meno	23.3				21	1	4		
Grg.	61.6				69	1	3		
Cra.	42.3				80	2	8		
Phd.	49.2				80		16		
IIa									
Smp.	39.3		2	1	55	2	8		
Lys.	14.9	1	4		17		(2)		
Phdr.	39.0	11	1	1	27	4	5		
Rep.	194.0	34	11	2	212	5	23		
Tht.	53.0	13	1	1	47	2	10		
IIb									
Prm.	31.2	6	2	5	9		(5)		
Phil.	43.2	26	2	7	9	27	3	1	3
Sph.	39.6	12	2	5	9	14	3	1	2
Pol.	43.2	20	3	8	16	34	5	3	3
Ti.	53.0			6	10	18	3	4	1
Criti.	11.2			1	2	5	1	1	
Laws	236.8	48	2	24	24	148	16	16	11

Notes: Different texts can produce different occurrences of a given word. The figures in the tables are those provided by the scholar concerned except for large errors, when the original figure is replaced by one in parenthesis; this always refers to the Oxford Classical Text. Further details are supplied in the tables of Brandwood 1990.

The ἕως(περ) figures for groups I and IIa, apart from those in parentheses, were provided later by Ritter.

ἴσως τάχ ἄν at Ap. 31a3 was ignored by Dittenberger, though he included the similarly inverted form at *Ti.* 38e2.

The last, comprising the *Philebus, Politicus, Timaeus,* and *Laws,* was characterized both by the complete absence of two of the synonyms, τῷ ὄντι and ὡς ἀληθῶς, and by the occurrence in it alone of a third, ἀλήθεια,[14] while the middle group, consisting of the *Cratylus, Euthydemus, Phaedrus, Theaetetus, Republic,* and *Sophist,* was distinguished from the earlier by the presence in it of ὄντως.

Comparison of his results with those of Dittenberger reveal only slight differences; indeed his allocation of the *Sophist* to the middle group on the basis of a single occurrence of τῷ ὄντι and three of ὡς ἀληθῶς is hardly justified, considering that their frequency in relation to the respective synonyms is the reverse of that found in the other works of this group. As for the *Cratylus* and *Euthydemus,* the argument for placing them in the middle group is weak, consisting of a solitary instance of ὄντως; in each case, furthermore, this is the reading of inferior manuscripts. In this connection it is also worth noting that ὄντως does not appear in the first four books of the *Republic,* casting further doubt on the reading of this form in the text of the *Cratylus* and *Euthydemus.* Unlike Dittenberger he found no evidence to suggest that the *Symposium* and *Lysis* belonged in the middle rather than the early group.

The next feature of Plato's style to be recognized[15] as useful for chronological purposes, his varying use of reply formulae, was to form the subject of several investigations during the following three decades.[16] Since these cannot all be treated here, that of Ritter, which was by far the most extensive, may be taken as representative. Convinced by the work of Dittenberger and Schanz that the *Sophist, Politicus, Philebus, Timaeus, Critias,* and *Laws* formed a discrete chronological group, he compiled a list of forty-three linguistic features, both reply formulae and others, which supported the view that these six dialogues marked the culmination of Plato's literary activity. A sample of these is reproduced in Table 3.3. By counting how many were present in each dialogue he was able to determine its degree of linguistic resemblance to the *Laws,* which he regarded as the last to be written. The result was as follows: *Laws* 40, *Phil.* 37, *Pol.*

Table 3.2 *Frequency of occurrence of three pairs of synonyms in the dialogues, used by Schanz as a means of ordering them chronologically*

	Pages (Didot)	τῷ ὄντι	ὄντως	ὡς ἀληθῶς	ἀληθῶς	τῇ ἀληθείᾳ	ἀληθείᾳ
				Schanz's first chronological group			
Ap.	19.7	5		2	1	3	
Euphr.	11.7	1		1	1		
Grg.	61.6	9		7		6	
La.	17.8	2		7			
Lys.	14.9	6		2			
Prt.	39.5	2		2	1	1	3[a]
Smp.	39.3	5		3			
Phd.	49.2	14		11	2		
				Schanz's second chronological group			
Cra.	42.3	1	1	3	1	4	
Euthd.	27.9	4	1	2	1	2	
Tht.	53.0	6	1	8	1	2	
Phdr.	39.0	8	6	7	1	2	
Rep. I–IV	80.5	13		19	2	3	
V–VII	60.5	18	5	6	3	3	

Table 3.2 (cont.)

	Pages (Didot)	τῷ ὄντι	ὄντως	ὡς ἀληθῶς	ἀληθῶς	τῇ ἀληθείᾳ	ἀληθείᾳ
VIII–X	53.0	10	4	3	3	9	
Sph.	39.6	1	21	3	6		
Schanz's last chronological group							
Phil.	43.2		15		7		1
Pol.	43.2		11		4	1	
Ti.	53.0		8		3	1	1
Laws	236.8		50		6	3	3
Works excluded by Schanz							
Chrm.	18.1			5			
Cri.	9.5			2		2	
H. Ma.	19.0	5				3	
Menex.	11.6	6			1	1	
Meno	23.3				2		
Prm.	31.2			1	1	1	
Epin.	14.1	1	16			1	1

Note: The last seven works were not included in his table by Schanz, some because, like *H. Mi.* and *Criti.*, they contained examples neither of τῷ ὄντι nor of ὄντως, others because they were considered unauthentic. The figures for these relate to the OCT.

a see note 14.

37, *Sph.* 35, *Rep.* 28, *Tht.* 25, *Phdr.* 21, *Prm.* 17, *Epin.* 12, *Cra.* 8, *Lys.* 8, *Phd.* 7, *La.* 5, *Euthd.* 4, *Prt.* 4, *Menex.* 4, *Smp.* 3, *Chrm.* 3, *Grg.* 3, *H. Ma.* 3, *Ion* 3, *Ap.* 2, *Meno* 2, *Cri.* 2, *Euphr.* 1. This seemed to confirm the view of his predecessors, that between the late works and the mass of early dialogues there was a middle group consisting of the *Republic*, *Theaetetus*, and *Phaedrus*.[17]

To determine whether the *Timaeus* and *Critias* belonged to the last or middle group, it was necessary to exclude from consideration those of the forty-three linguistic features, such as reply formulae, which were connected with dialogue, these two works being almost wholly narrative in form. Of the nineteen features remaining, the middle and late works possessed the following share: *Laws* 18, *Ti.* 17, *Phil.* 16, *Pol.* 16, *Sph.* 14, *Criti.* 11, *Rep.* 9, *Phdr.* 8, *Tht.* 6, *Prm.* 1 – indicating a position for the *Timaeus* and by implication its sequel the *Critias* in the last rather than the middle group.

Turning next to the question of the order of composition within each of these groups, Ritter first had to consider the possibility that an extensive work such as the *Republic* did not all appear at one time, but that the other dialogues were composed either contemporaneously with or in between parts of it. When to this end he produced statistics of his forty-three criteria for each of the ten books, it became apparent to him that, while Books II–X had a fairly uniform style, Book I exhibited a number of features that were typical of the early rather than the middle chronological group.[18] This seemed to justify the assumption that Book I was written separately some time before the rest, and the sporadic occurrence in it of expressions characteristic of the middle group[19] could be explained by the assumption that it underwent some revision before being incorporated into the larger work.

Of the dialogues in the final group Ritter considered the *Sophist* to be the earliest, since certain expressions characteristic of Plato's earlier style were still to be found in it before disappearing entirely, for example, τῷ ὄντι and ὡς ἀληθῶς (cf. Table 3.2). On the evidence of other

Table 3.3 Frequency of occurrence of selected linguistic features in the dialogues, used by Ritter as a means of ordering them chronologically

	La.	Chrm.	Prt.	Euthd.	Cra.	Ap.	Chr.	Euphr.	Grg.	Phd.	Meno	Smp.	Tht.	Phdr.	Rep.	Sph.	Pol.	Phil.	Ti.	Crit.	Laws	Ion	H. Ma.	H. Mi.	Menex.	Lys.	Prm.	Epin.
Pages [ed. Didot]	18	18	40	28	42	20	10	12	62	49	23	39	53	39	194	40	43	43	53	11	237	9	19	10	12	15	31	14
Total of reply formulae	77	110	50	107	203	10	22	64	336	176	182	36	285	69	1260	315	251	314	13		568	43	95	71	5	120	486	9
1. ἀληθῆ λέγεις	5	2	6	3	9		2	4	5	6	4	5	2	1	9	3	1	2			7	3	5	1		3	4	
2. ὡληθῆ	1	3	1							1			9		29	7	5	2			4		(1)			6	18	
3. ἀληθῆ (λέγεις), ὀρθῶς λέγεις	6	6	6	3	10		2	5	5	8	5	5	14	2	48	10	8	6			22	(3)	(5)	(1)		10	24	
4. ἀληθέστατα (λέγεις), ὀρθύτατα λέγεις	1				1					4		1	8	3	40	8	15	22			36						7	
5. πάνυ γε	10	16	3	20	38	3		12	48	23	27	6	5	1	40	10	7	9			4	4	12	3	1	18	28	
6. πάνυ μὲν οὖν	5	5	3	3	13			3	7	17	5		16	2	64	14	18	21			49		6			1	15	
7. πάντάπασι μὲν οὖν	1												9	3	38	10	4	4	1		13						7	
8. καὶ μάλα				1				1		1			4	3	47	4	2	7			6		5			1	2	
9. πῶς				1	1								4	2	31	20	17	18	1		14	1	4			1	10	
10. πῇ															4	7	6	3			3						3	
11. (τὸ) ποῖον (δὴ);	1				2				1	1			13	4	48	32	36	33			47						3	
12. δῆλον ὅτι	7	2	15	11	17	7		5	15	6	12	6	1		48	10	10	8	1	1	16	5	7	3	1	5	(3)	1
13. δῆλον ὡς												3	1		2		1	1									1	
14. σχεδόν τι	7	3	3	2	2		2	1	2	6	1	1	1		12		2	5			2	2	5			1	1	
15. σχεδόν		1			2	2	1		3	2		3			7	26	13	14	9	4	122	1	4		1	1	1	20
16. ἔνεσα	8	6	14	5	9	5	2	4	31	13	2	16	12	9	69	6	22	19	13	2	111		4	(1)	1	25	(1)	3
17. χάριν	1		1		(1)				3			1	4	8	12	1	3	3	7	2	33				1			4
18. τὸ/τὰ νῦν		1	1							1			1		1	5	5	9	7	3	79	1		(1)	1			4
19. χρεών (ἐστι)		1	1										1		1	1	3	3	7	7	57							2
20. Ionic dative form														3	6	1	4		3		85							2
21. πέρι (%)ª	13	0	2	10	3	11	0	8	10	4	10	8	12	23	23	22	26	34	16	10	31	3	0	4	20	6	7	19

Table 3.3 (cont.)

Note: 1. "You speak truly." 2. "Truly." 3. "(You speak) truly/rightly." 4. Superlatives of no. 3. 5 and 6. "Certainly." 7. "Most certainly." 8. "Very much so." 9. "How?" 10. "In what way?" 11. "What sort (indeed)?" 12 and 13. "It is obvious that." 14 and 15. "Just about." 16 and 17. "For the sake of." 18. "At the present." 19. "It is necessary." 20. Attic form with iota suffix. 21. "About."

The dialogues in the right-hand columns (*Ion*, etc.) were not included by Ritter in his main investigation on the grounds of unauthenticity.

[a] Numbers in this line indicate the anastrophic use of πέϱι, expressed as a percentage of the total occurrence of the preposition.

features that he considered particularly significant, he antedated the *Politicus* to the whole of the *Laws*, which he took to be the last work of all, and assigned to the *Philebus* a position contemporary with the first half of the *Laws*, and to the *Timaeus* and *Critias* one contemporary with the second half.[20]

Regarding the middle group, he refused to draw any conclusion from the fact that out of the forty-three expressions used as criteria for lateness of composition the *Republic* contained twenty-eight, the *Theaetetus* twenty-five, and the *Phaedrus* twenty-one, since the difference in the size of the figures corresponded to that of the works. A direct comparison of the *Theaetetus* and *Phaedrus* revealed that seven of the expressions favored a later date for the *Phaedrus*, only four the reverse order. Where the *Republic* stood in relation to the other two dialogues he could not say; on account of the time that the composition of such a lengthy work must have taken he was inclined to believe that the *Theaetetus*, and perhaps even the *Phaedrus* too, might have been written contemporaneously with it.[21]

About the chronological relationship of the rest of the works, which he assigned to the earliest group, he was not prepared to hazard any conjecture, since their style was generally uniform and such differences as were apparent were insignificant.

Toward the end of the last century the separate threads of research were pulled together by W. Lutoslawski.[22] His method was similar to that of Ritter, being an enumeration of the "late" linguistic features in each work, but whereas Ritter used only about 40 criteria, he amassed 500. This was made possible by the fact that for him a characteristic of Plato's later style did not necessarily mean an expression occurring in the *Laws*, as it did for Ritter, still trying to prove the lateness of the *Sophist*, *Politicus*, *Philebus*, *Timaeus*, and *Critias*, but one occurring in any of these six dialogues. To produce this larger total he selected what he considered to be the most important of the statistics published by earlier investigators of Plato's style, both chronologists and philologists, in the case of the latter determining himself which features were meaningful. To each he allocated a value of one, two, three, or four units, according to the degree of importance that it seemed to him to have, then after counting how many of the 500 features occurred in each dialogue, evaluated in terms of units of affinity its approximation to the final group or, in the case of the works in this group, to the *Laws*. Like Ritter he concluded that the last chronological group was preceded by one consisting of the *Republic* II–X, *Phaedrus*, *Theaetetus*, and also the *Parmenides*. His results, however, were vitiated by several flaws in his method, the most serious being the arbitrary nature of his evaluation of the importance of the various features and the use of some that were unsuitable, such as those which instead of being characteristic primarily of the last group were characteristic of another or of none.[23]

Contemporaneously with Lutoslawski's work, C. Baron published the results of research into Plato's use of the anastrophe of περί ("about"), that is, its occurrence after instead of before the substantive.[24] He discovered that its incidence was noticeably higher in works generally thought to be late (cf. Table 3.3, where it is expressed as a percentage of the total occurrence of the preposition),[25] though the behavior of the *Parmenides* was conspicuously deviant from this trend, as it had been in Ritter's investigation.[26] There appears to have been no one reason for the increasing use of anastrophe by Plato, but at least in works of the final group the avoidance of hiatus may plausibly be surmised.[27]

By the turn of the century, then, research into Plato's style had succeeded in separating the dialogues into three chronological groups, but had failed to determine the sequence within any of these, apart from some evidence to suggest that the *Sophist* was the earliest work of the last group. Shortly afterward new ground was broken, when G. Janell,[28] following comments made much earlier by F. Blass,[29] investigated the frequency of hiatus.[30] He began by distinguishing two types, permissible and objectionable. In the former he included two broad classes of hiatus: those which Plato could have avoided, if he had wished, by some simple means such as elision, crasis, or the choice of an alternative form, and those involving words of common occurrence, such as the definite article and καί ("and"), where avoidance seemed to be scarcely practicable.[31] The incidence of the rest, which he classed as objectionable, is shown in Table 3.4.

The conclusion that Janell drew from these figures was that Plato's treatment of hiatus differed considerably in two separate periods. In the first, comprising all the works down to the *Phaedrus*, Plato was not troubled by hiatus of any kind, but in the second, he carefully avoided those types of hiatus identified as objectionable. He made no attempt to deduce anything about chronology from the figures for the dialogues of the first period, and clearly there would be little point in it, since, if Plato's avoidance of hiatus was an abrupt, not a gradual development in his style, as the statistics would seem to indicate, then any variation in its frequency here would probably be accidental. With the last group of dialogues, however, one might well expect to find some development, either an increasing or a decreasing avoidance, or a third possibility, an avoidance that increased up to a certain point, then decreased. Janell himself, however, was not greatly concerned with chronology, his sole contribution in respect of the order of the last group of works being that "obviously Plato was prevented by death from applying the last touches to the *Phil.* and *Laws*. This seems to be the explanation of the difference in frequency of hiatus between these two and *Sph.*, *Pol.*, *Ti.*, *Criti.*"

Lastly he remarked on the frequency of hiatus in the *Phaedrus* being somewhat lower than in the rest of the earlier dialogues. To explain this he accepted Blass's view, that Plato later revised it, and in support of this thesis cited several passages where hiatus appears to be avoided more carefully than usual, such as (1) 250c ταῦτα μὲν οὖν – 251a τοῖς παιδικοῖς, (2) 259b οὐ μὲν δή – 259e μέλλῃ, (3) 265a ᾤμην σε – 263d ἄχαρι, and (4) 265e τὸ πάλιν– 267d τίθενται ὄνομα, with two, two, one, and ten instances of objectionable hiatus respectively.[32] It could be argued that similar passages may occur in other dialogues outside the last group. Without examining the whole Platonic corpus in detail it is impossible to refute this hypothesis absolutely,

Table 3.4 *Frequency of "objectionable" hiatus in the dialogues, as calculated by Janell*

	Instances of hiatus	Pages (Didot)	Average per page		Instances of hiatus	Pages (Didot)	Average per page
Lys.	685	14.9	46.0	Rep. II	607	18.8	32.3
Euthd.	1258	27.9	45.1	Rep. III	706	22.0	32.1
Prm.	1376	31.2	44.1	Rep. V	695	22.2	31.3
Chrm.	797	18.1	44.0	Cra.	1319	42.3	31.2
Rep. I	901	20.5	44.0	Menex.	327	11.6	28.2
H. Ma.	779	19.0	41.0	Phdr.	932	39.0	23.9
Phd.	2017	49.2	41.0	Laws V	126	15.9	6.7 (7.9)
Prt.	1591	39.5	40.3	Laws III	121	19.4	6.2
Rep. IX	601	15.1	39.8	Laws XII	152	21.1	5.7 (7.2)
Rep. IV	757	19.1	39.6	Laws X	108	19.5	5.6
Ap.	764	19.7	38.8	Laws II	89	16.3	5.5
Meno	892	23.3	38.3	Laws XI	172	19.4	5.4 (8.9)
H. Mi.	378	10.1	37.4	Laws I	95	18.6	5.1
Cri.	342	9.5	36.0	Laws IX	189	22.2	5.1 (8.5)
Smp.	1414	39.3	36.0	Laws IV	77	14.7	4.8 (5.2)
Grg.	2182	61.6	35.4	Laws I–XII	1389	236.8	4.7 (5.9)
Euphr.	413	11.7	35.3	Phil.	160	43.2	3.7
Rep. I–X	6833	193.7	35.3	Laws VIII	94	16.9	3.7 (5.6)
Rep. VII	661	18.8	35.2	Epin.	40	14.1	2.8

Table 3.4 (cont.)

	Instances of hiatus	Pages (Didot)	Average per page		Instances of hiatus	Pages (Didot)	Average per page
Rep. X	664	19.3	34.4	Laws VII	71	27.6	2.5
Ion	312	9.1	34.3	Laws VI	95	25.2	2.4 (3.8)
La.	598	17.8	33.6	Ti.	62	53.0	1.2
Rep. VIII	615	18.6	33.1	Criti.	9	11.2	0.8
Tht.	1733	53.0	32.7	Sph.	24	39.6	0.6
Rep. VI	626	19.3	32.4	Pol.	19	43.2	0.4

Note: For the figures in parenthesis, see CPD, 155 n.3.
The figures for H. Ma., Ion, and Epin., which Janell omitted from his investigation, are the author's.

but one may at least cast some doubt on it. On the basis of the figures in Table 3.4, *Menexenus* and *Cratylus* are the works in which there would be an expectation of finding passages with a scarcity of hiatus similar to that in the *Phaedrus*; yet in reading them one is not consciously aware, as with the *Phaedrus*, that some parts of the text contain fewer instances of hiatus than the rest.

This subjective impression can be given a numerical expression; if, for instance, with the first passage above one counts the number of words between the hiatus immediately preceding ταῦτα μὲν οὖν and that immediately succeeding τοῖς παιδικοῖς, the result is 210 (OCT). For purposes of comparison, therefore, it may be described as 2 instances of hiatus in 210 words. Similarly the second passage will be 2 in 211 words, the third 1 in 196 words, and the fourth 10 in 600 words. By contrast, in the *Cratylus* (a work of roughly equal length), there are only two passages of note: 400c7–401b7 with 5 in 217 words and 404e7–405c5 with 3 in 183 words. In the *Menexenus* there are three passages: 234c6–235b8 with 2 in 124 words, 242d8–243b4 with 3 in 151 words, and 240e3–242a7 with 10 in 285 words. Since neither can be said to match the *Phaedrus*, there is some evidence to support Janell's view of an apparent tendency on Plato's part to avoid hiatus more carefully in some parts of the *Phaedrus* than in others.

Janell's inquiry confirmed the unity of the final chronological group established by earlier research. Regarding a possible development of hiatus avoidance within this group, if one assumes that it was not haphazard and that the *Laws*, at least in part, was probably the last to be written, it would appear that toward the end of his life Plato was less strict in his approach. This would be psychologically plausible in that, having demonstrated his ability to match his rival Isocrates in this aspect of prose style, he could afford to adopt a more relaxed attitude. As the incidence of hiatus in the *Philebus* is similar to that in the *Laws*, one might argue that it is the closest to it of the other five or that it represents the first serious attempt to put Isocrates' principles into practice before achieving greater success in the *Timaeus*, *Critias*, *Sophist*, and *Politicus*.

Yet another aspect of Plato's style was revealed by W. Kaluscha, who examined the rhythm of his prose.[33] Since prior to the advent of computers it was impracticable to analyze the whole text in this respect, he confined his investigation to the part of the sentence considered in antiquity to be the most important rhythmically, namely the clausula, which he interpreted as the end of a period or colon. This, for the same reason of economy, was regarded as consisting of only five syllables, either long (–) or short (ᴗ) metrically, yielding thirty-two different combinations.

He first looked at the clausulae of the *Laws* in order either to corroborate or to contradict Blass's belief that in the latter part of his life Plato began, under Isocrates' influence, to prefer certain rhythms to others. He then compared with them the clausulae of the *Sophist, Politicus, Philebus, Timaeus,* and *Critias,* supposedly late works, on the one hand, and those of the *Protagoras, Crito,* and *Apology,* supposedly early works, on the other, to see which showed the greater similarity. Since his initial survey of the *Laws* indicated that the four most frequent combinations in every book were types ending in a long vowel and only in a few books did the fifth most frequent end in a short vowel, he decided that it was possible to regard the ambiguous quantity of the final syllable[34] as long in every case and reduced his statistics accordingly to cover sixteen combinations (Table 3.5).[35]

He observed a preference for five clausulae in the *Laws:* II 4, III 9, and IV 4, each of which represented one of the five highest figures in all twelve books; II 10 likewise with the exception of Books III and VIII; V, which had one of the five highest figures in half of the books. These five formed the following percentage of the total number of clausulae in each book:

I	46.9	IV	54.4	VII	54.4	X	60.1
II	55.3	V	53.1	VIII	51.2	XI	52.4
III	51.7	VI	55.9	IX	56.8	XII	54.6

That is to say, in all except Book I they were more frequent than the other eleven taken together. Conversely, there appeared to be a particular aversion to four clausulae: II 7, III 3, III 6, and III 8.

On comparing the *Protagoras*, *Crito*, and *Apology* with the *Laws*, Kaluscha noted the following differences: First, only two of the clausulae favored in the latter work (III 9 and IV 4) occurred frequently, but then they did so in every period of Plato's literary activity;[36] secondly, the clausulae to which there was an aversion in the *Laws* were not avoided – on the contrary, they were common, thus lending support to the view that their later avoidance was deliberate.

By contrast he found that the prose rhythm of the *Sophist*, *Politicus*, *Philebus*, *Timaeus*, and *Critias* was similar to that of the *Laws*. In the case of the *Philebus* it was practically identical, since its five most frequent clausulae were the same, and it avoided the four unpopular clausulae to an equal degree. In both the *Sophist* and *Politicus*, three of the five most common *Laws* clausulae also showed the highest frequencies, and the unpopular ones were avoided, though II 7 and III 6 not so carefully in the *Sophist* as in the *Politicus* and *Philebus*. In the *Timaeus* also, three of the five highest frequencies coincided with those of the *Laws*, but with a difference: whereas in the *Sophist*, *Politicus*, and *Philebus* the three highest-frequency positions were occupied by members of this favored group, here the top two positions were claimed by other clausulae, leaving only the third, fourth, and fifth places for the *Laws* forms. Moreover, the unpopular clausulae of the *Laws* were avoided less scrupulously than in the other three works.[37]

Kaluscha concluded that these works belonged together chronologically and that in accordance with the degree of similarity of their prose rhythm to that of the *Laws* the probable order of composition was *Timaeus*, *Critias*, *Sophist*, *Politicus*, *Philebus*, *Laws*. In support of this sequence he referred to the following: The *Politicus*, *Philebus*, and *Laws* were connected by their stricter avoidance of the four clausulae mentioned previously (II 7, III 3, III 6, and III 8), their combined occurrence as a percentage of the total number of clausulae

Table 3.5 *Prose rhythm in the dialogues: relative frequency by percentage of different types of clausula, as calculated by Kaluscha*

		Prt.	Cri.	Ap.	Laws I	II	III	IV	V	VI	VII	VIII	IX	X	XI	XII	Phil.	Pol.	Sph.	Criti.	Ti.
I 5	⏑⏑⏑⏑	4.2	2.6	3.4	5.6	6.4	**8.5**	6.4	9.1	7.9	6.7	5.6	5.1	3.6	5.2	4.9	7.3	4.5	5.3	**7.3**	5.9
II 4	⏑⏑⏑	3.8	1.9	3.6	**8.8**	**9.0**	**16.6**	**11.7**	**12.3**	**14.2**	**12.4**	**12.3**	**14.4**	**14.8**	**10.1**	**13.2**	**9.3**	6.5	5.9	**8.0**	**7.2**
7	⏑⏑⏑	5.2	3.1	6.1	4.1	3.0	4.1	2.1	3.7	1.4	2.2	1.6	2.7	3.9	2.6	4.3	2.8	4.2	6.4	4.0	**8.6**
9	⏑⏑⏑	4.0	3.8	4.2	4.4	3.8	6.0	6.8	7.8	5.2	4.7	6.3	5.4	6.4	5.2	6.6	4.5	5.6	5.7	4.7	4.1
10	⏑⏑⏑	4.2	6.3	6.6	**10.0**	**11.3**	6.6	**10.3**	**9.9**	**12.0**	**8.2**	**7.9**	**7.5**	**8.4**	6.0	6.6	**9.4**	**7.5**	**7.5**	**13.3**	**7.3**
III 3	—⏑⏑	6.3	5.1	6.1	5.6	2.6	2.2	4.6	4.1	5.1	2.7	2.4	2.7	3.1	6.0	3.6	4.7	3.9	5.5	6.0	6.7
5	⏑⏑	**8.0**	**7.6**	**7.5**	3.8	4.5	2.8	5.3	5.8	1.5	5.6	3.6	4.8	4.2	3.4	3.6	4.3	4.2	6.1	3.3	6.4
6	⏑	**7.3**	7.0	**8.6**	1.8	1.1	1.6	1.8	0.8	0.8	1.3	0.8	1.2	1.4	0.4	1.0	1.5	1.2	5.1	6.0	4.5
7	⏑	6.9	6.3	6.4	6.2	3.0	4.7	2.8	2.5	6.3	6.0	5.6	3.0	3.4	3.7	4.6	5.7	**7.7**	6.4	4.0	6.0
8	⏑	6.3	**9.5**	6.6	2.3	1.5	1.9	2.8	0.8	1.1	2.9	2.0	2.7	1.4	2.2	3.3	1.9	1.9	2.9	5.3	5.5
9	⏑	6.9	**9.5**	5.5	**11.1**	**10.2**	**11.0**	**10.3**	**9.5**	**12.0**	**12.9**	**9.5**	**15.3**	**10.9**	**11.2**	**13.5**	**12.0**	**9.7**	**7.8**	**8.0**	6.4
IV 1	⏑—	7.1	7.0	**7.7**	5.9	7.5	6.6	4.6	3.3	5.4	5.8	**9.1**	7.2	3.4	**9.7**	5.3	6.7	6.2	5.4	5.3	4.6
2	—⏑	**8.1**	7.0	**8.5**	**7.6**	5.3	**6.9**	5.7	5.3	6.3	4.2	6.7	5.4	5.0	6.7	**6.9**	4.5	**8.3**	**7.2**	4.7	6.3
3	—⏑	**7.6**	6.3	**7.4**	5.9	6.0	3.1	2.5	3.7	2.2	3.6	4.8	3.0	4.2	2.2	1.3	3.1	4.8	6.7	**8.0**	**9.7**
4	—⏑	**7.7**	**10.1**	5.6	**11.7**	**13.9**	**11.6**	**11.4**	**11.5**	**9.3**	**11.8**	**15.5**	**10.8**	**18.2**	**17.6**	**13.5**	**14.5**	**13.6**	**9.9**	4.7	**6.8**
V	—	6.3	6.9	6.6	5.3	**10.9**	6.0	**10.7**	**9.9**	**8.4**	**9.1**	6.3	**8.7**	**7.8**	**7.5**	**7.9**	**7.8**	**10.1**	6.0	**7.3**	4.0

Note: The figures of the five most frequent types of clausula in each work are in bold type.

being *Ti.* 25.3, *Criti.* 21.3, *Sph.* 19.9, *Pol.* 11.2, *Phil.* 10.9, *Laws* 10.0. On the other hand the *Timaeus*, *Critias*, and *Sophist* were connected by the small variation in frequency of their various clausulae, neither a strong preference for nor prejudice against particular forms being observable. This can be shown numerically by a calculation based on Table 3.5: taking 6.3 as the mean percentage frequency for the sixteen clausulae and observing the difference from this of the actual percentage of each, the average deviation is *Ti.* 1.3, *Criti.* 1.8, *Sph.* 1.0, *Pol.* 2.5, *Phil.* 2.9, *Laws* 3.1.

Turning to the remaining dialogues, Kaluscha discovered that they resembled the *Protagoras*, *Crito*, and *Apology* in lacking any consistent tendency to prefer certain clausulae and therefore concluded that together they belonged to an earlier period, in which Plato showed little or no conscious interest in prose rhythm.

This same subject was investigated again some years later by L. Billig,[38] who condemned Kaluscha's treatment of it as "unsatisfactory in many ways." Although he did not say what these were, they may have included the failure to mention the edition used, to specify the minimum length of sentence, and to define certain principles of scansion, all of which made it difficult to verify the accuracy of Kaluscha's statistics. He attempted to forestall similar criticism of his own inquiry by providing information about his procedure in these respects.

His primary reason for a reinvestigation, however, came from observing in the *Laws* the frequent occurrence of the fourth paeon (◡◡◡◡) as a clausula, the rhythm recommended by Aristotle (*Rhetoric* III 8) for this position. Unlike Kaluscha he did not restrict the clausula to the last five syllables of the sentence, but permitted such variation between four and six syllables as seemed appropriate, the basic fourth paeon, for instance, being extendable by one or two extra syllables (Table 3.6).

In the *Laws* Billig noted the high incidence not only of the fourth paeon and its variants but also of two other clausulae (–◡◡ and —◡). If

Table 3.6 *Prose rhythm in the dialogues: relative frequency by percentage of different types of clausula (broadly defined), as calculated by Billig*

						Laws												
	Ti.	Sph.	Criti	Pol.	Phil.	I	II	III	IV	V	VI	VII	VIII	IX	X	XI	XII
[I] ⏑⏑⏑⏑	12.0	11.5	16.2	14.2	17.1	16.2	14.0	22.8	18.8	23.5	21.8	19.7	17.4	22.4	17.5	15.5	18.6
⏑⏑–⏑	6.4	7.3	14.4	8.7	11.0	9.3	11.5	8.8	9.1	10.8	12.4	8.4	10.7	9.6	10.4	6.3	7.7
⏑⏑–⏑	2.9	3.9	1.8	3.7	4.4	3.8	2.0	8.0	6.6	8.3	4.9	5.5	6.2	6.9	6.3	6.3	7.7
⏑⏑–⏑	3.1	4.8	–	6.6	6.2	4.1	3.0	4.4	4.6	0.6	5.3	5.5	5.0	4.1	4.9	1.2	5.0
Total of [I]	24.4	27.5	32.4	33.2	38.7	33.4	30.5	44.0	39.1	43.2	44.4	39.1	39.3	43.0	39.1	29.3	39.0
[II] –⏑⏑	12.6	17.8	13.5	21.2	23.5	21.3	20.1	21.7	27.4	22.3	22.3	23.4	23.6	25.0	30.5	37.4	24.9
[III] –––⏑	8.6	10.5	6.3	16.3	16.0	14.2	23.2	11.6	12.2	10.8	13.6	13.9	18.6	16.8	11.1	11.5	13.6
Total of [I], [II] & [III]	45.6	55.8	52.2	70.7	78.2	68.9	73.8	77.3	78.7	76.3	80.3	76.4	81.5	84.8	80.7	78.2	77.5
–⏑–⏑	5.5	7.0	5.4	8.1	4.4	7.9	8.5	5.2	5.6	5.1	5.3	6.5	5.6	5.0	3.7	7.5	6.8
––⏑⏑	10.1	7.3	9.9	4.1	2.9	5.2	4.5	2.8	2.0	0.6	1.5	2.5	4.5	2.7	3.0	2.9	2.7
⏑–⏑⏑⏑	16.1	11.5	9.9	6.8	5.9	7.9	6.5	6.4	5.6	5.1	4.5	4.4	3.4	1.3	4.9	5.2	5.9
–⏑⏑–⏑	3.1	2.3	2.7	2.4	1.0	1.1	2.0	2.0	2.0	0.6	1.5	1.9	–	0.9	0.8	1.7	1.4
–⏑⏑–⏑	1.8	3.2	2.7	1.3	1.4	1.9	1.0	1.6	–	1.3	1.5	1.5	1.1	0.5	0.8	1.2	0.9
⏑–⏑–⏑	12.4	8.4	11.7	5.8	5.3	6.0	2.0	3.2	5.6	8.3	4.1	6.1	2.8	3.2	4.2	3.5	5.0
⏑–⏑⏑ / ⏑⏑–⏑	5.2	4.7	5.4	1.1	0.8	1.1	1.5	1.2	0.5	2.6	1.1	0.9	1.1	0.9	2.2	–	–
Total of remainder	54.2	44.4	47.7	29.6	21.7	31.1	26.0	22.4	21.3	23.6	19.5	23.8	18.5	15.5	19.6	22.0	22.7

Notes: The figures for the *Criti.*, which Billig did not include in his investigation, were calculated by the author in accordance with his principles; likewise those for the *Sph.*, since a check failed to substantiate Billig's own figures. The total occurrence for each work is not always exactly 100% owing to rounding up or down of decimals.

there were an even distribution of the fifteen clausulae, these six forms would constitute 40 percent. Perceiving that their actual occurrence in the *Timaeus* barely exceeded this, but was almost double in the *Laws*, and assuming an increasing expertise on Plato's part in achieving these preferred forms, he reached the conclusion that the chronological sequence corresponded roughly with their increasing occurrence: *Ti.* 45.6 percent, *Criti.* 52.2 percent, *Sph.* 55.8 percent, *Pol.* 70.7 percent, *Phil.* 78.2 percent, *Laws* 77.9 percent.

More recently, the use of statistical techniques to evaluate the significance first of Kaluscha's figures, then of data from a fresh examination of the clausulae has confirmed the results obtained by the two earlier investigations.[39]

The by this time somewhat hackneyed subject of reply formulae enjoyed a late revival through a second article by H. von Arnim, which reached book proportions.[40] The aim he set himself was to make the results of his new inquiry conclusive. Previous investigations had failed to achieve this because, while they showed that certain dialogues belonged together by reason of a common possession of particular stylistic features, they did not prove that an alternative arrangement according to others was impossible. Although it had been discovered, for instance, that a large number of such features connected the *Sophist* and *Politicus* to the *Philebus*, *Timaeus*, and *Laws*, no one had thought of finding out how many connected these same two dialogues to, say, the *Symposium*, *Phaedo*, and *Critias*. Yet it was theoretically possible that such an investigation would reveal a greater number than in the former case, necessitating a complete revision of the "established" chronology.

In order to eliminate any doubt in this respect, each work needed to be compared with every other, a task of several lifetimes if the material were to be all the possible features of style. However, an alternative was available in the smaller, yet self-contained material of affirmative reply formulae, which Arnim reexamined in order to acquire as accurate data as possible, even though the ground had been partially covered before by Ritter and himself. He then compared each pair of works in respect of both types of reply formulae employed and their relative frequency.[41] In this way he identified the following groups, arranged in chronological sequence:

1) *Ion, Prt.*
2) *La., Rep.* I, *Lys., Chrm., Euphr.*
3) *Euthd., Grg., Meno, H. Mi., Cra.*
4) *Cri., H. Ma., Smp., Phd.*
5) *Rep.* II–X, *Tht., Prm., Phdr.*
6) *Sph., Pol., Phil., Laws*

Despite the extensive nature of Arnim's material, which comprehended a much larger number of reply formulae than any previous investigation, the reliability of his results was diminished by methodological faults.[42] Nevertheless, it may be noted that the chronological sequence that he arrived at corresponded broadly with that obtained by his predecessors.

In his later years C. Ritter returned to the subject of research into Plato's style, which he had done so much to promote, for the specific purpose of determining the order of composition of the early dialogues.[43] By looking at the occurrence in them of five features[44] he was able to subdivide this group into an earlier and later set, the former comprising the *Hippias Minor, Charmides, Laches, Protagoras, Euthyphro, Apology,* and *Crito,* with the *Gorgias* and *Meno* at the end, the latter the *Hippias Major, Euthydemus, Menexenus, Cratylus, Lysis, Symposium, Phaedo,* and *Republic* I. It must be said, however, that this conclusion, based as it was on low-frequency figures in every case, should be regarded as no more than a probability.

Nearly a century after its inception through Campbell the stylistic method came full circle with an examination of Plato's vocabulary by A. Díaz Tejera.[45] His approach, however, was different: Whereas Campbell's standard of reference was internal, in that he measured the degree of affinity of the other dialogues to the *Laws*, Díaz Tejera's was external. Assuming that the development of the various Greek dialects into the *Koine* should be traceable, he collected together what he called "the non-Attic vocabulary,[46] which is well-documented in the *Koine*," then examined its occurrence in Plato's works.

Leaving aside the *Laws*, which he took for granted as the final work, he found the highest incidence in the *Timaeus* and *Critias*, followed by the *Politicus*, then the *Sophist* and finally the *Philebus*. In a "later middle group," which showed a considerably lower incidence, he placed the *Theaetetus*, *Phaedrus*, and *Parmenides*,[47] preceded in turn by an "earlier middle group" consisting of *Republic* II–X, *Phaedo*, *Symposium*, and *Cratylus*. Observing that the incidence in the latter three was roughly comparable with that in the early books of the *Republic* (as far as VI 502e), he inferred that the first part of the *Republic* was written between 388/7 BCE (Plato's return from Sicily) and 384 BCE (*terminus post quem* of the *Symposium*)[48] and was followed by the *Cratylus*, *Symposium*, and *Phaedo* before the *Republic* was resumed.

The main differences between Díaz Tejera's chronological order and that arrived at by his predecessors were the separation of the *Republic* by other works and the reversal of the positions in the final group of *Timaeus/Critias* and *Philebus*. If the investigation that produced these results had been sound, they would have required serious consideration, but it was seriously flawed in both concept and procedure. Starting, as it did, from the chronological divisions established by earlier research and accepting as evidence of late composition words common to the *Koine* and the final group of dialogues, its argument tended to be circular, and this basic fault was aggravated by various procedural errors, such as incorrect or inconsistent classification of words, incomplete statistics, and faulty calculations.[49]

The rhythm of Plato's prose was once more examined for chronological purposes by D. Wishart and S. V. Leach,[50] who analyzed in this respect not merely the clausula, as Kaluscha and Billig had, but the whole sentence. Owing to the exhaustive nature of the investigation, samples rather than whole works were looked at, and both the initial categorization of the text into long or short syllables and the subsequent assessment of the statistics were carried out by computer.

The authors took as their unit of measurement a group of five syllables, yielding thirty-two permutations. Every sentence was analyzed into such groups sequentially, that is, first syllables 1–5, then 2–6, then 3–7, and so on, after which the occurrence of each of the thirty-two types was expressed as a percentage of the total number of syllable groups in the sample. The works that they considered were as follows: *Smp.* (4), *Phdr.* (5), *Rep.* (3), *Sph.* (1), *Pol.* (1), *Phil.* (1), *Epist.* VII (1), *Ti.* (9), *Criti.* (3), *Laws* (5). The figures in parenthesis indicate the number of samples taken from the work in question, each sample comprising between two and three thousand groups of five syllables.

To determine the interrelationships of the various samples and works, five different statistical techniques were used: three of cluster analysis, one of principal components analysis, and one of multidimensional scaling. The purpose of cluster analysis was to identify groups of works or samples exhibiting a uniform use of prose rhythm. If it resulted in the clustering of separate samples from the same work, it would confirm that the work in question displayed consistent rhythms and so could be regarded as homogeneous; if, on the other hand, any sample could not be clustered with the rest, it would suggest either a difference of genre or a chronological separation or unauthenticity. The same would be true of whole works.[51]

It turned out that the thirty-three samples were grouped together according to their origin with the exception of those from the *Republic* and *Phaedrus.* In the former the sample from Book II appeared to be widely separated from those from Book X, which the authors were at a loss to explain, though they suggested as possible causes the shortness of the Book II sample and the fact that it came from a speech, whereas the other two were from a narrative. Another reason might be that the Book II sample contained several quotations in verse which clearly should not have been included in an analysis of prose rhythm (cf. *CPD*, 240). In the *Phaedrus*, while the four samples from Socrates' two speeches were grouped together, that from Lysias' speech was quite different. They considered that in view of the uniformity of rhythm in the four *Symposium* samples, despite their being parodies, imitation of Lysias' style would not account for its deviation and so concluded that it was probably Lysias' own composition.[52]

Regarding the ten works the authors decided that the chronological sequence was *Phdr.*, (*Smp.* and *Rep.*), *Ti.*, *Sph.*, *Criti.*, (*Epist.* VII and *Pol*), *Phil.*, *Laws*,[53] thus confirming the order arrived at by earlier investigators of Plato's prose rhythm, at least from the *Timaeus* onward.[54]

The most recent attempt [editors' note: at the time of this essay, published in 1992] to solve the chronological problems[55] was based on a computer analysis of the occurrence in words of certain letters, the occurrence being classified according to whether it was (a) anywhere in the word, (b) at the end,[56] or (c) in the penultimate position. The incidence of the significant letters, or variables, which were found to be thirty-seven in number,[57] was determined for sequential samples of 1,000 words from both Plato and other contemporary prose authors. The statistical profiles of the samples formed by these thirty-seven variables were then compared with one another by various techniques, such as cluster analysis and discriminant analysis, in the expectation of finding insignificant differences indicative of homogeneity between samples from the same author, but significant ones between those from different authors. While this expectation was for the most part fulfilled, there was a disturbing number of instances where statistical analysis failed to distinguish the works of two authors.[58] Nevertheless Ledger concluded that the results of comparisons with genuine works suggested the authenticity of *Alcibiades* I, *Theages*, *Epistle* VII, *Hippias Major*, *Epinomis*, and possibly also of *Alcibiades* II and *Hippias Minor*.

A comparison of the Platonic works using canonical correlation analysis to establish the chronological order indicated the existence of a sharply defined final group consisting of *Phil., Cleit., Epist.* III, VII, and VIII, *Sph., Pol., Laws, Epin., Ti.,* and *Criti.*, written in that order between 355 BCE and 347 BCE.[59] Prior to these came the *Phaedrus* and *Menexenus*. While accepting this fairly late position for the *Phaedrus* in compliance with his statistics, Ledger rejected it for the *Menexenus* in deference to the traditional view of an earlier date, based in part on a supposedly topical reference (245e) to the Peace of Antalcidas of 386 BCE. Immediately before these was a "middle group" of works written probably between 380 BCE and 366 BCE in the order *Euthd., Smp., Cra., Rep., Prm., Tht., Epist.* XIII,[60] preceded in turn by an "early middle group" consisting of *Grg., Menex., Meno, Chrm., Ap., Phd., La., Prt.,* written in this order probably between 387 BCE and 380 BCE. Finally, the earliest group comprised *Lys., Euphr., Minos, H. Mi., Ion, H. Ma., Alc.* I, *Theag.*, and *Cri.*, the *Lysis* being dated to 400 BCE before the death of Socrates on the basis of the anecdote in Diogenes Laertius (II 35).

The study of Plato's literary style has revealed two broad developments, an earlier one which was slow and gradual, and a later one, starting when he was about sixty, which was sudden and rapid. Regarding the former, where the changes concerned his vocabulary and were for the most part probably unconscious, one would expect the trend to be uneven and at times haphazard;[61] in the latter, which concerned the euphony of his prose and involved a deliberate choice in respect of hiatus avoidance and rhythm, a more rational and systematic evolution might be anticipated, with any aberrations in it explicable by known or deducible factors.

The early research on Plato's vocabulary by Campbell, Dittenberger, and Schanz, culminating in Ritter's book on the subject, identified in the *Sophist*, *Politicus*, *Philebus*, *Timaeus*, *Critias*, and *Laws* a group of dialogues distinguished from the rest by an exclusive or increased occurrence in them of certain words and phrases. Subsequent investigations into this aspect of style arrived at the same conclusion, and the dichotomy was confirmed by two further criteria with the discovery that only in these works, together with the *Epinomis* and *Epistle* VII, did Plato make a consistent attempt to avoid certain types of hiatus and achieve a different kind of prose rhythm.

It has been argued that Plato avoided hiatus changeably rather than consistently after a certain date.[62] This is to attribute to an elderly philosopher a fickle attitude, which is hardly compatible with the character of one who in his works emphasizes the importance of rational, consistent behavior. Of course Plato could change his style within a single dialogue, as in the *Symposium* and *Phaedrus*, but these changes were made for a specific purpose that is immediately apparent. No reason has so far been adduced why he should have employed the principle of hiatus avoidance intermittently, and in the absence of such a reason it is unsatisfactory to resort to the use of analogy, especially of Isocrates' forensic speeches, where the greater or lesser avoidance of hiatus is explicable on various grounds, not least temporal and commercial, considerations that hardly applied to Plato.

Regarding the question of sequence within the final chronological group, in comparing the various kinds of evidence particular weight should perhaps be attached to prose rhythm and the avoidance of hiatus, because unlike vocabulary they appear to be independent both of a work's form and of its content. Although the testimony of the data for hiatus avoidance was ambiguous, three independent investigations of clausula rhythm and one of sentence rhythm agreed in concluding that the order of composition was *Ti.*, *Criti.*, *Sph.*, *Pol.*, *Phil.*, *Laws*. In the light of this the ambiguity of the hiatus evidence regarding the place of the *Philebus* may be resolved in favor of its proximity to the *Laws*, a position supported by particular aspects of hiatus[63] and by other features, such as the reversion to longer forms of reply formulae after a predominance of abbreviated versions in the preceding works,[64] the culmination of a trend toward the more frequent use of superlative expressions,[65] the high proportion of περι,[66] and an increased preference compared with the *Timaeus, Critias,* and *Sophist* for a long final syllable in clausulae (*CPD*, 188–90).

The final position allocated by Ledger to the *Timaeus* and *Critias* would indicate a fluctuating level of hiatus avoidance in the final group: less strict in the *Philebus,* strict in the *Sophist* and *Politicus,* less strict in the *Laws,* strict in the *Timaeus* and *Critias.* Likewise with clausula rhythm: The forms preferred by Plato in the *Laws* would appear with similarly high frequency right at the start in the *Philebus,* with much lower frequency in the *Sophist,* increasing in the *Politicus* toward that of the *Laws,* but falling away again in the *Timaeus* and *Critias,* to the level of the *Sophist.* As both these linguistic features were adopted consciously by Plato, such indecisiveness would be remarkable. Since the *Timaeus* and *Critias* are for the most part continuous narrative compared with the dialogue form of the *Sophist, Politicus,* and *Philebus,* the difference in Ledger's statistics might be attributable to the same cause that he adduced[67] for the odd results obtained for the *Apology* and *Menexenus,* works of a rhetorical character, namely a difference of genre.

By comparison with the differences that distinguish the final group, those which separate the dialogues of Plato's middle period from all preceding it are not as sharp, connected as they are with the earlier, gradual development of his style. Ritter, incorporating the results of his predecessors' research with his own, found that many of the criteria used to identify the final group also served to separate the *Parmenides, Phaedrus,* and *Theaetetus* from the remaining dialogues,[68] and the same division was made by later investigators.[69] On the question of the unity of the *Republic,* Siebeck,[70] Ritter, and Arnim arrived independently at the view that Book I, which contains several features characteristic of the early dialogues, was originally a separate work written some time before the rest, but possibly revised at the time of its incorporation.

Despite the fact that there cannot be the same certainty about the sequence within this group as about that in the last, examination of Ritter's criteria (cf. *CPD*, 79ff.) suggests that the order of composition was *Republic, Theaetetus, Phaedrus*, which agrees with his own conclusion (cf. *CPD*, 77).[71] While the *Parmenides* unquestionably belongs in the same group (cf. *CPD*, 66), its peculiar character makes it difficult to determine its relationship to the above three works (cf. *CPD*, 84). On the other hand, if one also takes into account the apparent reference in the *Theaetetus* to the *Parmenides* and the fact that in the *Theaetetus* Plato renounces the use of the reported dialogue form, which seems to be merely an explicit declaration of a practice already implicitly adopted early in the *Parmenides* (137c), presumably induced by recollection of the wearisome repetition of ἔφη ("he said"), and so on, in the *Republic* and the prospect of its still greater occurrence in a dialogue with such frequent changes of speaker, then the correct place for the *Parmenides* would appear to be between the *Republic* and *Theaetetus*.

On the sequence of dialogues in the early group little can be said. Division into subgroups also seems out of the question. The difficulty is that the statistics produced by past research usually relate to linguistic features that are primarily characteristic of works belonging to Plato's middle and late periods; consequently, their occurrence in the early period tends to be slight and spasmodic.

The problem is compounded by two other factors: first, many investigations concerned the use of reply formulae, which was prejudicial to works containing little dialogue (e.g., *Menex.*, *Ap.*, *Cri.*); second, most scholars of the last century omitted certain works altogether from their inquiries, especially those suspected at that time of being unauthentic, making a general comparison impracticable. Nevertheless, if the frequency with which features characteristic of the middle and late works occur in the early dialogues is accepted as an indication of their chronological proximity, then the *Phaedo, Cratylus, Symposium, Republic* I, *Lysis, Menexenus, Euthydemus,* and *Hippias Major* would certainly have to be regarded as among the last of this group. Their relative order, however, cannot be determined on the basis of the stylistic evidence that has so far come to light.

NOTES

1 For a full discussion of the evidence, see Thesleff 1982: 7–66.

2 *Pol.* II 6, 1264b24–7.

3 Cf. *Prm.* 127b2, c4–5.

4 See the tables in Ritter 1910: 230–1, and Thesleff 1982: 8ff.

5 Grote 1867, 1: 185–6, 278–9.

6 Campbell 1867: introduction.

7 In the last century many dialogues now accepted as genuine were considered unauthentic. As scholars' views in this respect varied, so too did the number of works forming the subject of any investigation.

8 See Brandwood 1990: 5–7 (hereafter referred to as *CPD*).

9 Dittenberger 1881.

10 τί μήν, ("What else indeed?") and ἀλλά ... μήν, ("But what else indeed?"), the intermediate word normally being τί, are strong affirmative replies, while γε μήν ("but indeed") is usually adversative. The absence of the first two from *Ti.* and *Criti.* results from their lack of dialogue.

11 Dover 1965: 220.

12 *Acharn.* 757, 784.

13 Schanz 1886.

14 The three examples in *Prt.* occur in the analysis of a poem by Simonides and, being quotations, ought to be discounted.

15 Simultaneously and independently, it seems, by Siebeck (1888: 253ff.), and Ritter (1888).

16 *CPD*, chs. 10, 11, 13, 19.

17 At this time the *Prm.* was held by Ritter to be unauthentic. Otherwise his statistics would have required it to be placed in this group.

18 E.g., (1) the complete absence of καὶ μάλα ("very much so"), τί μήν, and ὀρθῶς ("rightly") together with its superlative, though they occur in all the other books; (2) six of the eleven instances in the *Rep.* of δῆτα ("indeed") with

a reply occur in this book, as do eight of the twenty instances of φαίνεται ("apparently"); (3) the preponderance of πάνυ γε over πάνυ μὲν οὖν (16 : 5) is the reverse of that in every other book (total 24 : 59).

19 E.g., one instance each of ἄριστα εἴρηκας ("Well said!"), καὶ πῶς ἄν; ("How might that be?"), Ionic dative (the Attic form with an iota suffix), γε μήν, παντάπασι μέν οὖν ("Most certainly"), together with a preponderance of ἀληθῆ over ἀληθῆ λέγεις (5 : 2).

20 His argument for these dispositions, however, is not convincing (CPD, 74–6).

21 A reassessment of Ritter's data (CPD, 77, 82) shows that there are reasonable grounds for concluding that the Phdr. was written after both the Tht. and Rep.

22 Lutoslawski 1897: ch. 3 ("The Style of Plato").

23 For a more detailed criticism see CPD, 130–5.

24 Baron 1897.

25 Instances of περί in the various forms of the phrase περὶ πολλοῦ ποιεῖσθαι ("to rate highly"), which never appears to admit of anastrophe, were excluded from the calculation. The figures are the author's and relate to the OCT. Baron's, referring to another text, sometimes differ, but only slightly.

26 The high percentage for the Menex. and La. may be explained by the low overall occurrence of the preposition in the former, and by special factors such as repetition in the latter (cf. CPD, 119).

27 See below and CPD, 120.

28 Janell 1901.

29 Blass 1874, 2: 426.

30 I.e., a word beginning with a vowel following one ending in a vowel. In the fourth century, with the advance of rhetorical technique, such a clash of vowels came to be regarded as detracting from the euphony of prose.

31 Reinvestigation showed that in his later works Plato did try to avoid hiatus with these too (CPD, 162).

32 Janell used Schanz's text. In Burnet's there are even fewer instances: only one in the second passage, none in the third.

33 Kaluscha 1904.

34 In the sense that even a short syllable would be lengthened by the pause in speech between the end of one sentence and the beginning of the next.

35 The true situation is a little more complex. Clausulae in works of the middle period show a preponderance of long final syllables; e.g., in *Rep.* VIII – X, 478 end in a long, 251 in a short syllable, an excess of long over short of 90%. Although in the *Ti.* the position is reversed, with a 2% excess of short over long, the preponderance of the long syllable reappears in the *Criti.* with a 20% excess (though in this case the low number of clausulae makes the calculation less reliable), and gradually increases through the *Sph.* (7%), *Pol.* (20%), and *Phil.* (34%) to the *Laws* (66%).

36 Cf. *CPD*, table 18.4.

37 About the *Criti.* he drew no conclusions owing to the limitations of its size and the resulting statistics, but contented himself with attaching it to the *Ti.*

38 Billig 1920.

39 Cf. *CPD*, 198ff.

40 Arnim 1912.

41 Counting the books of the *Rep.* and *Laws* separately there were forty-two works to be compared, the *Ap.*, *Menex.*, *Ti.*, *Criti.*, and *Laws* V and XI being excluded owing to their lack of dialogue.

42 Cf. *CPD*, 215ff.

43 Ritter 1935.

44 Four of these features are: (a) the particle μήν ("indeed"), (b) ὡς with a superlative adjective or adverb in the sense "as (e.g., great) as possible," (c) the change in use of ἕτερος ("other of two") to that of ἄλλος ("other"), (d) the interchange in function of ὥσπερ ("like") and οἷον ("like for example").

45 Díaz Tejera 1961.

46 By this he meant neologisms, Ionicisms, and poeticisms.

47 The incidence in the *Prm.* was less than half that in the other two, but he attributed this to the monotonous nature of its subject matter, especially in the ontological section.

48 Dover 1965: 220.

49 Cf. *CPD*, esp. 233–4.

50 Wishart and Leach 1970.

51 For an explanation of these techniques and their respective results see *CPD*, 238–46.

52 The absurdity of their further conclusion, that it was later than the other samples from the *Phdr.*, appears not to have struck them (cf. *CPD*, 247).

53 The relative order of works in parenthesis could not be determined.

54 Concerning the position allocated to the *Phdr.*, serious doubts arise from the choice of samples: All were taken from speeches rather than the dialogue section, and Socrates' two speeches, which provided four samples, are specifically denoted by Plato himself as poetical in character (241e1 and 257a4), a fact borne out by observation (cf. *CPD*, 57–8).

55 Ledger 1989.

56 Iota subscript was ignored, perhaps putting these statistics in some doubt.

57 Listed at Ledger 1989: 9.

58 Cf. Ledger 1989: 66–8 and 93ff. Discriminant analysis, for instance, attributed three of the eight samples from *Rep.* I to Xenophon (p. 103), while in a comparison of Xenophon's *Oeconomicus* and *Memorabilia* with several dialogues the *Phdr.* proved to be closer than the *Oeconomicus* in style to the *Memorabilia*, and the *Prt.* closer than the *Memorabilia* to the *Oeconomicus* (p. 160).

59 In this scheme the unfinished state of the *Criti.* was ascribed to Plato's death. However, one may also conjecture that the *Tht.*, with its apparent reference to the Isthmian war of 369/8 BCE, was the last work to be written before Plato's departure for Syracuse in 367; that the exuberant expression of delight in the attractions of the countryside near Athens, which has induced some to regard the *Phdr.* as a youthful work, may instead be attributed to Plato's relief on returning home a year later after being subjected to a period of virtual imprisonment; and that the reason for the interruption to the composition of the *Criti.* was his sudden departure for Syracuse again in 361.

60 Like several earlier investigators Ledger found the *Prm.* awkward to place, differing so much in style from the other dialogues that "most tests of authorship would lead us to conclude that it was not written by Plato" (1989: 213).

61 Nevertheless, in the case of individual linguistic features it is necessary to assume initially that the trend is, if not even, at least unilinear. Comparison of several such criteria provides the necessary correction.

62 E.g., Ryle 1966: 297; Waterfield 1980: 274–6.

63 E.g., the frequency in both works of addresses like ὦ ἑταῖρε ("my friend") and ὦ ἄριστε ("my good man"), six times in the *Phil.* and seventeen in the *Laws*, whereas in the other works of this group they are not found at all. If

the *Phil.* had represented Plato's first serious attempt at reducing the occurrence of hiatus, he would hardly have failed to eliminate such eminently avoidable instances. Moreover, in the *Ti.* and *Criti.* there is a temporary increase in "permissible" hiatus to a level exceeding even that in works where hiatus was not avoided (cf. *CPD*, 162–3), indicative perhaps of Plato's first serious attempt to avoid the "objectionable" kind, which at this transitional stage succeeded only at the expense of a rise in the former.

64 E.g., ἀληθῆ λέγεις and ἀληθέστατα/ὀρθότατα λέγεις instead of ἀληθῆ and ἀληθεστατα/ὀρθότατα (cf. *CPD*, 88 and 99ff.).

65 Only in the *Phil.* and *Laws* do the superlative reply formulae equal or surpass the positive forms (cf. *CPD*, 87–9).

66 See Table 3.3. Note also that its occurrence in *Ti.* and *Criti.* is much lower than in the other works of the late group.

67 E.g., Ledger 1989: 127, 145, 163.

68 *CPD*, 57–66.

69 E.g., Arnim (*CPD*, 97ff.) and Baron (*CPD*, 116ff.).

70 Siebeck 1888.

71 The late position of the *Phdr.* is further supported by its higher proportion of ὄντως to τῷ ὄντι (cf. *CPD*, 81), a percentage of rhetorical questions as reply formulae equaling that found in works of the last group (cf. *CPD*, 103), the frequency of πέρι (cf. *CPD*, 121) and passages in which there appears to be a conscious effort to avoid hiatus (cf. *CPD*, 155), leading to its lowest incidence outside works of the final group (cf. *CPD*, 156). In addition, the evidence of an interest in prose rhythm (cf. *CPD*, 158) together with mention of Isocrates (cf. *CPD*, 160) perhaps presages the development of this in subsequent works.

Plato's Socrates and his Conception of Philosophy

Eric Brown

I SOCRATES THE PHILOSOPHER

What is this thing called "love of wisdom" – "philosophy" – that Plato offers? Before Plato's time, many were hailed as wise (*sophos*, *sophistēs*), but surviving Greek texts written before the fourth century BCE rarely mention a "philosopher" (*philosophos*).[1] The word was common in Plato's time, though, and Plato contended with Isocrates about what it is to be a philosopher.[2] What exactly was Plato's contention? Despite apparently promising to do so (*Sph.* 216c–217c, *Pol.* 257a), he seems not to have written a dialogue dedicated to the question "What is a philosopher?"[3] But he does offer the unforgettable character of Socrates.[4] Because Plato presents Socrates as a philosopher[5] and as a deeply admirable human being (esp. *Phd.* 118a), this character offers a model of what Plato thinks philosophy is.[6]

Plato's Socrates contrasts his commitments with other clever talkers'. He says that he cares for truth and loves wisdom, whereas "eristics" such as Dionysodorus and Euthydemus seek to win debates and "sophists" such as Protagoras and Gorgias seek to persuade audiences.[7] Thus, Plato makes love of wisdom central to his

This chapter was first aired at a conference in honor of Hugh Benson, who has modeled an especially friendly version of Socratic inquiry while improving our understanding of Plato's Socrates. I thank him for all that and for many helpful comments on this essay. For lively feedback, I thank participants in the HughFest, the 2018 Biennial Chicago Conference in Ancient Philosophy, the St. Louis Ethics Workshop, and a Clark University colloquium, and for written comments, I thank Nich Baima, David Ebrey, Jeremy Henry, Richard Kraut, Keith McPartland, David McNeill, Casey Perin, Sandra Peterson, Ravi Sharma, Rachel Singpurwalla, and Nicholas D. Smith.

Socratic model of philosophy. But what is the wisdom that Socrates loves? Also, *how* does Socrates love wisdom? Scholars disagree about how to answer these questions,[8] and their disagreements are complicated by the fact that Plato's dialogues seem to offer more than one Socrates and thus more than one exemplification of philosophy. Our would-be model threatens to dissolve.

This chapter seeks solidity about what Plato's Socrates loves and what activities constitute his wisdom-loving. In search of answers acceptable to readers who distinguish sharply among Plato's Socrateses,[9] and especially those who distinguish between a "Socratic" Socrates who asks questions and a "Platonic" Socrates who develops answers,[10] I focus on the *Apology*.[11] This "dialogue" explicitly characterizes Socrates' philosophizing and, as a defense of his life, is widely thought to portray a very "Socratic" Socrates. But to amplify the *Apology*'s whispers, I give some voice to other dialogues, especially the more "Socratic" ones in which Socrates asks questions more than he develops answers.

II   THE WISDOM SOCRATES LOVES

On trial for impiety, Socrates spends the first third of his defense (17a–24c) ignoring the official charges against him, to concentrate on earlier accusations. He worries he has developed a reputation that falsely prejudices the jurors against him, and he wants to clear the air. In doing so, he distinguishes the wisdom he loves from the wisdom others misattribute to him.

The earlier accusers – including Aristophanes, in the *Clouds* (19c, 18d) – represent Socrates as one of the "nature-theorists" (*phusiologoi*) whom we often call "Presocratics" and as one of the "sophists" who teach rhetoric. Many fifth-century intellectuals counted as one or both of these,[12] but Socrates says he knows nothing of things in the heavens or under the earth and nothing of how to make the weaker argument stronger (19b–c). Elsewhere, he goes further to distance himself from these reputedly wise people by suggesting that the nature-theorists and sophists are pseudo-experts (*Phd.* 96a–99d; *Grg.* 462b–466a), although he acknowledges the possibility of genuine expertise in their fields (*Phd.* 97b–98b, 99b–c; *Grg.* 503a–b, 504d). In the *Apology*, he simply disavows their undertakings.

The earlier accusers also represent Socrates as someone who teaches the young how to be successful, for a fee. But Socrates says he lacks the expertise (*technē*) that would make him "a knower of human and political virtue" and enable him to teach others to live well (19d–20c, quoting 20b4–5). Elsewhere, he discusses this expertise obsessively, as something he and his interlocutors should want to find. In the *Apology*, he simply says such knowledge about how to live would be valuable, and claims not to have it.

Socrates' responses prompt a question: how did people come to such mistaken views about him (20c)? He answers by telling a story about the Delphic oracle (20c–23b).[13] Socrates' friend Chaerephon asked the oracle whether anyone was wiser than Socrates, and the oracle said no one was (21a). This pronouncement puzzled Socrates (21b) and inspired an unusual response that annoyed many but gave him the reputation of being wise (21b–23a).

To explain his puzzlement about the oracle, Socrates says, "I am aware (*sunoida*) that I am wise in nothing big or small (*oute mega oute smikron*)" (21b4–5). This phrase 'big or small' is not merely rhetorical. Socrates denies that he possesses the expertise the manual craftsmen do: they "know many honorable things" and are "in this way wiser than [he]" (22c–e). Such experts are another common obsession of the more "Socratic" dialogues, which are filled with talk of builders, doctors, and such (cf. *Grg.* 491a, *Smp.* 221e). Socrates treats each expertise (*technē*) as mastery of some particular work (*ergon*) – usually a product of activity but sometimes just an activity (*Chrm.* 165c–166a; *Euthd.* 290b–d) – and he assumes that the expert can make or do their particular work well, can correctly answer questions about their work, and can transmit their expertise to an apprentice.[14] In the *Apology*, while he admires such expertise as a kind of wisdom, Socrates contrasts it with something bigger:

> But I thought, men of Athens, that the good craftsmen and poets made the same mistake – because each practiced his craft well, he thought he was also very wise with respect to other things, the biggest things (*ta megista*) – and I thought this mistake of theirs overshadowed their wisdom. (22d4–e1)

So when Socrates disavows all wisdom, big or small, he disclaims both expertise focused on some small work and wisdom about "the biggest things."

What is this bigger wisdom? Translators often assume, reasonably, that the "biggest things" are especially weighty and thus important, and readers sometimes speculate that they include the cosmological matters that the nature-theorists explore (19b–c). But the context suggests another construal. The "biggest things" are contrasted with what a manual craftsman knows, which is a narrow domain defined by one particular kind of work. By contrast, then, the "biggest things" would be not simply important but also *broad*.[15] On this construal, big wisdom does not focus narrowly on one kind of work but concerns how to do everything one does – how to live. The most relevant earlier passage is not the one about the nature-theorists but the one about expertise concerning human and political virtue (20a–c; cf. 20d–e, 29e–30a). This construal certainly fits other, more "Socratic" dialogues, where Socrates finds people lacking wisdom not so much in cosmological matters as in questions of how to live virtuously and well.[16]

Given his own lack of wisdom big and small, Socrates' puzzlement is clear: why does the oracle credit him as the wisest? After failing to find anyone who has the bigger wisdom, Socrates arrives at an answer:

> What is likely, men, is that in reality the god is wise, and in this oracle he means that human wisdom is worth little or nothing. He appears to say "this one, Socrates" and to use my name in order to

use me as an example, as if he were saying, "This one of you, human beings, is wisest who, like Socrates, has recognized that he is in truth worth nothing in relation to wisdom." (23a5–b4)

Socrates interprets the oracle tentatively, but he makes sense of its claim by introducing a third kind of wisdom that consists in grasping that one lacks (big) wisdom. This is a wisdom he can claim, but those he has examined cannot. Socrates calls it *human* wisdom, as though it were what befits a human and not a god (cf. 20d–e). Moreover, Socrates does not take the oracle's point to concern only him. He takes the god to be saying that the wisest human being has the merely human wisdom that Socrates has, and he presents this as a perfectly general truth, applicable to any human being whomsoever. So the oracle means that no human *could* be wiser than Socrates, and Socrates follows the Delphic injunction "Know thyself" in a traditional way,[17] by understanding himself *as a human being*, a mortal incapable of immortal things (cf. 42a, *H. Ma.* 289b, *Phdr.* 278d).[18]

One might wonder whether Socrates identifies his human wisdom with some expertise, as he does the big and small wisdom he lacks.[19] He explicitly contrasts his general ignorance not with *all* expertise, but with the expertise *manual* craftsmen possess (22c–d; cf. *Grg.* 450a–e). Perhaps he intentionally leaves room to avow some non-manual expertise. Perhaps Socrates realizes he has some dialectical expertise (*Euphr.* 11d, *Grg.* 474a), including erotic expertise in how to desire well, by asking questions in pursuit of the truth (*Smp.* 177d; cf. *Lys.* 204c, *Phdr.* 257a), and midwifing expertise in how to test the fruits of good desire, by examining answers (*Tht.* 149a). Scholars typically ignore this possibility and attribute especially midwifery to a less "Socratic" Socrates.[20] But the possibility is not blocked by Socrates' disavowal of all wisdom big and small (21b) or his claim of general ignorance (22c–d). He qualifies these when he admits that he has some human wisdom, and nothing prevents him from identifying his human wisdom with some non-manual expertise. Nor is the possibility blocked by his assumption that expertise is teachable, since Socrates expresses confidence that he has inspired dialectical skill in others (39c–d, cf. 23c, 37d).[21]

Speculation about Socratic expertise aside, Socrates' story about the oracle helps us answer our first question. It reveals three kinds of wisdom – the narrow wisdom of craftsmen, bigger wisdom concerning human virtue, and human wisdom – and we can ask which Socrates loves. If love is not inexplicable – if it tracks what is good and beautiful, or at least what the lover perceives as good and beautiful[22] – then neither human wisdom nor the wisdom of limited technical expertise would be valuable enough to inspire Socrates' love. So understood, he must love the wisdom of the "biggest things," expertise about how to live. This certainly fits what he says in other, more "Socratic" dialogues, where he talks often about this expertise about living. In fact, in those dialogues, he usually calls such expertise "wisdom" full-stop and does not apply the word to any narrow expertise or his own awareness of ignorance. We, too, can use 'wisdom' without qualification to refer to the expertise about living that Socrates loves.

III   LOVING BY HONORING: PHILOSOPHY AS CRITIQUE

Socrates' story about the oracle also begins to answer our second question, concerning *how* he loves wisdom. After inferring what the god meant by saying that no one is wiser than he, Socrates infers what he should do:

> Thus even now I go around to inquire, in accordance with the god, and to seek among citizens and foreigners anyone I might think wise, and whenever he does not seem wise to me, I aid the god and show that he is not wise. And because of this work, I haven't had the leisure to do anything worth mentioning of the polis' business or of my household's, but I live in significant poverty on account of my service to the god. (23b4–c1)

Although Socrates understands the oracle to mean that no human could be wise, his interpretation is tentative, so he proceeds as though he could be mistaken, continuing to seek people who might be wise.

But he does this not merely to test his interpretation of the oracle. He also takes himself to be helping the god – presumably Apollo, the god of the Delphic oracle – when he shows that a person who seems to be wise is not. Socrates will later say that there is more to his service than this, but for now, he says that his examinations serve Apollo by disseminating the message that wisdom is divine, not human. That is, Socrates examines others to *honor* wisdom. But honoring wisdom is one way of loving wisdom. So Socrates has just identified critique as part of his wisdom-loving.

Socrates the critic has inspired skeptics,[23] but the Socrates of the *Apology* is no skeptic.[24] He does not even disavow all knowledge. He claims to know, for example, that his examinations annoy people (24a) and that were he to continue his examinations in another city, young people would flock to him (37d).[25] This need not contradict his disavowal of wisdom, big and small (21b), or even his claim of general ignorance, as compared to the manual craftsmen (22c–d). Those claims concern expert knowledge, and he might think that some things are knowable without expertise, by ordinary human experience.[26] Anyone can know who Chaerephon is (21a) or how to get to Larissa (*Meno* 97a).[27]

Still, the things Socrates knows without expertise are trivial (*Euthd.* 293b). He assumes that the "biggest things" concerning how to live are knowable only by the expert's systematic mastery. This explains why Socrates thinks Meletus is ignorant in charging him with corrupting the youth unless Meletus can explain what corruption is and identify other corrupters (24c–26b). Elsewhere, too, Socrates' assumption plays a prominent role, as he insists, for instance, that if Euthyphro knows that it is pious to prosecute his father, he must be able to explain what piety is (*Euphr.* 4a–5d).[28]

Given this assumption, and his lack of expertise about virtue, Socrates should disavow knowledge about virtue. Even if he has justified confidence in many claims about virtue, he should not think he *knows* them. But in the *Apology*, he says,

> ... and if I should affirm that I am wiser than anyone, it would be in this, that what I do not sufficiently know about things in Hades, so, too, I do not think that I know. But I do know that it is bad and shameful to do injustice and to disobey one's superior, whether god or human. (29b2–7)

Here and in three other passages (37b, *Euthd.* 296e–297a, *Grg.* 521c–d), a "Socratic" Socrates claims knowledge about virtue.[29] These passages are hard to square with a narrowly critical Socrates.

IV   LOVING BY PURSUING: PHILOSOPHY AS LEARNING

In fact, Socrates' account of the oracle has already assumed that critique does not exhaust his philosophizing. Consider again how he compares himself to the manual craftsmen. After noting that their limited wisdom was accompanied by a mistaken claim to be wise in the "biggest things," Socrates says,

> I asked myself on behalf of the oracle whether I would prefer to be in the condition I am in, not being wise in their wisdom or ignorant in their ignorance, or to have both the things they have. I answered, to myself and the oracle, that it profits me to be as I am. (22e1–e6)

Socrates prefers human wisdom without technical wisdom to technical wisdom without human wisdom. Why?

Human wisdom is worth "little or nothing" (23a, *Smp.* 175e). So it is not *by itself* more valuable than the limited wisdom the experts have. Perhaps it is instrumentally valuable because it fosters humility and a sensible conservatism. Elsewhere, Socrates finds something risky about prosecuting one's father without knowing what piety is (*Euphr.* 4a–b, 4e, 15d–e). He might think that someone aware of his ignorance would not be so bold.[30] After all, later skeptics often go for conservatism.[31] But Socrates is not at all conservative. In the *Apology*, he challenges ordinary Athenian values and insists that he will not give up doing so, even to escape death (*Ap.* 28b–30b, discussed in section V). So conservatism does not explain why Socrates is better off than the craftsmen.

Socrates' confidence in his own convictions suggests a more promising explanation. He thinks that his beliefs about how to live are better than theirs, and that it is better to have superior beliefs about how to live, without any limited expertise, than to have inferior beliefs about how to live, with some limited expertise.[32] This conclusion requires more than just human wisdom. If all he had was awareness of his own ignorance, without any grounds for confidence in his beliefs about how to live, he would not be justified in thinking himself better off. So what explains his confidence in his beliefs about how to live? For that matter, what explains his realization that he lacks wisdom, a realization that predates Chaerephon's visit to the oracle (because it explains Socrates' puzzled response)? Finally, what explains Chaerephon's thought that Socrates is especially wise, the thought Chaerephon took to Delphi?[33]

The simplest answer to these questions is that Socrates loved wisdom *and started pursuing it* long before Chaerephon went to Delphi.[34] There is no reason to suppose that Socrates always thought wisdom unattainable, since he presents this as a thought he reached *after* he tested the oracle. Nor need we suppose that he was initially motivated by any awareness of general ignorance. Mere curiosity or wonder (cf. *Tht.* 155d) about particular questions he could not easily answer could have stimulated Socrates, as some love of wisdom could prompt the pursuit of answers to such questions. Then, by pursuing understanding and falling short, he could have learned that he lacks wisdom – thus his puzzlement at the oracle – and that some attitudes are defensible without inconsistency whereas others are not – thus his confidence that he is better off than the craftsmen. Finally, because his continued pursuits prompted witnesses to attribute wisdom to him (23a), his earlier pursuits could have prompted Chaerephon to do the same.

So understood, Socrates' longstanding love and pursuit of wisdom made him confident that it is wrong to disobey one's superior

(29b, cf. 37b), that his way of life is better than other Athenians' (28b–32e, 37e–38a), and that his accusers cannot harm him (30c–d). He cannot consistently believe that he *knows* these things, since he takes such knowledge to require the wisdom or expertise that he lacks. But he can consistently suppose that his beliefs are well tested, unlike those of most people.

Why, then, does he sometimes claim to *know* something about virtue (29b, 37b, *Euthd.* 296e–297a, *Grg.* 521c–d)? Some readers suppose that when he wants to mark the fact that his beliefs are unusually well-tested, he exaggerates and says he knows.[35] But why would he do this *exactly when* he prides himself for *not* misconstruing his ignorance as knowledge (29a–b)?[36] Other readers suppose that Socrates' claims to ethical knowledge do not exaggerate at all, because he thinks his tested, coherent beliefs about virtue constitute a distinct kind of knowledge that lies between the mere opinion most people have and the full mastery only gods have.[37] But Socrates does not explicitly say any such thing, and if he really thought that his tested, coherent grasp of virtue constituted a kind of knowledge, he should claim to know a lot more about virtue than he does. It would make more sense of his practices if there were something special about the particular theses about virtue that he claims to know. Perhaps there is.[38] At their core, his problematic knowledge claims look like conceptual, necessary truths: the good obey the better (29b, 37b),[39] do not accuse the innocent (*Grg.* 521c–d), and are not unjust (*Euthd.* 296e–297a). Perhaps Socrates has inquired enough to be fully confident of these definitional entailments among goodness, justice, and obedience, even though he has not achieved complete mastery of what justice or goodness is, since that would include the ability to identify and explain instances. Thus, he might think his examinations establish that certain conceptual claims about justice and goodness are true, without establishing general knowledge, even of a secondary sort, of what justice or goodness is. Unfortunately, the more "Socratic" dialogues say nothing programmatic to encourage this suggestion.[40] Still, it both explains why Socrates avows ethical knowledge only when he does, and potentially justifies his doing so.

Speculation about Socrates' exceptional knowledge claims aside, the present account makes Socrates the philosopher a learner as well as a critic. His love of wisdom is longstanding; that love includes pursuit; and that pursuit has to some extent succeeded. While Socrates lacks wisdom and is thus not justified in claiming that he knows about how to live, he rightly takes himself to have acquired better beliefs – to have learned.

Some readers will doubt this. First, some will doubt that Socrates always pursues wisdom. Even if he pursued it for years before the oracle's pronouncement, once he interprets the oracle to mean that wisdom is unattainable for a human being, would he not drop the pursuit? What is the point of pursuing an unreachable goal?[41] It is true that some goals are not worth pursuing unless they can be attained. But not all goals are like this. Consider someone who thinks they could not perform Mussorgsky's *Pictures at an Exhibition* perfectly. They could still think it worthwhile to pursue this goal, because the pursuit could bring progress and it would be valuable to be able to play the piece *better*. Moreover, even if they should feel stuck in a rut, unable to make further progress, they might think that the attempt at progress – practicing – is intrinsically valuable. Socrates' pursuit of wisdom has earned him confidence in his beliefs about how to live. So he is well positioned to believe that he could make further progress by continued pursuit. But even if he had progressed as far as he could, given his limitations, he might have learned that pursuing wisdom is itself a valuable activity (see section V below).

Other readers will doubt that Socrates' pursuit has made any progress by wondering *how* his examinations foster learning. The fabled "Socratic method" of questioning and testing the answers with more questions is only briefly used in the *Apology*, where Socrates questions Meletus and finds him to have inconsistent beliefs (24c–28a). Elsewhere, Socratic examination is more fully on display, and such inconsistencies are the regular result. But how does this help anyone learn? Even if it is valuable to recognize that one's beliefs are inconsistent, this does not help settle what one should do next. At least one belief is false, but which (and how many)? So how does Socratic examination manage to make progress toward wisdom?[42] It is true that an isolated iteration of Socratic examination cannot yield a positive conclusion. But large sets of overlapping examinations establish patterns. Over time, little by little, Socrates learns that *these* beliefs cohere, whereas *those* introduce inconsistency, and he develops beliefs that hang together systematically.[43]

This might still seem insufficient. Even if, over time, Socrates can advance toward coherence, beliefs can cohere without being true. Unfortunately, in the most "Socratic" dialogues, Socrates simply assumes that by inquiring sincerely into what is true people tend to track what is true. But less "Socratic" dialogues suggest a way of potentially justifying this assumption: perhaps humans have some innate knowledge (*Meno* 81a–e, 85b–86b, *Phd.* 72e–73b).[44]

Whatever might explain (and justify?) Socrates' faith in learning by examination, we should note that the more "Socratic" dialogues are filled with evidence that he *claims* to learn. He repeatedly insists that in examining others, he also examines himself (28e, *Chrm.* 166c–d, *Prt.* 348c–e, *Grg.* 505e–506a).[45] Additionally, he reveals goals for his examinations – agreement with himself (*Grg.* 482a–c, *cf. H. Mi.* 376b), clarity (*Chrm.* 166d, *Prt.* 360e–361a, *Grg.* 505e) and stability (e.g., *Euphr.* 11b–c, *Prt.* 356d, *H. Mi.* 376c) – that offer criteria for assessing his progress. Finally, throughout the more "Socratic" dialogues, Socrates suggests he has made progress, by confidently insisting on certain turns in the inquiry. He suggests to Euthyphro, for instance, that piety is a species of justice (*Euphr.* 11e–12a), and he suggests to Charmides that temperance is good for a person as a feature of their character and not merely of how they behave (*Chrm.* 158e–159a, 160d–e). Repeatedly, he suggests that things are good only if they are honorable (e.g., *Chrm.* 159a–161b; *La.* 192c–d).

These features of Socrates' examinations give the lie to the impression that he is merely a critic, or worse, an unhelpful, hostile critic. They also help to explain why Socrates thinks he has gained some justification for the beliefs about how to live that he expresses so confidently in the *Apology*. After all, he presents himself as wise (though only humanly so, 23a–b), courageous (especially in the pursuit of wisdom, 28b–29d), temperate (in ignoring money and the pleasures it buys, 29d–30b, 31b–c, 36b–c), pious (by serving Apollo, 23b, 29b–d, 30e–31b), just (especially in politics, 31c–33a, 37a–b), and generally good (28a–b, 32e, 41d; cf. *Grg.* 521c–d). At first glance, this self-presentation conflicts with Socrates' admission that he lacks wisdom and his tenet, clearest elsewhere, that virtue is or requires knowledge or wisdom (cf. 29e–30a).[46] But if he has made enough progress to be confident that he possesses well-tested, true beliefs about how to live, and if he lives in accordance with those beliefs, he can reasonably conclude that he *approximates* wisdom and virtue.[47]

In fact, a third group of readers will doubt the present account by claiming that Socrates thinks he more than approximates wisdom and virtue. These readers suppose that he merely *pretends* that he lacks wisdom.[48] But this gives too much credit to Socrates' learning and neglects his insistence that wisdom belongs only to the gods.[49] Socrates might think that wisdom is "simply" knowledge of what is good and bad (e.g., *Chrm.* 174a–d, *La.* 194c–199e), but on his view, knowledge or expertise about a domain requires being able to survive examination about that domain. So if Socrates is not confident that he can survive examination about everything to do with good and bad – at least everything that it takes to be a knower[50] – he cannot be confident that he has wisdom. One further thing would give him pause. If he were wise about how to live, he would be able to transmit his expertise to apprentices. But Socrates doubts whether anyone can do this.[51]

V   LOVING BY LIVING: PHILOSOPHY AS TEACHING

According to Socrates' account of the oracle, he has honored wisdom by examining others and thus serving Apollo, and he has pursued wisdom, thereby acquiring better beliefs about how to live and thus improving his life. By honoring and pursuing wisdom, then, his love of wisdom has clearly benefited *him*. But what about the people he has annoyed with his examinations (22e–23a, 24a)? Is the love of wisdom a selfish enterprise? Later in the *Apology*, Socrates confronts this objection. After responding to the earlier accusations and clarifying his own relation to wisdom (17a–24c) and after briefly addressing the formal charges against him (24c–28b), Socrates imagines that someone might find something shameful about his love of wisdom (28b) and his avoidance of the political work that helps fellow-citizens (31c). In reply, Socrates insists that he will not quit philosophizing (*philosophein*) for any reason and that no greater benefit than his philosophizing has come to Athens. This full-throated defense transforms his model of philosophy.

Socrates' jurors find something shameful in philosophizing partly because they misidentify it. Socrates noted this earlier:

> And whenever someone asks them [viz., those charging Socrates with corrupting the young] what he [viz., Socrates] does and what he teaches, they are silent and ignorant, but in order that they not seem to be at a loss, they make the familiar charges against all who philosophize [*philosophountōn*], about "things in the sky and things below the earth," "not believing in the gods," and "making the weaker argument stronger." (23d2–7)

According to the "familiar" conception, philosophizers are atheistical nature-theorists and sophists. Socrates has distanced himself from those activities, but his audience has no other conception of philosophizing. To defend his philosophizing, Socrates must say what it is.

Thus, when he repeatedly insists that he will not stop philosophizing (28d–30b), Socrates never uses the verb *philosophein* by itself but always adds another verb, to explain what he means. The first time he does this, he says,

> I would do terrible things, men of Athens, if I had risked death and remained at my station (as anyone else would) when men you had elected to rule over me at Potidaea, Amphipolis, and Delium had stationed me, but now, when, as I have thought and supposed, the god stations me to live by philosophizing *and by examining* myself and others, I should leave my post for fear of death or anything else. (28d10–29a1, emphasis added)

Socrates is not saying that the god stations him to do two separate activities, philosophizing and examining himself and others. These participles are linked by an epexegetic 'and', which conjoins not two separate things but a second that explains the first.[52] Such conjunctions are common and occur several times in this chapter (e.g., Socrates "exaggerates *and* says he knows"). Socrates must be using an epexegetic 'and' here because he must be identifying philosophizing for his audience (and cf. 29c6–d1).

But Socrates is not content to explain philosophizing as examining. Soon after, he adds,

> Men of Athens, I am grateful and I am your friend, but I will obey the god rather than you, and as long as I breathe and am able, I shall not cease philosophizing *and exhorting you and showing* any one of you whom I happen to meet, saying in my customary way, "Best of men, since you are a citizen of Athens, the greatest city and a city most famous for wisdom and power, aren't you ashamed to care to get as much money, reputation, and honor as you can, while you do not care for or think about wisdom and truth and the best condition of your soul?" (29d2–e3, emphasis added)

Again, Socrates does not let the participle 'philosophizing' stand alone, where it might mislead his audience. Again, 'philosophizing' is followed by an epexegetic 'and' and then another participle to explain what he means. This time, though, the explanation is provided by a closely conjoined (by *te kai*) pair of participles, 'exhorting' and 'showing', which he *further* explains by a fourth participle ('saying', in simple apposition) that introduces the content of what he exhorts and shows. This sentence is complicated, but its point is simple: Socrates says that when he exhorts others to care about the right things, he is philosophizing (cf. *Euthd.* 275a).

In the ensuing lines, Socrates clarifies that exhortation is not subordinate to examination. He continues,

> And if one of you should dispute and insist that he does care [viz., about wisdom and truth and the best condition of his soul], I will not immediately let him go or leave him, but I will ask him and examine him and test him, and if I think that he does not possess virtue but claims to possess it, I shall reproach him because he makes the least of things worth the most and makes more of worse things. (29e3–30a3)

Some people whom Socrates exhorts to care about the best condition of their souls insist that they *do* care. This prompts Socrates to examine them, presumably in the hope of finding that they have successfully cultivated some virtue and put their souls into good condition. But when they prove to lack knowledge (and thereby virtue!), he exhorts some more, because he thinks that people who *claim* to care about virtue but do not cultivate it are failing to attach as much value to the cultivation of virtue as they should. Strikingly, the activity of examination here is *not* Socrates' ultimate focus. Rather, it is one part of a larger pattern of activity that aims at cultivating wisdom and virtue in others (cf. *Cleit.* 407a, 410b).

Examination remains important, of course. Examination can make Socrates' interlocutors aware of their ignorance and bring them closer to human wisdom. Human wisdom is not by itself valuable, but it does remove the conceit that one is already wise, which is an obstacle to the pursuit of wisdom. Indeed, awareness of one's ignorance might ignite desire for the wisdom one lacks.[53] But it might not: despair or hatred of inquiry might set in (21e, 22e–23a, 24a–b; cf. *Smp.* 215d–216b, *Phd.* 89c–91c). So examination and its product, human wisdom, are not enough. Socrates needs to exhort his interlocutors, too, so that they will pursue wisdom and seek improved beliefs about how to live.

Socrates immediately sums up his philosophizing activity and transforms his account of his divine mission:

> I will do these things [viz., exhort them to care about wisdom and virtue, test them if they say they do care, and reproach them if they turn out not to be virtuous] to anyone whom I meet, whether younger or older, whether citizen or foreigner, but especially to citizens, to the extent that you are closer to my people. For the god orders these things, know well, and I think no greater good has come to be for you in the city than my service to the god. For I go around doing nothing other than persuading the younger and older among you not to care for your bodies or money before or as intently as the best condition of your soul,[54] by saying "Virtue does not come to be from money, but from virtue money and all other things become good for human beings, both individually and collectively."[55] (30a3–b4)

According to his story about the oracle, he aids Apollo by examining people, which tests and disseminates the god's message about wisdom. Now, Socrates insists that he also serves Apollo by seeking to persuade others to care less for capital and more for virtue (cf. 36c–d). Moreover, he has now explicitly characterized both kinds of service as philosophizing. On Socrates' view, then, the god wants human beings to be virtuous but needs human help to achieve this goal, and philosophizing helps to achieve it by fostering both the awareness that wisdom belongs only to the gods *and* a commitment to trying, nonetheless, to become wise and virtuous like the gods.[56]

On this new account, philosophizing is clearly not a selfish enterprise. But the account prompts questions. First, how exactly can Socrates understand exhorting others as an instance of loving wisdom? To answer, Socrates could first clarify what it is to love and pursue wisdom. Some things that we love and pursue, we seek merely to be close to. One person, smitten, seeks to be in the company of another. Someone else seeks to own a beautiful vase. But wisdom is not like another person or an artifact. When Socrates pursues wisdom, he wants not merely to be in the company of wisdom or merely to have it in any old sense. He wants to *be* wise, and for him to be wise, as a living being, would be to live wisely.[57] So when Socrates loves and pursues wisdom, he loves and pursues living wisely.

With living wisely established as philosophy's goal, it would remain to explain why pursuing this goal includes exhorting others to virtue. The essential point is that trying to live wisely requires cooperation with others. This might occur especially naturally to Socrates, given his "love of humanity" (*philanthrōpia*, *Euphr.* 3d7), but insofar as Socratic examination is central to trying to live wisely, *anyone* trying to live wisely should see the need for cooperation. So Socrates' adherence to cooperative norms (29b, 32d), his strong preference for the company of good fellows rather than wicked ones (25c–d), and his exhortations are not extraneous to his wisdom-loving.

What Socrates says outside the *Apology* adds two important layers to this explanation. First, he suggests that virtue is or requires wisdom (see note 46, cf. 29e–30a), so helping people become virtuous must help them become wise. This tempts readers to think that Socrates has a narrowly intellectual conception of virtue, or that his conception of philosophizing outside the *Apology* is focused more on intellectual examination and less on exhortation. But even if every virtue is identical with wisdom, Socrates need not think intellectual achievement alone secures virtue. He might think the intellectual achievement requires some cultivation of affect and desire. Indeed, he *does* seem to think this. Throughout the *Apology*, Socrates shows sensitivity to others' emotions: the anger, humiliation, and envy of those he examines (21d, 22e–23a, 23c–d, 28a–b, 31a); the pleasure of onlookers (23c, 33c); the Athenians' ambition, greed, fear of death, and shame (23d–e, 28b, 29d–e, 30a–b); and the jurors' potential sympathies with him (34b–35b) as well as their surprise or even outrage at him (17c–d, 20e, 21a, 27b, 30c, 31e, 34b–d, 37a). Elsewhere, too, Socrates regularly appeals to his interlocutors' sense of honor or shame and confronts their emotions.[58] That is why, even if he thinks that every virtue is identical with wisdom, he does not limit his philosophizing mission to intellectual examination.

A second layer is added by Socrates' suggestion elsewhere that everyone has the ultimate goal of living well, that is, success (*eudaimonia*) (*Euthd.* 278e, 282a; *Smp.* 205a). This puts Socrates' commitment to living wisely in a new light. Either his goal of living wisely is subordinate to his ultimate goal of living well, or they are the same goal. The evidence in more "Socratic" dialogues suggests the latter: Socrates identifies living well with doing well, doing well with acting virtuously, and acting virtuously with acting wisely.[59] This helps to explain why Socrates prefers to die rather than to cease philosophizing. For him, there is no distinction between his ultimate goal of living well and the goal of acting wisely or being wise, so to cease philosophizing would be to give up on the point of living (cf. 38a). This also helps to explain why Socrates thinks philosophizing is so valuable. Because acting wisely is the ultimate goal, it is unconditionally valuable. Although only a god can be wise and live wisely, Socrates' philosophizing best approximates that goal, so nothing can be better for him than his philosophizing (cf. 38a).[60] Last, this additional layer helps to explain why *others* should philosophize. In the *Apology*, Socrates is on trial for impiety, so he frequently insists that he philosophizes because Apollo has told him to. This is a special reason to philosophize that others would not share (33c), but his general reason – that philosophizing best approximates living well – is available to others (cf. 38a).[61]

A second question about Socrates' expanded account of philosophizing concerns whether it answers the objection he faces. Even if his philosophizing aims to benefit others and so is not entirely selfish, does it fully replace the political work that he avoids? Socrates admits that he has largely avoided public affairs and gives two reasons why. He says that his service to the god examining people has left him with no time for political work (23b), and that if he had engaged more in public affairs, his commitment to justice would have led to his death long ago and thus cut short his help for others (31d–32a).[62] These are quite different reasons. The second suggests that public engagement would have been preferable had the Athenians been more just, whereas the first does not. Perhaps there is no inconsistency, though. Perhaps Socrates thinks that public work is *generally* preferable if one's community is just, but would not be preferable *for him* even if the Athenians had been just, because *he* has a special obligation to Apollo. So understood, he gives two reasons because he wants to record the second, but the first by itself was enough for him (cf. 28d–29d, 37b, 38a). Thus, Socrates *is* vulnerable to the charge that he has minimized his engagement with civic affairs.

Socrates answers, in effect, that his philosophizing – his examining, his pursuing, and his exhorting – does what politics is supposed to do, by striving to benefit others. His examinations foster clarity, which is a common good (*Chrm.* 166d, *Grg.* 505e), and pursue wisdom, which would also be shareable, and most importantly, both his examinations and his exhortations seek to move people toward virtue, which is good not just for the more virtuous but also for others. In the *Apology*, he does not call this political work, but he does say that he does more good for Athenians than anyone else (36c–d) and even that he is god's gift to Athens (30e–31b)! Elsewhere, he declares, more explicitly, that he, alone among Athenians, does the work of politics.[63] Socrates thus defines politics by its work of improving others' lives (cf. *Euthd.* 292d, *Rep.* I 347d) and challenges the assumption that locates politics in the business of ordinary civic institutions.[64] And because his philosophizing aims to help not just Athenians but also foreigners (23b, 30a), Socrates challenges anti-cosmopolitan assumptions, too.[65]

One last question about Socrates' extended defense is prompted by its suggestion that he teaches others to care about their souls, because Socrates insists in the *Apology* that he is *not* a teacher.[66] He asserts that he does not teach others as an expert would, transmitting expertise to an apprentice, or as a sophist would, in a formal relationship with a fee (19d–20c). But he also asserts broadly that he is not a teacher and that no one is his student (33a–b).

Socrates is aware that he teaches in some ways. At the close of his defense speech, he acknowledges that he *could* persuade the jurors to ignore their oath of office and thus "teach" them not to believe that there are gods (35d). This is teaching as persuading (35c2), and when Socrates examines and exhorts people, he is at least trying to teach them in this way (cf. 30a8). Also, Socrates knows that his examinations attract followers, who imitate him (23c, cf. 37d). He expresses confidence that after he is gone, there will be many others, younger and more difficult to deal with, examining the Athenians (39c–d). So he models and inspires – and in this way teaches – dialectical practices.

Why, then, does he deny that he teaches? He does so to insist that he is not responsible for what his interlocutors do (33b). This might seem objectionable: Is Socrates just evading responsibility? But he makes a good point about his philosophizing. The point is clearest in the case of his examinations, for when Socrates examines others, he does not seek to put thoughts into their heads that were not already there. He seeks to draw out their thoughts, to examine them. He is not so much teaching others as he is helping them rethink themselves (e.g., *Meno* 85b–86b, *Grg.* 495d–e).

This point is less apparent in the case of Socrates' exhortations. If many people entirely lack thoughts that incline toward temperance and justice, and away from wealth and status, then Socrates could hardly exhort others as he does without sometimes putting thoughts in their heads. But Socrates might think that people are *not* entirely without these thoughts. His experience examining others has taught him that some thoughts come easily from his interlocutors. He insists elsewhere that *everyone* wants to live well (*Euthd.* 278e, 282a, *Smp.* 205a) and that *everyone* thinks it is better to suffer injustice than to do it (*Grg.* 474b, 475e). Perhaps Socrates exhorts others not to give them values they lack but to redirect them toward values they already have.[67]

So understood, Socratic philosophizing does not teach by conveying new thoughts to people, but it does educate by inspiring and challenging others to examine themselves and reorient their priorities.[68]

VI   PLATO AND SOCRATES THE PHILOSOPHER

The historical Socrates certainly inspired Plato, and Plato's characterization of Socrates has inspired many others. But already in Plato's dialogues, there are questions about whether philosophy should be exactly as it is for the *Apology*'s Socrates. According to the Socratic model, a philosopher loves wisdom – the expertise about how to live, including understanding of good and bad – in three ways: by honoring wisdom as the gods' possession, examining others' false claims to knowledge; by pursuing wisdom, learning about how to live as one examines oneself alongside others; and by trying to live wisely, which includes helping others to pursue virtue. Many of the questions that arise in other dialogues involve relatively minor complications, such as how exactly to pursue wisdom (note 21), whether wisdom is attainable (note 49), what kind of thing (note 40) and how much (note 50) the wise must know, and the relation between intellectual and non-intellectual affect and desires (notes 54 and 58). But two questions involve deeper doubt about Socratic philosophizing. How well do Socratic examinations benefit those examined? And how well does the Socratic pursuit of wisdom cohere with the political work of helping others?

Both doubts are rooted in the *Apology*: Socrates is on trial in part because he has annoyed people and in part because his pursuits were ill-suited to ordinary politics. But he does not always shrug these doubts off as he does in the *Apology*. In the *Republic*, after Adeimantus records that Socrates' examinations fail to move most people (*Rep.* VI 487b–c), Socrates suggests that in an ideal city, they would keep such examinations away from the young and others who had not been carefully prepared for them, lest the examinations have the terrible consequences they have "nowadays" (*Rep.* VII 537d–539d, cf. VI 497e–498c, *Phil.* 15d–16a). Also, the *Republic*'s Socrates sees a conflict not just between philosophy and politics-as-usual, where the unjust threaten the just, but also between philosophy and politics-in-the-best-case-scenario, since politics is always messy and unappealing compared with the beautiful truths that the philosopher loves.[69]

Although the Socratic model of philosophy as a way of life is rarely manifest now,[70] many features of it survive. Strikingly, Plato's two concerns also survive. Today's worries about the effects of hostile criticism are not merely about practices alien to philosophy – eristic or sophistical practices – invading. They are also worries about *philosophical* practices misfiring. And today's debates about whether philosophy can or must be politically engaged are not boundary skirmishes about how to distinguish philosophy from other pursuits. They are debates that have been central to philosophy from the start. These questions, about how to examine critically in ways that help instead of hurting and about how to relate philosophy to politics, are living inheritances from Plato's reflection on the Socratic model of philosophy.

NOTES

1 Diogenes Laertius says, "The first to call himself a philosopher was Pythagoras" (I 12), but he cites Heraclides of Pontus, a follower of Plato who was probably pushing a Pythagorean origin for Platonic philosophy (Burkert 1960). (Isocrates credits Pythagoras as the first Greek to bring philosophy from Egypt, but does not say that Pythagoras called himself a philosopher [*Or.* 11.28].) Heraclitus fr. 35 DK includes the phrase "philosophical men" (*philosophous andras*), but this "fragment" looks like a paraphrase, by Clement of Alexandria, which leaves the origin of the key phrase uncertain (cf. Kahn 1979: 105; Laks and Most 2016, 3: 157). The earliest indubitable occurrence of *philosophos* or *philosophein* ("philosophize") is Herodotus I 30; other indubitable occurrences that probably predate the fourth century are Thucydides II 40.1; Gorgias, *Helen* (fr. 11 DK) 13; and the Hippocratic *On Ancient Medicine* 20.1 (with Schiefsky 2005: 300–2). To speculate

about origins, take up Moore 2020, note that Herodotus and Gorgias might have known Pythagoreans, from Herodotus' time in Thurii and Gorgias' in Sicily, and note that Gorgias and Thucydides likely knew of Socrates. I thank Robert Hahn, Rusty Jones, Christopher Moore, and Ravi Sharma for help.

2 Like Plato's Socrates, Isocrates sharply distinguishes philosophers from "sophists" and "eristics" (and cf. Xenophon, *Cyn.* 13.6–9). But Isocrates also denigrates some Socratic patterns of speech, and insists that philosophy should be more politically engaged than Plato's Socrates is. See especially the opening paragraphs of his *Encomium of Helen* (*Or.* 10) and *Antidosis* (*Or.* 15), with Nightingale 1995: 13–59. Cf. *Euthd.* 304d–306d, with Chance 1992: 200.

3 Cf. Gill 2012. See also the possibly Platonic *Lovers* with Peterson 2011: 201–5, and 2017.

4 This character was of course inspired by, and must resemble, the historical Socrates. For the problem of discovering the historical Socrates, see Lacey 1971 and Dorion 2011; cf. Jones and Sharma 2020.

5 See this chapter, section V; cf. *Grg.* 481c–482c, *Phd.* 60e–61a, *Rep.* VI 496a–c.

6 Cf. Peterson 2011, against Nehamas 1990 and Nightingale 1995.

7 See *Euthydemus* with Hawtrey 1981 and Chance 1992 and *Gorgias* with Shaw 2015: 102–42. Cf. Barney 2006, McCoy 2008, Irwin (this volume, ch. 2), and Asmis (this volume, ch. 11).

8 The vast literature includes Gulley 1968, Santas 1979, Kraut 1984, Reeve 1989, Vlastos 1991, Brickhouse and Smith 1994, Irwin 1995a: 3–147, Benson 2000, Weiss 2006, Wolfsdorf 2008, McNeill 2010, Peterson 2011, Belfiore 2012, Moore 2015, Ahbel-Rappe 2018, and Prior 2019. Wolfsdorf (2013) surveys one prominent strand. Taylor (1998), Brickhouse and Smith (2000), Ahbel-Rappe (2009), and Rudebusch (2009) provide introductions.

9 Wolfsdorf 2004: 76–9; Blondell 2002: 8–11.

10 This broad, fuzzy distinction is reasonable and potentially significant, but sharp divisions and chronological speculations are dubious. Cf. Ebrey and Kraut (this volume, ch. 1); Vlastos 1991; Nails 1995; Kahn 1996 and 2003; Gill 2006; Brickhouse and Smith 2010, 11–42; Brandwood (this volume, ch. 3).

11 When citing Plato's texts, I refer to the most recent Oxford Classical Text edition (Slings 2003, Duke et al. 1995, Burnet 1901–1907); I omit the title for the *Apology*; and I use my revisions of the translations in Cooper 1997a.

12 Irwin (this volume, ch. 2).

13 Cf. Brickhouse and Smith 1989: 87–100; Stokes 1992.

14 Cf. Reeve 1989: 37–45, Roochnik 1996.

15 Cf. the "biggest kinds" (*ta megista genē*) in *Sph*. 254b–257a.

16 The usual reading of "biggest things" as merely the most important supports the same conclusion, and agrees with other Platonic texts (e.g., *Alc*. I 118a; *Grg*. 527d–e; *Rep*. III 392a–b; *Laws* X 890b). But taking *ta megista* to be the broadest and not merely the most important things helps us notice one way in which eristics and sophists are a special threat to philosophy: they, too, claim the broadest scope for their endeavors (*Euthd*. 274d, 275e and *Grg*. 451d, 452d–e, 456a–c, respectively). I thank Emily Fletcher for this. Cf. Aristotle, *Met*. Γ2 1004b17–26.

17 Burkert 1985: 148; cf. Moore 2015: 22–31.

18 Forster 2006; cf. Benson 2000: 180–5.

19 These speculations are indebted to Verity Harte.

20 See, e.g., Burnyeat 1977b. Cf. Sedley 2004, LaBarge 2005, Reeve 2006, Belfiore 2012.

21 Socrates' dialectical expertise would be atypical, for it would be identified with the "worthless" product, human wisdom, that it creates and sustains, and Socrates teaches it not as a master transmits expertise to an apprentice but by inspiring imitation (see this chapter, section V). Also, this skill would differ from both the dialectic Socrates disavows in less "Socratic" dialogues (*Rep*. VI 506c–e with VII 531d–535a, 537c; *Phdr*. 262d with 259e–274b) and the dialectic the Eleatic Stranger of the *Sophist* and *Statesman* develops and calls "philosophy" (*Sph*. 249c d, 253c 254b, cf. 259d–260a).

22 See the *Lysis* (esp. 216d) with Obdrzalek 2013 and *Symposium* (esp. 201a–c) with Obdrzalek (this volume, ch. 7).

23 Cicero, *Acad*. 1.16, 1.44–6. Cf. Bett 2006.

24 That is, Socrates bears no resemblance to the "rustic" skeptic who suspends judgment about everything. He might resemble an "urbane" skeptic who suspends judgment only about non-evident matters. For the (contentious) distinction, see Burnyeat and Frede 1997.

25 Both times, Socrates uses the verb *oida* ("I know"), which is an ordinary way of making a knowledge claim, contrasted with "I opine" (*doxazō*), "I think" (*oiomai*), and "it seems to me" (*dokei moi*). The verb *epistamai* ("I know" or "I understand") is less common, but can be used interchangeably with *oida* (as at *Meno* 97a–b; cf. *Ap.* 22c–d).

26 Contrast the distinction between expert and non-expert knowledge drawn by Reeve (1989: 37–53) and Woodruff (1990). They distinguish two different ways of knowing the same facts or activities (and run into problems – cf. Reeve 1989: 58–62). I distinguish two sets of facts and activities. On my interpretation, a claim to knowledge is always justified by mastery, but for some facts and activities, this mastery is provided only by ordinary experience, and for others, only by expertise.

27 Socrates occasionally avows knowledge of epistemological or logical matters (e.g., *Meno* 98b and *Prt.* 360e–361a, respectively). Presumably, he puts these in the class of things knowable without expertise, or he treats them as parts of his dialectical skill that includes the erotic and midwifery arts. (Meno's response at *Meno* 98b might suggest the former.) Either way, he can similarly claim to *know* that he lacks wisdom, and we do not need to assume that his grasp (*sunoida*, 21b5; *egnōken*, 23b3) of this falls short of knowledge. Cf. Fine 2008.

28 Cf. Benson (2000: 112–41; 2013a) on "the priority of definition."

29 Cf. Wolfsdorf 2004.

30 Benson 2000: 245–6, retracted by Benson 2013b. Cf. Shaw 2015: 61–2.

31 Sextus Empiricus, *P.H.* I 23–4; Montaigne I 23 "Of Custom, and not easily changing an accepted law"; Descartes, *Discourse on Method* III.

32 I thank Nicholas D. Smith for clarification here.

33 Kraut 1984: 271 n. 43; Reeve 1989: 31–2; Brickhouse and Smith 1989: 87–100.

34 Socrates' response to the oracle – examining it (*elegxōn*, 21c1) to determine what it means – also suggests prior experience with examination. I thank Casey Perin for this.

35 Irwin 1995a: 29; Benson 2000: 236–8; Forster 2006: 15–16 nn. 35–6.

36 Vasiliou 2008: 37.

37 Vlastos 1985. Cf. Lesher 1987; McPartland 2013.

38 These speculations are indebted to Jeremy Henry. Cf. Vasiliou 2008: 27–39; Peterson 2011: 42–56.

39 The penalty Socrates knows to be evil (37b) is to cease philosophizing and thus disobey the god (cf. 29b–30b, 37e–38a). The other penalties Socrates

canvasses (death, exile, imprisonment, fine) are not evil for Socrates, at least not if evils harm their possessors (cf. 30c–d). Cf. Vasiliou 2008: 34.

40 In the less "Socratic" *Republic*, Socrates suggests that necessary, definitional truths are knowable but not opinable while contingent, perceptual matters are opinable but not knowable (V–VII 475c–535a). This recasts the distinction between things knowable only by expertise and things knowable only by ordinary experience (cf. note 26), restricting what can be known by the more demanding cognition to necessary, definitional truths and demoting the less demanding cognition based on ordinary experience.

41 Benson 2000: 182; Forster 2006.

42 For this "problem of the elenchus," see Vlastos 1983, Benson 2000: 32–95. Cf. Scott 2002.

43 Brickhouse and Smith 1994: 10–29; Gentzler 1994; Irwin 1995a: 17–30.

44 Note, too, the related concerns about how to start inquiring from a position of ignorance: see *Charmides* with Tuozzo 2011 and *Meno* with Scott 2006 and Fine (this volume, ch. 6).

45 Cf. *Sph.* 218b–d, *Pol.* 258b–c, 285c–d.

46 For this tenet and the related question of the "unity of virtues," see *Euthd.* 281e, *Meno* 88b–89a, and especially the *Laches* and *Protagoras* with Penner 1973b; Vlastos 1981: 221–69; Devereux 1992; and Brickhouse and Smith 2010: 154–67.

47 Shaw 2011.

48 Gulley 1968: 62–73; Senn 2013. Cf. *Rep.* I 337a.

49 Even the less "Socratic" Socrates who suggests wise philosopher-rulers are in principle possible (Burnyeat 1992) restricts the scope of their wisdom so that it does not include mastery over perceptibles (*Rep.* VIII 546a–b with note 40 above) and falls short of what the gods enjoy (*Rep.* X 613a–b).

50 Cf. *Euthd.* 293b–294a; Benson 2000: 162, 250–2. One might wonder how much one needs to know to be a knower about how to live. Does one need to know, say, the geometrical structure of nature? Compare *Grg.* 507e–508b with the less "Socratic" *Republic* VI–VII and *Timaeus*.

51 See the *Protagoras* and *Meno* with Kraut 1984: 285–304.

52 Cf. Strycker and Slings 1994: 134; Stokes 1997, *ad loc.*; Peterson 2011: 39.

53 Cf. *Meno* 84a–c, *Lys.* 218a–b, *Smp.* 203e–204a, with Obdrzalek (this volume, ch. 7).

54 "Bodies or money" replaces "money, reputation, and honor" (from 29d9–
e1). Cf. *Phd.* 68b–c and *Rep.* IX 580d–581c with VII 518d–e.

55 In translating the last clause, I follow Burnet 1924, *ad loc.*; Stokes 1997, *ad
loc.*; and Burnyeat 2003. Cf. Burnyeat 1971: 210; Strycker and Slings 1994,
ad loc. and 138–40; and Brickhouse and Smith 2010: 172–89.

56 *Euphr.* 13e–14c with Taylor 1982. Cf. Reeve 1989: 62–73; McPherran
1996; Burnyeat 1997; Forster 2007. Cf., too, *Rep.* X 613a–b, *Tht.* 176b, *Ti.*
90b–d, *Laws* IV 715e–718c.

57 Plato's Socrates often identifies being wise with acting wisely, and
sometimes means by 'virtue' or 'medicine' what the virtuous or doctors
know and sometimes what they do (e.g., *Grg.* 460a–c). Aristotle criticizes
this (e.g., *N.E.* I.8 1098b31–1099a7), but with the possible exception of the
comatose, no one who entirely fails to act wisely is wise.

58 Blank 1993, Devereux 1995, Singpurwalla 2006, Austin 2013. Brickhouse
and Smith (2010) reconcile this with "motivational intellectualism" – the
thesis that everyone always does what they believe to be best (cf. Reshotko
2006 and Penner 2011) – though perhaps they should not (Kamtekar 2017).
Cf. the less "Socratic" Socrates' division of the soul to explain non-rational
affect and desire, with Barney, Brennan, and Brittain 2012.

59 The first two identities are expressed at *Cri.* 48b; assumed at *Chrm.* 171e–
172a, *Grg.* 507b–c, and perhaps *Ap.* 28b; and used in *Euthd.* 278e–282d,
Meno 87c–89a, and *Rep.* I 352d–354a. For the third identity, see note 46,
with 29e–30a. Cf. Zeyl 1982; Irwin 1986; Brickhouse and Smith 1994: 103–
36; Morrison 2003; Bobonich 2011.

60 Whether Socrates approximates living well closely enough to count as
being successful (*eudaimōn*) is unclear. He might think that *eudaimonia*,
like wisdom, is beyond human reach during this life (cf. 41c). Cf. Smith
2016, Jones 2016. In any case, he should not say that he *has made* anyone
successful, although he could say that he *is making* people successful,
especially to insist that he has their genuine *eudaimonia* as his target (36d;
cf. *Grg.* 527c).

61 Cf. Ebrey 2017c.

62 Socrates also says his divine sign (*daimonion*) steered him away from
public affairs (31c–d), but it is unclear how much weight he gives the sign
apart from the reason he offers to explain why it was correct (31d–32a).
Although the *daimonion* probably bolstered Socrates' confidence in some
of his beliefs, and perhaps entirely underwrote his confidence in one (40b–

c with Austin 2010), Socrates does not suggest that a divine sign is essential to philosophy, for he encourages others to philosophize without saying they need a *daimonion*. Cf. Smith and Woodruff 2000, Destrée and Smith 2005.

63 *Grg.* 521d with Shaw 2011.

64 Brown 2009.

65 Brown 2000b.

66 Cf. Kraut 1984: 294–304; Reeve 1989: 160–9; Nehamas 1992; Scott 2000.

67 Compare the thought, mentioned in section IV above, that human beings innately possess the views drawn out by Socratic examination (*Meno* 81a–e, 85b–86b, *Phd.* 72e–73b).

68 Cf. *Phdr.* 261a; *Rep.* VII 518d *contra* I 345b (with *Smp.* 175d); and *Sph.* 228d–231b.

69 See *Rep.* VII 519c–521b, 540b with Brown 2000a. Cf. *Phd.* 78b–84b, *Tht.* 172c–177c, *Ti.* 89e–90d; Jenkins 2016, Peterson 2011.

70 Cf. Hadot 2002.

5   Being Good at Being Bad: Plato's *Hippias Minor*

Agnes Callard

The label "virtue ethics" usually serves to contrast Aristotle's approach to ethical theory with Kantian deontology or Mill-inspired consequentialism, but it would be more accurate to describe Aristotelian ethics as an ethics of "virtue-activation." For Aristotle's view is that (inner) virtue is for the sake of a further thing, namely, (outer) activity in accordance with virtue. The philosopher who valorizes the state of virtue as an end in itself is not Aristotle but Socrates; those looking to understand why he places virtue above virtuous activity should turn to the *Hippias Minor*.

The *Hippias Minor* is a short, neglected, strange dialogue; it is about the connection between being able to do something well, and being able to do it badly. In it, Socrates argues that the expert in any domain is also the person who has the power to (deliberately) go wrong in that domain. So, for instance, the expert archer can best ensure that her arrow misses the target; the novice archer, who might accidentally hit the target she's trying to miss, is not as good at being bad. Likewise, claims Socrates, the expert in justice is the only person who can, if he likes, make sure that he does something unjust. Socrates draws the shocking conclusion that if anyone deliberately does what is unjust, it's the just person.

Socrates uses the shock value of such a claim to redirect our attention from outward manifestations of success and failure – how someone behaves – to the inner source of that behavior. Socrates makes the case that the proper object of approbation and disapprobation is not the action but inner power underwriting both deliberate conformity to and deliberate deviation from the norm in question. The value of justice lies not in the just (or unjust!) things just people *do*, but in the power they *have*.

The *Hippias Minor* articulates the conception of power underwriting the distinctively Socratic approach to ethics: one that bottoms out in the value of the virtue one has, rather than the use to which one puts it.

I   FLOUTING AND FLUBBING

Even given its short length, the *Hippias Minor* is, at the level of argumentation, surprisingly simple. It proceeds by way of two waves of argumentation, the first at 365c–373b and the second at 373c–376b, each of which argues in roughly the same way for roughly the same conclusion. I will proceed in the order of the dialogue, discussing each wave; before doing so, however, let me explain the distinction that is central to the dialogue.

Over the course of the dialogue, Socrates and Hippias discuss a wide variety of opposed pairs: the truthful man and the liar, the fast runner and the slow runner, the strong man and the weak man, the archer who hits the target and the one who misses the target, the horse that one rides badly and the horse that one rides well, eyes that see well and eyes that see badly and finally, the just man and the unjust man. Socrates argues that these "opposites" are unified: it is *the same man* who speaks the truth and lies, *the same man* who hits and who misses the target. Or rather, it is the same man who *willingly* does both actions, because willingly doing something badly presupposes the ability to do it well.

Socrates calls on us to distinguish between two ways of violating the norms of a given activity. The person who lacks mastery with respect to the activity errs by, as I will call it, *flubbing* the activity. He doesn't control whether he breaks or follows the rule. Consider the norms associated with archery or race-running: hit the target, run fast. The flubber is the one who misses the target because he cannot keep his hand steady, or who runs slowly because he has a lame foot. When the person *with* mastery violates the norms of the activity, I will say she *flouts* them. The expert wrestler might lose a match on purpose to conserve energy; the Olympic runner might run slowly on purpose in order to allow his friend to win.

We can contrast intentionally/purposefully/willingly erring and accidentally/unintentionally/unwillingly erring in any domain; and this is exactly how Socrates draws the contrast in cases of running, wrestling, vision etc. But there are domains in which we do not need to *introduce* terminology to mark the distinction, because we already have the conceptual and linguistic resources to acknowledge the distinctiveness of the flouted activity, or the flubbed one. Examples of the former are losing at a sport because one "throws" the match, cheating at a game, breaking the law as an act of civil disobedience, and the phenomena of disobedience or rebellion more generally. Examples of the latter: negligence (as in a legal context), fumbling the ball (in a sports game), malfunctions, glitches, lapses, mistakes.

The basic principle to which Socrates wishes to secure Hippias' agreement throughout the dialogue is one that I will call *flouting over flubbing:*

> Those who flout some norm are better in relation to what is governed by that norm than those who flub it.

The first wave of the *Hippias Minor* discusses *flouting over flubbing* in the restricted domain of norms governing speech; the second wave covers any norm-governed activity, object, or condition. Both waves conclude by specifying that *flouting over flubbing* holds for moral norms as well as for nonmoral ones: the person who flouts the norms of justice (by intentionally speaking or acting in the most unjust way) is better with respect to justice than the one whose injustice is only accidental. This conclusion is sensational, and scholars have tried to resist it by faulting Socrates' argumentation: they accuse the first argument of trading on a verbal equivocation, and the second of an illicit employment of the craft analogy. I will defend Socrates on both fronts.

II THE FIRST WAVE: LYING VS. SPEAKING FALSELY (365C–373B)

The aim of speaking truly is internal to the practice of speaking, which is why it is appropriate to correct someone who says something false. Successful speech is truthful speech. But there is a very important difference between violating the norm of truthfulness accidentally, and violating it with the knowledge that what one is saying is false. Socrates' opening argument uses the distinction between flouting and flubbing to distinguish the mathematical falsehoods uttered by a mathematical expert such as Hippias from those uttered by an ignorant person:

> T1: Don't you think the ignorant person would often involuntarily tell the truth when he wished to say falsehoods, if it so happened (*ei tuchoi*), because he didn't know; whereas you, the wise person, if you should wish to lie, would always consistently lie? (367a2–5)

Those without mastery succeed, when they do succeed, by mere chance (*ei tuchoi*), and fail, when they do fail, by the same chance. If I say something true by chance, then I am also the kind of person whom chance leads to say false things. Likewise, if I had the mastery to speak falsely about math it follows that I had the mastery to speak truly.

In English, lying is one of those cases where the distinction between flouting and flubbing is built in to our terminology: we use "lie" for the case of flouting the norm of truthfulness; when we want to describe someone violating that norm unintentionally, by accident, without any intent to deceive, we say that they "made a mistake" or "misspoke" or "said something false." Greek does not, however, have two different words for "lie" and "speak falsely": in T1, "falsehood" and "lie" are translations of the same Greek word, *pseudesthai*. This creates a problem for Socrates' argument. The problem is not, of course, that Greek speakers lacked the *conceptual* distinction between lying and merely speaking falsely – that distinction is evident in the passage below:

> T2: HIPPIAS: When Achilles says false things (*pseudetai*), he's portrayed as doing so not on purpose but involuntarily, forced to stay and help by the misfortune of the army. But the lies of Odysseus (*pseudetai*) are voluntary and on purpose. (370e5–9)

The linguistic mismatch between Greek and English creates a little bit of awkwardness here, since if Hippias had the word "lie," he wouldn't have had to add the qualifications "voluntary and on purpose." Nonetheless, one virtue of translating the second *pseudetai* as "lies" is that it makes clear what Hippias is doing, namely, grounding the moral difference between Achilles and Odysseus on our familiar distinction between saying false things and lying. Greek speakers, like English speakers, have ample reasons to draw a *conceptual* distinction between lies and mere falsehoods.

The worry is not that Socrates and Hippias are unable to distinguish lying from truthtelling due to the fact that they are using only one word, the worry is that that word allows Socrates to slip from the unmoralized case of speaking falsely to the moralized case of lying. In T2, Hippias wants to contrast the case of Achilles and Odysseus, on the one hand, with the mathematical case described above. Hippias granted the mathematical superiority of the flouter, but he wants to assert the moral superiority of the flubber. Hippias wants to insist that precisely because Achilles merely flubs the rule of truth-telling, whereas Odysseus flouts it, Achilles is morally superior to Odysseus. Socrates responds by insisting that the mathematical and moral cases are parallel:

T3: SOCRATES : Then it seems that Odysseus is better than Achilles after all.

HIPPIAS : Not at all, surely, Socrates.

SOCRATES : Why not? Didn't it emerge just now that the voluntary liars are better than the involuntary ones?

HIPPIAS : But Socrates, how could those who are voluntarily unjust, and are voluntary and purposeful evil-doers, be better than those who act that way involuntarily? For these people, there seems to be much lenience, when they act unjustly without knowing, or lie, or do some other evil. The laws, too, are surely much harsher toward those who do evil and lie voluntarily than toward those who do so involuntarily. 371e4–372a5

When he compares the voluntary lies of Odysseus to voluntary injust-ice, Hippias is moved to recognize the distinctiveness of the category of intentional false speech that is *immoral*. He finds himself a moral context in which the claims he had been moved to agree on in the mathematical domain no longer seem true. He feels the tables have been turned on him, and this is difficult to convey in translation: while it is natural, in Greek, to set aside ethics and ask whether the person who speaks mathematical falsehoods is (mathematically) superior, in English "lies" is automatically moral, and the correspond-ing question – "is the person who lies about math better or worse?" – might prompt a response clarifying two senses of "better than."

It is not that the word "lie" *must* signify immoral false speech. For we are able, e.g., to ask a question such as "Are all lies immoral?" But such a use in English requires us to explicitly cancel the negative moral association. In Greek, the situation is reversed.[1] Because the base meaning of the word is false speech, the negative moral assess-ment must be explicitly attached. Thus it is not surprising that when he granted the superiority of the one who "lies" about math, Hippias allowed the context to present the word *pseudesthai* in a way that raised no moral questions, and was strictly about mathematical ability. In T3, by contrast, Hippias wants to promote Achilles' unin-tentional and moral false speech over Odysseus' intentional and immoral false speech. Hippias would not be wrong to protest that he agreed to the superiority of flouters *on the assumption that moral norms were not under discussion*. He has good grounds to resist extending his conclusion from the mathematical case to the moral one.

Many commentators have, consequently, charged Socrates' argument against the superiority of Achilles with equivocation.[2] Panos Dimas has defended Socrates by insisting that he uses "liar" in an exclusively nonmoral sense: "Socrates is not interested in, and, most importantly, not addressing Hippias' moral assessment of these Homeric characters ... he is concerned with the descriptive aspect of the proposition that someone is truthful or untruthful" (2014: 109).

But it is clear, surely even to Socrates, that *Hippias* does attach a moral sense to the *pseudesthai* of Odysseus in T3; if Socrates means to use *pseudesthai* only in a nonmoral sense, he is speaking, at best, misleadingly. Nor can we take the opposite path from Dimas, and insist that Socrates uses *pseudesthai* in a moral sense throughout. For the geometrical example is not naturally heard as a reference to the superiority of clever but evil geometers over decent but stupid ones.

In fact, it seems clear that Socrates holds both the moral and nonmoral position: mathematicians who say false things intentionally are mathematically superior to those who do so unintentionally; and, in addition, people who lie intentionally are morally superior to those who accidentally say what is false. The worry is, does he exploit the flexibility of Greek to use the plausibility of the former claim to secure Hippias' agreement to the latter?

If the dialogue had ended with the first wave, it might indeed have been fair to accuse Socrates of subterfuge in sliding between the nonmoral and the moral case. But as it stands, the exchange in T2–3 exposes a difference that needs to be further explored, and Socrates goes on to do precisely that: the distinction between moral and nonmoral cases of flouting is the central topic of the rest of the dialogue. In the second half of the dialogue, Socrates makes absolutely explicit the fact that he takes the rule that goes for the nonmoral cases to also apply to the moral ones. What might have been an equivocation if the dialogue had ended halfway is vindicated by Socrates' upcoming argument for a *principled* assimilation of the two kinds of cases.

III   THE SECOND WAVE: MORAL VS. NONMORAL FLOUTING

Let us, then, turn to some of the examples featured in the second wave (373c and following) of argumentation in the *Hippias Minor*:

> Which one is the better runner, then: the one who runs slowly voluntarily, or the one who does so involuntarily? (373d5–6)

So also in wrestling, one who voluntarily has worthless and shameful accomplishments is a better wrestler than one who has them involuntarily. (374a1–2)

Isn't the physically better person able to accomplish both sorts of things: the strong and the weak, the shameful and the fine? So whenever he accomplishes worthless physical results, the one who is physically better does them voluntarily, whereas the one who is worse does them involuntarily? (374a7–b3)

What about gracefulness, Hippias? Doesn't the better body strike shameful and worthless poses voluntarily, and the worse body involuntarily? (374b5–7)

So then one statement embraces them all, ears, nose, mouth and all the senses: those that involuntarily accomplish bad results aren't worth having because they're worthless, whereas those that do so voluntarily are worth having because they're good. (374d8–e2)

Is it better to possess a horse with such a soul that one could ride it badly voluntarily, or involuntarily? (375a3–5)

In these passages Socrates tries to establish that the point he made in the first wave – with reference to various forms of mathematical and scientific knowledge – is, in fact, a general point about flouting and flubbing. Those who have the power to act well in some domain don't flub the rule. In fact, insofar as they have the power, they cannot flub it. They can pretend to flub it, using their mastery to act exactly as one would act without it, but their pretend flubbing is real flouting. The flouter cannot violate the norm in a way that would indicate a defect in his capacity to obey the norm. It follows that if I criticize someone for a norm violation, I must be criticizing him for flubbing rather than flouting that norm.[3] For flouting of the norm is a sign of excellence in respect of that very norm. So, for instance, if I criticize someone who runs slowly on purpose, I do not criticize him in terms of his power of running, but rather in terms of getting his priorities straight, or being a good friend. I criticize him for flubbing norms of competition or friendship, not for flouting norms of running. This line of reasoning leads to a shocking conclusion when Socrates extends his argument from these explicitly nonmoral cases to the explicitly moral case of justice and injustice:

1) So the more powerful and better soul, when it does injustice, will do injustice voluntarily, and the worthless soul involuntarily? (376a6–7)

2) Therefore, it's up to the good man to do injustice voluntarily, and the bad man to do it involuntarily. (376b2–4)

3) So the one who voluntarily misses the mark and does what is shameful and unjust, Hippias – that is, if there is such a person – would be no other than the good man. (376b4–6)

Hippias and Socrates both recoil at the conclusion that associates voluntary injustice with goodness. And yet, this conclusion does seem to follow by analogy with the other cases: real injustice – violating the principles of justice by flouting and not mere flubbing – is the province of the one who has mastered justice. In the ethical domain, *flouting over flubbing* entails the disturbing conclusion that one who is being (fully, perfectly) unjust is the just person.

The remainder of this chapter constitutes an attempt to grapple with this conclusion. In section IV, I offer a brief overview of how the shocking conclusion has been read by other scholars. The general strategy has been to soften the claims of the *Hippias Minor* by interpreting them in the light of commitments drawn from other dialogues. I argue that this approach puts the attention in the wrong place: if we allocate the argumentative work elsewhere, we miss out on the dialogue's distinctive contribution.

My methodology is the opposite, in that I think the arguments at the core of the *Hippias Minor* are poised to shed light on the places where *flouting over flubbing* can be found outside the *Hippias Minor* (I present those texts in section V). In section VI I explain what I take to be the *Hippias Minor*'s distinctive argumentative contribution: instead of seeing (1)-(3) as the product of a craft analogy articulated more explicitly elsewhere, I show that the *Hippias Minor* contains an original argument for the existence of a craft analogy, an argument that gives *power* pride of place in Socratic virtue ethics. In section VII I offer some considerations to temper our shock at (1)-(3). In section VIII I consider Socratic virtue ethics from an Aristotelian point of view.

IV IMMORALISM IN THE HIPPIAS MINOR?

The apparent immoralism of (1)-(3) is so shocking, that, as Paul Friedländer once noted, these statements would long ago have relegated the dialogue to apocryphal status were it not for Aristotle's testimony (1964: 146).

Attention to the precise wording of (2) reveals an escape valve. That sentence is in fact a conditional, one whose antecedent ("if there is such a person") Socrates elsewhere claims to be necessarily false. Thus Taylor:

> On reflection we see that the key to Plato's meaning is really supplied by one clause in the proposition which emerges as the conclusion of the matter: "the man who does wrong on purpose, *if there is such a person*, is the good man." The insinuation plainly is that there really is no such person as "the man who does wrong on purpose," and that the paradox does not arise simply because there is no such person. In other words, we have to understand the Socratic doctrine that virtue is knowledge, and the Socratic use of the analogy of the "arts," in the light of the other well-known Socratic dictum, repeated by Plato on his own account in the *Laws*, that "all wrong-doing is involuntary." It is this, and not the formulated inference that the man who does wrong on purpose is the good man, which is the real conclusion to which Plato is conducting us.[4]

Most interpreters follow Taylor in understanding the phrase "if there is such a person" as a way of squaring the claim in the *Hippias Minor* with Socrates' many famous assertions that no one does wrong willingly.[5] Jones and Sharma offer one way to fill out the details of Taylor's rescue strategy: they read the *Hippias Minor* through the lens of an "interest" thesis that they find in other dialogues (2017: 130–3). Having noted that one would choose to violate a norm of an activity such as archery only because one takes doing so to promote one's interests, they then assert that Socrates holds that injustice never promotes a person's interests.

It is true that if there are no voluntary wrongdoers, this softens (1)–(3): the claim that voluntary wrongdoers are good, or better than involuntary wrongdoers, stops sounding like a paean to wickedness. But it is nonetheless hard to follow Taylor in reading "no one does wrong willingly" as the "real conclusion" of the *Hippias Minor*.[6] The subject of the *Hippias Minor* is not the willingness of wrongdoing or the advantageousness of justice, but rather the power to misbehave.

The *Hippias Minor* is filled with examples of rule-breakers: people intentionally giving the wrong answer to a math problem, running slowly on purpose, choosing to fall down while wrestling, shooting an arrow with the goal of missing the target, etc. Socrates' method of argumentation in the *Hippias Minor* suggests that he thinks those cases shed some light on the case of the just man – that the just man, too, has a kind of power to be unjust, even if, as Socrates will argue elsewhere, he won't use it. The thesis that no one does wrong willingly is, at best, gestured at in the *Hippias Minor*. We can invoke it to contextualize the shocking conclusion of that dialogue, but it neither supplants the conclusion nor does it entirely remove its sting. Even if Socrates is not actually claiming that good men do evil, the claim he is making – that good men (alone) are equipped or empowered or enabled to do evil – is difficult enough. Why does Socrates think this?

The standard answer, found in the quote from Taylor above, as well as in more recent work, is to take (1)–(3) as dividends of the craft analogy.[7] Most commentators take Socrates to presuppose that justice is a kind of craft, which opens up the following mode of argument: survey a number of crafts, find that they all have some property, inductively infer that all crafts have that property, then, *given that justice is analogous to craft*, conclude that justice has that property as well. The *Hippias Minor* would derive *flouting over flubbing* from the cases of archery, wrestling, etc., and then apply it to the case of justice. But this interpretation of the argument of the dialogue makes it mysterious why Socrates does not, instead, run *modus tollens* and conclude that he has discovered the limits of the analogy between craft and morality.[8] Indeed, one commentator, reading the dialogue ironically, concludes that this is what is happening beneath the surface.[9]

I will argue that the argument of the *Hippias Minor* does not so much exploit the craft analogy as underwrite it. Before doing so, I want to examine a few places where *flouting over flubbing* shows up outside the *Hippias Minor*.

V   TWO INSTANCES OF FLOUTING OVER FLUBBING OUTSIDE HIPPIAS MINOR

Consider Socrates' argument against Polemarchus' definition of justice in *Republic* I. Polemarchus says that the just man benefits his friends and harms his enemies.[10] Socrates points out that each craft allows one to benefit and harm in some area:

> SOCRATES : And who is most capable of treating friends well and enemies badly in matters of disease and health?
> POLEMARCHUS : A doctor.
> SOCRATES : And who can do so best in a storm at sea?
> POLEMARCHUS : A ship's captain. (332d10–e2)

Every craft can produce opposites, because the craftsman is the one who knows how to produce the distinctive kind of damage that is proper to the kind of benefit he also knows how to produce. A doctor can produce both health and sickness. After they identify the just man's particular province of benefit as the guarding of money, Socrates concludes: "If a just person is clever at guarding money, therefore, he must also be clever at stealing it ... A just person has turned out then, it seems, to be a kind of thief" (334a7–10). Here the conclusion is a kind of *reductio* – unlike in the *Hippias Minor*, Socrates seems to think that ascribing evil to the just person is absurd. Does this indicate that Plato is rejecting the argument of the *Hippias Minor*?

Many have thought that Plato uses *Rep.* II–X to expose the faulty reasoning characteristic of early Socratic dialogues. Reeve (1988: 22–4), for example, takes *Rep.* I to expose a "crippling defect in the craft analogy."[11] One might run this rejection of the craft analogy against the argument of the *Hippias Minor* as well: justice is not like archery, or running, or medicine, or navigation. Perhaps in *those* cases, intentional rule-breaking is a mark of mastery, but in the case of justice, intentional rule-breaking is a mark of *lack* of mastery.

Below, I will make the case that the argument of the *Hippias Minor* does not, in fact, work by presupposing the craft analogy. Even if it did, however, it would be important to distinguish Plato's perspective on Socratic argumentation from the line of thought contained in that argumentation itself. On the face of it, *Rep.* I has internal resources for explaining the error that has produced the conclusion that the just man is a thief. The problem is not that the craft analogy is invalid but that Polemarchus' definition of justice is wrong. Socrates thinks that justice cannot entail harming one's enemies because the just man never harms anyone (*Rep.* 335e1–5). Some have claimed, for this reason, that *Hippias Minor* and *Rep.* I line up perfectly: the just man has a power, the ability to harm, that he won't ever use.[12]

Even if the two dialogues can be reconciled in this way, I will argue that there is something to be gained from emphasizing the sharp rhetorical differences. In the *Hippias Minor* Socrates seems to embrace the possibility that the just man could be a thief, whereas in *Rep.* I he seems to view that as patently absurd. In the *Hippias Minor*, Plato doesn't have Socrates deny that just men harm, and this omission seems intentional – he seems to be flaunting the counterintuitiveness of saying that the just man does injustice.

Next, consider this exchange from the *Crito:*

T4: CRITO : Your present situation makes clear that the majority can inflict not the least but pretty well the greatest evils if one is slandered among them.

SOCRATES : Would that the majority could inflict the greatest evils (*ta megista kaka ergazesthai*), for they would then be capable of the greatest good, and that would be fine, but now they cannot do either. They cannot make a man either wise or foolish, but they inflict things haphazardly (*hoti an tuchōsi*). (44d1–10)

As in the *Hippias Minor*, Socrates connects the power to act well in a masterful (as opposed to haphazard) way with the power to inflict the greatest evils. This passage is important, because Plato represents Socrates espousing the connection between these two powers casually, as an established belief, rather than as a tentative (and suspect) conclusion. It is true that the *Crito*, like the *Republic*, seems to assert something weaker than the *Hippias Minor*, since only the latter traffics in actual floutings of morality. Nonetheless, some commitment to *flouting over flubbing* underlies all three passages.

The dominant interpretative strategy with reference to the problematic "immoralism" of the *Hippias Minor* has been to try to use statements outside the dialogue to soften its counterintuitive conclusions. I believe we will learn more from the dialogue by doing just the opposite: using it to shed light on a fundamental Socratic commitment – *flouting over flubbing* – that appears outside of but is nowhere so precisely articulated as within the *Hippias Minor*.

VI SOCRATES ON POWERS

Both the defenders and the skeptics of the argument in the *Hippias Minor* tend to see its conclusions as a product of the craft analogy. But notice, first, that the argument of the *Crito* passage (T4) does not rely on any claims about craft. Socrates seems to expect Crito to find it intuitively plausible that flouting entails expertise.[13] Furthermore, Socrates' methodology in the *Hippias Minor* suggests that he is not employing a craft analogy. For Socrates argues for *flouting over flubbing* by way of many activities or states that are not crafts: the practice of truth-telling (366aff.), having good eyesight (374d2–5), having good tools (374e3–6), possessing healthy horses or dogs (375a1–7), owning slaves with good souls (375c3–6). Even if some of these (e.g., the quality of one's tools) play a role in the practice of some craft, Socrates does not emphasize that fact. He doesn't seem to be employing a craft analogy so much as making a general observation about normativity, exploring the structure we find present whenever we speak of that in virtue of which someone is good or bad at something that she does. Crafts show up in this context, I suggest, because they are an arena where we can expect to find norms. It is evident to all, not merely to the practitioners of the craft, that in craft it is possible to do something well or badly. Socrates is, I believe, making a point about the larger genus, of which both morality and craft are parts. That arena is normatively assessable activity, i.e., what can go well or badly.

The distinction between flouting and flubbing describes two ways of violating a rule, but Socrates also takes it to illuminate two ways of conforming to a rule. The grounds of the distinction, both on the side of conformity and on the side of violation, is the question of whether the activity is based on desire or chance. Recall T1:

> Don't you think the ignorant person would often involuntarily
> tell the truth when he wished to say falsehoods, if it so
> happened (*ei tuchoi*), because he didn't know; whereas you, the

wise person, if you should wish to lie, would always consistently lie? (367a2–5)

The expert, Hippias, tells the truth when he wants to tell the truth, and does not tell the truth when he does not want to tell the truth. A non-expert, by contrast, says what is true when chance favors his saying the truth, and fails to tell the truth when chance fails to favor that outcome. The fact that it is *chance* that is the alternative to mastery comes out also in our *Crito* passage (T4), where the majority's lack of expertise is described in terms of their acting in a chance fashion (*hoti an tuchōsi*, 44d10).[14]

Socrates contrasts the case in which one's actions are the products of chance with the case in which one's actions are determined by one's desires. The latter state is what he calls *power*: "each person who can do what he wishes when he wishes is powerful" (*Grg.* 466b7–c1).[15] This conception of power is prevalent in the Socratic dialogues,[16] but it is articulated with special care and precision in the *Hippias Minor*. For Socrates takes the time to spell out what it takes to be in a position to do what you want to do: physical strength and, more generally, bodily health (no lame feet), skill at various handicrafts, cognitive endowment (memory), bodies of knowledge (geometry, arithmetic, medicine), well-functioning sense organs (eyes, ears, nose), well-crafted tools (rudder, bow, lyre) and animate helpers (dogs, horses, slaves) who themselves must have souls in good conditions in order to be of use. Socrates' list of examples is not unified by any relation in which they stand to craft. Rather, what the quality of one's eyes, one's memory, one's bow, and one's dog's soul have in common is that they are all forms of empowerment, which is to say, avenues of agency. Power consists in the tightness of the connection between what you do and what you want.

The argument of the *Hippias Minor* serves both to distinguish two forms of dependency, and to establish the one as superior to the

Table 5.1

	Conformity	Violation
Powerless	Mere conformity (chancy)	Flubbing (chancy nonconformity)
Powerful	Deliberate conformity (desire-based)	Flouting (desire-based failure to conform)

other. Socrates, in effect, invites us to consider a fourfold normative classification (Table 5.1).

Hippias is initially inclined to use the columns of this chart to classify agents as better and worse: Achilles is better than Odysseus because he does not lie. Socrates wants to show him that the division between columns in Table 5.1 is not so fundamental as the division between rows. The important comparison is not between those who follow rules and those who violate them, but between those who have, and those who do not have, the mastery that would allow their performance to depend on their desire. Agents on the left are not (necessarily) superior to those on the right; whereas agents on the bottom are necessarily superior to those on top. Whether one conforms to a rule is less important than *why* one conforms to or violates it. Hence flouters are better than flubbers.

To say moral flouters are better than moral flubbers comes uncomfortably close to saying that unjust action can be good. Socrates doesn't quite say that, but he doesn't quite deny it, either. As many commentators have noticed, one could block the route to immoralism by adding premises from other dialogues. Taylor (1937) couples *flouting over flubbing* with the thesis that everyone desires the good, Jones and Sharma (2017: 130–3) with the thesis that injustice is never in a person's interest, Irwin (1995a: 69–70) with the conception of virtue as superordinate craft and a commitment to psychological eudaimonism. By all of these routes, one can show that Socrates' adherence to *flouting over flubbing*, even in the ethical domain, doesn't force him to embrace injustice. Taylor, Jones and Sharma, and Irwin all offer reasons for thinking that, when it comes to ethical cases, the lower righthand corner of the chart above will never be populated with examples; it is a mere conceptual possibility.

Socrates can be rescued. But why does Plato put him in the position where he has to be? What is the force of asserting that good people have a power (to do evil) that they will never use?

It would have been simpler and more intuitive to assert that in the moral case there is no flouting. What is puzzling about the *Hippias Minor* is the lengths to which Socrates goes to make room for the possibility of a power to be immoral, instead of simply denying that there could be any such thing.

VII   SOCRATIC VIRTUE ETHICS

The first step toward solving this puzzle begins with consideration of dialectical context. Consider the care Socrates takes in excavating Hippias' view in this early section of the dialogue:

> SOCRATES : Do you say that liars, like sick people, don't have the power to do anything, or that they do have the power to do something?
>
> HIPPIAS : I say they very much have the power to do many things, and especially to deceive people.
>
> SOCRATES : So according to your argument they are powerful, it would seem, and wily. Right?
>
> HIPPIAS : Yes.
>
> SOCRATES : Are they wily and deceivers from dimwittedness and foolishness, or by cunning and some kind of intelligence?
>
> HIPPIAS : From cunning, absolutely, and intelligence.
>
> SOCRATES : So they are intelligent, it seems.
>
> HIPPIAS : Yes, by Zeus. Too much so.
>
> SOCRATES : And being intelligent, do they not know what they are doing, or do they know?

> HIPPIAS : They know very well. That's how they do their mischief.
>
> SOCRATES : And knowing the things that they know, are they ignorant, or wise?
>
> HIPPIAS : Wise, surely, in just these things: in deception.
>
> SOCRATES : Stop. Let us recall what it is that you are saying. You claim that liars are powerful and intelligent and knowledgeable and wise in those matters in which they are liars?
>
> HIPPIAS : That's what I claim.
>
> SOCRATES : And that the truthful and the liars are different, complete opposites of one another?
>
> HIPPIAS : That's what I say.
>
> SOCRATES : Well, then. The liars are among the powerful and wise, according to your argument.
>
> HIPPIAS : Certainly.
>
> SOCRATES : And when you say that the liars are powerful and wise in these very matters, do you mean that they have the power to lie if they want, or that they are without power in the matters in which they are liars?
>
> HIPPIAS : I mean they are powerful.
>
> SOCRATES : To put it in a nutshell, then, liars are wise and have the power to lie. (365d–366b)

Hippias wants to maintain that Odysseus says false things intentionally, where that mastery amounts to being clever at deceiving people. Unlike the geometer who gives a false answer, Hippias wants us to understand Odysseus' failings as specifically ethical. He is a cunning trickster, who wreaks evil (*kakourgousin* 365e8–9) on those around him, and the instrument of his destruction is his power of speech. Hippias understands Odysseus' ability to say false things as a power to be unjust. The commitment to the existence of a power to be unjust should thus be attributed to Hippias, rather than to Socrates.

Recall the conditional formulation of the ending of the dialogue –

So the one who voluntarily misses the mark and does what is shameful and unjust, Hippias – that is, if there is such a person – would be no other than the good man.

My suggestion is that the conditional aside refers to someone like Odysseus, as Hippias understands him. If Socrates grants to Hippias that it is possible to flout morality, then Hippias will have to concede that such flouting will both display mastery, and be the characteristic of the just person. In the *Hippias Minor* Plato is exploring what follows, if we hold fixed Hippias' commitment to the existence of voluntarily injustice.

If we let go of this commitment, a familiar argumentative alternative emerges. Instead of allocating to good people the power to act unjustly – to flout morality – Socrates could assert that all injustice is the result of flubbing. This would involve pointing to existent cases of injustice and noting that the people in question have no "power" or "ability" – they are incompetent. This is in fact what he seems to do elsewhere. Consider this passage from the *Theaetetus* (176d1–2):

> If, therefore, one meets a man who practices injustice and is blasphemous in his talk or in his life, the best thing for him by far is that one should never grant that there is any sort of ability about his unscrupulousness.

It is a persistent theme in Socratic dialogues that Socrates denies to wicked people even the trappings of goodness. He argues, against Meno, that wealth cannot be power (*Meno* 78c5–e5). He undermines Polus' veneration of tyrants and orators: The fact that they can put someone to death if they feel like it does not amount to power: "I think that orators have the least power of any in the city" (*Grg.* 466b9–10). In *Rep.* I, he argues that even a band of thieves requires justice, because injustice makes it impossible to achieve any kind of goal (351c7–352a8). The same is true in the *Crito* passage cited above: Socrates is saying that the many lack the power to harm. In all of these places, he seems to assert that bad people don't have the power to do what they do – i.e., there is no such thing as a power to be bad.

Thus it seems likely that Socrates' idiosyncratic commitment to the power to do evil in the *Hippias Minor* should be explained in terms of Plato's desire to engage dialectically with the relevant view. Socrates' hesitation and "wavering" would, then, signal the fact (372d, 376c) that the conclusions he arrives at come from a view he has accepted for the sake of argument. But this pushes the question back a step: why does Plato have Socrates hold the relevant claim fixed? My conjecture is that this device allows Plato to explore some truths that would otherwise lie on the dark side of normativity.

The problem here is one of explanatory overdetermination. There are many ways of construing Socrates' distinctive constellation of views about desire, the good, and justice; without wading into those interpretative waters, I hope it will be reasonably uncontroversial to claim he believes that everyone desires the good.

The "unadulterated" Socrates we find in *Theaetetus, Republic, Crito, Meno*, etc. says that because everyone desires the good, anyone who is *able* to be good will be good. In addition, since the relevant power turns out to be knowledge, all bad action is a result of ignorance. Bad people are incompetent at doing or getting what they want, and you can read their inner badness off of their bad actions. This would set up an apparent disanalogy with, e.g., running. If an action constitutes a "failure" running-wise – by being slow – it might nonetheless be the action of someone who is excellent at running. Unjust action is a reliable sign of ignorance, whereas slow running is an unreliable sign of poor running ability. Plato wants to make sure we understand that Socrates takes this superficial disanalogy to cover over a deeper analogy, which is that both in the case of justice and the case of running, what matters is not the outer behavior but the inner principle from which it springs.

It is in the *Hippias Minor* that he spells out this point, clarifying the Socratic position as one on which *even in the case of morality* the question of success or failure is a question about the state of a person's soul and not the actions that spring from that state. The dialogue offers up a general theory of how normativity works: deliberate (as opposed to chance) conformity is a matter of desire-dependence (power) rather than chance-dependence. The reason why power should involve *desire*, in particular, is not spelled out in the *Hippias Minor*, but it is easy to see the answer in the light of the "everyone desires the good" principle that features centrally in so many other Socratic dialogues: when something is determined fully by desire, it is determined by the good.[17]

Since desire-dependence is the crux both for craft and for morality, the argument of the *Hippias Minor* cannot be accused of uncritical reliance on a dubious analogy between craft and justice. Rather, it offers an argument for the existence of a similarity between craft and justice. What we praise or approve of is not the outer action – for that is something which could as well have come from chance – but the power to follow it. Power is the locus of value in both craft and morality.

Toward the end of the dialogue, Socrates moves to speaking of *souls* as the objects of value. He argues that one wants to possess animals (horses, dogs) and slaves with souls that are such as to conduce to flouting rather than flubbing; and similarly, one wants to possess one's own soul in such a condition that one flouts rather than flubs with respect to archery, flute playing, medicine (375a–d), and, likewise, justice. The most choiceworthy possession, the ultimate object of value, turns out not to be any of the visible things that Hippias can boast of having achieved with his many craft-abilities – the ring he engraved and sandals whose leather he cut, the tunic whose fabric he wove, the poems he wrote (368c–d) – but rather the invisible *soul* containing the *powers* that made it possible for all those accomplishments to depend on his desire to perform them. By directing our attention to the soul as the seat of power and value, the *Hippias Minor* effects the fundamental reorientation that is constitutive of Socratic virtue ethics.

VIII   ARISTOTELIAN VIRTUE ETHICS

It is crucial to the taxonomy in Table 5.1 above that one conceive of the very same normative violation – e.g., limping – as something that could have come about in two ways, and likewise for the case of conformity. But is that correct? One might push back against Socrates' assumption that the outer "action" constitutes a common denominator between the person with power and the one who lacks it. Is it really true that someone who deliberately limps counts as limping in the same sense in which the person with a lame foot limps? Is it really true that someone who does the just thing by chance does "the same thing" as someone who deliberately acts justly? This is precisely the line of questioning that Aristotle presses against the *Hippias Minor.*

In *Metaphysics* Delta 29, Aristotle objects that "a man who limps willingly is better than one who does so unwillingly" only insofar as "by 'limping' Plato means 'mimicking a limp'" (1025a11).[18] Aristotle's point is that we should draw a distinction between what the flubber is doing – actually limping – and what the flouter is doing – *imitating* a limp. In *Nicomachean Ethics* V.8 (1135b1) he argues that, although it is just to return a deposit, some-one who returns a deposit from fear does not do the just thing, "except in an incidental way." In the *Eudemian Ethics* (VIII.1, 1246b1–7) he argues that one cannot do the same action from knowledge and from ignorance, or from justice and injustice, even if there is some sense in which the outward aspects of the two actions might resemble one another. Only the first of the three passages – *Metaphysics* Delta – mentions the *Hippias Minor,* but Aristotle's strategy is clear. He wants to deny *flouting over flubbing,* on the grounds that the one who flouts and the one who flubs are doing substantively different things. And he notes in *Metaphysics* Delta 29 that in the case where they are not different – if someone is "deliberately limping" because he has intentionally damaged his foot – flouting may well be worse than flubbing!

Aristotle denies *flouting over flubbing* because he denies that we can classify "what was done" without reference to the inner state of the doer. This is, of course, part and parcel of his embrace of virtue-activation over virtue. Aristotle thinks that happiness consists not in merely having virtue – for one could do so and be asleep – but in the use one makes of that virtue, in the form of virtuous activities. When Socrates claims that "returning the money" can't be of value since one can do it without justice in one's soul, Aristotle responds that "returning the money justly" is the correct description of the action in question. And that is both valuable and lacking any counterpart in the domain of "powerlessness."

Aristotle and Plato both place great importance on the powers present in the soul, but Aristotle sees the empirical world – in this case, the action – as hospitable to the inscription of this psychic order. Plato, by contrast, sees an action as merely this or that bodily movement *caused* by the justice (or lack thereof) in the agent's soul. This dispute reflects the deepest divide between the two thinkers, as to the degree to which we can find order, value, and reality in the world we apprehend with our senses.

It is worth noting that the Aristotelian response – inscribing the power in the action – is least plausible in the case of speech. When the geometer intentionally gives the false answer to a math problem, it is hard to maintain that he is "imitating" the false answer of the ignoramus. It seems clear that what is said – e.g., "a triangle has 200 degrees" – is a common denominator between the two cases. So, although Aristotle can with some plausibility assert that two cases of "returning the money" can amount to actions with substantively different contents, he is on shakier ground when he must insist that two false utterances of "a triangle has 200 degrees" have different contents. And lying, as a form of flouting, relies on the identity of its outer aspect to sincere speech: I succeed as a liar only insofar as my lying intention is in no way perceivably inscribed in my action.

It may seem that the "first wave" of the *Hippias Minor*, in which Socrates and Hippias have an extended discussion of lying and truth-telling, is superfluous. For it is only the "second wave" overview of various crafts that provides the account of power underwriting the explicit assimilation of moral and nonmoral cases. But there is another way to look at the structure of the dialogue: Plato opens his presentation of virtue ethics by calling our attention to the one case in which it is most difficult to deny that the flouter and flubber must be understood as "doing the same thing." This is a very good way to introduce a theory on which the difference between right and wrong must be made solely by reference to an inner, imperceptible state.

NOTES

1 See Vlastos 1991: 276, and n. 130.

2 See Sprague 1962: 65–70; Hoerber 1962: 127; Mulhern 1968. See also Weiss' (1981) defense of Socrates against these various charges, with special emphasis on Mulhern.

3 Note that the culpably negligent person flubs norms of appropriate care-taking. Someone who knowingly decides not to take appropriate care is guilty of more than negligence.

4 Taylor 1937: 37 (emphasis original).

5 This way of taking the conditional is widespread. See Kahn 1996: 117; Shorey 1933: 471 (Shorey observes with evident relief at the escape clause: "Plato never forgets himself"); Hoerber 1962: fn. 2; Sprague 1962: 76; Irwin 1995a: 69; Penner 1973a: 140. Shorey and Hoerber both point us to helpful parallels at *Grg.* 480e and *Euphr.* 7d. See also *Cri.* 47d1–2 (cited in Weiss 2006).

6 Gould (1955: 42), criticizing Taylor: "There is more in the dialogue than a rather labored joke."

7 Jones and Sharma 2017: 123–8, and Penner 1973a: 136, Irwin 1995a: 69, Weiss 2006: 120–47.

8 Jones and Sharma's rescue strategy makes this question especially difficult to answer. For the interest principle (2017: 130–3) on the basis of which they secure just action for the just man relies, as they acknowledge, on a disanalogy between morality and craft.

9 Weiss 2006: 142–7.

10 Note that Polemarchus' claim (332d) is that the just man actually harms, not that he merely has the ability to do so.

11 See also Shorey 1903: fn. 38, Shorey 1933: 89–90, Gould 1955: 43, Hoerber
    1962: 131, Reeve 1988: 22–4. Shorey, like Irwin (1995a: 71–2), reads
    Aristotle's critique of the *H. Mi.* as emblematic of the failure of the craft
    analogy.

12 Jones and Sharma 2017: 133–5, Penner 1973a: 136–8.

13 Εἰ γὰρ ὤφελον, ὦ Κρίτων, οἷοί τ' εἶναι οἱ πολλοὶ τὰ μέγιστα κακὰ ἐργάζεσθαι,
    ἵνα οἷοί τ' ἦσαν καὶ ἀγαθὰ τὰ μέγιστα, καὶ καλῶς ἂν εἶχεν. νῦν δὲ οὐδέτερα οἷοί
    τε· οὔτε γὰρ φρόνιμον οὔτε ἄφρονα δυνατοὶ ποιῆσαι, ποιοῦσι δὲ τοῦτο ὅτι ἂν
    τύχωσι. I read Socrates as saying that the many can, accidentally, make
    someone wise; what they do not have is the *power* to make him wise
    or foolish. An alternative reading, on which Socrates is saying that the
    many *cannot* make anyone wise or foolish (even by accident) is
    rendered less plausible by the wording of the last clause: τοῦτο at 44d9
    is most naturally read as referring back to ποιῆσαι φρόνιμον/ἄφρονα.

14 Similar language is applied to the chancy (as opposed to good-dependent)
    quality of a low kind of love in Pausanias' speech in the *Symposium*
    (181b1–8): "he strikes wherever he gets a chance (ὅτι ἂν τύχῃ). This, of
    course, is the love felt by the vulgar, who are attached to women no less
    than to boys, to the body more than to the soul, and to the least intelligent
    partners, since all they care about is completing the sexual act. Whether
    they do it honorably or not is of no concern. That is why they do whatever
    comes their way, sometimes good, sometimes bad; and which one it is is
    incidental to their purpose (ὅθεν δὴ συμβαίνει αὐτοῖς ὅτι ἂν τύχωσι τοῦτο
    πράττειν, ὁμοίως μὲν ἀγαθόν, ὁμοίως δὲ τοὐναντίον)." Likewise *Prt.* 353a7–8,
    where Protagoras protests the need to investigate the opinion of *hoi polloi*,
    since they do not speak from expertise but rather from chance; they are
    people who say whatever strikes them (οἳ ὅτι ἂν τύχωσι τοῦτο λέγουσιν).

15 Δυνατὸς δέ γ' ἐστὶν ἕκαστος ἄρα, ὃς ἂν ποιῇ τότε ὃ ἂν βούληται, ὅταν βούληται.

16 *Grg.* 466d8–e2: If tyrants are shown not to do what they want, they are
    shown not to have power. This conception of power as doing what one
    wants also lies behind Glaucon's account of the state of nature in *Rep.* II
    359b1–4: someone who has the *power* to do justice and avoid suffering it
    does not form laws and covenants with others but simply does what he
    wants. In *Alc.* I 134e8–135a2, a different word for power (ἐξουσία) is also
    glossed as amounting to "doing whatever one likes" (δρᾶν ὃ βούλεται). At
    Laws 687a7–b8, wealth and strength, and more generally powers, are seen
    as attractive because they will get us what we want. See also *Rep.* VI,

where the two things that are given as possibly preventing someone from doing something are lack of willingness and lack of ability (497e3–4), and *Tht.* 177e5–6 where judgment and capacity stand in for willingness and ability.

17 For a discussion of whether this principle asserts that the object of desire is what really is good, or what the person takes to be good, see Callard 2017.

18 All translations of Aristotle are from Barnes 1984.

6　Inquiry in the *Meno*

Gail Fine

In most of the Socratic dialogues, Socrates professes to inquire into some virtue.[1] At the same time, he professes not to know what the virtue in question is. How, then, can he inquire into it? Doesn't he need some knowledge to guide his inquiry? Socrates' disclaimer of knowledge seems to preclude Socratic inquiry.[2] The Socratic dialogues don't explicitly address this issue. But, as we shall see, the *Meno* does so.

I　THE PRIORITY OF KNOWLEDGE WHAT (PKW)

Meno begins the dialogue by asking whether virtue is teachable (70a1–2). Socrates replies that he doesn't know the answer to that question; nor does he at all (*to parapan*, 71a7) know what virtue is. The latter failure of knowledge explains the former: for "if I do not know what a thing is, how could I know what it is like?" (*ho de mē oida ti estin, pōs an hopoion ge ti eideiēn*, 71b3–4). Nonetheless, he proposes to inquire with Meno into what virtue is. Here, as in the Socratic dialogues, Socrates both disclaims knowledge and proposes to inquire.

Socrates' disclaimer rests on his belief that he satisfies the antecedent of the following conditional, when "virtue" is substituted for x:[3]

(PKW) If one doesn't know what x is, one can't know anything about x.

Thanks to the editors for helpful comments on an earlier version of this chapter, which is a revised version of a paper with the same title that originally appeared in the first edition of the *Cambridge Companion to Plato*; that version is reprinted in my *Plato on Knowledge and Forms*, Ch. 2. I refer the reader to it for my initial acknowledgements.

Let's call this the Priority of Knowledge What (PKW). There's dispute about how to interpret PKW. One suggestion is that it means:[4]

> (A) If one has no idea what x is – if one is in a cognitive blank with respect to x – then one can't (intend to) say anything about x.

(A) is independently plausible; but it is difficult to believe it is what Socrates intends. For the self-confident way in which he examines Meno about virtue suggests he satisfies neither its antecedent nor its consequent: he appears to have some ideas about virtue, and he says things about it. For example, he says that everything that is virtuous is so because of some one form (72c6–8). Nor does he say that he has no *ideas* about virtue; he says that he doesn't at all *know (oida) what virtue is.*[5] Here there are two points: first, Socrates claims to lack *knowledge*, not all ideas or beliefs; second, he claims to lack knowledge of *what virtue is.* The second claim, taken in context, suggests that the knowledge he (believes he) lacks is knowledge of the definition of virtue: that is, he (believes he) doesn't know the answer to the Socratic "What is F?" question, which specifies the nature or essence (cf. *ousia*, 72b1) of F.

We might then try altering the antecedent of (A) so as to yield (B):[6]

> (B) If one doesn't know the definition of x, one can't (intend to) say anything about x.

In contrast to (A), (B)'s antecedent is one Socrates satisfies (or believes he satisfies). However, if it is a precondition of saying anything (intending to say anything) about x that one know what x is, and one does not know what x is, then it is difficult to see how one can inquire into x. How can one inquire into something if one can't even (intend to) say anything about it? Moreover, we have seen that Socrates doesn't satisfy the consequent of (B): he says things about virtue. If he is committed to (B), and (believes he) doesn't know what virtue is, yet continues to talk about virtue, his theory and practice conflict.

There is an alternative to (A) and (B) that is worth considering. Just as Socrates says, not that he lacks *beliefs* about what virtue is, but that he lacks *knowledge* of what it is, so he says that such knowledge is necessary, not for *saying* (intending to say) anything about virtue, but for *knowing* anything about it:[7]

(C) If one doesn't know the definition of x, one can't know anything about x.

In contrast to (B), (C) uses "know" in both clauses; so too does Socrates. He says that one needs to know what virtue is, not in order to *say* anything about it, or in order to have any *beliefs* about it, but in order to *know* anything about it. This leaves open the possibility that one can have beliefs about virtue, and (intend to) say various things about it, without knowing what it is; and if relying on beliefs that fall short of knowledge can guide inquiry, then, even if Socrates lacks all knowledge about virtue, he can still inquire if he relies on suitable beliefs.

Although (B) and (C) can thus be read so as to be quite different, it does not follow that Plato grasps, or exploits, their difference. For him to do so, he must be clear, among other things, about the difference between knowledge and belief. Yet it has been argued that he is unclear about their difference, at least in the Socratic dialogues.[8] We shall need to see whether this is true of the *Meno*.

Whether we read PKW as (B) or (C),[9] Socrates claims not to know what virtue is, in the sense of not knowing the definition of virtue. One might wonder why he does so. Doesn't his ability to pick out examples of virtuous actions, to use virtue terms coherently, and the like, show that he knows the definition of virtue?

If to know the definition of virtue were simply to know the conventional meaning of the term "virtue," it would indeed be odd were Socrates to claim not to know the definition of virtue.[10] But for Socrates, to know the definition of virtue is not simply to know the conventional meaning of the term "virtue"; it is to know what the thing, virtue, really is, what its essence and explanatory properties are. Knowing what virtue is, for Socrates, is more like knowing a Lockean real rather than nominal essence: more like knowing, say, the inner constitution, the atomic number, of gold, than like knowing, or having some idea of, the surface, observable features of gold, such as that it is yellow and shiny.[11] If this is right, then Socrates' claim not to know what virtue is is reasonable; for as the progress of science reveals, real essences are difficult to discover.

Even if it's reasonable for Socrates to disclaim knowledge of the real essence of virtue, one might wonder whether it's reasonable for him to claim that such knowledge has the sort of priority he accords it. Here (B) and (C) demand different verdicts. It's not reasonable to say, as (B) does, that such knowledge is necessary for *saying* (intending to say) anything about virtue. Presumably most of us lack knowledge of the real essence of virtue; but, for all that, we might have reliable beliefs about virtue. And Socrates seems to think we have such beliefs. For example, in *Meno* 87e1–3 he assumes, and Meno readily agrees, that virtue is good (*agathon*) and beneficial (*ophelimon*).[12] But (C) is more reasonable. For it says that knowledge of the real essence of virtue is necessary for *knowing* anything else about virtue. If we place strong conditions on knowledge – as Socrates does in 98a – and if we also clearly distinguish knowledge from belief, then it is reasonable if controversial to claim that knowledge of the nonessential properties of a thing requires, and is indeed grounded in, knowledge of its nature.[13] I shall, at any rate, from now on interpret PKW as (C).

PKW raises a *prima facie* problem. For it says that if one doesn't know what x is, one can't know anything about x. Socrates claims not to know what virtue is, yet he proposes to inquire into what virtue is. How can he inquire, or be justified in inquiring, given his disclaimer of knowledge? Doesn't inquiry require some initial knowledge?

It's not that PKW says that we need knowledge in order to inquire: it doesn't concern inquiry. Nor does it say that we need to know what F is before knowing anything else about F: it makes a claim about epistemological or explanatory priority, grounding one kind of knowledge in another; it makes no claims about chronological priority. For all it says, we might come to know what F is at the same time as we come to know something else about it. The point is just that, given PKW and Socrates' disavowal of knowledge of what virtue is, it follows that he knows nothing (takes himself to know nothing) about virtue. So, if one thinks one needs to have some knowledge about virtue in order to inquire into it, one will think he is not in a position to inquire into it; yet he claims to do so.

On some interpretations of his disclaimer and his practice, there is no difficulty. For example, on one interpretation, (a), Socrates is not really inquiring into virtue, at least, not in the sense of seeking knowledge of what virtue is; he seeks only to expose the ignorance of others, and this less demanding aim does not require moral knowledge. Hence, his disclaimer does not conflict with his practice after all.[14]

On another interpretation, (b), though Socrates wants to know what virtue is, he is hypocritical or ironical in disclaiming moral knowledge or, more charitably, he disclaims knowledge only in an effort to get interlocutors to think for themselves. If Socrates does not intend the disclaimer seriously, then, again, there is no difficulty in squaring his practice with his disclaimer.[15]

On a third interpretation, (c), both the disclaimer of knowledge and the desire to know what virtue is are genuine, but the disclaimer is less sweeping than it is sometimes thought to be. On one version of this view, (c1), Socrates disclaims knowledge in the sense of "certainty" but not in the different sense of "justified true belief"; and knowledge in this latter sense can guide inquiry. On another version of this view, (c2), Socrates disclaims knowledge of *what virtue is* – of its essence or nature – and of what it is like (e.g., of whether it is teachable), but he does not disclaim knowledge of what counts as an instance of virtue (e.g., that this action is just), and this knowledge can guide inquiry.[16]

If any of these interpretations is correct, the problem disappears. But whatever may be true of the Socratic dialogues (a matter about which there is dispute), none of them works for the *Meno*. Socrates claims in what follows that inquiry can lead us to knowledge (85c9– d1). It would then be perverse to suggest that its true goal is just to perplex interlocutors. Rather, as we shall see, Socrates elicits perplexity only as an interim stage in a journey whose ultimate destination is the acquisition of knowledge. (a) is thus inadequate.

(b) is also inadequate. Socrates' disavowal of knowledge of what virtue is, and his commitment to PKW, drive the whole dialogue; it would be perverse to think he is anything but sincere and serious. It is at any rate worth seeing whether we can take his disavowal of knowledge and commitment to PKW seriously, without that leading him into difficulty; and, as we shall see, we can do so.

Nor is (c1) adequate. At *Meno* 98a, Plato offers just one account of knowledge – as true belief that is tied down with reasoning about the explanation (*aitias logismos*) – and it is knowledge so understood that he disclaims; he doesn't countenance different senses of the term. Any cognitive condition that falls short of knowledge as explained in 98a isn't knowledge; it is at best mere true belief. Unlike some moderns, Plato places stringent conditions on knowledge; given those conditions, it's not surprising that he disavows knowledge.[17]

Nor is (c2) adequate. For Socrates claims not to know what virtue is; given PKW, it follows that he doesn't know anything about virtue. He can't then, as (c2) proposes, know some things about virtue.

So our problem remains. On the one hand, Socrates professes not to know what virtue is; given PKW, it follows that (he believes) he doesn't know anything about virtue. How, then, can he inquire into it?

II   MENO'S PARADOX

Although Socrates claims not to know what virtue is, and so not to know anything about virtue, he proposes to inquire into what it is. Meno makes several suggestions; but Socrates rebuts him at every turn, using his familiar elenctic method (which is a method of inquiry).[18] He asks an interlocutor a "What is F?" question: e.g., "What is courage?" (*Laches*), or temperance (*Charmides*), or piety (*Euthyphro*). He then cross-examines the interlocutor, appealing to agreed examples and principles. Eventually the interlocutor is caught in contradiction and realizes that, contrary to his initial belief, he doesn't know what F is after all.[19] Given PKW, it follows that he lacks all knowledge about F. The Socratic dialogues typically end at this stage, with the interlocutor at a loss (in a state of *aporia*).

When this stage is reached in the *Meno*, however, Meno, unlike the compliant interlocutors in the Socratic dialogues, turns to the offensive, challenging Socrates' ability to inquire into virtue if, as he says, he doesn't know anything at all about it:

> [A] How will you inquire into this [virtue], Socrates, when you don't at all know what it is? [B] For what sort of thing, from among those you don't know, will you put forward as the thing you are inquiring into? [C] And even if you really encounter it, how will you know that this is the thing you didn't know? (80d5–8)

Socrates reformulates Meno's questions as a dilemma:

> I understand the sort of thing you want to say, Meno. Do you see what an eristic argument you're introducing, that (1) it is not possible for one to inquire either into what one knows or into what one doesn't know? For (2) one wouldn't inquire either into what one knows (for one knows it, and there's no need for such a person to inquire) (3) or into what one doesn't know (for one doesn't even know what one will inquire into). (80e1–6)

Meno's questions, and Socrates' dilemma, are generally called "Meno's Paradox," and I shall follow suit.[20]

We can formulate Meno's questions as follows:

A) How can one inquire into something if one doesn't at all know what it is?
B) Which of the things one doesn't know is one inquiring into?
C) How will one recognize that one has found what one is looking for, even if one does so?

And we can formulate Socrates' dilemma as follows:[21]

1) For any x, one either knows, or does not know, x.
2) If one knows x, one cannot inquire into x.
3) If one does not know x, one cannot inquire into x.
4) Therefore, whether or not one knows x, one cannot inquire into x.

There are various differences between Meno's questions and Socrates' dilemma. For example, Meno doesn't mention (2), whereas Socrates doesn't mention (C). Further, Meno asks how one can inquire into what one does not know at all (to parapan, 80d6; cf. 71a7, 71b3, 5), whereas Socrates asks only how one can inquire into what one does not know: he doesn't repeat "at all." There's dispute about the significance (if any) of these and other differences.[22] I shall largely leave this issue to one side in order to focus on Socrates' dilemma.

We should note, to begin with, that the paradox does not ask whether, in general, one can acquire knowledge; it asks only whether one can come to know things like virtue through inquiry. The paradox does not question one's ability to come to know things quite unlike virtue (e.g., the road to Larissa: 97); nor does it question one's ability to come to know things in some way other than through inquiry (e.g., through perception or by being told). Hence it is not surprising that Plato's reply doesn't address these issues. It doesn't follow either that he restricts knowledge to things like virtue or that he takes inquiry to be the only way of acquiring knowledge.

Let's now look at Socrates' formulation. There's dispute about its logic. On the account I prefer, (1) is a harmless instantiation of the law of the excluded middle: one either does, or does not, know x; tertium non datur. (2) and (3) then tell us that whichever of these exclusive and exhaustive options obtains, inquiry is impossible. (4) then validly concludes that inquiry is impossible.

Is the argument, so read, not only valid but also sound? (1) is clearly true, but what about (2) and (3)? That depends on how we understand "knowledge." For, though (1) tells us that knowing and not knowing x are exclusive and exhaustive options, it doesn't tell us what knowing and not knowing are. Let's look at (2) first.

Suppose that to know something is just to have some minimal grasp of it. So read, (2) is false. I might know who Meno is, but inquire where he is; I might know something about physics, but inquire in order to know more about it. I might know p in the minimal sense of understanding what it means, but inquire whether it's true; or I might grasp, in a low-level way, that p is true, but inquire why it's true. However, if to know something is to know *everything* there is to know about it, one can't inquire about it: for, in this case, there is nothing left to inquire into about it. So (2) seems false if knowledge is understood weakly enough, but true if it is taken to involve complete knowledge.[23]

What about (3)? If knowledge, in (2), is complete knowledge, then, for the argument to remain valid, not knowing, in (3), has to be lacking complete knowledge. So read, (3) is false: lacking complete knowledge about something doesn't preclude inquiring into it. I might have partial knowledge, or true beliefs; relying on them, so far from precluding inquiry, enables it. If, however, not knowing, in (3), involves being in a complete cognitive blank, then I can't inquire; so understood, (3) is true. But then, for the argument to remain valid, knowing, in (2), has to be just not being in a cognitive blank; so read, (2) is false. Failing to be in a complete cognitive blank about something doesn't preclude inquiring into it: again, one might have partial knowledge, or true beliefs, about something; relying on them enables one to inquire.

So the reading of (2) that makes it true makes (3) false; and the reading of (3) that makes it true makes (2) false. But if we read (2) and (3) so that they are both true, the argument equivocates on "knowledge," in which case it is invalid.

At least, that's so if, as I've suggested, (1) is an instance of the law of the excluded middle. But one might argue that it says instead that, for all x, one either knows x (in the sense of having complete knowledge about it) or doesn't know x (in the sense of being in a cognitive blank about it); and one might take knowledge, in (2), to be complete knowledge, and not knowing, in (3), to be being in a cognitive blank. The argument is then valid. But it isn't sound, since (1) is now false. For, again, there are conditions other than complete knowledge and being in a cognitive blank, such as partial knowledge and true belief.[24] One could remedy this difficulty by taking (1) to be an instance of the law of the excluded middle. Then, if one continues to take (2) to involve complete knowledge and (3) to involve being in a cognitive blank, all the premises are true. But the argument is now invalid.

There is, then, no reading of the argument on which it's both valid and sound. At least, that's how it seems to me. But how does Socrates reply? We might expect him to reject (3), since he's disavowed knowledge yet claims to be able to inquire; and, as we've seen, there is a reading of (3) on which (3) is false. On the other hand, we've seen that (3) can also be read so as to be true, and that's how Meno seems to read it. That's why he says he is numb in both mind and tongue (80b1): he no longer has any views about virtue; he is (or takes himself to be) in a cognitive blank about it.[25] Hence it's reasonable for him to think he can't inquire about virtue.[26]

III   SOCRATES' REPLY: THE GEOMETRICAL DISCUSSION

Socrates replies in three stages. First he describes a theory of recollection. When Meno says he doesn't understand, Socrates says he'll explain (*endeixōmai*, 82b2; cf. *endeixai*, 82a6). This leads to the second stage: Socrates cross-examines one of Meno's slaves[27] about a geometry problem (82b–85d). According to Leibniz, this is "a fine experiment."[28] In the third stage, Socrates restates the – or a – theory of recollection (85d–86c).[29] How do these three stages fit together? How, and how well, do they reply to Meno's paradox? In this section, I consider the geometrical discussion. In the next section, I turn to the theory of recollection.

Socrates begins by asking the slave whether he speaks Greek (*hellēnizei*, 82b4).[30] Having ascertained that he does, Socrates then asks him whether he realizes (*gignōskeis*, 82b9) that a square is like this, or is this sort of thing: presumably he has drawn a square and is pointing at it. He then asks the slave how long a side is needed for a square with double the area of the original square (82c–e). The slave replies that we need a side with double the length of the original side (82d–e). Like most of Socrates' interlocutors in the earlier dialogues, and like Meno at the beginning of this one, the slave thinks he knows the answer to Socrates' questions, but he doesn't. Socrates then questions him further, until the slave realizes that he doesn't know what he thought he did; he is then puzzled and confused (84a–b), just as Meno was earlier, in his failed attempt to discover what virtue is.

This aporetic result is often reached in the Socratic dialogues too, as it was earlier in the *Meno*. The Socratic dialogues typically end at this point, which is one reason Socrates is often thought to be purely negative and destructive. That's why Meno compares him to a torpedo fish, who numbs those who come into contact with it (80a–b). But Socrates now points out that realizing that one doesn't know the answer is beneficial, for it makes (or ought to make) one more willing and able to inquire further (84b–c); and, if one does so, one can in the end acquire new true beliefs and even knowledge.

To illustrate this, Socrates questions the slave further; eventually the slave gives the right answer (84d–85b). He still lacks knowledge. But he now "has in himself true beliefs about the things he does not know" (85c2–8). Further, "if someone asks him the very same [sorts of] questions [alt.: "asks him questions about the very same things"] often and in different ways, you can see that in the end he will know these things as accurately as anybody" (85c10–d1). Hence, although the elenchus typically ends in *aporia* in the Socratic dialogues, and ended in it earlier in the *Meno* too, Socrates shows that it can lead to the discovery of true beliefs, and even knowledge.[31] However, he emphasizes that, though the slave has acquired a new true belief and can acquire knowledge, he doesn't yet have knowledge.

If the slave can inquire about geometry in the absence of knowledge, so too, Socrates assumes, can we all. Nor is there anything special about geometry; inquiry in the absence of knowledge is possible for "every other subject" (85e2–3), including virtue; and so, Socrates concludes, they ought to resume their inquiry into virtue, even though they don't know what it is (86c) or, therefore, anything about it.

In addition to vindicating the Socratic elenchus, Plato has also rejected (3) of the paradox. Contrary to (3), one can inquire even if one lacks all knowledge of the subject, for the slave has just done so.[32] The slave can inquire because, though he lacks knowledge, he has, and relies on his, true beliefs. To be sure, he doesn't initially have a true belief about the answer to Socrates' question: he acquires that as a result of inquiry. But he starts off with *other* true beliefs; and relying on them enables him to inquire. For example, he realizes that squares have four equal sides. Similarly, Socrates was justified, both in the Socratic dialogues and earlier in the *Meno*, in claiming to be able to inquire into virtue in the absence of knowledge. For, though he disclaims all moral knowledge, he never claims to lack true moral beliefs; and, as we've seen, he seems to believe he has them. Moreover, in clearly distinguishing knowledge from true belief, and in insisting that having, and relying on, the latter is sufficient for inquiry, Plato shows that PKW is not self-defeatingly strong, that he can distinguish (B) from (C), and accepts only (C).[33]

So Plato rejects the paradox as unsound by arguing that, contrary to (3), we can inquire even if we lack knowledge, if we have and rely on true beliefs. At least, he rejects (3) when knowledge is understood as Plato explains it in 98a. He doesn't mean that one can inquire into something even if one is in a cognitive blank about it – which, as we've seen, is how Meno understood (3). Socrates is pointing out that being in a cognitive blank isn't the only way to lack knowledge; one can also lack knowledge by having mere true beliefs. Even if the former precludes inquiry, the latter doesn't do so. Though (3) is true as Meno understands it, it is false as Socrates understands knowledge.

Before turning to the theory of recollection, I consider two objections to my account of the geometrical discussion.

First, one might argue that Socrates has not shown that inquiry is possible in the absence of knowledge. For even if the slave lacks knowledge, Socrates, in this case if not in the moral case, has the relevant knowledge; and that is what makes progress possible.[34] However, Socrates doesn't say that he *knows* the answers to the questions he asks, and it is not clear that (he believes) he does; perhaps he has (or takes himself to have) just true beliefs. To be sure, he thinks he is cognitively better off than his interlocutors are. But this isn't because (he thinks) he has knowledge; it's because (he believes) his true beliefs are better justified, or are closer to being knowledge, than are those of his interlocutors. Not all true beliefs are on a par. Given Socrates' high standards for knowledge, it's not surprising if he doesn't think he has it even in the geometrical case. Perhaps, for example, he thinks knowledge is synoptic, such that one can't know one thing in isolation from others; and that, in the case of geometry, knowledge requires proof. Perhaps Socrates doesn't think he can prove enough in the geometrical case to count as having geometrical knowledge. And if he doesn't think he has it, that would explain why he claims not to be teaching the slave (82e4–6; cf. 82b6–7, 84c10–d2). For, in his view, one can teach something only if one knows it.[35]

On an alternative view, Socrates uses "teach" in two different senses or ways and, though he claims not to teach in one of them, he teaches in the other of them. On one version of this general view, the two senses or ways of teaching are imparting information that the learner passively receives, and causing someone to recollect. When Socrates denies that he teaches, he has the first sort of teaching in mind; but that's compatible with his teaching in the second way.[36] However, if Socrates thinks that *all* teaching requires knowledge and denies that he has knowledge, then we need not import two senses or ways of teaching. Rather, he straightforwardly denies that he teaches, period, since he doesn't (take himself to) have knowledge but takes having knowledge to be a necessary condition for teaching.[37]

But even if Socrates knows, or believes he knows, the answers, the point of the geometrical discussion is not undermined. For, though Socrates asks the slave leading questions, he does not feed him the answers. On the contrary, Socrates emphasizes that the slave should not rely on Socrates' authority, but should say what he believes (83d); this point is brought home by the fact that the slave twice offers wrong answers by relying uncritically on what Socrates says (82e1–2, 83d4–e1). The slave's progress – from initial misguided confidence, to a realization of his ignorance, to the discovery of the right answer – ultimately comes from his own independent reflection. At each stage he decides to resolve a conflict in his beliefs by discarding the ones that seem less reasonable, just as other interlocutors do in moral inquiry.[38]

A second objection asks how we can know which of our beliefs are true, which false. Beliefs don't come neatly labelled "true" and "false." What's to stop us from relying on the false ones instead? The mere fact that I have true beliefs is not sufficient for me to inquire.[39] Here it's important to note that Plato's claim is that one can inquire, even if one lacks knowledge, so long as one in fact relies on one's true beliefs. He does not claim that one can inquire, even if one lacks knowledge, only if one *knows* that one is relying on true beliefs. Of course, from a first-person perspective, I will be subjectively justified in inquiring only if I believe that I am relying on true beliefs. But we need to distinguish the question of what makes inquiry possible from the question of what subjectively justifies one in thinking one is in a position to inquire. Of course, one might not inquire if one thought one couldn't do so. But even if thinking one is in a position to inquire is a necessary condition for actually inquiring, the overall conditions for the first might differ from the overall conditions for the second. Be that as it may, in neither case do I need to know (or even have true beliefs about) which of my beliefs are true, which are false. In the first case, I need to rely on beliefs that are in fact true; in the second case, I need to believe that I have some true beliefs. Neither of these ways of appealing to true beliefs requires one to know (or have true beliefs about) which of one's beliefs are in fact true.[40]

Of course, someone might rely on false, rather than on true, beliefs. As in science, one can follow a false track; progress requires luck. Socrates seems to assume, however, that everyone, or at least everyone rational, will, if they inquire systematically, progress in the same direction. That's because he thinks that, when we realize that various beliefs, or claims, conflict, we tend, upon reflection, to reject the false ones.[41] This is a substantial, and optimistic, claim about human nature – one that requires and, as we shall see, receives, further explanation.

IV SOCRATES' REPLY: THE THEORY OF RECOLLECTION

The geometrical discussion seems to be a good, and complete, reply to Meno's Paradox. Why, then, does Socrates supplement it with the theory of recollection? What role does it play in replying to the paradox?

Let's look first at Socrates' initial account of the theory of recollection, according to which:

> Since the soul is immortal, has been born many times, and has seen (heōrakuia) all the things both here and in Hades, there is nothing it has not learned (memathēken). So it is not at all surprising that it can recollect the things it knew before, both about virtue and other things. For since the whole of nature is akin, and since the soul has learned (memathēkuias) everything, nothing prevents one, when one has recollected one thing – which men call learning – from discovering everything else for oneself, if one is brave and does not tire of inquiring. For inquiring and learning are, as a whole, recollection. So one shouldn't be persuaded by that eristic argument; for it would make us lazy, and is pleasant for fainthearted people to hear. But this one [sc. the argument just described] makes them hard working and eager to inquire. Being convinced that it is true, I want to inquire with you into what virtue is. (81c5–e2)

This is sometimes taken to say that inquiry is impossible: rather than inquiring, we recollect instead.[42] As against this, however, Socrates says that he is eager to inquire because the theory of recollection is true. This suggests that recollection *enables* inquiry: it explains how it is possible.[43] In saying that "inquiring and learning are, as a whole, recollection" (81d4–5),[44] Socrates doesn't mean that there is no such thing as learning or inquiry. He means that they consist in – or essentially involve or are explained by – recollection: since recollection is possible, so too is inquiry.

The theory of recollection posits prenatal knowledge; but it's not clear exactly what we knew prenatally. At 81c6–7 (cf. d1), Socrates says that (a) the soul saw everything, which is sometimes taken to imply omniscience.[45] However, at 81c8 he mentions (b) "virtue and other things"; and at 81d4–5 he mentions (c) all *zētein kai manthanein* ("inquiry and learning"). It's reasonable to think that (b) and (c) restrict the scope of (a), in which case our prenatal knowledge was just of such things as virtue and geometry; there's no implication that our prenatal knowledge extends to, for example, what whoever is President in 100 years will wear on a given day. Nor do we need to assume that we have prenatal knowledge of everything there is to know about such things as virtue, including, for example, who instantiated it when. Perhaps our prenatal knowledge was just of what such things as virtue are: we knew the answers to "What is F?" questions about them.

Though the first statement of the theory of recollection posits prenatal knowledge, it doesn't posit current or innate knowledge; neither of them is mentioned or implied.

It's often thought that the first statement of the theory of recollection says that we acquired our prenatal knowledge.[46] This is because of its claim that since the soul "saw" all things, there is nothing it has not learned (81c6–7). If we acquired our prenatal knowledge, the question arises of how we did so. If the answer is "through inquiry," we can raise Meno's paradox again; and we might then seem to be launched on a vicious infinite regress.[47] But there is no regress, vicious or otherwise; for the first statement of the theory of recollection isn't committed to the claim that we acquired our prenatal knowledge. The claim that we saw things prenatally just means that we grasped, knew, or understood why they are as they are.[48] And the claim that there is nothing the soul has not learned might mean that the soul was, for the whole of its prenatal existence, in a learned condition, i.e., it always knew; there need not have been any episodes of learning.[49] The passage is neutral about whether the soul acquired its prenatal knowledge or always had it. The second statement of the theory of recollection, however, clearly claims that the soul always had its prenatal knowledge (86b1). In defending that view, it doesn't contradict the first statement of the theory of recollection.

Socrates seems to suggest, not just that we had prenatal knowledge, but also that our having had it explains how we can inquire. He makes this clearer in the second statement of the theory of recollection, so let's now turn to it.

As we've seen, he's argued that the slave inquired and thereby acquired a new true belief, though he still lacks knowledge. He then says:[50]

1) Won't he know without having been taught by anyone, but by being questioned, taking up (analabōn) the knowledge himself from himself? (85d3–4)
2) Isn't it the case that to take up (analambanein) knowledge oneself in oneself is to recollect (anamimnēskesthai)? (85d6–7)
3) Isn't it the case that he either acquired the knowledge he now has at some time, or else always had it? (85d9–10)

Analambanein can mean "to recover." But Plato sometimes uses it to mean "to take up," in a sense that is compatible with, but doesn't imply, learning for the first time;[51] and I think that's how it's used here. The point in (1) is just that the slave will acquire knowledge, not by being taught, but by working things out for himself. This is just what we'd expect Socrates to say, given the geometrical discussion.

In (2) Socrates says that to *analambanein* knowledge in this way is to recollect. That is, the best explanation of what the slave does is that he is recollecting: that's what enables him to make progress, to acquire his new true belief and eventually, if all goes well, to acquire knowledge. The geometrical discussion shows *that* inquiry in the absence of knowledge is possible, by providing an example of it. The theory of recollection explains *how* it is possible. For example, the geometrical discussion assumes that, in inquiring, we tend to rely on our true beliefs: when faced with a contradiction among his beliefs, the slave abandons the false ones. In Plato's view, the theory of recollection is the best explanation of this remarkable tendency. We can all inquire, and tend toward the truth in doing so, because, though we currently lack the relevant knowledge, we had it prenatally. Like advocates of innate knowledge, Plato believes that certain remarkable features of human beings should be explained in terms of prior knowledge though, so far, he's posited only prenatal knowledge, not innate or current knowledge.

However, Plato is generally thought to posit not just prenatal knowledge, but also latent innate and current knowledge.[52] Yet doing so seems to contradict 85b8–d2 where, as we've seen, Socrates says that the slave *doesn't* know.

But why, then, does (3) mention the knowledge the slave "now" has (85d9)? The usual answer is that there is no contradiction because the point in 85b8–d2 is that the slave lacks explicit conscious knowledge, whereas (3) means that the slave has latent innate and current knowledge.[53] An alternative I prefer is that "now" is forward referring: it indicates the time when, if all goes well, the slave will acquire the knowledge he so far lacks.[54]

Whatever we make of "now," it's generally thought that (3) offers us two options – either we at some time acquired the knowledge we "now" have, or else we always had it; Plato goes on to eliminate the first and endorse the second (86b1). But if we always – for all time or for as long as we exist – have knowledge, we have it from birth and so have it innately and currently.

On an alternative I prefer, the second option in (3) isn't that we had knowledge for all time or for as long as we exist, but that we had it for the whole of our prenatal existence.[55] Nor does 86b1 say that *knowledge* has always been in us; it says that *the truth* about beings has always been in us. Again, I think Plato is just discussing our prenatal state. But even if he's discussing our state for as long as we exist, still, saying that the *truth* is always in us falls short of saying that *knowledge* is always in us. Perhaps the truth is always in us as mental representations that are suitable for serving as the content of knowledge or true belief even if they don't so serve now; or perhaps it is in us just as a disposition to favor truths over falsehoods.[56] Similarly, Leibniz says that innate ideas are in us in something like the way in which Hercules is in rough marble before it has been carved, because its veins make it easier to carve a Hercules shape than various other shapes.[57]

86a8 has also been taken to say that we have innate and current knowledge: the slave's soul "has for all time been in the state of having once been [in a] learned [condition]." However, I take this to say that it is always true of him (and so it is now true of him) that he was once in a learned condition, i.e., once had knowledge. To claim that it is always (and so is now) true of him that he once knew is not to claim or imply that it is now true of him that he now knows.[58]

So the *Meno* doesn't argue that we all have latent current or innate knowledge. It posits only prenatal knowledge; and that's what makes inquiry possible.[59] But what Plato says is compatible with – though it doesn't imply – the view that our prenatal knowledge was lost when we were born, in such a way that we no longer know.[60]

But if the knowledge was lost when we were born, how can it explain our current ability to inquire? Why not say that, rather than inquiring, we are learning for a second time?[61] If we're recollecting, musn't there be a persistent entity that causally relates our past knowledge to our ability to inquire?[62] It's not clear that, in the *Meno*, Plato is committed to that view. But even if he is, it doesn't follow that he's committed to innate *knowledge*: the persisting entity might be something else: perhaps a disposition to favor truths over falsehoods, or something about the structure of the mind that grounds, or gives rise to, such a disposition.

Though the theory of recollection doesn't posit innate knowledge, its motivation is similar to the motivation for positing innate knowledge. In both cases, the root intuition is that a remarkable ability must be grounded in knowledge. Usually those who favor this view take the relevant knowledge to be latent and innate. Chomsky, for example, thinks that our remarkable ability to acquire language, and to understand sentences we've never heard before, can't be a brute fact and can't be wholly explained by ordinary processes of learning such as induction and experience. Rather, they can only be explained, or are best explained, by positing innate knowledge of the rules of grammar. Since this innate knowledge clearly isn't explicit, Chomsky takes it to be latent.[63]

Plato agrees that we don't have explicit innate knowledge. But he doesn't think we have latent innate knowledge either. For he accepts an accessibility condition on knowledge, according to which we know something only if we are able to explain, relatively easily, why what we know is true.[64] Since we can't do that at birth, we don't have innate knowledge, period. Nor do we currently have knowledge of, e.g., virtue since, again, we can't say relatively easily what it is. But, like Chomsky, Plato thinks that having a certain ability requires knowledge. Hence, he thinks the knowledge must be prenatal.

The view that having a certain ability requires knowledge – whether prenatal, innate, or current – is open to criticism. Many would prefer to say that even if it is remarkable that we have a certain ability, still, it is just a brute fact that we have it; there is no further explanation. Or, if there is one, it consists – not in any sort of knowledge but – in, for example, evolution.

However we spell out the details of the theory of recollection, few nowadays are likely to believe it. But the second stage of Socrates' reply – the geometrical discussion – remains convincing; and it can be accepted even if we reject the theory of recollection. We can agree that we can inquire in the absence of knowledge if we have and tend to rely on true beliefs, without accepting Plato's account of what makes this possible. Perhaps Plato agrees. For he seems to place less weight on the theory of recollection than on the elenchus. He introduces the theory as something said by priests and priestesses and by Pindar and other poets (81a5–6, a10–b2); later he makes it clear that he thinks such people lack knowledge (99c). Socrates says he would not like to take an oath on all that he has said (86b); but later he says that if he were to claim to know anything, one of the few things he would claim to know is that knowledge differs from true belief (98b1–5).[65] And it is the difference between knowledge and true belief that is crucial to the second stage of his reply.

NOTES

1 The Platonic dialogues are often divided into four groups: (i) early Socratic dialogues: *Ap., Cri., Euphr., Chrm., La., Lys., H. Mi., Euthd., Ion,* and *Prt.*; (ii) transitional dialogues: *Grg., Meno, H. Ma.,* and *Cra.*; (iii) middle dialogues: *Phd., Smp., Rep.,* and *Phdr.*; and (iv) late dialogues: *Prm., Tht., Ti., Criti., Sph., Pol., Phil.,* and *Laws.* Some scholars favor a tripartite division into early, middle, and late dialogues. The dates of some dialogues are disputed, but it is generally agreed that the *Meno* belongs after the dialogues in (i), and before the dialogues in (iii). For discussion of the dating of the dialogues, see L. Brandwood, "Stylometry and Chronology," ch. 3 of this volume.

2 There are two questions here: (a) Does Socrates need to have some knowledge in order to inquire? (b) Does he need to believe he has some knowledge in order to be subjectively justified in inquiring? If Socrates believes he lacks knowledge but in fact has knowledge, (b) but not (a) arises. If he believes he has knowledge but does not in fact have it, (a) but not (b) arises. I shall generally ignore the difference between (a) and (b), but see my reply to the second objection to my interpretation of the second stage of Socrates' reply, at the end of section III. I take inquiry to be a directed, intentional search for knowledge one lacks. Hence, perceiving, happening upon an object one is looking for, and being told are not forms of inquiry;

but ordinary scientific research is. Inquiry can take various forms. In the Socratic dialogues and, I shall suggest, in the *Meno*, it takes the form of elenchus, on which see further below.

3 It might be better to formulate PKW as: "All knowledge about x is grounded in knowledge of what x is; and so, if one doesn't know what x is, one can't know anything about x." The first clause makes it clear that PKW is not just a necessity but also a priority claim. But it will be simpler to use the formulation in the text. Thanks here to Richard Kraut.

4 See Nehamas 1985: 5–6.

5 Unfortunately, many translations obscure this crucial point. For example, Grube (2002) translates 71b3 as: "I blame myself for my complete ignorance of virtue." "I blame myself for not knowing at all about virtue" would be more accurate. Although Guthrie (1956) translates 71b3–4 accurately enough, he translates 71a5–7 as: "The fact is that far from knowing whether it can be taught, I have no idea what virtue itself is." "I have no idea" should be rendered as "I do not know (*eidōs*)." He translates 71b4–6 as: "Do you suppose that somebody entirely ignorant who Meno is could say whether . . ., " when he should have: "Do you suppose that someone who does not at all know (*gignōskei*) who Meno is could know (*eidenai*) whether . . . ." Nehamas (1985: 8) translates 80d–6 as "in what way can you search for something when you are altogether ignorant of what it is?"; but the last clause is better rendered as "when you don't at all know what it is."

6 See Geach 1966.

7 He says that one needs to know what (*ti*) x is to know what x is like (*poion*). Knowing what x is is knowing its real essence; knowing what x is like is knowing its non-essential properties. More precisely, this is the relevant contrast in the case of knowing things like virtue. It may be that one can know, e.g., who Meno is (71b) or the way to Larissa (97a) without knowing their real essence. But since, in this chapter, I focus on cases like virtue, I leave such cases to one side. I discuss PKW further in Fine 2014: 31–42. In the case of virtue, an example of knowing what virtue is like is knowing whether it is teachable. It's not clear whether knowing instances (e.g., that Socrates is virtuous, if he is) also counts as knowing what virtue is like; but even if PKW doesn't include such cases, the *Meno* seems committed to the view that one can't know whether something is an instance of F unless one knows what F is. For the sake of simplicity, I'll write as though PKW includes such cases. For discussion, see Scott 2006: 20–2, 85–7.

8 See, e.g., Beversluis 1974.

9 I assume PKW should not be read as (A), so I shall not consider it further here.

10 This might be disputed. For example, Bostock (1986: 69–72) argues that knowing the meanings of terms is difficult. That is no doubt true on some views about meanings. But if we take meanings simply to articulate ordinary usage, then, even if not everyone can readily state them, it would be odd for Socrates to believe that knowledge is as difficult to come by as he seems to take it to be.

11 For Locke on real vs. nominal essences, see Locke 1975 (originally published in 1690), III.iii; III.vi; III.x; IV.vi.4–9; IV.xii.9. For a defense of the view that Socrates is more interested in something like the real essence of virtue than in the conventional meaning of virtue terms, see Penner 1973b; Irwin 1977, esp. ch. 3; Irwin 1995a, esp. ch. 2; and Fine 1993: 46–9, and chs. 8–9.

12 See also *Chrm.* 159c1, 160e6; *La.* 192c5–7; *Prt.* 349e3–5, 359e4–7. That virtue is good and beneficial is a general principle about virtue. Socrates also relies on examples of virtuous behavior, insofar as he regularly tests definitions against them (though he doesn't think definitions consist in or even mention examples). See Irwin 1977: 38–43, 61–8, and 1995a: 48–9; Burnyeat 1977a.

13 I consider Socrates' 98a account of knowledge shortly. In *Posterior Analytics* 1.1–10 Aristotle defends a version of (C), claiming that one can know the nonessential properties of a thing only by deducing propositions about them from its real definition.

14 For (a), see Vlastos 1956: "Introduction," esp. xxvi–xxxi; contrast Vlastos 1983, esp. 45. Vlastos 1991: ch. 4 rejects (a) for the Socratic dialogues; but he argues that in the *Meno* Plato believes that elenchus (a type of inquiry practiced in the Socratic dialogues) can do no more than detect contradictions.

15 For (b), see, e.g., Robinson 1953: ch. 2.

16 (c1) distinguishes two senses of "knowledge" ("certainty" and "justified true belief"); (c2) distinguishes different ranges of things known or not known (what virtue is and what it's like, vs. instances of virtue), in a single sense of the term. For (c1), see Vlastos 1985. For a version of (c2), see Kraut 1984: ch. 8. There are traces of (c2) in Vlastos' article, but he focuses on (c1). Nehamas (1987: 284–93) also seems to endorse a version of (c2). One

might try to defend (c1) by appealing to two senses of "knowledge" other than those Vlastos appeals to: see, e.g., Woodruff 1990; and Reeve 1989: 53–62. The consideration I adduce below against (c1) applies to all versions of it. I discuss Socrates' disavowal of knowledge in the *Apology* in Fine 2008. See also Taylor 1998.

17   The definition, or account, of knowledge in 98a uses *epistēmē*; PKW, as formulated in 71, uses a form of *eidenai*. One might argue that the conditions for one to *eidenai* something are weaker than are the conditions for having *epistēmē* of it. However, 95d5ff. uses forms of *eidenai*, *epistasthai*, and having *epistēmē* interchangeably. It would be misleading if 71 used *eidenai* differently. I discuss the 98a account of knowledge in detail in Fine 2004. For criticism of my account and defense of a different view, see Schwab 2015 and Judson 2019.

18   For discussion of the elenchus, see, e.g., Vlastos 1983; Irwin 1995a: ch. 2.

19   One might argue that even if one has contradictory beliefs about F, it doesn't follow that one doesn't know anything about F. However that may be in general, given what a correct answer to a "What is F?" question is, it seems reasonable to suppose that the interlocutors don't know it; given PKW, it follows that they have no knowledge about F.

20   I discuss various labels for the paradox in Fine 2014: 25–7; and ch. 3 discusses the paradox in detail. I refer the reader to Fine 2014 for more discussion than I can provide here.

21   (2)–(4) are explicit; (1) is implicit. In addition to stating (1)–(4), Socrates offers support for (2) and (3); I leave discussion of this support to one side.

22   For discussion, see Fine 2014: 84–7; Benson 2015: 55–63. Benson and I are in broad agreement that the differences between Meno's questions and Socrates' dilemma are not philosophically significant. Contrast Moravscik 1978; Weiss 2001; Scott 2006: ch. 7; and McCabe 2009.

23   What if "knowledge" in (2) is understood as Plato explains it in 98a? Then it seems false. For example, even if one knows the real essence of x, one can still inquire about x, e.g., to discover its non-essential properties.

24   For this "all or nothing" conception of how the paradox goes, see Bronstein 2010, and Charles 2010: 116.

25   For criticism of the view that Meno takes himself to be in a cognitive blank about virtue and understands (3) accordingly, see Ebrey 2014b: 1–4.

26   Since Meno doesn't address the possibility of inquiry if one has knowledge, it's not clear what his attitude to (2) is.

27 *Pais.* This can mean "slave" (of any age) or "boy" (whether or not a slave); but it doesn't mean "slave boy." It's not clear what age the slave is.

28 *Discourse on Metaphysics* 26.

29 There's dispute about how the two accounts of recollection fit together. For discussion, see Dancy 2004: 221–36, esp. 234–5; Scott 2006: 97.

30 He doesn't say that the slave *knows* Greek, just that he speaks Greek. Hence the remark isn't evidence that Socrates thinks the slave has any knowledge.

31 For the view that the whole of the discussion with the slave – including the positive phase in which the slave emerges from his *aporia* and acquires a true belief about the answer to Socrates' question – is a standard Socratic elenchus, see Irwin 1995a: 132–5; and Gentzler 1994. For the view that only the negative phase, which issues in *aporia*, involves the elenchus, see Vlastos 1991: ch. 4, esp. 123.

32 I take it that not only does the slave not know the answer to Socrates' question, but neither does he have *any* geometrical knowledge – a claim that is reasonable given PKW and Socrates' strong standards for knowledge as explained in 98a. Contrast Charles 2006, to which I reply in Fine 2014: 99–103 and 128–34. Cf. Franklin 2001. It's true that at 82b9 the slave is said to *gignōskei* that a square is like this, or is this sort of thing; and *gignōskein* can be used for knowledge. But it can also be used for recognition that falls short of knowledge; and that's how it's used here. For one thing, if the slave has some geometrical knowledge, his cognitive condition with respect to geometry doesn't match Socrates' condition with respect to virtue; but it is supposed to.

Since the slave can inquire about the answer to Socrates' question despite not already knowing it, the geometrical discussion rejects a *matching* version of a foreknowledge principle, according to which one can inquire into something only if one already knows that very thing. Since the slave lacks all geometrical knowledge, the geometrical discussion also rejects a *stepping-stone* version of foreknowledge, according to which one can inquire into something only if one knows something else relevant to that thing. (One might argue that even if the slave lacks all geometrical knowledge, still, he has other relevant knowledge, e.g., of logic. However, again, given Socrates' strong conditions on knowledge, it seems unlikely that the slave has knowledge of logic; nor does the text ascribe it to him.) On foreknowledge, see Fine

2014: 12–14, and *passim*. I owe the distinction between matching and stepping-stone versions of foreknowledge to Brown 2008.

Nor does the geometrical discussion involve a stepping-stone version of a prior *true belief* principle. For it says that having and relying on relevant true beliefs is *sufficient* for inquiry, not that it is *necessary* for it.

33 We saw above that one difference between Meno's and Socrates' formulations of the paradox is that Meno asks whether one can inquire into what one doesn't know at all, whereas Socrates asks only whether one can inquire into what one doesn't know. This difference is sometimes thought to indicate that Plato believes that, though one can't inquire into what one doesn't know at all, one can inquire into what one doesn't know in a way (so long as one knows it in some different way); see, e.g., Moravcsik 1978: 57. On my account, however, Plato allows that one can inquire into what one doesn't at all know, since one can inquire on the basis of true beliefs. Hence his omission of "at all" is not significant. Plato is cavalier in his use of *to parapan* elsewhere too: though it is used in 71a6 and b3, 5, it is omitted in the statement of PKW at 71b3–4. This suggests that the geometrical discussion not only rejects (3) of Socrates' dilemma, but also responds to Meno's questions. In particular, in saying that the same method can lead to knowledge, Socrates responds to Meno's third question (C above).

34 For the view that Socrates has, or takes himself to have, geometrical knowledge, see Devereux 1978; Kraut 1984: 297.

35 That Socrates thinks knowledge is needed for teaching is suggested by 96b. It's true that he proceeds to argue that true belief is as good a guide to correct action as knowledge is. But he doesn't say that someone with mere true belief can teach; the ability to teach requires more than the ability to act correctly.

36 See, e.g., Devereux 1978; Scott 2006: 142–4.

37 See Fine 2014: 114–19. At 87b7–c1, Socrates says that another way to ask whether virtue is teachable is to ask whether it is recollectable; since some things are recollectable, he thinks some things are teachable. But even if virtue, or geometry, is teachable, it doesn't follow that Socrates is in a position to teach them, as he understands teaching.

38 See Vlastos 1965: esp. 158–9, and 1988: 374 n. 42.

39 See Nehamas 1985: 16–17; McCabe 2009.

40 See note 2. One might argue that it is not necessary to have true beliefs in order to inquire; all that is necessary is that one's use of a term be on a suitable causal chain. See Kripke 1980 (originally published in 1972) and Putnam 1975. Be that as it may, it's sufficient for inquiry that one have and rely on one's true beliefs; since Socrates thinks that's our actual condition, he focuses on it.

41 See Irwin 1977: 41–2, 66–70; 1995a: ch. 9 at, e.g., 133–4.

42 Ryle 1976: 4; Dancy 2004: 209, 222.

43 The passage just quoted also suggests that recollection shows how discovery is possible. This responds to Meno's third question, C.

44 I take it that "and," in "inquiry and learning," is epexegetic: inquiry – or, more precisely successful inquiry – is a type of learning.

45 See, e.g., Ryle 1976: 4; Vlastos 1983: 61 (pagination from Fine 1999a); Kraut 1984: 298 n. 79.

46 See, e.g., Sharples 1985: n. on 81c6; Scott 2006: 96–7; Dancy 2004: 223f.

47 See, e.g., Leibniz 1981: Book I, ch. 1, 79, also cited by Scott 2006: 116. Even if the soul went through an initial process of learning, a regress can be avoided – even if the process was simply inquiry all over again. Plato might argue, e.g., that when the soul was discarnate, it was not hampered by perception and bodily desires; without such distractions, it could acquire knowledge through inquiry even if it did not know in some still earlier life. On this account, the theory of recollection would be introduced to explain not how inquiry in general is possible, but how it is possible when we are incarnate. Another possibility, suggested by Scott (2006: 116), is that if there is a regress, Plato would view it as virtuous, not vicious, since it would help establish the view that the soul is immortal.

48 Plato uses the imperfect, which need not indicate any episode of seeing; it might indicate that we saw, i.e., knew, for the whole of our prenatal existence.

49 Plato uses the perfect – *memathēken* – which need not imply an act of learning.

50 I have omitted Meno's positive responses to Socrates' questions.

51 LSJ, s.v. *analambanō*; see *Ap.* 22b, *Meno* 87e5, *Smp.* 185e1, *Rep.* 606e4, *Tht.* 203a1; *Sph.* 255e9; *Pol.* 261c5. See Irwin 1995a: 132–6, and 372 n. 15.

52 The view that Plato posits innate knowledge has a long pedigree; see, e.g., Leibniz 1981, Book I, ch. 1. Among many others, see also Scott 2006: 108–12;

Dancy 2004: 228–336. (However, whereas Scott seems to think Plato thinks we have always been in the cognitive condition of knowing, Dancy seems to think that only content innatism is at issue. For this distinction, see Dancy 2004: 228–32; Fine 2014: 140–2.) It's one thing to posit innate knowledge, another to posit current knowledge. Perhaps the slave was born with knowledge, but lost it at some point and so no longer knows. Or perhaps he was born without knowledge but acquired it at some point, if only in the form of latent rather than explicit knowledge. It usually seems to be assumed, though, that we have latent innate knowledge and retain that knowledge in latent form, though we can make it explicit by recollecting.

53 See, e.g., Scott 2006: 105–12.

54 For criticism of my alternative, see Scott 2006: 110–12. I reply in Fine 2007: 358–61.

55 See Fine 2014: 153–63.

56 Another possibility is that the truth is always in us as true beliefs. But, in my view, Plato doesn't posit innate true beliefs or, for that matter, innate concepts: see Fine 2014: 160–1. Contrast Gentzler 1994: 293.

57 Leibniz 1989: 27.

58 Cf. Vlastos 1965: 153 n. 14. In general, all the passages that mention having knowledge are either forward-referring, to the time when the slave will acquire knowledge (85d1, 3–4 [epistēsetai], d6, 9) or backward-referring, to prenatal knowledge (81c9).

59 If Plato thinks we can inquire and discover only because we had prenatal knowledge, he accepts a version of foreknowledge. Whether it is a matching or stepping-stone version depends on what we had prenatal knowledge of. But accepting what we might call *Prenatal Foreknowledge* doesn't commit Plato to the view that we have latent innate or current knowledge.

60 Though the claim that we forgot our prenatal knowledge isn't made in the *Meno*, it is compatible with it, and it is explicit in *Phd.* 75d–76e. For criticism of my interpretation of what forgetting involves, see Castagnoli 2018. For detailed criticism of my view that the *Meno* isn't committed to innate knowledge, see Bronstein and Schwab 2019.

61 Cf. Aristotle, *De Memoria* 451b9–12.

62 See Moravscik 1978: 58.

63 See, e.g., Chomsky 1988; on 4 he compares his view with Plato's. See also Chomsky 1965: e.g., 27. Plato would argue that what Chomsky calls

"knowledge" doesn't count as genuine knowledge. Chomsky sometimes seems to agree. For in Chomsky 1980: 92, he suggests it would be better to speak of innate cognition; see also Chomsky 1965: 25.

64 Chomsky, by contrast, doesn't accept an accessibility condition on knowledge. Nagel (1974) appeals to an accessibility condition on knowledge to argue that we don't have innate knowledge of the rules of grammar. The accessibility condition implies not only that we don't have latent innate knowledge but also that many of us lack latent current knowledge of many things.

65 The passage can be read to say that one of the few things Socrates claims to know is that knowledge and true belief differ, in which case it provides even stronger support for my view that he places more weight on the distinction between knowledge and true belief than on the theory of recollection. But if the passage is taken that way, Socrates would be claiming, contrary to PKW, that he knows something about knowledge and true belief (that they differ) without knowing what they are. Even if he does not claim to know that knowledge and true belief differ, he expresses considerable confidence in that claim, saying that he does not issue it on the basis of *eikasia*. In *Rep.* V–VII, he distinguishes *eikasia* from *pistis*, where both are beliefs, but *pistis* is a higher-level sort of belief. So perhaps Socrates thinks he has *pistis*.

7 Why *Erōs*?

Suzanne Obdrzalek

I INTRODUCTION

I want you to think back to the first time you fell in love. I'm talking about falling hard, head-over-heels, crazy in love. I want you to remember that feeling: how the whole world seemed transformed, how every moment seemed more intense, how this person seemed to be more wonderful than anyone you had ever met before – to be perfect, almost divine, and how it felt like all meaning derived from being near them, and receded when you were apart. I now want you to take all those vivid emotions and imagine feeling them toward a philosophical theory or concept, toward Gödel's incompleteness theorem or Kantian things-in-themselves. One of the ways in which Plato has captured the popular imagination is with his claim that philosophy is grounded in love, that the philosopher can feel *erōs* (passionate love)[1] for the objects of knowledge. But I want to draw attention to what a startlingly odd claim this is. It is an odd claim to make, first, because for many of us it is hard to imagine what it would be like to direct the sorts of emotions we feel for human love-objects toward abstract, intellectual objects. But Plato's claim is even stranger than that. For he is not simply claiming that the best philosophers feel toward intellectual objects whatever it is most of us feel for human love-objects. He also appears to be making a developmental

Though this chapter is unworthy of its predecessor, I would like to dedicate it to my friend and teacher, John Ferrari. I would also like to express my gratitude to David Ebrey and Richard Kraut for the invitation to write this chapter and to my audience at the Chicago Area Consortium in Ancient Greek and Roman Philosophy for their thoughtful comments.

claim: that one path to becoming a Platonic metaphysician is by falling for a really physically beautiful human being, and that this erotic response can then be redirected toward intellectual objects. But how could this redirection occur, how exactly might one extract a beautiful boy from one's affections and swap in a form? The question, then, that I wish to address in this chapter is, why erōs? Why should Plato propose that erōs – and here I take him to mean precisely passionate interpersonal love[2] – is an appropriate model and starting-point for philosophical engagement?

In fact, when we consider this question, a parallel question suggests itself: why philosophy? In depicting philosophy as erotic, Plato is seeking to answer the question of why we should do philosophy. This question has been largely ignored among contemporary Anglo-American philosophers: we propose all sorts of philosophical theories but pay surprisingly little attention to the question of what the value or purpose of philosophy itself is. In what follows, I argue that in suggesting that philosophy is potentially erotic, Plato is addressing precisely this question. He is claiming that philosophy can and perhaps should begin with erōs because the appropriate response to the forms is not purely cognitive but also desiderative and affective. In short, it is love. This, because the forms are the best of all objects, due to their ideal natures – their perfection, eternality, changelessness, and independence.[3] These ideal properties not only make them epistemologically and metaphysically significant, but also ethically significant; they make the forms worthy of love and awe. As the best objects, they have the potential to transform our lives. As humans, we are by nature mortal and imperfect; our mortality and imperfection give rise to erōs, the desire for immortality and perfection. This desire achieves its highest form of satisfaction in the philosopher's contemplation of forms, objects that are truly eternal and perfect. Thus, our yearning for the forms is not simply a desire for understanding; it is a desire to stand in an intimate relation to something greater than ourselves, grounded in a perhaps inchoate sense of our own mortality and imperfection.

Here is one way to frame the puzzle I wish to address in this chapter. Though Plato makes passing reference to the philosopher as erotic throughout his dialogues, he only really makes good on this claim in two, the *Symposium* and the *Phaedrus*.[4] Elsewhere, he proposes paths to philosophy that appear to be entirely non-erotic. For example, in the *Phaedo*, he describes how one might begin to recollect the form of equality by seeing two equal sticks (74a9–b6). Once one recognizes that they are both equal and unequal, this has the potential to cause one to recollect the form through a purely intellectual process. Likewise, in the *Republic*, he proposes an educational curriculum that appears to be entirely non-erotic, that begins with mathematics and ends with dialectic. In this context, he describes the sorts of things that awaken our interest in philosophy, referring to them as summoners (523a5–4d5). Whereas no one is prompted to philosophical exploration through observing a mere finger, since it is not deficient in being a finger, one's philosophical curiosity might be awakened by observing two fingers, and how one is larger than the other. The larger finger will inevitably be found to partake of opposites – perhaps by appearing smaller than some other finger – spurring the would-be philosopher to inquire into the nature of the large itself. But whereas the largeness of fingers and the equality of sticks may prompt philosophical inquiry, they appear to do so in a manner that is entirely non-erotic. And this leads us to my central puzzle. Plato clearly has the conceptual resources to describe non-erotic paths to philosophy. So why should he present us with erotic paths as well? What distinguishes the erotic paths from their de-eroticized cousins?[5] My exploration centers on Plato's *Symposium* and *Phaedrus*; though there are significant differences between these dialogues,[6] my focus is the story they tell in common, of how we can go from loving a beautiful body to falling for the forms.[7]

I address this puzzle by proposing three ways in which erotic paths to philosophy differ from non-erotic.[8] First, I consider the source of philosophical *erōs*. I argue that it is grounded in our mortality and imperfection; this gives rise to a desire for immortality and the immortal. Second, I turn to the object of philosophical *erōs*. I suggest that philosophical *erōs* is an arresting response to beauty through which we are brought to recognize and value the ideal properties of the form of beauty and, indeed, of all the forms. Finally, I address the nature of *erōs*. I claim that it is a focusing desire, a desire that overrides other concerns and aims and causes us to overwhelmingly focus on its object.

II IMMORTALITY

Let us begin by considering the source of philosophical *erōs*. There are, after all, many paths to philosophy: In the Socratic dialogues, Plato emphasizes how we are drawn to philosophy by a sense of puzzlement and a desire to explore and eradicate inconsistencies within our beliefs. But in Plato's erotic dialogues, he considers a quite different source for the drive to do philosophy, namely our sense of our own mortality and imperfection and our desire to become or to enter into a relationship with the immortal and perfect. We see this if we consider an initially puzzling feature of the *Symposium* and *Phaedrus*. Both are, not just erotic, but also, and strikingly, theological dialogues. The passages that arguably serve as the philosophical core of each – Socrates' speech in the *Symposium* and his second speech in the *Phaedrus* – are addressed to divine beings.[9] Socrates' speech in the *Symposium* is a paean to the *daimōn* (spiritual being), Erōs; it concludes: "every man must honor Erōs and I myself honor him and especially practice the erotic arts and call on others to do so, and both now and forever I eulogize the power and courage of Erōs to the best of my ability" (212b5–8).[10] Socrates' second speech in the *Phaedrus* is a palinode to the god, Erōs, offered in supplication for having offended him with his earlier speech which exalted the non-lover.

This in itself is virtually unique within the Platonic corpus,[11] but this religious theme is amplified within the speeches themselves. Both speeches make extensive reference to mystery rites, using both linguistic and structural cues to develop an analogy between mystical initiation and philosophical enlightenment. In the *Symposium*, the ascent to the forms is referred to as the initiation into *ta telea kai epoptika* (the final and epoptic [rites], 210a1); the *epopteia* were the highest grade of initiation into the Eleusinian mysteries. This stage of initiation came to a climax when torchlight broke through the darkness to reveal sacred objects. Bury suggests that the way in which Plato presents the philosopher's vision of the form in the ascent – he beholds it suddenly (*exaiphnēs*) and at the culmination of a series of initiatory stages – is meant to develop a parallel to the mystical initiate's sudden vision of the sacred objects.[12] This exact parallel recurs in the *Phaedrus*. At 250b5–c5, Plato describes our prenatal vision of the forms: "Then, beauty was radiant to see, when with a happy chorus they saw the blessed and divine vision, we following Zeus, others other gods, and were inducted into the mysteries that are rightly called most blessed ... we were initiated into whole, simple, stable, and happy visions, and we were initiated (*epopteuontes*) in a pure light, being pure ourselves." Again, our vision of the forms is likened to the sight of the sacred objects in the *epopteia*; Yunis (2011: 149) draws attention to Plato's extravagant use of imagery associated with illumination that is reminiscent of the use of torchlight to reveal the sacred objects. Though little is known about the Eleusinian mysteries, it seems that their purpose was to bring the initiate into a more intimate relationship with the gods, to purify his soul, and to provide him with a better fate in the afterlife.[13] It might seem quite odd that these speeches about *erōs* should be interwoven with religious imagery and couched in the language of mystical initiation. But this feature becomes less surprising once we recognize that Plato takes *erōs* to be, at its heart, a desire to enter into a close relation to the immortal and divine.

Socrates begins his account of *erōs* in the *Symposium* by providing a general analysis of *erōs* as a psychological state: *erōs*, he argues, desires its object; as a species of desire, it necessarily originates in lack (200a2–b1). Embedded in this account of *erōs* is an account of human nature: to the extent that we are desiring, erotic creatures, we are creatures that are lacking. This, in turn, implies a contrast between humans and gods – whereas humans are needy, gods are beings that lack nothing. Socrates goes on to develop this contrast when he shifts his focus from the psychological state, *erōs*, to the spiritual being, Erōs. Erōs, he argues in opposition to Agathon, cannot be a god: gods, by definition, forever possess the beautiful and the good, whereas Erōs desires and hence lacks these (202c6–d7). But this is not to say that Erōs is mortal, nor that he is ugly: Erōs, Socrates proposes, is a *daimōn*, existing between the mortal and the immortal, its function to connect man to god (202d11–3a8). If Plato's portrayal of the *daimōn*, Erōs, is at once a characterization of the psychological state, *erōs*, then this implies that the deficiencies that give rise to *erōs* are reflective of our status as mortals and express an aspiration to the divine. This suggestion is further developed in the myth of Poros and Penia: Erōs is portrayed as existing in a state of metaxy, neither immortal nor mortal. Plato adds that Erōs is a *philosophos*, a lover of wisdom, both because wisdom is beautiful and because he is aware that he lacks this beauty (204a8–b5). Thus, the psychological state, *erōs*, appears to arise in us not simply from a deficiency in our mortal natures, but from a perhaps unarticulated awareness of this deficiency; this gives rise to a desire to overcome that deficiency by seeking to gain the beautiful and good and thereby approach the state of the gods.

In what follows, Plato – temporarily, at least – shifts his focus from the pursuit of beauty to the pursuit of immortality.[14] The means by which he accomplishes this is by proposing that *erōs*, broadly construed, is the desire to possess the good always. But we can only possess the good always if we exist always and hence are immortal. In connecting *erōs* to the pursuit of immortality, Diotima engages in a subtle argumentative legerdemain:[15] until 206e7, immortality is given an implicitly adverbial role – we seek immortality because it enables us to possess the good always, but in itself, immortality is not treated as an object of desire. But at 206e8–207a4, in the context of proposing that *erōs* aims at reproduction, she begins to treat immortality and the good as if they were each an object of desire: "according to what we agreed, immortality, together with the good, must be desired, if in fact *erōs* is of the good belonging to oneself always. For it is necessary from this account that *erōs* be of immortality as well." But in what follows, Diotima provides no discussion of how the good is to be acquired; her focus is solely on the pursuit of immortality, *tout court*, and by 208d7–e1, talk of the good has all but disappeared – though *erōs* pursues virtue, it pursues it under the guise of *immortal* virtue and as a means to undying glory: "it is for the sake of immortal virtue and this sort of glorious reputation that everyone does everything, the more so the better they are; for they are in love with immortality." This slide might be puzzling if we had not already noted the theological focus of the *Symposium*: Plato is able to treat immortality as an end, and not simply as a means to happiness, because immortality is one of the essential features of the gods; in aspiring to be immortal, we aspire to the condition of the gods.[16]

At 207c9–208b6, Plato couches our pursuit of immortality, yet again, in terms of a contrast between mortal and divine nature. Whereas the divine is immortal "by always being absolutely the same" (208a8), this is impossible for mortal creatures, as we are subject to constant flux; we must therefore pursue a mortal form of immortality via reproduction. This pursuit is ubiquitous: according to Plato, even the sexual intercourse of irrational animals is driven by an unconscious drive toward immortality. Plato thereby addresses what we might call the homonymy objection: Is he not guilty of taking the name of one phenomenon, sexual desire, and applying it to quite another, the pursuit of immortality? Not so, for Plato's proposal is that brute sexual desire, conceived of teleologically, is in fact the desire for immortality.[17] But in shifting the focus of *erōs* to immortality, Plato thereby dethrones beauty. Whereas Phaedrus proposed that Erōs is beautiful (195a7), Socrates begins by arguing that it is not itself beautiful but rather that it is the desire for the beautiful; he then revises that claim, proposing that it is not the desire for beauty at all, but rather for immortality. Beauty retains a role in Socrates' account, but it is purely ancillary, its function is to serve as a medium which facilitates reproduction. Diotima thus chastises Socrates: "*Erōs* is not ... as you think, of the beautiful ... It is of generation and birth in the beautiful" (206e2–5). As we shall see in the next section, it is only in the ascent passage that beauty resumes its central role as the object of *erōs*; I shall argue that it does so precisely because of its immortality and perfection.

On the face of it, Plato's account of human nature in the *Phaedrus* appears to stand in opposition to that of the *Symposium*: Whereas in the *Symposium*, he emphasizes our current deficiency, in the *Phaedrus*, Socrates' second speech begins with an account of our prenatal bliss. Prior to incarnation, each of our souls followed in the chorus of its god, assisting them in ruling the universe and joining them in contemplating forms (246b–248b). But upon closer examination, we can uncover a treatment of human nature in the *Phaedrus* that is not so far removed from that of the *Symposium*. Even in his account of our prenatal state, Plato emphasizes the gap between human and divine souls – our souls, like the gods', are composed of a winged team of a charioteer and horses, but whereas all of the gods' horses are good, one of ours is white, the other black (246a6–b4). This black horse, roughly corresponding to appetite, represents our souls' inbuilt pull toward incarnation. When our souls are winged and perfect, we are each able to follow our god and observe the forms. But the unruly nature of the dark horse leads most souls to shed their wings and fall into a solid, earthy body. And it is once a soul is imprisoned in a body that it becomes part of the composite that is a human. Thus, even as Plato creates a beatific portrayal of our souls' divine potential, he emphasizes that our current state, as embodied humans, is one of fallen-ness.

In the *Symposium*, Plato proposes that *erōs* is the desire for immortality. It might appear that Plato cannot sustain this analysis in the *Phaedrus*: at 245c5, he declares outright, "all soul is immortal." But as we have seen, Plato also contrasts disembodied and embodied souls: he writes that when a soul has lost its wings, it "is carried along until it takes hold of something solid, and settling there, it takes on an earthy body that seems to move itself on account of the soul's power, and the whole thing is called an animal (zōon), the soul and body made fast together, and it has the name, mortal. Immortal it is not, not on the basis of any account that has been reasoned through" (246c2–7). Thus, to the extent that we are soul–body composites, we are mortal beings. However, our souls never lose their latent capacity to regrow their wings, become disembodied and immortal, and reascend to the forms. When, as incarnate, mortal beings, we encounter something beautiful, this causes the wings of our soul to throb and pulse and itch to grow. The result is a mad desire to regrow our wings, reascend to the heavens, and see the forms. The name of this desire, Plato proposes, is erōs (249e3–4, 252b1–3). To the extent that erōs is the desire to regrow our wings, it is a desire to escape our incarnate, mortal condition and to regain our blessed, disincarnate, immortal condition.

As in the Symposium, so in the Phaedrus, Plato's emphasis on immortality brings with it an implicit demotion of beauty. Though the lover's erōs is sparked by his attraction to a beautiful boy, his ultimate aim does not concern the boy; rather, it is to regrow his wings, reascend to the heavens, and contemplate the forms. Just as, in the Symposium, beauty assists in the process of giving birth, a process that aims at immortality, so in the Phaedrus, Plato assigns it the role of nourishing the regrowth of the wings of the soul (246d6–e4). However, once he regrows his wings, what the lover ultimately wishes to grasp is not the form of beauty per se, but, rather, the set of all the forms; though beauty plays a special role in prompting recollection, its value lies in the ideal nature that it shares with all the forms.

III   BEAUTY

What we see, then, in the Symposium and Phaedrus, is the proposal that erōs is a desire that arises due to an awareness of our deficient, mortal human nature; it is a desire to achieve immortality and to stand in relation to the immortal and divine. This is a radical and ambitious claim for Plato to make. Whereas *erōs* is commonly under-stood to consist in sexual desire, Plato proposes that it is, in fact, something quite different. And he is not just taking the term, *erōs*, and using it to describe an entirely different phenomenon; instead, he is claiming that what we mistakenly identify with mere sexual desire is, in fact, a significantly wider phenomenon, that lies at the root of our desire for sex, but also, potentially, at the root of our desire to do philosophy. To return to my original puzzle: What, then, distin-guishes *erōs* as a path to philosophy from non-erotic forms of ascent? This desire is more fundamental and ethically significant than mere intellectual curiosity. It arises from an awareness of what sorts of creatures we are and of what we might aspire to become; as such, it concerns what we ought to aim at in life. But granting that *erōs* is a desire for immortality, why should this desire find its ultimate expression in philosophical contemplation? This brings me to my second proposal, that *erōs* is distinguished by the role of beauty. It is an arresting response to beauty that causes us to recognize and value the ideal attributes of the form, which, in turn, promise to address our sense of mortality and imperfection.

Earlier, I observed that in treating *erōs* as the desire for immor-tality, Plato sidelines beauty; beauty facilitates reproduction and birth, it eases the regrowth of the soul's wings, but it is no longer the primary focus of *erōs*. It is in the ascent passage of the *Symposium* that beauty resumes its status as the object of *erōs*.[18] On its surface, the ascent passage of the *Symposium* appears to conform with Diotima's earlier statement that *erōs* is not of beauty, but of "birth in beauty," as she enigmatically calls it: As the initiate shifts his attention from one kind of beauty to the next, he is thrice depicted as giving birth to ideas (210a7–8, c1–2, d4–5), and the passage culmin-ates with his giving birth to virtue (212a3–5). But at the same time, throughout the ascent, the focus appears to shift back to the beauty of the beautiful objects as valuable in itself, and as leading to the ultim-ate goal of *erōs*, the vision of the form of beauty. The ascent passage opens with a twenty-eight-line long sentence, consisting of a series of purpose clauses, which describe how the initiate rises from one level to the next; this syntactic structure serves to emphasize the directionality and even urgency of the ascent. It is broken off with a sudden warning to pay attention, that serves to offset the purpose at which the entire ascent is aiming. Plato next writes: "Whoever is led thus far in erotic matters, contemplating beauties correctly and in the right order, approaching the end (*telos*) of these erotic matters, will suddenly catch sight of a beauty amazing in its nature, and this is the very thing ... that all his earlier toils were for the sake of" (210e2–6). Plato here states outright that the *telos* (goal, end) of *erōs*, at which all the earlier stages aim, is the sight of the form of beauty. He refers to the sight of the form, again, as the *telos* of *erōs* when he recapitulates the ascent at 211b5–d1, and claims at 211d1–3 that to the extent that human life is worth living, it is worth living in the contemplation of the form of beauty. But all of this raises the following question: Why should Plato have been at pains to argue earlier that *erōs* is not of beauty, but rather of birth in beauty, only to vividly and emphatically reintroduce beauty as the proper object of *erōs* in the ascent?

The solution to this puzzle lies in the fact that what has been introduced as the proper object of *erōs* is not simply another beautiful particular; it is the form of beauty. And the form of beauty, *qua* form, fully possesses the eternality and perfection that we lack and that give rise to erotic longing. Thus, when Plato describes the form, he has little to say about what its beauty consists in; instead, his description focuses entirely on its ideal attributes. The first thing that Plato tells us about the form is that "always existing, it neither comes to be nor passes away, neither waxes nor wanes" (211a1–2); this represents exactly the condition that Plato earlier identified with true immortality.[19] Just as the form of beauty serves as the proper object of *erōs* in the ascent *qua* immortal form, so the successive beauties are objects of *erōs* to the extent that they point toward and progressively approximate the ideal nature of beauty. If we look carefully at the stages of the ascent, at no point does Plato describe the higher objects as more beautiful than the lower. It is true that the lover comes to view his attraction to a particular body as a small thing and to look down on it, but this is not to say that he no longer finds the body to be beautiful; indeed, it is his realization that what beauty it has is shared by other bodies that occasions his derision. Later, the lover recognizes that the beauty of souls is more valuable (*timiōteron*, 210b7) than the beauty of bodies, and that bodily beauty is of little worth. But none of this is equivalent to claiming that the higher objects are more beautiful than the lower, only that they are somehow more worthwhile. What makes the higher objects more worthwhile than the lower and thereby causes the lover to ascend? In his description of the form, Plato focuses entirely on its unchanging and perfect nature: it does not come into existence and cease to exist and it is not located in or conditioned upon anything particular. This suggests that, correspondingly, the value of the successive beauties in the ascent is connected, not to their being more beautiful, but to their better approximating the ideal properties of the form. Whereas a body is a concrete, corporeal particular, subject to decay, its beauty lasting a mere moment, a soul is incorporeal and its beauty longer-lasting.[20] Customs, laws, and knowledge are progressively less connected to the corporeal world and, correspondingly, longer-lasting. Thus, in the ascent passage, the form of beauty can serve as the ultimate object of *erōs* in virtue of its being a form, an object that is fully perfect and immortal;[21] the successive beauties of the ascent lead us to the form by progressively sharing in its ideal nature.

But if the ascent is driven by the beauties' increasing participation in the ideal nature of the form of beauty, then this raises the question of why the form of beauty in particular should play this role. Why might we not ascend by considering increasingly abstract and unchanging examples of, say, equality? What makes beauty so special? Plato addresses this question in the *Phaedrus*, in one of the most evocative but obscure passages in his corpus:

> Now there is no illumination in the likenesses down here of justice
> and moderation and the other things that are of value to souls, but

through dim organs and with difficulty, only a few, approaching their likenesses, behold the original that is imaged in them. But beauty was radiant to see then, when, with a happy chorus, they saw the blessed and divine sight, we following Zeus, others other gods, and were initiated into the mysteries that are rightly called most blessed ... concerning beauty, as we said, it was shining with those things, and now that we have come here, we grasp it through the clearest of our senses, glistening most clearly. For of all the sensations that come to us through the body, sight is the sharpest, but it does not see wisdom, for it would cause terrible feelings of love in us if it allowed some such clear image of itself to approach sight, and so, too, with the other objects of love; but now beauty alone has this privilege, to be most evident and most loved. (250b1–e1)

What is Plato trying to say here; what does it mean to say that beauty is "most evident and most loved"? This is not a claim about the form of beauty considered on its own and apart from its instances; when we grasped beauty in our disembodied state it shone with all the other forms and there is no implication that at that time it shone brighter than its brethren. Nor again is it a claim about particular beauties considered in isolation from the form; Plato is not claiming, say, that a beautiful object is more readily identifiable as beautiful than a large object as large.[22] Instead, as Lear (2006: 117) has suggested, this is a claim about the relation between the form of beauty and its instances. The unique power of the form of beauty lies in its capacity to shine through its instances and reveal "the original that is imaged in them." In other words, the form of beauty is somehow distinguished by the manner in which it reveals itself through its instances, prompting recollection. But why should this be the case?

Here, we might return to the comparison I drew earlier between, on the one hand, the erotic ascents of the *Symposium* and *Phaedrus* and, on the other hand, the sticks passage of the *Phaedo* and the

summoners passage of the *Republic*.[23] The *Phaedo* passage implies
(74b4–75b8) and the summoners passage states outright (523a10–c4)
that it is the deficiency of particulars that prompts dialectical investigation into forms. But in the *Symposium* and *Phaedrus*, there is no
suggestion that it is the deficiency of particular beauties that spurs
philosophical discovery. Indeed, if that were the case, we would be
best off falling for a partially ugly boy rather than one who is excep-
tionally beautiful. What, then, is it about the beautiful boy that
inspires the lover to recollect his pre-incarnate vision of the form of
beauty? To see the form reflected in a particular is to recognize that,
over and above particular beauties, such as the boy one has fallen for,
there is something that it is to be beautiful, a form of beauty that is
eternal, changeless, and independent, by approximating which all
beautiful particulars come to be beautiful. Thus, to the extent that
we see the form of beauty imaged in the boy, we do not just see in him
the proper attribute of the form, its beauty, but we also somehow see
its ideal attributes, its changelessness, perfection, and eternality,
reflected in him.[24] It is the fact that we see these ideal attributes
reflected in its instances that distinguishes the form of beauty from
the other forms.[25]

But what does it even mean to see the ideal nature of the form
reflected in the boy? Plato continues our passage as follows:

> the recently initiated, who saw much of the things then, when he
> sees a godlike face or a bodily form that imitates beauty well,
> first shivers and undergoes some of his former fears, and then,
> beholding him, he reveres him like a god, and if he did not fear
> a reputation of complete madness, he would sacrifice to his
> beloved as to a divine statue and to a god. (251a1–7)

What we see here is a phenomenon that Freud would later term
overvaluation: Through falling in love with the boy, the man sees
him as if he were perfect and is even inclined to worship him as a god.
Part of the madness of love is a tendency to be so overwhelmed by the
beauty of the beloved that we experience his beauty as if it were

perfect, timeless, and universal.[26] Though this reflects a metaphysical confusion, it also enables us to see the ideal nature of the form reflected in spatiotemporal reality. So long as our memory, and with it our *erōs*, passes from the boy to the form, this offers us a potential path to philosophy.[27]

Thus, the surprising result is that, even as Plato proposes that *erōs* aims at immortality and perfection rather than at beauty per se, he retains a central role for the form of beauty: It is in virtue of its being a form, and a form that reveals its ideal nature through its instances, that the form of beauty can serve as the ultimate object of *erōs*. Broadly speaking, the object of *erōs* is all of the forms, conceived of as perfect, immortal objects, but it is the form of beauty that first inspires love and that eventually draws the philosopher to all of the forms. But granting that the forms are perfect, eternal objects, how does the sight of the forms address the philosopher's erotic yearning for immortality and perfection? The answer is twofold. First, in the *Phaedrus*, Plato claims that the sight of the forms causes our soul to grow and maintain its wings (248b5–c2); indeed, it is their sight of the forms that serves to make the gods divine (249c5–6). Thus, Plato appears to propose that grasping the forms causes one's soul to approximate the forms' incorporeal, eternal natures. Though this proposal is puzzling, it is one that Plato pursues throughout his corpus – for example, in the *Phaedo*, he claims that contemplating forms makes one's soul assimilate to their unchanging natures (79d1–7), and in the *Timaeus*, that thinking immortal thoughts causes one's soul to partake of immortality (90b6–d8).[28] But there is also another possible role played by the philosopher's grasp of the forms. The *Symposium* and *Phaedrus* both suggest that our erotic longing is not solely a desire to become immortal ourselves, but also to behold that which is fully immortal and divine. Thus, in the *Symposium*, Erōs is a *daimōn* that connects man to god, and in the *Phaedrus*, our longing is not simply to assimilate to our god, but also to follow him. In enabling us to grasp objects that are fully immortal and perfect, philosophy can satisfy *erōs*, conceived of as a desire not simply for becoming immortal and perfect ourselves, but also as a desire for contemplating and admiring that which is greater than ourselves, that which is fully perfect and divine, namely the forms.[29]

IV MADNESS

I opened this chapter by asking what distinguishes erotic from non-erotic paths to philosophy. I proposed that philosophical *erōs* originates in our sense of our own mortality and imperfection and aims at our becoming or standing in relation to the immortal and perfect; I then examined how the form of beauty both awakens and fulfills this desire. My final task is to examine the nature of erotic desire – granting that *erōs* is a species of desire and that it is in some way directed toward beauty, what distinguishes it from other forms of desire? Plato raises this question in Socrates' first speech in the *Phaedrus*: "That *erōs* is some sort of desire is clear to everyone; we also know that men desire what is beautiful even when they do not feel *erōs*. How, then, shall we distinguish the man who feels *erōs* from the one who does not?" (237d3–5). The answer he proposes is that *erōs* is a species of hubris, in which the desire for pleasure overpowers one's judgment about what is best; while hubris takes on many names, the name of *erōs* derives from its forcefulness: "The unreasoning desire that has overpowered the belief that urges one to what is correct, borne toward pleasure in beauty and forcefully reinforced by kindred desires for bodily beauty, overpowering them in its course, and taking its name from this very force (*rhōmē*) – this is called *erōs*" (238b7–c4). In his second speech, Socrates rejects certain aspects of this analysis: its assumptions that the only kind of beauty is corporeal, that the only object of desire is pleasure, and that the pursuit of beauty stands in opposition to reason. But he does not reject the proposal that *erōs* is distinguished by its overriding force; thus, at the conclusion of the *Phaedrus*, Socrates states that his two speeches in fact carved out two species of madness, one the product of human illness, the other the result of divine inspiration (265a2–11). In treating *erōs* as a form of madness (*mania*), Plato is signaling that it is what we might call a focusing desire, a desire that overrides other concerns, causing us to focus overwhelmingly on its object.

Plato depicts this aspect of *erōs* vividly in Socrates' second speech:

> [The lover's soul] is sorely troubled by this mixture of [pleasure and pain] and it rages, confused by the strangeness of his condition, and maddened, it is unable to sleep by night nor remain in place by day, but it runs to wherever it thinks it will see the one who has the beauty it longs for; and seeing him, it opens the sluicegates of longing, and it frees what was blocked up before, and finding a breathing-space, it leaves off from its stinging birth-pains, and enjoys for the moment the sweetest of all pleasures. This it is not willing to give up, and it does not value anyone more than the beautiful [boy]. (251d7–252a2)

The lover is overwhelmingly focused on his love-object, to the extent that all other aims and interests vanish. As the lover's recollection begins to turn from the boy to the forms, he even appears to exit this world and to be out of his mind: "Standing outside of human concerns, and drawing close to the divine, he is admonished by the many for being disturbed, unaware that he is possessed by a god" (249c8–d3); "looking upward like a bird, ignoring the things down below, he is charged with being mad" (249d7–e1). *Erōs* is a focusing desire in the sense that it commands our attention; the result is not simply that we feel compelled to pursue it, but that other considerations and aims recede, to the point that the agent can even cease to be aware of himself. Though, for Plato, the beautiful and the good are coextensive, to respond to something as beautiful can be quite different from responding to it as good.[30] When we respond to something as good, we see it as an end to be pursued, and we deliberate as to how to pursue this good and how to balance its pursuit with other goods that we might wish to obtain as well. By contrast, an erotic response to beauty has a kind of tunneling effect, where all other ends recede, and the beloved object becomes one's dominant focus.[31] While Socrates' second speech provides a striking portrayal of how this erotic response can belong to reason, his first speech does not miss the mark in treating it as opposed to what he later calls "mortal self-control" (256e5), to reason's prudential functioning.

In opposing "mortal self-control," philosophical erōs presents significant moral risks. Even in Socrates' second speech, Plato does not shy away from this; he describes how the lover's soul "forgets mother and father and friends altogether, and it thinks nothing of losing its wealth through neglect, and it looks down on the standards of propriety and decorum in which it once took pride, and is even ready to act the part of a slave" (252a2–7). Plato elaborates on these risks in the Republic, when he proposes that a soul becomes tyran-nical when erōs is implanted within it (572e4–573a2); in a passage that echoes the Phaedrus, he notes that the tyrannical man is even willing to enslave his beloved parents for the sake of some new boyfriend (574b12–c5). It is perhaps due to this socially destructive potential that Plato provides an entirely non-erotic curriculum for the guardians in Book VII.

But in the Phaedrus, we see how, provided that it is directed toward beauty and not toward bodily pleasure or mastery over others, the overpowering force of erōs also has a significant positive potential. In the Phaedrus, Plato appears to claim that we can only fully grasp the forms when we are disembodied; our disembodied condition and capacity to recollect the forms are metaphorically represented as the state when our souls are fully winged. In depicting the philosopher's recollection of the form of beauty, Plato deftly interweaves imagery of the regrowth of wings, divine possession, and metaphysical insight:

> For this reason, it is just that only the mind of the philosopher grows wings. For he is always as close as possible, through memory, to those things proximity to which makes a god divine. The man who uses such reminders correctly, always completing perfect mysteries, alone becomes truly perfect. Standing outside of human

concerns, and drawing close to the divine, he is admonished by the many for being disturbed. (249c4–d2)

Plato later signals that we cannot fully regrow our wings while embodied (249d4–e1);[32] thus, to the extent that the philosopher's soul begins to regrow its wings, it must be achieving some proxy of disembodiment while still embodied, which enables it to at least grasp the forms through memory. Plato goes on to characterize those souls that are capable of recollecting the forms as "struck from their senses and no longer in themselves" (250a6–7). What Plato is describing is how the philosopher's overwhelming attraction to beauty enables his reason to at least temporarily shed its mortal nature, to turn away from its embodied, social existence, from its internal role as ruler of a partite soul and its external role as a member of society. In this moment, his reason solely identifies with its contemplative capacity; the philosopher thereby comes as close as possible to achieving disembodiment while still embodied and he attains a mortal approximation of immortality.

But the intensity of the lover's response to the form of beauty has another aspect that I wish to explore: it opens the possibility of his *erōs* transforming from a self-centered, acquisitive response into a disinterested one. We see this shift within Socrates' speech in the *Symposium*. He begins by treating *erōs* as an acquisitive desire to possess what is beautiful. With his proposal that *erōs* is, in fact, the desire for birth in beauty, it becomes productive, but its focus is still self-directed, at achieving eternal possession of the good for oneself. In the ascent passage, however, we see the lover shift from treating beauty as a means to treating it as an end, to recognizing its intrinsic value, a value that is, in fact, radically independent of human interests and concerns (211a5–b5); he now does not seek to possess it, but rather to contemplate it (211e4–12a2). In focusing on a perfection that is outside of himself, the lover ceases to be self-directed; his *erōs* transforms into a disinterested state of awe. Nehamas has suggested that the disinterested response to beauty is a Kantian invention, and that Platonic *erōs* is not disinterested in Kant's sense (2017: 1–13). To the extent that Plato continues to view the philosopher's response as erotic, Nehamas' observation may be apt, but it is worth noting that *erōs* bridges the senses of desire and of love; inasmuch as the philosopher responds to the forms with a love that borders on religious devotion, it does not appear to be motivated by self-interested desire.[33] This form of disinterested reverence is precisely what we see in the philosopher's response to beauty in the *Phaedrus*. Plato describes how the charioteer's memory is "carried back to the nature of beauty, and it sees it once again, standing together with moderation on its sacred pedestal; seeing it, he becomes frightened and falls back in sudden reverence" (254b5–8). Though *erōs*, as we see in the case of the tyrant, can give rise to the greatest selfishness, for many of us, falling in love is our first and most significant experience of being arrested by a value that we recognize outside of ourselves and that we may even come to care about more than ourselves. For Plato, this radical shift in value can serve as a first step to philosophy, since it enables us to overcome our limited, self-centered perspectives, and since it mirrors the reverence that we ought to direct toward the forms.

But even if the philosopher's attitude toward the forms is ultimately disinterested, this is not to say that he does not stand to gain from his grasp of the forms. There is, in fact, a significant ambiguity in how Plato understands the philosopher's *erōs*: Does it aim at immortality, in other words at the perfection of the philosopher's soul, or at the immortal, in other words at the contemplation of the immortal forms? In the *Symposium*, immediately after Plato presents the sight of the form of beauty as the *telos* of the philosopher's *erōs*, he surprisingly reverts to the birth-in-beauty model:

> in that life alone, looking at the beautiful with that by which it can be seen, will it be possible for him to give birth, not to images of virtue, because he is not grasping images, but to true virtue, because

he is grasping the truth; and it belongs to the one who has given birth to true virtue and nurtured it to become god-loved and, if any human can, immortal. (212a2–7)

A similar puzzle arises in the *Phaedrus* as well, where it is unclear whether the philosopher seeks to grasp the forms in order that he may regrow his wings or to regrow his wings in order that he may behold the forms. On the one hand, Plato claims that "the reason there is so much eagerness to see the plain where the truth is is that the pasturage which is fitting for the best part of the soul comes from the meadow there, and that the nature of the wings, by which the soul is lifted, is nourished by it" (248b5–c2). This would seem to suggest that the primary reason we wish to grasp the truth is in order that we may regrow our souls' wings. But we wish to regrow our wings in order that, returning to the heavens, we may follow in the path of our god, and the gods' ultimate aim appears to be to contemplate the forms. What we have then, is a virtuous circle: Our contemplation of the forms sustains our soul's wings, but the purpose of our wings is to enable us to see the forms. Perhaps Plato's thought is that, paradoxically, it is only when we cease to focus on our own imperfection, and forcefully recall the forms, that we are fully able to grasp and assimilate to them; in forgetting ourselves and contemplating the perfection of the forms, we stand our best chance of perfecting our human natures.

V   LOVE

Before concluding, I would like to briefly consider a question that has occupied a central place in philosophical responses to Plato's theory of *erōs* over the past fifty years: What are we to make of this as an account of love, a paradigmatically interpersonal state?[34] In his seminal article, "The Individual as Object of Love in Plato," Vlastos develops a powerful critique of Plato: He argues that Plato's theory of love is a failure, because it is incapable of accommodating disinterested love for other persons. This, because love, for Plato, is fundamentally egoistic: "if A loves B, he does so because of some benefit *he* needs from B and for the sake of just that benefit."[35] To the extent that Platonic love is ultimately directed at the form of beauty, this entails that we are to treat human love-objects as mere placeholders for the form, to be abandoned once they serve their philosophical function. If I am correct that Platonic *erōs* can result in the disinterested admiration of what is beautiful, as depicted in the lover's worship of the beautiful boy in the *Phaedrus*, then Platonic love is not as egoistic as Vlastos makes out: even if his admiration for the boy serves the purpose of leading him to the form of beauty, it needn't follow that the lover admires the boy for this purpose. But this still leaves us with Vlastos' concerns that the lover objectifies the boy in loving him for his beauty and that he will readily abandon the boy when he encounters something more beautiful still.

In a recent response to Vlastos, Sheffield (2012) has argued that Vlastos' critique misses the mark: Plato's theory of *erōs* is not intended as a theory of interpersonal love at all, but as a theory of the pursuit of happiness; it is thus inappropriate to subject it to the expectations we might have of an account of interpersonal love. Sheffield is certainly correct in observing that Plato takes *erōs* to be a broader phenomenon than mere interpersonal love. But that does not entail that Vlastos' objection misses the mark. First, just because Plato takes *erōs* to be a broader phenomenon than interpersonal love, it does not follow that it does not contain within it a treatment of interpersonal love, conceived of as a means of pursuing happiness. I have argued that Plato takes *erōs* to be an overwhelming and arresting response to beauty. In this light, it is of the utmost importance to Plato that philosophical *erōs* should begin with interpersonal love: it is because we have an overwhelming response to the beauty of a person and not, say, a pencil, that *erōs* is awoken, that we begin to experience a longing for immortality, to see the divine in our love object and eventually to recollect the form of beauty. But in that case, the person who initially awoke our *erōs* might quite justifiably ask, what about me? A boy might understandably feel abandoned and devalued if his erstwhile lover should throw him over once he grasps the form. Second, to the extent that Plato is offering an account of how we ought best to live our lives, it is reasonable to ask what role, if any, persons should play in providing our lives with meaning. Sheffield claims that "Socrates' move away from individuals as the focus of a happy human life is laudable" (2012: 127–8). But if Plato is indeed claiming that persons ought not to be a source of meaning in life, and that we should find happiness in philosophical wisdom, but not inter-personal love, then I suspect that many of us would strenuously object.

In order to address Vlastos' critique, we need to ask what the philosophic lover will be like, once he has grasped the form. Plato's answer is, in fact, equivocal. On the one hand, in the ascent passage of the *Symposium*, Plato suggests that the philosopher's grasp of the form will result in an extreme devaluation of all earthly particulars, includ-ing his boy. The boy's body is compared to a step that the lover climbs over in order to reach the form; upon seeing the form he "no longer measures beauty in terms of gold, clothing, beautiful boys or youths" (211d3–5), but recognizes it as "pure, clean, unmixed, and uncontamin-ated by human flesh, colors, or any other mortal nonsense" (211e1–3). To see the boy's beauty as being as worthless as that of a fancy cloak, and to see the form's value as residing, in part, in its being uncontam-inated by mortal nonsense, surely implies that whatever value the boy once had is now eclipsed by that of the form. But at the same time, Plato's portrayal of Socrates in the *Symposium* suggests a quite differ-ent picture. It is a matter of controversy whether we should take Socrates to have completed the ascent; his description of himself in the opening of the dialogue as having knowledge of erotic matters (*ta erōtika*, 177d8), suggests that perhaps he has.[36] But if he has indeed grasped the form, then his resulting state is complex. On the one hand, he appears to no longer be erotic: Alcibiades describes in excruciating detail how Socrates was utterly impervious to his attempted seduction. But Socrates' state is not one of total interpersonal detachment; indeed, one of the most moving aspects of Alcibiades' speech is the friendly concern that Socrates directs toward him. Perhaps this is due to Socrates' merely mortal nature. In the opening of the dialogue (175b1–2), as well as in Alcibiades' speech (220c3–d5), Plato depicts Socrates as entering into philosophical trances, but these are merely temporary. Perhaps, to the extent that Socrates is unable to sustain his contemplation of forms, he finds value, albeit lesser value, in engagement with particulars, including the beautiful Alcibiades.

But I do not think that this does justice to Plato's portrayal of Socrates. For what Socrates manifests toward Alcibiades and his other companions does not appear to be watered-down *erōs*, but rather, an ironic pretence of *erōs* as a veneer for an attitude of friendly concern, or *philia*. Though the *Symposium* does not have much to say about *philia*, two points in the ascent passage are noteworthy. First, though Socrates earlier claims that the gods, as beings that lack nothing, are beyond *erōs*, at the conclusion of the ascent, in describing the initiate as *theophilēs* (god-loved, 212a6), he implies that they are capable of *philia*. Second, he describes the initiate as giving birth to beautiful and glorious ideas *en philosophiai aphthonōi* (in unstinting philosophy, 210d6). His use of *aphthonos* here is picked up in the *Phaedrus*, where the gods are described as allowing all who wish to follow in their chorus, since they are completely lacking in *phthonos* (envy, 247a7). The lover, in turn, is described as training his boy to become godlike, because he manifests no *phthonos* toward the boy (253b7). The lover's unstinting generosity toward the boy is the result of his gratitude toward the boy for causing him to recollect the god (253a5–b1); in adopting this attitude toward the boy, the lover appears to imitate that of the gods toward the mortal souls that follow in their chorus. Later, in the *Timaeus*, Plato describes the demiurge as ordering the universe because he is good, and hence lacking in *phthonos*; being without *phthonos*, he desires that all things should resemble him to the extent possible (29e1–3). It is not clear what should motivate a god who can contemplate forms to order spatiotemporal reality, given that his grasp of the former will reveal the insurmountable inferiority of the latter. In a sense, this is the problem of the return to the cave, writ large.[37] But this attitude is the one that we see reflected in the lover of the *Phaedrus* and, for that matter, in Socrates in the *Symposium*. Thus, at the completion of the ascent, the lover will indeed no longer feel *erōs* for the boy, but he may, instead, develop a godlike attitude of beneficent concern.

If this is correct, then the boy is indeed initially loved as an imperfect instantiation of beauty and ceases to be loved once the philosopher grasps the form of beauty. This is not to say that the lover will abandon him altogether, but the boy will cease to be an object of love and become, rather, an object of goodwill. To many, this will seem objectionable – the passionate love we feel for persons can seem like an incomparably valuable part of a good human life, and not something to be bypassed. But I would suggest that to the extent that we find Plato's position objectionable, it is not primarily because we think his account of love is wrong, but because we think his account of value is. For Plato, the forms are the most loveable objects because they alone are unqualifiedly good, where their goodness resides in their ideal natures, in their eternality, changelessness, and unqualified being, properties that humans can never hope fully to instantiate. This is an account of value that many of us might find puzzling. But if we were to share this view of value, then we would surely think it obvious that if we are able, we should spend our lives in relation to objects that fully instantiate it. If we think that we should primarily love humans rather than forms, then this reflects another theory of value – perhaps that subjectivity or the capacity for rational thought give humans special worth. Plato simply does not recognize these as ultimate sources of value; in this regard, the bridge between Plato and us may appear to be insurmountable. But perhaps Plato's position is not as outlandish as it may initially appear. For many people do seek meaning in something bigger than themselves, something that transcends their merely mortal existence, whether it be art, religion, or a political ideology.[38] In proposing that philosophy can, and perhaps should, begin with *erōs*, what Plato is really telling us is that the value of philosophy lies in the path it opens to the contemplation of truths that are timeless and universal.

NOTES

1 As many have noted, the Greek word, *erōs*, does not map precisely onto any English term. In Plato's time, its primary sense is passionate sexual or romantic love, but Plato uses it in an extended sense throughout his corpus to denote the intensity of the philosopher's attraction to the forms. I use the term, "*erōs*," interchangeably with "love" throughout the chapter; though "*philia*" can also be translated as "love," for purposes of clarity, I typically translate it as "friendliness" or "goodwill."

   Plato's treatment of interpersonal *erōs* focuses on romantic relationships between older men and adolescent boys. Such relationships were typically asymmetrical: the man felt *erōs* for the boy, whereas the boy typically felt *philia*, affectionate non-sexual love, for the man. Such relationships are assumed to have served an important social and educational function, with the man serving as a mentor to the boy, providing him with political connections and/or moral, philosophical, and athletic training, in exchange for the boy's companionship and, possibly, sexual favors. For further discussion, see, e.g., Dover 1978 and Halperin 1990.

2 *Pace* Sheffield 2012; I develop my arguments against her in the final section of this chapter.

3 For the distinction between proper and ideal attributes of forms, see Santas 2001: 182–3. Proper attributes of forms are attributes that the form has in virtue of being the particular form that it is (e.g., beauty is the proper attribute of the form of beauty), whereas ideal attributes of forms are attributes that the form has simply in virtue of being a form (e.g., perfection and changelessness are ideal attributes of the form of beauty and, indeed, of all forms). I also follow Santas in identifying the goodness of the forms with their ideal attributes (2001: 180–7). Santas argues that the forms are the best objects of their kind in virtue of their ideal attributes; they owe their possession of these ideal attributes to their participation in the form of the good. For a contrasting position on the goodness of the forms, see Kraut's contribution to this volume (ch. 10).

4 Plato's most extensive use of erotic imagery to characterize the philosopher outside of the *Symposium* and *Phaedrus* occurs in Book VI of the *Republic* (e.g., 485a10–b8, 490a8–b7, 499b2–c2, 501d1–2).

5 One might maintain that the erotic and non-erotic paths differ in their intended audiences: the former use beauty as a hook to awaken an interest in truth in those without prior philosophical leanings, whereas the latter are directed at those who are already disposed toward philosophy. But in fact, the erotic ascents in the *Symposium* and *Phaedrus* are aimed at those who are already philosophically inclined. The ascent passage in the *Symposium* is presented as esoteric – Diotima warns that even Socrates may be incapable of partaking in it (210a1–2). Likewise, in the *Phaedrus*, Plato specifies that only those who had the greatest prenatal vision of the forms are capable of recollecting them through their earthly instantiations (250a1–5).

6 Among the more significant differences: whereas the *Symposium* treats *erōs* as a species of the more general desire for the good, the *Phaedrus* treats it as a species of *mania*. However, this might simply reflect a difference in focus – whereas Socrates' speech in the *Symposium* provides an analysis of *erōs* from the outside (as Ferrari [1992: 249–50] and others have observed, the context of the dialogue is strangely de-eroticized), the *Phaedrus* is largely focused on what *erōs* feels like on the inside, on what sort of psychological state it is.

7 As my focus in this chapter is Plato's treatment of philosophical *erōs*, I do not discuss the *Lysis*. Readers interested in Plato's treatment of *philia* in that dialogue might turn to Vlastos 1981: 3–42, Price 1989: 1–14, Kahn 1996: 258–91, and Penner and Rowe 2005; Obdrzalek 2013 provides a critical overview of much of the literature on the dialogue.

8 Cf. Sheffield (2017), who also seeks to explain the connection that Plato develops between philosophy and *erōs* by proposing a set of hallmarks of *erōs*.

9 One complication is that, whereas in the *Symposium*, Socrates is adamant that Erōs is not a god but a *daimōn*, in the *Phaedrus*, he appears to treat him as a god, though 242e2 (*theos ē ti theion*) may signal an attempt to reconcile the two views.

10 Translations are my own, though at points I borrow the phrasings of Nehamas and Woodruff 1989 and 1995 and of Rowe 1998a and 1986.

11 One exception is Critias' speech in the *Timaeus* (21a2–3).

12 Bury 1932: 128.

13 See Burkert 1985: 276–90. For extended analysis of Plato's incorporation of the imagery and structure of the mysteries into his representation of the philosophical life, see Betegh's contribution to this volume (ch. 8); for discussions more narrowly focused on the *Symposium*, see Edmonds 2017, as well as, e.g., Bury 1932: 124, 128; Des Places 1964; Morgan 1990: 80–99; and McPherran 2006.

14 It is a topic of considerable interpretive controversy whether, in the *Symposium*, Plato takes *erōs* to aim at immortality. Those who claim that he does include Bury 1932: xliii–xlvi; O'Brien 1984; Santas 1988: 47–8, 41–2; Rowe 1998a: 184, 192, 202; Lear 2006; Nightingale 2017; and Price 2017. Sheffield argues that Plato does not take *erōs* to aim at immortality for its own sake, but only as a means to eternal possession of the good (2006: 82–6; see also Price 1989: 17 and White 1989a: 154). In Obdrzalek 2010, I argue that while Plato depicts *erōs* as aiming at immortality prior to the ascent passage, he portrays this form of *erōs* as deeply misguided, since what it aims at, self-perpetuation, is not worthwhile; in the ascent passage, he describes a higher form of *erōs*, that aims at contemplation of forms, but not at immortality. I have since come to reconsider my position, since it does not attend to the possibility which I explore in this chapter, that we might pursue immortality not in order to perpetuate ourselves, but rather, in order to resemble the immortal forms, which are the best objects.

15 See also Price 1989: 17 and Rowe 1998a: 184 and 1998b: 248–9.

16 One might object that Plato cannot take immortality to be desirable in itself, since it is not unconditionally good – as Plato observes in the *Phaedo*, it would be a blessing for the wicked if their souls should perish with their bodies, since they would thereby escape post-mortem punishment (107c5–d2). However, this difficulty can be avoided if we distinguish between the claims that immortality is intrinsically good and that it is unconditionally good. For Plato, immortality is intrinsically good insofar as it is one of the characteristics, such as perfection and changelessness, in virtue of which the forms are the best objects. However, this does not entail that immortality is unconditionally good – indeed, its intrinsic goodness can be overridden should it be conjoined with a significant evil.

17 Cf. *Laws* 721b6–d8.

18 Neumann (1965: 42–4) and White (1989a: 152–3 and 2004: 373) argue that beauty is not reintroduced as the object of *erōs* in the ascent; for critical response, see Obdrzalek 2010: 440. Even among interpreters who take beauty to reemerge as the object of *erōs* in the ascent, my position in this chapter is somewhat unusual in taking beauty to be the object of *erōs* in light of its ideal attributes.

19 While Plato portrays the forms as *athanata* (immortal) at, e.g., *Phd.* 79d1–2 and 80b1–3, in the *Timaeus*, he introduces an important refinement to his position. Though he describes the forms as *aidia* (eternal), he also claims that the forms do not exist in time (37c6–38c3); their eternality is a matter of their existing timelessly, rather than of their existing forever. Thus, the kind of immortality that we aspire to – endless existence in time – will always be an inferior approximation of that which the forms necessarily possess.

20 This is not to say that souls last longer than bodies – indeed, 207d4–208b2 can be taken to imply that souls are as perishable as bodies. My point is more minimally that, whereas a body's beauty begins to wane by middle age, a soul's beauty – i.e., wisdom and virtue – can potentially extend throughout one's life.

21 Here I oppose, e.g., Vlastos (1981: 24), who argues that the form's loveability resides in its being unqualifiedly beautiful. While I see no reason to deny that beauty in the ascent is narrowly and fully self-predicating, I claim that what makes it loveable are its ideal, not its proper characteristics.

22 In this I am opposing, e.g., Santas (1988: 69), who claims that what distinguishes beauty from the other forms of value properties (e.g., justice, moderation) is that its earthly instances can be directly perceived. Against Santas, it is not clear why one cannot directly perceive that, say, an artifact is good or a warrior brave.

23 See also Burnyeat 2012: 255–6.

24 For a similar line of argument, see Lear 2006: 117–18.

25 Is Plato claiming that we see the ideal attributes of the form in the boy or in his beauty? *Phaedrus* 251a1–7 would seem to suggest the former – it is the boy who is worshipped as a god, not the boy's beauty. But perhaps Plato does not intend for us to draw a sharp distinction; perhaps the lover worships the boy as godlike because he possesses godlike beauty.

26 On the role of idealization in *erōs*, see also Lear 2006: 117–18 and Sheffield 2017: 132.

27 This still leaves us with the question of why beauty, and not other properties, occasions love, causing us to see the ideal properties of the form in its instances. I take it that Plato views this as a brute psychological fact, not admitting of further explanation: We are just constituted such that, for us, beauty, and not other forms, shines brightest through its instances.

28 Other interpreters who take the philosopher's immortality to result from his grasp of the form include Bury (1932: xliv–xlv), Cornford (1971: 127), O'Brien (1984: 196), and Kahn (1987: 94). For an opposing argument, see Hackforth (1950: 44). A more common strategy is to argue that the spiritual ascent in the *Symposium* is continuous with the discussion that precedes it, and that the philosopher achieves immortality-by-proxy, through giving birth in beauty. This can take the form of his giving birth to virtue in the boy's soul, or to ideas and discourse or constitutions and laws that outlive him. For this strategy see, e.g., Kraut 1973a: 339–41; Santas 1988: 41–2; Price 1989: 49–54; Reeve 1992: 102–3, 109; Rowe 1998a: 192, 201; and Nightingale 2017. For opposing arguments, see O'Brien 1984: 196–9, Ferrari 1991: 181–2 and 1992: 260, Sheffield 2006: 106–8, Sedley 2009: 160, and Obdrzalek 2010: 441–3.

29 One might wonder whether *erōs* ought to count as a single psychological state, insofar as it can be expressed both via the pursuit of immortality and via the attempt to stand in close relation to the immortal. I maintain that it still counts as a single state, insofar as both forms of expression arise from a common source: our sense of our own mortality and imperfection.

30 See also Lear 2006: 97.

31 See also Irwin 1977: 240.

32 See also 248e5–249a5.

33 Kant's treatment of disinterestedness is admittedly obscure. To the extent that the philosopher's *erōs* for the forms is grounded in his incomplete, needy nature, it would presumably fail to count as disinterested in the Kantian sense. The point I wish to make is simply that for Plato, even if *erōs* arises from and seeks to address our mortal deficiency, it eventually shifts in focus. It transforms from a hunger to acquire something for ourselves or to become a certain way into an appreciative reverence for the forms as objects that are entirely independent of us.

34 The literature on this topic is vast. Interpreters who advocate an inclusive interpretation of the ascent, according to which the philosopher's grasp of the form is compatible with his continuing to love his boy, include Kosman (1976), Irwin (1977: 169), Price (1989: 43–9), Reeve (1992: 109), Rowe (1998a: 7, 193, 195, 197, and 1998b: 257), and Kraut (2008). Interpreters who advocate an exclusive or intellectualist interpretation of the ascent, according to which the philosopher's grasp of the form causes him to devalue, or at least lose interest in, his boy include Moravcsik (1972: 293), Vlastos (1981), Ferrari (1992: 258–60), and Obdrzalek (2010). Nussbaum's interpretation of the ascent falls within the exclusive camp, though she argues that both Alcibiades' speech and the *Phaedrus* express Plato's reservations about the excessive rationalism he attributes to Socrates in the ascent (1986).

35 Vlastos 1981: 8.

36 For a contrary view, see Rowe 1998a: 200 and Sheffield 2006: 196 n. 27.

37 See *Republic* 516c4–521b10. The problem is that of why the philosophers should agree to rule the city when they are able to engage in an activity they find infinitely more rewarding, contemplating forms.

38 See also, e.g., Vlastos 1981: 27, Nussbaum 1986: 161–3 and Kraut 2017: 246–52, as well as Kraut's contribution to this volume (ch. 10).

8   Plato on Philosophy and the Mysteries

Gábor Betegh

This chapter aims to explore Plato's reflections on Greek religion, as it was lived and practiced by his contemporaries. My focus is on mystery cults, which constituted a particularly intense form of religious experience, and were conceived by many as the highest form of piety. I try to show that Plato's engagement with these rites is deeply connected to, and can help to illuminate, such centrally important topics as his conception of the philosophical life, its relation to the human good, the role of memory in the knowledge of the Forms, and the soul's kinship to the divine.

Public rituals, codified in the sacred laws and festival calendars of cities, were the principal occasions for communities to reaffirm and channel their relationship to gods, and to express their civic identity and unity. Although primary in importance, "polis religion"[1] did not cover important aspects of the religious life of Plato's contemporaries: there were also institutions, sanctuaries, festivals, and cults that transcended the level of individual cities. Most important, all cities and individuals could turn to the oracle of Apollo at Delphi, which enjoyed unparalleled authority in the Greek world.[2] There were other forms of religious activities, often referred to collectively as *mustēria* (the origin of our word "mystery") or as *teletai*, "(initiatory) rites," which were less strongly integrated in the institutions of the polis – although the level of integration and acceptance varied to a considerable extent. The term *mustēria* originally referred to the festival of Demeter and her daughter Kore in Eleusis, but gradually came to cover a set of other religious activities, including Bacchic rites, rites conducted by itinerant

I would like to thank Richard Kraut, Suzanne Obdrzalek, David Sedley, Frisbee Sheffield, Verity Platt, Giulia Corsino, Richard Cook, and Solveig Gold for their help with this chapter. I am particularly grateful to David Ebrey for many in-depth discussions.

priests under the name of Orpheus, as well as the rites of a group of minor divinities called the Corybantes. A common feature of these cults was that they offered a particularly strong religious experience, which required special ritual preparation. Participation was not linked to membership in the political community since all Greeks could take part in them. This openness was, however, combined with a strong sense of exclusivity, emphasizing the distinction between the in-group of those who have already gone through the rites and the out-group of the "uninitiated."[3]

Plato frequently refers to various mystery cults, such as the Corybantic rites.[4] Yet, explicit mentions and more subtle allusions to the Eleusinian mysteries, as well as ideas and practices connected to Orphic and Bacchic cults, are particularly prominent in passages in which he discusses the nature and ultimate goal of philosophical contemplation, its connection to the best life, the relationship between soul and body, the soul's immortality and its relationship to the divine. Remarkably, while mentions of these cults are practically absent from Plato's early dialogues, they suddenly become frequent in the dialogues of his middle period, which gravitate around precisely these topics.

The secrecy surrounding these cults makes a precise reconstruction of the ritual actions and the religious ideas sustaining them well-nigh impossible. There is no scholarly consensus about what happened at the various stages of the Eleusinian mysteries. Even though there is a growing body of archaeological finds from all over Greece that provides us with further snippets of information about the eschatological ideas connected with Orphic/Bacchic rituals, the interpretation of the evidence remains debated. Notably, for both the reconstruction of the Eleusinian mysteries and the interpretation of new pieces of evidence related to Orphic/Bacchic practices, scholars often rely on information scattered in Plato's dialogues – an indication of how important these cults were for Plato. On the other hand, this fact also raises the possibility that our perception and reconstruction of the mysteries is already filtered through Plato's perspective.

For these reasons, trying to work out precisely Plato's engagement with mystery cults is fraught with methodological difficulties, and interpretations are bound to remain speculative and tentative. I will try to show that it is, however, a risk worth taking.

I MYSTERIES AND THE PROMISE OF PHILOSOPHY

A discernible pattern common to the mysteries can already reveal why they could be of particular significance for Plato. (i) The shared premise of these cults was that, on the basis of a personal choice and by going through a well-defined process, individuals could establish a privileged relation to divine powers, going beyond what could be achieved in the framework of the cults of the polis. (ii) The promise of the mystery cults was that on the basis of this special relationship, the individual could expect extraordinary prerogatives and rewards from the relevant divinities. These rewards were, moreover, framed as a "blessed" state, the best a human can expect for this life and the afterlife. (iii) The individual had to reach and maintain a certain condition in order successfully to go through the mysteries. Traditional religious language most often referred to this condition as "purity," which could be achieved by carrying out certain pre-scribed actions and avoiding some others.

At this general level, Plato could fully agree with all three elements and their interrelation. He shared the view that one has the possibility to establish a special relationship with divine beings, becoming "dear to the gods" to a degree higher than what was available through communal forms of worship. He also agreed that it is through this special relationship that a human can achieve the best life and, moreover, maintain high hopes for a good afterlife. He concurred, too, that only those can reach this state who, by a certain behavior – by doing certain things and by avoiding others – are in a condition that can be characterized as "purity."

So far, the mysteries appear to hold the key to the ultimate human good. Plato, however, also held that the mysteries, as they were conceived and conducted by his contemporaries, relied on and fostered mistaken assumptions at each of the three steps – it is philosophical inquiry, and philosophical inquiry only, that can put those misbeliefs aright. Philosophy can bring us beyond traditional conceptions of the gods, operative also in the mysteries, and lead us to a better, and indeed fundamentally novel, understanding of the divine entities with which we have to enter into a special relationship.[5] One of Plato's central tenets expounded in his middle period dialogues – the *Phaedo*, the *Symposium*, the *Republic*, and the *Phaedrus* – is that the ultimate goal and achievement of philosophy is to lead us to the knowledge of the eternal, transcendent, divine Forms. Phrased in terms of the scheme sketched above: instead of the traditional gods, the Forms are the divine entities with which we need to enter into a special relation in order to realize our highest abilities and to have the best life. It is, moreover, philosophy that can help us to understand better who we ourselves are. As we will see in more detail, Plato argues that a crucial part of our self-understanding is that we are naturally more closely related to the divine than traditional conceptions would suggest. This understanding in turn shows that what had been conceived of as a "special" relationship can in fact be achieved by fostering some of our natural tendencies, and by letting our natural relationship to the divine develop to the fullest.

Plato moreover maintains that this double understanding of the divine and what it is in us that naturally links us to the divine doesn't simply provide us with a set of instructions about how to establish the desired relationship. Rather, philosophy conceived of as the intellectual effort to understand these divine entities and ourselves *is* the activity by which we can realize our highest abilities, it *is* the realization of what is divine in us, and thereby it *is* what brings us close to the divine. Moreover, insofar as our bodily desires are the primary obstacle to engaging fully and persistently in philosophical contemplation, we can put ourselves in the required state, achieve "purity," not by going through ritual actions and observing ritual taboos, but by controlling our bodily desires and avoiding, and developing the right attitude toward, bodily pleasures and pains.[6] Plato also argues that because philosophy brings us close to the divine, it is also the best preparation for the afterlife. Moreover, there is a hope that the project of the philosophical life can be carried on and brought to fulfillment in the afterlife when our souls are no longer hindered by our bodies.

The outcome is that what the mysteries promise, philosophy can fulfill: it brings us closest to the divine, it is what offers us the best human life on the basis of that relationship, and it is also what can dispel most effectively our eschatological anxieties. Finally, it is what specifies how to achieve all this – what to do and to avoid. One can then either say that philosophy is a direct competitor of the mysteries in offering the best life through closeness to the divine or – and this appears to be Plato's preferred way to conceive the relationship – that philosophy *is* the truest mystery.

Picturing philosophy as a mystery cult is not new with Plato. Aristophanes in the *Clouds* presents Socrates' school as a cultic association,[7] where "sacred mysteries" are imparted to the "initiates" for a fee (*Clouds* 140–3). Socrates parades as the high priest, who proclaims himself able to disclose knowledge about the "true gods," officiates initiations with a travesty of traditional rites, and promises material gains and overall success in life by teaching how to employ specious arguments to turn any situation to one's advantage. In Aristophanes' lampoon, Socrates denigrates and challenges traditional cults by setting up an alternative that masquerades as the true mystery.[8] Viewed against this background, Plato's presentation of philosophy as the truest mystery acquires a further dimension. He appears boldly to accept some elements of Aristophanes' pasquinade: Yes, philosophy can lead you to realize that there are divine entities distinct from the traditional gods, and, yes, philosophy is the route to the best life, and, yes, in this sense it is more effective than traditional forms of piety and the mysteries in particular. Nevertheless, Plato makes a firm corrective: Philosophy never promises material gain, and economic advantage has no role in the good life that philosophy offers. More important, the philosopher is motivated by a love of truth and knowledge, and therefore, misleading arguments with no concern for the truth, such as the ones Socrates teaches in the *Clouds*, are fundamentally opposed to the philosophical enterprise.

The Socrates of the *Clouds* moreover requires that members of his cult renounce the existence of traditional gods (*Clouds* 423–6). This was echoed at Socrates' trial, when he was charged with inventing new gods and not acknowledging the traditional gods of the city (*Ap.* 24b–c; *Euphr.* 3a–b; Xenophon, *Ap.* 10–13).[9] The same charge might have been leveled against Plato, now with respect to his introduction of Forms. Yet, Plato also wants to make clear that considering the Forms as divine entities is not incompatible with acknowledging the gods of the city and honoring them in ways sanctified by tradition. The philosopher doesn't want to claim authority on how to worship the traditional gods: Ancestral custom sanctioned by Apollo's oracle in Delphi must remain the ultimate source for setting up and sanctifying laws regulating civic cults (*Rep.* IV 427b–c; *Laws* V 738b–d; for the Socratic origin of this principle, see Xenophon, *Mem.* IV 3.16). In such matters as the identity of and narratives about traditional gods, the best we can do is to rely on tradition and the poets, without making these stories mundane and uninteresting by means of a "rationalizing" allegorical interpretation, which eliminates the divine and the sacred. Rather, we should fully embrace the sense of awe and wonder expressed in them and use them as an inspiration for exploring further the divine and its relation to the human (*Phdr.* 229b–230a; also *Ti.* 40d–41a). This does not mean that we should accept these stories uncritically; many of these narratives, and even those that figure prominently in cults, conflict with Plato's fundamental theological tenets, and most importantly with the principle that "the god is really good" and therefore only does good and never harms or deceives humans (*Rep.* II 378e–383a; *Euphr.* 14c–15a). These theological principles provide us with strong criteria for which stories we can accept from tradition and the poets. The same principles give firm ground for censoring religious practitioners who promise, under the auspices of Orphic texts, to acquire the pardon of the gods for anyone who is ready to pay a fee and to go through some rituals, no matter whether the person otherwise leads a virtuous and good life. These practitioners even claim to be able to persuade the gods to destroy the life of their clients' enemies, no matter whether the enemy is just or unjust, fostering a pernicious image of the gods (*Rep.* II 364b–365a; cf. *Laws* X 888c).

Plato thus never suggests that taking the Forms as divine, and conceiving philosophy as the highest mystery leading to them, should be concomitant with a deprecation of the traditional gods or a desacralization of sacred rites, and the traditional mysteries in particular – as long as they are in line with his theological principles.[10]

Indeed, in the very same texts in which Plato presents philosophy as the highest mystery, he also allows that poets, priests, diviners, and founders of *teletai* can have direct access to information about divine matters – or more precisely, that gods can choose to communicate with humans through select individuals (*Smp.* 202e–203a, *Meno* 99c–d). Plato appears to accept that on such important topics as the soul–body relationship and the immortality of the soul, or what might happen to the soul after death, the divinely inspired pronouncements of such people might contain crucial insights. Once we make a genuine effort to understand what these pronouncements really mean, and subject them to a thorough critical examination, they can galvanize and feed into philosophical investigation.[11]

II KNOWLEDGE OF THE FORMS AND THE CLIMAX OF THE MYSTERIES

If acquiring knowledge of the Forms is the goal of the entire process, it is natural to expect some account of what awaits the philosopher as a result of a life of intellectual inquiry and contemplation (cf., e.g., *Phdr.* 247c). Such an account could turn potential candidates toward the philosophical life; this is clearly one of Socrates' motivations when he attempts to describe the summit of philosophy to his young interlocutor in the *Phaedrus*. It can also function as an encouragement and orientation for those who are already on the road, but haven't as yet seen what is at the end. Diotima's description of the highest stage of philosophical life, as reported by Socrates in the *Symposium*, seems to have had such an effect on Socrates.

But who can give such an account, and how should it be given? The trouble is that the only ones who could do so authoritatively are those who have already come to know the Forms. Plato, however, does not present Socrates as having reached that stage in either the *Symposium* or the *Phaedrus*; and according to the *Phaedo* the process might only be completed after the end of our earthly life when our souls are unimpeded by our bodies (cf., e.g., *Phd.* 66c). Moreover, in the *Republic*, Socrates argues that full understanding of the Forms is dependent upon the knowledge of the Form of the Good, which is in turn achievable only by completing the entire educational curriculum of the guardians – and no one, so far, has ever had an opportunity to do this. For Socrates, full knowledge of the Forms thus remains a yet unachieved ideal.[12] Accordingly, in the *Republic* he reverts to images and analogies, and in the *Phaedrus* he needs divine inspiration to come up with an avowedly fanciful narrative about the soul's prenatal encounter with the Forms. Again, in the *Symposium*, he retells what he, as he says, heard from Diotima – but once again it is not entirely clear whether Diotima herself is able to speak in such an enthralling manner about the encounter with the Form of Beauty because she has systematically completed the entire philosophical path, or (also) because she is one of those "daimonic" persons who are able to act as channels of communication between gods and humans, like seers, "priests, and ... those concerned with sacrifices, rites (*teletai*), incantations (*epodai*) and all of divination and of magic" (*Smp.* 202e–203a).[13] Be that as it may, just as no description of the mysteries can replace the personal experience of being initiated, no account can be a substitute for the necessarily personal achievement of full understanding on the basis of the knowledge of the Forms (*Rep.* VII 533a).

At this point, the mysteries can become interesting in yet another respect. If we try to convey some approximation of the culmination of philosophical life, one promising way can be to picture it in terms of the most intense, overwhelming, and transformative religious experience available to Plato's contemporaries: what the initiate experiences when, after careful preparation and with the highest expectations, she can feel herself personally in close proximity of the divine and have an epiphany at the climax of the rites, the *epopteia*.[14] This is precisely what Plato is doing in the *Symposium* and the *Phaedrus*, where he not only casts the progress of the philosopher in terms of initiation in the mysteries, but refers to the culmination of the process specifically as *epopteia* (*Smp.* 210a–e; *Phdr.* 250b–c).[15]

Plato does not merely think that the Forms are *like* divine beings – he maintains that they *are* divine entities.[16] In that respect, getting to know them directly is not only comparable to, but is indeed a form of epiphany. As Andrea Nightingale has shown, Plato in the *Phaedrus* extensively and systematically uses the language and narrative structure of literary and religious descriptions of epiphanies.[17] Although the language and the imagery is different in each case, the same could be shown about Socrates' speech in the *Symposium* and, to a certain extent, the allegory of the Cave in the *Republic* as well. The outcome is thus the following: Going through the Eleusinian mysteries was the most well-established, controlled, and structured way a Greek could prepare for and expect personally to experience an epiphany at the moment of *epopteia*.[18] By using the language of *epopteia* and epiphany, Plato is now suggesting that philosophy is a structured way to lead us personally to experience the epiphany of the Forms. Importantly, these are *controlled* ways to epiphany, and this is true in at least two senses. The strictly regulated ritual preparation and sacred setting in the mysteries prepare the participants' sensitivity to experience the orchestrated scene at the high moment of the rites *as* an epiphany. Moreover, Greek mythological narratives contain numerous examples when sudden, unprepared epiphanies lead not merely to bedazzlement and reverential awe, but to catastrophic results: blindness, death, or derangement. Similarly, Plato makes clear that knowledge of the Forms can only be reached if it is preceded by an enduring and systematic preparation of study and inquiry, and the philosopher can behold the Forms only after having habituated her eyes not to be "blinded by their brilliance" (*Rep.* VII 515e–516a).

Further features of epiphany and the initiatory experience might mold the way we think of what it means to acquire knowledge of the Forms. Some of these features may help us achieve a better sense of the phenomenon; however, as is often the case in complex analogies, some other features may lead us astray. It remains open to interpretation – and has been debated by scholars – what aspects and how much of the imagery of the mystical, non-verbal, and possibly non-verbalizable religious experience is to be transferred back to what it means to reach the summit of philosophical understanding.

For instance, the account in the *Phaedrus* echoes the over-powering emotive component of encountering the divine at the *epopteia*: getting to know the Forms is described as being accompanied by awe, fear, astonishment, and wonder, mixed with exhilarating joy and happiness (*Phaedrus* 247c; 250c, cf. *Smp.* 211d–212a; *Rep.* VII 516a–e). Plato might well have thought that these emotive responses are natural concomitants of coming into close contact with divine beings in general, and must therefore apply to the Forms as well, even if these emotional responses to encountering the Forms are proper to reason itself.[19]

Moreover, as recent studies have emphasized, the climactic moment of the mysteries centered around intense sensory and in particular visual experiences: disorienting darkness, followed by the dazzling light of torches in which Demeter and Kore, and probably sacred objects (*hiera*), suddenly appear to the initiates.[20] The very term *epopteia* ("beholding") indicates that it was conceived as primarily a visual experience, and this denomination in turn could reinforce the expectation that *seeing* the goddesses and the sacred objects was the central element of the mysteries. The initiate is most often described as someone who has "seen" (e.g., Hom. *Hymn to Demeter* 480; Pindar Fr. 137.1 Maehl.). Studies that focus on the sensory and emotive elements of the initiatory experience customarily also evoke

Aristotle's claim that "those who go through the initiation rites are not to learn (*mathein*) anything but to experience (*pathein*) something and be put into a certain condition (*diatethēnai*)" (F 15 R^3 = Synesius, *Dio* 48A). This picture is then sometimes projected back onto Plato's depictions of philosophical *epopteia*, suggesting that it was also primarily the emotive and sensory (or more precisely quasi-sensory) aspects of the summit of philosophy that Plato wanted to convey in these descriptions.[21]

Yet, contrary to Aristotle's characterization of the initiate as not concerned with learning, Platonic lovers of wisdom do want to understand and to learn something; indeed, they want to learn the most that can be learned and understood through getting to know the Forms – they are not there just for a transformative sensory and emotional experience.

Even if the phenomenology of an epiphany can justifiably be described as a "sensory extravaganza" (Platt 2011: 56), exclusive focus on this and the corresponding emotive aspect of *epopteia* conceals important cognitive elements, which, as I will try to show, might be crucial for Plato's purposes. In general, epiphany is not reducible to a mere perception of a god. As Petridou puts it, in an epiphany "*idein* ['to see'] is not enough; the aim is always to comprehend and acknowledge (*gignōskein* or *noein*) the divine" (Petridou 2015: 21; cf. Platt 2011: 57). And as she goes on to stress, even the language of "seeing" and "beholding" points beyond mere sensory experience: "the passage from ritual blindness to ritual sight, the transformation from being a *mustēs*, who is sightless and blind, to true knowledge, to being an *epoptēs*, insightful and sensitive viewer, was the basic conceptual framework" of the mysteries (Petridou 2015: 254). In an epiphany, the god made herself *enargēs*, fully present and vividly manifest, to selected mortals, and through experiencing the *enargeia* of the god, the mortal could get acquainted with, get to know the god, in an immediate way, and acquire knowledge of something essential about the nature and the power of the god.[22] These considerations strongly suggest that when Plato describes the culmination of philosophy in terms of *epopteia* and the epiphany of the Forms, the comparison was not meant merely to convey the emotive and the experiential. Just as in the case of an epiphany, experiencing the Form of Beauty, beauty in its *enargeia*, full clarity and manifestness, is to get to know Beauty to as great an extent as is possible for a human.[23]

Direct encounter with the gods through epiphany was thus conceived as the privileged way of getting to "know" them. In fact, the effect of initiation was sometimes described with a verb of knowing (e.g., *oiden* in Pindar Fr. 137 Maehl.). However, it remains unclear how to characterize more specifically the type and content of knowledge about Demeter that the experience of "seeing" her in the *epopteia* was supposed to impart. And although Plato frequently and systematically describes knowledge of the imperceptible Forms on the analogy of vision, not only when he describes it explicitly as the *epopteia* of the Forms, but also in the analogies of the Sun and the Cave in the *Republic* (cf. also *Rep.* VII 532b–533d), he is much more specific about the nature of this knowledge.[24] Knowledge of the Form of F enables us to give an account (*logon didonai*, e.g., *Phd.* 78d) of F and to formulate a fully satisfactory answer to the Socratic question "What is F?" (cf., e.g., *Phd.* 75c–d), which captures and describes the nature and essence of F. Can such knowledge be acquired on the basis of a mental act that can be justifiably described as, or on the analogy of, "seeing," and be modeled on directly encountering or experiencing something in its full *enargeia*?

Plato seems to allow such a move, for instance, in the *Meno*. In that dialogue, he does not speak in terms of the transcendent Forms, but develops the view according to which what we call learning and discovery is, in fact, the recovery of knowledge that the soul acquired before we were born. Socrates approvingly reports what he says he learned from priests and priestesses:

> since the soul both is immortal and has been born many times, and has *seen* [*heōrakuia*, a form of the same verb as *idein*] both what is here and what is in Hades, and in fact all things, there is nothing it

has not *learned* (*memathēken*). And so it is no matter for wonder that it is possible for the soul to recollect both about virtue and about other things, given that it *knew* (*ēpistato*) them previously. (*Meno* 81c, trans. Long)

In this passage we see all the relevant cognitive acts together. "Seeing" things is thus not merely "learning" about things – it puts us in possession of knowledge of all kinds of things, including virtue, which, as is clear in the context of the *Meno*, enables us to give fully satisfactory answers to questions like "What is virtue?" This knowledge is forgotten but is recoverable through intellectual inquiry. In the *Phaedo* and the *Phaedrus* Plato specifies that the objects of this prenatal "seeing" must in fact be the Forms. In the *Phaedrus*, he extensively uses the language of "seeing" and *epopteia* to describe that original encounter with the Forms,[25] whereas in the *Phaedo* he refers to it as "learning" and acquisition of knowledge (*epistēmē*) that, once recollected, enables us to give philosophical accounts and real definitions of the relevant properties (*Phd.* 72e–73a, 76c). Through encountering or "seeing" the Form of Beauty, we don't merely become acquainted with it, but also grasp the truth about beauty, come to know all the relevant true propositions about it, and come to know the answer to the question "What is beauty?" In fact, this leads us to one of the most vexed questions of Platonic epistemology: whether knowledge for Plato is of objects ("knowledge by acquaintance" or "experiential knowledge") or of propositions, or whether he simply did not make that distinction – or at least not until his later dialogues.[26] This is not the place to argue for any of these options. I hope, however, to have indicated why Plato found it particularly promising to depict the knowledge of the Forms on the model of the epiphanic experience of a god's *energeia* and getting to know the god, and how he could nevertheless combine this with his strict requirements as to what counts as knowledge.

There is, however, more. As Verity Platt has argued, epiphanies had a crucial epistemological role also with respect to the representations of the gods: What could validate the representations of gods, of which the "prototypes are, by nature, incorporeal, elusive and inaccessible," was "the gods' ability to render themselves visible independently of their material representations – on the authority of epiphany as a seemingly *unmediated* visual encounter with divinity" (Platt 2011: 48). In other words, although epiphanic visions were themselves conditioned by traditional pictorial and literary representations, what conferred value, authority, and trustworthiness on these representations was that the gods could, and sometimes did, reveal themselves directly. Plato confirms that epiphanies of traditional gods (*phasmata theōn, Laws* V 738c) can validate representations and cults of them. To apply this scheme to the Eleusinian mysteries: What could be seen at the *epopteia* must have corresponded to and been prepared by representations of the goddess with which the initiate had already been familiar; yet the vision of the goddess in her *enargeia* gave confirmation to those representations, and made the goddess recognizable with further certainty in representations. Subsequent encounters with representations of the goddess could also remind the viewer of what he had seen at the *epopteia*. At the same time, viewing an *agalma*, a cult statue, of the goddess even in a ritual setting must have fallen short of the overwhelming intensity of the direct encounter with her at the *epopteia*. The viewer thus acquires a preliminary, ordinary acquaintance with the god through her culturally validated representations; and most people will remain at this stage. The select few are, however, allowed a direct vision of the divine prototypes in an (epoptic) *epiphany*, which then leads to a recognition of the ways in which the representations give something back of the god's features, but are still paltry images compared to the full power and radiance of the god. This scheme could serve Plato as a model for describing the relationship between everyday acquaintance with different properties in the physical world and the stable recognition of instantiations based on knowledge of the Forms, which, at the same time, makes us realize that the physical manifestations fall short of the divine original.

This scheme can be cashed out in multiple ways. After having described the ascent from the cave, and how the philosopher finally sees real humans and trees in the bright light of the sun, Socrates continues by expressing the sentiment of the philosopher who has to return to the dim world of the prisoners. The philosopher who witnessed divine spectacles (*theiai theōriai*) in the outside world is now compelled to contend in courtrooms and other places "about the shadows of justice or the *agalmata* of which they are the shadows" (*Rep.* VII 517d). Previously, Socrates referred to the puppets casting shadows on the cave wall simply as artifacts or statues depicting men (*andrias*, 514b). But once the philosopher has had the "divine spectacle," she recognizes them as *agalmata*, representations of originals outside the cave. She can only recognize that there is a relationship between objects in the outside world and the puppets once she has seen the world outside. This allows her to establish a threefold relationship of representation between things in the outside world, puppets as representations of real objects, and the shadows of puppets.

In the *Phaedrus*, Socrates singles out beauty: this is the character the earthly manifestations of which retain to the highest degree the *enargeia* of the divine original that we beheld before our incarnate life (250d). This is why someone whose memory of *epopteia* is still fresh recognizes divine beauty in the "godlike" face or form of his beloved. This recognition makes him relive the experience of the awe and fear he felt at the epiphany, and he is thereby taken by an urge to worship the beloved as an *agalma* or even as a god (251a; cf. *Charmides* 154c). Socrates' topic in this speech is love, but the model is the same, expressed once again in terms of the relationship between epiphany and *agalma*: a direct encounter with the Form enables one to recognize the relevant character in the physical world, and recognize it as a manifestation of the original. Recognizing instances of a property in its physical instantiations is a centrally important function and consequence of knowing the corresponding Form.[27]

At a later point of the speech in the *Phaedrus*, Socrates comes back to the same image: the lover treats the boy as if he were the god the lover had encountered in the prenatal epiphany and constructs from the boy "an *agalma* for himself, and decorates it in order to worship his god and celebrate his rites" (252d, trans. Waterfield, slightly modified). The encounter with the divine original not only enables us to recognize its manifestations in the physical world; remembering the epiphany motivates and enables us to create instantiations of it in the physical world – just as it was sometimes claimed that Praxiteles and Phidias created their astonishing cult statues on the basis of epiphanies. By remembering the Form of Virtue one can give a fully satisfactory account of virtue, and also produce truly virtuous acts, as *agalmata* of the Form. Such truly virtuous acts, based on remembering the Form, are extraordinary, even to a much higher degree than the stupendous cult statues of Praxiteles and Phidias. This pattern can also shed light on a vexed passage of the *Timaeus*. As Timaeus says, the divine craftsman models the physical cosmos as an "*agalma* of the everlasting gods" contained in the everlasting living being, which serves as the divine prototype for the demiurge's creation (*Ti.* 37c). It is precisely his direct observation and knowledge of the divine prototype that enables the demiurge to create a valid "*agalma*," which represents as well as possible the relevant features of the divine original. It is on the basis of his direct knowledge of it that he can also perfect his creation, making the *agalma* an appropriate likeness of the model in as many respects as possible.[28]

III   THE ELEUSINIAN MYSTERIES, THE HUMAN GOOD, AND "GIVING BIRTH" IN THE SYMPOSIUM

As I indicated above, Plato maintains that philosophical contemplation and knowledge of the Forms is the best and the highest form of life a human can achieve. In this section, I will show in more detail how Plato uses this framework to bring out a distinct feature of the good life in the *Symposium*.

The Homeric *Hymn to Demeter* contains the foundation myth of the Eleusinian mysteries and is thus an important source of information for us concerning the religious ideas operative in them. However, apart from a generic promise of a better fate in the afterlife, the only thing it says about the "blessed life" of the initiate is that those who are dear to the gods can expect a visit from Ploutos, the son of Demeter, the personification of agrarian abundance and economic wealth (486–8). According to one authoritative reconstruction of the rites at Eleusis, the birth of Ploutos, represented by the dramatic appearance of an ear of grain (and possibly of a child) constituted the climactic moment of the mysteries (Clinton 1992: 91–3; Bremmer 2014: 19). If so, the promise of material prosperity was at the very core of the ritual action as well. It is highly significant, then, that the *Symposium*, which presents the philosophical life as initiation, starts precisely with a contrast between philosophy and material wealth. The young Apollodorus joined the circle of Socrates only recently, but already values listening to philosophical conversations above all else, and is confident enough to declare to his rich interlocutor that material abundance will never make a life worthwhile (*Smp.* 173c–d). Apollodorus then relates the speeches that the guests at a drinking party gave in honor of Erōs, the personification of love and desire. In the sequence of speeches, Erōs gradually emerges as the driving force that leads us toward things that we deem worth pursuing and that can make our life happy.[29] The topic of wealth (*ploutos*) comes up repeatedly, and the speakers – their different conceptions of the good life notwithstanding – agree that the desire for material fortune is ignoble and cannot lead to a good life (*Smp.* 178c; 184e–185a).[30] The crowning speech of the party, in which Socrates recalls the teaching of the wise woman Diotima, brings us then to the mysteries. But in order to reach that point, we first need to understand better the role of Erōs in the philosophical life.

Diotima explains that we are motivated by *erōs* "to give birth in beauty." Some people beget children, while others are more focused on carrying out virtuous actions, creating poems, coming up with technical inventions, or engaging in political activity and making laws. All these are expressions of our quest for a good life: We "give birth" to what we value most and what we find the ultimate source of our happiness. It is also through these progenies that we seek immortalization – either through our children, who can preserve our memory and legacy and pass them on to the next generation, or through the "immortal glory and fame" that our spiritual offspring can bring to us (*Smp.* 209d). Diotima, however, hastens to add that these manifestations of love of honor (*philotimia*) still only aim at securing reputation and fame among humans (*Smp.* 208c–d); it is only through the true love of wisdom (*philosophia*) that humans can go beyond the ever-changing sphere of the mortal and reach the divine. Diotima expresses the difference between the two attitudes in terms of the difference between the Lesser and Higher Mysteries.[31]

The initiand to the Higher Mysteries first apprehends beauty in a single body, then recognizes the commonality of beauty in all beautiful bodies, and becomes a lover of beauty in all these bodies (210a–b). Going higher, he then perceives and becomes lover of all beautiful souls, all beautiful practices and laws, and all beautiful branches of knowledge. Importantly, he is also able to give an account (*logos*) of the common quality that he recognized at each stage, and also of the fact that each successive stage is more valuable than the preceding one. These accounts are expressions of the love of wisdom and are testimonies of an increasingly better understanding of the nature of beauty. So the cognitive aspect we discussed earlier is emphasized throughout. The ultimate goal of this process, however, is only reached in the *epopteia* of Beauty itself, which transcends all other beautiful things encountered on the way.

As has been shown by scholars, the stages of the philosophical life can be mapped on to the ritual stages of the mysteries.[32] However, it has not been remarked that *epopteia* in Eleusis did not consist in simply catching sight of the goddesses, but – as mentioned at the outset of this section – in the dramatic event of the goddess giving birth to a child, announced at high voice by the hierophant, the leader of the rites, and marked by the appearance of an ear of grain (and possibly of a child).[33] As we have seen, the child born must have been Ploutos, the personification of the promised reward for the initiates. Remarkably, in Diotima's teaching, too, the culmination of philosophical mysteries does not consist in catching sight of the Form of Beauty (*Smp.* 211b), but in the act of "giving birth."[34] The goal of the process is reached when, having beheld Beauty itself, the philosopher-*epoptēs* gives birth to the highest form of virtue, the best of offsprings, compared to which the progeny of those initiated in the Lower Mysteries are mere shadows (*Smp.* 212a). In Diotima's account, it is not the divine that begets – the Form does not change in any respect – but the *epoptēs* through the transformative encounter with the divine. What is born at the climactic encounter with the divine is still the highest reward: The life of the highest virtues is the best possible life and possibly the closest a mortal can get to immortality. Ploutos is thus reinterpreted not as material abundance, but as a life of true virtue based on philosophical knowledge.[35]

The centrality of "giving birth" as the culmination of philosophical life is a striking feature of the *Symposium*, and interpreters of the dialogue sometimes have a hard time explaining it. As we now understand, this special focus is in a way overdetermined. It is naturally linked to the topic of erotic desire, the overarching theme of the dialogue. Giving birth is also the way to achieve "immortality" through one's biological or psychic progeny. But for someone who knew what happened at the mysteries, Diotima's pronouncement had deeper meaning and powerful connotations, echoing and reinterpreting the culmination of the rites. At the same time, the reference to the mysteries can help us better understand the relationship between the goal of the process and the "reward." The ultimate goal of going through the process of the mysteries is the experience of *epopteia*, just as the ultimate goal of a philosophical life is to acquire knowledge of the Forms. Yet, what makes a life good, the "reward" of the initiate, is also born at that moment.

Finally, echoing and giving new meaning to the coda of the *Hymn to Demeter*, Diotima's speech ends in expressing that those who take part in the highest mysteries of philosophy, and have "given birth to true virtue and nourished it," have the gods' love (*theophiles*) and are liberated from eschatological anxieties by attaining as much immortality as is possible for a human being (*Smp.* 212a).

Diotima offers a coherent, self-contained, and philosophically sophisticated account of the complex relationship between the (im)possibility of reaching immortality for human beings,[36] how this is connected to the endless cycles of death and birth in nature, the transformative experience of getting close to and beholding the divine, and giving birth in that very moment to what makes a life good – indeed, we wouldn't need to know anything about what happened at Eleusis to understand and appreciate all this. Yet, as I have tried to show, the conjunction of these themes is conspicuously close to the key elements of the rites; these elements now receive new meaning as part of Plato's substantive account of the quest for the best human life. We see once again that Plato's attitude toward the mysteries is not confrontational but integrative.

IV   THE IMMORTALITY OF THE SOUL, MEMORY, AND KINSHIP WITH THE DIVINE

In this section, I explore how Plato, by conceiving of philosophy as the highest form of initiation, had a framework that allowed him to connect apparently disparate ideas: the relationship between the soul and the divine Forms, the role of memory in this relationship, and the fate of our soul in the afterlife.

A better afterlife is consistently listed among the chief rewards for the Eleusinian initiate. Yet that promise remained somewhat vague, and, as far as the available evidence allows us to see, was not sustained by more specific eschatological ideas. The post-mortem existence of the soul is left aside also in Diotima's teaching. In a set of dialogues, which, according to the standardly accepted chronology of

Plato's works, were composed both before and after the *Symposium*, Plato emphatically affirms and formulates arguments for the immortality of the individual soul. He often accompanies these arguments with imaginative narratives about the post-mortem and prenatal journey, judgment, rewards, and punishments that await the soul. Both the more argumentative discussions and the eschatological myths show that Plato kept thinking about these topics through the lens of religious tradition.

In the eschatological myths in the *Gorgias*, *Phaedo*, *Republic*, and *Phaedrus*, Plato picks up, develops, and transforms themes and images from religious and literary representations of the afterlife.[37] Plato's descriptions show considerable variation both regarding how justice is meted out and in the topography of the places where souls dwell before and after incarnation. Yet one feature is constant: The myths express the firm conviction that the structure of the world must be such that it makes the rule of divine justice and the moral betterment of the individual soul possible. In traditional representations, Tartarus is a horrifying place, which makes it a suitable location to confine those who revolt against Zeus' order. We also find occasional mentions of the "Isle of the Blessed" as the designated dwelling place of those few who deserve an exceptional afterlife. These references, however, are not developed into a comprehensive cosmic topography connected with a system of afterlife judgments, as in Platonic myths. By contrast, it is central to Plato's myths that there is a stratified system of inherently better and worse regions apt for rewards and retribution, creating a wider cosmic landscape for the functioning of an all-encompassing moral order.[38] Similarly, his mythical accounts of afterlife judgments, focusing on how a person lived her life on earth, are considerably more elaborate than anything we find in the surviving traditional representations.

Even more important, the experiences of the soul before and after incarnation, and outside the earth inhabited by humans, extend the possibilities of individual development and obtaining knowledge.[39] The *Meno*, the *Phaedo*, and the *Phaedrus* put the acquisition of knowledge prior to our life. And while the *Symposium* and the *Republic* indicate that, when a set of stringent criteria are met, knowledge of the Forms is possible during our life, in the *Phaedo* Socrates argues that the completion of philosophical progress, a renewed encounter with the Forms, is only possible when our souls leave the prison of the body, and for this we can only get prepared, "purified," during our embodied life.

Apart from the metaphysical thesis of the prenatal and post-mortem existence of the soul, this model involves a set of epistemological conditions. First, that the soul has the capacity to gain and retain knowledge before incarnation. Second, that this knowledge, although "forgotten" at incarnation, can be recovered through intellectual inquiry during our present life. In fact, progress in philosophy, on any construal, needs strong cognitive capacities, among which memory is paramount (*Rep.* VI 486c–d, 487a; *Tht.* 194d). Third, if the philosophical project is to be carried on and completed in the afterlife, the soul after death must be able to build on what it has achieved during incarnate life and be able to (re)acquire full knowledge of the Forms. Memory, the capacity to retain and recover knowledge, becomes central at all stages of this framework. Indeed, Plato often describes memory as a divine capacity and forgetfulness as a curse of embodied existence, which requires constant rehearsal for retaining knowledge (*Phdr.* 249c–d; *Smp.* 207c–208e; *Pol.* 273d–e). Recollection through inquiry (*anamnēsis*) and continuous intellectual practice, exercise, and repetition of what one has learned (*meletē*) are the means by which we can reconnect, and retain the connection, with the Forms.

There are clear indications that Plato drew on and creatively repurposed religious ideas when exploring the relationship between the prenatal and postmortem existence of the soul and retaining and recovering memories during and beyond our embodied life. Socrates explicitly introduces the doctrine of the immortality of the soul, reincarnation, and the additional epistemological doctrine of recollection in tandem, and as something he learned from divinely inspired poets and priests and priestesses. According to the view propounded by them, the soul has been reincarnated many times, and is able to remember what it experienced in its previous lives, and in Hades between incarnations (*Meno* 81c–d).[40] In the immediate context, this tenet is presented as an alternative to skepticism about the possibility of inquiry and discovery. The view adduced, however, not only offers a *possibility* of engaging in inquiry through recollection, but presents it as the pious (81b) and brave choice, what one *ought* to do. In fact, the priests and priestesses are described as not merely divinely inspired, but as ones "who have taken care to be able to give an account" (*logon didonai* 81a–b) – the mark of an attempt to gain knowledge, which in the light of their own doctrine can be done through recollecting.

Remarkably, those whom Plato could take as the main proponents of reincarnation, Pythagoras and Empedocles (and, as we shall see, in a different way the Orphics[41]), indeed put a premium on memory and recollecting what was learned and experienced in previous lives. According to a set of early testimonies, Pythagoras claimed to be able to remember his previous incarnations and used this as "proof" of the doctrine. According to some later testimonies, Pythagoras could transmit the ability to remember past lives to his followers (Porph. *VP* 45), who used systematic daily exercises (Iambl. *VP* 63) to enhance their memory. For Empedocles, the ability to remember "ten or even twenty human lifetimes" (B129) was both the sign and the source of epistemic superiority, insofar as it meant that one's knowledge is not limited to what one experiences in a single life-span and from the perspective of a single life-form.[42] He himself claimed to be able to recall that he was "a boy and a girl and a bush and a bird and a fish traveling in the sea" (B117).[43]

While agreeing about the paramount importance of knowledge gained before our birth, and the ability to regain it, Plato could still strongly disagree about what the relevant knowledge is and where and how we acquired it. For Plato, what counted as knowledge was not what the soul could experience in previous embodied lives, not what Pythagoras could see from his previous incarnation as a Delian diver or a Homeric hero, and what Empedocles could recall from his experiences as a "bush and a bird and a fish." There is only one thing worth recalling: knowledge of the Forms, and as we have seen, and at least in the *Phaedo* and the *Phaedrus*, the full encounter with the forms happens outside the sphere of ordinary experience: in the realm of the "unseen" (Hades) or in the "region above the heavens."

That the soul can retain and gather knowledge before and after death was not part of traditional eschatological ideas. In the most gripping and influential descriptions of the afterlife in Homer, the souls of the deceased linger in Hades, but they have lost (most of) their cognitive abilities, and, relatedly, their agency and connection with the world of the living.[44] Persephone, the queen of the underworld, granted only Teiresias the ability to retain his memory (*Od.* 10.494–5). At the end of the *Meno*, Plato quotes this passage from Homer but reverses the image: He likens the many who have right opinions to the witless dead souls, and the one who has been able to recollect knowledge to Teiresias (100a).

As the Homeric description of the souls of the dead also shows, one of the main eschatological anxieties was that even if the soul continues to exist after the death of the human being, it loses its memory. It seems that some Orphic practices promised a better afterlife by revealing to the initiate how she could retain her memory after death. Tiny gold lamellae, dozens of which have been unearthed in tombs in ancient Greek territories, from Southern Italy and Sicily to Crete and Thessaly, give us some glimpse of Orphic ideas of the afterlife,[45] and the largest cluster of them, traditionally called the B tablets, focus on memory. They contain precise directions about how the initiate, on her arrival to Hades, can access the refreshing water of Mnēmosynē, the goddess of Memory.[46] The earliest and longest version puts the role of Memory in even sharper relief by announcing already at the outset: "This is the work of[47] Mnēmosynē" (B10 = *OF* 474, Hipponion, fifth century BCE). Drinking from the water of Mnēmosynē grants one the ability to retain all the knowledge and experience one has gathered throughout one's life and to recognize, converse with, and join the procession and eternal feast of other initiates and heroes, semi-divine and divine beings. This is what it means to say that after death a new, full, and even better, life awaits the initiate.

Indeed, from the perspective of this newly acquired immortal life, earthly life now appears to be a reduced form of existence, much like that of the shadowy souls in the Homeric Netherworld. This reversal of the traditional notions of life and death is expressed in the catch phrase, also used by Plato with reference to the Orphics, according to which through our earthly life, our bodies are tombs of the soul (*Grg.* 493a; *Cra.* 400c; cf. *Phdr.* 250c).

Aspects of this picture could appeal to Plato. As he says in the *Phaedo*, the philosopher's soul has good hopes "just as is said of the initiates" to "truly spend the rest of time with gods" (*Phd.* 81a). Of course, the Orphic image of the afterlife also has to be corrected. The philosopher does not want to join the company of gods and "other initiates" in order to feast with them and be in a constant state of inebriation (*Rep.* II 363c–d; cf. Pelinna 1 *OF* 485; cf. Aristophanes, *Frogs* 86; with Edmonds 2004: 84–6), thereby absurdly replicating the fulfillment of bodily desires in a disembodied state, but in order to continue the philosophical project unhindered by the body. Moreover, once again, what puts us in the requisite condition to have such a good afterlife is not the performance of initiation rites conducted by an Orphic/Bacchic priest, but being initiated into philosophy. And of course, we cannot take any written texts with us, on gold lamellae or otherwise, as reminders capturing the core of philosophical initiation.[48]

But, yet again, Pythagoras, Empedocles, and even the Orphics might still have a crucial insight in store for us: for in different ways, they all maintained that by remembering, we also realize our divine origins. Pythagoras apparently claimed that in his previous incarnation he was the son of Hermes and received the gift of memory from him; the ability to remember everything that happened to him through his incarnations was the best substitute for complete divine immortality his father could give him (D.L. VIII 4, quoting Heraclides

Pontus = fr. 8.89 Wehrli).[49] It is also due to his memory that
Empedocles was able to declare his ultimate origin and identity: He
was one of the *daimones*, who has to go through these incarnations,
locked in various "alien garments of flesh" (B126), because of a sin he
had committed, but he was hopeful that his wanderings are close to an
end and that he would soon be able to rejoin the happy gathering of
other immortals (B146, B147). Empedocles' narrative about the wanderings of the *daimones* was circulated under the title *Purifications*,
indicating that his return to the company of other *daimones* and gods
is conditional upon being purified.

The recognition of one's divine origin, and that one is ready to
return to where one naturally belongs because one has attained purity,
is central to the Gold Tablets as well. For on the other main cluster, the
A tablets, the deceased has to affirm his purity ("Pure I come from the
pure," *OF* 488–91) and that he has paid a penalty for (some unspecified)
unjust deeds (*OF* 489–90; cf. *OF* 485–6, 493). Moreover, on both clusters, the deceased has to be able to declare his divine origin to pass the
test. According to the standard formula on the B tablets, to the
prompting of the guardians of the netherworld the deceased has to
answer "I am the son of Earth and starry Heaven," to which one version
adds "But my race is heavenly" (*OF* 476; cf. *OF* 477). On the A tablets,
the deceased has to announce to the gods and *daimones* he meets
thereafter that "I am of your blessed race (*genos*)." That the human
soul has a divine origin and nature, and that, if purified, it is ready to
return to its true kin, are ideas that go beyond the traditional assumption that the separation of gods and humans is (almost) absolute.

The interrelation between the elements I outlined above – the
immortality and reincarnation of the soul, the importance of memory
during and beyond incarnate life, and the kinship of the soul with the
divine – might be reflected in the series of the first three arguments in
the *Phaedo* that aim to show that the soul exists before and/or after
human life. The first, customarily called the "Cyclical Argument"
(70c–72d), seeks to offer a proof of reincarnation on the basis of
a general theory of change. The second, the "Recollection

Argument" (72e–77a), aims to establish that prior to perceiving things in our embodied life we knew the Forms, so that our souls have cognitive powers also when not embodied, and that the proper objects of recollection are not what we experience during embodied existence, but the Forms. Finally, the objective of the "Affinity Argument" (78b–80b) is to show that our souls are "of the same kind" (*sungenes*) as the divine Forms, so that there is hope that at the end of our earthly life, those who are properly "purified" – that is, those who have harnessed their bodily desires and, through systematic and sustained philosophical inquiry, have aimed at the recovery of the knowledge of the Forms – can rejoin these divine beings with whom they are *sungenes* in the company of other philosophical souls (cf. 82b).

Again, Orphic initiators and Empedocles are mistaken about most of the details, but they are right in their intuition, possibly divinely inspired, that the fact that we are of the same *genos* as the gods makes it possible for us to become better and regain as much as possible our divine nature, and that a recognition of this fact sets the ultimate goal for our lives: to put ourselves in a condition that prepares us, as far as possible, to (re)assume our position among the gods by reinforcing what is divine in us, and repressing, ignoring and avoiding all that would forestall that endeavor. It is on this basis, and with these crucial modifications that Socrates can finally ask:

> So does a soul in this condition go off into what is similar to it, the unseen, the divine, immortal and wise, where after its arrival it can be happy, separated from wandering, unintelligence, fears, savage sorts of love and the other human evils, and just as is said of the initiates, does it truly spend the rest of time with gods? (*Phd.* 81a, trans. Long)[50]

This scheme, based on an adaptation of the mysteries, might set our highest goals and can soothe some of our eschatological anxieties, but it cannot be the final proof for the immortality of the soul – as Socrates acknowledges in the *Phaedo*. Moreover, by focusing exclusively on the Forms, it might ignore something essential about the nature of the soul and at least partly misidentify the divine with which the soul is akin: The Forms are completely immutable whereas the soul, although it needs stability, is also changing. Indeed, Socrates argues in the *Phaedrus* that the soul is essentially a self-mover, and constructs an argument for its immortality precisely on that basis (245c–246e). But in the context of the same argument Socrates also explains that our souls are of the same kind, only less perfect, as the souls of cosmic gods, now identified as the traditional Olympians. These gods are "nourished by intelligence and pure knowledge" of the Forms (247d), "the proper nourishment for the best part of the soul" (248b). According to a less metaphorical, but more striking formulation, these gods "are divine by being close to" the Forms (249c): The gods derive their divinity from the contemplation and perfect knowledge of the Forms. Human souls, before their first incarnation, joined those gods, and "as part of a happy company they saw a wonderful sight and spectacle and were initiated into what we may rightly call the most wonderful of the mysteries" (250b). This is the condition to which the philosopher tries to get back as much as possible, by reconnecting with the Forms through recollection and dialectic (249c). Beyond the confines of single embodied lives, ordinary souls have to wait for 10,000 years to get out of the cycles of reincarnation and return to that divine state (248e), but it is promised that the philosopher's soul can much sooner rejoin the gods, being nourished on truth and knowledge, or, as the Orphics would say, "to feast in the company of gods."[51] The *Phaedrus* brings a new understanding of the nature of the soul, and correspondingly a novel interest in a class of divine beings distinct from the Forms, whose characteristic activity is intellection, to contemplate and have full knowledge of the Forms; now these are the divine beings to which our souls are presented as "akin," serving as paradigms for the proper, highest activity of our souls, and whose company it is our final goal to rejoin.[52] The theory thus shows significant modifications. Remarkably, Plato once again readapts the framework of the mysteries to express this modified theory, and to capture the relationship to the divine and the ultimate goal of human life.

V   EPILOGUE: THE PHILOSOPHICAL INITIATE AND CIVIC RELIGION

Where does all this leave us with those who are not initiated into philosophy – the majority of citizens? How can they be pious, "dear to the gods"? In the *Republic* the philosopher-ruler leaves traditional forms of worship and traditional narrative and visual representations of the gods untouched, as long as they are sanctified by the oracle at Delphi and are not in conflict with Plato's theological principles. In the *Laws*, Plato voices the same rule,[53] but explores more deeply the role and responsibility of the political leader in regulating public forms of worship. The aim is clear: to create a framework in which citizens can develop what is most godlike in them and get assimilated to the divine, and thereby become virtuous, even without an understanding of philosophical theology. The solution Plato comes up with is a life completely imbued with the divine. Myths about the gods composed under the supervision of the lawgiver and used in early education lay the foundations for a correct, even if non-philosophical conception of the divine, while daily sacrifices and especially frequent religious festivals, with joyful choral performances involving the active participation of citizens, establish and constantly refresh the contact with the gods. In all these formats, the gods appear as "exemplary fellow-celebrants" and role models for developing and perfecting virtues (Prauscello 2014: 130; Morrow 1960: 469; Bartninkas 2019: ch. 3). At the same time, citizens can feel that through these activities they please and make themselves dear to the gods (e.g., VI 771d–e; VII 809d).

Two key moments of the dialogue subtly signal that Plato hasn't left behind the conception of philosophy as the highest mystery. In his first address to the new citizens, which will also serve as the preamble for all the subsequent laws of the city, the lawgiver sets out the fundamental principles that govern the lives of the members of the community, explaining why it is their utmost task to become moderate and just by emulating the gods, and how they can achieve this by honoring the gods in the sanctified rituals and by observing the laws of the city. The entire speech starts by evoking the "god who, according to the ancient account, holds the beginning and the end and the middle of all beings" (IV 715e). As has often been noted, these words echo the Orphic hymn to Zeus (cf. [Arist.] *De Mundo*, 401a27–b29; *P.Derv.* col. XVII.12), in all probability used also by Orphic initiators.

But there is another important clue that is rarely picked up. The "head" of the whole city, its highest-level advisory institution, is customarily referred to as the Nocturnal Council. Yet, when Plato first mentions it, he calls it the "council *tōn peri nomous epopteuontōn*" (951d), which in the most commonly used English translation is rendered as "the council which muses on legislation" (trans. Saunders). On the basis of our previous discussion we can see that this does not quite capture the force of the phrase. In fact, apart from the passages in the *Symposium* and the *Phaedrus* that we considered earlier, it is the only time Plato uses the *epopt-* root. Moreover, in the context of the *Laws*, "law is the embodiment of divine reason" (Laks 2000: 271), and the word-play between intellect (*nous*) and law (*nomos*) often recurs. We can then also understand the phrase as expressing that this council is the association of those who have an *epopteia*, the highest insight not into human laws, but into the ultimate laws, the laws of the divine *nous*. What gives this council authority is precisely this insight. The Nocturnal Council is the interface between the highest-level knowledge of the divine and human legislation. In the *Laws* Plato finally shows how a philosophical understanding of the divine, exclusive to a small group of "initiates," can trickle down and mold civic religion so that other citizens can also benefit, as far as possible, from the philosopher's *epopteia*.

NOTES

1 On polis religion, see esp. Sourvinou-Inwood 2000; Parker 1996 and 2005. For an important corrective, see Kindt 2012.

2 On the importance of the Delphic oracle for Plato, see section I, with note 9.

3 For more on this see below, section II. On mystery cults in general, see in particular Burkert 1987, Graf 2006, Bowden 2010 and Bremmer 2014. Throughout this chapter, I will use the term "mystery" in this technical sense. On Bacchic rites and Orphism, see Parker 1995, Bernabé and Casadesús 2008, Edmonds 2013. On Orphic elements in Plato, see in particular Bernabé 2011. On the Eleusinian mysteries, see in particular Mylonas 1961, Dowden 1980, Clinton 1992 and 2005.

4 Cf., e.g., *Cri.* 54d; *Euthd.* 277d–e; *Ion* 533e–534a; *Smp.* 215e; *Phdr.* 228b, with Linforth 1946 and Wasmuth 2015.

5 On Plato's theology, see, e.g., Bordt 2006, Lefka 2013, Van Riel 2013, and Sedley 2019.

6 For a recent discussion of Plato's conception of "purity" as a systematic avoidance of bodily pleasures and pains, and its relation to the Orphic and Pythagorean notions of purity, see Ebrey 2017b.

7 Cf. esp. Adkins 1970 and Dover 1968 *ad loc.*

8 Cf., e.g., Marianetti 1993.

9 Socrates' trust in and probing of what the Delphic oracle might have meant when it pronounced that no one was wiser than him (*Ap.* 21a–b), leading him to important recognitions about himself and the nature of wisdom, could provide a template for this attitude. On the religious views of Socrates, and the charge of impiety against him, see, e.g., Vlastos 1991, McPherran 1996, Burnyeat 1997, and the essays in Smith and Woodruff 2000, and now Denyer 2019: 15–20.

10 Plato acknowledges that things might go wrong. Two prominent characters from the dialogues remind us of this fact. A year after the dramatic date of the *Symposium*, Alcibiades and his friends, including Phaedrus, were convicted on the charge that they repeatedly enacted the rites in private houses, assuming the roles of the high priest and those who were sanctioned to officiate various roles in the ritual (Plut. *Alc.*, 22.3–4; Andocides 1.15).

11 Nightingale (2021) became available after the completion of this chapter, so I was not able to engage with her interpretations here. I am, however, very pleased to see that at some important points she and I have independently arrived at similar conclusions.

12 At, e.g., *Phd.* 64d–e Socrates and his friends agree that there are Forms of Just, Beautiful, and Good, but there is no suggestion that all, or indeed, any member of the company would have knowledge of all these Forms.

13 Diotima has proven her skills in such matters when she mediated between gods and humans through ritual means, prescribing the correct sacrifices to postpone a plague for ten years (*Smp.* 201d).

14 As, e.g., Burkert (1987: 90) shows, one of the primary aims of mysteries was to prepare for and create a sacred setting for an "immediate encounter with the divine."

15 That Plato characterized the high point of philosophy as *epopteia* was recognized also by his ancient readers; cf., e.g., Plut. *De Is.* 32D–E, *Quest. conviv.* 718C; Clem. *Strom.* 1176.2.

16 Plato regularly calls the Forms divine (e.g., *Phd.* 80a–b; *Rep.* VI 500c; *Phdr.* 246e). Forms possess the most important features which characterize gods for Plato's contemporaries: they are eternal, have great causal power, and are not available to the senses. In the *Phaedrus*, Socrates says that the traditional gods "are divine by being close to" the Forms (249c); in view of Plato's theory of causation, the Forms can confer divinity on the gods only by being divine themselves. At the same time, this also establishes a hierarchical relationship between Forms and other types of divine beings.

17 Nightingale 2018, drawing on Platt 2011; Petridou 2015.

18 On the Eleusinian *epopteia* as the clearest case of collective epiphany, see Graf 2004: 126.

19 Cf. Burnyeat 2012: 238–58.

20 See, e.g., Bowden 2010, Edmonds 2017, building on the work of the anthropologist Whitehouse, who distinguishes between "doctrinal" and "imagistic" modes of religiosity and correspondingly "doctrinal" and "imagistic" revelations; see esp. Whitehouse 2000. Petridou (2013) applies Elsner's concept of "ritual-centred visuality" to the Eleusinian rites. Perhaps the most gripping ancient description of the experience of the initiates is given by Plutarch (Fr. 6 Dübner = fr. 178 Sandbach; Stob., *Anthologion* IV 52.49). It has been debated whether Plutarch is speaking about the Eleusinian mysteries in particular or about initiatory experience more generally, and how much his description is already influenced by the Platonic passages.

21 Dinkelaar (2020) argues that Plato used the images and vocabulary of the mysteries for their emotional appeal.

22 "Epiphanies are sources of knowledge: knowledge about human and divine nature and morphology; knowledge about the limited abilities of humans and the limitless abilities of gods" (Petridou 2015: 124).

23 Experiencing the Forms in their *enargeia*: *Phdr.* 250d; cf. *Rep.* VI 484d, 511a; *Phd.* 77a.

24 On the relationship between *theōria* as viewing religious festivals and *theōria* as philosophical contemplation, see the analyses in Nightingale 2004: 72–139 and 2005.

25 For the more complex image that by "seeing" the forms the soul is "fed" with what is its proper nourishment, knowledge and truth, see *Phdr.* 247c–e; 248b–c.

26 For classic statements of the first two options, see Fine 1978 and Gonzalez 1996; for the view that Plato did not make the distinction, see Taylor 2019. For a book-length attempt to show that, for Plato, acquisition of knowledge consisted in grasping concepts pictorially or "iconically," see Rowett 2018.

27 On Alcibiades' reference to Socrates' speeches as *agalmata* of virtue (215b; 216e; 222a), and that it shows that Alcibiades has made progress, cf. Destrée 2011: 202 and Steiner 1996.

28 For an alternative interpretation, suggesting that the genitive should be rendered not as *agalma* "of the gods," but "for the gods," see Cornford 1937 (1997): 99–101, which is followed in Zeyl's translation.

29 Cf. in particular Sheffield 2006 and Obdrzalek in this volume (ch. 7).

30 Note also that when Diotima presents the mythical genealogy of Erōs, she says that his mother was Penia, the personification of poverty and need. However, the father is not Ploutos, material abundance, as one might expect, but Poros, the personification of intellectual resourcefulness. I owe this point to Suzanne Obdrzalek.

31 Gaps in our knowledge of the relationship between the Lesser and the Higher Mysteries have led to different construals of the relationship between these two paths. According to an influential reconstruction, the two festivals were linked as stages in a continuous progression, so that the Lesser Mysteries was a preparatory stage for the Higher Mysteries. Accordingly, interpreters of the *Symposium* tried to make *philotimia* a stage on a path leading to *philosophia* (Riedweg 1987: 2–29; Ionescu 2007). Yet, as an alternative reconstruction shows, there is no need to assume this. The Lesser Mysteries were probably an independent festival, and taking part in them constituted an act of piety complete in itself, although of lower prestige than being initiated at Eleusis (Dowden 1980; Bowden 2010: 32–3; Edmonds 2017); lives devoted to poetic creation or

giving good laws to one's city are complete in themselves, although of lower value than the pursuit of philosophy. In fact, Diotima describes the successive stages of the ascent of the Higher Mysteries, from its starting-point in youth to its ultimate end, without including honor-loving.

32 See, e.g., Sattler 2013.

33 Hippolytus, *Ref.* 5.8.39–41.

34 The verb used in the hierophant's dramatic announcement, *eteke*, runs through Diotima's speeches, and she uses the same word repeatedly at the climax to describe "giving birth" to true virtues.

35 Empedocles B122 DK, according to which "blessed is the one who has acquired the *ploutos* of divine thoughts" is a possible precursor.

36 It is a vexed question whether Diotima only allows the immortality of the soul, or only immortality through our biological and/or intellectual progeny. See Sedley 2009: 158–60.

37 See in particular Edmonds 2004; Bernabé 2007.

38 Notably, Plato includes a value distinction between cosmic regions even in the *Timaeus*: Returning to one's star is the ultimate reward, whereas the murky depths of the sea are an inherently bad place, fitting for those who are reincarnated as dumb fish.

39 Sedley 2009: 145.

40 Cf. also *Phaedo* 70c, where the theory of reincarnation is introduced on the basis of an "ancient account," which is interpreted by ancient and modern interpreters as a reference to Orphic and Pythagorean tenets.

41 The direct evidence is inconclusive on how far Orphic initiators professed reincarnation. It seems that Plato, like Herodotus (Hdt. II 123.1 = *OF* 423), took it to be also an Orphic doctrine.

42 Empedocles B115, B117, B127, B146, with Tor 2017: 321–7.

43 Plato perhaps took a bow to this approach: In the preceding section of the *Meno* he gives an object lesson on how to provide adequate answers to a "What is X?" question, and as examples of at least partially successful attempts he evokes the account of color by Empedocles and one that might be attributed to Pythagoreans (Arist., *Sens.* 439a33–4).

44 Cf., e.g., *Il.* 23.103–4; *Od.* 10.493–5. As Sourvinou-Inwood (1995) reminds us, however, depictions of the afterlife allowed a fair amount of variation in and outside Homeric epic.

45 For recent editions and discussions of the Gold Tablets, see Bernabé and Jiménez San Cristóbal 2008, Graf and Johnston 2013, Edmonds 2011.

46 Zuntz 1971: 380, Edmonds 2004: 52–5, Bernabé and Jiménez San Cristóbal 2008: 15–19.
47 Or, according to alternative readings: "consecrated to" or "gift of."
48 The criticism of writing at the end of the *Phaedrus* (274b–277a) as unsuitable for storing knowledge, and deleterious to proper memory, can also apply as a rejection of the Orphic gold plates: We cannot rely on any such written aides-mémoire.
49 On Heraclides' testimony, see Casadesús Bordoy 2013: 164–8, arguing that Pythagoras' later incarnations underline his privileged connection to Apollo.
50 Cf. also *Phd.* 79d, 81b–d, 84b. *Phd.* 79d emphasizes that the soul acquires stability through contemplating the immutable Forms.
51 For contemplating what is true and divine as a "nourishment" for the soul, cf. also *Phd.* 84b.
52 In the *Timaeus*, we can discern the application of the same scheme with the difference that what our rational souls are said to be *sungenes* with and ought to emulate is the divine soul of the cosmos; cf. Betegh 2018.
53 Cf. V 738b–d; VIII 828a; on the revision of traditional representations IV 719b, V 727d, VII 801c–d, X 905d–907; Delphi: VI 759c–d; VIII 828a; IX 865b; XII 946d. On religion and theology in the *Laws*, see esp. Morrow 1960: 399–499; Schofield 2006: ch. 7; Mayhew 2010.

9 The Unfolding Account of Forms in the *Phaedo*

David Ebrey

Perhaps Plato's most famous idea is that things like justice, beauty, largeness, and smallness are in some fundamental way different from ordinary, perceptible things. While this idea is famous, it is difficult to find an account in the dialogues of why he thinks it, and how, exactly, these things – which he sometimes calls "forms" – are supposed to be different from the ordinary objects we touch and see. Intuitively, there is clearly a difference between largeness and a large thing, such as Mount Olympus, but why and how does Plato think these are different? We should not assume that he thinks of the differences the way that we do, especially since he seems to be the first Greek philosopher to provide a general account of things like largeness and beauty – which we might call "abstract entities." As one might expect, he also seems to be the first to develop a contrasting category that corresponds, at least roughly, to what we might call an "ordinary physical object." Plato's most extensive discussions of forms are in the *Phaedo* and the *Republic*. Since there are good reasons to think the *Phaedo* was written first, it seems like a promising place to look for his account of why they are fundamentally different from ordinary physical objects.[1]

In the *Phaedo*, Socrates does not use the term "physical object" or other terms that we might use for such things, such as "body" or "material thing."[2] The first time he contrasts such things with forms,

I would like to thank for helpful written feedback Gábor Betegh, Joseph Bjelde, Ian Campbell, Sylvain Delcomminette, Emily Fletcher, Dhananjay Jagannathan, Richard Kraut, Connie Meinwald, Stephen Menn, Robert Mordarski, Giulia Weißmann, and James Wilberding. I have also received valuable feedback from audiences at University of Chicago, Charles University, Federal University of Goiania, University of Groningen, Humboldt-Universität zu Berlin, University of Colorado-Denver, UCLA, University of Wisconsin-Madison, Harvard, and the University of Oslo.

he simply gives examples – a stick equal to another stick or a stone equal to another stone or "anything else of that sort" (74a10–11); the next time, he refers to them as "the many beautiful things, such as people or horses or cloaks or any other such thing, or equal things, or any other thing that shares a name with those things [the forms]" (78d10–e2, cf. 102b).[3] While our notions of abstract object and physical object arise out of an intellectual tradition going back to Plato, he is in a radically different position from us, inheritors of millennia of reflections on these topics, along with a developed terminology. Understanding his reasons for thinking that forms are different from "ordinary objects," as I will call them, helps clarify how he thinks about each category.

The most common interpretations are either (1) that in the *Phaedo* Socrates simply assumes the existence of so-called "Platonic forms" – that is, entities that have a number of features, including being in some strong sense distinct from ordinary objects – or (2) that the dialogue's recollection argument contains one of Plato's few arguments for them.[4] In this chapter I present a new interpretation of why and how forms are different from ordinary objects, according to Socrates in the *Phaedo*. Rather than identify one particular passage as the key to understanding the *Phaedo*'s account, I argue that the explanation unfolds across the dialogue, so that Socrates' claims near the end are needed to fully understand what he says near the beginning.[5] According to this reading, Socrates asserts some claims early in the dialogue without providing the underlying explanation for them. This is part of why some interpreters claim that he is simply assuming the existence of Platonic forms. I argue instead that each time he returns to forms and ordinary objects he further explains the claims made the previous time he discussed them.

Socrates' basic description of the forms is that they are what he is looking for when he asks his "what is it?" question. He mentions this the first three times he brings them up in the *Phaedo* (65d–e, 75c–d, and 78c–d). For example, in the recollection argument he says that he is talking about "everything to which we attach this label, 'what it is,' both in the questions we ask and in the answers we give" (75d1–3). The fourth time he discusses them – his discussion of forms as causes – he says that what he is talking about "isn't anything new, but what I've never stopped talking about, on any other occasion or in the discussion thus far" (100b1–3). Socrates is making new claims about the same things he has always sought. Several of the dialogues typically called "Socratic" are devoted to answering such "what is it?" questions, but none of them contrasts forms with ordinary objects. There are several possible reasons for this difference between the *Phaedo* and the Socratic dialogues, each compatible with the account provided here.[6] The important point for this chapter is that Plato does not portray Socrates as talking about some entities that he does not normally discuss, but rather as making new claims about the things he has always been interested in.[7] In this chapter I use the term "form" simply as a name for this thing Socrates has always searched for – without building into this term any contrast with ordinary objects or the idea that the forms are somehow "transcendent."

Aristotle lies in the background of any discussion of why and how Plato distinguishes forms from ordinary objects. Aristotle's discussions of Plato's forms can be useful for understanding Plato's dialogues. For example, I think Aristotle is right when he notes (*Met.* Alpha 6, Mu 4, 9) that Plato's commitment to ordinary objects being in flux is part of why he thinks that they are distinct from forms.[8] But we can also be misled by Aristotle if we try to use him to understand Plato's dialogues.[9] In particular, Aristotle frequently distinguishes his own view of forms from Plato's by saying that Plato "separates" forms from ordinary things, whereas Aristotle does not (*Met.* Alpha 6, 9; Mu 4–5, 9; and the *Peri Ideōn*). Plato does not describe forms as "separate" in the *Phaedo*.[10] This idea plays no role, I shall argue, in the *Phaedo*'s reasons for viewing forms as fundamentally different from ordinary objects. The goal of this chapter is to understand the *Phaedo*'s reasons for this contrast on their own terms. Moreover, Aristotle focuses on what arguments there are for the existence of Platonic forms – that is, for the existence of forms that are separate from ordinary objects (*Met.* Alpha 9, Mu 4, and the *Peri Ideōn*). In my view, the *Phaedo* has been misunderstood by seeking such arguments in it. Instead, it treats separately the questions (1) whether there are forms and (2) why and how they are different from ordinary objects. This chapter focuses on the latter question. As for the former: Socrates thinks that there are forms, in the first instance, because he thinks that there are things like justice, holiness, and largeness – the things he is searching for when he asks his "what is it?" questions. But the *Phaedo* does not ultimately rely on Socrates' (and his interlocutors') commitment to there being such things. In the fourth stage of his unfolding account of forms, he famously lays out a method of hypothesis, and adopts as separate hypotheses the existence of individual forms, each of which serves as a cause (100a–101e). How this works is its own story. My question here is, given that there are forms, what is the *Phaedo*'s account of why and how they differ from ordinary objects?

The primary contrast Socrates draws in the *Phaedo* is between a given form and ordinary objects with the corresponding feature – for example, between the form of beauty and ordinary beautiful things. Across the dialogues, a basic feature of forms is that the form of *f*-ness is that by which any *f*-thing is *f*. In the fourth stage of the *Phaedo*'s unfolding account, Socrates uses this basic feature of forms to identify the form of beauty as the cause of beautiful things being beautiful. I argue here that, at the end of the *Phaedo*'s unfolding account, we learn that the nature of any ordinary beautiful thing does not allow it to be such a cause. Thus, the *Phaedo* provides an account of causes and of the nature of ordinary objects that means that no ordinary object could be a cause, and hence none could be a form. Most of the key differences between forms and ordinary objects can be traced back to this basic difference. I argue for this interpretation by considering each section of the dialogue where Socrates discusses the forms and ordinary objects; however, my focus is on the later sections, since these, on my interpretation, provide the *Phaedo*'s ultimate account of why forms and ordinary objects are fundamentally different. The end of the chapter considers Socrates' account of what I call "bringers" – things like fire, snow, and three, which bring some opposite with them. Considering them anticipates an objection to my interpretation as well as clarifying why and how ordinary objects differ from forms.

I   FIRST STAGE: ARE FORMS PERCEPTIBLE?

Socrates first mentions forms in his defense speech (63b–69e), the part of the dialogue where he defends his shocking claim that the philosopher desires to be dead. In defending this, he describes both why the philosophers avoid pleasure and why they do not inquire using the senses. His initial discussion of forms arises after Socrates gives some preliminary considerations for not inquiring with the senses (65a–d). It begins as follows:

> "Well now, what do we say about things like the following, Simmias? Do we say that there is such a thing as a just itself, or not?"
>> "Indeed we do!"
>> "Yes, and such a thing as a beautiful, and a good?"
>> "Of course."
>> "Now have you ever actually seen with your eyes any of the things of this kind?"
>> "Not at all," he said.
>> "Or have you grasped them with one of the other senses that are through the body? I'm talking about all of them, such as largeness, health, and strength and, to sum up, about the being of all the rest – what each one turns out to be. Are they viewed at their truest through the body, or ... ?" (65d4–e2)

First, note that Socrates does not refer to these using the term "form." It is not until the fifth and final stage of the unfolding account that Socrates first uses the term "form" (*eidos*, 102b1) as a name for the thing referred to by the correct answer to a "what is it?" question. Here in the first stage he refers to them first as "an *f* itself", then he uses abstract nouns – *f*-ness – then as the being (*ousia*) of all other such things, and finally as "what it is." These are all expressions used for justice, beauty, and holiness in the *Protagoras* (330c–e), *Euthyphro* (5c–6e, 11a–b), *Meno* (72b–e), and *Hippias Major* (286d–e, 289d); in the last three dialogues, Socrates refers to this as a "form" (*eidos* or *idea*). In none of these dialogues are forms explicitly contrasted with ordinary objects, although in the *Hippias Major* some such contrast seems implicit. A form – both in these dialogues and in the *Phaedo* – is what we are looking for when we ask the "what is it?" question. It is the being of a thing. It can be referred to as "the large itself" or as "largeness." What we find in the *Phaedo* – unlike the *Protagoras*, *Euthyphro*, *Meno*, and *Hippias Major* – is a sustained discussion of what one can say about forms in general, independently of what the correct answer to the "what is it?" question turns out to be.[11]

Note that Socrates asks Simmias whether there are forms before asking whether they are perceived – treating the latter as a separate question. Socrates seems to be suggesting that it would be a sort of category mistake to think that one could use the senses to perceive a form, but we should be careful not to assume that he puts largeness into the same category that we might put it – perhaps, "abstract entity." Moreover, Socrates does not explain here why forms are not the sort of thing to be perceived. If one merely wanted an argument that forms are different from ordinary objects, Socrates all but gives one here: Forms are not perceived through the body, ordinary objects are; hence, forms are not ordinary objects. This, I think, is the most intuitively gripping argument the dialogue has to offer: Justice simply is not the kind of thing that we see or touch. But there is no reason to think that being perceptible is the fundamental difference between forms and ordinary objects.

In general, one should ask what the goal of an argument is. Is it supposed to start from premises that seem obviously true? Or provide an underlying explanation for why the conclusion is the case? There is no reason to expect that an argument could do both. Here, in the first stage, Socrates provides premises that are easy to accept.[12] But do they identify the underlying explanation for why forms are not ordinary things? Of course, not everything has an underlying explanation, so it is conceivable that forms could belong to a different category than ordinary objects without there being any explanation for why this is. But there would be something dissatisfying about this scenario and so good reason to be cautious before accepting it. One would be asked to accept the existence of the forms – a category we probably do not have clear intuitions about and at least many of whose members have never been discovered – and then accept as a brute fact that they cannot be ordinary objects. I will argue, instead, that by the end of the dialogue it turns out that the basic description of what one is searching for, when searching for a form, requires their nature to be fundamentally different than that of ordinary objects. This underlying explanation for their difference, as we shall see, does not have to do with whether or not they are perceptible.

Since Socrates does not, at this stage, explain why forms are distinct from ordinary objects, we can see why some interpreters think that he simply assumes the existence of Platonic forms from the beginning. Instead, I suggest that Socrates begins by getting Simmias to agree to an intuitively plausible claim about the forms, a claim not made in the Socratic dialogues: One cannot grasp them with bodily senses.[13] But we need to read on to see why and how the nature of forms must differ from that of ordinary objects.

II   SECOND STAGE: THE RECOLLECTION ARGUMENT

Socrates next refers to forms in the recollection argument (73b–77a), which argues that everyone had knowledge of the forms before birth. Perhaps no other argument in ancient philosophy has received as much attention over the last seventy years.[14] In my view, this argument's key claims about forms are further explained by what comes later, and so my discussion of it here is very brief.

The most famous section of this complicated argument is the part where Socrates argues that equal stones and sticks are not the same as the equal itself (74b–c). Regardless of how this subargument is supposed to work, it clearly is supposed to argue *that* the form of equality is distinct from ordinary equal things, such as equal sticks. Socrates later clarifies that his claims are meant to apply not only to the form of equality, but also to the rest of the forms (75c–d). Does this subargument also provide an underlying explanation for why forms are distinct from things like sticks and stones? According to some readings it does not.[15] However, most think that it is supposed to illuminate an underlying difference between them. Soon after this subargument, Socrates says that the equal sticks are deficient and fall short of equality itself but want to be like it (74d–75b). This strongly suggests that there is supposed to be something about the nature of ordinary objects that makes them not simply different from, but in fact inferior to the forms. Nonetheless, it is obscure how to understand this inferiority. The route taken by many in the secondary literature is to understand ordinary objects' inferiority by going back to the two sentences where Socrates contrasts the equal sticks with equality itself (74b7–c2).[16] Often, such interpretations also look to other dialogues (such as the *Hippias Major* and the *Republic*) to fill in Socrates' reasoning. Let me suggest that the two sentences contrasting equal sticks with the equal itself do not contain a fully satisfying account of the fundamental difference between them. But at the same time we do not need to go to other dialogues to fill in the reasoning. We simply need to wait for the next stages of the unfolding account.

III   THIRD STAGE: THE AFFINITY ARGUMENT

The so-called "affinity argument" (78b–80b – which I think would be better named the "kinship argument") comes directly after the recollection argument. Socrates argues here that the soul is more like and akin to "the unseen" – a category whose only identified members are the forms – than to "the visible," and so there are good reasons to expect the soul to be indestructible, like the unseen. In arguing for this, he provides his most detailed account in the *Phaedo* both of forms and of ordinary objects. But, in stark contrast to the recollection argument, the affinity argument has received relatively little scholarly attention.[17]

Socrates' primary description of forms in the affinity argument is the following:

> "Then let's turn," he said, "to the same things as in the previous argument. Take the being itself which is the object of our account when in our questions and answers we give an account of what it is. Is each of them always in the same state and the same condition or in different states at different times? The equal itself, the beautiful itself, what each thing itself is, that which is – does that ever admit of change of any kind at all? Or is what each of them is, since it is uniform itself through itself (*auto kath hauto*), always in the same state and the same condition, and does it at no time, in no way, in no manner admit of any difference[18]?"
>
> "It must be in the same state and the same condition, Socrates," said Cebes. (78c10–d9)

This is a complicated description of the forms. I focus here only on those aspects that are directly relevant to my overall interpretation. Note first that Socrates says that he is talking about the same things as in the previous (recollection) argument, which again he describes as the object of their search when they ask, "what is it?" He says that these things, the forms, are in the same state and the same condition.[19] Socrates' last sentence, I take it, explains why this is so: because each is uniform, itself through itself (*auto kath hauto*).[20]

A careful account of the notoriously difficult expression "*auto kath hauto*" would require its own essay.[21] Let me suggest an interpretation that could result from a number of different ways of understanding what this expression literally means. The suggestion is that Socrates is saying that each form has each of its features insofar as it is what it is. In other words, the nature of each form entirely determines how it is. By contrast, most of an ordinary thing's features – for example, whether it happens to be beautiful or ugly – are not determined by its nature. Thus, in the above passage, Socrates is saying that since each form is uniform and its nature determines the way that it is, it is always in the same state and the same condition.

What does it mean to describe the forms as uniform (*monoeides*)? Socrates later says that ordinary objects are, by contrast, multiform (*polueides*) (80b4). Our evidence suggests that Socrates is using "uniform" here to indicate that the forms are single, partless wholes, so that they have no (even non-spatial) parts with independent functions or roles. In saying that forms are "uniform," Socrates is thus saying that anything attributable to a form is not attributed to some part of it (since it has no such parts), but to the entire form.[22] One piece of evidence for this way of understanding "uniform" comes near the end of *Republic* X, where the question of whether or not the true nature of the soul has several parts is put in terms of whether the pure soul is "uniform" or "multiform" (611b–612a). Similarly, in the *Phaedrus* Socrates asks whether the soul is "simple" or "multiform," where this is determined by whether or not it has different parts with different functions (270d–271a). In considering the possibility that the soul is uniform or simple in the *Republic* and *Phaedrus*, Socrates is not doubting that it has several things attributed to it, but saying that anything attributed to it would be attributed to the whole soul.

Drawing together the account so far: Socrates is saying that since each form is a simple whole and has all of its features insofar as it is what it is, it is always in the same state and the same condition. This is a much more determinate characterization of the forms than we had in the previous stages.

Before turning to the next stage, we should consider the contrasting description of ordinary objects:

> What about the many beautiful things, such as people or horses or cloaks or any other things whatsoever that are of that sort? Or again, equal things, and so on for all the things that share the names of those things? Are they in the same condition, or, quite the opposite to those things, are they virtually never in any state

or in the same condition as themselves or as one another?
(78d10–e4)

Again, Socrates' claims are very difficult to decipher. He describes a group as "the many beautiful things, such as people, horses, cloaks," and so forth. These are the many ordinary objects that we call beautiful. These many beautiful things – and equal things, and so forth – are virtually (hōs epos epein) never in any state or the same condition; specifically, they are never in the same condition as themselves nor the same condition as one another.[23] By contrast, the forms are always in the same state and condition. Socrates cannot simply mean that the many beautiful things change over time, given that he says that they are virtually never – literally at no time (oudepote) – in any state or the same condition. Nor can he mean that there are simply some states that they are not in, since he says that they are virtually in no state. Why think that each beautiful person, horse, and so forth is virtually never in any state or same condition as itself? Earlier in the argument Socrates said that such things are composite (78c) and later he will say that they are multiform (80b). Let me suggest that beautiful things are each like a statue that is beautiful (as a whole) in virtue of its eyes – perhaps the eyes' color nicely complements that of the rest of the statue – but ugly (as a whole) in virtue of its arms – perhaps the arms are out of proportion with the rest of the statue. The statue is both beautiful and ugly (as a whole) at the same time, in virtue of its different parts, and so not in the same state as itself. As we will see, Socrates provides another way in which they are not in the same state as themselves in the fifth stage of his unfolding account.

Socrates draws this strong contrast between forms and ordinary objects in the affinity argument before saying anything about them being perceptible or imperceptible. It is only after this description of the "many beautiful things" that Socrates notes that they are perceptible and the forms are unseen (79a). While it is tempting to think that anything perceptible must have spatial extension and this is why perceptible objects are multiform, Socrates makes no such claim, and it is not clear that Plato in the *Phaedo* is thinking in terms of a category like "spatial extension." Nonetheless, it is now much clearer how the nature of forms differs from that of ordinary objects: (1) The form of *f*-ness, since it is uniform and itself through itself, is entirely unchanging and in the same state and the same condition. By contrast, (2) the many *f*-things are changing, multiform, and virtually at no time in the same state or condition as themselves or as one another. Yet again, we have a clear argument that forms are distinct from the ordinary objects: From (1) and (2), one can easily conclude that the form of *f*-ness is not any *f*-thing. This account, unlike that in the defense speech, provides an underlying explanation for why the forms have features that distinguish them from ordinary objects, but it does not rest on intuitively obvious claims. Instead, its claims are further clarified and explained in the following stages.

IV FOURTH STAGE: FORMS AS CAUSES

Near the end of the section known as Socrates' autobiography (95e–102a), Socrates puts forward as a hypothesis the existence of the form of the beautiful, which he says causes each beautiful thing to be beautiful, and similarly hypothesizes the existence of the other forms (100a–102a).[24] He says that to know a cause would be to know, "because of what?" (*dia ti*, 96a) and he regularly treats causes as that *by which* (causal dative) things are as they are. Hence, the form of *f*-ness, as a cause of something's being *f*, is that because of which and by which that thing is *f*. So, for example, it is because of the form of beauty that a sunset is beautiful. While Socrates may be applying the term "cause" to forms for the first time in the *Phaedo* (see also *H. Ma.* 296e–297d), there is nothing new in the idea that things are the way they are because of the forms. Neither the *Euthyphro* nor the *Meno* call forms "causes," but they both describe the form of *f*-ness as that because of which and by which something is *f* (*Euphr.* 6d–e, *Meno* 72c–e; cf. *H. Ma.* 289b–d, 294a–e, and 296e–297d). As noted in the introduction, Socrates himself emphasizes when introducing his hypothesis that what he is talking about "isn't anything new, but what I've never stopped talking about, on any other occasion or in the discussion thus far" (100b1–3). What is new here is that Socrates discusses what must be true of forms, given that they are causes.

A topic of considerable debate since Vlastos' 1969 article – particularly in the 1970s and 1980s – was whether to translate "*hē aitia*" and "*to aition*" with the traditional translation, "the cause," or instead with something like "the reason" or "the explanation." I retain here the traditional translation, although it is important to recognize that Socrates is operating with a concept for which there is no perfect English translation. A Platonic cause need not be an event, it need not be temporally prior to what it causes, nor need it have several other features some contemporary philosophers require of causes – though contemporary philosophical views of causation are also fairly different than they were in the 1960s–80s, when Vlastos' position was developed and most thoroughly discussed.[25] A Platonic cause is something that answers, "because of what?" or, more colloquially, "why?" Anything that could be taken to answer this question is a candidate cause. Thus, if we ask, "why is that large?" we can answer, "because it meets the requirements for being large" – something like, "it exceeds in height." Forms are candidate causes precisely because an answer to a "what is it?" question can function as an answer to a "why?" question.[26] Michael Frede, David Sedley, and others have emphasized that in the original legal context, as well as ordinary Greek, one of the terms typically translated "the cause" (*to aition*) is the person or thing responsible for a crime.[27]

With this background in place, let us consider one of Socrates' descriptions of the causal role of the form of the beautiful:

> I keep the following at my side, in my straightforward,
> amateurish, and perhaps simple-minded way: nothing makes it
> [some beautiful thing] beautiful other than that beautiful's presence,
> or association, or whatever its mode and means of accruing may
> be. For I don't go so far as to insist on this, but only that it is by
> the beautiful that all beautiful things are beautiful. (100d3–8)

Although forms have been discussed several times earlier in the dialogue, the autobiography is the first place where Socrates mentions this basic feature of them: that it is because of the form of f-ness that f-things are f.[28] This focus on forms' causal role helps to clarify the idea in the recollection argument that forms are superior to ordinary objects. Part of the reason for this superiority is that the form is causally prior to ordinary objects: Equal things are equal because of the form, not the other way around.[29] Moreover, turning to the affinity argument, we now have a positive characterization of the forms, which clarifies what it means to describe each as itself through itself (auto kath hauto) and uniform. They do not have different parts with different activities or functions; the only thing the form of beauty explains is why each beautiful thing is beautiful. This is the nature it does not depart from. There is no chance that the thing by which all beautiful things are beautiful will change its nature and start explaining instead why all large things are large. In sum, Socrates' characterization of the forms here helps us understand the claims made in the previous two stages. In doing so, it clarifies the characteristics that distinguish them from ordinary objects.

So far I have emphasized that in calling forms causes, Socrates is characterizing them in the same basic way that he does in the Euthyphro, Meno, and Hippias Major.[30] But the Phaedo further examines causes, which turns out to be crucial for understanding the underlying difference between forms and ordinary objects. In the Phaedo, Socrates seems committed in general to the requirement that x cannot be the cause of something if x's opposite has an equal claim to causing this same thing. He defends this when he first rejects his initial candidate causes (97a–b). He argues that neither addition nor division can be the cause of two because each has an equal claim to causing two: Sometimes we say that something is two because of addition and other times because of division. The idea seems to be that a minimal requirement on a cause is that the opposite thing cannot do an equally good job of explaining the same effect. Of course, it may be that without addition there would not have been two in some particular case, but that is compatible with addition being merely "that without which the cause could not be a cause" (99b3–4) – that is, a necessary requirement, but not the thing ultimately responsible. We must not have identified the thing genuinely responsible if the opposite thing could explain the same thing equally well. Socrates' alternative is that twoness is the cause of things being two (101c). Twoness is responsible precisely for things being two. Twoness has no opposite, but even something like halfness (the opposite of double at *Rep.* 479b) has no claim on causing things to be two. While I can divide an apple and end up with two halves, the halfness does not cause these to be two; halfness is only responsible for each being a half. People sometimes find Plato's focus on opposites archaic or simplistic. Instead, this argument at 97a–b makes clear that focusing on opposites brings out the most extreme cases, where it is especially clear that we must not have identified the thing responsible.

The important requirement for us will be an inverse requirement that Socrates also seems to accept: Nothing could be a cause if it makes an equal claim to causing one thing and its opposite. For example, a head cannot be the cause of a person's being large since it could just as well be the cause of someone's being small (101a; cf. 99a). I take this requirement to be justified by parallel reasoning: The fact that x is an equally good candidate to explain two opposite things indicates that it must not really be responsible for either of them. The head might be a necessary requirement for someone's being large, but it is no more responsible for being large than being small. By contrast, the form of largeness only explains things being large, never small.

To sum up, in the fourth stage we gain a positive account of a form's nature: Since it is what *f*-ness is, it causes all *f* things to be *f*. Moreover, this stage introduces important constraints on causation: The form of *f*-ness, as the cause of things being *f*, will never be responsible for something being un-*f*. There is no explicit contrast with ordinary objects in this stage; however, such a contrast is found in the fifth and final stage.

V FIFTH STAGE: CAUSATION AND COMPRESENCE
OF OPPOSITES

Immediately after Socrates' discussion of forms as causes, in the lead up to the final argument, he describes how an ordinary thing is both large and small at the same time (102b–103c). Socrates connects this phenomenon of being characterized by opposites – typically called "the compresence of opposites" – to not being a cause. I argue in this section and the next that the fundamental explanation for why forms are different from ordinary objects is that forms are causes whereas ordinary objects cannot be.

The passage comes after Socrates has presented his method of hypothesis and used it to hypothesize that forms exist. It begins with Phaedo, the narrator of the dialogue, speaking in his own voice:

> When these points of his [Socrates] were accepted and it was agreed that each of the forms exists and that other things receive a share of and are named after the forms themselves, I think that he next asked: "So if that's what you are saying, whenever you say that Simmias is larger than Socrates but smaller than Phaedo, aren't you saying that at that time both of these, both largeness and smallness, are in Simmias?"
>
> "Yes, I am."
>
> "However," he said, "do you agree that 'Simmias exceeds Socrates' does not express in words as it in fact truly is? For presumably it isn't in Simmias' nature to exceed by this, by being Simmias, but rather by the largeness that he happens to have. And do you agree that, again, he does not exceed Socrates because Socrates is Socrates, but because Socrates has smallness relative to his largeness?"
>
> "True."
>
> "Right, and again that he is not exceeded by Phaedo because Phaedo is Phaedo, but because Phaedo has largeness relative to Simmias' smallness."
>
> "That's so."

"In that case, this is how Simmias is named both small and large, by being in between the pair of them, offering his smallness to Phaedo's largeness to be exceeded, but providing to Socrates his largeness, which exceeds Socrates' smallness." (102a11–d2)

Socrates provides here a concrete example of how an ordinary thing can be rightly called both large and small at the same time. This example does not have to do with change over time (e.g., *Cratylus* 439d–440d)[31] or being *kata* (perhaps "through" or "according to") different things in the same object (*Republic* 436d–e). Instead, this case of the compresence of opposites arises because of how ordinary objects are in relation to (*pros*) one another (*H. Ma.* 289b–d, *Tht.* 154c).[32]

In order to think through this example, we should consider Socrates' introduction here of "the largeness in Simmias," which he later discusses alongside "largeness itself" (102d6). This is a particularly fraught topic, since Aristotle criticizes Plato for thinking that there is a type of largeness that does not exist "in" anything. Again, it is important to approach the *Phaedo*'s account on its own terms, not through Aristotle's lens. At this stage in the dialogue, Simmias and Cebes have agreed to the existence of forms many times, and Socrates has defended this claim with his method of hypothesis in the autobiographical section. Phaedo begins the above quotation by saying (in the outer frame of the dialogue) that Socrates and the others agreed that there are forms themselves and that other things receive a share of them. Socrates then says that "if you say these things" (102b3–4), then when you say that Simmias is larger than Socrates, you are saying that there is a largeness in Simmias. Thus, Socrates thinks that if you are committed to (a) there being the form of largeness and (b) something having a share of this form, then you are committed to (c) there being largeness in this thing. Nonetheless, he treats largeness itself as distinct from largeness in something.[33] Socrates is emphatic in the affinity argument that the forms themselves are completely unchanging and indestructible (e.g.,

78d, 80b). By contrast, the forms in things – which I will call "imma-nent forms" – either retreat or perish when their opposite approaches (102d–e). The heat in me perishes when I become cold; by contrast, heat itself will never perish or change in any way. Hence, heat itself must be distinct from immanent heat.[34]

I suggest that we understand this as follows. Largeness itself is what Socrates is looking for when he asks, "what is largeness?" It does not change over time, nor is it destructible, since there is always something that it is to be large and this stays the same. In addition, when something has a share of largeness, there is something about it – something "in it" – that makes it appropriate to call it "large" in certain situations. It is tricky to identify what this largeness is that is in Simmias. Suppose that Simmias is six feet tall and Socrates five feet tall. We do not want to say that the largeness in Simmias is his being six feet tall, because six feet tall can also be small, whereas Socrates says that the largeness in Simmias is never willing to be small (102d–e). We might then be tempted to identify the largeness in Simmias as his having a greater height than Socrates. But it is strange to think of this relation to Socrates as "in Simmias," and Simmias would then need a different largeness in him for each person and thing that he is larger than. However, Socrates only speaks of Simmias having a single smallness in him and a single largeness in him (102c–d). There is thus much to be said for Sedley's suggestion that we draw on the discussion of largeness in the *Parmenides* (150c–e) (cf. *Hippias Major* 294a8–b4, *Laches* 192a–b).[35] The proposal is that the largeness in Simmias is his power to exceed. Simmias exercises this power only when he exceeds someone, never when he is exceeded. Being six feet tall gives Simmias' power its specific charac-ter, explaining why it is exercised at some times but not at others.

Simmias only has a share of largeness when his immanent largeness is appropriately related to someone (or something) else's immanent smallness. Whereas a thing is only large in relation to something else, Socrates treats heat and cold, odd and even, and living and dead as non-relational features. These non-relational features are simpler: If something has heat in it, it will have a share of the form of heat. Hence, we can think of immanent heat as the manifestation of having a share of the form of heat. I say this to offer a way to think of immanent forms. But for purposes of this chapter, the crucial point is that Socrates thinks that a commitment to the forms themselves and to things that have a share in these forms brings with it a commitment to immanent forms.

Now that we are clearer about the immanent forms, let us return to the above passage. Socrates emphasizes that it is not in the nature of something like Simmias or Phaedo to be that *by which* things are large or small. Neither Simmias nor Phaedo is the cause of their being large or small. Rather, it is by the largeness Simmias happens to have that he exceeds. Why is it not in Simmias' nature to exceed? Socrates says that instead Simmias just "happens" to be large. He could have been smaller. If someone put Simmias himself forward as a cause of his being large, one could object that he could have been a cause of being small, and so, by the same reasoning about opposites that Socrates used earlier, he should not be identified as the cause of either being large or small. If one wants what is really responsible for Simmias' being large, it is his largeness. This is responsible only for his being large, with no claim on making anything small.

After Socrates provides his account of how Simmias is both large and small, he further clarifies the difference between Simmias, on the one hand, and the largeness in him and largeness itself, on the other (102d–103a). This is the last place in the dialogue where Socrates contrasts a form with an ordinary thing. He says that he is able to admit both opposites, largeness or smallness, whereas the largeness and smallness in him and largeness and smallness themselves are not able to admit (*dechetai*) such opposites (102e–103a). Whether Socrates is large or small in relation to something is determined by which form he happens to have admitted. Socrates already said in the affinity argument that the forms do not admit (*endechetai*) of any difference (78d). This is one of the fundamental features of ordinary objects that distinguishes them from forms: Ordinary objects admit opposites, whereas forms do not. Even if some ordinary object managed not to be characterized by some opposite – even if it were somehow entirely smooth, in no ways rough – its nature would admit of both. It would not be responsible for its being smooth; it would just happen to be that way. But forms, as causes, are precisely what are responsible for things being the way they are, and so cannot be receptive of opposites.[36] Reflecting on ordinary objects' receptivity to opposites helps clarify why forms must not have such receptivity, but rather always are the same way by virtue of their own nature.

VI BRINGERS

After discussing how Simmias is both large and small, in preparation for the final argument, Socrates describes a group of things that include fire, snow, three, and soul (103c–105e). He does not give a name to these, but I call them "bringers," since one of their key characteristics is that they always bring a member of a pair of opposites to whatever they occupy. (I will henceforth refer to a member of a pair of opposites simply as "an opposite.") Some bringers are ordinary, perceptible objects, such as fire and snow, and some not, such as three and soul. Each is unable to admit some specific opposite: cold, heat, even, or death. While bringers that are ordinary objects admit many opposites – large and small, beautiful and ugly, etc. – each does not admit some specific opposite, and so they do not face the same obstacle that other ordinary objects face to being a cause. In fact, bringers are generally taken to be causes – called "sophisticated causes" by Vlastos.[37] If that were correct, then the account of this chapter could not be correct: Socrates' ultimate explanation for forms not being ordinary objects could not be that forms are causes and ordinary objects cannot be. If fire were a sophisticated cause, then at least some ordinary things would be causes. As the last step in my argument, I will argue that the bringers are not causes for Socrates and he has good reasons to not make them causes. This will further clarify Socrates' account of why forms are not ordinary objects.

Socrates gives a complicated description of the bringers; it is important to consider carefully the different claims he makes about them. After distinguishing fire from the hot and snow from the cold, he notes that fire does not admit cold, nor snow hot; if hot approaches snow, snow flees or is destroyed, just like the cold in us (103c–d). Next, he says that bringers always are characterized by one member of a pair of opposites and they do not admit the other member of the pair: fire is always hot, and does not admit the cold, and snow always cold, and does not admit the hot (103e–104b). Then, Socrates notes that the bringers have in them the opposite that always characterizes them (104b–c). He refers to this opposite several times as a form;[38] the bringers have in them the immanent forms that Socrates introduced immediately before introducing the bringers. Fire has the form of heat in it and snow the form of cold in it. Next, Socrates says that they bring this opposite that is in them to whatever they occupy: Whatever fire occupies will be hot, and whatever three occupies will be odd (104d). Sometimes, Socrates is reported as saying that fire is "essentially hot" or the soul "essentially alive."[39] But he never uses such language and instead emphasizes that fire always has the form of heat in it and brings this to whatever it occupies.

In Socrates' account of forms as causes, he repeatedly indicates that anything caused by a form is not caused by anything else; for example, he says that "what is smaller is smaller because of nothing other than smallness" (101a4–5). When making these claims, he emphasizes that doing so means not identifying other things as causes (100c–d, 100e–101a, 101c).[40] He never takes back these claims and he refers back to his hypotheses of forms after his discussion of bringers (107b). We might have expected that any ordinary object that moves, alters, or changes another thing must be a cause. But since Socrates says that nothing other than the form is a cause, these ordinary objects that change another thing must not be causes. If only forms are causes, then bringers are not causes. This explains why he never describes bringers as causes, nor does he use causal language to describe what they do. He never says that they "make" (poiein) things some way, nor says that things are some way "because of" them, or "by" them. Instead, he says that the bringers bring with them the form of an opposite, which is in them: Fire has heat in it; snow has cold in it; and they bring heat and cold to other things. There is a very tricky grammatical construction at the end of Socrates' discussion of bringers, which is often translated as if it were a causal dative. However, no commentator has defended reading it as a causal dative, and Denyer and Bailey have both argued that it is not one.[41] I agree with them, although for my purposes it is only necessary that it need not be a causal dative and that the broader context suggests that it is not one. On my reading of the tricky construction, Socrates says that both "fire" and "heat" could be used to answer the question, "What is such that, anything in which it arises, in the body, will be hot?" (105b8–9).[42] He is not saying that it is *because* of fire that this thing is hot. He is saying that fire is a sufficient condition for something to be hot. Bringers bring an opposite with them, but they are not the cause of things having this opposite.

Given that Socrates never says that bringers do this causal work and given that he never takes back his claim that anything explained by a form is not explained by anything else, we should conclude that he does not think of bringers as causes. But why not? According to his method of hypothesis, he should put forward whatever theory seems strongest and count as true about cause and everything else that seems to harmonize with that theory (100a). He thinks that it harmonizes with his theory that things are beautiful because of *nothing other than* beauty. Identifying bringers as causes would be a different theory from the one he has adopted and defended.

We can see why this theory appeals to Socrates, both intuitively and theoretically. Intuitively, bringers are not what is truly responsible. Those are the forms – either the forms in us, or the forms themselves. Instead of themselves being responsible, bringers bring what's responsible: the forms that are in them. A bringer is like the accomplice who brought the killer to the scene, rather than the murderer himself – the one genuinely responsible. If one wants what is "proximate" to the effect, that is the heat that is in the bringer. If one wants the cause described in full generality, that is the form of heat itself. Neither is the bringer.

Furthermore, ordinary objects are characterized by countless features that are entirely irrelevant to anything they might putatively cause. Fire is large and small, beautiful and ugly, loud and quiet, and so on. The relevant feature that fire possesses, heat, is what is responsible for something's being hot, rather than fire as such. The form of heat, being uniform, is exactly what is responsible for a thing's being hot, whereas any ordinary object (whether a bringer or not), being multiform, will have many parts that are in no way responsible for being f. This, then, clarifies why Socrates thinks that the forms are uniform. If the forms had a part that were irrelevant to their being the cause of f, the relevant part of the form would have a better claim on being the cause. Since what it is to be a form is to be a cause, they have no such irrelevant parts.

VII CONCLUSION

Plato's historical context is very different from our own. He seems to have been the first philosopher to discuss, in general, how to think of things like "largeness" and "justice," as well as how to think about a contrasting class of ordinary objects. So we should not be surprised if his way of distinguishing these groups from each other is very different from our own. In the *Phaedo*, Socrates does not stop at the idea that forms simply do not seem like the kind of thing that we can perceive, nor is he driven by puzzles about how an unlimited number of large things could have a share of the same thing, largeness. Those sorts of puzzles are very important to Aristotle, and Plato discusses them briefly in the *Euthydemus* (300e–301a) and at more length in the *Parmenides* (130e–134e).[43] But he does not present them as reasons for thinking that the forms are distinct from ordinary objects; instead, they are puzzles once one views them as distinct. Socrates also does not distinguish forms from ordinary objects by some process of abstracting one feature common to many ordinary objects, nor does he say that forms are not bodies or not material. Instead, Plato's approach in the *Phaedo* is for Socrates to argue that, independently of what the correct answer is to any "what is *f*-ness?" question, we know the sort of causal work the form of *f*-ness must do. It must be because of it that all *f*-things are *f*. A minimal requirement on causing something to be *f* is not making as good a claim on causing the opposite, un-*f*. But ordinary objects are receptive to opposites, and so make equally good claims on causing *f* and un-*f*. Hence, ordinary objects are not the sort of things that could be causes, and so not the sort that could be forms. The form of *f*-ness must not be receptive of opposites and must not have parts, but rather be simple, so that it as a whole – rather than some part of it – explains why *f*-things are *f*. It must do so for all time and so be eternal. In sum, in order to meet the basic requirements for being a form, it must be uniform and eternally have all of its characteristics through its own nature. This makes forms fundamentally different from ordinary objects.

NOTES

1 See Brandwood (this volume, ch. 3) for reasons to think the *Republic* was in a second chronological group, after the *Phaedo* and before the late dialogues.

2 The word "body" is generally used to refer to living or once-living bodies in the *Phaedo* (except once, at 86a) – just as it is in all texts before Plato. By the *Sophist*, a late dialogue, "body" can refer to anything tangible (246a–b). I have learned much about Plato's development of the notion of body from Betegh (unpublished).

3 Translations from Sedley and Long 2010, occasionally modified. Text is Duke et al. 1995. Ordinary objects "share a name" with the forms because in Greek one can refer to either beauty or an individual beautiful thing as "*to kalon*" ("the beautiful").

4 Examples of the first group include Burnet 1911, Gallop 1975, Scott 1995, Sedley 2007c. Examples of the second group include White 1992, Irwin 1999, Kelsey 2000, Dimas 2003, and Tuozzo 2018.

5 Irwin (1999) takes the approach closest to mine, though our accounts differ in a number of significant ways. I argue in Ebrey (2023) that this unfolding structure also applies to the *Phaedo*'s ethics and account of the soul. In this book, I also consider each of these discussions of forms in more detail, situating each within its broader context in the dialogue.

6 Three possibilities, compatible with one another, are: (1) that the Socratic dialogues were written before the *Phaedo* and other so-called "middle period" dialogues, and reflect an earlier stage in Plato's thinking; (2) that Plato intended the Socratic dialogues to be read before the Platonic dialogues, and hence the differences reflect a pedagogical structure; and (3) that Plato has Socrates express different views in different dialogues because Socrates is speaking to different interlocutors on different topics, leading him to approach issues in different ways. Regarding (3), note that the *Phaedo* is a conversation between Socrates and his closest companions on the last day of his life, so he may be making "new" claims about the forms not only because they are relevant for his arguments (which they are not in many other dialogues), but also because he thinks his close companions will be able to understand these claims, whereas other interlocutors might not. For a further discussion of these broad interpretive possibilities, see the introduction to this volume.

7 One could accept most of what I say in this chapter and think that Socrates begins by assuming the existence of Platonic forms, but that over the course of the dialogue he explains this assumption by explaining why and how forms are distinct from ordinary objects.

8 This is a common view. See, e.g., Irwin 1999, Kelsey 2000, Dancy 2004. Aristotle refers to what I am calling "ordinary things" as "perceptible things," which Socrates does not in the *Phaedo*. As I discuss below, in the affinity argument Socrates identifies a group as "the visible," but only does so after contrasting members of this group with the forms in ways that have nothing to do with visibility.

9 In most of the relevant passages, Aristotle attributes views to Plato without explicitly referring to any of Plato's dialogues. Perhaps Aristotle is correctly reporting views that Plato presented in his Academy. I am simply claiming that his claims can be misleading when used to interpret the dialogues, in particular the *Phaedo*.

10 He uses the term "separation" in the *Parmenides* (first at 129d), though it is unclear whether he means by it what Aristotle means. See, e.g., Fine 1984, Meinwald 2016: 301–6.

11 Socrates asks Simmias in the above passage whether he agrees that there are such things as a just itself and a beautiful itself and so on. In the so-called "Socratic" and "transitional" dialogues, Socrates similarly asks his interlocutors to agree that there are forms. For example, he asks whether Euthyphro thinks that there is such a thing as the form of unholiness (*Euphr.* 5c–d) and whether Protagoras agrees that there is such a thing as justice and holiness (*Prt.* 330c–d; cf., *Meno* 72a–73c, *H. Ma.* 287c–d). In the same way, Socrates repeatedly asks his interlocutors in the *Phaedo* whether they agree that there are forms (65d, 74a–b, 100b–c) or notes that his arguments rely on their earlier acceptance (76d–e, 78c–d, 107b; cf. 92d–e). While it is natural to assume that there are the things that we are searching for when we ask a "what is it?" question, Socrates does not think it is an innocuous assumption. For one way that the assumption could be denied, see *Meno* 71d–73a.

12 By contrast, Dancy (2004: 250) suggests that Socrates is implicitly making an explanatory argument here.

13 For a similar idea, see Irwin 1999: 144. For a broad defense of the idea that Socrates in the *Phaedo* is starting with intuitive claims, see Dimas 2003, esp. 179–81.

14 See Tuozzo 2018 for a recent extensive bibliography. Further secondary literature on the recollection argument and other parts of the *Phaedo* are in Ebrey 2017a, an annotated bibliography on the dialogue.

15 This is true of most of the so-called "epistemological readings," such as Sedley 2007c. For a list of such readings, see Tuozzo 2018: 5 n. 13.

16 This is the view of a diverse group of interpreters, which includes, for example, Nehamas 1975a and Kelsey 2000. For a partial (but lengthy) list, see Tuozzo 2018: 5 n. 13.

17 Apolloni 1996 is a rare article devoted to it. Mann (2000) and Ademollo (2018) have significant discussions of it.

18 Cf. *Rep.* 454c9 for "ἀλλοίωσις" meaning difference, not alteration. Even at a given time the forms do not admit difference in way or manner.

19 It is a difficult question what it means for the forms "to be in the same condition" (*echein kata tauta*). I argue in Ebrey (forthcoming) that this

standard translation does not capture its meaning, but there is not space to address this here.

20 For the translation of this participial phrase as explanatory, see Mann 2000: 107–8 n. 50.

21 The phrase "*auto kath hauto*" is first applied to the forms at 66a. For a discussion of its role in the ethics of the *Phaedo*, see Ebrey 2017b. For a discussion of "*kath auto*" in the *Sophist*, see Frede's contribution to this volume (ch. 14). My translation "itself through itself" is meant to capture two ideas. First, *auto kath hauto* is frequently connected to purity: there is nothing else through(out) it; it is simply itself through(out) itself. Second, if something is *auto kath hauto*, it is the way that it is on the basis of its own nature, and so is itself through (i.e., on the basis of) itself.

22 Mann (2000) says it is "natural" (81) to suppose the form of x is uniform just in case the form of x is *only* x, having no other features. But Socrates includes "uniform" in a list of several other features that all the forms have: unseen, immortal, indestructible, always in the same state, etc. (80b). My account allows the forms to have several features, so long as these features apply to it as a whole, not some part of it.

23 Ademollo (2018: 38–40) argues persuasively that not being in the same state is what "virtually" is meant to soften.

24 In Ebrey (forthcoming), I argue that Socrates in the *Phaedo* distinguishes between two expressions translated "the cause" here: *hē aitia* and *to aition*. Strictly speaking, the form is *to aition* and *hē aitia* is: having a share of the form. For simplicity, I ignore this distinction here.

25 Vlastos 1969 – picked up, for example, by Gallop 1975, Frede 1980, and Bostock 1986. Deep disagreements in the contemporary debate about causation are made clear in Schaffer 2016.

26 One reason not to call these "reasons" is that this often suggests something psychological, but Platonic causes are not, in general, psychological. Similarly, "explanation" suggests a linguistic utterance of some sort, whereas candidate causes for Plato are often things or processes picked out with nouns, such as "a head" or "division" or "the large itself" or "intelligence." Nonetheless, we do sometimes say in English, for example, that the air in the radiator explains the loud noise you are hearing – and in this sense a cause explains something.

27 Frede (1980) thinks we should not call them "causes" in Plato, whereas Sedley (1998) thinks we should.

28 One important difference between (i) the *Phaedo* and (ii) the *Euthyphro* and *Meno* is that in the latter dialogues Socrates says that, for example, the holy things have (*echein*) the form of holiness in them (*Euphr.* 5d and *Meno* 72c–73a). He also never suggests that they might be at the same time unholy. In the *Phaedo* Socrates does not commit himself to what the relation is between forms and ordinary objects, but he says that they have a share of (*met-echein*) the forms. This change in terminology may, at least in part, be because he maintains in the *Phaedo* that ordinary *f* things are both *f* and un-*f*.

29 Another part of their superiority is likely related to the so-called "compresence" of opposites that the ordinary objects have. The form of *f*-ness is entirely what it is and in no way its opposite, unlike ordinary objects.

30 Note that in later dialogues, such as the *Philebus* (26e–27b) and *Timaeus* (28a–29a), Socrates does not identify forms as causes; he simply identifies there the maker or craftsman as the cause. This chapter only aims to explain Socrates' account in the *Phaedo*.

31 Depending on which manuscript reading one takes of the key sentence about equal sticks in the recollection argument, it may have to do with change over time. See Verdenius 1958, Dixsaut 1991, Ebert 2004, and Sedley 2007c.

32 These correspond to the three different ways in which something can undergo opposites, according to the principle of non-opposition in the *Republic*: "the same thing will not be willing to do or undergo opposites through (*kata*) the same thing, at least in relation to (*pros*) the same thing and at the same time" (436b8–9). In Ebrey (forthcoming), I argue that in the recollection argument Socrates says that ordinary objects, unlike forms, undergo opposites at different times, and that in the affinity argument he says that ordinary objects, unlike forms, undergo opposites through (*kata*) different things. Here he says that they undergo opposites in relation to (*pros*) different things. And so, over the course of the dialogue, he attributes all three types of compresence of opposites to ordinary objects and denies that each type applies to the forms.

33 Fine (1986) argues that in the *Phaedo* largeness itself could be the same as the largeness in Simmias. If so, this could simplify my interpretation; however, in my view, Devereux (1994) provides decisive arguments against Fine, which I briefly summarize here.

34 At 106b–c Socrates explicitly says that odd perishes when the even comes into three. Moreover, 106a very strongly suggests that the hot and the cold in things are perishable.

35 Sedley 2018: 211.

36 It might seem possible that forms could admit some opposites, if these are irrelevant to what they cause. I explain why Socrates does not allow this at the end of the next section. On a separate note, Aristotle says in *Categories* 5 that it is most characteristic of substance/being (*ousia*) that it is receptive of opposites (4a10–4b19), using the same term for receptive (*dechetai*) used in the *Phaedo*. As we saw, the beings (*ousiai*) for Plato are the forms. Hence, precisely the feature of ordinary objects that disqualifies them as forms, and hence beings, for Plato is the feature that Aristotle says is most characteristic of beings.

37 Vlastos 1969.

38 Using the term "*idea*" (rather than "*eidos*"), which seems to be his term in the *Phaedo* for the immanent forms (so Devereux 1994: 71 n. 16). See for example 104b9, 104d2, 104d9.

39 E.g., O'Brien 1967 and 1968, Frede 1978, Sedley 1998.

40 For a further discussion of Socrates' commitment to there being just one cause, see Ebrey 2014a.

41 So Denyer 2007: 91–3, and Bailey 2014: 24–6. See next note.

42 The Greekless reader will probably want to skip this note. Here are the first two occurrences of the construction, with a slightly more literal translation:

εἰ γὰρ ἔροιό με ᾧ ἂν τί ἐν τῷ σώματι ἐγγένηται θερμὸν ἔσται, οὐ τὴν ἀσφαλῆ σοι ἐρῶ ἀπόκρισιν ἐκείνην τὴν ἀμαθῆ, ὅτι ᾧ ἂν θερμότης, ἀλλὰ κομψοτέραν ἐκ τῶν νῦν, ὅτι ᾧ ἂν πῦρ· οὐδὲ ἂν ἔρῃ ᾧ ἂν σώματι τί ἐγγένηται νοσήσει, οὐκ ἐρῶ ὅτι ᾧ ἂν νόσος, ἀλλ' ᾧ ἂν πυρετός· (105b8–c4)

For if you should ask me, what is such that, whatever it arises in, in the body, this thing will be hot, I will not give you that safe, ignorant answer, that it is heat, but rather a more ingenious one, based on what we now said, that it is fire. And if asked what is such that, whatever body it arises in, this body will be ill, I will not say that it is illness, but fever.

The interrogative (τί) is embedded within the relative cause (ᾧ ... ἐγγένηται). This construction cannot be translated directly into English, hence the "what is such that" at the beginning of the translation of each question. My translation takes the dative relative ᾧ to be governed by ἐγγένηται; its antecedent is the omitted subject of ἔσται. The ἐν τῷ in Socrates' initial question makes for a somewhat strange question and so Stephanus omits it, but there is no need to do so: Socrates is asking about something (fire) that arises in something else (e.g., the blood, or the brain), which in turn is in the body (so Burnet 1911 and Rowe 1993).

O'Brien (1967) translates it similarly and offers a reasonable explanation for what it means (223–4); and Gallop (1975: 237) in a note (n. 75) also gives a similar "literal translation" (cf. also 204) as does Rowe (1993). But most translations (including Gallop's) read as if Socrates is saying that fire is that *by which* something is hot (for a list of such translations, see Denyer 2007: 93–4 n. 6). However, the Greek cannot literally mean this (so also Denyer 2007 and Bailey 2014). To think through how such a reading would need to work, note that there would be an omitted τούτῳ in the clause θερμὸν ἔσται, which refers back to the relative ᾧ. Such readings could take the ᾧ to be attracted to the dative, but need not. Next, note that "fire" is the answer to the question "what?" (τί;). Since the interrogative pronoun (τί) is in the same clause as the relative ᾧ, they must refer to different things. Hence, even if this sentence somehow were mentioning something "by which the body will be hot" (τούτῳ θερμὸν ἔσται), whatever this is would not be fire, since fire is the referent of τί and this other thing would be the referent of ᾧ. For example, if we take τί as the subject of the ἐγγένηται and ᾧ as its object, ᾧ would be whatever fire arises in. But that does not identify fire as that by which something is hot, but rather whatever fire arises in would be that by which something is hot. If we took the ᾧ to be a causal dative within the relative clause, then whatever causes fire to arise in the body, by this same thing the body would be hot. Again, this does not identify fire as that by which the body is hot.

43 For a discussion of one of these puzzles, see Meinwald's contribution to this volume (ch. 13).

10 The Defense of Justice in Plato's *Republic*

Richard Kraut

In this chapter I will try to identify and explain the fundamental argument of Plato's *Republic* for the astonishing thesis that justice is so great a good that anyone who fully possesses it is better off – even in the midst of severe misfortune – than a consummately unjust person who enjoys the social rewards usually received by the just.[1] Plato's attempt to defend this remarkable claim is of course the unifying thread of the dialogue, but his argument ranges so widely over diverse topics that it is difficult to see how it all fits together, and anyone who attempts to state his argument must take a stand on interpretive issues about which there is considerable scholarly controversy.[2] The dialogue's difficulty is increased by Plato's failure to give any explicit justification for the complex moral equation he boldly announces: Justice discounted by pain and dishonor is more advantageous than injustice supplemented by the rewards of justice (580b–c with 367b–e). Even if he manages to show that justice is the greatest single good, we are still left wondering whether its value is high enough to make this equation come out right. My main thesis is that the theory of Forms plays a crucial role in Plato's argument for that equation, but that the precise way in which that theory contributes to his defense of justice is difficult to recognize. It is hard to overcome a certain blindness we have to one of Plato's principal theses – a blindness we can find in one of Aristotle's criticisms of Plato's conception of the good. My goal is not to show that Plato's theory is defensible against all objections, once we correct for the

I am grateful to audiences at Clark University, Johns Hopkins University, Northwestern University, the University of Michigan, and Wayne State University for their comments on earlier drafts of this essay. In addition, I profited from the criticism of Christopher Bobonich, Sarah Broadie, Shelly Kagan, Ian Mueller, Constance Meinwald, and David Reeve. I am grateful to David Ebrey for his contributions to the present revised version.

mistake Aristotle makes. But I do think that there is something powerful in Plato's argument, and by criticizing Aristotle I hope to bring this feature to light.

I PLATO'S FUNDAMENTAL ARGUMENT FOR JUSTICE

I said that I will focus on Plato's "fundamental" argument that justice is in one's interest, but it might be wondered why any one argument should be singled out in this way and given special attention. For on the surface, the *Republic* seems to present four independent attempts to support the conclusion that justice pays apart from its consequences.[3] First, at the end of Book IV, we learn that justice is a certain harmonious arrangement of the parts of the soul. It is therefore related to the soul as health is related to the body, and since life is not worth living if one's health is ruined, it is all the more important to maintain the justice of one's soul (444c–445c). Second, in Book IX, Plato compares the five types of people he has been portraying in the middle books – the philosophical ruler, the timocrat, the oligarch, the democrat, and the tyrant – and declares that the happiest of them is the philosopher, since he exercises kingly rule over himself (580a–c). Third, Book IX immediately proceeds to argue that the philosophical life has more pleasure than any other, since the philosopher is in the best position to compare the various pleasures available to different types of people and prefers philosophical pleasures to all others (580c–583a). And fourth, the pleasures of the philosophical life are shown to be more real and therefore greater than the pleasures of any other sort of life (583b–588a).

Does Plato single out any one of these arguments as more fundamental than the others? It might be thought that his fourth argument – the second of the two that concern pleasure – is the one he thought most important, for he introduces it with the remark that "this will be the greatest and supreme fall [of injustice]" (*megiston te kai kuriōtaton tōn ptōmatōn*, 583b6–7). This could be taken to mean that pleasure is the most important good in terms of which to make the decision between justice and injustice, and that the argument to come is the one that most fully reveals why justice is to be chosen over its opposite. But I think that such a reading would give this argument far more significance than it deserves, and that Plato's words can and should be given a different interpretation. As I read the *Republic*, its fundamental argument in defense of justice is the one that comes to a close in Book IX *before* anything is said about how the just and unjust lives compare in terms of pleasure. This is the argument that Plato develops at greatest length, and if it is correct it makes a decisive case in favor of the just life. It shows precisely what it is about justice that makes it so worthwhile. By contrast, the two arguments that connect justice and pleasure are merely meant to assure us that we do not have to sacrifice the latter good in order to get the former. They add to the attractiveness of the just life, but they are not by themselves sufficient to show that justice is to be chosen over injustice, as is the lengthier argument that precedes them.

Why should we read the *Republic* in this way, despite Plato's statement that "the greatest and supreme fall" of injustice comes with his final argument? The answer lies in the way he poses, in Book II, the fundamental question to which the rest of the dialogue is an answer. The thesis he there undertakes to prove is phrased in various ways: It is better (*ameinon*) to be just than unjust (357b1); justice must be welcomed for itself if one is to be blessed (*makarios*, 358a3); the common opinion that injustice is more profitable (*lusitelein*) must be refuted (360c8); we must decide whether the just man is happier (*eudaimonesteros*) than the unjust (361d3);[4] justice by itself benefits (*oninanai*) someone who possesses it whereas injustice harms (*blaptein*) him (367d3–4); we must determine the advantages (*opheliai*) of justice and injustice (368c6). Plato does not give any one of these phrases a special role to play in his argument, but moves back and forth freely among them. And he surely must be assuming that once the consummately just life has been shown to be more advantageous than the consummately unjust life, even in the midst of misfortune, then he has given decisive reason for choosing the former over the latter.

Notice, however, that Plato never promises, in Book II, to show that justice provides greater pleasures than does injustice, and never even hints that he would have to defend this thesis in order to show that we should choose the just life. This suggests that the question whether the just or the unjust life has more pleasure will still be an open one, even after the greater advantages of the just life have been demonstrated. And of course, this suggestion is confirmed in Book IX: Having shown that the just person is happiest, Plato thinks it requires further argument to show that the just person also has the greatest pleasure. So, in order to accomplish the task Plato assigns himself in the *Republic* it is both necessary and sufficient that he show why justice is so much more advantageous than injustice. But he never says or implies that if he can show that justice brings greater pleasures, then that by itself will be a sufficient or a necessary defense of justice. By supporting justice in terms of pleasure, Plato is showing that there is even more reason to lead the just life than we may have supposed. But the fundamental case for justice has been made before the discussion of pleasure has begun.[5]

What then should we make of his statement that the "greatest and supreme fall" for injustice occurs in the battle over pleasure? We might read this proleptically – an anticipation of the claim made at the end of passage, where the philosopher's pleasure is said to be 729 times greater than the tyrant's (587e).[6] In no other argument had Plato tried to portray the gap between justice and injustice as so great. But perhaps a better interpretation is this: Plato does not mean that, of the three arguments *considered separately*, this last one, adverting to the illusory nature of the tyrant's pleasures, gives us the single weightiest reason to choose justice over injustice. Rather, the point is that with the other two arguments in place, adding this third one (not the third one on its own) shows that there is *every* reason to be just and *none* to be unjust. We might have assumed that pleasure is one point in favor of injustice, but now we see that there is *nothing* to be said for injustice, and *everything* for justice.

II   JUSTICE AND THE PHILOSOPHER-KING

I will therefore set aside the two hedonic arguments Plato gives in Book IX and concentrate entirely on the single complex defense of justice that precedes them. But it might be thought that this material contains two separate arguments, for by the end of Book IV Plato already seems to have come to the conclusion that since justice is a harmony of the soul comparable to physical health, it is far superior to injustice.[7] We might therefore suppose that after Book IV Plato launches on a second and independent defense of justice, one that concludes in Book IX with the pronouncement that the most just and "kingly" life is happiest. But Plato himself makes it clear that these two segments – Books II–IV on the one hand, Books V–IX on the other – cannot be isolated from each other in this way. For at the beginning of Book VIII we are told that the victorious pronouncement of Book IV – that the best person and city had been found – was premature (543c7–544b3). This means that the argument of Book IV is not complete after all, but is in some way strengthened by additional material presented somewhere between Books V and IX. For by admitting that Book IV did not yet discover who the best person is, Plato indicates that he had not at that point presented a full enough picture of the just life.[8] It would therefore be a mistake to examine the argument of Books II–IV in isolation from later material as though they were meant to provide a complete defense of justice.

Nonetheless, Plato clearly thinks that he has given at least a partial defense of justice by the end of Book IV; the fact that he goes on to strengthen the argument by giving a fuller picture of the just life does not mean that by the end of Book IV we have no reason at all to think that justice is superior to injustice. To understand the single argument that runs from Book II through Book IX, we must see why Plato arrives at a preliminary conclusion in Book IV and how the additional material that comes in later books strengthens that argument.[9]

To make progress on this interpretive question, let us begin with an observation with which all scholars would agree: One of the fundamental ideas that Plato puts forward in his defense of justice is that we should look for a *general* theory of goodness. His proposal is that when we say of a human body, or a human soul, or a political community, that they are in good condition, there is some common feature that we are referring to, and it is because they share this common feature that they are properly called good.[10] He expects his audience to agree with him that the goodness of a body – health – consists in the control certain parts naturally have over others; and he appeals to this point to support his claim that one's soul is in good condition if it too exhibits a certain order among its components (444c–e).[11] But the analogy between health and psychic well-being is by itself only of limited value, because it does not tell us anything about what sort of order we should try to achieve in the soul. What Plato needs, if he is to give a stronger argument from analogy, is a structure that has the same kind of components and can exhibit the same kind of balance as the soul. He thinks he can accomplish this by examining the question of what the best possible city is, for he believes he can show that the tripartite structure of the best political community corresponds to the structure of the human soul.[12] If he can convince us that these correspondences do exist, and if he can get us to agree that the city he describes is ideal, then he has some basis for reaching the conclusion that the ideal type of person is someone whose soul exhibits the same kind of order that is possessed by an ideal political community.[13]

But in Book IV Plato has not yet given us all of his arguments for taking the political community he is describing as ideal. For one of his main reasons for favoring the kind of city described in the *Republic* is that it alone is governed by individuals who have the wisdom needed to rule well; and that kind of political expertise is only presented in Books VI–VII. This is one reason for saying that the argument from analogy presented at the end of Book IV is incomplete. Furthermore, Plato has not yet said in Books II–IV everything he wants to say about the kind of order that should be established in the soul. He tells us that reason should rule and look after the well-being of the rest of the soul, that spirit should be its ally, and that the appetites should be kept in check (441e–442a). But how should reason be trained, if it is to rule the soul well? What would it be for spirit to rule instead? Or for the appetites to grow too large? Of course, Plato has already given some content to these notions, for he has been describing the proper education of these elements of the soul since the end of Book II, and this gives us some sense of how they should be related to each other. But that education has not yet been fully described; the most important objects of study have still to be presented. When we find out more about what reason must occupy itself with, we will have a fuller idea of what its rule involves.[14]

III   THE PHILOSOPHICAL LIFE

We must now turn to Books V through VII to see how Plato's depiction of the philosophical life contributes to the argument that justice pays. We want to know what it is about the philosophical life that makes it so much more worthwhile than any other; and we must understand how this new material is connected to the argument from analogy that comes to a preliminary conclusion at the end of Book IV.

An answer to these questions must in some way or other appeal to Plato's belief in Forms – those eternal, changeless, imperceptible, and bodiless objects the understanding of which is the goal of the philosopher's education.[15] For the philosopher is defined as someone whose passion for learning includes a love of such abstract objects as Beauty, Goodness, Justice, and so on (474c–476c). And as soon as Plato introduces this conception of who the philosopher is, he lets us know that it is precisely because of the philosopher's connection with these abstract objects that the philosophical life is superior to any other. Those who fail to recognize the existence of Forms have a dreamlike kind of life, because they fail to realize that the corporeal objects they perceive are only likenesses of other objects (476c–d).[16] In a dream, we confusedly take the images of objects to be those very objects. Plato's claim is that non-philosophers make a similar mistake, because they think that the beautiful things they see are what beauty really is; more generally, they equate the many observable objects that are called by some general term, "*A*," with what *A* really is.[17] The philosophers are those who recognize that *A* is a completely different sort of object, and so they rid themselves of a systematic error that in some way disfigures the unphilosophical life. This is of course the picture Plato draws in the parable of the cave (514a–519d): Most of us are imprisoned in a dark underworld because we gaze only on the shadows manipulated by others; to free ourselves from this situation requires a change in our conception of what sorts of objects there are.

Plato's metaphysics is of course controversial, but our present problem is to understand how it contributes to the defense of justice. Suppose we accept for the sake of argument that at least these central tenets of his metaphysics are correct: There are such objects as the Form of Justice, and to call acts or individuals or citizens just is to say that they bear a certain relationship to this Form. Calling an act just is comparable to calling an image in a painting a tree: The image is not what a tree is, and it is correct to speak of it as a tree only if this means that it bears a certain relation to living trees; similarly, just acts, persons, and cities are not what justice is, and it is correct to call them just only if this means that they participate in the Form of Justice.

If we accept this theory, we avoid the errors of non-Platonists; we recognize that a wider variety of objects exists than most people realize, and that our words constantly refer to these objects. Even so, we should still ask: Why would having this Platonic conception of the world make our lives so much better than the lives of non-Platonists? One answer Plato might give is that since knowledge is a great intrinsic good, a life in which we know the truth about what exists is far superior to one in which we know nothing, or know only some portion of reality. But is Plato entitled simply to assume that knowledge is good? Should he not have something to say about *why* it is good? I believe he does address this question – by telling us what the objects of knowledge are, and explaining why they are valuable.

It might be thought that for Plato knowledge of the Forms is valuable precisely because it is a means to some further goal. For example, he might claim that unless we study the Form of Justice, we are likely at some point to make errors in our judgment of which acts, persons, or institutions are just; and when we make errors of this sort, we will also make bad decisions about how to act. But if this is Plato's argument, he assumes the thesis that he sets out to prove: that acting justly is good for the agent. We are trying to see how the material he presents in the metaphysical and epistemological sections of the *Republic* strengthen the case he began to make in Books III and IV for the great value of justice. If that additional material merely supplements the earlier argument by telling us that we must know the Forms in order to act justly, then Books VI and VII do not enhance our understanding of *why* we should strive to have just souls in the first place.

Perhaps he assumes that knowing the Forms is worthwhile not merely as a means to action but because in coming to understand the Forms we develop our capacity to reason.[18] Human beings are not just appetitive and emotional creatures; we also have an innate interest in learning, and if this aspect of our nature is not developed our lives become narrow and impoverished. One problem with this answer is that intellectual curiosity and a thirst for learning can be satisfied in many different ways. Why, Plato might be asked, is it best for us to train reason to contemplate Forms rather than to understand the visible cosmos, or human nature, or music and theater? Furthermore, as Plato is aware, it is possible to devote oneself to intellectual matters without ever arriving at the realization that the Forms exist. Those who study the universe and seek to explain all phenomena without appealing to Forms surely develop the reasoning side of their nature; it is not sheer emotion and appetite that leads them to their theories. Even so, they are not leading the philosophical life, according to Plato's narrow conception of philosophy, and so they don't have the best kind of life. If he thinks that intellectuals who deny the existence of Forms thereby fail to develop their capacities and therefore fall short of happiness, he owes his reader some argument for this thesis.

IV THE GREATEST GOOD

I believe that Plato's answer to this question is staring us in the face, but that we fail to recognize it because initially it strikes us as doubtful or even unintelligible. My suggestion is that for Plato the Forms are a good – in fact they are the greatest good there is.[19] In order to live well we must break away from the confining assumption that the ordinary objects of pursuit – the pleasures, powers, honors, and material goods that we ordinarily compete for – are the only sorts of goods there are.[20] We must transform our lives by recognizing a radically different kind of good – the Forms – and we must try to incorporate these objects into our lives by understanding, loving, and imitating them, for they are incomparably superior to any other kind of good we can have. This is why Plato thinks that the philosopher is so much better off for having escaped the confines of the dreamlike existence of the ordinary person: The objects with which the philosopher is acquainted are far more worthy objects of love than the typical objects of human passion. These are the objects a fully just person is acquainted with, for the full understanding of justice that guides such an individual has as its object the Form of Justice and its relationship to Goodness and the realm of Forms.

So Plato is not claiming that it is intrinsically good to have a complete inventory of what exists or that developing and satisfying our intellectual curiosity is inherently worthwhile, regardless of the sorts of objects to which our curiosity leads us. Rather, he takes the discovery of the Forms to be momentous because they are the preeminent good we must possess in order to be happy, and he takes reason to be the most worthwhile capacity of our soul because it is only through reason that we can possess the Forms. (What is it to "possess" a Form? I will soon explain.) If there were nothing worthwhile outside of ourselves for reason to discover, then a life devoted to reasoning would lose its claim to superiority over other kinds of life.[21]

The interpretation I am proposing has some resemblance to the way Aristotle treats Plato's moral philosophy. According to Aristotle, we can discover what kind of life we should lead only by determining which good or goods we should ultimately pursue. He considers competing conceptions of this highest good and takes the Platonists' answer to be that it is not some humdrum object of pursuit like pleasure or virtue but is rather the Form of the Good (*N.E.* I.6). Aristotle of course rejects this answer, but it is significant that he takes the Platonists to be saying that a certain Form is the highest good and should therefore play the role non-Platonists assign to pleasure, honor, or virtue. So interpreted, the Platonists are not simply saying that the Form of the Good is an indispensable means for determining which among other objects are good; it itself is the chief good.[22] My interpretation is similar in that I take Plato to treat the Forms in general as a preeminent good; the special role of the Form of the Good will be discussed later.

At this point it might be asked whether the theory I am attributing to Plato is intelligible. For perhaps a Form is simply not the sort of thing that a person can have or possess. Of course, a Form can be studied and known, but studying something does not by itself confer ownership. The moon, for example, might be a beautiful object worthy of our study, but no one in his right mind would say that it is a good he *possesses* by virtue of studying it. Similarly, the claim that the Form of the Good is not the sort of thing that can be possessed is one of Aristotle's many objections to the Platonists' conception of the good (*N.E.* 1096b35). He takes Plato to be saying that the ultimate end is the Form of the Good, and objects that it is disqualified from playing this role because it is not an object of the right type. It might be thought that this objection is so powerful that out of charity we should look for a different interpretation from the one I am proposing.[23]

But I think Aristotle's objection is weak. Of course it is true that if we take the possession of a thing to be a matter of having property rights to it, then studying the Form of the Good does not confer such rights, and it is hard to understand what it would be to possess a Form. But we can speak of having things even though we have no property rights in them; for example, one can have friends without possessing them. And we can easily understand someone who says that in order to live a good life one must have friends. What it is to *have* a friend is quite a different matter from what it is to possess a physical object; it involves an emotional bond and activities characteristic of friendship. What it is to have a certain good varies according to the kind of good it is; different types of goods do not enter our lives in the same way. And so the mere fact that a Form cannot be possessed (that is, owned) gives us no reason to reject Plato's idea that if one bears a certain relationship to Forms – a relationship that involves both emotional attachment and intellectual understanding – then one's life becomes more worthwhile precisely because one is connected in this way with such valuable objects.

In fact, there are similarities between the way in which persons can enter our lives and improve them and the way in which Plato thinks we should be related to the Forms. We can easily understand someone who says that one of the great privileges of his life is to have known a certain eminent and inspiring person. Even if one is not a close friend of such a person, one may have great love and admiration for him, and one may take pleasure in studying his life. That is the sort of relationship Plato thinks we should have with the Forms – not on the grounds that loving and studying are good activities, whatever their objects, but on the grounds that the Forms are the preeminent good and therefore our lives are vastly improved when we come to know, love, and imitate them.

Suppose it is conceded that if the Forms are a good, then they are the sorts of things that can improve our lives when we are properly related to them. Nonetheless, it might still be asked whether we can make sense of the idea that they are good. If someone says that water is a good thing, we might be puzzled about what he has in mind, and we might even be skeptical about whether water is the sort of thing that can be good in itself (as opposed to a mere means).[24] Similarly, we might have doubts about Plato's Forms: How can such objects, which are so different in kind from such mundane goods as health and pleasure, be counted as good? And if he cannot convince us that they are good, then of course he has no hope of persuading us that they are vastly better than such ordinary goods as pleasure, health, wealth, power, and so on.

For Plato's answer to our question, What is it to say of something that it is a good thing? we might turn for help to his discussion of the Form of the Good. But although he insists on the preeminence of this Form, he does not say precisely what he takes goodness to be; he simply says that it is not pleasure or knowledge (505b–506e). There is a marked contrast here between the fullness of his account of what justice is and the thinness of his discussion of goodness. We learn what it is to call a person, act, or city just, and we see the feature that they all have in common, but Plato points to no common feature of all good things. So he does not take up the project of showing that Forms are preeminent by stating what property goodness consists in and arguing that they exhibit that property more fully than anything else.

Perhaps we can discover why Plato thinks of Forms as goods if we focus on their distinguishing characteristics and ask which of them Plato might put forward as points of superiority over other objects. For example, he thinks that Forms are more real than corporeal objects, and presumably he counts this as evidence of their superiority in value.[25] But this point will not take us as far as we need to go, because he thinks that objects that are equally real can nonetheless differ greatly in value. Consider two bodies, one of them healthy, the other diseased: One is in better condition than the other, but Plato never suggests that one of them must therefore be more real than the other. Though Forms are more real than other types of objects, we cannot treat differing degrees of reality as what in general constitute differences in value.

But our example of the healthy and diseased bodies suggests another line of reasoning: Plato equates health, the good condition of the body, with a certain harmony among its elements; and he argues that justice, the good condition of the soul, is also a certain kind of harmony among its parts; and so the thought suggests itself that he takes the goodness of anything of a certain kind to be the harmony or proportion that is appropriate for things of that kind. According to this suggestion, the goodness of Forms consists in the fact that they possess a kind of harmony, balance, or proportion; and their superiority to all other things consists in the fact that the kind of order they possess gives them a higher degree of harmony than any other type of object.[26]

Clearly Plato does think that the Forms exhibit the highest kind of orderly arrangement. He says that the philosopher looks away from the conflict-ridden affairs of human beings to things that are unchanging and ordered (tetagmena, 500c2); by studying the divine order (kosmos, c4) her soul becomes as orderly and divine as it is possible for a human soul to be (c9–d1). Even the beautiful patterns exhibited in the night sky fall short of the harmonies present in true shapes and numbers, since the corporeality of the stars makes deviation inevitable, whereas the incorporeality of the Forms ensures that the orderly patterns they exhibit will never deteriorate (529c7–530b4). But he does not say precisely what the orderliness of the Forms consists in; bodies, souls, and political communities exhibit order (and therefore goodness) when their parts or components are related to each other in suitable ways, but we are not told whether the Forms have parts or whether they achieve their order in some other way. Perhaps this explains Plato's refusal to say what the Form of the Good is (506d–e); though goodness simply is some kind of harmony, he had not yet reached a firm grasp of what this harmony is in the case of Forms, and so he could not put forward a general characterization of harmony that would apply equally to the various kinds of harmony exhibited by living bodies, souls, stars, and Forms. But in any case, we can now see how Plato would try to address doubts about whether Forms are the sorts of objects that can intelligibly be called good. He would reply by appealing to his discussion of politics, the soul, and health: In all of these cases, the goodness of a thing consists in a kind of order; and so if the Forms can be shown to have the kind of order that is appropriate for things of that kind, they too will be good. And if they necessarily have a higher degree of order than anything else, then they are the best goods there can be.[27]

V   THE PHILOSOPHICAL LIFE IS THE JUST LIFE

It may now be asked how any of this provides Plato with a defense of the virtue of justice. Even if we see why he thinks that the philosophical life is best, we still can ask why this should be regarded as a defense of *justice*. Why is the philosopher the paradigm of the just person? Part of Plato's reply, as I understand it, is as follows:[28] When the ideal state properly educates individuals to become philosophers, their emotions and appetites are transformed in a way that serves the philosophical life, and these affective states no longer provide a strong impetus toward antisocial behavior, as they do when they are left undisciplined (499e–500e). Someone who has been fully prepared to love the orderly pattern of the Forms will be free of the urge to seek worldly advantages over other human beings or to engage in the sort of illicit sexual activity to which people are led by unchecked appetites.

Not only will antisocial motivation be lacking; there will be a passionate drive to produce orderly and harmonious relations both among the parts of one's own soul and among the members of one's political community (500c–d). Justice, as Book IV revealed, is a kind of order and harmony (443d). That is what the Forms exhibit; and the philosopher, as a lover of the system of Forms, will seek to reproduce those harmonies in his soul and city.

Furthermore, such a person is in the best possible position to make wise political decisions; having understood the Forms, she can see more clearly than others what needs to be done in particular circumstances (500d–501a). One of the things we look for, when we seek a paradigm of the just person, is someone who has these intellectual and affective skills.[29]

It is tempting to protest at this point that Plato is being extremely naïve. After all, we all know people who have impressive intellectual abilities but who are hardly models of justice. And of course there is nothing to prevent such individuals from recognizing the existence of abstract objects, and even loving the contemplation of the orderly pattern among such objects. Consider a Platonist mathematician who occasionally gets drunk and indulges in other behavior that conflicts with Plato's description of the just individual. Aren't such individuals living refutations of Plato?

The mistake made by this objection to Plato's theory is that it overlooks the special features of his conception of Forms that I have been emphasizing. He is not claiming that anyone who studies objects that are now called "abstract" (numbers, universals, sets, and so on), and takes these objects to exist independently of the mind, will be a paradigm of justice and other moral virtues. Plato's Forms are conceived as *moral exemplars*; this is not how mathematicians think of numbers. Of course, Forms do not borrow from each other or make promises. But Plato holds that at bottom justice in the soul is a love of proper order, harmony, right relationships, and the like. If one really does have a general love of and admiration for the perfect structures of the Forms, one must also love justice and other right relations among human beings.

We should recall, however, that Plato promises to do more than merely show that justice is a great good. He has to show that it is a greater good than injustice, so much so that even if the normal consequences of justice and injustice are reversed it will nonetheless be better to be just than unjust. The paragon of justice must be punished because he is thought to be unjust; and the paragon of injustice is to receive the honors and rewards because he appears to be just. How can Plato show that even in this situation it is better to be just?

The answer lies partly in the way he describes the situation of the completely unjust person, that is, the tyrant. Such a person is allowed to live out his fantasies of power and eroticism without restraint, and Plato's case against such a life is that this lack of restraint will inevitably exact a devastating psychological toll.

When erotic desires are allowed to grow to full strength, they become impossible to satisfy; rather than leading to a life of peace and fulfillment, they leave one with a chronic feeling of frustration (579d–e). Similarly, tyrannical power inevitably gives rise to continual fear of reprisals and an absence of trust in one's associates (576a, 579a–c). The failure to impose any order on one's appetites makes one the victim of frequent and disorganized internal demands (573d). So, in order to achieve great power and intense sexual pleasure, the tyrant must lead a chaotic life filled with anguish, fear, and frustration. No one who reads this account of the tyrannical life could seriously hold it up as a model of how human beings should live. When the immoralist praises the life ruled by unrestrained desires for power and pleasure, he simply fails to think through the consequences of giving these desires free rein. He responds to something in human nature, for Plato agrees that no one is completely free of the impulses that the immoralist champions (571b–572b). The presence of these illicit urges seems to lend some credibility to the immoralist's doubts about whether justice is a virtue, for the praise of immorality answers to something within us. Plato's response to the immoralist is that when we seriously consider the psychological consequences of magnifying the power of our illicit urges, the life of maximal injustice loses its appeal. This is something he thinks we will be able to see without having the benefit of the theory of Forms; he invokes the Forms because they are the objects around which the best kind of human life must be built, but he makes no appeal to these objects when he tries to convince us that the tyrannical life is miserable.

Again, it is possible to protest that Plato's argument is naïve. It seems to rest on the empirical assumption that anyone who possesses tyrannical power will also have sexual obsessions, and this makes it easier for him to make such a life look unattractive. But in fact such an empirical assumption is unwarranted: It is certainly possible to tyrannize a community and hold all other passions in check.[30] Here too, however, I think Plato is less vulnerable to criticism than we might have thought. His portrait of the tyrant is not meant to be an exceptionless empirical generalization about what such individuals are like. Rather, he is developing the portrait of the unjust life that is presented in Book II when Glaucon and Adeimantus try to make such a life look attractive. According to their portrait, the unjust man can seduce any woman who appeals to him; he can kill anyone he wants (360a–c). Plato's idea is that if these features of injustice capture its subrational appeal, then it is fair to describe the paragon of injustice as someone whose sexual appetites and murderous tendencies are extreme. If that is how he is proceeding, then it is irrelevant that in fact tyrants need not be dominated by sexual appetite.

Plato's portrait of the tyrant makes it clear that his argument for justice does not rest solely on the metaphysics of the middle books and the political theory of the early books but also relies on various assumptions about human psychology. Certain desires, if unchecked, lead to the sorts of consequences – frustration, fear, pain – that every-one tries to avoid and that no one regards as compatible with a fully happy human life. What Plato is assuming is that the life of the completely just person is not marred by these same features. Fear, frustration, and chaos are not the price philosophers must inevitably pay for having a love of the Forms and for giving this passion a dominant role in their lives. On the contrary, those who are in the best position to study the Forms will have modest and therefore easily satisfied appetites, and will be free of the competitive desire for power that typically sets people at odds and destroys their tranquility. So the philosophical life will include the felt harmony of soul that everyone can recognize and value, as well as the more complex kind of harmony that one can understand only through a philosophical investigation of the parts of the soul and of the metaphysical objects that enter one's life when reason rules.

We can now see why Plato is confident that he can prove that justice pays even when he allows the just person and the unjust person to reverse their roles in Book II. Even if the just person is mistakenly dishonored and punished, she will still be at peace with herself; she will be free of the chaos and frustration that make the life of the tyrant so repellent. In place of the great physical pain imagined for the just person, the tyrant must endure great psychological pain. Neither is in an enviable condition, but there is a major difference that Plato thinks counts decisively in favor of the just person: Her understanding and emotions gain her entrance into a world of completely harmonious objects, and so she possesses the greatest good there is. We have finally answered the question with which we began: The consummately unjust person has troubles that counterbalance the pain and dishonor imagined for the just person, and if these were the only factors involved in their comparison, it might be difficult to decide whose situation is worse; but once the possession of the Forms is added to the just person's side of the equation, the advantage lies with her, overwhelmingly so because of the great worth of that non-sensible realm.[31]

VI   THE PHILOSOPHER'S OBLIGATION TO RULE

One important feature of Plato's theory has not yet been discussed, and it is best brought to light by considering a well-known internal difficulty in his argument. He says that the philosophers of the ideal city must not be allowed to study the Forms without interruption, but must instead return to the darkness of the cave and help administer the political community (519d–521b, 540a–b). Why won't the philosophers be tempted to resist this requirement, however just it may be, since it seems to conflict with their self-interest?[32] After all, life in the open air illuminated by the Form of the Good must be better than life in the subterranean atmosphere in which one must rule the state. Won't the philosophers be strongly tempted to think of ways in which they can escape such service? If so, they cannot be held up as paragons of justice. Furthermore, this example seems to show that justice does not always pay: If one could unjustly escape service to the community and continue contemplating the Forms, one would do what is best for oneself, but one would not act justly.

Plato is completely confident that the individuals he has trained for the philosophical life will accept this requirement to rule. After all, he says, they are just, and the requirement is just (520e1). But why doesn't he see any problem for his theory here? Why doesn't it leap to his eye that ruling is contrary to the philosopher's interests, so that this feature of his ideal state presents a clear counterexample to his thesis that justice pays? One possible answer to this question is simply that Plato is willing to make exceptions to this generalization.[33] But it is unlikely that he would restrict himself to the weak claim that justice is *usually* in one's interests. It is more fruitful, I think, to look at the problem in the reverse manner: Plato thinks that ruling the state is a just requirement, and since he believes that justice is always in one's interest, he must think that somehow it does pay to rule the city. The question is how he could believe this.

He tells us at one point that when philosophers look to the harmonious arrangement of the Forms, they develop a desire to imitate that harmony in some way or other (500c). And then he adds that if it becomes necessary for the philosophers to imitate the Forms by molding human character in their likeness, they will be in an excellent position to do this job well. So it is clear that when the philosophers rule, they do not stop looking to or imitating the Forms. Rather, their imitative activity is no longer merely contemplative; instead, they start acting in a way that produces a harmony in the city that is a likeness of the harmony of the Forms. Furthermore, were they to refuse to rule, they would be allowing the disorder in the city to increase. Were any single philosopher to shirk her responsibilities, and let others do more than their fair share, then she would be undermining a fair system of dividing responsibilities. The order that would be appropriate to their situation would be undermined. And so failure to rule, whether in an individual philosopher or in a group of them, would create a certain disharmony in the world: Relationships that are appropriate among people would be violated. And in creating this disharmony, the philosopher would in one respect cease to imitate the Forms. She would gaze at the order that is appropriate among Forms but would thereby upset an order that is appropriate among human beings.

What this suggests is that Plato has the resources for showing that justice is in one's interests even when it requires forgoing some purely philosophical activity. What he must hold is that one's highest good is not always served by purely contemplating the Forms;[34] rather, one's highest good is to establish and maintain a certain imitative relationship with the Forms, a relationship that is strained or ruptured when one fails to do one's fair share in a just community. The person who is willing to do her part in a just social order, and whose willingness arises out of a full understanding of what justice is, will see the community of which she is a part as an ordered whole, a worldly counterpart to the otherworldly realm of abstract objects she loves. When she acts justly and does her fair share, she sees herself as participating in a social pattern that approximates the harmony of the Forms, and she therefore takes her good to be served by acting justly. In making this connection between social harmony and the harmony of Forms, Plato offers an account of the positive appeal that justice in human relationships should have for us. We are – or should be – attracted to justice in human relationships; when we act justly, we should do so not merely because of the absence of such motives as greed, sensuality, and the desire to dominate others. Rather, we should see something attractive about communities and relationships in which each person does his or her appropriate part, and we should be loath to violate these relationships because of our love of justice. If I have understood Plato correctly, he recognizes that justice as a relationship among human beings can have this positive appeal.[35]

VII   WEAK AND STRONG PLATONISM

I said at the beginning of this chapter that there is something powerful in Plato's argument that justice pays. What I have in mind is his thesis that the goodness of human life depends heavily on our having a close connection with something eminently worthwhile that lies outside of ourselves. To live well one must be in the right psychological condition, and that condition consists in a receptivity to the valuable objects that exist independently of oneself. If one is oblivious to these objects and devotes oneself above all to the acquisition of power, or the accumulation of wealth, or the satisfaction of erotic appetites, then one will not only become a danger to others but one will fail to achieve one's own good. Psychological forces that lead to injustice when they become powerful are forces that should in any case be moderated for one's own good, for when they are too strong they interfere with our ability to possess the most valuable objects.

Even if we reject Plato's belief in Forms or his thesis that goodness consists in harmony, we should recognize that there are many different ways of trying to sustain his attempt to connect the goodness of human life with some goodness external to one's soul. The Abrahamic religions provide obvious examples, for they hold that the external good is God and that no human life is worth leading unless God is somehow present in it. Another example can be found in Romantic conceptions of nature, according to which a person who is cut off from the beauty of the natural order has been excluded from his home and must lead an alienated existence. We can even see some similarity between Plato's theory and the idea that great works of art so enrich human lives that the inability to respond to their beauty is a serious impoverishment.

In this last case, the valuable objects are created by human beings, but nonetheless it could be held that one's good consists in learning how to understand and love these objects. Someone can reasonably say that her life has been made better because she has come to love one of the cultural products of her society – a great novel, for example. This does not have to mean that the novel has taught her lessons that have instrumental value or that it has brought forth psychological capacities that would otherwise have lain dormant. It is intelligible to say that a relationship to a certain object – something beautiful in nature, or some work of art, or a divinity – by itself makes one's life better. And that seems to represent the way many people view their lives, for it is difficult to sustain the belief that one's life is worthwhile if one sees and feels no connection between oneself and some greater object.

Plato would of course reject these alternatives to his theory: He claims that the natural world for all its beauty is no model of perfection and that the works of poets are of lesser value still. Perhaps then we should distinguish a weak from a strong form of Platonism: Weak Platonism holds that the human good consists in having the proper relationship to some valuable object external to oneself, whether that object be a work of art, one's family or political community, the natural world, or a divinity. Strong Platonism goes further and holds that the valuable object in question must be eternal and unchanging. What is distinctive of Plato's own view, of course, is that the Forms, or at least some of them, are such objects. But even if his particular version of Platonism is rejected, it should be recognized that some form of this doctrine, strong or weak, is deeply appealing. Plato might be pleased and not at all surprised that watered-down forms of Platonism have had such a long history.

NOTES

1 See *Rep.* 360e–362c for the contrast between the just and unjust lives. (All future page references will be to this dialogue, unless otherwise noted.) It should be emphasized that Plato is not trying to show that it is advantageous to *act justly* regardless of one's psychological condition. His claim is that it is advantageous to be a *just person.*

2 I have learned most from these studies: Irwin 1977; White 1979; Annas 1981; Reeve 1988. Among older treatments still worth consulting are Murphy 1951; Nettleship 1962; Cross and Woozley 1964; Joseph 1971. More recent important works include: Irwin 1995a; Ferrari 2007; Vasiliou 2008; Reeve 2013; Scott 2015; Brown 2017; Kamtekar 2017; Thakkar 2018.

3 Here I am setting aside the arguments of Book I of the dialogue and concentrating entirely on the issue as it is reintroduced at the beginning of Book II. Plato must have believed that the arguments of Book I were in some way deficient; otherwise there would be no need to reopen the question in Book II. Perhaps their deficiency lies principally in their schematic nature: They need to be buttressed by political theory, metaphysics, and psychology. An alternative reading is that in Book II

Plato thinks that the earlier arguments are entirely of the wrong sort. For this interpretation, see Irwin 1995a: 181–202; Reeve 1988: 3–24. I also set aside the further considerations Plato mentions in Book X at 612b ff.: These are the worldly and otherworldly rewards the just can expect to receive. It is precisely these rewards that Plato agrees to overlook when he promises in Book II to show that justice is in our interest, apart from its consequences. It should be emphasized that Plato thinks these rewards make the just life even more desirable. He agrees that the just person who suffers the torments described at 361e–362a suffers a loss of well-being and is no paradigm of happiness. When he refers to wealth and other "so-called goods" at 495a7, his refusal to call them goods outright should be taken to mean that these ordinary objects of pursuit are not in all circumstances good; he cannot hold the stronger thesis that they are never good, for then the social rewards of justice would be a matter of indifference. For discussion of what Plato means by saying that justice is good *in itself*, see Foster 1937; Mabbott 1937; Sachs 1963; Cross and Woozley 1964: 66–9; Kirwan 1965; Irwin 1977: 184–91, 325–6; Annas 1981: ch. 3; White 1984; Reeve 1988: 24–33.

4 Readers of the *Republic* should bear in mind that Plato does not use *eudaimonia* (often translated "happiness") and its cognates to refer to the feeling of pleasure. For Plato, to seek one's own happiness is simply to seek one's own advantage, and so to discover what happiness is one must determine where a human being's true interests lie.

5 At 589c1–4 Plato distinguishes between praising justice for its advantages and praising it for its pleasures (cf. 581e7–582a2, 588a7–10). This implies that the two arguments from pleasure in Book IX are not addressed to the issue of whether justice or injustice is more advantageous. For an alternative reading, see Gosling and Taylor 1982: 98–101; their interpretation is endorsed by Reeve 1988: 307 n. 33. For further discussion of this alternative, see my review of Reeve 1988 (Kraut 1990). For yet another alternative, see Vasiliou 2008: 272–81.

6 So I proposed in the first version of this chapter. For discussion of Plato's calculation, see Reeve 1988: 150–1. He argues that the correct figure should be 125. The interpretation I suggest in the remainder of this paragraph is similar to the one adopted by Vasiliou 2008: 278.

7 Or, following Annas 1981: 168–9, we might think that Plato is arguing for two different conclusions: The earlier material is designed to show that

justice is good in itself, apart from happiness; whereas the later material does try to link justice and happiness. But we should reject her statement that "the notion of happiness has not occurred" in Book IV. When Plato asks at 444e7–445a4 whether justice is more profitable (*lusitelei*) than injustice, he is in effect asking whether the just person is happier. As Book II shows, the thesis Plato is trying to prove can be formulated in several terms that are treated equivalently.

8   See 472b7 and 484a7–8 for evidence that Plato does not take himself to have fully revealed in Book IV what justice is.

9   For the contrary view – that Plato does not attempt to give *any* argument in Books II–IV for the thesis that justice is advantageous – see White 1986. But I think 444e7–445b7 rules this out: The interlocutors here agree that justice is advantageous and that injustice is not; and surely they think that they have some reason for this conclusion. I take 445b5–7 to mean that the conclusion has not been supported as fully as possible, and that the fuller argument is now to come. Despite this difference, White and I agree that Books II–IX should be read as a single continuous argument in defense of justice.

10   This is of course a consequence of Plato's general principle that whenever we call a group of things by the same name there is something they all have in common. See, for example, *Meno* 72b–c and *Rep.* 596a. Plato's assumption that goodness is a single thing is attacked by Aristotle in the *Nicomachean Ethics* 1.6.

11   More fully, the argument is this: (1) Health is the preeminent good of the body, in the sense that life is not worth living when one's body is completely lacking health. (2) What makes health so worthwhile is that it involves a natural balance of elements – certain elements appropriately dominate certain others. (3) Justice involves an analogous balance in the soul. (4) Since justice has the same good-making characteristic as health, it must be equally true that life is not worth living if one is greatly deficient in justice. The crucial premise is (3), and to support it Plato appeals to the analogy between city and soul. But even if Plato had completely left aside the idea that health involves a balance, the main argument from analogy of Books II–IV would still remain: What is best for the polis is an internal balance, and so we should expect the same to hold true of the individual. The appeal to health is an attempt to strengthen the argument by adding one more case in which advantage can be equated with proper balance.

12 On the divided soul, see Irwin 1995a: 203–22; Lorenz 2006; Barney, Brennan, and Brittain 2012. Earlier studies include Penner 1971; Irwin 1977: 191–5; Cooper 1984; Reeve 1988: 118–40.

13 Plato's strategy would fail if it were impossible to say anything about what a good city is without first knowing what a good person is or what human happiness is. Books II–IV try to convince us that we can discover a good deal about how a political community should be organized, even before we address the question of human virtue and happiness.

14 The limitations of Plato's argument as it develops from Book II to Book IV are emphasized by Cooper 1977: 152–3; White 1986: 39; and Irwin 1995a: 256–61. More recently, Dominic Scott has argued that although the material in Books VIII and IX, portraying degenerate cities and correspondingly inferior individuals, is a continuation and elaboration of the sketchier argument of Books III and IV, Plato's text gives no indication that we are to add the metaphysical and epistemological theories found in Books V–VII to the reasoning that concludes in the pronouncement (580a–c) that the most just city and individual is happiest and the tyrannical city and soul least happy. See Scott 2015: 54–70. For Scott, that argument, Plato's longest defense of justice, builds entirely on psychological and political premises, and makes no appeal to the existence and nature of otherworldly Forms. I believe, against this, that the text does invite us to include the Forms, and philosophical love of Forms, among the material we are to assemble in our understanding of this lengthy argument. First, at 543d–544a, Glaucon notes that although the city and man portrayed up to the end of Book IV was good, there was a still finer city and man – and this of course must be Kallipolis as portrayed in Books V through VII and the philosopher who rules that ideal city. It must be this still finer individual (the philosopher) who is compared to the tyrant at 580b–c, where the most just person is placed at the height of happiness and the tyrant in the depths of misery. Second, this way of reading the text is confirmed by Plato's use of the term *basileus* (king) or its cognates to designate the individual who is placed opposite the tyrant in terms of justice and happiness. The rulers of Kallipolis are called guardians (*phylakes*) in Books III and IV (414b, 428d), but starting in Book V they are designated kings (473c). When Book IX pronounces the kingly individual (576d, 580b) most just and happy, the tyrant least so, the word "kingly" indicates that it is the philosopher-king (no mere guardian) who figures in Plato's argument.

15 Among the most important passages characterizing the Forms are *Phd.*
    65d–66a, 74b–c, 78c–80b; *Phdr.* 247c; *Rep.* 477a–480e; *Smp.* 210e–211e; *Ti.*
    27d–28a, 38a, 52a–b; *Phil.* 59c. For a thorough examination of Plato's
    reasons for postulating the existence of Forms, see Penner 1987 and David
    Ebrey's chapter in this volume (ch. 9).

16 For a lucid interpretation of this aspect of Plato's theory, see Patterson 1985.

17 See Penner 1987: 57–140.

18 See Irwin 1977: 236, for the claim that Plato's defense of justice depends on
    the idea that we must develop all of our capacities. His interpretation is
    more fully developed in Irwin 1995a: 302–17.

19 The principal textual support for this reading derives from the many
    passages in which Plato describes the Forms as the proper objects of love:
    476b, 480a, 484b, 490a–b, 500c, 501d. They could not be such unless they
    are good (*Smp.* 204d–206a). (See the contribution of Suzanne Obdrzalek in
    this volume, ch. 7, for related themes.) I am not claiming that according to
    Plato each Form counts as a separate good; rather, it is the ordered whole
    constituted by the Forms that is a good, although some of the individual
    Forms (Goodness, Beauty, etc.) may by themselves be goods. Of course, if
    my interpretation is to be an improvement over the ones just considered,
    then Plato cannot simply *assume* that the Forms are a great good. His
    argument for this claim will be discussed later. It might be asked how the
    Forms can be the greatest good, since that distinction is reserved for justice
    (366e9). But there is no real conflict here. When Plato says that justice is the
    greatest good, he does not mean that the universe has no better object to
    show than a just human being; the Forms are superior to this. He means
    rather that possessing justice is better for us than possessing any other type
    of good; and this is compatible with the claim that the Forms are the
    supreme objects. For on my reading, being fully just and fully possessing the
    Forms are the same psychological state, and so there is no issue about which
    state it is better to be in.

20 It is widely recognized that according to Plato happiness consists in
    possessing good things – a point he takes to need no argument. See *Smp.*
    204e–205a. What is distinctive of my interpretation is the suggestion that
    Plato defends the philosophical life (and therefore the life of consummate
    justice) by adding to the conventional list of goods.

21 The pattern of argument in the *Philebus* is similar: Reason is declared to
    be a more important component of the good human life than pleasure

because it is more akin than pleasure to the good. Here, as in the *Republic*, something outside of human life is taken to be ideal, and those elements of human life that most fully approach this ideal are to receive priority.

22 This is why his discussion in *N.E.* I.6 of the Platonic conception of the Good is not out of place. Aristotle also considers the possibility that for the Platonist the Good is not itself a desirable object but is instead a tool for gaining the knowledge we need to make practical decisions. See 1096b35–1097a6. But this is an alternative to the main conception of the Good that he considers in I.6.

23 Thus Santas 1989: 154. He takes Aristotle to be obviously right that a Platonic Form is not the sort of thing that can be possessed, and defends Plato by denying that his theory makes any such claim. Instead, he takes Plato merely to be saying that the Form of the Good must be known, the better to possess other goods. A related view seems to be presupposed by Martha Nussbaum (1986: 148), who takes Plato to believe that "the bearers of value are activities." On this view, the Forms themselves cannot be "bearers of value," since they are not activities. Rather, they have value because they are the objects of pure, stable, truth-discovering activity. See Nussbaum 1986: 145–8.

24 See Ziff 1960: 210, 216. His view is that when we call something "good" we are saying that it "answers to certain interests" (p. 117). Unless we are provided with further information, it is not clear how water can meet this condition. Of course, on my reading, Plato is not merely saying that the Forms answer to certain interests. They are good quite apart from our interests, and because of their great goodness it is in our interest to possess them.

25 The analogy of the cave (514a–517c) and the critique of artistic imitation in Book X (see esp. 596a–597d) bring out this aspect of the theory most fully. See too 477a, 478d, 479d. For discussion, see Vlastos 1981: 58–75. Vlastos holds that the Forms are fully real in two senses: they have the highest degree of cognitive reliability, and they have a kind of value that "transcends the usual specifications of value" (p. 64). Of course, Plato cannot simply lay it down without argument that Forms have this transcendent value, nor can he infer that they have it merely because of their greater cognitive reliability.

26 So read, the arguments of Books II–IV and of V–IX are mutually supporting: The later material adds content and support to the thesis that justice is

a psychological harmony, and that thesis in turn supports the identification of being in good condition with being harmoniously arranged.

27 Some support for this interpretation comes from the *Philebus*, since Plato there appeals to measure and proportion to explain the nature of goodness (*Phil.* 64a–e). Throughout the cosmos, and not merely in human affairs, wherever limit is imposed on the disorder inherent in the unlimited, a harmonious unification is achieved, and this harmony is what makes things good. See *Phil.* 23c–26d. I take Plato to be saying that a thing of one type is better than something of the *same* type if it has a greater degree of the harmony appropriate for things of that type; and a thing of one type is better than something of a *different* type if things of the first type can achieve a higher degree of harmony than things of the second. Harmony is for Plato a form of unification, and so on my view he connects goodness and unity. Note his emphasis on unity as the greatest civic good: 462a–b; cf. 422e–423c. On the role of unity in Plato's argument, see White 1979: 31, 38–40. For further discussion of the Form of the Good, see Cooper 1977: 154–5; Irwin 1977: 224–6; Santas 1983; and Reeve 1988: 81–95.

28 In section VI, I will discuss another part of Plato's answer: Some acts of justice imitate the Forms.

29 For further discussion of the ways in which Plato's novel understanding of justice is related to the ordinary Greek conception, see Vlastos 1981: 3–39. This is a response to Sachs 1963, which argues that these two conceptions are unconnected. Some other responses to Sachs are Kraut 1973b; Irwin 1977: 208–12; Annas 1981: ch. 6; Demos 1984; and Reeve 1988: ch. 5.

30 The criticism of Plato discussed in this paragraph is made in Annas 1981: 304. The kind of defense of him I give here is more fully developed in Arruzza 2019: 15–183.

31 Here my reading differs from that of White 1989b.

32 The philosophers' motivation for ruling has received much discussion but no consensus has emerged. For some of the conflicting views, see Kraut 1973a; Cooper 1977: 155–7; White 1979: 44–8, 189–96; Annas 1981: 266–71; White 1986; Reeve 1988: 95, 197–204; Irwin 1995a: 298–317; Brown 2000a.

33 For the view that Plato makes an exception in this one case, see White 1986.

34 I do not believe that Plato ever claims or commits himself to the thesis
   that the best human life is the one that has the greatest amount of purely
   contemplative activity. What he does clearly hold is that such activity is
   better than political activity (520e–521a); but this does not entail that pure
   contemplation that creates injustice is more advantageous than political
   activity that is justly required.

35 For a fuller presentation of the interpretation I have given in this section,
   see Kraut 1999.

11 Plato on Poetic Creativity: A Revision

Elizabeth Asmis

In Book X of the *Republic*, Plato expels the poetry of Homer and his followers – "the poetry of pleasure," as he calls it – from his ideal state by observing that there is an ancient quarrel between philosophy and poetry. At the same time, he expresses a willingness to put aside the quarrel. His spokesman, Socrates, throws out a challenge: If the poetry of pleasure or its defenders can show that it is "not only pleasant, but also useful for cities and human life," it will have a receptive audience (607a–e). Plato returns to this challenge in his last work, the *Laws*. The tragic poets approach the lawmakers and ask, May we bring our poetry to your city? The lawmakers reply that they, the lawmakers, are "poets" too, rivals and competitors in making the "most beautiful drama." Their drama is the political order (*politeia*) they have created, an "imitation of the most beautiful and best life." If the tragedians can show them dramas that agree with theirs, they will be allowed to perform; otherwise not (817a–d).

In the *Laws*, Plato takes the more conciliatory stance of one who admits rather than expels, but the quarrel persists. Only the type of poetry that is politically correct is permitted; the rest is banished. The reason is that poets and lawmakers are rivals in fashioning human life. Both are at once "makers" (the etymological meaning of *poiētai*, "poets") and "imitators" of moral values; and in a well-ordered society they must speak with one voice.

This subordination of poetry to politics has offended many readers of Plato from antiquity to the present. Plato sees the poet primarily as a maker of ethics, and this concern appears strangely one-sided. What

This is a revision of my chapter "Plato on Poetic Creativity" in the first edition of *The Cambridge Companion to Plato*. It owes a special debt of gratitude to David Ebrey for his careful reading of my revision and his many insightful suggestions.

makes his position especially jarring is that he was himself a consummate literary artist. Yet Plato has a much more complex view of poetry than his moral strictures suggest. Along with his censorship goes a far-ranging exploration of poetic creativity. Trying out various approaches in different dialogues, Plato enters into a dialogue with himself; and the tensions and variations in his own thinking lay the foundation for a much richer conception of poetic aesthetics than is ordinarily recognized.

This chapter seeks to illuminate Plato's contributions to the history of aesthetics by focusing on the topic of poetic creativity. While giving a central place to the false creativity analysed in such detail in the *Republic*, it will embed it in a context that shows how to replace it by genuine creativity. In the process, it will outline a path from a traditional view of divine inspiration to a new kind of inspiration, which transforms the poet into a philosopher.

I HISTORICAL BACKGROUND

Plato's quarrel with poetry takes its start from the traditional role of poets as teachers of mankind.[1] Poets, like prophets, were thought to be inspired directly by the gods with wisdom about the human and divine condition. It was their prerogative to make known the past, present, and future to their contemporaries and future generations by oral performances. Prose writings and books did not become common until the fifth century BCE, and even then the primary method of publishing a work was oral performance. The poems were chanted or sung, usually to instrumental accompaniment, at gatherings that ranged from private affairs to celebrations held by an entire community or region, such as the dramatic festivals in honor of Dionysos. Most occasions had a religious setting, and many poetic performances were a form of religious worship. To grasp the role of poetry in ancient Greece, one might think of Hindu religious drama, in which gods confront the audience directly in terrifying struggles between good and evil.

The values transmitted in poetry evolved continuously. While many poems – most prominently those of Homer – were passed on with little or no change from one generation to the next, poets and performers were continually reinterpreting their past. Poets not only preserved values, but also questioned and subverted the traditions they inherited, and long before Plato's attack on poetry, there were poets who condemned poets. The first known critical attack on poetry was by the poet Xenophanes in the sixth century BCE. In the same epic meter used by Homer and Hesiod, Xenophanes denounced these poets for "attributing to the gods everything that is a shame and reproach among humans – to steal, commit adultery, and deceive one another."[2] The quarrel continued with Heraclitus' stern verdict that Homer and Archilochus "deserve to be thrown out of the contests and beaten with the rod."[3] Heraclitus used prose, but his attack belongs to the same tradition of criticism as that of Xenophanes. About the same time, Parmenides laid the foundations of metaphysics and logic in a poem modeled in part on Homeric epic. The dramatists of the fifth century quarreled with their poetic predecessors no less vehemently than earlier poets did.

Plato's view of the quarrel between poetry and philosophy involves a third group, the sophists. Their name, "wise men" (*sophistai*), which soon became a term of derision, shows that they considered themselves heirs and rivals to the poets. In Plato's *Protagoras*, Protagoras (fl. c. 450 BCE), leader of the first generation of sophists, proclaims that he was the first person to claim a place openly within the tradition of Greek educators (316c–317c). As heir to the poets, he considers the most important part of education to be the criticism of poetry (338e–339a), and he illustrates his contention by attacking a well-known poem by Simonides. In their challenge to the poetic tradition, the sophists used a new weapon, prose. Partly, they discovered new possibilities of language in prose; partly, they attempted to capture the power of poetry by modeling their prose on poetic usage. One new use of prose was to engage the listener in an exchange of questions and answers, with the aim of scoring a victory by forcing the respondent to agree with whatever is proposed. Socrates' dialectical method is a development of this invention. The sophists were also the first to teach methods of argument. Unlike the poets, they claimed no authority for their teachings except their own "wisdom." They emphasized the practical utility of their teaching, which they regarded as the culmination of a series of inventions devised by humans for their own advancement.

Along with their new use of language, the sophists developed theories of language. We are fortunate that one of the few extant writings of the sophists contains a brief theory of language – the first in the Western tradition. In the *Encomium of Helen*, Gorgias (fl. c. 430 BCE) personifies language, *logos*, as a "great potentate, who with the tiniest and least visible body achieves the most divine deeds."[4] The "deeds" (*erga*) created by language are, remarkably, its effects on the hearer. When *logos* is accompanied by persuasion, it "shapes the soul as it wishes." Just as drugs can drive various humors from the body and end either illness or life, so language can set up various emotions in the soul, and "drug and bewitch with an evil persuasion."[5] As evidence, Gorgias cites poetry and magical incantations as well as scientific, forensic, and philosophical prose. Defining poetry as "language with meter," he points out that by implanting intense fear, pity, or yearning in the listener, it makes the soul "suffer an affection of its own" at the fortunes and misfortunes of others.[6] Elsewhere, Gorgias singles out tragedy as a kind of deceit. In this case, the speaker is justified in practicing the deceit, as the listener is wise for being deceived.[7] In the *Encomium*, Gorgias explains that *logos* would not have the power it does if there were not such a wide field of ignorance. As it is, we have only partial knowledge of the past, present, and future; language fills this gap by supplying fallible beliefs to the soul.[8]

In this theory of language Gorgias classifies poetry as a subdivision of language, while extending its power to all of language. He adopts a simple scheme of cause and effect: a message is sent from speaker to a recipient who accepts it passively by a change in his soul. The listener is momentarily put in the power of another, as demonstrated most vividly by the effect of poetry and magical spells.[9] The speaker controls the listener not by any insights that he has, but by the language that bears his message. In general, what language creates is neither knowledge nor proposals by themselves, but beliefs and emotions imprinted in the souls of others. It is not an instrument of learning, but of persuasion. This theory of language fits within a general theory of the effect of the perceptible environment on a person. Just as language shapes the soul by being heard, so objects of sight shape the soul by being seen. Examples adduced by Gorgias are the terror produced by the sight of enemy soldiers as well as the delight caused by paintings and statues.[10] Artistically fashioned objects, whether heard or seen, have the same kind of impact on the soul as other objects of experience.

II   DIVINE INSPIRATION IN PLATO'S EARLY DIALOGUES

In his response to the poets and sophists, Plato sought to change language into an instrument of investigation and moral reform. He aimed in short to replace the *logos* of the poets and sophists with the *logos* of the philosophers – those who love wisdom, rather than those who pretend to it. He generally draws a distinction between the disinterested creativity of the poets and the sophists' self-interested manipulation of language; but at times his criticisms of the poets and the sophists merge. In the *Apology* and *Meno* very briefly, and in the *Ion* at length, Plato takes the additional view of the poet as a divinely inspired individual and finds a flaw in it: poets speak by divine inspiration without knowing what they say. In the *Apology*, Socrates tells that when he went to the poets to test the Delphic oracle, he found that, although they said "many beautiful things," they were utterly incapable of explaining what they said. Thereupon he concluded that they composed "not by wisdom, but by some natural talent and inspiration," like prophets.[11] He suggests in the *Meno* that poets are inspired with correct beliefs by a god.[12] Having such beliefs, he maintains, is not sufficient for having knowledge or being a teacher. In the *Ion* Socrates extends the poet's inspiration to the performer and the listener: All hang in a chain from an original divinity – poet first, then performer, then listener – like successive iron rings from a magnet. None of these human links has a "craft" (*technē*) because none has any knowledge of what he is doing.[13]

This is a picture of innocence as well as ignorance. In both the *Apology* and the *Ion*, however, ignorance is accompanied by delusion. In the *Apology*, Socrates points out that poets think they are wise about matters in which they are not. In the *Ion*, Plato exemplifies this delusion by the rhapsode Ion, who starts by claiming that he knows everything that Homer does and ends with the ridiculous assertion that he knows at least how to be a general. Ion is a false teacher, Plato implies, because he claims to be able to explain what Homer said, when he cannot.[14] The link with deity, moreover, does not preclude a poet's words from being false, as Socrates insinuates when he requires that the correctness of poems be judged by an expert. Nothing indeed prevents the poet, or any other inspired creature, from being as fatuously ill-informed as Ion. Although Ion bears the brunt of Socrates' attack, Plato indicates that divine possession is a bad reason to regard anyone – even "the best and most divine of poets," Homer (*Ion* 530b10) – as an authority.[15]

III   THE POWER OF SPEECH IN PLATO'S GORGIAS

By conjoining divine inspiration with human ignorance in these early dialogues, Plato begins to dissolve the link with divinity into an all-too-human purpose. Thus he suggests already in the *Ion* that the rhapsode does not hang wholly from a divine source; for Ion acknowledges that he pays great attention to the crowd, to see whether they hang on his words, since otherwise he will lose money (535e).

In his concern for money and reputation as well as his practice of poetic exegesis, Ion has much in common with the sophists. It is not surprising, then, that in another early dialogue, *Gorgias*, Socrates associates poetry with the rhetoric of the sophists. The whole dialogue is an attack on Gorgias' theory, as put forward in his *Encomium to Helen* (8–14), that language is a great power; and incidentally

Socrates brings poetry into the attack. Socrates does not indeed dispute Gorgias' contention that language has a great impact on the hearer; his whole attack rests on a tacit acceptance of this view. Instead, he argues that those who use language unjustly have no power; for they lack the power to accomplish what they really want – justice in their own souls. The rhetoric of the sophists, Socrates charges, is a pseudo-craft, a mere "semblance" (*eidōlon*) of the political craft of justice. It is a flattery of the soul, just as cookery is a flattery of the body. Instead of seeking what is best, it only seeks to gratify the crowd by taking their likes and dislikes as a standard.[16] Rhetoric shares this aim with poetry. For when stripped of melody, meter, and rhythm, poetry is a form of "public speaking" (*dēmēgoria*, a term whose meaning verges into "demagoguery") – a "rhetoric" of the theater – that merely aims to flatter the populace.[17]

Socrates subverts in this way not only the newly advanced claim of the sophists to have a craft that improves human life, but also the traditional claim of the poets to be teachers of mankind. This is an abrupt change from the qualified respect that Socrates shows the poets in the other early dialogues. Socrates builds up to his conclusion by an inductive chain in which he argues that public musical performances, from flute playing and lyre playing to choral productions, dithyrambic poetry, tragedy, and finally all poetry, aim only to gratify the audience. In constructing this sequence, Socrates has the respondent agree that the "revered and wondrous" poetry of tragedy (502b1) also aims at the pleasure rather than the improvement of the spectators. The respondent's ready assent is surprising in view of the respect traditionally bestowed on poets; but it also fits contemporary criticism of new forms of tragedy, as composed by Euripides.[18] As in the *Ion*, Socrates does not attack the most respected of all poets, Homer, directly. Instead, he attacks theatrical productions and infers that all poetry plays to the crowd.

Having broken the link with deity, Socrates suggests a new reason why poetry, in common with rhetoric, has such great power over the listener: *Logos* shapes the soul by indulging the listener's craving for pleasure. Conceived in this way, *logos* has no autonomous power; it is parasitic upon the desires of the listener, and the author's creativity is nothing but an adaptation of words to the beliefs of the listener. The ostensible power of the *logos* consists, paradoxically, in strengthening the weakness of the listener; in short, it is so devoid of power as to feed on the weakness of another. With an allusion to Socrates' trial, Plato has Socrates suggest that he may be the only person to practice the true craft of politics (521d). His *logos* cannot but offend the crowd since it aims at moral improvement. What, then, is the source of its strength?

IV   POETIC CREATIVITY IN PLATO'S SYMPOSIUM

The *Symposium* marks an important change from the early dialogues. Plato now tries out a new approach to poetry. Using a new conception of love, together with a theory of Forms, he now presents the poet as a creator, producing his poems as an act of private communication between himself and an intimate friend. Divinity returns, transformed into both a stimulus and a goal.

This entire proposal is attributed to Diotima, the prophetess who acts as Socrates' teacher. She begins her analysis with a complex definition of love, *erōs*, as an intermediary between gods and human beings, consisting of a desire for the creation of an immortal good in something beautiful.[19] Drawing a distinction between those who are creative in body and those who are creative in soul, Diotima exemplifies the latter by poets and "inventor" craftsmen, along with lawmakers (208e–209e).[20] All are creators of "prudence" (*phronēsis*) and other forms of "goodness" (*aretē*); the "greatest and most beautiful" kind of prudence is the "ordering of cities and households." Being "divine" in soul, these creators are pregnant with their offspring from an early age and give birth to them when they come upon a beautiful soul joined to a beautiful body. The act of creation consists of an abundance of words (*logoi*), spoken to the beautiful friend, about what a good man should be and what he should "practice" (*epitēdeuein*); this is an attempt to "educate." Both the creator and his friend promote this attempt by joining in a close and stable union to rear what has been created. Examples of such offspring are the poems of Homer and Hesiod and the laws of Lycurgus and Solon.

From this of type of creativity, dubbed by scholars the "lower mysteries," Diotima proceeds to what she calls the "perfect" mysteries (210a1). She reveals an ascent from love for one beautiful body to love for all beautiful bodies, then to a love of the beauty of souls and practices (*epitēdeumata*), then to a contemplation of the beauty of knowledge, and finally to a vision of beauty itself. Each of these four main stages, except the last, is said to be attended by a creation of discourse (*logoi*, 210a–d); the last creates, not "semblances of goodness" (*eidōla aretēs*), but the immortality of "true goodness" (212a). Although Diotima does not assign a place to poets in this ascent, there are sufficient similarities with her previous account to suggest that there may be a place for poets even here. In particular, Diotima's description of the second main stage, love of psychic beauty, as "giving birth to and seeking words that will make the young better" (210c) echoes her description of the lower mysteries. The next main stage of the ascent is the creation of philosophical discourse, as stimulated by the beauty of the various kinds of knowledge. Can poetic discourse reach this stage? Diotima does not say so. Still, it is possible to see the creativity of poets, lawmakers, and the rest, as depicted in the lower mysteries, as a preliminary stage, capable of being transformed into the philosophical type of discourse that belongs to the perfect mysteries. As we shall see, Socrates suggests such a transformation in the *Phaedrus*.

Throughout the progression from the lower to the perfect mysteries, Diotima offers a new interpretation of divine inspiration as the power of love, impelling humans along a path that leads from semblances of goodness to the ultimate goal, genuine goodness. Assigned by Diotima to the level of semblances, the poet first makes discoveries within himself, then is inspired by the beauty of another to bring them into creation as poems; subsequently, he keeps developing his creations in communication with the other. Poetic creation thus becomes a joint enterprise, nurtured by the love that binds the poet and his friend in a common pursuit of moral goodness. Interestingly, Diotima blurs the distinction between the creation of a poem and the creation of moral goodness. The reason is that these two types of creation coincide; for a poem serves as a vehicle for the transmission of goodness. The distinction itself, however, is fundamental to Plato's conception of poetry: A poem is the linguistic expression of a psychic disposition, which is transmitted to another.

Plato is often thought to have lacked a notion of poetry as an expression of personal feelings and beliefs.[21] Between his theory of imitation, as developed in the *Republic*, and the traditional view of divine inspiration, he seems to leave no place for self-expression in poetry, as advocated much later by the Romantics. Yet in the *Symposium* Diotima comes close to formulating a conception of art as self-expression. Although this is an expression of views about moral goodness in general, it originates within the poet as a communication to be shared with another. The poet continues to reflect on his discoveries as he develops them in cooperation with another; and he will himself grow in this process along with the other. All of this is an intensely personal endeavor, aided by an interpersonal bond. Like the other "inventors" and lawgivers, the poet gives voice to his own aspirations as he attempts to attain a kind of immortality by union with another.

In the *Gorgias* Socrates took theatrical poetry as the paradigmatic type of poetry. Diotima now implicitly proposes love poetry as a paradigm. This is surprising; for the privacy of love poetry seems to put it at the opposite extreme from public performances. Diotima, however, connects the two types: Love poetry lies at the origin of the publicly disseminated poetry of Homer, Hesiod, and other "good poets" (209d). Similarly, private discourse lies at the basis of the laws created by such renowned legislators as Lycurgus and Solon. In general, Diotima underpins public discourse with a theory of private communication, as inspired by love. As a result of this conversion from private to public discourse, men have produced "many beautiful deeds" among both Greeks and barbarians, together with "every kind of goodness" (209d–e). Ironically, this turns out to be a mere semblance. The process of creation, it appears, needs to be revised from the bottom up, starting at the level of private erotic discourse.

Love poetry thus becomes a model for intellectual creativity in general. Prose may be used for the same purpose; but it looks to love poetry as a paradigm for how to create moral value in union with another. All the speeches spoken at the banquet, including Alcibiades' crowning tribute to Socrates, may be understood as prose versions of Diotima's analysis of poetic creativity. All reveal moral discoveries made by the speaker in response to the beauty of one or more people at the gathering. All, too, may be viewed as preliminary to a philosophical ascent. Alcibiades attests the difficulty of making the transition to philosophy. Comparing Socrates' words to carved *sileni* – uncouth on the outside, but "most divine" on the inside (222a) – he credits them with the power to bewitch and possess the listener, like the music of Marsyas or the Sirens. In his own case, Alcibiades testifies, Socrates' words so reduced him to a frenzy of self-recrimination that he felt that his life was not worth living as it was (215d–216c). Alcibiades transfers to Socrates the power of enchantment traditionally assigned to poets, with the crucial difference that Socrates' words incite the listener to look into himself and that Socrates himself has far outstripped anyone else in his ascent to genuine goodness.

V   POETRY AS IMITATION IN PLATO'S REPUBLIC

(a) Books II–III

It is easy to overlook Diotima's remarks on poetry in the *Symposium* in view of the much more extended treatment in the *Republic*. In this dialogue, Plato considers poetry in the first place as a means of educating children to be guardians in his ideal state. Since Plato believes that children's souls are especially malleable, he is especially concerned with the impact of poetry on them; but he soon extends his concern to adults.[22] The public returns as the primary listener. Plato first purges poetry in Books II and III; then he returns to this purge in Book X by explaining in detail what is wrong with the poetry that he eliminated. In the two parts, Plato builds a powerful new theory of poetry as "imitation," *mimēsis*.

The purge takes its beginning from the fact that Socrates' initially healthy city, the "city of pigs," has become bloated and feverish by the admission of a vast throng of people, including imitators such as painters, poets, rhapsodes, actors, and dancers (*Rep.* II 372d–374a). Socrates responds with a program of education whose first concern is the reform of poetry. Like a physician, he reconstitutes poetry as a health-giving drug. This endeavor is in agreement with Gorgias' view, as discussed previously in this chapter, that poetry has the power both to heal and to poison the soul, and that it is especially powerful because it can make a person assume the identity of another. Socrates argues, first, that poets must present the truth about the gods and heroes, who are to serve as models of goodness (377d–392c) and, second, that poets must "imitate" only good individuals or individuals engaged in good action.[23] The first requirement concerns the content of a poem; the second concerns the diction (*lexis*). By "imitation" (*mimēsis*), Socrates here means what has traditionally been called "impersonation" (392d–394c). The poet "imitates" another whenever he speaks the words of a character in direct speech, as though he were that character. By contrast, the poet "narrates" whenever he reports in his own person what a character is doing or saying. As moral educator, the poet must imitate only what is morally good, and he must narrate all the rest. The reason is that the poet's imitations are passed on to the listener in such a way that if they continue from childhood on, they become rooted in the listener as habits (395c–d).

The right kind of poetry, therefore, will have only a small amount of imitation, consisting in the imitation of what is good, and it will have much narration (396e). This requirement automatically eliminates traditional tragedy and comedy, as Socrates' interlocutor recognizes. As Socrates hints, it also eliminates Homeric epic (394d). Socrates completes his type of pharmaceutical activity by prescribing melodies and rhythms that suit the content. Just as the diction must signal the difference between good and bad, so the melodies and rhythms must underscore the contrast by resembling the simplicity and restraint of moral rectitude. With its kernel of "imitation," the new poetry is carefully designed to confer a maximum of moral benefit by immersing the listener in an experience that resembles that of a good person as closely as possible.

Just as the physician will resort to an extreme remedy, the excision of a diseased limb, if other treatments are insufficient, so Socrates ends up with the ultimate remedy of expelling the sort of poet who corrupts the city. In a resounding statement, he proclaims: If "a man who is able to become every kind of individual (*pantodapos*) because of his wisdom and to imitate all things" were to come to our city, wishing to perform his poems, we would honor him as "sacred (*hieron*), marvelous, and giving pleasure," but say that "there is no such man in our city nor is it lawful that he should come to be, and we would send him off to another city, pouring myrrh on his head and crowning him with a chaplet" (398a). There is no such man in the city because none is allowed to assume more than one role, and this must be beneficial. As befits the sanctity of the occasion, Socrates does not name the man; but all his previous criticisms point to Homer. The "sacred" poet is a blight upon the city, and he is sent off, consecrated to a god like a scapegoat.[24]

From the purge of poetry, Socrates moves to a general cleansing of the city and a general theory of the crafts (401a–d). This theory, I suggest, may plausibly be regarded as the first theory of aesthetics in the Western tradition. Joining poetry to the other crafts, Socrates demands: not only poets "must be directed and forced to implant the likeness of a good moral character (*tēn tou agathou eikona ēthous empoiein*) in their poems," but also "the other craftsmen must be directed and prevented from implanting what is morally bad (*kakoēthes*)" in what they produce (401a1–b6).

The other craftsmen are exemplified by painters, weavers, house-builders, makers of equipment, and all who deal with "the nature of bodies and plants"; the latter subgroup presumably includes physicians, trainers, and farmers. Concerning non-poets, Socrates does not make a positive demand for implanting the likeness of a good character; instead, he prohibits bad character and, on the positive side, demands a seemliness (*euschēmosynē*) and harmony that he says are "akin" to, and "imitations" (*mimēmata*, 401a8) of, "good character." Presumably, poetry is especially suited to creating a "likeness" of good character; the other crafts imitate (in a broad sense) good character as much as possible. In general, Socrates demands of both poets and non-poets the ability to track down the "nature of the beautiful and seemly," so that the young will be led from childhood by the impact of "beautiful works" on the sight and hearing into "similarity, friendship, and harmony with the beauty of reason" (401c4–d3). Still showing the concerns of a physician, Socrates compares this aesthetic environment to a place in which gentle breezes waft health to the inhabitants. He assumes that just as a location has a direct effect on health, so visual and acoustic impressions have a direct effect on the moral condition of the soul.

In sum, Plato offers a bold new aesthetic theory that is distinguished by three main features: the perceptual impact of beautifully crafted things on the sight and hearing; the extension of beautiful craftsmanship to the sensory environment as a whole, including not only man-made objects but also things that grow by nature; and the direct influence of this environment on the moral configuration of the soul. Like Gorgias, Plato assumes that sensory impressions can shape the soul directly by triggering certain emotions and beliefs. What he adds is a certain affinity of such impressions with moral character, leading in the end to a lasting effect on the moral character of the percipient.[25] This position anticipates the metaphysical system that will be proposed subsequently in the *Republic*, according to which the sensible world contains degrees of resemblance to the Form of the

Good and the human craftsman must create sensible objects that resemble as much as possible what is good.

(b) Book X

In Book X of the *Republic*, Socrates' reform of poetry fades from sight, so much so that one might think it has been abandoned altogether. Although Socrates ends by keeping "hymns to gods and praises of the good" (*Rep.* X 607a3–5), he now proposes to ban all "mimetic" poetry; and it is not at all clear what kind of poetry is left.

The problem begins with Socrates' introductory claim that they were right, in founding the city, "not to admit in any way any [part of poetry] that is mimetic (*mimētikē*)" (595a5). This announcement is clearly a reference to the purge of poetry in Book III. But in Book III Plato certainly did not ban all poetic *mimēsis*; he merely banned *mimēsis*, defined as impersonation, of the type that impersonates bad character, while demanding the impersonation of good character and actions. Is there a discrepancy then? There has been much disagreement on this question. I agree with those who hold that there is no clash. For although Socrates previously defined *mimēsis* as impersonation, the kind of poetry he banned in Books II and III is "mimetic" in the wider sense of "given to imitation," or "imitative of anything at all"; in other words, it is "indiscriminately imitative" or "all-mimetic."[26] This sense appeared in Socrates' final description of the expelled poet as one who "is able to become every sort of individual because of his wisdom and to imitate all things" (398a1–2). Socrates here uses "mimetic" in the sense of "all-mimetic" to sum up his previous arguments. In short, the type of poetry he previously expelled is "mimetic" in the sense of "all-mimetic"; and in Book X he defends this expulsion.

This is not to deny that Book X marks a shift from the earlier discussion. Plato now returns to the problem of poetry because the metaphysics and psychology that he proposed in the meantime provide a new justification for the expulsion. He develops his answer in three stages, in which he successively reduces mimetic poetry into an object of detestation. First, he offers a new definition of "imitation" (595c7–598d6); second, he shows that the poetry of Homer and his successors fits this definition (598d7–602b11); and third, he argues that Homer and all other imitative poets corrupt even morally decent individuals and therefore deserve to be banished (602c1–607c3). In all three stages, Plato bases his conclusions on an analogy between the painter and the poet; as it turns out, poetry is beset by an acute moral problem of its own.

First, then, Plato builds his new definition of "imitation" directly on the conclusions of Book III. There he banished the all -mimetic poet, as we saw, who "is able to become every sort of individual because of his wisdom" (398a1–2). Plato now explains this "wisdom" (*sophia*): It is no wisdom really, but fakery, because it is just like taking a mirror and reflecting all things in it. The person who looks as though he can make all things is a "marvelous sophist" (*sophistēs*, 596d1), but he only seems "all-wise" (*passophos*) to the ignorant (598d3–4). He looks like a "maker" (*poiētēs*); in fact, he is an "imitator," not a real maker or craftsman, but a pseudo-maker of pseudo-creations. Plato brings in his metaphysics of Forms, together with God as the maker of Forms, in order to reduce this amazingly prolific "maker" to a mere shadow of a maker.[27]

Apart from one reference to the "maker of tragedy" (597e6), the "poet" (*poiētēs*) is present in this first stage of the argument only implicitly – though very obviously – as "maker." The "imitator" is represented by the painter, who makes all things by making appearances of them, just like the person with the mirror. He imitates objects made by human craftsmen, such as the bed made by the carpenter. Above the carpenter is God, maker of the Form of the bed, on which the carpenter models his creations. The painter's imitations are at two removes from real being, the Forms; and the painter is at two removes from the one truly genuine maker and craftsman, God. To this basic scheme Plato adds a refinement that will be of crucial importance later (597e–598d). The painter does not imitate the objects of human craftsmanship as they are, but as they appear. For example, he imitates the bed as it appears from the side or the front, not as it is. His imitation, therefore, and all imitation in general, is the imitation of an appearance, not of things as they are in this world. In short, an imitation is a "semblance" (*eidōlon*, 598b8) that is far from the truth, and the imitator knows nothing about any of the crafts that he imitates.

Plato's mirror simile has had an overwhelming influence on the interpretation of his aesthetics and on aesthetic theory in general. It stands as a compelling symbol of the view that it is the job of the artist to copy nature. But Plato's use of the simile needs to be interpreted with some care. In the first place, Plato thinks that merely copying things of the sensible world is not the same as to show the truth, as Socrates required of the poet in Books II–III; it is what the mimetic poet does. In the second place, the mimetic poet does not aim to copy things as faithfully as possible; he reproduces his own impressions of it. The commonplace contrast between mirroring and self-expression in the arts does not really fit Plato's use of the mirror simile. In the *Republic* Plato combines the two approaches by requiring both external models and a personal response. Just as the painter renders aspects of reality as they appear to him, so the poet renders his own impressions of reality. These appearances prompt the ignorant to take them for the real thing; instead, they are distortions produced by the imitator's own view of the world. Even though the poets of the *Symposium* come much closer to the Romantic notion of self-expression, the mimetic poet of the *Republic* also draws on his own inner resources – in particular, as will become clearer, his emotional inclinations – to give an interpretation of the external world. As Plato fills in gradually, the mirror is the poet's own soul: the external world is refracted by the poet's soul, not cast back as a faithful reproduction.

Plato's hierarchy of being has also proved misleading. It might seem that the poet can escape the shadowy unreality of his pseudo-craft by moving higher on the scale, either to an imitation of the Forms themselves or, at least, to a faithful replica of sensible reality. The first alternative is barred by the argument, which is presented later, that if the poet did model his creations on the Forms, then he would be a maker of human conduct in this world, taking his place among the craftsmen of the world; he would not devote himself to making mere semblances of goodness (598e5–601c2). This argument has been perceived as a serious difficulty for the view that in Book X Plato leaves open the possibility of a morally beneficial craft of poetry, as proposed in Books II and III; and we shall return to this problem. The second alternative is also barred. As Collingwood has argued, since imitations and sensible things are distinct categories of being, there is no way in which the imitator can attain the truthfulness of his particular model.[28] Just as the carpenter cannot recreate a Form, neither can the imitator recreate a sensible object. It might be objected that, like painters, poets can make more or less realistic copies. But a photographic type of realism is what Plato most decries, as the most perfect illusionism. Although Plato indicates in the third stage of his argument that a poet would err less if he did approximate sensible reality more closely, he nowhere proposes that a poet should model his work more closely on the actual world. His reason is that hanging on sensible reality, without independent guidelines, can only produce further distortions of reality.[29]

In the second stage of his argument (598d7–602b11), Plato launches a direct attack against poetry by reducing Homer and his followers from their traditionally exalted position as educators of the Greeks to the level of ignorant imitators. There are those, he mentions, who assign a knowledge of all crafts to Homer; he will not address this claim (598d7–599c6). What he will investigate is whether Homer had any knowledge of "the greatest and most beautiful things" about which he attempts to speak, that is, "about wars, generalship and the administration of cities, and about the education of a human being" (599c6–d2). The whole of this list is an allusion to the *Ion*, where Socrates shows up the rhapsode Ion (and implicitly Homer) as not knowing any crafts, with special attention to generalship.[30] The part that Socrates now singles out for discussion has special reference to Diotima's depiction of poets in the *Symposium* as creators of prudence, of which "the greatest and most beautiful" kind is the "ordering of cities and households," and other forms of goodness (209a). As we saw, Diotima groups poets with lawmakers and other creative craftsmen in this type of creativity. Citing Homer and Hesiod, together with Lycurgus and Solon, Diotima pairs all of these creators with an intimate friend in an effort to educate others by telling them what to "practice." Plato now expels Homer and his successors from this group.

With a point-by-point refutation of Diotima's account, Socrates argues that Homer did not know what "practices" (*epitēdeumata*, 599d5) make humans better either as members of a community or as private individuals.[31] Homer was not a good lawmaker like Solon or Lycurgus, or an innovator in the crafts such as Thales (599d7–600a7). Nor was he a private educator; in particular, his "companion" Creophylus would provide a laughable example of an educated disciple (600a9–c1). This obscure reference to Creophylus fills in a gap in Diotima's account by supplying an example of someone allegedly loved and educated by Homer. In the *Republic*, Socrates also brings Hesiod into his attack by suggesting that Homer's and Hesiod's contemporaries would hardly have let them roam around singing if they really had been able to help them become good (600d5–e2). His conclusion that all "poetic persons starting with Homer" are "imitators of semblances of goodness" (600e4–5) assigns a new depth of meaning to the expression "semblances of goodness," as used in the *Symposium* (212a4). Homer and other poets are demoted to a status below that of craftsmen and lawmakers because they are imitators of the sort that produce nothing but semblances at two removes from the truth.

In this part of the argument, then, Plato corrects Diotima's view of poetry by placing it at the bottom of a theory of imitation. In effect, he drives a wedge between Diotima's view of poetic creativity and the "perfect" mysteries of the upward ascent. Instead of occupying a stage on the way to knowledge, poets are exposed as cultivating ignorance; they are merely adept at faking wisdom. This is a new explanation of the ignorance imputed to poets in the *Apology* and *Ion*. At the same

time, Plato keeps in mind the possibility that he canvassed in the
Meno (96d–98c), that correct belief may be just as good a guide as
knowledge. "So as not to leave things half said," Socrates goes on in
the *Republic*, mimetic poets also lack the correct belief that comes
from taking instructions from a user (601c–602a). Socrates now offers
a tripartite division among user, maker, and imitator. Resorting once
more to the analogy of the painter, he pairs the painter with craftsmen
who make reins and bridles; he also brings in the maker of flutes, with
an implicit reference to mimetic music or poetry. Although the maker
of the physical object lacks knowledge, he makes a good product by
acquiring correct belief from a user who has knowledge. By contrast,
neither the painter nor any other imitator has knowledge himself or
acquires correct belief by associating with a user who knows. In his
ignorance, the imitative poet, now viewed as a tragic poet producing
either tragedy or epic, imitates what appears beautiful to the ignorant
masses (602b), as suggested previously in the *Gorgias.*

The third main stage of the argument (602c1–607c3), as I have
distinguished it, follows directly on this conclusion. Exploring further
the ignorance of the poet and his appeal to an ignorant crowd, it
consists of several sections, culminating in the "greatest charge"
(605c) against mimetic poetry – that it corrupts even decent persons.
The climax is a reiteration of the expulsion order, now directed explicitly against Homer and his successors.[32]

This third stage is initiated rather abruptly: there is just a "by
God," followed by a new line of thought. Socrates now uses the
analogy with the painter for the last time. Just as the painter creates
impressions that are accepted uncritically by the beholder without
any attempt at calculation, so all imitation appeals to the non-
rational, worthless part of our soul (602c–603b). This use of the
painter analogy is perhaps the weakest part of Plato's entire progression of arguments. The beholder of a painting, it is claimed, does not
measure the impressions before him against reality; instead, he is
seduced by appearances to accept them as they are, without bothering
to calculate how close they are to the real thing. In one stroke, the

argument empties imitation of rationality by removing the everyday practice of measurement. One would expect much more discussion. Still, the argument has some merit: The response to a work of art differs fundamentally from the response to a real-life situation. Plato here touches on the notion that a work of art is valued for its own sake, separated from real-life concerns by a suspension of disbelief. He spurns this outlook because he thinks that make-believe is harmful unless it agrees with an ultimately transcendent reality.

After taking away reason from the imitator as such, Socrates devotes all the rest of the discussion to poetic imitation. He finally reveals what the reader has been waiting for all along, an explanation of what sort of semblances are produced by the mimetic poet. What he imitates, Socrates now spells out, are humans engaged in action and having feelings of pain or joy at the thought of faring badly or well (603c). Further, the mimetic poet tends to dwell on such feelings instead of their control by reason; for he has a "natural" propensity to this part of the soul, since it is easy to imitate, and it is also easy for listeners, especially a crowd in the theater, to appreciate this type of imitation. Therefore, in order to win fame among the many, the imitative poet fixes his attention on uncontrolled feelings (604e–605a).

In case the mirror simile, along with the examples of the painter, carpenter, and bridle maker, misled the reader into thinking that the poet creates word pictures, as it were, of objects such as couches and bridles, he is now set straight. The poet imitates moral goodness and badness, as shown in human actions, beliefs, and feelings. The depiction of Achilles driving a chariot or running around the plain of Troy, for example, is incidental to the imitation of his moral character. Corresponding, therefore, to the Form of the couch or table are the Forms of the virtues – justice, moderation, courage, and wisdom.[33] The mimetic poet creates nothing but distortions of the virtues, since he looks only to how humans actually respond to circumstances and he is drawn, moreover, to the opposite of virtuous behavior – the disorderly rule of the emotions. It would be bad enough if he merely imitated human conduct as it is; instead, he imitates it as it appears to the worthless part of his and everyone else's soul. Instead of showing us Oedipus, let us say, bringing order to the city by his wisdom, he dwells on the agony of his downfall. Oedipus' success would be too boring to most people.

As in the *Gorgias*, so in the *Republic* Plato condemns poetry as theatrical demagoguery, aiming to please the crowd by indulging its ignoble desires, although he now uses a wealth of new arguments. He also takes back the view of poetic creativity that Diotima sponsored in the *Symposium*. Substituting negative terms for Diotima's language of love and goodness, Socrates claims that all imitation "consorts with and is a companion (*hetaira*) and friend (*philē*) to something far from prudence in us for the purpose of nothing healthy or true"; in short, "being worthless, it associates with something worthless and creates worthless things."[34] In contrast with Diotima's poet, who is said to join in love with a beautiful soul and create prudence, the mimetic poet prostitutes himself in the service of the worthless part of the human soul and creates nothing but worthlessness.

In many respects, Plato's mimetic poet stands for what many of us value most in poetry. He creates his poems in response to the spectacle of human action and feelings. Immersed in this world, he derives all his inspiration from it, ranging over it with a full engagement of his emotions, entrancing others as he is entranced by life. Plato casts out this poet on the ground that his emotional intensity "feeds" (606b–d) and strengthens the emotional part of the listener's soul, like a malignant cancer, while weakening the rational part. In opposition to what he demanded in Book III (401b), Socrates accuses the mimetic poet of "implanting (*empoiein*) a bad constitution privately within the soul of each person" (605b7–8). Worst of all, this poetry is so powerful that it corrupts not only the many, but the better sort (with very few exceptions) who ordinarily try to control their emotions by reason (605c–606d). For they are seduced into gaining pleasure by letting go of their emotions, with the excuse that it is not disgraceful to share the emotions of someone else.

There are many ways of resisting Plato's diagnosis of the bad effects of poetry while accepting much of his analysis of what the poet does. Aristotle takes the view that the emotionality of poetry cleanses instead of corrupts. Without denying the power of poetry to shape moral habits, we might look for an escape in Plato's analogy of the painter. In creating his illusions, one might argue, the painter does in fact carefully measure appearance against reality. In foregrounding one aspect of the table or couch, for example, he calculates how this aspect is related to the whole and indicates its relationship to the beholder. This sort of measuring, it seems, is intrinsic to the work of art; it belongs to its very essence. Similarly the poet, even though he may emphasize the emotions, sets them in the wider context of a moral order. Oedipus' suffering is the more acute because of his search for wisdom; and when the theatergoer suffers with him, his suffering is a measure of his recognition of the nobility of Oedipus' character. By separating off an emotional part of the soul from rational insight, Plato closes off this way of defending poetry as a genuinely creative endeavor.

In Plato's view, how can the poet escape degradation? This question takes us back to our first problem. What room is left for the type of poet who implants "the likeness (*eikona*) of a good moral character" in his poems (Book III, 401b2–3)? At that point, Socrates said that poets must be "directed and forced" to do so. This remains an option: the poet, now viewed as a maker of semblances at two removes from the truth, must be required to follow the sort of prescriptions that were set out in such great detail in Books II and III. This would make him a special kind of imitator – not the "mimetic" kind who will imitate anything at all, with an inclination toward the worse, but a selective imitator, directed by an overseer to imitate only what is good. There is also another possibility. As we saw, the mimetic poet does not look to the Forms, nor does he have correct beliefs. What prevents a poet, on the other hand, from looking beyond sensible things to the Forms or, at any rate, deriving correct beliefs from a lawmaker? He would still present semblances; but they would be of the correct type, created from within himself on the basis of his own insights (whether knowledge or beliefs), with a view to educating others. A revision of this kind would raise a type of poetry, along with other types of imitation, to the level of a genuine craft, creating real goodness by means of semblances rooted in the poet's own goodness.

Plato does not take any steps toward developing this kind of answer in the *Republic*, although, I suggest, he lays a foundation for it. As it is, he presents just two options: The poet either follows his own inclinations and corrupts, or is directed by an overseer to a selective imitation of what is good. Nor does the painter or any other imitator fare any better. In common with other craftsmen, they must create a good moral environment for the citizens; and what makes the task especially difficult for them is that they are drawn by their own nature to a fascination with the sensory impressions of this world.

VI   THE TRANSFORMATION OF POETRY IN PLATO'S
     PHAEDRUS

Plato reconsiders the place of poetry in human life in the *Phaedrus*. As though dissatisfied with his coercion of poetry in the *Republic*, Socrates proclaims that no one can become a good poet unless inspired with divine madness (*Phdr.* 245a). In words that recall Diotima's analysis of poetry in the *Symposium*, he explains that possession by the Muses gets hold of a "tender" soul and "educates" later generations by celebrating the deeds of the ancients (*Phdr.* 245a). At the same time, he takes up a possibility that was barely a hint in Diotima's discourse. Developing a new theory of soul and a new theory of discourse, Plato now supplies detailed guidelines on how to transform poetry into philosophy.

Let us start with a puzzle. In the *Phaedrus*, poetic inspiration is one of four types of divine madness, along with prophecy, ritual, and love; love is the best madness of all (244a–245a, 265b). Divine madness in general is said to be responsible for the "greatest goods" to humans (244a), and all four kinds are said to produce "beautiful works" (245b). On the basis of Diotima's view of poetry, we might expect poetry to have some role in the soul's ascent to the Forms, as depicted by Socrates in his palinode; instead, Socrates explains this ascent as motivated entirely by love. Moreover, he places the "poetic person" (*poiētikos*) surprisingly low in his ranking of lives (248d–e). The best life is that of the "philosopher or lover of beauty or a certain musical and erotic person (*philosophou ē philokalou ē mousikou tinos kai erōtikou*)." Next is the lawful king or military commander, followed by the politician or businessman, then the trainer or physician. Fifth is the life of the prophet or conductor of rites; sixth is the "poetic person or another who is concerned with imitation (*mimē-sis*)"; seventh is the craftsman or farmer; eighth is the sophist or demagogue; and ninth and last is the tyrant (248d–e). The "poetic person," cast as an imitator, is lowest of the four types of divinely inspired persons, with the prophet and conductor of rites just above him. The terms "poetic" and "imitation" recall the *Republic*. Divine inspiration, it seems, is no more a guarantee of enlightenment than it is in the *Apology* or *Ion*; nor does it save the poet from the low ranking he received in the *Republic*. Even though the poet is now placed a step above the craftsman, he is far removed from the "musical person" who shares first place with the philosopher and the lover.

In the *Phaedrus*, then, Plato appears to drive another wedge between poetry and philosophy. At the same time, he offers a fundamentally new proposal: the transformation of all types of discourse – in particular, poetry, political rhetoric, and legal language – into philosophical discourse. The underlying topic of the *Phaedrus*, like that of the *Gorgias*, is rhetoric. But "rhetoric" is now taken explicitly in the broad, etymological sense of the "art of speech" in general, so as to subsume both public speaking and private discourse. Defining "rhetoric" as a "leading of the soul (*psychagōgia*) by words" in both public and private (261a), Socrates gradually transforms the basic meaning of *psychagōgia*, "conjuring" and "enchantment," which fits the sophistic view of language, into the sense of "leading the soul" to the truth, as befits philosophical discourse. In the course of Socrates' examination, rhetoric becomes the art of dialectic, devoted to the purpose of guiding another to the truth. It requires, first of all, the dialectical ability to define and divide the subject matter correctly, and, further, a knowledge of the types of souls and their particular occurrences, together with a knowledge of the kinds of language, so that the speaker will be able to adapt his language to the soul of the listener (276e–277c). Socrates exemplifies this genuine art of rhetoric throughout the *Phaedrus*. Using various kinds of language, including a "mythic hymn" adorned with "poetic" words, he leads his companion, Phaedrus, to an understanding of the proper use of language.[35] Genuine rhetoric may include prose speeches and poetry, but it is essentially an act of communication between two individuals.

Plato's newly comprehensive theory of language is accompanied by a new psychology, which integrates love within the tripartite division developed in the *Republic*. Revising Diotima's ascent to the Form of Beauty in the *Symposium*, Socrates now proposes that, confronted by the similarity (250a6), or imitation (251a3), of beauty in his beloved, the lover is reminded of the genuine beauty that he saw previously as a disembodied soul above the heavens. By "using such reminders correctly," the lover is initiated into "perfect" rites and becomes "truly perfect" (249c7–8). The first task is to conquer one's physical erotic impulses; after this, the lover is ready to fashion his beloved into whatever kind of deity he discovers within himself. The best kind of initiation, it turns out, is to fashion one's beloved as much as possible into Zeus, in agreement with one's own nature (252c–253a). This is the nature of a "philosopher and leader" (252e3).

Socrates draws together his new thoughts on rhetoric and love in a message that he asks Phaedrus to convey to his "beloved" (*paidika*, 279b2), Lysias, at the end of the *Phaedrus*. This is a message to Lysias and any other speechmaker, as well as to Homer, along with any other poet, and to Solon along with any other writer of laws: If they know the truth about what they wrote and can defend it by speaking about it, while showing that what they wrote is worthless, then they deserve the name of "philosopher" rather than the name that corresponds to their written texts – that is, "speechwriter," "poet," or "writer of laws" (278b–e). Plato's dialogues may be regarded as attempts to exemplify this use of language. Described by Plato as "play" and "reminders for his old age" (276d2–4), they signal, through their configuration as conversations, the way in which all language – poetic, political, legal, and the rest – may be transformed into philosophical discourse.

A poet's written compositions, then, are but moments of thought, frozen in language and worthless in themselves. The serious part of his endeavors consists in a philosophical defense of them. Like islands in a sea of reflection, the texts that have been passed down are merely stages on the philosophical quest for wisdom. This is indeed how Plato uses traditional poetry in his dialogues. As for the poet, his transformation into a philosopher catapults him from sixth place into first place in the ranking of lives. As a truly "musical" person, he is no longer fettered by laws nor blinded by appearances, but is inspired by love to search for wisdom in communication with another.

I shall close with the *Laws*, where Plato not only reduces the imitative poet once more into a servant of the lawmaker but also proposes to transform the poet, together with the maker of laws, into a philosopher.[36,37] The old Athenian who has replaced Socrates as Plato's chief spokesman suggests that the discussion that he and his companions have had about the laws is a kind of "poetry": It is the most suitable of all poems and prose works, he says, for children to hear and teachers to approve (811c–e). This completes the transformation of a poet into a philosopher by transforming the philosopher himself into a kind of poet.

NOTES

1 In his pioneering study *Preface to Plato*, Havelock (1963) emphasizes the importance of oral poetic teaching in Greek society. See also Murray 1981: 87–100.

2 DK 21 B 11.

3 DK 22 B 42.

4 DK 82 B 11.8. See Wardy 1986: 38–47.

5 DK 82 B 11.13–14.

6 DK 82 B 11.9.

7 DK 82 B 23.

8 DK 82 B 11.11.

9 Gorgias sought to recreate the enchantment of poetry in his own prose by using balanced clauses and sound patterns to emulate the rhythms of poetry. See de Romilly 1975: 8–11.

10 DK 82 B 11.15–19.

11 *Ap.* 22a–c.

12 *Meno* 99c–d.

13 *Ion* 533d–534d, 535e–536d. See further Murray 1992: 27–46. Scott (2011) identifies divine inspiration (as treated primarily in *Ion* and *Meno*) as one of three sources of poetic creativity recognized by Plato; the other two sources are, in his view, internal inspiration (as presented in the *Symposium*) and the external crowd (as treated in *Grg.* 501–2 and *Rep.* VI 493).

14 Ion prides himself not only on being able to recite Homer's poems, but also on being able to explain his meaning better than anyone else (*Ion* 530b–d).

15 See further Woodruff 1982.

16 *Grg.* 464b–465d, 500e–501c; the term *eidōlon* occurs at 463d2 and e4.

17 *Grg.* 501d–503b, with the term *dēmēgoria* at 502c12 and d2.

18 In the *Frogs* (1009–10), Aristophanes has Euripides say that poets are admired because they make the citizens better. Iris Murdoch (1977: 13) makes the sweeping claim that "like all puritans Plato hates the theatre."

19 See esp. *Smp.* 206e–207a and Obdrzalek's contribution to this volume, ch. 7.

20 There is no need to emend *theios* ("divine," 209b1), which occurs in all the manuscripts. This entire section deals with what Price (1989: 27–9) calls "educative pederasty." Sheffield (2001; and 2006: 90–153) offers a detailed analysis. See further Dover 1980 and Rowe 1998a.

21 M. H. Abrams discusses the distinction between imitative and expressive theories of art in his highly influential book *The Mirror and the Lamp* (1953).

22 *Rep.* 377a–b, 378d–e, 380c1, 387b4.

23 At 396c5–e2, Socrates specifies that the poet must imitate good characters most of all when they act prudently and less when they err, and that the poet will imitate unworthy characters only briefly when they do something worthwhile. Socrates does allow that "for fun" (*paidias charin*, 396e2) a poet may occasionally imitate someone unworthy. Gabriel Lear (2011) proposes that *mimēsis* in Book III should not be understood in the traditional sense of "impersonation," as implying an identification with a character, but as "appearance-making" of a sort that does not imply such an identification.

24 On the purification (*katharmos*) of a city by the expulsion of a human scapegoat (*pharmakos*), see Burkert 1985: 82–4. In one text, the scapegoat is "decked in boughs and sacred vestments" before being chased away. Socrates uses *diakathairein* and *kathairein* at *Rep.* 399e5 and 399e8. In his far-ranging study "Plato's Pharmacy," Derrida (1981) suggests that Socrates is a scapegoat, *pharmakos*, as well as *pharmakeus* ("sorcerer," see esp. *Smp.* 203d8), expelled from Athens by poison. Homer's banishment may be viewed as an ironical counterpart to Socrates' execution.

25 See further Bosanquet 1892: esp. 49.

26 Belfiore (1984: 126–7) argues for this meaning, which was first proposed by Menza (1972: 161–3). Menza (1972: 132, 161–2) reasonably takes the occurrence of μιμητικός at 395a2 as an implicit definition of the term. Following Menza, Belfiore translates μιμητική as "versatile imitation." Ferrari (1989: 124–5) also adopts this interpretation. See further Moss 2007.

27 *Rep.* 607c5. At 607a5, he calls this poetry the "sweetened Muse" (ἡδυσμένην Μοῦσαν). At 600e4–6, Socrates claims that "all poetic persons (*poiētikous*), starting with Homer, are imitators of semblances of goodness" and the rest; cf. 601a4. This has often been interpreted as a general claim about "poets." In my view, this is a claim about the traditionally celebrated poets of the Greeks. Although *poiētikos* may be used as a synonym of *poiētēs*, "poet," Plato appears to use the term in the *Republic* (and, as I shall suggest, also at *Phaedrus* 248e) in the same way as "mimetic," with the special connotation of "given to poetry," that is, "given to imitations"; see esp. 607a2, where Homer is described as "most poetic" *(poiētikōtaton)*.

28 As Cherniss (1932) has argued, Plato is not here revising his theory of Forms by making God their creator, but brings in God merely for the sake

of the analogy. Socrates himself qualifies this stratagem by the tentative "we might say" at 597b6.

29 Collingwood 1925: esp. 157–9. For a different view, see Nehamas 1982: esp. 60–3.

30 In the *Sophist*, Plato develops his ideas on imitation further by dividing *mimētikē* into (a) the making of likenesses (*eikastikē*), which consists in preserving the proportions of the "paradigm," and (b) the making of appearances (*phantastikē*), which changes the proportions of the paradigm so as to make it appear beautiful (235b–236c). In the *Republic, mimētikē* does not include (a), which may be taken as a philosophical descendant of the craft of making a "likeness" (*eikona*) of goodness, as proposed in Book III of the *Republic*. In the *Sophist* Plato explores the connection between poetry and sophistry by identifying the sophist in turn as an imitator of appearances. The poet does not appear explicitly, but fits the category of the simple-minded imitator who wrongly thinks he knows; by contrast, the sophist is a dissembling imitator (268a).

31 The crafts come into the discussion at 537a; generalship enters as the culminating craft at 540d. See also 536e1–3, where Ion claims that Homer speaks well about "everything whatsoever."

32 The *Symposium* is generally thought to be close in date of composition to the *Republic*. It seems to me that the much more elaborate account of the Forms and of the ascent to knowledge in the *Republic* is subsequent to the account in the *Symposium*, and that Socrates' criticism of Homer and all traditional poetry in Book X is additional evidence for dating the *Symposium* before the completion of the *Republic*.

33 Annas (1982) argues that there is a serious discontinuity in the argument; for Plato regards poetry as trivial in everything except the very last part of the argument (605c–608b), where it suddenly appears as a danger to mankind.

34 See further Battin 1977.

35 *Rep.* 603a12–b4; cf. 605a9–b2.

36 *Phdr.* 265c1 and 257a5; cf. 241e1–3. See Asmis 1986; and Moss 2012.

37 For further discussion of the entire dialogue as "poetry," see Asmis 2015: esp. 491–3.

12 Betwixt and Between: Plato and the Objects of Mathematics

Henry Mendell

In *Republic* VI and VII, Plato has Socrates present the outlines of an educational program for the rulers of his ideal state. Preliminary to the study of dialectic, the pure activity of intellect, they are to study five mathematical sciences. These sciences differ in degree of clarity and truth from dialectic and from opinion, the cognition of the senses. The mathematical sciences had developed in the previous hundred years in the Greek world along lines very different from ordinary mathematical practice in the Greek world and, more broadly, the Middle East. Plato attempts a philosophical account of this new practice that is sometimes descriptive and sometimes prescriptive. We expect from Plato an account of the methodologies of these sciences, their relation to the perceptible world and to Forms, and how they provide knowledge.

In *Republic* VI, Socrates distinguishes the visible world of things that merely are becoming from the intelligible world of things that are. Within the visible world, he contrasts the objects of conviction, animals, plants, stars, artifacts (certainly including mathematical diagrams), with the images of them in shadows and reflections. However, for the intelligible world, he uses only differences in methodologies, and not objects, to distinguish reasoning (*dianoia*), which encompasses the mathematical sciences, and the truer science of dialectic, which makes use of Forms. We

This paper is dedicated in memory of Ian Mueller. It has had a long gestation, with section VII first presented at Columbia University (1986), section V initially in a reply to Richard Foley at an A.P.A. (2004) and fully at Clarke University (the resulting paper being way too long to be included in BACAP), and the general approach at Florida International University as well as at the conference for this volume at Northwestern in 2018. I thank, especially, Gisela Striker, Julius Moravcsik, John Driscoll, Nick White, Hera Arsen, Sophia Stone, Richard Kraut, but most of all David Ebrey, in patience, generosity, and insight a true mensch.

might well expect that there should be special objects for the mathematical sciences, given that earlier (V 477c–d) Socrates has stated that powers, specifically cognitive powers, differ in their objects *and* the ways in which they work with them. Yet, other than to state that the objects of the science cannot be the objects of conviction, he explicitly avoids ascribing any special objects to the mathematical sciences. This raises for all readers of Plato the difficult question, how, on his view, mathematical propositions are true, and what, if anything, they must be true of, given that they provide a sort of understanding, albeit one inferior to the knowledge of Forms that dialectic provides.

Aristotle famously provides Plato with an answer, that Plato postulated a tripartite ontology with objects between Forms and perceptibles, which he calls 'the betweens' (intermediates) and 'the mathematicals', the ancestors of most modern mathematical Platonisms, or perhaps we should say Speusippanisms, if, alternatively, Plato's nephew, Speusippus, is the originator of the view. Mathematical propositions are true of these objects. Since there are no passages in Plato's dialogues that unequivocally support Aristotle's claim, many twentieth-century readers of Plato have rejected Aristotle's attribution as based in a polemically motivated misunderstanding of Platonic metaphysics.[1] In agreement with older interpretations, others have defended Aristotle, whether the doctrine stands apart from dialogues or provides a deeper insight how to read them.[2] I shall defend neither approach. Whether or not Aristotle has distorted Plato's beliefs, we can find in Plato's writing traces of the very metaphysical concerns that Aristotle points to, although Plato's characters also avoid taking that extra step of addressing the question of the ontology of mathematics, that is, what mathematical statements are about. Nonetheless, in some dialogues, characters present a tripartite ontology with intermediate objects that partially – but only partially – satisfy the conditions for intermediates that Aristotle attributes to Plato. In fact, the view is nearest to an account that

Aristotle discusses but does not associate with Plato. We are left with quandaries.

Before I proceed, I should make clear five principles I employ in reading the dialogues. First, I read the text linearly and don't assume a thesis at the beginning of a dialogue that is only introduced later. More generally, I ask how one character could naturally understand what another says at every step of a dialogue, Fine's 'Dialectical Requirement'.[3] I also extend this to Plato's contemporary reader, a 'Reader's Requirement', in particular, how such a reader would understand some mathematical practice or concept. Since these requirements often amount to the same, I shall speak of them together as the Audience Requirement. Also, when a character says something ambiguous or clearly problematic or omits something, that ambiguity or omission may well be a salient feature of the text. Finally, when a character explicitly avoids a discussion or skips a postponed one, I don't try to put a hidden thesis into the character's mouth, but just accept that Plato doesn't want to discuss the issue, for whatever reason. Of course, these principles may be violated, just not with impunity.

I SOME FEATURES OF GREEK MATHEMATICS RELEVANT TO THE STUDY OF PLATO

Because Plato is responding to the mathematics of his own time, it is important for anyone approaching his views on mathematics to have some understanding of it. As there are no surviving Greek mathematical treatises from the time of Plato or earlier, we must infer their basic characteristics from the little Plato allows his characters to present, some quite sophisticated,[4] presentations scattered through Aristotle, fragments of Aristotle's follower, Eudemus, and traces in Hellenistic treatises. This was a period of fast development of the Greek mathematical style, so that we cannot naively rely on works from half a century later to understand mathematical practices in Plato's time.[5] Besides developments in arithmetic, geometry, and stereometry, several mathematical sciences were also emerging in

Plato's time: astronomy, harmonics, mechanics and statics, and optics, all in the context of a rich and ancient mathematical and astronomical tradition in the Middle East.[6]

In Plato's *Laws* VII, the Athenian Visitor describes geometry as measurement[7] and urges an Egyptian style of education in calculation and measurement, when introducing the basic education in arithmetic, geometry, and astronomy for citizens in the new city (817e5–818b5). He does not imply that Greeks do not teach their children these things, only that they do not do it as well.[8] The Visitor is not recommending that the hoi polloi study Greek mathematics. Despite the Visitor's complaint, it is likely that ordinary Greek mathematical education was not very different from the Egyptian and Mesopotamian metrical practices. Students would learn the appropriate number systems and operations, including the use of an abacus, with an emphasis on conversion from one measure to another.

They would have learned by imitating paradigmatic procedures. A typical metrical procedure text in the Egyptian and Babylonian traditions stipulates a situation, e.g., a square field of 100 square cubits, and asks the student to find the diameter of a round field of the same size.[9] The text then walks through the calculation of the diameter. It may finally verify the answer, here by calculating the area from the diameter. The student would then use the procedure to solve similar problems. Unlike texts in the Greek mathematical style, such texts are common in Greek papyri, albeit from a later period.[10]

Instead of stating a problem metrically, with numerical measures, a Greek-style text, with a few notable exceptions, will state its objects abstractly, with letter labels. So, a line might be introduced, "Let-there-be a line, that on which the AB is."[11] Even where the text discusses numbers, e.g., where, clearly from context, the series is: 2, 4, 8, 16, the text will maintain a charade that these are arbitrary, "the A, B, C, D."[12]

In Plato's time (and later?), there seems to be a middle ground between this abstract form and the metrical tradition. At least, this is what we see in the two discussions in Plato closest to presenting Greek mathematical work. The unlabeled square to be doubled in the *Meno* 82b–85b is 2 × 2 feet. Theaetetus, at *Theaetetus* 147d–148b, starts his discussion of incommensurability with the square of three-square feet, although his account quickly becomes abstract, with 'feet' dropped, when he turns from describing what Theodorus did in their joint work.[13]

The overall structure of a Greek problem is not all that different from a metrical problem. It requires one, here in general terms, given certain objects, to construct or find something, e.g., "Given a cone or cylinder, to find a sphere equal to it."[14] The given objects are then hypothesized, followed by a procedure for constructing/finding the required objects. Instead of a brief, optional verification of a particular solution, here is a demonstration that everything so constructed has the required property, that the procedure always works. So, the demonstration now becomes a centrally important justification. However, like their metrical ancestors, Greek problems are not existence proofs. Their importance lies in their providing methods for getting objects. Furthermore, the methods of construction go beyond the straight line and circle of Euclid's *Elements* I–VI.[15]

In extant treatises, there are two typical forms of propositions, the problem form above and the theorem, which puts forward a statement to be shown true, e.g., "Every triangle has internal angles equal to two right angles."[16] Although this distinction between problem and theorem probably was not solidified until a half century after Plato's death, the conceptual difference certainly goes back to the beginning of Greek mathematics. In problems the goal is a procedure: given some object A one gets an object B such that B is always F (to construct F given A), while in a theorem the goal is the proof of a statement, that B always is F (whether or not one has a procedure for getting B). The demonstration or justification will be the same, to show that every B is F.

Although we have nothing of the early attempts at organizing elementary treatises before Euclid (early third century BCE), by Hippocrates of Chios (late fifth), Leon, and Theudius,[17] the latter two little more than names, one could get a fairly good sense of the arrangement of such a book by tracking mathematical examples in Aristotle and the fragments of Eudemus.[18]

In *Republic* VI 510d–511a, in the analogy of the Divided Line, Socrates says that in mathematics we hypothesize the odd and the even, the shapes and the three species of angles and the siblings of these in each procedure, without giving an account of them, but proceeding from these to conclusions. By contrast, dialectic, he says, proceeds from hypotheses to what's unhypothetical, and without the use of diagrams. The one common sense of 'hypothesis' throughout Plato's works is: what is set down at the beginning of a discussion. I will not speculate on what Plato here means by hypotheses, whether objects, definitions, initial construction rules of a treatise, other sorts of principles, or the hypothesis of things given at the beginning of a proof. Even if his readers knew, we do not. It is enough that Plato envisages a body of mathematics as having certain starting points (objects or principles) without giving an appropriate account of them (of what sort?) and that the science proceeds deductively from these. It is plausible, though not much more than that, that a 'problem' for Plato in *Rep.* VII is a mathematical question – "Can this be constructed/found?", "Is that the case?" – which will become an established proposition when answered with a construction and proof from the hypotheses of the science.

Another striking characteristic of Greek mathematics is the use of diagrams, an essential part of Greek proofs, to visually represent the mathematical configurations described in the verbal part of the text, both in illustrating constructions indicated and in marking out things cited in the demonstration, which would usually be nigh incomprehensible without the diagram (to some degree they are part of the text).[19]

Now, naively, one might think a diagram presents an arbitrary instance, an exemplar (*paradeigma*), of a circle, a polygon, etc. In general, the function of an exemplar determines the type of detail required. A perfect 1:1 three-dimensional exemplar of a column for a building is an instance, even if it is never used.[20] A 1:1, but two-dimensional architectural plan, no matter how precise,[21] is not. If, unlike architectural plans, geometrical and arithmetic diagrams were never metrically precise, as Netz has argued,[22] or at least never needed to be metrically or shape-wise precise, since the inaccuracies in the diagram do not enter into the proofs, as Aristotle claimed,[23] one might still think that a diagram of a triangle, even if drawn free-hand, is still a triangle – albeit an imperfect one. On the other hand, an astronomical diagram depicting the ecliptic, equator, horizon, stars, and sun at different points on the ecliptic, cannot be even an imperfect instance. It is not a heavenly system at all.

The second feature of mathematics that Socrates mentions in *Republic* VI 510d–511a is that mathematicians make arguments about visible objects, which they contrive and draw (and label), but they reason, not about these, but about things that these resemble (and represent). "Line AB" in the argument or text will refer to the drawn line AB, but the reasoning concerns what drawn line AB resembles (what that is for Plato is the principal concern of this chapter).

It is obvious that Socrates is here speaking of diagrams but not just diagrams alone. Later, he alludes back to this when he explains the use of the heaven[24] as an exemplar:

> Accordingly, I said, one must make use of the heaven's adornment as exemplars (*paradeigmasi*), for the sake of coming to learn those things, just as if someone were to happen upon diagrams[25] excellently drawn or labored over by Daedalus or some other craftsman or drawer. For in seeing such things, someone experienced in geometry, I suppose, would consider them as holding most beautifully in their execution, but doubtless would

consider it laughable to examine them carefully with the intent of getting the truth in them of equals or doubles or any other commensurability. (529d7–530a1)

Though not a diagram, the heaven corresponds to a diagram. It would be as laughable to measure carefully the heaven as to measure a diagram of the diagonal and side of a square to see if they are the ratio of two numbers. As with the geometrical diagram, the astronomer can make arguments that refer to objects of the visible heaven (harder to label), but the reasoning will concern the proper objects of astronomy, which, Socrates argues, are not visible.

This does not answer our question: whether, for Plato, the visible representations used in mathematical arguments need to be instances, but mathematical reasoning does not concern those instances. One can, with some implausibility, read Plato as committed to treating the diagram as a visible exemplar;[26] however, it is of no importance for actual mathematical practice that representations also be instances.

As to Greek arithmetic in the time of Plato, it is commonly stated that Greek number theory is about whole numbers (usually larger than one), and this is largely true, if for no other reason than that in the time of Plato, Greeks, unlike their Babylonian and Egyptian neighbors, had no general system for representing fractions and for working with them. It is likely that fractions were conceptually tied to subunits, e.g., one Greek foot into 16 inches, with the effect that a fraction is conceived as taking some part, e.g., a sixteenth, and treating it as a subunit. The common way of representing numbers in Plato's world was a Greek version (origin?) of Roman numerals (with IIII = 4, etc.), which we call acrophonic because numbers above one get represented by the initial letter of the name for the number: five (Γ for 'pente'), ten (Δ for 'deka'), etc., with fifty a combination of ten and five (ΓΔ). This system worked seamlessly with abaci or counting boards, which could be divided up according to the numerals, a units area, a five area, a tens area, etc., even a subunit area, and manipulated by shifting pebbles about. In ordinary parlance, a combination of superunits and subunits might be considered a number.[27] It is a natural annex to this treatment of numbers to represent numbers by pebble units and look at their properties by shifting configurations of pebbles, working with whole numbers, although we do not know how mathematicians would represent numbers in proofs in the time of Plato.[28]

Bluntly put, everyone in the world of Plato would have conceived and understood a number as a collection of units of some sort.

II   THE PROBLEM: ARISTOTLE

Aristotle says of Plato:

> Furthermore, besides the perceptibles and the Forms he says that
> the mathematicals are between things, differing from the
> perceptibles by being eternal and lacking motion and from the
> Forms by these being many similar particulars, while the Form
> itself is each only one. (*Met.* Alpha 6 987b14–18)

The mathematicals then have four properties:

1) They are eternal
2) They lack motion
3) They are many (infinite[29]) instances in cases where there is one Form
4) They are similar to one another, whereas there is one Form.

The first two we can call Parmenidean, in that we readily recognize them as features of the objects of a Parmenidean epistemology (e.g., *Phaedo* 80a–b). The last two we recognize as echoing a one-over-many principle, that where several things are similar, there is one Form over them.[30] I separate the plurality and the similarity merely for our convenience. There is one Form, say, of triangle, but lots of mathematicals that are similar in virtue of being three-angled rectilinear figures.

Besides being plural and transitory, there is another way in which perceptibles may differ from Forms and which will play out in our discussion. Whereas the Form just exemplifies itself (the F is F), a perceptible F is F only with a qualification. In the case of relational Forms and Forms of things that go into comparisons, this may seem obvious. This stick is *equal-to* that stick. This horse is *finer-than* that one as a racehorse but less fine as a cavalry horse (building on *Rep.* V 478e–479b, cf. *Phaedo* 74a). However, the Beautiful/Fine itself just is beautiful/fine. In this regard, mathematicals will have to be like perceptibles: Intermediate triangle ABC will be *equal to* triangle DEF, and it will not be the case that it is just equal. But they will perfectly exemplify the Form triangle. Whereas no perceptibles are simply two, since they may be counted in different ways, two fingers, six finger segments, etc., it is open to a Platonist to develop a theory of special units such that only aggregates of such units are numbers, where any two such units (uu) are a number two, but two triplets (uuu, uuu) of such units might be a multitude of two, but not a number. At least this is Euclid's conception of number in *Elements* VII–IX, and this may well be the conception of mathematical number that Aristotle attributes to Plato in *Met.* Mu 6.

III   TWO APPROACHES TO TRUTH AND KNOWLEDGE

Consider a theorem in geometry, "The diagonal of a parallelogram bisects the parallelogram,"[31] where, on any interpretation, there will be Forms of Diagonal, Parallelogram, Bisection, Two, Triangle, Equal, etc. We can ask, "What is it that we know?"

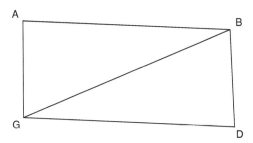

FIGURE 12.1 Parallelogram bisection

At the heart of Aristotle's analysis of Plato on mathematics is a view about the necessary conditions for scientific knowledge, that the objects of its principles and theorems be adequate. The text of the theorem talks about parallelogram AGDB, diagonal BG, and two equal triangles ABG, BGD.[32] But to be objects of knowledge, what these resemble must each exist as stipulated by the theorem, and strictly so. I shall call this the 'subject centric view'. It is tempting to see in this view insights familiar from *Sophist* 263a–e, where the Eleatic Visitor analyzes the truth of the sentence "Theaetetus is sitting," as saying of something about Theaetetus that it is about Theaetetus. On the subject-centric view, we know of any parallelogram that it is bisected by a diagonal, and there must be parallelograms to know this of, precise exemplifications of the Parallelogram Itself. Moreover, this cannot be the Parallelogram Itself, as it would then be divided into two Triangles Themselves.

Anyone interpreting Plato as accepting (1) the subject-centric view and (2) that perceptibles are inadequate as mathematical objects will, I suspect, commit Plato to intermediates.[33]

Another variation on the subject-centric view would be that there are adequate, perceptible subjects of mathematical understanding. The visible heaven is an adequate subject for astronomical theorems, the triangles and regular polyhedra of *Timaeus* 53b–89d are the elements for geometry and stereometry,[34] or perhaps perceptible triangles are only defective exemplifications in their being ephemeral.[35]

There is another way of thinking about these sentences, which I'll call 'the Form-centric view'.[36] The theorem concerns relations between Forms, which we come to reason about through AGDB, resembling Parallelogram itself, and GD, resembling Diagonal itself, so that the entire figure resembles Bisection itself, through ABG, BGD resembling Triangle and Equal. Although it may be merely a poor likeness, in the mathematician's reasoning AGDB becomes idealized, as if it were a perfect exemplification. These Forms are so related to each other that they impose structure on things resembling them, *to the extent that* they do, but the science really reasons about relations between Forms, however these relations are to be conceived.[37] Hence, there is no need for either special objects or perfect perceptibles. Anyone who rejects intermediates as components of Plato's ontology and holds that Plato considers perceptibles inadequate exemplifications probably commits Plato to some version of the Form-centric view.[38]

On the subject-centric view, there are two features that mathematical objects of knowledge satisfy. They must be stable so as to remain objects of knowledge, and they must instantiate the propositions of the science. When we grasp this theorem about parallelograms through reasoning, we grasp a geometrical configuration that the theorem and proof holds true of. If this is not the diagram itself, there must still be some parallelogram with a diagonal that we are reasoning about. The theorem does not merely state the conditional: If AGDB were a parallelogram, it would be bisected. For in going through the proof, we are reasoning about an actual parallelogram (that drawn parallelogram AGDB, referred to in the text of the proof, represents), and this must exist. Likewise, the theorem cannot be based on a hypothesis that is unjustified, as Socrates says the hypotheses must be justified in dialectic. Hence, the geometer reasons about real perceptible parallelograms or, if they are inadequate, imperceptible intermediates. However, for propositions outside the mathematical sciences, which lack their deductive rigidity (medicine?), there is no need for intermediates (an intermediate human?[39]).

The subject-centric view immediately brings us to the **precision problem**: what requirements are there for the objects of mathematics to exemplify basic properties discussed in the science? I think that there are actually three precision problems relevant for understanding Aristotle and Aristotle on Plato:

a) All objects of a science should have certain general **Parmenidean properties** required of objects of knowledge: They are eternal and lacking change.

b1) The **generic condition**: There should exist objects that instantiate the genera of the science, for geometry: points, lines, surfaces; for arithmetic: units.

b2) The **attribute condition**: The objects of the science should have the qualities and features employed in the science, for geometry: straight, circular, etc.

In Aristotle's introduction of Plato's view, as we saw, he only mentions Parmenidean properties, but elsewhere the generic condition also figures prominently, especially in his own account of mathematics in *Met.* Epsilon 1 and Mu 3. However, there are only two places in the entire Aristotelian corpus where the attribute condition appears at all.

The fifth puzzle of *Met.* Beta primarily concerns intermediates. After presenting arguments against intermediates, Aristotle turns to his one and only argument for intermediates, which employs attribute precision (2.997b34–998a6): the circle does not touch a ruler at a point (Protagoras), the motions and spirals of the stars are not as the astronomer describes, nor do points have the nature of stars. Later (*Met.* Nu 3 1090a35–b5), he claims that the proponents of intermediates think the axioms of mathematics are not true of perceptible numbers and magnitudes but must hold true. Clearly, Aristotle is attributing to the Platonists the subject-centric view. So, we have another feature of mathematicals:

5) There are mathematical objects that perfectly instantiate every property discussed in the science (with respect to genera and attributes), whereas perceptibles do not perfectly exemplify them.

Given his own lack of interest in the attribute condition, it is plausible that Aristotle is taking attribute precision from Academic discussions.[40]

Furthermore, there is one last feature of mathematicals. Without invoking Plato's name, Aristotle says that those who postulated intermediates and Forms also held:

6a) The mathematicals are separate from the perceptibles.[41]

However, Aristotle also mentions an alternative view, which he considers yet more vulnerable to objection:

6b) The mathematicals are in the perceptibles.[42]

Thus, Aristotle holds that Plato has a tripartite ontology:[43] Forms, perceptibles, and intermediate mathematicals. Given his antipathy to a Platonic account of participation of perceptibles in Forms, he has little to say about the relations between the intermediates and the other two levels except that Plato's Forms and intermediates are separate from and prior to perceptibles.[44] However, on the view that they are separate, the relation between all three levels is obscure within the tripartite ontology. This obscurity will not dissipate in my discussion. I shall argue that Plato does present us with tripartite ontologies, but that they fit with (6b), immanent mathematicals, rather than (6a), separate ones. In this, I am pursuing a line suggested by Madigan (1999) in his commentary on *Met.* Beta 2. Will this imply that Aristotle has misrepresented Plato's views?

IV DIVIDED LINES

The most natural place to look for intermediates is the Divided Line, a complex analogy at the end of *Republic* VI and in VII 533c–534b, where Socrates compares four segments of a divided line to different levels of psychological states, methods of acquisition, objects of the states, as well as objects on their own. Although it may prove unreasonable to insist that Socrates and Glaucon presume intermediates, the text also does not require a bipartite ontology. Rather, Plato is not setting up doctrines so much as arguments about the nature of mathematics, problems to inspire the reader to develop views about mathematics.

The very opening words of the Divided Line bring this out:

Socrates : Anyhow, you have these two forms, visible, intelligible.

Glaucon : I have them.

Socrates : Well, then, just like taking a line bisected into unequal [or equal] segments; again cut each segment in the same ratio, the segment of the seen kind and that of the intellected kind, and you will have in clarity and unclarity in relation to one another in the seen realm one segment as images ... (VI 509d4–e1)

It is always ignored in modern translations that the line is said to be not merely cut in two but bisected,[45] which is surely why some manuscripts[46] break up the word, 'unequal' (ἄνισα) into two words, a grammatical particle and 'equal' (ἂν ἴσα), although in Plato's time both would be written: ΑΝΙΣΑ (could this be word play?).[47]

Modern discussions of the Divided Line have also been stunted by a misleading translation of the analogy going back to November 12, 1855,[48] where it is alleged that because the segments are cut in the same ratio as the initial line, the middle sections of the line must be equal. The Cambridge Interpretation, as I call it,[49] is a *possible* interpretation of the text, which has even become inexplicably explicit in Grube's popular translation,[50] but Socrates' initial description of the line requires merely that they be cut in the same ratio as each other, while there is ample evidence that it does not *necessitate* that they be cut in the same ratio as the initial line.[51]

There are many possible divisions of the line.[52] If we label the segments in order A, B, C, D, and require that A : B ≈ C : D, the only

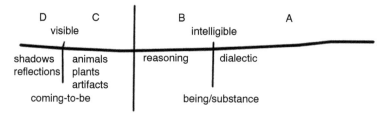

FIGURE 12.2 Divided Line

explicit stipulation throughout, and attend to the different claims about the realms of the line in truth and clarity, besides the Cambridge Interpretation, where A : B ≈ C : D ≈ AB : CD (so that B = C[53]), there are actually forty-two mathematically distinct possible ways of dividing the line, including a division in mean and extreme ratio,[54] i.e., where AB : A ≈ A : B ≈ CD : C ≈ C : D (so that B = CD), which actually fits all of Socrates' claims better. If one takes the opinable (*doxaston*) as CD, one can get the Cambridge Interpretation by taking the knowable (*gnōston*) as AB, and the Mean/Extreme by taking the knowable as A and C as an imitation of B.[55] Does Plato want us to play with these or are they unimportant? If the Mean/Extreme interpretation requires intermediates, does the Cambridge eliminate the need?[56]

Additionally, discussions of the Divided Line are occasionally muddled by attempts to read more into its mathematics than can plausibly be part of Socrates' analogy. For example, the line has no particular orientation if it is drawn in a horizontal sandbox surrounded by the dialogue's characters. Nor is it evident what difference it would make for an unequal division which segment is longer. Another, more clever interpretation[57] suggests that the sections of the line compared in truth and clarity are actually the areas determined by a triangle formed in the construction of its divisions, although, even if Socrates draws a line, he could just as easily do it freehand,[58] or with any variety of implements.[59] How is the reader to know?

Furthermore, whatever may be the placement of the analogy itself, or any other part of the *Republic*, in Socrates' division, the division of the line in ratios is itself just a piece of mathematics and so belongs to section B.[60]

What should we make of the possible interpretations? If Plato is just playing around with ratios, mere idle musings or embellishments, and does not intend this seriously, especially if he sneaks incoherencies into the account, then why has he bamboozled his reader? Alternatively, if the details are supposed to help us understand the relations between the different objects, states, etc. represented in the Line, we are still left to guess without guidance. The difficulty with both, and many variations in between, is that we just cannot know without knowing Plato's mind. But there is something that we can know, something important for understanding Plato. The text underdetermines interpretations, and Plato knows that. If he had wanted to be more precise, he was not short of papyrus to do so. He leaves it to the reader to do the work.

In fact, there are five divided lines, two by Socrates (509e6–511c2, 511d6–e5) and, in between, one by Glaucon (511c3–d5) in VI, and two by Socrates in VII (533e7–534a5, 534a3–9). Each divided line puts forth different relations, sometimes with conflicting or indeterminable terminology, where sections of the line are determined by a cognitive state or by the objects of the cognitive state or by a methodology used or by the objects on their own.

Even though Socrates characterizes sections AB, CD, C, D, and even A as either objects or objects of cognition, he is careful not to characterize section B of the intelligible realm by anything other than reasoning, that is by its method. This does not imply that he might not characterize it differently elsewhere in book VII, as we shall see, but that will not lead us to a determinate Platonic doctrine.

I have already discussed some aspects of Socrates' description of the method involved in reasoning in section I, and, while there are many questions about the ontological import of the methodology, we should resist expansive interpretation. The basic question whether there is a commitment to or against intermediates in the initial presentation of the Divided Line in *Rep.* VI turns first on the claim:

> Accordingly, as you also know, they [mathematicians] make use of seen forms and make their arguments *about* them, reasoning not *about* these but about those these resemble, making their arguments *for the sake of* the square itself and diagonal itself, but not *of* this one which they draw, and the others in this way, these

themselves that they fashion and draw, of which both shadows and things in liquids are images, then making use of these as images, seeking to see those things themselves which someone could see in no other way than by reasoning. (510d5–511a1)

Four things are contrasted: (1) the drawn figure (in realm C) that the mathematician makes the arguments about, on which the labels are written; (2) what the drawn figure resembles and which the mathematician reasons about; (3) that for the sake of which the mathematician makes her arguments; (4) the things that themselves can only be seen by reasoning. One way to bring intermediates into this passage is to presume in (3) that the square itself and diagonal itself are intermediates.[61] While there is no necessity that 'the square itself and diagonal itself' signify Forms,[62] the only thing to prepare the audience for anything but Forms and ordinary perceptible objects in this passage is the earlier introduction of the reflections of ordinary objects. Bringing in a whole new sort of entity in this way would violate the Audience Requirement. However, the natural reading is compatible with both subject-centric and Form-centric views. Socrates later fills out the very odd expression of (3) as 'for the sake of apprehending' (525d2 on arithmetic, 527a7 on geometry) and 'for the sake of learning with respect to those things' (529d8 on astronomy), in contrast with using things for the sake of trade or war, some pragmatic activity. On any interpretation of the Divided Line, the goal of reasoning is the apprehension of Forms, even if the methodology of reasoning is inadequate.

The crux of the passage lies in the difference between what the mathematician *makes* her arguments about, the artifact/diagram, and what the mathematician *reasons* about, what the diagram is a likeness of. Nor is (3) recapitulating (2) – 'for the sake of X' does not mean 'about X', but gives the reason for the activity. There is also no necessity that what the mathematician reasons *about* be the same as that *for the sake of which* she makes her arguments, although the audience might well expect them to be the same. But here the reader might also feel discomfort, since he also expects the argument produced, a geometrical proof, to match exactly the reasoning (verbal argument matched with mental content?), and so for the diagram about which the argument is made (2) to be *structurally* like whatever the reasoning is about, and this could not be a Form for the sake of seeing which she reasons. Are the objects themselves that can only be "seen" by reasoning (4) therefore not "seen" by dialectic and so are special objects of reasoning, or are they Forms which must initially be "seen" by reasoning? Are the objects of (4) the same as those of (3)? A thoughtful reader might well conclude that he really does not understand perfectly what Socrates is saying.

Glaucon, however, seems to draw the inference that the objects of A and B are different in his version of the line:

> ... that you want to distinguish the [part/aspect] of what both is and is intelligible that's contemplated by the science of dialectic as being clearer than the [part/aspect of it contemplated] by the so-called crafts ... (511c4–6)

Socrates accepts the description, so that if we wish, we may interpret him as introducing objects under each craft (the objects of 4) distinct from Forms, each a part of being. But it is also possible that Glaucon sees the objects as the same, but in different relations to the methodologies, different aspects of what is and is intelligible.[63]

V   MATHEMATICAL COMMITMENTS
IN THE EDUCATIONAL PROGRAM OF REPUBLIC VII

In *Rep.* VII, Socrates surveys five sciences for the education of the guardians of Kallipolis: arithmetic, geometry, stereometry, astronomy, and harmonics. Each science, except for the jejune science of stereometry, is shown to be practical for the guardians and is able, more importantly, to summon the student away from looking at perceptibles toward contemplation of the Forms. I shall focus on the discussions of arithmetic and, more briefly, astronomy. Arithmetic directs us toward contemplating pure units, while astronomy will lead us to abandon the visible heaven to contemplate true slowness and fastness. Although nowhere in these accounts do any characters speak of special mathematical objects, and Socrates forgoes any account concerning objects of reasoning, it is very difficult to understand, in particular, the accounts of arithmetic and astronomy without at least worrying about what the objects of the science are. There are clear tensions in his account.

Socrates begins his discussion of sciences with 'arithmetic' or 'calculation' (*logistikē*) (he does not here distinguish them[64]). We can distinguish three levels of arithmetic. Simplest is mere knowledge of counting, and secondly basic calculation, whether with a counting board or in some other way, and conversions of measures.[65] The difference of measures can even be explicit in the acrophonic system (see section I), that while two generally are ||, two drachmas are often ⊦⊦. Third, at a sophisticated level, are analyses of numbers based on classifications into even and odd, associated, for better or worse, with Pythagoreans,[66] the study of relative primes, proportion, and especially continuous proportion,[67] underlying solutions to basic numerical puzzles, the theory of irrationals, as well as some combinatorics.[68]

Socrates' description requires more than the first two levels, something of relative primes, certainly enough proportion theory for the astronomy and harmonics to be discussed, and enough to understand the notorious nuptial number, 60^4 (*Rep.* VIII 545c–e). Kept away from commerce, the guardians will only study calculation for military purposes and for the sake of knowing and "touching" on being, where, as we expect from the Divided Line, calculation leads the guardians toward the "observation of the nature of numbers by intellection itself (A or AB)," where reasoning (B) is distinct from that (525a–d). Socrates now explains why calculation for the sake of intellection is useful:

> Just this which we were now saying, that it very much leads the
> soul upward hither and compels it to discuss about numbers

themselves, in no way accepting it if someone should propose discussing by it numbers having visible and tangible bodies. For you know, I suppose, that those clever in these things, moreover, if someone undertakes to divide the one itself in the ratio (or: argument), they ridicule him and do not accept it, but if you break it up, they multiply, taking care lest the one should ever appear as not one, but as many portions.

You are speaking most truthfully, (Glaucon) said.

And so, what do you think, Glaucon, if some should ask them, "O wondrous ones, concerning what sort of numbers are you discussing, in which the one is such as you assume, each equal, everyone to everyone, and not differing in a small way, and having no portion at all in it?" What would you think they would answer?

I (think) this, that they are speaking about these (numbers) which it is possible only to be reasoned about, but which it is in no way at all possible to get a grip on in any other way. [*Glaucon echoes Socrates at VI 511a1*]

And so, you see, friend, said I, that it is likely that the lesson really is necessary for us, since it appears as compelling the soul to make use of intellection itself (to go) at the truth itself. (525d5–526b3)

Our primary concern is the nature of the clever experts' calculation. Clearly, it is not about physical units and numbers, drachmas, feet, humans. Yet, numbers are units aggregated, and we can assume that these must be such here.

Cherniss argued that the ones that do not differ are the Forms of numbers.[69] The motivation behind this interpretation is his belief that since the numbers cannot be physical numbers, they must be the only thing left, Forms of numbers, but Plato's Forms are simple, so that they are not composed of units and must, each of them, be a unity. This interpretation, which requires a heavily revisionist approach to Greek mathematics, is nigh impossible.[70]

Let us start with the audience's understanding at that moment of the discussion and what they can expect. The experts cannot be Platonic philosophers; otherwise, Socrates would have to say something to indicate that they are not just the ordinary experts that one might find in a school, who would know nothing about the theory of Forms. Unless Socrates presumes a totally unfamiliar notion of multiplication,[71] the numbers they talk about can be multiplied, i.e., so-many units added to themselves so-many times, which Forms cannot be, as they cannot be duplicated. Moreover, Glaucon is depicted as understanding Socrates perfectly, which would be odd if some special notion of multiplication were intended. The experts are teaching and using numbers, just not numbers tied to volumes, coins, weights, etc. Furthermore, we expect that the example itself has some meaning: What is the operation where one multiplies to avoid breaking?

Although the operation in question cannot concern money, weights, or distances, there is nothing in the text to suggest that the operations for these disappear when one treats numbers abstractly. There is a straight-forward operation where one multiplies to avoid dividing. One has a drachma and wants to take half and so switches to a subunit, the obol, multiplies by 6 and then takes half to get 3 obols. It is no accident that the verb that Socrates uses, 'break up' (*kermatizō*), is also an expression for breaking up a coin, getting change (*kermata*).[72] Of course, this need not be the precise operation that Plato wants, but it is not difficult to find many families of puzzles where one multiplies to avoid dividing, e.g., in using Euclid, *Elements* VII 39: "to find the least number having given parts," e.g., 30 for two-fifteenths and a sixth, which allows one to avoid fractions in solving problems like finding a number such that when these parts are taken out, the remainder is 42.[73]

The claim that the units do not differ in any way from one another must refer back to Glaucon's remark that sight reports the seen one to the intellect as one and its contrary, unlimited in number, and to Socrates' reply that this also holds for the whole of number (525a3–7, cf. 524e2–3). Again, readers and characters would understand that the three of the experts should appear only as three things (see section II for a comparison with Euclid). It may well be that an expert teacher uses perceptible units, perhaps pebbles, as diagrams. We can even imagine her explaining the pebbles as equal units, unlike the pebbles on a counting board, which have different values according to position. However, Socrates also undercuts the expert if she thinks the units just are perceptible units. Even well crafted pebbles would inevitably differ in many ways and, though you wouldn't want to smash them, they are not partless, as we can infer from the previous argument that all perceived numbers are summoners.[74] We readers might well wonder whether Socrates' question what these units are is also a question for the expert teacher, who may only have reflected that the units are pure without asking what this might entail.

We should not, then, completely dismiss the motivation for Cherniss' interpretation. In the preceding discussion, only two sorts of items have been in question, the perceived and the intelligible, as in the lead-up example of the large and small (524c10–13). So, the reader is not prepared for some special sort of mathematical objects. Nor is the reader prepared for some special interpretation of perceptibles that would make them adequate objects of theorems. In other words, the audience expects Socrates to be speaking about the sort of abstract calculations in the ordinary Greek way, but also doesn't have an ontology to explain how. Rather than inferring Cherniss' implausible Form-units or more plausible perceptibles *qua* units alone (Aristotle's gambit) or even somehow idealized perceptible units (where do these explicitly appear in Plato?) or units of a new sort, we can observe instead that these equal, partless units, that can only be reasoned about (not seen), leave deep tensions in the account. It may well be intentional.[75]

We see similar tensions in the accounts of some of the other mathematical sciences. The fourth science that Socrates examines is astronomy. Socrates presents a revisionist account of astronomy based in a contemporary astronomy, although any account beyond noting how one might extrapolate to the true celestial motion will be mere speculation. More significant for us, whatever that extrapolation may be, we lack an account of how the objects of astronomy could be either Forms or perceptibles. Again, we will be left with tensions and a question about what sort of ontology is required.

It is unlikely that Eudoxus did any of his important work on creating spherical models of complex planetary motion before the writing of the *Republic*.[76] However, some of the audience would know the two-motion model depicted at *Rep.* X 616b–617d, namely where the band of fixed stars rotating east/west turns the bands of the planetary stars (moon, sun, planets), themselves moving slowly west/east. The ordinary astronomy that Socrates describes and regards as inadequate for the advanced astronomy of the guardians is calendrical, finding periods in which two or more bodies complete a whole number of cycles, not by measuring them meticulously (torturing the phenomena, as the empirical harmonists at 431b2–3), but using arithmetical techniques to determine, for example, that 19 years (solar cycles) = 235 months (cycles of the moon relative to the sun) = 6,940 days (turnings of the fixed stars), that is, 110 hollow (29-day) months and 125 full (30-day) months.[77] Socrates here and Timaeus (*Timaeus* 38e–39e) also include the joint periods of any two stars. These are the commensurabilities that Socrates mentions. Moreover, having earlier stated that the visible adornments may be the most precise of visibles, but are deficient from the true ones (529c8–d1), he elaborates how:

> But the commensurability of night to day and of these to a month and of a month to a year and of [the periods of] the other stars to these and to each other, do you believe, will he not consider it absurd to believe that these come about always in the same way and that nothing deviates anywhere, although they have a body and are seen, and to seek in every manner to get the truth of them. (530a7–b4, but see Glaucon at 527d2–4)

Without a rich account of variations in lunar and solar motion, such as begins to appear in Greek astronomy with Eudoxus, the perceived distributions of whole and full months will often deviate from the theory, and so for any other celestial period.[78] The *Timaeus* and *Laws* may well present different views.[79]

The advanced astronomy will then involve theorems from hypotheses (see section I on advancing to problems), such that:

> ... the true (adornments), with which motions the real fastness
> and the real slowness[80] move in true number and all the true figures
> in relation to one another and move [that is, carry] the things in/on
> it [i.e., the true heaven], which are to be grasped by an account
> [or 'in a ratio'] and *reason* (*dianoia*), but not by sight.[81] (529d1–5)

I won't attempt here to flesh out Socrates' description and resolve its many difficulties (the Audience Condition is barely fulfilled), although one can imagine how it might proceed as an analysis of periods with some spherics. As we saw in section I, the adornments of the heaven are to be used as exemplars, like a diagram. Socrates also says that we should leave these alone (530b7), but this must be in the sense that one leaves any perceptible diagram alone,[82] as a representation to reason about something else (and not as the object of study), here periods of so many revolutions.[83] Yet, if 19 units cannot be Forms, so much the more, 19 revolutions connected to 235 revolutions cannot be Forms. Without Socrates' setting out an account of intermediates or some account of how the visible heaven can be the subject of the theorems, as idealized[84] or as something else, as well as being in awe of the magnitude of the enterprise, Glaucon ought to be perplexed, and Plato's readers as well, as to what these objects are. It is worth pointing out, however, that in *Met.* Beta 2 997b12–20 and Mu 2 1076b39–7a4, Aristotle treats the need for an intermediate heaven as an objection to the theory of intermediates, not as an obvious feature of it.

VI   THE SUMMARY OF THE CAVE AT REPUBLIC VII 532
AND THE LINE REDUX

The analogy of the Cave has many elements that come in between, on
the one hand, the prisoners and the shadow motions on the wall, and,
on the other hand, the plants, trees, stars, and the sun outside the cave.
These include the puppets, the light source in the cave, puppeteers, the
walls and pathways of the cave, the shadows and reflections in pools of
water outside the cave. All of these elements are part of the educational
progress of the cave prisoner to knowledge and understanding. None of
these is identified with mathematical objects nor is anything specific
implied about their relation to sections of the Divided Line, i.e., any
and all can represent objects of the process leading to understanding of
the Forms. Later, however, after the presentation of mathematical
education, Socrates summarizes the Cave:

> The release, said I, from bonds and turning from shadows to the
> representations[85] and the light and the trip back up from what's below
> ground to the sun, and there the further inability to look at the animals
> and plants and light of the sun, but at the divine[86] images in waters and
> shadows of real things, but not shadows of the representations through
> a different light of this sort, which are as shadows cast, to compare it to
> the sun – all this occupation of the crafts which we went through has
> this power and progression of what's best in a soul toward seeing
> what's best among beings, just as then it was toward seeing what's
> clearest in a body in relation to the seeing of what's most radiant in the
> bodily and visible place. (532b6–d1)

Here we have most of the elements mentioned in the cave, and here
Plato comes closest to committing Socrates to special mathematical
objects in the progression from the cave shadows to the sun.[87] Clearly,
gazing at images in waters and shadows is the activity of the crafts and
is something the traveler does because she cannot look at the trees
and animals. And these shadows and reflections are separate from the
shadows on the walls of the cave and even ontologically distinct, as

they derive from things outside the cave and not puppet representations of these. So, Plato is hinting to the cognoscenti at the doctrine of separate intermediates. However, the speech does not quite do this. Everything from release prior to seeing animals, plants, and the light of the sun is the activity of these crafts. Perhaps the reflections and shadows outside are the mathematicals. Or perhaps we need to include the puppets (intermediates prior to wall shadows?). Surely, one might conclude, Plato thinks that all these are the objects discussed in the mathematical sciences.

The difficulty with this approach is that Plato provides neither his characters nor the readers with any guidance about what to think of these objects. We have seen philosophical tensions that might push the reader in one direction or another, and intentionally so. However, if we try to match up the objects of the Cave with the levels of the Divided Line, we can make only partial claims. It is clear that the shadows on the wall are semblances of the puppets (compatible with the Mean/Extreme interpretation of the Divided Line), and the puppets are artificial semblances of things in and out of the cave, people, animals, plants, etc., while the reflections and shadows outside the cave are natural semblances of them. It is uncontested that the plants and animals outside the Cave correspond to Forms, the fire to the sun, and the sun to the Good. From these one could easily have Socrates fit the rest into all four sections of the Divided Line, or into three, or even two. Does Plato intend us to play a hermeneutical guessing game? Or does he want us to take hints from the presentation to ask and ponder real and deep philosophical questions?

Indeed, Socrates undercuts any hope of guessing right in the very next discussion, where he gives yet two more versions of the line. Having stated that the objects of the intelligible realm and the visible realm are proportional to the cognitive states and repeating the initial proportion of the line,[88] he says:

> But let us leave aside the proportion and division in two of each (being and coming-to-be) over which these (knowledge, conviction,

reasoning, imaging) are, Glaucon, so that it does not fill us up with multiply more accounts than all those which have just passed. (534a5–9)

When Socrates skips over the relation between the objects within divisions, does Plato mean for his characters and us to fill in the proportions with objects for each sort of cognition, but that to examine this would be an enormous discussion? And if so, what are these objects? Or does Socrates not tell us because he is aware that the section for objects of reasoning is "a blank"?[89] Or maybe he is telling us that they are merely hypothesized (e.g., if there are parallelograms, then ...). Or maybe the objects are fictional, ironically described as true.[90] Or maybe they are perceptibles somehow idealized.

Socrates may postpone the discussion, but the author, Plato, is in control and has the choice to tell us more, to lengthen the discussion however he pleases, or genuinely to omit any further discussion. Why not just presume that Plato means what Socrates says? We see a similar avoidance in the introductions to the discussions of the Good at VI 506d–e (cf. 509c, VII 517b–c) and dialectic at VII 533a. A more modest interpretation, I submit, is that Plato allows his characters to speak in a way that may raise questions for the moderately astute reader, but that he does not want to discuss the issue further in the Republic. He explicitly avoids having his characters commit to any ontology of the two intellected realms beyond that the principal objects are Forms (of the entire realm or of knowledge).[91] The very fact that, instead of 'Forms', he uses 'being' (ousia) for the intellected realm in contrasting it with the 'coming-to-be' of the world of opinion confirms that he really is avoiding all commitments. For although being is always the goal (523a3, 524e1, 525b5, 525c5–6 [with truth], 526e6–7), the open issue is whether "to be" applies only to Forms. Or better, the issue is not even raised. The objects of imaging and conviction are clearly explained; the only thing one knows about the upper realm is that there are Forms and that one uses objects of conviction as images of Forms and uses hypotheses differently in the crafts and in dialectic. We find an enormous gap in the story, that is explicit and intended. Plato invites us to fill in the gap, maybe even to find inspiration in puppets and puddles, but Plato's people provide little direction how to do this.

VII   INTERMEDIATES OF A SORT IN THE PHAEDO AND TIMAEUS?

If in the *Republic* there are at most hints of separate mathematical objects arising from tensions in its accounts of mathematical sciences and its analogies, there is a sort of mathematical object that does appear more explicitly in the dialogues. The *Phaedo* presents, in addition to the soul, a sequential tripartite ontology of perceptibles, Forms-by-nature, and, in between, Forms-in-us: the small Socrates, the Small itself, and the small in Socrates. The small in Socrates satisfies some of the properties that Aristotle ascribes to intermediates, but it fails to meet three of them. While it cannot undergo any change in what it is and cannot accept its contraries, Socrates does not preclude its moving around with its host and allows that it can cease to exist. Nor is it separate.

At *Phaedo* 99d–107a, Socrates produces two models of explanation, with the first two concerning two sorts of Forms, that the beautiful is beautiful due to the Beautiful Itself (the Form-in-nature) (99d4–102a9, cf. 103b6), that Socrates is smaller than Simmias because he has smallness (the Form-in-us) compared to the tallness in Simmias (102a10–103c9).[92] Each of these sorts of Forms must self-exemplify and so cannot receive its contrary but must retreat or cease to exist at its approach.[93] Socrates then identifies an ontological principle, that, for example, any three must similarly have odd and cannot receive the even (103c10–105b4). The ontological status of the subject is not specified, but it is clear that the even and the odd designate

Forms-in-us. Moreover, anything that Socrates calls 'an idea' in the *Phaedo* is a Form-in-us.[94] So, when Socrates says:

> that, things that the idea of three occupies, it is necessary for them not only to be three, but also odd (104d5–7)

he is saying that there are some triple, *abc*, the idea of three that they have (i.e., the Form-in-us of three that is in them), and the idea of odd (i.e., the Form-in-us of odd). Hence, for some things:

1) The idea F is F (self-exemplification).
2) If something (perceptible or whatever) has idea F, then it has idea G.

This is compatible with both the subject-centric view and the Form-centric view. To establish that Socrates has a subject-centric view and so the possibility that the idea three is an intermediate mathematical object, we need to show additionally:

3) The idea three is odd.

Now, Socrates does not explicitly say this, but it is very difficult to understand a step in the argument that the soul is deathless without it (105b5–107a1).

> By being in a body, the soul makes the body alive.
> Hence, the soul cannot receive the contrary of life, i.e., death.

One of Socrates' illustrations before making this inference is (105b4–6):

> By being in a number, the unit makes the number odd.[95]

The only way this can be used to justify the inference about the soul is if there is some general principle which will also allow the inference:

> The one cannot receive the even (and so is odd)

Given that two is the first number, this might seem peculiar (but cf. Aristotle, *Met.* Mu 8 1083b28–30, 1084a36). It is enough for us that the one here is an idea and that it rejects (and receives) arithmetical properties. Hence, the Forms-in-us satisfy some of the basic requirements for being mathematical objects, receiving neither their contrary nor the contrary of a necessary property, and they satisfy the multiplicity condition. On the other hand, they can be destroyed and move with the things they occupy (and so are not separate).[96]

There may well be intermediates in two accounts of the *Timaeus*. Closest to the *Phaedo* would be the distinction between the Form, the copies of the Forms in the receptacle, and the receptacle (49b–53a), where the perceived object is a congeries of copies located together. In neither dialogue do we have any account of the relation between the ideas or copies and the Forms-in-nature (part–whole, image, identity, or something else); however, since Timaeus postpones the question about the relation between copies and Forms (50c5–6), Plato there leaves it to us.

Immanent, intermediate astronomicals of a different sort may appear in the account of the world soul at *Timaeus* 35a–40d. After concocting soul-Being, soul-Same, and soul-Different out of the unchanging and the changing sorts, the crafter creates a diurnally rotating band of the Same (the motion/soul of fixed stars) and seven rotating circles of the Different (the motion/soul of planetary stars). Nonetheless, though invisible, the soul has length and circular shapes and motion, prior to its being endowed with body (36b–37a).[97] This might provide an answer to the question what the true heaven is in *Republic* VII, as opposed to the visible, embodied heaven.

VIII SKEPTICAL CONCLUSIONS

Aristotle's discussion of Plato's views on mathematics poses a challenge for readers of the dialogues. Do we dig into the dialogues to find the doctrines Aristotle attributes to Plato, perhaps merely interpreting texts to fit our expectation? However, Aristotle has one advantage over us all – he was there. Aristotle's interpretation of Plato as endorsing a tripartite ontology presumes the subject-centric view, where there must be objects distinct from perceptibles, having the requisite properties, but it is also possible that Plato held to a Form-centric view. Should we conjure a story of how Aristotle could have come to misrepresent Plato so profoundly on an issue of such importance in the Academy?

In examining the *Republic*, we saw that Socrates and Glaucon create tensions: there are different ways of understanding the Divided Line; it is hard to understand what the expert's aggregated, undifferentiated units are or the new astronomer's true motion/periods. They give no account of them. True, Socrates goes on to suggest that the reflections and shadows of goats outside the cave are aids to seeing the real goats. If one has Aristotle's account, these reflections could well be the intermediates, completely separate from the shadows on the walls of the cave. However, Socrates describes the entire process from being untied to seeing the puppets (and puppeteers?) to seeing the outside shadows and reflections as reasoning. The reader is invited to think through many interpretations. However, when, immediately after, Socrates has the opportunity to identify objects for reasoning and dialectic, he demurs. Should we try to construct the tripartite ontology in a metaphor?

The account of Forms-in-us in the *Phaedo* and copies in the receptacle in the *Timaeus*, as well as its heavenly soul, are certainly better candidates for constructing a Platonic account of mathematics. There are the three *humans*, Socrates, Simmias, and Phaedo, differing in size. However, the unit-in-Socrates does not differ from the unit-in-Simmias at all, as each just is a unit. These might qualify as the experts' units.

Aristotle mentions a theory that places mathematicals in things, and he loathes this theory.[98] One basic objection claims that the immanent, unchangeable mathematicals will change with the object they occupy.[99] They fail the basic Parmenidean condition. Of course, Platonic responses abound, e.g., that while they exist they have essentially only the requisite properties.[100] In objecting that on this view Forms will also have to be immanent, he may be implicitly placing it within someone's tripartite ontology with separate Forms.[101] Despite what Aristotle elsewhere suggests (see note 41), there would then be two alternative tripartite ontologies in the

Academy. It seems, nonetheless, more likely that he attributes separate mathematicals to Plato.[102] Could he have been wrong?

We have a quandary. If Plato believed in separate intermediates, why doesn't he make them appear more explicitly? And if he thought of the Forms-in-us as encompassing mathematical objects, why doesn't he say, for example, that the soul in the *Timaeus* is the true subject of astronomy (or maybe some will claim that he does say this)? And if he held to both (puppets and outdoor shadows and reflections?), our quandary intensifies. And if he believes neither, how could Aristotle have been so wrong?

While these are legitimate historical questions, they may be missing an important point, that, as important as mathematics is for Plato, he is not interested in directing his reader to precise ontologies of it. As readers of Plato, we want desperately to know what he thinks. He just prefers us to think.

NOTES

1 Among many others, Shorey 1895, Cook Wilson 1904, Cherniss 1945, Tarán 1981, Moravcsik 2000.

2 Among many others, Adam 1902, Wedberg 1955, Burnyeat 1987 and 2000. Annas (1975 and 1981: 249–51) is something of a skeptic, arguing that the texts do not commit Plato to intermediates, but that they create a tension. Hers is closest to my approach here.

3 Fine 1990: 87.

4 For a collection of passages, Frajese 1963.

5 Netz 1999: esp. ch. 7.

6 For contemporary Egyptian mathematics, see Imhausen 2016: ch. 17 and Parker 1972. For contemporary Mesopotamian mathematics, see, with Høyrup 2002 for background, Robson 2008 and Friberg 2007, but the last only with the deep reservations expressed by Unguru 2008.

7 On geometry as numerical measurement in late Plato, see also *Pol.* 283c11–285d2, 299e1–2, *Phil.* 55e1–57d8, as well as *Alcib.* I 126c–d, if it is genuine.

8 The almost universal mistranslation of μετρητὰ πρὸς ἄλληλα (measurable with respect to one another) and ἄμετρα (unmeasurable) as 'commensurable' and 'incommensurable' at 819e10 and 820a8, c4 (I have found no

exceptions) might mislead one into thinking that the Visitor recommends advanced mathematics. The issue is just measuring planes by lines, etc.

9 See Parker 1972, prob. 32 from P. Cair. 89127 (third century BCE).

10 For a survey of both sorts, see Fowler 1999, to which add P. Oxyrh. 5299, a list of propositions from *Elements* I.

11 "That on which AB is" is used occasionally by Aristotle, Eudemus, and Archimedes and may be older than the standard, "the AB."

12 Cf. Euclid, *Elements* IX 36.

13 Additionally, in referring to the role of a diagram, Aristotle speaks of a mathematician as speaking of a line as foot-length when it is not (*Pr. An.* A 41 49b34–7, *Post. An.* A 10 76b41–3, *Met.* M3 1078a19–21, N2 1089a22–3). See *inter alia* Acerbi 2008 and Mendell 1998a: 181–2. See note 7 in this chapter.

14 See Archimedes, *Sphere and Cylinder* II 1; c.f. Euclid, *Elements* I 1.

15 At *Phil.* 51c3–6 and 56b7–c2, we find mentioned compass, peg and string, straight edge, angle, square, and plumb-line listed as tools of construction and as carpenter's, builder's, and shipwright's tools, but these would hardly be all of them. At the very least, in Plato's world, there would be free rotation of figures, constrained movements, convergence (fiddling a ruler from a given point, so that a fixed length is cut off by a line), and point-wise constructions, as well as intersection of two solids.

16 Euclid, *Elements* I 32b.

17 As reported by Proclus, *In Euclidis Elementa* 66–7.

18 No one has actually published such a study, although Heiberg 1904 makes much headway. Lasserre 1987 provides much of the material for such a study, and Mendell 1984 provides further material.

19 See Netz 1999: ch. 1.

20 On exemplars in architecture, see Coulton 1977: 55–8.

21 See Haselberger 1997.

22 Netz 1999: ch. 1. For example, in medieval manuscripts, lines drawn to represent unequal magnitudes or numbers often have the same length.

23 See the references in note 13, where it doesn't matter that the line is not a foot long or not straight. No one would draw a 100′ diagram to represent a 100′ length.

24 It is important to translate ὁ οὐρανός as 'the heaven'. We say 'the heavens' because it is plural in Hebrew and Greek texts influenced by Hebrew,

which reflect a view that there are many distinct heavens – ultimately, from late antiquity on, some collection built out of each star system (moon, sun, planets, fixed stars, precession) as well as the strictly theologically required heavens. The singular is important to emphasize that we are speaking of a single entity, albeit with many components. (Note that, though it usually uses the plural with the article, the King James version of Genesis begins with God creating "the heaven"). Despite the OED, the article is necessary, as people typically understand by 'Heaven' one of the theologically required heavens, and not simply the world from the moon up.

25 Although διάγραμμα is commonly used as a synecdoche for a proof, e.g., *Euthd.* 290c, it cannot be that here, as clearly the diagram is drawn or labored over.

26 At *Sophist* 235d–236c, the Eleatic Visitor divides the craft of imitation into the representative (εἰκαστική, a word used only in the *Sophist* and *Laws* II 667d–668a), which preserves the commensurabilities (measurements) of length, width, depth, color, etc., and the imaginative, which distorts the copy to make it appear better. If these are the only two choices, the drawn square should be an exemplification of the Square itself, even if its relation to the Square itself is as the reflection in water of the drawn square to it. But then which should the drawn heaven be? We could imagine other objects serving a similar function, a bronze sphere in stereometry or a scale in harmonics (with difficulty).

27 As in some mid-fourth-century BCE inscriptions at Delphi, e.g., CID 2:77 (335/334 BCE): "in number two minae 12 staters 5 obols a half obol." Cf. CID 2:75, 76, 78, 82, 84, 86, 87.

28 For a defense of pebble arithmetic in the late fifth and fourth centuries BCE, see Knorr 1975: ch. 5.

29 *Met.* B6 1002b21–2: "For things of the same form also are there infinite."

30 See *Met.* B6 1002b14–16, M6 1080a22–3. The expression used, τὰ πόλλ᾽ ἄττα ὅμοια/ὁμοειδῆ (the many particulars being similar/of-a-common-form), is probably a stock Academic phrase.

31 Euclid, *Elements* I 34, second part.

32 The diagram is based on codex Vaticanus Gr. 190 (P) f. 32^r.

33 Explicitly, Wedberg (1955: 48–62, for geometry, and 66–8, for arithmetic), who builds an argument for intermediates out of a semantic view that

mathematical statements must be precisely true of objects. See too Arsen 2012.

34 This would be a very limited geometry, only figures built from two sorts of right triangles, the isosceles and the bisected equilateral (and possibly a third for the regular pentagon), unless one can build other figures out of an infinity of progressively tiny triangles, but it seems very unlikely that Plato has thought out the mathematical implications of *Timaeus* 58a4–7, that all things are packed tight and admit no empty area.

35 See Pritchard 1995: 127–49. This also seems to be the view of Smith (1981).

36 The clearest presentations may be found in Tait 1986 and 2002 and Moravcsik 1992 (esp. 74–81), and 2000. For how the interpretation plays in astronomy, see Vlastos 1980: esp. 21 n. 14; and Mourelatos 1980.

37 How this non-semantic structure of relations is supposed to work is not easy to grasp. Moravcsik 2000: 192–3 attempts such an account of numbers.

38 There is a notable hybrid of both views, where the Forms as self-exemplifying are the units of arithmetical theorems. See notes 69 and 71 below.

39 As Aristotle objects, *Met.* B2 997b15–24, M2 1076b39–1077a9.

40 In *Met.* N3, his principal concern is with units and numbers where, arguably, the attribute precision problem does not arise.

41 See *Met.* Λ1 1069a33–5, M6 1080b11–14.

42 See *Met.* B2 998a7–19, M1 1076a32–M2 1076b11.

43 In calling this a tripartite ontology, I am not addressing many other objects one might find in Plato's world, such as souls and images of perceptibles.

44 In *Met.* M2 1076b11–39, 77a14–20, Aristotle implies that the separate intermediates are prior to perceptibles, which may imply that they can exist without perceptibles, but not perceptibles without them (cf. Plato's notion of priority at *Met.* Δ11 1019a1–4). Is Plato a target here?

45 I know of no Classical or Hellenistic text where a quantity can be described as divided in-two (δίχα) where it is not thereby bisected, including in Plato, e.g., *Meno* 85a1, *Laws* 895e1–8; imprecisely Crat. 396a–b, 410d, Symp. 190d–191a. At *Laws* 745c5, land is bisected according to value and not area. The merely apparent exceptions in Plato all involve dividing kinds (cf. Pol. 264e12–13). Proclus, *In Rem Publicam* 288.18–20, who reads 'unequal', sees the need for explanation: "And so for these reasons he takes one line, and bisects this, although not cutting into two

equal parts, but into unequal, but nevertheless two parts." Lloyd (1992)
sees a similar tension in the *Meno*.

46 The F group (seven manuscripts). See Boter 1989, esp. 99–110 and the
stemma, p. xviii.

47 Plato would not have separated words, while the smooth breathing mark
or accents that would have indicated the beginning of IΣA are innovations
of ca. 200 BCE, although Aristotle mentions a way of indicating accent
outside the word (*Soph. El.* 4.166b1–9, 20.177b2–7). On the history of
accentuation, see Laum 1928: 99–118, and for smooth breathing also 128–
30 with 21–4.

48 Whewell 1856: 601. The interpretation that the segments are cut in the
same ratio as the initial line may be found in Proclus, *In Rem Publicam*
288.18–20, while one may find a line drawn approximately in the ratio
from the images, 1 : 2 : 2 : 4 (or more precisely, 13 : 18 : 21 : 42) in codex
Paris. Gr. 1807 (A) f. 72^r, the basis for the diagram here.

49 Where its principal advocates in the nineteenth century worked: William
Whewell, followed by Henry Jackson, its first publicist (1882), and James
Adam, for his influential commentary (1902).

50 Grube and Reeve (1992): "Then divide each section . . . in the same ratio *as
the line*" (my italics).

51 So, for example, Euclid, *Elements* V 7.3–7, where A = B, and G any
magnitude, "each of A, B has the same ratio to G and G to each of A, B."
One would never infer that they are in the same ratio as A : B!

52 The content is based on the first version of the line and the last. I write
'AB' to indicate the segment composed of A and B.

53 A : B ≈ C : D iff AB : B ≈ CD : D iff AB : CD ≈ B : D. Hence, C : D ≈ B : D.

54 A line XY, with X > Y, is divided in mean and extreme ratio if XY : X ≈ X : Y
(cf. Euclid, *Elements* VI def. 3).

55 A : B ≈ B : C ≈ C : D ≈ A : CD ⟶ B = CD & AB : A ≈ CD : C ≈ B : C ≈ A : B ≈ C : D.
The continuous proportion appears at 511e3.

56 I present a survey of all possibilities in an unpublished paper.

57 Echterling 2018.

58 See Netz 2010: 429–32 on free-hand drawing, as well as Haselberger 1997
for free-hand drawing in architectural plans.

59 On tools see note 15. Imagine an ancient or modern carpenter going
through the procedure of *Elements* I 2 to copy a length! The interpretation

also requires that 'segment' be a line at 509d7 and e1 but an area at 511b2 and d7.

60 On this, Hahn (1983) is certainly right, regardless of the rest of his interpretation that puts the Divided Line and Cave analogies in the realm of reasoning, on which one might well be agnostic. For a different view, see Foley 2008: 19–22.

61 Adam 1902 *ad loc.* and vol. II: 159–60 (VII Appendix 1).

62 Burnyeat 1987: 219–20, cf. n. 19, and 2000: 35–7.

63 Those who advocate intermediates, however, might well turn the tables on those who argue that we would never read the Divided Line their way, were it not for Aristotle. The partitive reading with (4) is more natural to someone ignorant of the dispute but understanding Glaucon as introducing the new kind implicit in Socrates' (4). So too, one might think that in Socrates' second line (511b6–c6), as degrees of clarity cover cognitions, degrees of truth cover objects, each in continuous proportion.

64 Socrates distinguishes counting (*arithmētikē*) and calculation (*logistikē*) at *Gorgias* 451a8–c5, 453e1–454a1 and *Charmides* 166a4–10.

65 See Lang and Crosby 1964.

66 See Euclid, *Elements* IX 21–34, X Appendix 27 (Heiberg) and Knorr 1975: chs. 5, 6.

67 Euclid, *Elements* VII–IX 20.

68 Consider the number 5,040 at *Laws* V 737a–738b and perhaps Euclid, *Elements* IX 35–6. For background, see Acerbi 2003.

69 Cherniss 1947: 238 n. 79, 1944: 497, 1945: 34–7. Cherniss holds that Aristotle's interpretation of Plato derives from his misunderstanding texts such as this. Tarán (1991: 210 n. 28) suggests Cherniss is following Shorey, e.g., 1927: 215. One passage central to Cherniss' argument (cf. Cherniss 1945: 34), *Cratylus* 432a–d, is importantly irrelevant. Socrates makes here a simple contrast, that whereas if you add anything to a number or take something away, *it* becomes a different number, with images they can lose or gain properties of the original in different degrees and still be images. Socrates cannot be speaking about Form-numbers, where a Form cannot become something different at all. Epicharmus (DK 23 B 2) and Aristotle (*Cat.* 6 6a19–25) make similar points. Socrates treats numbers as aggregates.

70 Besides Mueller 1986, cf. also Pritchard 1995: 120–5, and Mendell 2008: 152–3.

71 Building on Cherniss 1947, Tarán (1981: 13–18) attempts to give an account of Platonic Forms where adding Forms constitutes something like adding ordinal numbers: Form n + Form m is the mth number Form after n, rightly criticized by Mueller (1986) and so far as I can tell, not defended in Tarán's reply (1991). Not only would no reader think of addition in this way, Plato would be a very poor writer had he left both reader and characters in the dark. It is very difficult to know what a similar revisionist version of the other sciences would look like.

72 Aristophanes, *Wasps* 785–92, fr. 208, cf. fr. 15: ἀκερματίαν (lacking coinage, anything to break up).

73 Let lcm be the least number with the given parts, and f the sum of these parts of lcm, N the sought number and R the required remainder, then $N : lcm \approx R : (lcm-f)$. The technique is behind the manageable part of Archimedes' *Cattle Problem* and solutions in the scholia to *Greek Anthology* XIV. See Mendell 2018 and also 2009.

74 This is the point of the discussion of summoners, 523–5. Pritchard (1995: esp. 128, 132–3, 145) rightly points out that, even for Plato, once one gets that one is counting fingers, the units are precise and unproblematic, but they will still be fingers, divisible and differing in many ways, just what makes perceptible units inadequate. This is the principal difficulty for taking perceptible units as objects of arithmetic.

75 Similar points may be made about *Philebus* 55e1–3, which also distinguishes two sorts of counting, measuring, and weighing, that of crafts and the philosopher's, wherein the philosopher posits (55e2–3) "a unit that doesn't at all differ from each of ten-thousand units, anyone from anyone."

76 Eudoxus arrived in Athens sometime around 370 to 365 and presumably wrote his work, *On Fast Things*, on planetary motion sometime later. When was the *Republic* written?

77 The system of Meton (432 BCE). See Fowler 1999: 41–3, 50–3, 121–5 for how this might be done. Bowen and Goldstein (1988) speculate that Meton's system is a Babylonian borrowing.

78 The anomalies of motion are handled at *Rep.* X 620e, by the three daughters of Necessity: Clotho, Atropos, and Lachesis (Knorr 1990: 316–17). Franklin (2012: 501) thinks that the difficulty is that the heavens cannot maintain a perfect motion in the future (for which see *Pol.* 269a–274c), but the verbs are all in the present. *Rep.* VIII 546a1–3 on the

corruption of perceptibles, is thus not relevant. For Eudoxus' lunar theory, see Mendell 1998b: 188–94, and 2000: 100–4.

79 Timaeus (40c3–d5) suggests more complicated models to explain the motions of the planets, its details postponed, and in the *Laws* VII 821b–822c the Visitor says that their motions do not deviate at all.

80 Since motions are distances travelled, we should understand the fastness (the daily motion?) and the slowness (the planetary motion?) as *quantitative relations*, namely so many rotations in a given time.

81 This sentence is a minefield. See Adam 1902 *ad loc.* and Book VII Appendix X, 186–7.

82 See esp. Mourelatos 1980 for a careful comparison of the discussion of geometry with the discussion of astronomy.

83 The basic idea of Mueller (1980) that Plato envisages something like the works of Autolycus is surely right, except that we expect an emphasis on periods. Fowler (1999: 118–21; 2000) sees the importance of periods. It may be ironic that the abstract study of cycles closest to what Socrates seems to suggest would be a late Hellenistic treatise, Theodosius, *On Days and Nights*, which treats of commensurable and incommensurable cycles.

84 Vlastos (1980: 21–2 n. 14) and Mourelatos (1980) attempt some such account of the visible heaven idealized, but these are not positions even hinted at by Socrates.

85 The common translation 'statues' is slightly anemic, as the word εἴδωλον signifies an image or representation, sculpture, or painting, of something. The puppets used to create the shadows on the walls are themselves representations of other things.

86 Slings (2003) athetizes 'divine' (θεῖα) and prefers 'seeable' (θεατά), but see Shorey 1890 and Adam 1902: VII App. XIII, 190.

87 Burnyeat 1987: 227–8; more hesitantly, Burnyeat 2000: 34.

88 Being : becoming ≈ Intellecting : Opinion ≈ Knowledge : Conviction ≈ Reasoning : Imaging (534a3–5), where Intellecting is divided into Knowledge and Reasoning; Opinion into Conviction and Imaging. However, $AB : CD \approx A : C \approx B : D$ is equivalent to the initial proportions for the line, $A : B \approx C : D$. For $A : B : C : D$ iff $A : AB \approx C : CD$ iff $AB : CD \approx A : C$, and iff $A : C \approx B : D$.

89 So Shorey 1895: 235.

90 Franklin 2012: 504–5.

91 Adam (1902, *ad loc.*), who rightly criticizes Shorey 1895 and advocates eschewing giving an answer to the question, yet at VII App. I, 159–62 and throughout his commentary on the Divided Line and mathematical sciences treats the text as presupposing the doctrine of intermediates.

92 For a further discussion of these two models, see Ebrey's contribution to this volume (ch. 9).

93 For a discussion of this self-exemplification in Plato, see Meinwald's contribution to this volume (ch. 13).

94 Devereux 1994: 70–2.

95 See *Elements* VII def. 7.2 "differing from an even number by a unit."

96 The Form-in-us appears again in the *Parmenides* (130b2–5) in a distinction between Similarity itself as existing separately from the similarity we *have*. It may be implicit at *Rep.* V 476b5–8, where each Form, though one, "by appearing everywhere through its communality with actions, bodies, and one another seems to be many."

97 Aristotle (*De An.* I.3 406b26–407b13) objects to the *Timaeus* for making the soul have magnitude.

98 *Met.* B2 998a7–19, M1 1076a32–33, M2 1076a38–b11.

99 *Met.* B2 998a14–15. This is the third of four very brief arguments.

100 Aristotle holds this view in his own account of mathematicals.

101 *Met.* B2 998a11–13. Since it is an objection, it should be distinct from a theory of immanent Forms that Aristotle attributes to Anaxagoras and Eudoxus (*Met.* A9 991.14–20). It is also possible that Aristotle thinks that a cogent argument for one bad theory, immanent mathematicals, would force anyone holding to Forms to accept another bad theory, immanent Forms.

102 Whatever Aristotle means elsewhere by 'separate', in *Met.* B2 and M2 the contrast is between mathematicals being (locatively) in and being separate from perceptibles, although his arguments presuppose that separate mathematicals are, like the Cave's puppets, prior to perceptibles.

13 Another Goodbye to the Third Man

Constance C. Meinwald

I INTRODUCTION

Plato's commitment to sentences like:

> Bravery is brave

is characteristic. It appears throughout his career and is at the foundation of Platonism. (See, e.g., *Prt.* 330c2–e2, *Phd.* 100c4–6, *Sph.* 258b9–258c.[1]) Scholars mark this commitment with the special tag "self-predication." Yet these sentences produce negative reactions in us. The one above seems clearly false: it seems to be attributing a feature to Bravery[2] that it could not have – we cannot imagine it performing deeds of valor or bearing up under adversity. As Plato moves into the late period and writes of forms for living things, the situation becomes worse; he now has to accept:

> The Fox is (a) fox.

(On the variants "the F" and "F-ness," see section III.) Does the Fox go out on a chilly night for missions of predation like the title character of the folk-song – except for somehow doing it perfectly, eternally, and changelessly? Plato's thinking seems confused. Aristotle's rude dismissal, "Goodbye to the forms. For they are nonsense" (*Post. An.* 83a32–3; see also *Met.* 997b5–12) seems correct.

I have revised my original "Good-bye" to give some indications of how I arrive at my interpretation and to take account of recent secondary literature. This has left insufficient space to treat the "Greatest Difficulty"; redressing my (not wholly successful) treatment of that must wait. Thanks to the volume editors. I am most particularly grateful to Elizabeth Asmis and Jan van Ophuijsen for advising me on matters of Greek. I owe much as well to other test readers in both the old millennium and the new: Mahrad Almotahari, the late Charles Chastain, the late Dorothy Grover, Wolfgang Mann, Pamela Meinwald, Sandra Peterson, Marya Schechtman, and the members of Northwestern University's Ancient Philosophy Workshop.

Our suspicion that Platonic forms are not philosophically respectable makes the *Parmenides* intriguing. Its first part contains an exchange between a young Socrates and a venerable Parmenides; the core statements of Socrates are reminiscent of presentations of forms by a character of the same name in the *Symposium*, *Phaedo*, and *Republic*. The main topics of those widely-read works were *erōs*, the prospects for our souls after death, and whether we are better off being just or unjust. But Socrates also indicated that full success in understanding the matters at hand and, indeed, in living required a reorientation of one's attention to focus on forms. These were entities with special status; he in effect described sensible things and said: Forms are not like that. These remarks on forms propose a research program and motivate us to take it up. They are brief and sketchy, and rely heavily on images.[3]

It is the *Parmenides* that, for the first time,[4] takes on forms as its main topic. In recognition of this it bore in antiquity the alternative title "On the Forms." Yet in our dialogue, Socrates fails repeatedly to uphold his views when questioned by the senior philosopher, and acknowledges perplexity. This passage has seemed to generations of readers to show sensitivity to problems they themselves associated with Platonism. Had Plato himself come to think his research program was misguided, or did he see some way forward?

Plato composed the dialogue so that immediately after showing the limitations of Socrates, Parmenides commends the youth for his interest in forms, suggests that an able person could deal even with the "greatest difficulty" he has raised, and declares that forms are necessary if one is not to make thinking and dialectic impossible; the venerable philosopher says Socrates has gotten into trouble because he has posited his forms too early, before having "exercised" (135a7–e4 with 133b6–9). He then describes (135d3–137c3) a complicated exercise evidently consisting on any occasion of multiple sections, and says this exercise must be done repeatedly, taking in turn a variety of forms as subjects. Socrates says he cannot understand the description (136c6–8), so the company prevail on the senior philosopher to demonstrate. This inaugural exercise, the second part of the dialogue, is the longest stretch (thirty Stephanus pages!) of uninterrupted argument in the Platonic corpus.

We should look to the exercise if we wish to know Plato's response to the problems. Yet this approach is difficult to take. The surface strangeness of Parmenides' demonstration is maximal: It seems full of bad arguments to bizarre conclusions. Moreover, there appears to be massive and systematic contradiction between what is said to follow from the hypothesis Parmenides takes up in the first section of his exercise and what is said to follow from the same hypothesis in the second section, and so on. And the same thing happens with what follows from the negation of that hypothesis! At the end of the exercise, Parmenides sums up its results as follows:

> If the One is or if it is not, it and the others are and are not, and
> appear and do not appear all things in all ways, in relation to
> themselves and in relation to each other. (166c3–5, tr. based on Gill
> and Ryan)

Unlike Parmenides and Socrates in the first part of our dialogue or the participants in Socratic dialogues, Parmenides and his respondent for the demonstration (a person named "Aristotle," but not the one we know) express no dissatisfaction.[5] Indeed, the respondent goes to an extreme in accepting this summary with the superlative *Alēthestata* ("Most true") – literally the dialogue's last word.

All these indications create the presumption that Plato thinks these results are established in the exercise.[6] Yet because they seem initially so intractable, it is out of the question that he wants us *simply* to accept them. Rather, he is setting us a philosophical task. The *Phaedrus* passage (274c5–277a4) about the naivety of thinking wisdom is transmitted automatically by written formulae shows why Plato designed texts that challenge us to work to achieve understanding of whatever points are at issue. And Myles Burnyeat has developed in detail the idea that different clusters of dialogues require different levels of independent work on the part of readers.[7] It should thus be no surprise that the second part of the *Parmenides* challenges us to engage in considerable philosophical activity of our own in response to the text. Indeed, its interpreters generally take this sort of line. Of course, since we are interpreting Plato, our activity must be securely based in what he has written.

The unintelligible methodological remarks and the seemingly bad arguments to puzzling conclusions can appear as independent problems that together amount to a total mess. In reality, their being together holds promise. In composing methodological remarks that describe a schema for exercise and then creating an illustrative demonstration to help Socrates understand those remarks, Plato indicated we should read each in light of the other. Having done that systematically, I find the second part of the *Parmenides* intelligible. A positive and crucial innovation – a distinction between two kinds of predication, going hand-in-hand with a distinction between two kinds of facts – emerges as what allows us to see that the exercise consists of good arguments to reasonable conclusions which are not contradictory after all.

The exercise was introduced to help aspiring Platonists handle the problems of the first part of the dialogue. For this present chapter, I have selected the most notorious of these, the "Third Man Argument." (The name derives from Aristotle's tag *tritos anthrōpos* – his version of the argument was based on what we would now be careful to translate as the Human itself, but which has long been known under more sexist translations. Plato's example is the Large.) We will start with a general treatment of the first part of the dialogue and an initial look at this particular problem. This will lead to a question that I will address with some key background. We will then be in a position to proceed to the main innovation of the second part of the dialogue. Finally, we will return to our title argument, with deeper understanding of every move in it. An Appendix explains how my interpretation of the distinction developed in the *Parmenides* coincides with Michael Frede's pioneering reading of the two uses of "is" in the *Sophist*. Thus each strengthens the case for the other.[8]

Working through the exercise prescribed to Socrates will show that Plato continues to uphold self-predication sentences. But he helps us distinguish a use for them on which their truth conditions are entirely different from the ones that come most readily to mind. Thus I characterize self-predication sentences as those *of the grammatical form* "The F is F" (or of course the variant form "F-ness is F"); it is important not to build in the interpretation that the F *has* F-ness.[9] All this affects decisively our understanding of how Plato's forms do their jobs. They are not what I shall call "exemplars," the sort of entities invoked by phrases like "the Platonic ideal of the banana split."

II THE EXAMINATION OF SOCRATES

I have mentioned that the first part of the *Parmenides* (perhaps up to 135d3) resembles a Socratic dialogue. There a presumed expert in some area enters into conversation with Socrates, answering a series of questions, and turns out to lack expertise, being unable to avoid contradiction. In our dialogue, Parmenides is the questioner and Socrates the respondent. When Parmenides questions him about forms, Socrates falls into difficulties.

Here as with the Socratic dialogues, some interpreters assimilate the failure of the respondent to a *reductio ad absurdum* of one of the claims in play, meant to motivate rejection of that claim and so to function as an indirect proof of the targeted claim's negation. To serve this purpose effectively, an argument must be explicit enough to establish that its unacceptable conclusion is due solely to the targeted premise and cannot be laid to the account of either another premise or an illicit inference. The arguments in our present passage are far from matching this description: There is not even enough information to indicate how we should make them fully determinate. The passage is so far from following effectively the strategy we have been considering that we should doubt that this was Plato's purpose.

Even if it does not fulfill the indirect proof strategy, Plato considers the type of examination depicted here a test of the expertise of an individual. To contradict oneself when discussing some subject betrays that one is no expert, even if it will require investigation to determine the source of the problem. In the case in our dialogue, working through the exercise Parmenides prescribes will enable us to see how the research program Socrates advocates can be developed successfully. But in his immaturity, he embraces key formalism without being clear about its true interpretation; thus he is led into unviable readings and disastrous inferences from them.

Socrates' aggressive criticism of Parmenides' Eleatic comrade Zeno (127d6–130a2) is what leads into the examination of the young man by the senior philosopher (130a3–135c7). Because of the resemblance of the core views of Socrates in these passages to statements by the character Socrates in the *Symposium*, *Phaedo*, and *Republic* (and indeed because the spokesman for forms here as before *is* "Socrates"), the first part of the *Parmenides* has long been regarded as a comment by Plato on his own work. (Plato uses literary elements to indicate that the *Republic* in particular is in view.[10]) Disagreement has centered on the content of his comment. As I see it, there is something correct in the formulation of Gregory Vlastos, that our passage is a "record of honest perplexity."[11] But while Vlastos attributed the perplexity to Plato as he wrote the *Parmenides*, we should not rush to do that. Rather, I believe Plato is showing that his previous sketches of forms did not themselves contain answers to many important questions about these entities. Nevertheless, Parmenides' advice to Socrates indicates that Plato still considers the program promising. I have explained that we will have to engage with the second part of the dialogue to identify Plato's way forward. But first let us take an initial look at our title argument to get some sense of the issues in play.

*

We now come to Plato's "Third Man Argument" (132a1–b2). Some information concerning what is being talked about here will be useful. The Greek *idea* and *eidos* lie behind the translation "form"; I am one of those who think we needn't make a big technical distinction between them. These terms, cognate with each other (and with English *vision*), appear in Greek well before Plato. Early on, they referred to an aspect of a thing that can be presented to our sight. Over time, each word comes to have occurrences in which it definitely refers to something general which can be common to a number of things as redness is common to red objects, and the semantic range was extended so that what is picked out need not literally meet the eye. Ordinary speakers could use this vocabulary without making any commitments on philosophical questions about the status of these items. Plato's usage from the Socratic dialogues on is continuous with and develops gradually from this.

Parmenides starts by confirming Socrates' commitment to thinking every form is one (i.e., single, unique) and then gets the youth committed to a result in tension with this. The key moves flash by, leaving the exact formulation the argument should receive and, in particular, the grounds for taking many of the steps underdetermined. I offer a translation and initial discussion with the proviso that there cannot be a single "correct" way of doing this. In any case I think it is wrong in principle to make up our minds about this passage before considering how the second part of the dialogue bears on it. (My discussion will apply with small adjustments to many of the translations others have offered.[12])

Parmenides' prompts run as follows:

A) I suppose you think that every form is one on the basis of something of this kind. When a number of things seem large to you, presumably there seems to be a single form that is the same as you look at them all, whence you suppose the Large to be one ....

B) Now what about the Large itself and the other large things, if you look at all of them in the same way with the *psychē*? Again, won't a single Large appear,[13] by which all these things appear large? ...

> C) Therefore another form of Large will appear plainly, produced in addition to both the Large itself and the things participating in it. And over all these again another, by which all these will be large. And each of your forms will no longer be single, but unlimited in multitude (132a1–b2, my trans. with reference letters added)

Parmenides starts off, in (A), by articulating a basis for Socrates' thinking every form is single: when he looks at, e.g., large things, it seems to him that there is some aspect of all these cases that is the same – so the Large is one. Socrates cannot have done the parallel thing for every form separately – he isn't even sure of exactly how many there are (130c1–d9). Nevertheless, his accepting Parmenides' suggestion indicates that he takes this case to be representative.

Parmenides in (B) speaks of "the Large itself and the other large things," which builds in the commitments that the Large is distinct from the original sensibles, and is itself a large thing. Socrates acquiesces in considering the things in this heterogeneous new group "in the same way" (as the original group).[14] So he agrees that a single Large will appear, which makes all the things in this new group appear large.

I take (C)'s "form of Large" that "will appear plainly" to pick up on (B)'s "won't a single Large appear?" In (C), Parmenides is making explicit as his conclusion ("Therefore") that (B)'s "single Large" is in fact *another* form, distinct from all members of the heterogeneous group it accounts for, including the original Large itself. And (presumably by reiteration of the same reasoning), there will be another new form after that. This parade will go on without end, and the same thing will happen with each of Socrates' forms.

Socrates agrees, in (A), to a sequence of thoughts that Parmenides carefully shows him, and that causes no problem so far. Parmenides then, in (B) and (C), induces the young man repeatedly to leap before he looks at any corresponding rationales – or pitfalls. In being led to treat the heterogeneous group introduced in (B) in "the same way" he had treated the original group of visible things, Socrates ends up assimilating his treatment of the Large itself to that of the sensible large things. Can it possibly be right to think of forms in this way? We are not even clear exactly why we should take Largeness to be a large thing; we may well question whether it is an exemplarily large item. We have seen that Bravery and the Fox cannot be understood as exemplars.

Thus one may think to stop the train of Parmenides' argument by rejecting self-predication.[15] Yet to do that would be to give up on Socrates' program – is that really what Plato should do? In the next section, some philosophical time-travel will help us reanimate the dialectical situation at the time of the dialogue's composition and realize why it is so important to preserve that commitment in *some* way. Linguistic information will then help us appreciate that Socrates glimpses correctly that self-predication sentences must express truths, though – like ourselves – he is not clear initially how to identify what truths they express. It is exciting to realize that, in building self-predication into his theory, Plato does not make an unmotivated slip. He is heir to a program that gave a central explanatory role to sentences of this type. Moreover, the very form of words guarantees that each such sentence expresses *some* truth.

III   SELF-PREDICATION: THE BACKGROUND

The thread we now trace originated with the historical Parmenides of Elea – in making "Parmenides" the leader in our dialogue Plato acknowledges this debt. The historical man is among the greatest of philosophical bullet-biters: His message is that, unless we can find out what is wrong with his argument, we must accept all of its conclusions. His position rules out any commitment to or thought about "not-being/what is not"; we must cleave only to "being/what is." Because of this, he argues we must repudiate as illusory the world we ordinarily believe in, a world in which real things undergo generation, destruction, and change. For all of these mix being with not-being.

Parmenides offered what was for generations "an argument that nobody could fault" to "a conclusion that nobody could believe."[16]

A group of Presocratic philosophers of nature (including the Atomists, Empedocles, and Anaxagoras) found a productive way to cope. Their theories are two-tiered. They explain the so-called generation, destruction, and change of ordinary "objects" in terms of rearrangement of "things that are" (each purely what it is, and meant to be free from mixing being and not-being in virtue of not suffering generation, destruction, or change). These theorists aimed in this way to rescue our ordinary world from the imputation of being illusory. Their strategy involves seeing what we ordinarily think of as individuals – the trees and horses, the fish and lakes of our daily world – as composites. Thus, ordinary "things" are derived from and explained in terms of fundamental beings.

At the level of fundamental reality, Eleatic rules are indeed close to being preserved. The "things that are" of these Presocratics are all but free from not-being: They are eternal and unchanging, except in position. (Whether these cosmologists had any reason for allowing themselves a plurality of elements and for allowing the elements to change in location is unknown.) Anaxagoras in particular is "footnoted" by Plato as relevant to the *Parmenides*.[17] A look at some details of his system will reveal ancestral versions of key Platonist tenets.

Anaxagoras took the Eleatic proscription on coming to be from what is not to rule out even coming to be F from what is not F. He is quoted as asking "For how can hair come from what is not hair, and flesh from what is not flesh?"[18] This committed him to putting a tremendous number of items on his list of fundamental beings: The hot, the cold, the bright, the dark, flesh, hair, air, and aether are just some items from just some of the fragments (B4, B10, and B1). Familiar objects are composed of shares or portions of these pure elements – thought of as basic stuffs or "quasi-stuffs."[19] These shares stand to the composite objects in a simple relation: we can think of them as physical ingredients.

We ourselves think about *some* cases in a broadly Anaxagorean way (bracketing our atomism). For example, we think a piece of gold

jewelry is a composite: a gold bracelet is one that has enough pure gold
in its makeup to be considered as gold. Pure gold actually is gold in the
same way as composites except without the admixture of competing
elements, so it is easy to see how the portion of gold that is
a constituent of a bracelet accounts for the characteristics of the
composite. In effect, a straightforward sort of self-predication puts
the elemental ingredients of Anaxagoras in a position to endow composites with their own qualities. That is what makes the elemental
stuffs explanatory.

The theory of Anaxagoras was a wonderful one in its place and
time. He managed to do cosmology while "heroically adhering to the
strictest interpretation of the Parmenidean code"[20] – or at least the
strictest interpretation compatible with his primary project. Plato (in
the *Sophist*) and we ourselves as well eventually came to find some
cases of "not-being" or "what is not" tractable; people identify in
various ways where "father Parmenides" went wrong. In any case,
and in particular whether or not the reasoning that originally motivated him was entirely sound, the theory of Anaxagoras holds considerable attraction. This is due largely to the appeal of his explanatory
scheme. But while his approach works well in many cases, there is
a limit to how far it can be extended. Plato drew attention to this in
the *Phaedo* (96d–e with 100e–101c). The context was Socrates' narration of how he, initially attracted to Presocratic philosophy of nature,
ultimately found it confused and launched instead on a "second sail-
ing," his own proprietary type of explanation.

A variant of one of the *Phaedo* puzzles (on being taller "by
a head"), occurs at *Parmenides* 131c12–e1. Socrates gets into trouble
because he is not in command of any definite alternative to the
problematic part of Anaxagoreanism his *Phaedo* analogue had
meant to leave behind and falls back into using the old approach
(cf. 132d9–e1). On the Anaxagorean scheme, what makes, e.g.,
a mountain large should be its share of the large, and this share should
do its job by bringing its largeness with it. But considering how very
many mountains there are in the world, not to mention large deserts,

large oxen, large temples, large countries, and so on and on and on, the share of largeness available even to the world's largest mountain would have to be quite a small one. Being a small thing prevents this share, in Socrates' eyes, from having the requisite largeness to bring to the mountain, so that he can no longer see how the share can make the mountain large.

Given that Plato wants to explain not only the aspects of the world Anaxagoras focused on[21] but moral and aesthetic phenomena as well, much that interests him will resist an approach on which the fundamental entities and the shares of them that ordinary things get are Anaxagorean ingredients. One obviously cannot claim that when a singer's sound becomes beautiful this is because of the mere physical addition of a share of some elemental stuff, the beautiful, qualitatively identical with what the Manhattan skyline loses as it becomes overbuilt. Nevertheless Plato, like Anaxagoras, undertakes to explain everything about derived entities – ordinary objects – in terms of their *having shares of*, that is, *participating in* fundamental ones: pure stuffs in one theory and forms in the other. We actually have the Greek *metechein* in Anaxagoras B6 and B12,[22] though translation can obscure the overlap in vocabulary with such Platonic texts as the famous declaration Socrates made in the *Phaedo* even as he introduced his own approach in contrast to the confusing Presocratic work:

> I think that, if there is anything beautiful besides the Beautiful itself, it is beautiful on account of nothing other than that it has a share of/participates in [*metechei*] that Beautiful, and I say so with everything .... I simply, naively and perhaps foolishly cling to this, that nothing else makes it beautiful other than the presence of, or the communion with [*koinōnia*], or however you may describe its relationship to that Beautiful we mentioned, for I will not insist on the precise nature of the relationship, but that all beautiful things are beautiful by the Beautiful. (100c4–d8, tr. based on Grube)[23]

To sum up, as early as the *Phaedo*, Plato showed that we can't understand having a share of a fundamental entity in the same way Anaxagoras did. Largeness is not adequately conceived of as transferable, homogeneous large stuff, portions of which are physical ingredients in ordinary objects. While one might respond to this recognition simply by throwing up one's hands, Plato more optimistically sought to retain the basic explanatory scheme. That is, he retained the abstract tenets:

Things are F because they have a share of (= participate in) the F.
The F is itself F.

And he did this even while recognizing that the intertwined issues of how to think of the fundamental entities and their self-predication would need rethinking.

*

To carry forward this program would be idiotic unless Plato had some reason for thinking there indeed was an alternative and safe interpretation of "The F is F." In fact, the metaphysically unloaded usage with which he starts already provides this reason. To see how, we start from the fact that the Greek analogues of "the beautiful," "the just," etc. are commonly used in two different ways. "The just" used one way refers to something or everything that happens to be just; used the other way it refers to justice, i.e., to what it is about those things that is *just* (as opposed perhaps to cheerful, popular, or what have you). "The beautiful" can refer to something, say an urn, that happens to be beautiful or to all such things; used the other way it refers to beauty, i.e., to what is *beautiful* about those things. Abstract nouns come to be used increasingly in Plato's time and are unambiguous; Plato uses both forms of words.

Even in our English (as just now), glosses such as "what it is about just things that is just" and "what is beautiful about beautiful things" work perfectly well – as long as one reads naturally without getting caught in the toils of philosophical questions. In fact, we can immediately make an important observation.[24] By substituting such a gloss for the expressions it cashes out, we can recognize that to say:

The just is just

or:

Justice is just

is to say something tantamount to

[What it is about just things that is just] is just.

And using this version, we can see that the predicate *has to apply* as long as the subject term (in square brackets) refers: simply look at the last bit within the subject term, and compare it with the predicate.

This explains otherwise unaccountable passages in the *Protagoras* and *Hippias Major*, in which even characters who cannot be taken as subscribing to Platonism accept self-predication: linguistic competence assures them that the relevant formulations express truths, even if they are not in a position fully to explicate those truths.[25] "Bravery is brave" is of course false as we ordinarily read it, so that reading cannot be the relevant one; work will be required to identify the interpretation of ancient Greek self-predication sentences Plato needs.

Earlier in this section, we saw that the theory of Anaxagoras relied for its explanatory power on what we might call the obvious form of self-predication for his elemental beings (the hot, the cold, the bright, the dark, and so on). The hot (the totality of heat in the world) was itself hot, and so were the shares of it composites got. But the way in which Anaxagorean quasi-stuffs are what they are purely does not work if one wants to take account of goodness, justice, and beauty or even largeness, triangularity, and unity. We now know that Plato was justified in being confident about the prospects for developing a successor-theory. Self-predication sentences are guaranteed to be true on some reading. It would be of paramount importance to identify that reading of these explanatorily crucial truths about forms. Since we are at a loss to identify how "The F is F" could hold without the F having F-ness, Plato needs to provide us with guidance on this point. In the next section, we will see how the *Parmenides* does that.

IV PLATO'S INNOVATION

We have seen that Plato set us as homework to interpret the remarks that prescribe exercise to Socrates and the demonstration that illustrates those remarks by reading each in light of the other. Thus, we will be going back and forth between them. This section contains some samples of the much more extensive evidence I have developed in lengthy study of the second part of the dialogue. My reading shows, among other things, how the exercise enables us to identify the interpretation of self-predication central to Plato's theory.[26]

The Structure of the Exercise

Parmenides' methodological prescription appears at 135c8–137c3. This long passage describes what the exercise would amount to with a variety of initial hypotheses (we are to exercise taking in turn each of the forms), and culminates in a general description, quoted below. What exactly Parmenides is recommending and why is, when one reads the passage on its own, stunningly opaque:

> ... in a word, concerning whatever you might hypothesize as being or as not being or as suffering any other affection, you must examine the consequences in relation to itself and in relation to each one of the others, whichever you pick out, and in relation to several and in relation to all in the same way, and then you must examine the others in relation to themselves and in relation to whatever other thing you pick out on occasion; and all this must be done on the supposition that what you originally hypothesized is the case, and again on the

> supposition that it is not (136b6–c4, changing Burnet's
> semicolon in 136c2 to a comma; my translation)

This general description, taken together with the particular ones that precede it, indicates a schema for generating instances of the exercise.

The beginning and the end of the quotation tell us that, on each occasion, we start from some hypothesis and examine the consequences of supposing first that our hypothesis obtains and then that it does not. The demonstration we actually get does this, in eight clearly marked sections.[27] We can see that the description above has the resources to account for this number: We can read it as operating crucially with three pairs of qualifications: "if one's hypothesis obtains/does not obtain," "what follows for the subject/for the others," and "in relation to itself/in relation to the others" (pros heauto/pros ta alla). (This is confirmed by the summary of the results at 166c2–5, which we looked at earlier.) There are eight possible combinations of one member from each of the three pairs, since $2 \times 2 \times 2 = 8$. Taking all this together with the particular descriptions of the exercise taking sample subjects (136a5–b4), it is natural to suppose that the exercise is structured so that each of the eight combinations characterizes one of its sections, with the first considering "If the subject is, what follows for the subject in relation to itself."[28]

The members of the first two pairs of qualifications figure obviously in setting the agendas of the sections in the demonstration we get ("the others" are other forms). Not so with the third pair. The agenda-setting questions opening the sections do not include "in relation to itself" or "in relation to the others," nor are those phrases prominent within the individual arguments. Nevertheless, we need to give them a role if we are to respect Plato's description of the exercise and use its elements to account for the number of sections we actually get. (Two pairs of qualifications would yield only $2 \times 2 = 4$ combinations.)

Some think the phrase "in relation to itself" must pick out assertions we could schematize as aRa, and "in relation to the others" those we could schematize as aRb (where a ≠ b). Though the most obvious way to understand the phrases on their own, this makes it impossible to read the methodological remarks as describing the exercise and so fails to meet a basic interpretative constraint.[29] We should focus our efforts on finding a different way of understanding the "in-relation-to" phrases.

Tree Predication

We can find a way toward a different interpretation of Plato's "in relation to itself" by using ideas from earlier in this chapter.

1) The arguments of the demonstration work.
2) Given that Parmenides starts from the hypothesis "If the One is," the first section (137c4–142a8) should investigate: If the One is, what follows for the One [in relation to itself].

Now, we read in that section that if the One is, it is not the same as itself, not other than anything, and so on. Bizarre results, if interpreted the usual way! Surely everything must be the same as itself and other than some things. But (2) tells us that the consequents are implicitly:

> The One is not the same as itself [*in relation to itself*].
> The One is not other than anything [*in relation to itself*].

How does adding that qualification to each change its force? The entire section is evidence. For given (1), we should be guided by what its arguments actually achieve in tailoring our understanding of "in relation to itself."

Here's a sample:

> ... it won't be other by being one [*tōi hen einai*: on this see below]. Or do you think so? – Certainly not. – But if not by this, it won't be by itself (*heautōi*), and if not by itself neither [will] *it* (sc. be other); and it being in no way other will be other than nothing. – Right. (*Parm.* 139c6–d1, my tr.)

The skeleton is:

> it won't be other by being one ... and if not by itself, neither will *it* be other.

The idea that this section explores what holds of the One *in relation to itself* is consonant with this passage's invoking what the One is "by itself." We can see what that might be by reflecting that it is connected with what the One is *tōi hen einai* ("by being one" or more literally "by the to-be-one").

This usage belongs to a network of terms derived from *einai* (to be) that Plato associates with natures. Starting with *Euthyphro* 11a6–b1, we see the nominalization *ousia* used to designate the nature that an account answering a Socratic "what *is* it?" question is supposed to set forth; such an account can also be described as the account of a "to be."[30] These accounts articulating natures – alternatively styled in English as "definitions" though of course not merely dictionary definitions – will continue to be central in Plato's search for understanding. After all, the forms are eternal, unchanging, and immaterial items each identified with a nature. (We too can regard sweetness – what is common to all sweets – as the nature that one analyzes when inquiring into what it is to be sweet, and which makes edible sweets sweet.) Such a nature is a universal property or quality where that is understood as nontechnically as possible, and understood so that Cathood, Whiteness, Heat, and Multitude all count. The idea that investigation of a subject in relation to itself in the *Parmenides* is a study of natures gets confirmation immediately after the passage we are working with, from remarks cast in terms of the unambiguous *phusis* in 139d1–e4 and 139e7–140b5.

So our passage suggests that truths about a form F-ness/the F *in relation to itself* hold (in some way) because of what the nature F-ness *is* (in a strong sense).[31] I suggest we characterize predications about F-ness/the F *in relation to itself* as articulating what it is to be F (i.e., the nature F-ness) in whole or in part. (I sometimes speak of being "involved in" a nature so as not to keep repeating the disjunction.) The F will be G [in relation to itself] if being G is part or all of what it is to be F. In fact, Plato only requires that the nature associated with the term "G" is part or all of the nature associated with the term "F." The endings of the words used may vary, and this allows for the sentences in question to read normally. Thus, assuming that Excellence, i.e., Virtue is part of Justice (that is, assuming that being virtuous is part of being just),

Justice is virtuous

will hold [in relation to itself].

Notice that the core mission of this type of predication does not require Justice to *have* Virtue. And we should not add that require-ment – to bake such a commitment into predications of a subject in relation to itself would destroy our whole interpretative enterprise.[32] We have also seen that "The One is not other [in relation to itself]," on the interpretation we are now stopping with, is well-supported by Plato's argument for it. On the understanding I propose, the assertion is not denying that the One has Otherness as a property. Rather it holds because the nature Otherness is not involved in the nature Unity: being other is neither the whole nor a part of what it is to be one.[33] (I have shown elsewhere how the arguments of this first section are doing very interesting work on this reading, and how a natural extension of the reading works well for the investigations in our exercise that concern the others in relation to *them*selves.[34])

We've been connecting the kind of predication under study with the project of understanding a nature by knowing what is *involved in* it. Plato increasingly recommended doing this through a project scholars call "collection and division." This appeared in kernel in the *Euthyphro* (11e–12e), and is developed and used exten-sively in the *Phaedrus, Sophist, Statesman,* and *Philebus.* The aim is to map relations among genera and species (more and less general kinds[35]) using differentiae so as to produce genus–species "trees." The results achieved by the descendants of this project include the familiar biological classifications of living things. In Plato's scheme, the nature of a species involves those of its genus and its differentia, and this is transitive. For example, the nature Humanhood perhaps involves both Animality and Rationality (or to put it the other way, being human perhaps involves being animal and being rational). So on my interpretation, predications "in relation to itself" are those that hold in virtue of relationships between natures shown through the mapping of genera, species, and differentiae. To help us remember this, I sometimes call them "tree" predications.

Let's consider some examples. Assuming that to be a triangle is to be a three-sided plane figure (i.e., that Triangle is the species of the genus Plane Figure that has the differentia Three-Sided),

Triangularity is three-sided [in relation to itself]

must hold. We can also see that

Angling fishes

is correct when made as this type of predication since Angling is a kind of Fishing. If Motion figures in the account of what Dancing is,

Dancing moves

will hold of Dancing in relation to itself. Finally, consider:

The Just is just.

Though not as useful as a detailed articulation of that nature, this is safe all the same: it is trivially true that being just is involved in being just. Self-predication sentences are the limit case of in-relation-to-itself predications.

We've been able to explore this understanding of "in-relation-to-itself" only briefly. But we can already begin to see its philosophical payoff. In developing the "tree predication" reading, we make some of the progress needed for Plato's Anaxagorean program. The reading makes self-predication sentences come out true by diverging completely from the obvious reading ordinarily given to them. Moreover, we can now identify Plato's parallel for the pure stuffs of Anaxagoras. Since what it is to be S either involves or does not involve being P, we will never find among tree predications pairs of the form "S is P" and "S is not P." For Plato the totality of tree truths (including but not confined to self-predications) is the realm of pure being.

Ordinary Predication

What then of our dialogue's predications "in relation to the others"? These will turn out to be what we might previously have taken to be *all* predications: those that we might describe as holding in virtue of their subjects' having the properties associated with their predicate terms. (I thus call them "ordinary predications.") We can start to see that by considering the second section of arguments, which ought to consider the One "in relation to the others." That section provides a host of ordinary results: If the One is, it is one and many, same and different, like and unlike, etc. – as anything must be.[36] Indeed there is general agreement about the force of the section's results.[37]

Our work now is to appreciate in detail how these ordinary predications of a given subject involve a variety of forms. In a later section of the exercise,[38] when discussing a scenario in which the One and the others are unlike in the ordinary way, Parmenides adds:

> The One would have Unlikeness *in relation to which* the others are unlike it. (161b3–4, my trans.)

Compare 161c6–d1, concerning an ordinary scenario in which the One and the others are unequal; Parmenides adds that this is *in relation to Inequality*. Why these supplements? We've already seen that Plato's Anaxagoreanism posits having a share of F-ness/the F itself as what makes things F in the ordinary way; the supplements register this aspect of Platonism. If we write the whole class of ordinary predications this way, they will include:

> Socrates is just [in relation to Justice].
> Northern Dancer is a horse [in relation to Horsehood].
> The Triangle is Intelligible [in relation to Intelligibility].

My proposal is that these are our dialogue's predications "in relation to the others." The phrase presumably marks that subjects stand in the relation in question to all sorts of natures, generally "other" than themselves.[39]

Having identified the second class of predications the *Parmenides* apparatus marks, can we make further progress in understanding them? Remember that in the theory of Anaxagoras, what enabled ingredients to play their roles was their status as pure beings. Now Plato allocates that status in a different way: to natures (for example Justice, i.e., what it is to be just) as articulated by their accounts. So it is no surprise that the *Parmenides* should give the starring role in explaining ordinary facts to them. And this works well. Suppose that Justice is the Excellence in which each part – the rational, the spirited, and the appetitive – does its job in the functioning of the overall entity (as the *Republic* suggested). It is obvious how explanatorily useful this is. It immediately enables us to understand why a character like Socrates in the *Apology* and *Phaedo* was so unconflicted. Similarly, since Northern Dancer is a horse *in relation to Horsehood*, fundamental truths articulating Horsehood will have application. If that nature involves being herbivorous, this will determine much about all horses: e.g., they won't do well if fed steak, or plastic.

In all such cases, what exactly the nature associated with the predicate term amounts to will determine (some of) the ordinary facts about the subject. We will in effect have the ancestral of the Aristotelian "formal cause." Plato's previous dialogues had long gestured at this sort of application of knowledge of accounts. We heard as early as *Euthyphro* 6e3–6 that being in possession of the account of piety would let us decide correctly whether a particular case is pious or impious. Socrates in the *Republic* made clear the need to understand what Justice *is* in order to figure out whether or not we are better off being just. He went on to apply his proprietary account to work out how to help the young develop in accordance with this nature.

Because the "others" that ordinary predications are "in relation to" are the very natures that (on other occasions) are the subjects of "in-relation-to-itself" articulations, it turns out that tree truths are what ultimately explain and ground ordinary ones. The "formal-cause" way in which the articulation of underlying natures is explanatory of ordinary facts is Plato's new and improved substitute for Anaxagorean explanation in terms of physical transfer of portions of homogeneous fundamental stuffs. To have fundamental entities that in some important way are purely what they are, and then to use this to explain ordinary facts is in order for a successor-program to the two-tiered cosmologies that we saw arose in response to the challenge of Parmenides the Eleatic.

V THE INNOVATION APPLIED

Let's now prepare to return to the first part of the dialogue by recalling the general situation. Socrates' views there have always reminded readers of certain passages from the *Symposium*, *Republic*, and *Phaedo*. The position produced by concretizing the suggestions of those passages in the most simpleminded way posits forms as perfect exemplars. We have seen how bizarre this view is.

Engagement with Parmenides' demonstration has led us to read its juxtaposition of paired sections of argument apparently presenting massive and systematic contradictions as challenging us to develop a distinction between two kinds of predication and a corresponding one between two kinds of facts. "In-relation-to-itself" (tree) predications function as a compact verbal way to present the results of inquiry into what each nature is. A tree predication "The F is G" articulates some or all of what is involved in F-ness: The nature associated with the term "G" is part or all of the nature associated with the term "F." These predications are Plato's domain of pure being, and are of surpassing value to grasp on their own. Moreover, in articulating how natures are structured, they provide grounding and explanation for ordinary facts. "In-relation-to-the-others" (ordinary) predications have the complementary role of allowing us to fill out our portrait of each form by registering what properties it has. And ordinary predications also register the facts about items around us in the sensible world.

With this distinction in hand, we see clearly why we need no longer think Plato's theoretically central self-predication sentences commit him to forms that perform their roles by being perfect exemplars. No longer embarrassed by the prospect of these superexemplifiers, we were able to put together and develop many suggestions from the dialogues in a satisfying way. In effect, we've seen that the *Parmenides* apparatus isn't so much introducing new projects as it is giving us a way of organizing and being clear about ones present in much of Plato's work.

To transition to our remaining challenge by bringing out some points of detail that will be essential: We can readily see that "The A is B" made as a tree predication and the same words, "The A is B," used on a different occasion to make an ordinary one will always have different truth conditions, and often different truth values as well. Thus, if using sharp teeth to gnaw prey is part of being a fox, then

The Fox uses sharp teeth to gnaw prey

is perfectly in order as a tree predication – and it is one we can make without having to countenance the form running around with grease and blood on its jaws.

Let's also dwell a moment on the circumstance that in-relation-to-itself facts, identified as Plato's realm of pure being, are cordoned off by our distinction from occlusion by ordinary ones. Thus, Plato is as free as anyone to agree that the Fox doesn't have Foxhood, nor does Triangularity have Triangularity. On the other hand, Unity does have Unity (144e8–145a3). That is, different forms exhibit different patterns when it comes to the ordinary truths about them. This will come into play when we return to our title problem.

*

Since the exercise Parmenides prescribed was meant to help with the problems of the first part of the dialogue, the work we've done should prepare us for a return engagement with the "Third Man." Let's start by seeing how the distinction we've been exploring blocks the regress in the case of typical forms like the Human.

The analogue of the base level in the text would be that when a number of things seem human to us, there seems to be a single aspect which is the same as we look at them all, so we suppose that the Human is one and is what makes all the sensibles in question human.[40] On to the next stage. Should we accept a purported new group of humans (the original visible humans plus the Human itself) and treat it "in the same way" as the original group?

The Human is human

is ridiculous if we read it as concerning the same sort of fact as

Socrates is human.

And now we can say why: one is a tree predication, the other an ordinary one. Of course, Plato wants to maintain *tree* predications including:

The human is vertebrate

and

The human is human.

But the crucial point is that in maintaining these, he does not take the Human to be a member of our species. With no new group of humans to treat "in the same way" as the original group, there is no question of having to crank up our machinery again to produce a new form, and then another, and another . . . . A single form of Human is all that is needed. "The Third Man" is not only outmoded as sexist language – in terms of the underlying philosophy as well, Plato can say goodbye to the Third Man.

Of course, for some forms, "The F is F" does hold as an ordinary predication.[41] The basic insight we have achieved about how Plato's theory handles explanatory/causal responsibility enables us to deal with these as well, with only a slightly more involved exposition. Let's take the example of Beauty. We start off with a base group of visible things each of which is beautiful. Since it seems to us there is some aspect of all these ordinary "beauties" that is the same, we suppose Beauty is one (i.e., single) and makes each of the ordinary cases beautiful (i.e., it has causal/explanatory responsibility for the relevant facts). Here as before Plato will maintain the "in-relation-to-itself" predication

The Beautiful is beautiful.

And of course, that is not a matter of Beauty being beautiful in the same way as sensible beauties are. So in accepting that self-predication we do not yet create a new group.

Now we need to address the fact that the ordinary self-predication

Beauty is beautiful

also holds; Beauty is a property every form has. So in fact, we *will* have a new group (the original beauties plus Beauty itself) that all have the property of being beautiful. Will we have to treat this group "in the same way" as the base group of sensible beauties – and so confront a new, unwelcome Beauty, a Third Beauty, and so on forever?

Of course not. On the one hand, Plato *does* have to say there is a single Beauty by which all the things in this new group (which includes Beauty itself) appear beautiful. But we should now be able to see why the single Beauty in question will not have to be a *distinct* Beauty produced in addition to both the original form and the visible things that were participants in it.

Why might it have seemed that we *would* need an additional entity? Let's get a running start by thinking about the base step, where we had the sensible beautiful things and we recognized the single form, Beauty itself, by which the sensibles appeared beautiful.

Obviously, none of the sensibles could sustain the causal/explanatory role; we needed something additional to do that work: Beauty. This turns on the explanatory inadequacy of the sensibles, and therefore does not license the claim that *nothing* can ever explain anything about itself. Nor does that claim appear in the *Parmenides*.

Our exercise has put us in a position to say how Beauty out-classes any sensible item in this respect. For we are now clear that there are two different kinds of facts about any form F-ness/the F: fundamental facts articulating what is involved in the nature F-ness (that is, what it is to be F) as well as ordinary facts about F-ness (that is, facts about what features the F has). It is the articulated natures that, in Plato's formal-cause scheme, have causal/explanatory responsibility for ordinary facts. So in particular, what was explanatory and metaphysically grounding of sensible beauties at the base level was the nature: what it is to be beautiful.

Let's now resume with the augmented group consisting of the original sensibles plus the form by which they were beautiful. As we saw, Plato is committed to there being a single Beauty by which all the things in the augmented group are beautiful. But now we can see that there is no reason to think that this must be *another* form *produced in addition to* the first one. The same nature (what Beauty *is*: what it is to be beautiful) that explained the base group also explains the new group formed by recognizing that Beauty has Beauty. The key point is that the articulation of that nature is fundamental in a way none of the ordinary facts can be. We are appealing to an explanatory *fact* that is distinct from the ordinary facts that it explains, but there is no need to import a *form* distinct from the original one in order to do so. Beauty can account for the fact that it itself appears beautiful in the same way it accounts for everything else that does so. One form here is enough; no Third Beauty threatens.

VI PLATO AND THE THEORY OF FORMS

Attempts to interpret the *Symposium*, *Phaedo*, and *Republic* as con-taining a determinate theory of forms (whether individually or together) face a trade-off between on the one hand giving a natural reading of Plato's remarks concerning the self-predication and pure being of forms and on the other hand attributing to him a non-ridiculous view. The crux of the matter is whether each form, the F, must have F-ness without qualification to perform its role in the theory. Some interpreters give a natural reading to Plato's language, but make confusion the basis of his main tenets.[42] Others bend over backward to avoid committing Plato to what Terry Penner has called "Literal Self-Predication."[43] But while this latter family of readings may not be *incompatible* with the texts of the relevant passages, Plato could hardly have expected people reading those remarks in context to understand them this way. I advocate avoiding both of these options, by letting the force of self-predication sentences be less than fully interpreted in Plato's works before the *Parmenides*. (Thus any "theory of forms" will be underdetermined by those dialogues.)

We have seen that the *Parmenides* is the first dialogue in which we can securely ground an unproblematic interpretation of the sentences at issue in Plato's own text. Helping us with this is what Plato was doing in suggesting acceptance of massed results apparently in pervasive, systematic contradiction with each other (i.e., the results of paired sections of Parmenides' dialectical exercise). In this work, for the first time, Plato is showing over and over that sentences of the type "S is P" have two systematically different readings. These were marked by the two "in-relation-to" qualifications in Parmenides' prescription for exercise, and his thirty-page demonstration consti-tutes a treasure-chest of evidence to guide our interpretation of them.

This gives the story of Plato's career a hopeful narrative arc. In the dialogues most closely modeled on the activity of the historical Socrates, he showed that people who were supposed to possess expert-ise on various matters did not have it. Plato then explored these matters, including *erōs*, the soul, and the virtues. This exploration was associated with some metaphysical remarks. But the brevity of these remarks indicates that spelling out dogmatically a mature the-ory in all its detail was not their task. Rather, Plato used his skill as a writer to sweep us along, gaining our assent on the points needed for the primary inquiry of each work while leaving many difficult issues about forms in the shadows.[44] I believe that Plato composed the first part of the *Parmenides* in order to exhibit where his previous remarks called for further work. The dialogue as a whole gives the best possible evidence for how he thought we should respond to the problems it introduces.

APPENDIX: THE PARMENIDES AND THE SOPHIST

As I mentioned above, my reading of Parmenides' distinction between *pros heauto* and *pros ta alla* predication coincides with the Eleatic Visitor's distinction in the *Sophist* between the *kath' hauto* and *pros allo* uses of "is," as interpreted by Michael Frede. Assertions using Frede's "is$_1$" correspond to what I have called here "tree" predications, and those using his "is$_2$" correspond to my ordinary ones.[45] Our being able to make independent cases for this from two different dialogues is a significant strengthening of the evidence for our interpretations.

The two uses of "is" coincide with the two kinds of predication because of the philosophical equivalence of, e.g., "Samantha walks" and "Samantha is walking" (see Aristotle *Met.* 1017a; we ourselves can use a single symbolic form to translate both natural-language sentences – whether that looks like "Fa" or "a is F," etc.). This brings out something that the *Parmenides* does not resolve: the question of whether and how the form Being is involved in all predication. This is manifested in the localized, atypical confusion concerning whether or not to accept the last few conclusions in the first section of arguments (perhaps 141e7–142a8).[46] One hopes that the study of Being in the *Sophist* will help us sort out these few atypically confused results in our dialogue.

Finally, the starring role of the distinction in the *Parmenides* explains why Plato felt able to rely on it without much fanfare elsewhere.[47] That had come with the distinction's debut in the

Parmenides, with the entire dialogue serving as material to be used in its exploration and application.

NOTES

1 Citations throughout are to Oxford Classical Texts available at time of writing in 2019.

2 We can no longer follow the orthographic conventions of Plato's time: texts were all in capital letters and without spaces or punctuation between words. Among other modern conveniences, I use initial capitals when it is important to mark that the entities being considered have a special role in Plato's theory. This is useful as long as one doesn't give the choices in question more authority than is appropriate.

3 The *Phaedo* (76d7–e7, 107b4–9) and *Republic* (506c2–507a5) themselves signal that their presentations of forms need to be supplemented by more work.

4 On the chronology of Plato's works see Meinwald 2016: 18–21.

5 There is brief confusion in 141e7–142a8; see Appendix for an explanation.

6 In the first instance, the results are conditionals (whose antecedents are either the positive or the negative hypothesis). We will see why genuine contradictions do not follow from either hypothesis. On ways to obtain unconditional results, see Peterson 1996: 173–8.

7 Burnyeat 1990.

8 See Frede 1967; and this volume, ch. 14. Frede's work was the starting-point for mine; I argue for my reading of the *Parmenides* initially without using the *Sophist* because the *Sophist* is and the *Parmenides* is not in the clearly established group of late dialogues. Plato could not have expected readers to bring understanding of the *Sophist* to the *Parmenides*.

9 The latter idea is often put in terms of instantiation (and I have done this myself) – though there is the complication that some people may think that concept admits narrower and broader construals.

10 On Plato's use of literary elements for philosophical "footnoting" in the dialogue see Meinwald 2005, following Proclus on this point.

11 Vlastos 1954: 343.

12 For discussion of possible translations, see Gazziero 2014. Notable discussions of the argument include: Vlastos 1954; Sellars 1955; Geach 1956; Strang and Rees 1963; Cohen 1971; Peterson 1973; Frances 1996; Pelletier and Zalta 2000; Peacock 2017. On Aristotle's version of the argument as well as Plato's see Fine 1993. Treatments of our argument that contain detailed study of the *Parmenides* as a whole include Cornford 1939; Proclus 1987; Meinwald 1991; Sayre 1996; Rickless 2007; Brisson 2011; Gill 2012.

13 Taking *ti* in 132a6 as an indefinite pronoun nominalizing *mega* to yield "a Large." David Sedley (2007c: 73–4) points out that for Plato, phrases like "We say ... there is *an* Equal" (*Phd* 74a9–10) are a "standard existential formula for introducing a Form." So readers would have been used to taking *ti mega* as a unit (as in the footnoted alternative in the Hackett volume). This unit is destroyed by the rendering: " ... again won't some one thing appear large?" (Gill and Ryan tr., Hackett main text). This severs *ti* from *mega*, making *hen ti* the subject of *phaneitai*, and *mega* the complement. It also undermines the intended correspondence (indicated by *au*) between the present phrase and what we had in (A).

14 I don't think Socrates necessarily had in mind from the start preferred versions of what scholars call One Over Many, Self-Predication, and Non-Self-Explanation/Non-Identity, all cast in such a way as to apply at every stage of the argument; he need not have thought about this sort of case at all. (Especially on my reading since I take him to stand for the *presentations* of forms in previous dialogues.) If this is what Gazziero (2014) means in saying the argument is not deductive but recursive, I am in sympathy with him.

15 So Bostock 1990: section 1.

16 Annas 1986: 235.

17 See Meinwald 2005: 10–11 and 14–15 following Proclus on this point.

18 Fragment B10, tr. Curd (2007: 53–4, with judicious assessment of the authenticity of the quote). On Anaxagoras, see for present purposes Furley 1976; Meinwald 2016: 219–26, 257–9.

19 We find items like "the hot" assimilated to a stuff like air, hence commentators' use of "quasi-stuff." On the commitment of this theory to pure elements, see Strang 1963.

20 Furley 1976: 83, incorporating a remark of Montgomery Furth's.

21 Anaxagoras does mention smallness, largeness, and large and small (things), e.g., in frs. 1 and 3.

22 The closely related *moiran echein* occurs frequently in the fragments.

23 For further discussion of this passage and related topics in the *Phaedo*, see Ebrey's chapter in this volume (ch. 9).

24 Modifying Michael Frede's original way of putting this with help from Walter Edelberg and Mahrad Almotahari.

25 For more detail, see Mann 2000: 17–18, 120–4.

26 Meinwald 1991: chs. 2–8; 2014a; and 2016: chs. 8–10 treat many issues there is not space for here.

27 The chunk of text at 155e4–157b5 starts not from the regular positive hypothesis, but from "If the One is such as we have said." I agree with the majority that it is an appendix to what has come before; I believe it is needed only this first time around. The most important nine-section interpretation is Proclus 1987.

28 Meinwald 1991: ch. 2.

29 See Meinwald 2014b; 1991: ch. 2.

30 See, e.g., *Phd* 78d1–4 and Burnet 1911, *ad loc.*; Kahn 1981. Kahn also says (109–10) that the *Phd.* prepares for the *Rep.* sense of "essence" or "whatness," and he points out the close relation of Plato's terminology to the Aristotelian *to ti esti* ("the what-it-is") and *to ti ēn einai* ("the what-it-is-to-be ___").

31 Plato won't include putative natures like "Round-Square-hood." On not every expression of the grammatical form "F-ness"/ "the F" corresponding to a Platonic form, see Denyer 2007.

32 This is a crucial difference between, on the one hand, the distinction between attributes a form possesses *qua* form and those it possesses *qua* the particular form it is and, on the other, my suggestion. For problems with relying on the former, see Keyt 1992; Meinwald 2014a: 490–2.

33 I am pleased to note that S. Rickless now agrees (email, 2011) that he was mistaken in claiming that the argument I identify in 139c3–d1 is invalid (Rickless 2007: 105).

34 For more detail on the first section of arguments, see Meinwald 1991: 63–70, 76–94; on how to understand what it means to take the others than the subject "in relation to themselves," Meinwald 1991: 139–42, 150–2.

35 In ancient philosophy "genus" and "species" can be used for any pair of a kind and one of its subkinds – the terms are not associated with a fixed

level of the classification scheme. "Kind" and "species" in English can both render *eidos*, one of the two words that underlie the translation "form." Note that a Platonic kind is not just the set containing its members. Of primary importance is *what makes them members*. Thus it makes sense that Plato sees his study of relations between kinds as a continuation of his study of forms.

36 See Meinwald 1991: ch. 5; with more on the philosophical issues in Meinwald 2016: 278–87.

37 There is disagreement on a strategic level – many interpreters think this pattern of results is characteristic of sensibles and so unacceptable for a form. I am able to embrace these "rolling around" results because they are cordoned off from disturbing Plato's realm of pure being – the realm of tree truths.

38 See Meinwald 1991: 146–7 on why this section comes before the "in relation to itself" consequences for the One from the negative hypothesis.

39 Indeed Socrates, without being a nature at all, is in a position to have Musicality, Pallor, Justice and Humanity. But nothing prevents, e.g., Beauty bearing the same relation to Beauty itself that it does to Unity.

40 For the last bit see 132a7–8; *au* in line 7 indicates that it applies to the base level as well.

41 I omitted to spell this out formerly, thinking that it would be obvious once one had got this far. That led to some misunderstanding of my position. See now my fullest discussion, Meinwald 2016: 259–60 with 269–71. I am gratified that, even without divining (or agreeing with) my views on all details, others have applied versions of my interpretation of Parmenides' exercise to address the TMA to their satisfaction – the main purpose of my paper had been to draw attention to Parmenides' exercise as a resource for addressing the famous problems of the first part of the dialogue. See Frances 1996; Pelletier and Zalta 2000, Peterson 2019: 251–3.

42 Vlastos 1954 and many other papers; Owen 1957; other authors too numerous to mention.

43 Nehamas 1975b, 1979; Patterson 1985; Penner 1987.

44 As Jowett wrote (1953: 13), "Plato's doctrine of ideas has attained an imaginary clearness and definiteness which is not to be found in his own writings. The popular account of them is partly derived from one or two passages in his Dialogues interpreted without regard to their poetical environment."

45 Frede's interpretation is often assimilated to the one advanced by Owen (1970 and elsewhere). In fact, they expressed agreement because both rejected the view that the *Sophist* distinguishes between existence and a two-place notion. But their positive interpretations do not agree. Owen constantly puts his view in terms of a contrast between identity and predication; he illustrates (1965: 71) with the sentences "Arrowby is mayor of Margate" (identity) and "Arrowby is idle" (predication). For Frede, *neither* of these sentences illustrates the *kath 'hauto* use of "is." More generally, we should recognize that Frede did not think that "is$_1$" claims attribute a feature to an individual. While he said that "is$_1$" and "is$_2$" have the same meaning, that was because he thought it anachronistic to use one's own theory of meaning in this connection, and he thought sameness of meaning was guaranteed in Plato's eyes by sameness of Platonic form. Thus, Frede agreed that if *we* think the truth conditions of assertions, the way in which one entity is predicated of another, etc. affect meaning, then we will not regard "A is$_1$ B" and "A is$_2$ B" as having the same meaning.

46 Adapting a suggestion made by Peterson (1996).

47 Contra Vlastos 1981: 288–90 n. 44.

14 Plato's *Sophist* on False Statements

Michael Frede

In Plato's dialogue the *Sophist*, the main interlocutors, the Eleatic Stranger and Theaetetus, are trying to determine the nature of the sophist. Given that the phenomenon of the sophistic movement is so many-faceted and somewhat amorphous, it is not surprising that the first attempts in the dialogue to get a grip on the elusive reality underlying this phenomenon turn out to be not particularly successful, since they at best capture some superficial feature of the sophist. These features are recapitulated at 231c8–e7.[1] Then, in 232a1ff., a renewed attempt is made to capture the sophist; this attempt seems to go more to the heart of the matter, but runs into difficulties whose resolution occupies the remainder of the dialogue. The suggestion is that the sophist has a remarkable ability to represent things in a way that makes this representation, the sophist's statement about things, appear and seem to be true, though, in fact, it is not. This raises a series of difficulties, first alluded to in 235d2, then again in 236c9ff., and spelled out in considerable detail in 236d9ff. These problems the sophist will exploit to the fullest to reject the characterization suggested and thus again to elude capture (cf. 239c9ff., 241a3). The difficulties, in brief, amount to this: There are problems about the very possibility of false statements. For a statement, in order to be a statement at all, has to manage to say something, that is, there has to be something that gets said by it. But both in ordinary Greek and in the language of Greek philosophers a false statement is one that says what is not (or: what is not being).[2] Yet what is not being does not seem to be something that is there to get said. Hence it would seem that there is nothing that gets said by a false statement. But in this

I am particularly indebted to the following papers: Owen 1970, vol. 1: 223–67; McDowell 1983: 123; Bostock 1984.

case it fails to be a statement. So it seems that there can be no false statements. But, if there is a problem about the possibility of false statements, there is – *a fortiori* – also a problem about the possibility of false beliefs (of false *doxa*), about something's seeming (*dokein*) to somebody, but not being a certain way. And if there is a problem about the possibility of false beliefs, there also is a question concerning the possibility of false appearances. Indeed, there is a problem about appearances as such; given that they are not the real, the true thing itself, but just an appearance of it, they in some way do lack reality and, in some special sense, which is difficult to pin down, truth (cf. 236e1–2, 239c9–240c6).

In the *Sophist* Plato tries to deal with most of these problems. But he does focus on the central problem of false statements. Here he primarily tries to show that and how there can be such a thing as a false statement, and in the course of this he tries to clear up the confusions that give rise to doubts about the very possibility of false statements. His view seems to be that these confusions have at least two sources. First, they rest on a misunderstanding of the negative particle "not" in "not being"; because of this misunderstanding one tends to think that what is not, or what is not being, is nothing whatsoever and hence not something that, for example, could get said in a statement. Secondly, there is considerable confusion about what a statement is. Hence one fails to realize that the truth or falsehood of a statement is a matter of what gets said in the sense of what gets said about, or predicated of, a subject. Once we realize this, and once we understand how the expression "not being" is to be construed, Plato thinks, we also see that it is entirely unproblematic to say that what gets said by a false statement is something that is not. It is something that is perfectly real, it just happens to be something that is not (true) in the case of the particular subject in question that it gets said of.

Given this diagnosis of the problem, Plato proceeds in two stages. He first (241c7–259c4) tries to show that it is unproblematic to say that there is something that is not. He then (259c5ff.) turns to statements to show in which way it is unproblematic to say of a statement that it asserts something that is not. In this way he tries to accomplish the task he had set himself at the outset when he said (236e4–237a1): "For how one should put the matter when one says or thinks that there really are falsehoods and, in uttering this, not to get involved in contradiction, that, Theaetetus, is altogether difficult." We should note that the aim Plato sets himself in a way is a rather modest one; it is not to solve all difficulties one might want, or be able, to raise concerning false statements, but to find a coherent way of thinking about them such that, thought of in this way, they no longer seem to pose a problem.

The discussion of what it is to be something that is not, that is, to be something that is not being, takes up a much larger space, though, than the discussion of what it is to be a false statement. At least in part this is so because Plato thinks that the notion of something that is, of a being, is no less puzzling than the notion of something that is not, and that the two puzzles are related. So the problems about not being, on Plato's view, are not just due to problems about the proper understanding of the function of "not" in "is not being," they are also due to problems about the proper understanding of being. What is more, the problems about being stand in the way of properly understanding what a statement is. Hence when Plato finally at 242b6ff. actually sets out to refute Parmenides and to show that there is something that is not, he does so by first calling into question our understanding of "being" (cf. 243c2–5, 250e5ff.), which turns out to be as problematic as "not being." He then (251a5ff.) turns to at least a partial resolution of the problems about being before he returns to the problem of not being. Hence the considerable overall length of the discussion of how we should understand the phrase "not being" or "what is not."

Instead of discussing all this, though, I want in what follows to focus on the discussion of false statements. Hence I will, only very briefly, comment on the remarks about being, and, in somewhat more detail, consider the remarks about what it is to be not being, to the extent that this seems necessary to understand Plato's resolution of the difficulty concerning false statements.

I   THE PROBLEM OF BEING

The problem about being, in a nutshell, seems to be this. Suppose we follow the philosophers in their attempt to determine and identify what is to count as a being (cf. 242c5–6); and suppose we decide in the end that we have to recognize as being whatever is in motion and whatever is at rest, and that these two classes exhaust what there is (cf. 249c10–d4). There still is a problem about what being is (249d6ff.). Though it is true that whatever is is in motion or is at rest, being itself is neither in motion nor at rest. Neither to be in motion nor to be at rest is what it is to be; and hence what is, as such, in itself, by itself, is neither in motion nor at rest. It is by itself just what it is to be. But if it is neither in motion nor at rest, it does not seem to be a being (250c1–d5).

To see the solution to this problem, we have to see how each thing can be said to be lots of things, not just what it is by, or in, itself (if it is the kind of thing that is something by itself), but also other things that it is not by itself, but by standing in the appropriate relation to something else. Thus being, of itself, is just whatever it is that it is to be. But this does not prevent it from being at rest, or from being in motion, by standing in the appropriate relation to rest, or to motion. What makes it difficult to see this is that this problem is entangled with a problem about statements. There is the view of some of Plato's contemporaries (perhaps, e.g., of Antisthenes) that it does not make sense to say of something that it is something else, to say of something that it is something that it is not. It is fine, they seem to argue, to call a man "man" and what is good "good"; but how can one say of a man that he is good, if a man is not what is good, but something else (cf. 251a5ff.)? This involves a misunderstanding of what statements are. To make a statement is not just a matter of calling a thing by its own specific name. It is rather a matter, as Plato will point out later (262d2–6), of naming something so as then to go on to say something about it. But this failure to understand what statements are, to understand how something can be said to be lots of things and can be called by many different names (cf. 251a5–6), gets aggravated by, as it in turn aggravates, a failure to understand being.

The crucial point to understand here is a point Plato makes in a much-debated passage in 255c12ff. The being that we attribute to things is of two kinds (cf. 255d4–5). Some of the things we say something is, it is by itself; other things we say something is, it just is with reference to something else, it is by standing in the appropriate relation to something else. Thus Socrates is or is a being, for instance, in being white. But white is not something Socrates is by himself; it is something he only is by being appropriately related to something else, namely the color white. He only is a being in this particular way, or respect, namely in being white, by standing in a certain relation to something else, namely color. He is white, not by being this feature, but by having this feature. He is white, as we may say, by "participation" in something else. The color, on the other hand, is said to be white, not by participating in, by having, this feature, but by being it. Similarly the color is a color, not by having this sort of feature, but by being this sort of feature. Hence it is not just white, but also a color, by itself. On the other hand, it is different from the color pink. And though there is a sense in which it is different from the color pink by being the color white, this is not the relevant sense here. It is not part of being the color white not to be the color pink. So the color white is different from pink by being appropriately related to something else, namely to difference. And so, quite generally, the color white is a being in two quite different ways. It is a being by being whatever it is by itself, for example, white and a color; it also is a being by being appropriately related to other things, such as difference, so as to be, for example, different from pink. Once we understand that being takes these two forms, we also understand how it is possible that we can tell a thing not only by its specific name, but by many names, how, for instance, we can say of the color white not only that it is white, but also that it is a being, that it is different from pink, and that it is identical with itself. Moreover, we can explain how being itself can be in motion or at rest, though of itself it is neither.[3]

But, what is more, we begin to see how the solution of the problem concerning being sheds light on the problem concerning not being. It lies in the very nature of being that whatever is, is many things that it is not, namely whatever it is with reference to something else.

This interpretation crucially rests on the assumption that Plato in 255c12–13 distinguishes two uses of "... is... ."[4] Since I want to assume that Plato in what follows continues to rely on this distinction, but since this interpretation of 255c12–13 has been challenged, I want to make a few remarks in its defense. It has been attacked, for instance, by David Bostock (1984: 89). To begin with, it should be noted that the distinction is not supposed to be the distinction of two senses of the incomplete use of "... is ... , " let alone the distinction between the "is" of identity and the "ordinary" copulative, predicative "is." What speaks decisively against this is that Plato recognizes just one idea of being and that he talks throughout the dialogue as if this one idea was involved both in saying that not being is, namely not being (258b11–c4), and in saying that something is, namely different from something (263b11). It is one and the same being (255d5) that we are attributing to something in both cases. Moreover, the two uses are such that "... is ..." in its first use could not be replaced by "is identical with" without changing the meaning. To say that man is a rational animal is not to say that man is identical with a rational animal. To say that man is a vertebrate or that white is a color clearly is not to make an identity statement, though it is a case of saying what man is of himself or what white is of itself.

It also would be a mistake to think, as Bostock seems to suppose, that the distinction of the two uses is supposed to be a grammatical or logical distinction, if by this we mean a distinction that can be made independently of the metaphysics we rely on. Thus, contrary to what Bostock (1984: 92) seems to think, "Socrates is a man" and "Socrates is the man in the corner" for Plato clearly are

cases, not of the first, but of the second use of "... is ...," given that
Socrates, on Plato's view, is not a human being in himself, but only by
participation in something else, namely the form of a man. But
though Socrates and man, on this view, are two different items of
which the first participates in the second, we are not even tempted to
think that "Socrates is a man" means that Socrates is different from
man, or that Socrates participates in man. Hence we also should not
be tempted to think that "not being is not being" means that not being
is identical with not being. Indeed, it is not the case that the identity
of X and Y constitutes either a necessary or a sufficient condition for
the truth of "X is Y" in the first use of "... is ...." It does not constitute
a necessary condition since white of itself is a color. And it does not
constitute a sufficient condition, given that, for example, "The same
is the same (i.e., with itself)" should be a case of the second use of "...
is ...," as "The different is the same (i.e., with itself)" clearly is. This
also allows us to distinguish different kinds of self-predication and to
claim that the kind of self-predication Plato had been interested in all
along, and continues to hold on to, is the one that innocuously
involves the first use of "... is ...."

With this unfortunately rather brief and sketchy account of the
resolution of the problem about being, let us turn to how Plato tries to
deal with the problem of not being.

II   THE PROBLEM OF NOT BEING

The resolution of the difficulties concerning what is not begins at
255e8. It clearly falls into four parts:

1) 255e8–257a12: Plato shows that things, indeed the form of being
   itself, can be said to be not being.
2) 257b1–257c3: Plato tries to show that the difficulties concerning
   what is not have their source in misconstrual of the word "not" in
   the phrase "not being."
3) 257c4–258c5: Plato tries to show not only that there are things that
   are not, but what the nature of not being is.

4) 258c6–259c4: Plato gives a summary that leads to the discussion of statements.

Let us first consider 255e8–257a12. In the preceding section Plato had shown that there are five distinct genera or forms of particular import-ance: being, motion, rest, the same, and the different. In 255e8ff. he singles out motion and argues that motion, being different from rest, the same, the different, and being, is not rest, is not the same, is not different,[5] and hence also, *pan ratione*, is not being (cf. 256c10–d10). For this he relies on the single fact that if X is different from Y we can say that X is not Y. From this, in 256d11–12, he draws the following inference: "Hence, of necessity, not being is in the case of motion and all other forms." The following lines (256d12–e4) make it clear how this inference is to be understood. Given that not only motion, but all other forms (except, of course, being itself) are different from being, it will be true of all of them that they are not being. So "something that is not being," far from being a phrase that cannot possibly be applied to anything correctly, does at least characterize all forms other than being. We should also note in passing the language of the conclusion; Plato seems to be using an expression like "F (or: F-ness) is in the case of a" if it is true that a is F. Underlying this language there seems to be the notion that one way for F to be is for there to be some a that is F.

In 256e6–7 Plato draws a further conclusion from the argument that begins with 255e8: "Hence, with reference to each form there is much which is being, but an immense amount which is not being." Here we seem to have the same manner of speaking that we noted in the preceding conclusion, except that we now not only talk about something that is, or is being, with reference to a given subject, but also about items that are not, or are not being, with reference to a given subject. It seems that this language is to be understood in the following way: Just as F-ness is said to be in the case of a if a is F, so F-ness is said not to be, to be something that is not, or to be not being, with reference to a, if a is not F. At least on this assumption we can see how the conclusion would follow from the preceding argument.

There are lots of things that motion is not, for example all the other forms. And what is true of motion is, of course, true of all other forms. So it is true with reference to each form, that there is an immense number of things that it is not, or is not being. So here is a second apparently quite problematic way in which even forms can be said to be not being. It is not only that each particular form is not the form of being, it also is the case that any other form is not this particular form and that, in that sense, it is not being with reference to any form other than it.

Finally, at 257a1ff., Plato shows that even the form of being itself can be said not to be or to be something that is not, namely all the things that are different from it. From the way Plato talks here it is also clear that he regards something's not being F as a further way in which something is not, that is to say as something that is not being. For he says (257a4–5), "Being, hence, is not in as many ways as there are other things." If, with this in mind, we return to 255e8ff., we notice that Plato already there, when he argued that motion is not rest, the same, the different, or being, apparently had taken these as ways in which motion is not or is not being. For in each case he had paired off the negative statement about motion with a positive state-ment that was supposed to show that motion is, as by being different, or the same, or being. Thus there is yet a further way in which things are not, or are not being, namely just by not being this, that, or other.

Let us summarize the results of this section. There are various ways in which we can say of something that it is not being that seem entirely innocuous. It is generally accepted that if X and Y are differ-ent, we can say "X is not Y." Hence, since all other things are different from the form of being, each of them can be said to be not being. This seems to be unproblematic. But there are more interesting ways in which something can be said to be not being. For X not to be Y is for X in a way not to be, namely Y; at the same time this also is for Y in a way not to be, namely with reference to, or in the case of, X. But that X is something that in this way is not, obviously does not mean that X is nothing. It is something, for example, different from Y. Indeed, it would not have this way of being something that is not, namely Y, unless it was being, namely different from Y. Similarly, that Y is something that is not in this way obviously does not mean that Y is nothing. Y, as we have shown, is lots of things, for example different from X. So there are here two further ways in which something can be said to be not being: (i) the way an X can be said not to be insofar as it is not some Y, and (ii) the way a Y can be said not to be insofar as it is not with reference to some X. Obviously, the second way is just the converse of the first. In any case, it is clear that there is an entirely unmysterious way in which there are things that are not being.

With this we can turn to the next section, 257b1–257c3, in which Plato tries to explain where people got confused when they came to think that there is no such thing as what is not. The claim is that they came to think "what is not" or "not being" must refer to the contrary of what is. What is, is something of which it is true that it is in some respect. Instead of realizing that what is not, by contrast, is something of which it is not true that it is in this respect, they assumed that it is something of which it is not true that it is in any respect. But this understanding is not justified by the use of expressions of the form "not X." What is meant by expressions of this form is not something that somehow is contrary to X.

This much, perhaps, is rather uncontroversial. But interpreters have had great difficulty with Plato's own positive characterization of the use of expressions of the form "not X" and in particular his elucidation of the expression "not being." To understand Plato's remarks, we have to keep in mind the close connection between these remarks and the preceding passage. Plato begins with a remark about "not being" (257b3–4). He says, "Whenever we talk of what is not being, we do not, it seems, talk of something contrary to being, but only of something different." The qualification "it seems" indicates that the remark is to be understood in light of what precedes. But what is meant also becomes clearer when we look at the next sentence (257b6–7): "When, e.g., we speak of something as 'not big,' do we then seem to you to indicate by this phrase the small rather than the equal?" As is clear from the fact that this is presented as an elucidation of the preceding sentence (cf. Theaetetus' question in 257b5 to which this is a response), but also from the "e.g." (*hoion*), talking of something as not big is supposed to be a case of talking of something as not being. It seems immediately obvious in which way it is a case of talking about something as not being: It is a case of talking about something as not being in a certain way, namely as not being big. And that this is the correct way to understand the text is supported by the following considerations. In light of 255e8–257a12, we should assume that the not being we talk about in 257b3 is either (i) the not being of something which is not the form of being, or (ii), more generally, the not being of something that is not something or other, or (iii), finally, the converse of (ii), the not being of something that is not with reference to something or other. Now it is quite true that something that is not being insofar as it is not the form of being, is not the contrary of being, but just different from it. But what is not big is not an example of what is not being by not being the form of being. Nor is the not big a straightforward example of what is not being with reference to something or other. Plato here does not seem to think of a case in which it would be false to say of something that it is not big, but rather of a case in which it would be true to say of something that it is not big, and he seems to be saying about this case that to say of something that it is not big is not to say that it is small. Hence it seems that the not being Plato is talking about here in 257b3 is the not being of something that fails to be something or other, for example to be big. And this fits the fact that this was the kind of not being Plato had last talked of in the preceding passage, when he had said that even the form of being itself in many ways is not being, namely in not being all the things that differ from it. Moreover, it is true that what is not being in that way, for example by being not big, is not the contrary of what is being in this way, but simply different. For what is not big is not contrary to what is big, but merely different from what is big. This is clear because, though one way of being different from what is big (relative to something) is being small (relatively), another way of being different from what is big is to be of equal size. Quite generally, then, "not X" applies to something that merely differs from what is X.

Now the crucial difficulty is how Plato can assume, as I have just taken for granted, that the kind of not being that is involved in something's not being big, or in something's being not big (Plato does not seem to distinguish the two) is the same as the kind of not being that is involved in motion's not being rest, the same, the different, being, or any other form. Interpreters are agreed that Plato in 257b3 or in 257b6 shifts to a different kind of case. Up to this point he has been talking about cases in which something straightforwardly is different from something else, more specifically about cases in which a form is different from some other form. The feature smallness, for instance, is different from the feature bigness. And thus smallness, we can say, is not bigness, or, if we grant Plato his language, the small is not the big, or even smallness is not big. But at 257b3 Plato begins to talk of what is not being, for example about what is not big, as if this at least covered the case of what fails to be big, not by being different from the feature bigness, but by failing to have it. And this seems to be a radically different kind of case. That Plato moves, without warning, from one kind of case to the other, might make us suspect that he is just confused. This is what Bostock is arguing. Less charitably we might think that Plato is cheating. But most interpreters have tried to be charitable and, moreover, to find some way to free Plato of the charge of confusion. Yet it is difficult to see how we can avoid attributing some confusion to Plato.

The problem cannot be solved by claiming that Plato in 257b3ff. is *just* making a point about the use of "not" in expressions like "not big," quite generally in expressions of the form "not F," and hence also in the expression "not being," namely the point that "not" does not signify contrariety. It is true enough that he does make a point about the use of "not" in expressions of the form "not F," but it also seems to be true that, in making this point, he believes he has made a point about what is not something or other. It is misleading to say, as Owen does (1970: 232, 237, 238), that Plato here offers an analysis of expressions like "not big" and tries to explain "not being" in analogy to them. Talking of something as not big is, at the same time, treated as a case of talking of something as not being rather than as a mere analogue of it.

The difficulty precisely is that Plato moves from talking about motion's not being rest to something's not being big, as if the not being in both cases were the same kind of not being. And this does, indeed, seem to be his considered view. For when in 257c4ff. he moves on to explain what the nature of not being is, he specifies (258a11ff.) *one* nature that supposedly is involved in all cases of not being we have been considering, that is to say, on anybody's interpretation, both in cases of simple non-identity and in cases of what we would regard as ordinary negative predication. It is also clear from this that Plato cannot mean to solve the problem by distinguishing two senses of "... is not ..." or "not being." He must assume that there is one sense of "... is not ..." involved both in "motion is not rest" and in "Theaetetus is not flying." The problem obviously is how he can assume this.

We make this a hopeless task if we think of Plato as moving from negations of identity to considering falsehood in predicative statements, as Owen does (1970: 237). To begin with, the move in question here is not the move to falsehood in predicative statements, but rather the intermediate move to, as it seems to us, negative predicative statements, a move Owen tellingly glosses rather too quickly (1970: 237–8). But, more importantly, it is a mistake to assume that Plato thinks of the earlier statements simply as negations of identity. If he did, the task would be hopeless. He rather must think that if X and Y are not identical and we thus say that X is not Y, we are not, in saying this, denying the identity of X and Y, but are attributing not being to X. And he must equally assume that to say of a small thing that it is not big is to attribute the very same not being to it; it is to say of it that it is not, namely big.

Nevertheless it seems that Plato must want to make some distinction here. For consider the following. The small is different from the big. Hence the small is not the big. Plato allows himself to move from this to "The small is not big" (presumably relying on the fact that this is the denial of "The small is big" in the use of "... is ..." in which this is true if "The small by itself is big" or "The small by its very nature is big" is true). So we have both "The small is not big" and "This (a small thing) is not big." There seems to be a clear difference between the two statements. The first seems to deny that something is a certain feature, the second that something has a certain feature. What means does Plato have to locate this difference?

Even without getting into the details of the subsequent section 257c4ff., we can note already here that Plato does not identify not being with difference, but with a particular form or kind of difference, with "a part of the different." Hence he cannot assume that "The small is not the big" or "The small is not big" means, or should be analyzed as, "Smallness is different from bigness." I take it that he thinks it should be analyzed as "The small is different from what is big." And I also take it that he thinks that "This (a small thing) is not big" should similarly be analyzed as "This is different from what is big." This explains why he thinks that there is just one account for the use of "not," that there is no ambiguity in "big" or "the big," that there is no ambiguity in "difference" or in "... is not ...." But we can also readily see how Plato can, if he wants to, distinguish the two kinds of cases we want him to distinguish. He can do so by distinguishing the two uses of "... is ..." in "... is big."

In a third section (257c4–258c5), then, Plato tries to show that what is not or is not being, far from being nothing at all and unthinkable, far from being an impossible and illegitimate subject of discourse, constitutes a definite, specifiable kind. At the same time we are supposed to see that, given the way this kind is constituted, what is not is as real as what is. Take what is not beautiful. It is constituted, to begin with, by difference. Difference is something that is. But difference always is difference from something, just as knowledge is knowledge of something. Thus there is difference from the beautiful, that is, from what is beautiful. It sets off a class of things, namely all those things that are not beautiful, over against another class of things, namely all those things that are beautiful. Since difference is perfectly real and the beautiful is perfectly real, difference from the beautiful, and hence being not beautiful, is perfectly real and unproblematic, as real as the beautiful. So in this sense the not beautiful constitutes an unproblematic class of things, no less real than the beautiful. Similarly with not being. It involves a difference, and, more specifically, a difference from what is or is being in a certain way. There is nothing mysterious about this. And this specific difference sets off a class of things, namely all those things that are not in the same way, over against another class of things, namely all those things that are in this way. To be not being just is to be something that is set off from what is in a certain way, something that is different from what is being in this way. In this sense not being is as real as being and hence a nature of its own.

One may be worried here about the phrase "in a certain way" which I have introduced into the account. It reflects the fact that being for Plato always is a matter of being something or other. And correspondingly not being always is a matter of not being in a certain regard, respect, or way. There is no such thing as unqualified not being. This seems to be captured by Plato in the summary that follows, where he talks of not being as the part of the different that is set over against a particular kind of being (*pros to on hekaston*, 258e1).[6] So to be not being is to be something that is different from something that is in a certain way, in a certain regard.

What is clear now, as a result of the discussion of this section, is something that was not clear in the previous section about the use of "not," and that we, at best, could have gotten out of that section by a prejudicial interpretation of the words that "'not' put in front signifies one of the things which are other than the name which follows it, or rather, which are other than the things which are designated by the name which is applied to them and which follows the negation" (257b10–c2). What is clear now is that Plato understands "not being" and "... is not ..." in such a way that it covers the case in which something fails to be something in that it fails to have a certain feature. It is clear now that "not being" is intended to cover the case of what we would call ordinary negative predication. Given all this, we have no difficulty in understanding what Plato has to say when we turn to the next section, 258c7ff., the recapitulation of the argument. But this recapitulation also is puzzling and, indeed, must be confusing, if one has not been able to see how Plato takes the cases discussed in the first section to be cases of not being precisely in the sense at issue here, that is to say at issue in statements like "Theaetetus is not flying." For in 259a5ff. Plato explains again how unproblematic it is to say of something that it is not or that it is not being. Take the form of the different; it is different from being; hence it is not being (259a6–b1). The form of being is different from all other forms; hence it, too, is not, namely all these other forms (259b1–5). Similarly each of the other forms is different from the rest; hence each of the other forms in many ways is not (259b5–6). Now it is true that this shows that there is a use of "... is not" or "... is not being" that is innocuous, but the question is whether this is going to help us much if we want to understand how statements can be false. All along, down to the end of the summary, Plato is relying on the fact that if X and Y are different we can say that X is not Y. And on the basis of this he has thought that we are justified in saying that X is not or that X is not being, namely Y. He also has relied on the fact that in the case in which Y is the form of being itself, it will be true immediately of anything other than being that it is not being.

Now if one believes that the negative statements in the first section (255e8–257a12) are non-identity statements, that they have to be analyzed as stating of some form X that it is different from some form Y, then this summary must be very confusing. For the sense of "X is not Y" that we need in order to understand false statements clearly is not the sense of "X is different from Y." For if it is false that some particular object a is beautiful, we want to say something to the effect that "a is beautiful" is false because a, in fact, is not beautiful. And a's not being beautiful is not a matter of a's being different from beauty or the beautiful. It would be different from beauty even if it were beautiful by participation in beauty. So the account of not being that we need for false statements has to be more complex than an account according to which to say that X is not Y is just to say that X is different from Y. So, if the summary is supposed to give us the result that we will need to explain false statements, it seems that it does not even come near to giving us what we need, as long as we hold on to the assumption that Plato regarded the negative statements in the first section as non-identity statements.

What this, I take it, shows is that it was wrong all along to assume that Plato takes statements like "The different is not the same" to be non-identity statements to be understood in the sense of "The different is different from the same." He takes them to be attributing not being to the subject in the same sense in which he takes "a is not beautiful" to attribute not being to a. But even if one sees this, it has to be granted that it is puzzling that Plato in the summary returns to the cases of not being that do not seem worrisome and that, in any case, we are not worried about if we are worried about false statements. Perhaps the explanation is that Plato in the summary wants to emphasize again how unproblematic it is to talk of something as not being, and that to talk of something that is not is not to talk of something that is nothing at all.

For our purposes we may sum up the result of the discussion so far in the following way. Plato thinks that there is a use of "... is not..." in which X can be said to be not Y if X is different from what is Y, where both the form Y-ness and whatever participates in this form count as something that is Y. Correspondingly he finds it unproblematic to claim that X is something that is not, for instance in not being Y. He, correspondingly, introduces (256e6–7) a converse use of "... is not...." If X is not Y, Y-ness can be said to be not with reference to X. And this, correspondingly, is to say that Y-ness is different from what is with reference to X. And this again is to be understood in such a way that both difference and difference from the same count as what is with reference to difference, though in different ways. This, Plato thinks, suffices to understand the not being involved in false statements. But to understand the way in which false statements involve not being we have to have a better understanding of statements. And so this is the topic he turns to next.

III   FALSE STATEMENTS

Now the crucial move Plato makes to arrive at a more adequate understanding of statements is to point out that to make a statement we have to do two things: (1) identify an item we mean to say something about, and (2) specify something we mean to say about it. Hence a statement will minimally consist of two parts, a part identifying a subject of discourse and a part by means of which something gets said about the subject. That a statement manages to single out a subject is a condition for having a statement in the first place. Hence its truth or falsehood is a matter of what then gets said about this subject; that is, the locus of truth or falsehood, as it were, is not the statement as a whole, but the predicative or stating part of it. To put the matter differently: To make a true statement is to say something about something that is true of that something; correspondingly, to make a false statement is to say something about something that is false about, that is not true of, that something. So the problem about a false statement is not that it is about nothing. It is about whatever the subject expression names as the subject of the statement. Now the fact that something is true of a given subject, of course, does not mean that it is true of any subject. It will, at least as a rule, be false of some subjects. Conversely, what is false of a given subject will not, at least as a rule, be false of all subjects, but be true of something. So there is no problem about what gets attributed in a false statement as such, either. If there is a problem at all, it must be a problem about attributing it to a subject it is not true of. But this now does not seem to be problematic anymore, either. For to say something false about something, that is, to say something about something that is not true of it, now just seems to be a matter of saying something that is a perfectly good thing to say about something, except that it happens to be different from what is true about this particular subject. So if we know what it is for a statement to be about something, if we know what it is to be true of or about something, and if we know what it is to be different from what is something, we should have no problem understanding how there can be false statements. Or we can put the matter thus: Once we have seen that to be what is not is just a certain way of being different, and if we know what it is to be a statement and what it is to be what is not, we should have no problem seeing the possibility of false statements. This, in a nutshell, seems to be Plato's solution.

But let us look at the details of Plato's discussion concerning statements more closely. Central to it is the claim that a statement minimally has two parts, a name (*onoma*) and a verb (*rhēma*), as Plato identifies the two kinds of parts (262c4ff.). The function of the name is to name, to refer to, something. But it is only by adding a verb that we "get somewhere," as Plato puts it rather vaguely (262d4), that we can be said to say (*legein*) something (262d5), whence also the resulting complex expression is called a *logos* (262d5–6). Obviously there are all sorts of problems here about the identification and characterization of the two kinds of expressions that minimally constitute a statement. Thus, if, as seems likely, "name" (in the sense of the ancient grammarians) and "verb" here are supposed to refer to the respective word-classes, we, strictly speaking, only get a characterization of an irrelevant subclass of statements, whereas it seems that Plato is aiming at a characterization of simple (i.e., nonmolecular) statements quite generally and really is looking for syntactical categories. The semantic characterization of the two kinds of expressions seems inadequate (cf. 262a3–7), however we interpret their classification, whether by word-class or by syntactical category. But whatever the difficulties and the problems may be, this much seems to be right – and noting it seems to constitute a major advance – that simple statements are constituted by two parts with radically different functions, one part whose function is to name, refer to, to identify a subject, and another part by means of which we say something, state something, predicate something of or about the subject.

Having clarified this, Plato turns to two features of statements of which he obviously supposes that they need to be kept strictly apart: (1) they are statements about something, and (2) they have, as he puts it, a certain quality, that is, they are true or false (262e4ff.). A surprising amount of attention is given to the first feature (cf. 262e11–263a10, 263c5–12). It is made clear that these not only are two different features, but that the first is independent of the second. In order to have a statement that is true or false we first of all have to have a part of the statement that manages to specify a subject, and which subject it does specify, at least in principle, is settled independently of what gets said about this subject and, *a fortiori*, of its truth or falsehood. Plato quite pointedly lets the Eleatic Stranger settle the question of reference for the sample statements discussed before he lets him go on to consider their truth or falsehood.

Some of the relevance of the care and detail with which this is discussed becomes apparent, if we turn to the historical background. As we noted above there was some unclarity and confusion about the object of the verb "to say" (*legein*). This could lead to the view that what a statement said was what a statement was about. Thus, for example, Euthydemus, in the dialogue of his name (*Euthd.* 283e9–284a1), asks Ctesippus: If one says something false, "does one do so in saying the thing the statement is about?" And Ctesippus answers in the affirmative. From this Euthydemus infers that there cannot be such a thing as making a false statement. For the statement must be about something that is, whereas what gets said by a false statement is something that is not. To clear up this puzzle we need to be clear that what a statement is about is something independent of its being true or false, and that what gets said about this subject is another thing, and that it is this latter thing that is true or false.

There is another historical puzzle, or perhaps rather set of puzzles, that Plato seems to have in mind here. There was the view, which Aristotle repeatedly attributes to Antisthenes, that there is no such thing as statements contradicting each other (*Met.* 1024b26ff.; *Top.* 104b20ff.). In fact, in the *Metaphysics* Aristotle links this view to the view that there can be no false statements. Antisthenes' view, according to Aristotle's testimony in the *Metaphysics* (1024b32–4), was that each thing has its unique *logos* or statement, which identifies or spells it out. This has always reminded scholars of the view expounded at the beginning of the last section of the *Theaetetus*, according to which, if a statement can be made about something at all, it must be its own statement, a statement proper and peculiar to it (cf., e.g., *Tht.* 202a6–8). And it also reminds one of the view attacked in the *Sophist* itself (251a5ff.), according to which each thing should be addressed only by its own name, and not by the name of something else, so that we should not call, for example, an object "white," since "white" is the name of a color and an object is not a color. But, however this may be, we can see how, if each thing has its own statement and all statements have to be the statement of some one thing, contradiction will be impossible. For, of two apparently contradictory or even just contrary statements only one can be the statement of the thing in question. In this case the other statement will fail to be a statement of the thing in question, and thus will be a true statement about something else or will fail to be a statement of anything, and hence will also fail to be false.

In the *Euthydemus*, 285d7ff., we get a somewhat different version of this *antilogia* argument, which here is said to be quite common and attributed to associates of Protagoras or even earlier dialecticians (286c2–3). Here it is argued that for two persons to contradict each other they could not be producing the statement of the same thing, which would be the same statement and hence not yield any disagreement (286a4–7). Nor would there be any disagreement if neither of them produced the statement of the thing in question (286a7–b3). So if there is to be even the appearance of a disagreement, it must be the case that one person is producing the statement of the thing in question, whereas the other produces a statement that disagrees, that is in conflict with the first statement. But in that case the second person must be producing a statement of something else, in which case there is no contradiction. Or he fails to produce the statement of anything, in which case he does not manage to say anything, let alone to contradict the first speaker (286b3–6). In what follows Socrates takes this, too, to be an argument concerning the possibility of false statements. It may be noted in passing that this and similar arguments somewhat gain in plausibility if they are associated with certain metaphysical views, for example the denial of nonsubstantial change.

Now one reason why one may suspect that Plato here, too, is thinking of a version of this argument is, apart from its relevance and appropriateness, a striking linguistic detail in the passage we are considering: Instead of just using the language of "The statement is about *(peri) X*," for example, "about you," it also talks of "the statement of *X*" and "*X*'s statement," e.g., "the statement of you" and "your statement" (cf. 262e6, e14; 263a4, a5, a9, c7), sometimes combining both ways of talking (cf. 263a4, a5, a9–10), without in these cases maintaining a definite order that would allow us to say that one way of speaking was supposed to elucidate the other (cf. "about me and mine" in 263a5 and "mine and about me" in 263a9–10). Given this, given that the language of "about" is perfectly clear, and given that the language in terms of possessive pronouns is neither ordinary nor natural, it is difficult not to see in it an allusion to the way of thinking about statements underlying the *antilogia* argument and, indeed, to the *antilogia* argument itself. The point, then, would be that what a statement is about and what gets said about it in the statement are two things to be distinguished, which in fact may be, and normally are, different even if the statement is true. Thus there may be conflicting statements about the same thing, and one of them may be true and the other false. Nor does it follow from the fact that what gets said by the false statement is false, and something that is not, that what the statement is about is something that is not, let alone that it is about nothing.

It also becomes clear what we have to say about a view that is related to Antisthenes' position or to the one reflected in the *Euthydemus*, but that in one regard significantly differs from them. Antisthenes' view was that each thing at best has one statement. At this point in the *Sophist* we have already argued that "Each thing has many statements," to stay with the language of Antisthenes and the sophists (cf. Aristotle, *Met.* 1024b32ff.). But somebody might still want to hold on to the view that there are no conflicting or false statements, that an apparently conflicting or false statement in reality is a true statement about a different subject. Thus, if Socrates is healthy, somebody might take the view that this was a statement about Socrates, but more precisely about a healthy Socrates, and that the statement "Socrates is ill" was not in conflict with it, let alone false, since it was about a different Socrates, namely one who was ill. Note that in 263c7 the Eleatic Stranger assures himself that Theaetetus is going to grant that the statement "Theaetetus is flying" is about himself, who actually is sitting (cf. 263a2), rather than about somebody else. To take such a view, again, among other things, is to fail to see that it is one thing for a statement to be about a certain subject and quite another thing for this subject to have something said about it that is true or false of it; it is a failure to realize that what the statement is about in theory is settled independently of what then gets said about it, whether it is true or not.

So, to conclude our review of Plato's discussion of this feature of statements, Plato is quite willing to grant that a statement cannot be a statement about nothing, that a statement has to be about something (263c9–11). But he resists, as relying on some confusion about statements, any move to argue that false statements as such are about what is not and hence about nothing. Having a better understanding of statements and having a better grasp of what it is to be something that is not, we now are in a position to understand precisely in what sense a false statement is a statement that states something that is not, and this in such a way that we can see that this is entirely unproblematic.

We can thus, finally, turn to the discussion of the crucial feature, the quality of statements, their being true or false (cf. 263a11–d5). To begin with, though, a brief comment on the term "quality" here (cf. 262e5, e9; 263a11, e2). The mere language, relying on the familiar contrast between the what it is, or essence, of a something (cf. 260e4–5, 263c2) and the what it is like, suggests that a statement is a statement independently of its being true or its being false. A statement is a statement by (1) managing to specify a subject and (2) saying something about this subject. Once these two conditions are satisfied we have a statement, and the question whether the statement is true or false only arises – Plato, in using this language, is claiming – once both conditions are satisfied. Moreover, he is claiming that to understand truth and falsehood we have to focus on what gets said in the sense of what gets said about the subject, that is to say we have to focus on the predicate.

Plato first turns to the (ex hypothesi) true statement that Theaetetus is sitting, but considers it quite generally as a true statement about Theaetetus. What he seems to aim at is a general characterization of true statements. In *any* case, he characterizes the statement about Theaetetus in the following way (263b4–5): *legei ... ta onta hōs estin peri sou.* This, taken by itself, is ambiguous in various ways. Given the ambiguity of *hōs*, it might mean that a true statement says things that are *as* they are, or that a true statement says of things that are *that* they are. The parallel uses of *hōs* in 263b9, 263d1, and 263d2 suggest that the latter is meant. There is a further ambiguity, depending on whether *onta* refers to predicates that are affirmatively true of the subject or whether the claim is supposed to cover all predications, whether affirmative or negative. Given that this seems to be intended as a characterization of at least simple true statements in general, we should assume that *onta* is to be taken in the latter sense. There is yet a further question, namely whether *peri sou* goes with *onta* or *estin*. A comparison with 263b11 shows that it certainly goes with *onta*, though possibly with both. Given this disambiguation, the claim seems to be that a true statement says of what in fact is, namely about, or with reference to, the subject, that it is. The phrase "what is about, or with reference to, X" obviously is a bit of quasi-technical language that needs some elucidation. We readily recognize something like the converse use of "... is ..." which we discussed earlier in connection with 256e6, a passage Plato himself seems to be referring to a few lines further down (263b11–12) to explain his language here. I say "something like," though, because there seems to be a slight difference. If we assume that Plato is trying to explain here the truth of true statements in general, and not just the truth of affirmative statements, we have to assume that he now allows "F" in "F is something that is with reference to a" to be itself of the form "not G." Plato's view about true statements, then, seems to be this. Corresponding to the set of true simple statements about a, there will be a set of Fs that are with reference to a. And a true statement will be one that says of such an F that is with reference to a that it is, or that it is with reference to a.

Consider "Theaetetus is sitting." For this to be a statement in the first place it has to be about something, it has to manage to refer to, to name something, which then we can go on to say something about. It does so in referring to Theaetetus. For Theaetetus is something that is there to be talked about. So there is no problem in this regard. There also is no problem about sitting. There is such a thing as sitting. One can give a coherent account of what it is, and (let us assume) a complete account of the world would be impossible without some reference to sitting. Moreover it is clear that there is such a thing as sitting insofar as there are things that are sitting, and so also in this regard sitting is something that is, namely with reference to them. So there is no problem, as far as sitting is concerned. The only question is whether sitting is something that is with reference to Theaetetus, or – to put the matter the other way around – whether Theaetetus is sitting. And the claim is that "Theaetetus is sitting" is true precisely if sitting is something that is with reference to Theaetetus.

But if all this is clear, we should have no problems with false statements, either. Take "Theaetetus is flying." There is no problem about what the statement is about. It is about Theaetetus, and he is something that is. There is no problem, either, about what gets said about the subject, that is, about flying. There is such a thing as flying. One can give a coherent account of it. A complete description of the world will have to make some reference to it. There surely is such a thing as flying, insofar as there are plenty of things that are flying. The only question is whether flying is something that is with reference to Theaetetus. If it is not, then the claim is false. But this now is not a problem, either, given what we have said earlier about not being, or what it is to be not. That flying is not with reference to Theaetetus just means that flying happens to be different from what is with reference to Theaetetus, that is, flying is not one of the *F*s that are with reference to Theaetetus. But this does not mean that flying is nothing at all. We have already seen that it is something that is, and this in more than one way. Indeed, its not being in the case of Theaetetus itself is just another regard in which it is something that is, namely different from whatever is with reference to Theaetetus.

But, given that this is the point that Plato has been working up to so carefully from 236e onward, let us consider in detail how he himself now resolves the question of false statements and how he deals with this particular example. He turns to the false statement in 263b7. This is what he says: *ho de dē pseudēs hetera tōn ontōn*. It is clear that this sentence is elliptical and has to be understood as parallel to the corresponding "*men*" clause about the true statement "Theaetetus is sitting" in 263b4–5. Thus understood, it will be rendered in the following way: The false statement then speaks of (*legei*) things other than those that are. For the claim about true statements had been that they say of those things that are that they are. There is a slight difficulty here: It holds of true statements in general that they say of those things that are that they are; but when we are talking about a particular statement, as we are here, it, strictly speaking, only says of one of the things that are that it is, and not, as Plato puts it, of the things that are that they are. But this should not particularly worry us. Plato could have said in 263b3–4 that the true statement says of something that is that it is (*on ti hōs esti*). But he wants to get a reference to the whole class of things that are, relative to a given subject, into the characterization of the true statement, as this will be needed to get an adequate characterization of the false statement. This corresponds to the need for a universal quantifier in a proper characterization, first, of the use of "... is not ..." along Plato's lines, and then of falsehood, a need several commentators rightly have insisted on.[7] Only thus can Plato say that the false statement says, speaks of, something other than *any* of the things that are, that is, something other than any of the things that are in relation to the given subject. For it is clear that it will not do simply to say of a false statement that it speaks of something other than something that is. To be false it has to speak of something other than any of the things that are, namely with reference to the given subject. Moreover, it is clear, given the parallel to 263b4–5, that 263b7 has to be understood in this sense: The false statement says of something other than whatever is in relation to a given subject that it is, namely in relation to that subject. Hence Plato can move on to claim in 263b9: "Hence it says of what is not that it is." Obviously, all he does here is (a) to supply the "that it is" that had to be understood with 263b7 from 263b3–4, and (b) to move from "other than whatever is" to "what is not." That latter move is covered by our earlier explanation of how, for example, what is not beautiful or big is just what is other than whatever is beautiful or big. Correspondingly what is other than whatever is being is not being.

We now have allowed ourselves for the first time in the dialogue since the problem arose to say that a false statement states, says, speaks of (*legei*) what is not. But we also know in what sense this has to be understood, and why, thus understood, it does not pose any problems. To say what is not is to say of something other than whatever is in relation to a given subject that it is. To do away with any residual qualms we may have, Plato in 263b11–12 goes on to explain the phrase "what is not" as it is used in 263b7. There is a minor textual problem here that hardly affects what Plato means to say. The first word in 263b11 is given by the manuscripts as *ontōs*. If we follow the transmitted reading, Plato would be explaining that, though a false statement says, or talks of, what is not, what it is talking of is something that really (*ontōs*) is, namely different. To be more precise, he would be explaining that the false statement says about the given subject something that really is, namely different. We would have to understand this in the following sense: The false statement says about the given subject something that really is, namely different from whatever is with reference to this subject. But we could have Plato say something that comes much closer to this, if, instead of the received text, we followed Cornarius' conjecture, adopted by all modern editors, and read *ontōn* for *ontōs*. We would get closer still, if we conjectured *tōn ontōn*.[8] But whichever text we adopt, the point Plato is trying to make is clear enough. To say what is not is to say something that is not altogether nothing, but something that is; in fact, it can only be called "not being" insofar as it is, namely different from what is with reference to the given subject. And at this point (263b11–12) Plato reminds us of our earlier finding that with reference to everything there is much that is and much that is not. Given the language he must be referring back to 256e6–7. But this has constituted a major problem for scholars that we need to look at in some detail.

Plato's thought here in 263b seems to be the following. Take the false statement that Theaetetus is flying. It says of Theaetetus something that is not with regard to him, namely flying. It presents, talks of, something that is not, namely flying, as if it were in relation to Theaetetus. This is supposed to be unproblematic, because we have already seen earlier that in relation to anything there are lots of things that are not. And so flying is just one of those things that are not with reference to Theaetetus. And this is what makes the statement that Theaetetus is flying false; it presents flying as something that is with reference to Theaetetus, when, in fact, it is not, when, in fact, flying is different from whatever is with reference to Theaetetus (cf. 263d1–2), or, to put the matter yet differently, when, in fact, Theaetetus is not flying.

But if we look back at the claim in 256e6–7, to which Plato seems to be referring in 263b11–12, it was arrived at by considering cases in which X and Y are different, in which we hence can say that X is not Y, and, moreover, hence can say that Y is not being with reference to X. And, given that for any X there are lots of things X is different from and that hence X is not, we were able to say that with reference to everything there are lots of things that are not being with reference to it. But this, it is thought, does not help here, since, though it is true enough that Theaetetus and flying are not the same thing, that Theaetetus is different from flying and hence that Theaetetus is not flying, this is not the sense we need in order to explain why it is false to say that Theaetetus is flying. For even if it were true that Theaetetus is flying, it still would be the case that Theaetetus and flying are not the same thing and that hence in that sense Theaetetus is not flying. So this cannot be what explains the falsehood of "Theaetetus is flying."

Given their understanding of 256e6–7 and of the preceding section, given in particular their assumption that in this section statements of the form "X is not Y" express non-identity statements, commentators also are rightly puzzled why Plato here in 263b does not refer to the later part of the discussion of not being, where – on anybody's interpretation – Plato tries to come to terms with what we would regard as ordinary negative predication (cf. McDowell 1983: 122ff.; Bostock 1984: III). It should be clear by now that Plato's reference back to 256e6–7 only makes sense because Plato all along did not understand the statements of the form "X is not Y" in that section as non-identity statements, not as statements of difference, but as statements of not being, that is to say as statements of a particular way of being different. And Plato even there must have thought that this way of being different was exhibited not only in those cases in which two forms are different from each other, but also in those cases in which something fails to have a certain feature. So already 256e6–7 has to be understood as involving the use of "... is not ..." that Plato needs to rely on in 263b. What the subsequent discussion, 257b1ff., added was an understanding of this use that allowed one to see that it also covered the case of negative predication. It took the subsequent discussion to determine the nature of the very not being whose being we had ascertained by 256e6–7. This is what allows Plato in 263b to refer back to 256e6–7, rather than to, say, 258b. So, though there are details of the text that require further clarification, and though it seems that even with further clarification we would wish Plato to have been clearer and more precise on certain points, the outline of his argument and his general position are reasonably clear and do not seem to be vitiated by confusion.

IV   CONCLUSION

In fact one thing that is striking about the *Sophist*, in comparison to the earlier dialogues, is its "dogmatic" and systematic character. It sets out carefully constructing a series of puzzles, *aporiai*. In this respect its first half resembles the early dialogues or even its immediate predecessor, the *Theaetetus*. But then it turns toward a resolution of these *aporiai*. In this regard the procedure of the dialogue reminds one of the methodological principle Aristotle sometimes refers to and follows, the principle that on a given subject matter we first of all have to see clearly the *aporiai* involved before we can proceed to an adequate account of the matter, which proves its adequacy in part by its ability both to account for and to resolve the *aporiai* (cf. *De An.* I.2, 403b20–1; *Met.* Beta 1 995a27ff.). And the *Sophist* proceeds to resolve these difficulties in a very systematic and almost technical way. By careful analysis it tries to isolate and to settle an issue definitively. In this regard it does stand out among all of Plato's dialogues. And because of this it also is more readily accessible to interpretation. If, nevertheless, we do have difficulties with this text, it is in good part because in his day Plato was dealing with almost entirely unexplored issues for whose discussion even the most rudimentary concepts were missing. Seen in this light, Plato's solution of the difficulty presented by false statements is a singular achievement.

NOTES

1 I quote the text in Dies' edition in the Budé series; its line-numbers at times differ from those of Burnet's text.

2 In Greek: *mē on*; in what follows, I will render this and *ouk on* indiscriminately by "what is not" or "what is not being" or even just "not being."

3 For a different interpretation of the problem, see Roberts 1988.

4 I developed and argued for this interpretation at great length in Frede 1967: 12–36. It was then, following a suggestion by R. Albritton, adopted by Owen (1970); Owen had originally taken a different view of the passage (1957: 107 n. 25). Cf. Owen's first footnote to the reprint of "Plato on Not-being" in Owen 1986: 104.

5 There are technical reasons why Plato here moves back and forth between "different" and "the different." As I noted earlier, there is, according to Plato, a (self-predicational) way of being different, and generally of being *F*, such that difference or the different is different in this way (and generally *F*-ness or the *F* is *F*); thus not to be different in this way is not to be the different, just as being different in this way is to be the different.

6 Translators tend to construe *hekaston* with *morion*; wrongly, as the preceding part of the sentence shows. Difference is distributed among all things that are with reference to each other, i.e., it is distributed among things that are not beautiful with reference to things that are beautiful, among things that are not big with reference to the things that are big, etc.; the *pros to on hekaston* clearly picks up the *pros allela*.

7 Cf. Wiggins 1971: 299; McDowell 1983: 123; Bostock 1984: 113.

8 There are yet other possibilities, e.g., *ontōs de ge onta hetera tōn ontōn peri sou*.

15 Cosmology and Human Nature in the *Timaeus*

Emily Fletcher

I INTRODUCTION

In the *Timaeus*, the eponymous character Timaeus gives a lengthy speech about the origin of the cosmos.[1] Human beings play an integral role in Timaeus' cosmology, because the completion of the cosmos depends on the transformation of human beings into nonhuman animals. In this chapter, I argue that Timaeus views human nature as lying on a continuum with other mortal beings, such that human beings do not differ in any fundamental way from nonhuman animals.[2] Those features that distinguish human beings from other mortal (and immortal) beings are, by Timaeus' own standards, relatively superficial; they can change without destroying the identity of the individual, and they obscure more fundamental differences between individual human beings. One feature that apparently sets human beings apart from other mortal beings is their functional role in Timaeus' account of how the cosmos as a whole came to be.[3] However, this special role cannot serve to distinguish human beings from nonhuman animals, because it does not apply to human beings beyond the first generation, nor does it apply to any women (42c, 90e–91d). Human

First and foremost, I am grateful to David Ebrey for his invaluable support and feedback throughout this project, both on written drafts and in countless conversations. I would also like to thank Ursula Coope, Thomas Johansen, Sean Kelsey, Richard Kraut, Stephen Menn, Alesia Preite, Jason Rheins, David Sedley, and John Wynne for comments that significantly improved this chapter. I am grateful for the opportunities to present earlier versions of this chapter at the Northwestern Late Plato conference in March 2016, the Annual Ancient Philosophy Conference at Renmin University of China in May 2018, Oxford University in May 2018, the Chicago Area Consortium in Ancient Greek and Roman Philosophy in October 2018, and McGill University in January 2019.

beings have a more immediate potential than other mortal creatures for living a godlike life and ultimately escaping mortal embodiment. However, even this difference is merely one of degree, for every mortal animal possesses an immortal soul and is in principle capable of restoring this soul to its original, godlike condition.[4]

Understanding Timaeus' view of human nature requires digging into the details of his cosmology, because the two are tightly intertwined. According to Timaeus, the cosmos is the product of divine craft, and he argues that the gods crafted it to be as good as possible.[5] In addition to being as ordered, beautiful, and intelligent as possible, the cosmos must also be "complete." For it to be complete, the cosmos must contain three types of mortal creatures: those which live on land, those which live in the air, and those which live in the water.[6] The gods do not craft these three types directly; instead, they craft the first generation of all-male human beings, and the three types of mortal creatures come to be, in part, through the cognitive and moral failure of these first humans. The very purpose for which the gods crafted human beings places them on a continuum with the three kinds of mortal beings, all of which come to be from male human beings.

The three types of mortal beings, which the cosmos must contain in order to be complete, all lack intelligence to varying degrees. The criterion of completeness thus raises a puzzle, because it would seem that in becoming more complete the cosmos thereby becomes less ordered, beautiful, and intelligent. Even if we can dispel this apparent tension among the criteria for a good cosmos,[7] the crafting of mortal creatures calls into question the goodness of the gods; after all, the gods place immortal souls in mortal bodies in order to complete the cosmos, foreseeing that foolishness and vice will inevitably result. Timaeus addresses this apparent inconsistency by distancing the gods as much as possible from the emergence of foolishness and vice in the cosmos.[8] Thus, rather than crafting fish and other inherently foolish creatures directly, the gods craft human beings, who have some chance of achieving and maintaining intelligence and moral virtue in their initial embodiment. Of course, most human beings fail at this task, and the completion of the cosmos depends on their failure. The degeneration of human beings into less intelligent animals provides a mechanism by which the gods ensure that the cosmos becomes complete without directly producing any bad results.

In the first half of the chapter, I articulate in more detail the central tension in Timaeus' cosmology (section II) and how the crafting of human beings helps to alleviate it (section III). In the second half, I examine the account of human nature that emerges from Timaeus' speech. I highlight the differences between mortal beings and immortal beings, in order to bring out the broad similarities between human beings and all other mortal creatures (section IV). I then argue that Timaeus presents a view of human nature according to which human beings lie on a continuum with other mortal beings; on this account, human beings differ merely in their bodily form from other animals, and they do not have any distinctive moral or cognitive characteristics (section V). In the conclusion (section VI), I observe that human nature does not contain a normative ideal for human beings in the *Timaeus*. Since being human does not guarantee any significant (i.e., cognitive or moral) superiority over other mortal beings, to the extent that human beings strive to live well, they should aim to live like gods.

II   COMPLETING THE COSMOS

The *Timaeus* is one of Plato's most ambitious dialogues. Timaeus is asked to give a speech "beginning with the origin of the cosmos and concluding with the nature of human beings" (27a3–6).[9] In his speech, the origin of the cosmos and the nature of human beings are inextricably linked. The reason the gods craft human beings is to "complete" the cosmos, but crafting human beings also requires subjecting intelligent, immortal souls to the disruptions associated with mortal embodiment. In this section I argue that foolishness and vice, far from being accidental, regrettable features of the cosmos, are in fact necessary for its completion. In order to see why this is the case, we need to consider Timaeus' basic account of the construction of the cosmos.

Throughout his speech, Timaeus frequently refers to the world as a "cosmos" (kosmos), which means "order."[10] According to the cosmology Timaeus presents, the world does not come to be from nothing; instead, he tells the story of how a craftsman god brings everything that is visible[11] into a state of order from a previous state of disorder (30a).[12] Timaeus refers to the god that orders the visible world as the craftsman (demiourgos, 28a6) or the assembler (sunistas, 29e1) of the cosmos. Scholars traditionally refer to this god as the "Demiurge" (from demiourgos, the Greek for "craftsman").[13] I will adopt this convention in what follows, in order to clearly distinguish the main craftsman of the cosmos from the subordinate gods, who construct human beings under this original god's direction. However, as Stephen Menn (1995) has noted, "Demiurge" is not the god's name. In fact, Timaeus says that it is not possible to name (legein) "the maker and father of the universe" (28c3–5).[14]

The Demiurge is good, and his very goodness explains why he constructed the cosmos. Timaeus states that the Demiurge "wanted everything to become as much like himself as was possible" (29e3). Since the Demiurge orders the visible world, rather than creating it from scratch, the starting conditions are a good god and a visible world that is not as good as it could be. To understand the Demiurge's motivation, we need not assume that it is better for the visible world to exist rather than not exist, but rather that it is better for the visible world to become orderly rather than disorderly.[15]

Timaeus characterizes the goodness of the cosmos in four ways. First, he claims that a good cosmos must have an eternal, changeless model (28a–29a). He does not entertain the possibility that the Demiurge constructed the cosmos without a model, but he considers whether he used an eternal model or "something that has come to be" as a model (28a6–b2). Timaeus appeals both to the evident beauty of the cosmos (29a2) and to the goodness of the Demiurge (29a3) to confirm the use of an eternal model. Second, a good cosmos manifests as much order as possible, because the Demiurge believed that "order (*taxis*) was in every way better than disorder (*ataxia*)" (30a5–6). A third feature Timaeus attributes to a good cosmos is intelligence (*nous*), because "in the realm of things naturally visible, no unintelligent thing could as a whole be better than anything that does possess intelligence as a whole" (30b1–3). Imbuing the cosmos with intelligence also requires the construction of soul, because "it is impossible for anything to come to possess intelligence apart from soul" (30b3).[16] Possessing a soul is what makes something alive (77b), and so it is impossible to make the cosmos intelligent without making it a living being. Finally, Timaeus says that the cosmos must be "complete" (*teleion*), which in this context means that the cosmos must contain within it everything contained within its model (30c2–31a1).[17] In this passage, Timaeus describes the eternal model of the cosmos in more detail, referring to it as "that Living Thing of which all other living things are parts" (30c5–6) and "the best of the intelligible things" (30d1–2). In order for the cosmos to be complete, it must be a living thing that contains within it all of the living things that are contained within the model.[18]

These four ways in which Timaeus describes the goodness of the cosmos are not equivalent, and it is not clear they are entirely consistent. It is plausible to think of the first two features as closely linked, given the association of beauty with order in the *Timaeus* and throughout Plato's dialogues.[19] The third feature, intelligence, adds something new, because intelligence is not merely a beautiful and ordered thing; it is a cause of beauty and order (46d–e). The first living beings that the Demiurge constructs are intelligent gods, who later imitate the Demiurge's craft activity and make other beautiful and ordered things, including human beings. Similarly, intelligent human beings can impose order on their own mortal parts, and in this way make themselves "the most beautiful, the most desirable of all things to behold" (87d8). However, the fourth characteristic of completeness is a very different sort of criterion, which seems to pull against the other three. The cosmos is not complete until the generation of the three kinds of mortal creatures, which are of necessity less orderly, beautiful, and intelligent than the cosmos itself.

The generated cosmos inevitably falls short of its model; however, it is not clear exactly why and in what way it falls short. One explanation for the imperfection of the cosmos is its metaphysical status. As a generated thing, the cosmos does not have the stability and permanence of an eternal thing (27d–28a). Another, closely related, explanation is the tendency of the cosmos to revert to its original, disorderly, condition. Timaeus refers to this tendency as "Necessity"[20] (47e5) and the "Straying Cause" (48a6–7). The cosmos is in a non-stop process of becoming; absent the guidance of intelligent craft, these changes inevitably tend toward disorder.

It would be natural to assume that Necessity is responsible for everything bad and nothing good in the cosmos, and likewise that intelligent craft is responsible for everything good and nothing bad. However, Timaeus' account is not so tidy. Foolishness and vice are both bad, but their presence in the cosmos cannot be attributed solely to Necessity, understood in contrast with intelligent, divine craft. The Demiurge specifies that the cosmos will not be "complete" (*teleion*) until three kinds of mortal creatures come to be within it (41b–c). However, the three kinds of mortal creatures necessarily possess foolish and vicious immortal souls; thus, the cosmos must contain foolishness and vice in order for it to be complete. Spelled out in this way, the characteristic of completeness apparently conflicts with every other characteristic of a good cosmos. The presence of unintelligent and vicious mortal creatures in the eternal model of the cosmos challenges the purported goodness of this model. Completeness also conflicts with being ordered and intelligent, because to the extent that the cosmos contains foolishness and vice, it lacks both order and intelligence. While the Demiurge need not aim at foolishness and vice in order for the three mortal kinds to come to be, it is also not accurate to characterize foolishness and vice as unfortunate and unintended consequences of divine craft activity. The Demiurge chooses to subject immortal souls to the forces of Necessity, fully expecting – requiring even – that many of them will become foolish and vicious.[21]

We are now in a position to see why human beings play a vital role in completing the cosmos. The first generation of mortals consists of male human beings, and all other human and nonhuman animals come about through the cognitive and moral failure of these first mortals. Timaeus distances the Demiurge himself from the emergence of foolishness and vice in at least four ways: (1) The Demiurge constructs the immortal souls of mortal beings, but he delegates to the subordinate gods the tasks of crafting the mortal body and mortal soul, as well as weaving the immortal and mortal parts of these beings together (41c–d; cf. 42d–e). (2) Even the subordinate gods do not craft foolish or vicious mortal creatures directly; instead, all such creatures, including women and nonhuman animals, come to be from those human males who lived badly in their first mortal embodiment (42b–d; 90e–92c). (3) Foolish and vicious immortal souls are responsible for their own failure to master the disorderly motions[22] to which they are exposed in mortal life (42d–e). (4) Finally, Necessity, not divine craft, is the source of the disorderly motions that disrupt the intelligent motions of immortal souls from without (48a).

Mortal embodiment itself is what makes immortal souls vulnerable to disorderly motions in the first place. The world soul and the souls of subordinate gods are not threatened by such motions, because they are not subject to mortal embodiment. Were it not for the Demiurge's instructions to join immortal souls to mortal bodies, so that the cosmos could become complete, the cosmos would contain neither foolishness nor vice. That is not to say that cognitive and moral failure is inevitable for mortal beings; some individual immortal souls are able to restore and maintain their intelligence, despite the initial disruption of mortal embodiment (44b–c).

Timaeus describes the cosmos as an offspring of intelligence and Necessity, but he gives intelligence the leading role: "Intelligence prevailed over Necessity by persuading it to direct most of the things that come to be toward what is best, and the result of this subjugation of Necessity to wise persuasion was the initial formation of this universe" (48a2–5). Intelligence may prevail over Necessity in most matters; however, in the case of at least some immortal souls, intelligence must give way to Necessity in order for the cosmos to be complete.

III THE TWO ENDS OF CRAFTING HUMAN BEINGS

Human beings are central to Timaeus' explanation of how the cosmos came to be, because they are the initial point of contact between immortal souls and the disruptive motions associated with inanimate bodies. The immortal soul of a human being is the locus at which intelligence gives way to Necessity, and foolishness and vice emerge – apparently for the good of the cosmos as a whole. Despite being necessary ingredients in a complete cosmos, foolishness and vice cannot be among the Demiurge's ends in crafting it. These states are bad, while the Demiurge is good and aims to make everything else as much like himself as possible. Furthermore, the Demiurge explicitly denies responsibility for the moral failing of individual immortal souls at 42d. The Demiurge must somehow ensure that foolishness and vice come to be, despite neither aiming at nor being responsible for the cognitive and moral failure of individual immortal souls.

The solution is for the gods[23] to aim at two distinct ends when crafting human beings. One end is to complete the cosmos, which must contain three kinds of mortal beings. This is the reason the Demiurge decides to craft human beings in first place (41b–42a). The second end is to give every immortal soul the best possible chance of restoring and maintaining intelligence after entering a mortal body. This second end is in tension with the first, because the completion of the cosmos requires that many immortal souls fail to restore and maintain their intelligence while embodied as human beings.[24] The opposition between the pressures of mortal embodiment and the striving of individual souls (with the support of the gods) to regain their intelligence provides a mechanism by which the gods are able to construct a cosmos that contains foolishness and vice, all the while aiming at only good ends.

According to Timaeus' account, human beings are composed of parts that have radically different natures: an immortal, rational soul, crafted by the Demiurge (41d–42a) and a mortal kind of soul and a mortal body, both formed by the lesser craftsmanship of the subordinate gods (41c–d, 42e–43a, 69c–72d). Thus, human beings are the product of two levels of craftsmanship. Timaeus explains that the products of the Demiurge's craft cannot be destroyed, except by the Demiurge's will; at the same time, the Demiurge would never consent to the destruction of anything that was well put together. As a result, everything that is the direct product of the Demiurge's craftsmanship has a contingent kind of immortality: Despite being the sort of thing that admits of destruction, it will never in fact be destroyed (41a–b). The very excellence of the Demiurge's craftsmanship is a limitation when it comes to creating the mortal beings that are contained within the cosmos, because the Demiurge cannot craft anything with a mortal nature.[25] This means that the Demiurge does not, and in fact cannot, complete the cosmos solely through his own craftsmanship.

The Demiurge mixes a new batch of immortal souls and delegates to the subordinate gods the task of "weaving what is mortal to what is immortal" (41d1–2). The Demiurge does not instruct the subordinate gods to craft human beings in particular; instead, he provides general instructions for the crafting of all three kinds of mortal beings (41b–c). Human beings are not mentioned until 41e–42a, where we learn that the gods assign to all of the new immortal souls crafted by the Demiurge "one and the same initial birth" as male humans (41e3–4). When the subordinate gods join immortal souls to mortal parts of their own making, the result is a temporary whole: "they bonded together into the same thing the parts they had taken, but not with those indissoluble bonds by which they themselves were held together" (43a1–2). Despite the generic character of the Demiurge's initial instructions, Timaeus' account focuses on how the subordinate gods crafted the first generation of all-male human beings in particular. Presumably, the subordinate gods play a similar role in the crafting of subsequent generations of mortal beings, as instructed by the Demiurge.[26] The condition of the immortal soul after its first embodiment, for which the subordinate gods are not responsible, dictates what kind of mortal body they join it to next, and so what kind of mortal being they produce.[27]

The three mortal kinds differ by degrees of foolishness (91d–92c), and so the completion of the cosmos requires the emergence of at least three degrees of foolishness, which correspond to the three mortal kinds. This requirement gives rise to a practical dilemma: The Demiurge requires the subordinate gods to craft mortal creatures, but the subordinate gods in turn require a supply of appropriately foolish immortal souls in order to craft each mortal kind. It is against the nature of the gods to directly produce foolish immortal souls, and doing so would conflict with the Demiurge's insistence that the gods are not responsible for the cognitive and moral failures of individual human beings (42d–e). But it seems equally problematic to leave the generation of the three mortal kinds to chance.

It seems that mortal embodiment is itself sufficient to ensure that some immortal souls become foolish and vicious, due to the violent onslaught of disorderly motions that an immortal soul faces on first being joined to a mortal body (43a–44c). In fact, after placing immortal souls in mortal bodies, the gods do everything they can to help immortal souls master the disruptive forces associated with mortal embodiment, so that some of these souls can maintain a degree of intelligence. Helping those immortal souls subjected to mortal embodiment is a second end that the gods have in mind as they craft human beings, in addition to their primary[28] end of completing the cosmos.

The Demiurge and the subordinate gods help immortal souls restore and maintain intelligence in different ways. The Demiurge prepares the immortal souls of human beings by showing them the nature of the cosmos (41e),[29] as well as instructing the subordinate gods to guide human beings (42e). In addition to providing this guidance, the subordinate gods craft the mortal body and mortal kind of soul with the well-being of the immortal soul constantly in mind. In these ways, the gods mitigate as far as possible the negative consequences of mortal embodiment.

The second end of supporting immortal souls facing mortal conditions may appear to conflict with the gods' end of completing the cosmos. After all, if the gods were too effective in their help, and all immortal souls were able to restore their intelligence and escape mortal embodiment, the cosmos would never become complete. However, on further examination, it may be that completing the cosmos requires the gods to simultaneously pursue the second end of helping the immortal souls within mortal creatures. Counteracting disorderly motions is not trivial for any immortal soul, and Timaeus' comment that those immortal souls that enter mortal bodies differ from divine souls in purity (41d) provides further reason to doubt that all immortal souls, or even a large number of them, will ultimately escape mortal embodiment. Perhaps it is the very opposition between the pull toward foolishness due to mortal embodiment and the striving of individual souls (with the help of the gods) for intelligence that produces the full spectrum of intelligent and foolish immortal souls required for all three kinds of mortal creatures to come to be.[30]

As I have shown, the two ends of the gods in crafting human beings, completing the cosmos and supporting the intelligence of immortal souls under mortal conditions, are not strictly incompatible; both can be at least partially fulfilled. Eventually, some of the immortal souls embodied in mortal bodies will reestablish their original motions, whereas most of these souls will become distorted to various degrees and transform into the three kinds of mortal beings. The second end may even be necessary for the fulfillment of the first, since without the aid of the gods, immortal souls would have less chance of maintaining even the low level of intelligence required to become a bird or land animal. However, these two ends are still in tension with one another, in the sense that they cannot both be fulfilled completely. In particular, the gods cannot fully succeed at the second without failing at the first, though they can fully succeed at the first while also partially succeeding at the second. When it comes down to it, the gods still rely on the moral and cognitive failure of some individual immortal souls in order to complete the cosmos.

In highlighting the role of human beings in completing the cosmos, I am not raising an objection to the account of human beings in the *Timaeus*. The tension between the two ends that the gods pursue in crafting human beings provides a practical resolution to the deeper tension within the criteria for a good cosmos identified in section II. There may be no way to resolve the tension between the criterion of "completeness," which requires the generation of foolish and vicious mortal beings, and the characterization of the cosmos as ordered, beautiful, and intelligent. Whether or not we can resolve this deeper tension, the tension between the two ends of human beings serves as an elegant solution to the problem of how the gods can complete the cosmos, without admitting that foolishness and vice are products of divine craft.

One possible solution to the deeper tension is to posit that the cosmos as a whole is made better by containing mortal creatures with varying degrees of intelligence. The world soul ensures that the heavens move in an intelligent and orderly way, and yet the body of the cosmos still contains plenty of disorderly motion. Mortal creatures are a battleground between the intelligent motions of immortal souls and the disorderly motions characteristic of the simple bodies, and even the most foolish water-dwelling creature represents at least a limited victory on the side of intelligence. The motions of any immortal soul, no matter how badly distorted, may better approximate the motions of the heavens than do the motions of inanimate bodies. If this line of speculation is correct, then by containing mortal creatures with varying degrees of intelligence, the cosmos as a whole becomes "more like the Demiurge" than it otherwise would be. Timaeus describes all of the living things contained within the cosmos as "akin to [the cosmos] by nature" (30d3–31a1). Perhaps they are akin not merely in being living things, but also in possessing at least some degree of intelligence.

IV MORTAL BEINGS AND THE COSMOS

Timaeus describes the crafting of human beings in much more detail than that of any other mortal being. However, this unevenness of treatment does not signal that human beings differ fundamentally from other mortal beings; on the contrary, it is the similarity of all forms of mortal embodiment that allows Timaeus to provide such a brief description of the three mortal kinds at the end of the dialogue (91d–92c). At 42c–d, Timaeus describes a series of transformations between different types of mortal beings from the perspective of a single immortal soul, suggesting continuity between the various forms of mortal embodiment.

All mortal beings differ from the gods in being susceptible to disease, old age, and death, but these differences are almost entirely due to the possession of mortal bodies. Like the gods, mortal beings possess immortal souls, and these souls have the same kinds of ingredients and structure as the world soul.[31] Timaeus does mark a difference in the quality of the ingredients the Demiurge uses to craft the souls of immortal and mortal beings, commenting that the ingredients used for the latter were "no longer invariably and constantly pure, but of a second and third grade of purity" (41d6–7). Timaeus does not explain the significance of these differences in purity among immortal souls; one possibility is that they represent different aptitudes for achieving intelligence under mortal conditions. These differences may even be necessary to ensure that all three types of mortal creatures come to be. On the other hand, any differences in the starting conditions of the immortal souls threaten to undermine the Demiurge's claim that each immortal soul is responsible for its own moral and cognitive failings.[32]

The main explanation for the differences between mortal beings and the gods is the difference between their bodies. The Demiurge crafts the body of the cosmos so that it is "as whole and complete as possible and made up of complete parts" (32d1–33a1).[33] Since the body of the cosmos is complete and encompasses everything, there is nothing that can attack it from without, bringing about disease or old age. The cosmos is self-sufficient, with no need for organs for sense perception, breathing, or nourishment, for there is nothing outside for it to perceive, breathe, or eat (33c–d). Finally, the cosmos has no feet, for there would be nothing for them to stand on; instead, the cosmos engages in a spinning motion that is perfectly suited to its body (34a). It is striking that Timaeus describes the body of the cosmos by listing the parts and capacities it lacks as compared with mortal bodies. This comparison serves to emphasize the self-sufficiency of the gods in comparison with mortal beings, who require additional organs for perception, nourishment, and locomotion.

The subordinate gods craft mortal bodies for life under very different conditions. Crucially, mortal embodiment exposes immortal souls to the impact of disorderly motions (43a–b). Sense perception and nourishment, both necessary capacities for the survival of mortal beings, are among the sources of these disruptive motions (43b–d). The subordinate gods craft mortal bodies with a view to protecting the immortal soul as much as possible from distortion as a result of these motions, but they cannot insulate it completely.[34] In crafting human bodies, the gods begin by copying the shape of the universe, thus forming the head, but they must also fashion a torso and limbs, which serve as a vehicle for the immortal soul (44d–45a). Furthermore, in order to mitigate the effects of disorderly motions on the orbits of the immortal soul, the gods provide organs of sight and hearing, so that humans can imitate the revolutions of the heavens (46e–47e).[35] In all these ways, the subordinate gods help human beings restore and maintain intelligence; however, they cannot change the fact that immortal souls are fundamentally unsuited to mortal life. No matter how well the subordinate gods craft the mortal body, it is better for an immortal soul to escape mortal embodiment altogether. Even if an immortal soul is able to restore its original condition under these adverse conditions (90b–d), as long as it possesses a mortal body it remains vulnerable to disruption from disease, violent death, and negative societal influences.

In addition to the mortal body, the subordinate gods construct a second, mortal kind of soul. Timaeus describes the formation of the mortal soul only in the second, more detailed, account of the crafting of human beings (69c–72d). The significance of the fact that human beings have two kinds (genē) of soul, as opposed to a single soul with multiple parts, has not been fully appreciated by scholars.[36] The immortal and mortal kinds of soul are products of different types of craft (that of the Demiurge versus that of the subordinate gods), and they have different characteristic motions.[37] Furthermore, the association of the immortal soul with the mortal soul is just as temporary as the association of the immortal soul with the mortal body; both are bound to the immortal soul with dissoluble bonds (43a).

The Demiurge does not specifically instruct the subordinate gods to craft a distinct, mortal kind of soul; he simply tells them to "make whatever else remained that the human soul still needed to have" (42d7–e1). The subordinate gods craft the mortal soul to fulfill some need resulting from mortal embodiment that cannot be met by the mortal body alone. One possibility is that the mortal soul is necessary as the subject of all the non-cognitive living functions of human beings. The construction and motions of the immortal part of the soul make it suitable for thinking, but given that they live under mortal conditions, mortal beings must also engage in activities of nourishment, locomotion, and sense perception.[38] In support of this suggestion, Timaeus explicitly locates pleasure, pain, sense perception,[39] desire, and various other affections in the mortal part of the soul: "And within the body they built another kind of soul as well, the mortal kind, which contains within it those dreadful but necessary disturbances" (69c7–d1). Moreover, since these disturbances disrupt the immortal soul from without, it is hard to see how they could come from it. The mortal soul provides a source for these necessary but disruptive psychic motions.

We now have a better view of how mortal beings differ from the immortal cosmos: whereas the cosmos is complete, self-sufficient, and immortal in body and soul, mortal beings possess an immortal soul that is bound to a mortal body and a mortal soul. The structure and motions of the world soul are perfectly suited to its body, but the immortal soul of a mortal being resides within a body designed for nourishment, locomotion, and sense perception, as well as the motions characteristic of the immortal soul. The subordinate gods aim to insulate the immortal soul from disorderly motions, but they cannot protect it entirely. At best, a human being can achieve an uneasy alliance between immortal and mortal parts; still, the immortal soul is our "original nature," and it is the life of this part of us, the immortal life, that we want to live (42b–e, 90d).[40]

V   HUMAN NATURE IN THE TIMAEUS

Critias initially instructed Timaeus to describe "the nature of human beings" (27a6), which might lead one to suppose that human beings differ in some fundamental way from other mortal beings and the gods. Instead of offering such an account, Timaeus places human beings on a continuum with all other mortal beings, and the only features that distinguish human beings from nonhuman animals turn out to be superficial bodily differences. The most significant difference between mortal beings in general is the relative intelligence or foolishness of their immortal soul, and yet human beings are not essentially more intelligent than other types of animals.[41] The mortal body reflects the intelligence of the immortal soul at the moment of birth, but the condition of the immortal soul changes in the course of a mortal life. Subsequent embodiment as nonhuman animals results from the fact that human beings come to manifest very different levels of intelligence, depending on the way they live. Ultimately, human beings share little more than an upright, bipedal body, which allows them to look at the stars (47a), as well as the ability to reproduce with one another (91a–d).[42]

Timaeus' speech contains four references to "human nature,"[43] along with eight additional references to general characteristics of human beings.[44] Rather than setting human beings apart, these passages highlight the continuity between human beings and other mortal creatures. Timaeus repeatedly contrasts human and divine cognition.[45] But of course, the distinction between human and divine cognition is compatible with the lack of any sharp distinction between the cognitive faculties of humans and other mortal beings. According to Timaeus' account of reincarnation, human cognition can unfortunately sink to the level of a wolf or a fish (91d–92c). The gods make plants "congenial to human nature" (77a3–4) in order to serve as nourishment for human beings; however, it is as mortal beings, not as human beings in particular, that we become depleted and require nourishment. The Demiurge instructs the subordinate gods to make additions to the "human soul" (42d7), but the resulting mortal soul is common to humans, nonhuman animals, and even (partially) to plants.[46] While Timaeus ascribes two types of desires to human beings, the desire for nourishment and the desire of the immortal soul for wisdom (88a–b), neither of these desires is uniquely human. All mortal creatures, even plants (remarkably), desire nourishment (77b). Timaeus says that birds originate from men who "believed that the most reliable proofs concerning [the heavenly bodies] could be based upon visual observation" (91d8–e1). These human beings became birds not because they lacked a desire for wisdom, but because they failed to pursue it in the right way. If desiring wisdom in the wrong way leads to being reborn as a bird, then even the desire for wisdom does not clearly distinguish human beings from other mortal beings.

Timaeus calls human nature "twofold" because it contains both men and women (42a1). Women differ from men in many of the same ways as nonhuman animals, further blurring the distinction between humans and other mortal beings. Despite the multiple references to human beings and human nature in the speech, Timaeus' account focuses on the crafting of male human beings. The gods do not receive the immortal souls of women directly from the Demiurge; instead, like nonhuman animals, women come to be through the moral or cognitive failure of immortal souls initially embodied as human males (42c, 76d8–e1, 90e–91d).[47] Again like nonhuman animals, women differ from men in their bodily form, given that they possess different sex organs. The capacity of sexual reproduction between male and female human beings is one feature that links men and women together, providing some basis for speaking about "human nature." Near the end of the speech, Timaeus claims that "human nature" can to some extent share in immortality by caring for the immortal soul, and that this is the best life offered to human beings by the gods (90c–d). Despite the reference to "human nature" and "human beings," the consistent male pronouns suggest that Timaeus is speaking primarily about the masculine half of human nature.[48]

Timaeus provides two separate accounts of reincarnation in his speech, which give different impressions about the relationship between men and women, as well as between human beings and other animals. The first account suggests that women differ from men along the same dimension as the three mortal kinds, though to a lesser degree. After initial embodiment as a male human being, an immortal soul is born a second time as a woman as a result of failing to live justly (42b–c). A further transformation into "some wild nature" (i.e., one of the three mortal kinds) occurs if the immortal soul "still cannot refrain from vice" in its life as a woman (42c1–4). Thus, all inferior forms of mortal embodiment seem to result from varying degrees of injustice (adikia) or vice (kakia) more generally. By suggesting that the immortal souls reborn as women and nonhuman animals differ along a single dimension, this account implies that, at least with respect to the condition of the soul, the distinction between women and nonhuman animals is one of degree rather than kind.

The second, more detailed, account of reincarnation indicates that there may be two separate dimensions along which an immortal soul can become worse, one resulting in female embodiment, the other in embodiment as a nonhuman animal (90e–92c). Timaeus describes the transformation of men into women in terms of moral failure, whereas he describes the transformation of men into the three mortal kinds exclusively in terms of cognitive failure. Women come to be from men who "lived lives of cowardice or injustice" (90e7). Timaeus later characterizes this account as an explanation of how "women and the whole female kind" came to be (to thulē pan, 91d5–6), suggesting that moral failure explains the generation of all females, whether human or nonhuman. By contrast, transformation from human embodiment to embodiment as a nonhuman animal results from cognitive defects, such as mindlessness (aphrōn, 92a4–5), foolishness (anoētos, 92b1–2), and ignorance (amathēs, 92b2, 92b7). Timaeus even describes the immortal souls embodied as birds as "unknowing of evil" (akakōn, 91d7), because their cognitive mistake of relying too much on sense perception to study the heavens results from being "good natured" (di' euētheian, 91e1).[49] In this account, the three mortal kinds do not come to be from women; instead, all three come to be directly from men as the result of cognitive failure.[50] Of course, some immortal souls fail both morally and cognitively, which presumably explains the generation of female, nonhuman animals.

There is additional evidence that Timaeus distinguishes between cognitive and moral defects in the account of psychic disease (86b–87b), which supports the proposal that there are two dimensions of decline for immortal souls. He introduces "foolishness" (anoia) as a generic term for disease of the soul, of which there are two subtypes, "ignorance" (amathia) and "madness" (mania) (86b2–4). It is not clear where moral defects, such as injustice and cowardice, fit into this categorization, because it seems to encompass cognitive defects only. Even the person suffering from madness caused by excessive pleasures and pains has a primarily cognitive problem, being "least capable of rational thought" (86c3). Timaeus first mentions moral defects when he names the variety of diseases caused by bodily motions in "the three regions of the soul" (87a3–4). Here he lists "bad temper and melancholy" and "recklessness and cowardice," as well as the cognitive defects "forgetfulness and slowness of learning" (87a5–7). One possibility is that cognitive defects are proper to the immortal soul, whereas moral defects reflect the bad condition of one or both parts of the mortal soul.

Another, compatible, possibility is that moral defects concern the way the immortal soul responds to the disruptive motions generated by the mortal soul, whereas cognitive defects concern the immortal soul's relationship to the objects of cognition. In support of this, Timaeus identifies injustice as a failure of the immortal soul to master emotions and the other necessary disturbances associated with mortal embodiment (42b–c; cf. 88d–e). Someone might struggle to fully master these disturbances and yet still exercise their immortal soul correctly in studying the heavenly bodies. This could explain why women, despite representing an inferior form of mortal embodiment, still resemble men in standing upright and being able to gaze at the heavens.

By distinguishing the types of failures that produce women, and nonhuman animals, the second account of reincarnation provides a basis for distinguishing those immortal souls reborn as human beings from those reborn as other mortal beings. However, even if human-born immortal souls share certain cognitive capacities, this similarity holds only at the moment of birth. Each human being's immortal soul inevitably undergoes further changes, depending on how well or badly it fares under the hostile conditions of mortal life. Thus, there do not seem to be any psychic features that distinguish human beings from other mortal animals; instead, humans share at most superficial bodily features, such as possessing an upright, bipedal body.

VI   CONCLUSION

Human beings play an indispensable role in the completion of the cosmos, and the fact that human beings can play this role reveals how much they have in common with all other mortal beings. According to Timaeus, human beings cannot claim absolute moral or cognitive superiority over nonhuman animals, so it is not surprising that human nature does not contain a normative ideal for human beings. Every human being should aim to live an excellent human life, and yet the ultimate payoff for succeeding in this aim is to transcend mortal embodiment altogether (42b). No one should aim to be a human being, even a perfectly virtuous and intelligent human being, forever, because mortal embodiment always comes with the risk of cognitive and moral decline. Near the end of his speech, Timaeus articulates the goal of human life as follows.

> To the extent that human nature can partake of immortality, he can in no way fail to achieve this: constantly caring for his divine part as he does, keeping well-ordered the guiding spirit that lives within him, he must indeed be supremely happy. Now there is but one way to care for anything, and that is to provide for it the nourishment and the motions that are proper to it. And the motions that have an affinity to the divine part within us are the thoughts and revolutions of the universe. These, surely, are the ones that each of us should follow. We should redirect the revolutions in our heads that were thrown off at our birth, by coming to learn the harmonies and revolutions of the universe, and so bring into conformity with its objects our faculty of understanding, as it was in its original condition. And when this conformity is complete, we shall have achieved our goal: that most excellent life offered to humankind by the gods, both now and forevermore. (90c2–d7)

Even in this passage Timaeus does not praise the supremely happy and rational human life in unqualified terms. For example, the human being who achieves such a life partakes of immortality "to the extent that human nature can," but this falls short of the immortality of the gods. Timaeus does suggest that human beings can bring the faculty of understanding "into conformity with its objects." However, as Timeaus' accounts of disease, old age, and death make clear, this achievement is under threat as long as the immortal soul resides in a mortal body. At the end of this passage, Timaeus identifies the life he has described as "the most excellent life offered to humankind by the gods." Again, Timaeus qualifies his praise of the most excellent human life. It is not the most excellent life of all, nor is it the most excellent life that is possible for the immortal part of our nature.[51]

NOTES

1 The *Timaeus* has enjoyed increased scholarly interest in the past thirty years. Recent monographs dedicated to the *Timaeus*, or with substantial discussion of the dialogue, include Johansen (2004), Carone (2005a), and Broadie (2012). Important collections of essays on the *Timaeus* include Calvo and Brisson (1997), Wright (2000), Southeast-European Association for Ancient Philosophy (2005), and Mohr and Sattler (2009). Modern commentaries and translations (in English) of the *Timaeus* include Taylor (1928), Cornford (1937), Archer-Hind (1973), Brisson (1994), Zeyl (2000), Lee (2008), and Waterfield (2008). Ancient commentaries include Plutarch (1976), Calcidius (2016), and Proclus (2007–2017). Cornford's classic (1937) commentary is still widely cited, despite significant shifts in scholarly attitudes toward the dialogue. For example, scholars now take seriously aspects of the dialogue that Cornford was quick to dismiss as mythical, and so not to be taken literally, or that he viewed as for the most part derivative of other thinkers, such as the Greek medical writers. See Betegh 2009 and Burnyeat 2005 for recent approaches to myth in the *Timaeus*. Recent treatments of the philosophically rich accounts of health and disease in the *Timaeus* include Gill (2000), Grams (2009), Lautner (2011), and Prince (2014).

2 The phrase "human nature" appears four times in the *Timaeus* (29d1, 42a2, 77a2–4, 90c2–3), and I am not challenging the idea that human beings share some distinctive features on account of which they are all human, as opposed to some other type of living being. The question remains how weighty a notion of "nature" is at play here. In what respects do human beings differ from other animals and the gods, and what is the normative or other significance of these differences?

3 In particular, male human beings are the first mortal creatures crafted by the gods, and as such they are the only kind of mortal being produced solely

by divine craft, without the influence of the disorderly motions associated with mortal embodiment.

4 Broadie (2012) calls Timaeus' claim that we are made up of contrary things, immortal and mortal, "the paradox of human nature" (87). Note that human beings share this paradoxical nature with all nonhuman animals, because all mortal creatures (with the exception of plants) consist of both mortal and immortal parts.

5 For another discussion of craft in late Plato, see Verity Harte's contribution to this volume (ch. 16).

6 Why are there three types of mortal beings, and why are they categorized based on where they live (39e–40a)? The bodies of the gods are made of fire, and so Timaeus seems to associate the four types of living beings (one immortal, three mortal) with the four simple bodies (fire, earth, air, and water). Perhaps soul needs to penetrate all four types of bodies in order for the cosmos to be complete. Similar divisions of animals appear in Plato's *Politicus* (264d–e) and Aristotle's *Topics* (6.6, 143a34–b2).

7 See the last paragraph of section III for discussion of one way we might resolve this tension.

8 Timaeus' strategy of explaining how foolishness and vice emerge in a cosmos crafted by good gods can be seen as a way of responding to a version of the problem of evil.

9 Translations are from Zeyl 2000, with occasional modifications.

10 E.g., 32c1, 40a6, 42e9, 48a1–55d8, 62d4, 92c6. In addition, Timaeus frequently refers to the activity of the gods in crafting the world and what it contains as "ordering" (*diakosmein*, 24c4, 37d5, 69c1, 75d7; *katakosmein*, 47d6, 88e3; or simply *kosmein*, 53b1).

11 Timaeus indicates that the world was already visible before the Demiurge ordered it: "he took over all that was visible" (πᾶν ὅσον ἦν ὁρατὸν παραλαβών, 30a3–4). This is surprising, given that the goal of making the cosmos perceptible, and in particular visible and tangible, explains why the god crafted it out of fire and earth at *Timaeus* 31b.

12 See Broadie 2012 for an illuminating comparison between the cosmology of the *Timaeus* and the creation theology of the Abrahamic tradition, according to which God creates the world *ex nihilo* (7–12).

13 This is not an honorific. The same word is used throughout Plato's corpus to refer to any ordinary craftsman (e.g., *Apology* 22d6, *Protagoras* 322c7).

14 Menn 1995: 6.

15 For an in depth discussion of the connection between the Demiurge and order, see Johansen 2004: ch. 4.

16 There is debate among scholars about whether this passage rules out *nous* existing apart from soul. Hackforth (1936) and Menn (1995) argue that this restriction applies only to things that come to be (*genesthai*), and so does not rule out identifying the Demiurge as intelligence (*nous*) that exists apart from soul. An alternative view is to identify the Demiurge as the *nous* of the world soul. Cornford (1937) raises, but does not fully commit to, this interpretation (38–9). Carone (2005a) provides a recent defense of the view (42–6). Scholars agree that the Demiurge either is, or possesses, *nous*. *Timaeus* 47e4 refers to the cosmos as "what has been crafted by *nous*," and this fits with the identification of *nous* with the cause of mixture in the *Philebus* (31a).

17 The Greek word translated here "complete" (*teleion*) can also mean "perfect" or "final" (referring to an end that is not pursued for the sake of a further end). Cf. *Phil.* 20d1–2 and Aristotle, *N.E.* I 1097a25–b6, where the adjective *teleion* serves as a criterion for the happy human life.

18 It is not clear in what sense intelligible living things and generated living things are both "living," given that intelligible living things are changeless, whereas the souls of generated living things move themselves and the bodies they inhabit. For the question of how to think of both intelligible living things and generated living things as living, see Meinwald in this volume (ch. 13).

19 At *Timaeus* 46d–e, Timaeus contrasts beautiful and good things produced by intelligence (καλῶν καὶ ἀγαθῶν, 46e4) with the disorderly result of chance (τὸ τυχὸν ἄτακτον, 46e5). Cf. *Grg.* 506d and *Phil.* 26b.

20 I capitalize Necessity here in order to distinguish this tendency toward disorder from other forms of necessity potentially at work in the *Timaeus*. For example, at 31b–32a Timaeus seems to appeal to a form of mathematical necessity to explain the construction of the cosmos out of four primary bodies. He does not similarly associate this mathematical notion of necessity with a tendency toward disorder – quite the opposite! Johansen (2004) argues that there are two forms of necessity present in the *Timaeus*, what he calls hypothetical and simple (or material) necessity (145–8).

21 Why need the three types of mortal creatures, all of which are nonhuman animals, possess immortal souls at all? Only the immortal soul is capable of intelligence, and it seems also of non-ideal forms of cognition.

22 The natural, orderly motions of the immortal soul are perfectly circular. At 43a–b, Timaeus identifies disorderly motions as rectilinear motion in six directions.

23 Including both the Demiurge and the subordinate gods to which the Demiurge delegates the task of crafting the mortal parts of human nature. I discuss the significance of these two levels of divine craft in what follows.

24 Two ends are in tension when they cannot both be fulfilled completely. To achieve one, you must accept less of the other. I would like to thank Richard Kraut for suggesting this formulation.

25 The limitation of the Demiurge's craftsmanship raises a puzzle about the crafting of the four simple bodies, because the Demiurge gives them their distinctive structures (53a–c), and yet they are not immortal but are regularly destroyed, and three of the four kinds can be transformed into one another (54b–d). Rather than identifying the simple bodies as independent products of the Demiurge's craft, we can view the ordering of these bodies as a stage in crafting the body of the cosmos as a whole, which is immortal (32a–b). Cf. 69b8–c2: "All of these things [i.e., earth, water, air, and fire] the god first gave order to (διεκόσμησεν), and then out of them he proceeded to construct (συνεστήσατο) the universe." The same sort of move would not work in the case of mortal creatures, because they are not (merely) parts of a larger, indestructible whole.

26 It is not entirely clear whether mortal creatures beyond the first generation come to be through divine craft, reproduction, or some combination of the two. The gods craft both male and female sex organs, thus making sexual reproduction possible (91a–d). The gods also craft aspects of human bodies in anticipation of the needs of wild animals that would come to be in future generations, suggesting that the human body contains a blueprint for the bodies of all nonhuman animals (76d8–e4). It is not clear why this foresight would be necessary if the gods directly crafted the mortal body appropriate for any given immortal soul. On the other hand, the descriptions of the mortal bodies of various nonhuman animals suggest the direct operation of divine craft activity: "The god placed a greater number of supports under the more mindless beings so that they might be drawn more closely to the ground" (92a3–4).

One issue with reproduction as an explanation of how mortal beings come to be is that it makes reference to unintelligent causes, such as sexual desire, rather than divine, or even human, craft. This complicates

Timaeus' argument near the beginning of the speech that "[the cosmos] is a work of craft, modeled after that which is changeless" (29a7–b1).

27 In addition to crafting a mortal body that suits the condition of each immortal soul, the subordinate gods may also have the additional task of punishing immortal souls for their transgressions. Timaeus describes reincarnation in the form of a water-dwelling animal as a "penalty for ignorance" (δίκην ἀμαθίας, 92b7). Kamtekar (2016) argues that in the *Timaeus*, reincarnation is both a direct consequence of an individual's choices and a method of divine punishment for wrongdoing (127–30).

28 I identify completing the cosmos as the gods' primary end, because this is their explicit motivation for crafting the first generation of human beings.

29 Broadie (2012) claims that the immortal souls of human beings are "essentially oriented toward mortal embodiment and moral responsibility for embodied action" (84). She observes that the precarnate life of immortal souls is preoccupied with "preparation for mortal embodiment" (88). While I agree that the education of immortal souls prior to mortal embodiment prepares them for their future life, I disagree that it is ultimately for the purpose of their mortal embodiment in particular. Instead, this education provides immortal souls with the possibility of escaping mortal embodiment and returning to their original home in the stars.

30 I would like to thank Jason Rheins for suggesting this picture.

31 See Fronterotta 2007, Pitteloud 2019, and Betegh 2020 for discussion of the composition and structure of the immortal soul in the *Timaeus*.

32 The Demiurge states that each immortal soul receives the "same initial birth" (41e3–4), but this is compatible with differences in purity between the immortal souls themselves. It is not clear how to reconcile the attribution of responsibility for moral failing to individual immortal souls with Timaeus' later declaration that "no one is willfully bad" (86d7–e1).

33 I focus on Timaeus' description of the body of the cosmos, because he does not describe the bodies of the gods contained within the cosmos in any detail. The Demiurge crafts the bodies of the gods, and so they cannot be undone by disease, old age, or death due to the guarantee of the Demiurge's will (41a–b). The cosmos is invulnerable to these marks of mortality for the additional reason that it contains everything, so there is nothing that can attack it from without.

34 In the rest of this paragraph, I focus on the construction of human bodies, but any mortal body exposes the immortal soul to similar challenges. The differences between the mortal bodies of human beings and those of nonhuman animals are due to differences in the condition of the immortal soul. For example, the gods must give the heads of land animals elongated shapes, in order to accommodate the distorted orbits of individual immortal souls (91e–92a).

35 The second, more detailed, account of the human body contains many additional examples of ways in which the gods mitigate the effects of disorderly motions on the immortal soul (69c–81e). For example, they build a neck to separate the immortal soul from the mortal soul, which is a further source of disorderly motions (69e).

36 Zeyl (2000) points out that the *Timaeus* differs from the *Republic* in treating spirit and appetite as two parts of a distinct, mortal kind of soul created by the lesser gods (lxxviii–lxxix), and yet he speculates that the gods make the mortal parts by adapting the immortal soul to perform the functions of the body (footnote 155). Carpenter (2008) similarly argues that we should not view the mortal soul as distinct from the immortal soul, but rather as "one way the immortal soul manifests itself" when embodied in a mortal body (47). To my mind, this interpretation does not take seriously enough Timaeus' account of the crafting of the mortal soul by the lesser craftsmanship of the subordinate gods. According to this account, the subordinate gods craft a distinct product, the mortal soul, not simply additional capacities for the same, immortal soul crafted by the Demiurge: "And within the body they build another kind of soul as well, the mortal kind" (69c7–8). Carpenter (2008) also argues that the mortal soul is not mortal in the sense of "dying" but rather means "concerned with the dying bit" (46), which requires interpreting the adjective "mortal" as ambiguous in the *Timaeus*.

The possibility that mortal and immortal souls are more distinct than scholars have generally supposed complicates the question of how the soul relates to the body in the *Timaeus*; for example, the body may have a different relationship with the mortal soul than it does with the immortal soul. For a recent debate about how to understand the soul–body relationship in the *Timaeus*, see Carone 2005b and Fronterotta 2007.

37 The two parts of the mortal soul also have different characteristic motions from one another and are located in different parts of the body, so one

might question the unity of the mortal soul itself. Similarly, one could question the unity of the mortal body, which also has separable parts. These questions do not undermine the strong unity of the immortal soul and its distinctness from both the mortal soul and the mortal body. Even though the immortal soul has "parts" (e.g., the circles of the same and the different), these are bound together by the will of the Demiurge. By contrast, the immortal soul will separate at death from all of the mortal parts to which it is temporarily bound.

38 Cf. 91a1–3, where Timaeus states that the gods "fashioned the desire for sexual union, by constructing one ensouled living thing in us as well as another one in women." Here, the gods construct a new living being, which possesses some sort of mortal soul, in order to accommodate a new desire. Similarly, I suggest they construct the two parts of the mortal soul, spirit and appetite, to accommodate the psychic activities required for living a mortal life.

39 See Brisson 1997, O'Brien 1997, Lautner 2005, Fletcher 2016, and McCready-Flora 2018 for recent debate about the account of sense perception in the *Timaeus*, including the relationship between sense perception and the immortal and mortal kinds of soul.

40 Cf. the reference to the true and primary nature of the soul in *Rep.* X 611a–d.

41 Cf. Kamtekar 2016: "Yet the idea that the human soul's reincarnation into nonhuman animals depends on our character and intellectual qualities ... undermines the absolute difference between humans and other animals that might be suggested by the claim that human beings alone are rational, other animals non-rational" (130). I argue in this section that the account of reincarnation in the *Timaeus* undermines any fundamental distinction between human nature and the nature of nonhuman animals, including one based on rationality.

42 Cf. Carpenter 2008: "Psychically (or psychologically), in both character and intellect, animals are identical to confused, ignorant human beings" (51).

43 29d1, 42a1–2, 77a3–5, 90c2–3.

44 42d, 51e, 68d, 71e, 75b, 76e, 88a–b, 90d.

45 29c–d, 51e, 68d3, 71e3.

46 There is no indication that the eternal model of the cosmos contains plants, and unlike the three mortal kinds, plants do not possess an

immortal soul. The subordinate gods craft plants independently of the Demiurge by producing a mortal soul (corresponding to the appetitive part of the mortal soul in human beings) and weaving it together with a mortal body. Carpenter (2010) argues that plants bear a relation to the world soul that is analogous to the relation a human being's appetite bears to their immortal soul. In Fletcher 2016, I challenge the view that in the *Timaeus* sense perception always requires an immortal, rational soul, a crucial premise of Carpenter's argument.

47 Most directly, at 76d8–e1, Timaeus says the gods understood that "women and wild animals would come to be from men" (ἐξ ἀνδρῶν γυναῖκες καὶ τἆλλα θηρία γενήσοιντο). The use of the gendered "men" indicates that Timaeus regards the first generation of mortal creatures as male, rather than sexless, despite the fact that the gods do not craft either male or female sex organs until after the generation of women (91a–d).

48 This passage also occurs right before Timaeus describes the origin of women (90e–91d).

49 Zeyl translates *akakōn* here as "simpleminded" and *euētheian* as "naiveté" (*ad loc.*). Regardless of how one translates these words, Timaeus describes the immortal soul's failure in this passage primarily in cognitive, rather than moral, terms.

50 See ἀνδρῶν at 91d7, which is also implied at 91e2–3 and 92a7–b2.

51 For further discussion of the ideal of godlikeness in Plato's dialogues, see Sedley 1999a, Armstrong 2004, and Mahoney 2005, as well as Betegh (ch. 8) and Obdrzalek (ch. 7) in this volume.

16. The Fourfold Classification and Socrates' Craft Analogy in the *Philebus*

Verity Harte

I. INTRODUCTION

Viewed from 40,000 feet, the *Philebus* has a clear structure, organized around two contests, each concerned with the competing claims of pleasure and intelligence to play the key role in determining the best human life. Here and in the dialogue, "pleasure" (*hēdonē*) and "intelligence" (*nous*) each does duty for a family of hedonic or intelligent states and activities (11b).[1] The dialogue's first contest is settled early, when Socrates and his principal discussant, Protarchus, agree that neither pleasure nor intelligence *is* the good, the best human life being some mixture of both in ways yet to be specified (20b–22c). The second contest, which continues to the end of the dialogue, is framed in light of this agreement and considers which of pleasure and intelligence is more akin to and more responsible for whatever does constitute the good of such a mixed life (22c–e). At the close of the dialogue, after a brief sketch of the constituents of the best human life, five good-making features of that life are ranked (66a–c). No form of intelligence or pleasure ranks higher than third, but every variety of intelligence is more highly ranked than any form of pleasure. Only certain forms of pleasure feature in the ranking at all, others being excluded from the life as inimical to happiness.

Work on this chapter benefited from comments upon presentations to a Chicago Area workshop organized by the Editors and to the 42nd Annual Ancient Philosophy Workshop at Trinity University, San Antonio, Texas. In addition, I am deeply grateful for feedback on an earlier draft from the Editors and from Liz Asmis, Rachel Barney, Amber Carpenter, M. M. McCabe, David Sedley, Justin Vlasits (and, through his agency, Zhe Wang), and Raphael Woolf.

While this overarching structure is clear, in close up, the *Philebus* is a puzzle. Famously compared to "a gnarled and knotted old oak-tree" (Bury 1897: ix), its granular organization seems at best opaque, at worst a loose aggregation of topics only tangentially related. Widely agreed to be among Plato's later writings, alongside his *Sophist, Statesman, Timaeus, Critias,* and *Laws,* it is unique amongst these peers in having Socrates as lead speaker. This "return of Socrates" seems well suited to the dialogue's ethical focus on the character of the best human life.[2] But this suitably Socratic project can seem either enriched or engulfed – according to one's persuasion – by having grafted onto it the obscure methodological and metaphysical preoccupations of Plato's old age.

In this chapter, I shall take up one piece of this puzzle. My focus will be the first move that Socrates makes in the dialogue's second contest: his fourfold classification of "all the things now in the universe" (23c4) into four broad forms (*eidē*) or kinds (*genē*):[3] what is without limit (the *apeiron*), limit (*peras*), mixtures of these two (the *meikton*), and the cause of said mixtures (*aitia*). Typically treated largely independently of the rest of the dialogue as a window onto Plato's late ontology, the passage (23b–27c) has preoccupied scholars as to whether its use of two, probably Pythagorean-inspired terms – "*peras*" (limit) and "*apeiron*" (without limit) – is or is not consistent with Socrates' use of these terms earlier in the dialogue and as to its implications for Plato's "later theory of forms."[4] I will make the case that, whatever its broader horizons, Socrates' classification proves to be very specifically tailored to the context and project of the dialogue in which it appears and that obscure aspects of its metaphysics emerge more clearly when seen in this light.[5]

There is a methodological moral here: Plato's dialogues are carefully constructed unities such that it is always worth investing time to consider how local context may shed light on seemingly extraneous obscurities. There also proves to be a striking continuity in the Socratic approach to ethical investigation across the corpus that may go further to explain the character's late return. The continuity involves his use of analogies from the crafts (*technai*), especially for virtuous activity.[6] I will argue that Socrates' fourfold classification in the *Philebus* is directed toward an analysis of the metaphysics of craft objects and that, in developing and explaining the classification, Socrates puts in place, without directly defending, material for an analogy drawn from the craft of medicine. According to this analogy, as health stands to body, so stands to soul that good condition of soul responsible for human happiness; further, as medicine stands to health, so stands some as yet unidentified craft to the relevant good condition of soul.[7] In this way, the *Philebus* makes distinctive progress toward articulating a framework for the recognizably Socratic and historically influential idea of a craft of human living.[8]

"Craft" will be my routine translation of the Greek term "*technē*," for which alternatives might be "art," "skill," or "expertise." In general, a *technē* may be thought of as an organized body of knowledge oriented toward some kind of good or benefit. In the *Philebus*, the notion seems strikingly broad. It includes evidently productive crafts, both familiar (medicine or carpentry, 56b) and less familiar (a divine intelligence argued to be responsible for the organized cosmos, 28a–31a).[9] But it also extends to forms of knowledge without obvious practical product external to themselves, such as mathematics, perhaps even dialectical knowledge.[10] I take such breadth not to weaken the force of talk of a *craft* of living, but to point to the very wide range of knowledge that Plato takes to have potential import or benefit for human living.[11] If I am right in my account of the project of Socrates' classification, the diversity and seeming abstraction of some of the topics that he and Protarchus take up in the dialogue is itself evidence of this.

II.   THE PROJECT OF SOCRATES' CLASSIFICATION

Prior to their second contest, and in response to certain general puzzles regarding the compatibility of unity and complexity, Socrates had advanced a method, attributed to "some Prometheus" and credited with all discoveries pertaining to craft (*technē*) (16c–17a). Importantly, this method is premised on a characterization of reality, passed on to us by "the ancients," according to which "whatever things are said to be are made up of one and many, having limit (*peras*) and lack of limit (*apeiria*) naturally together within them" (16c9–10). Mention is made here of two of the four forms that Socrates will posit when, embarking on their second contest, he advances an initial fourfold classification of all the things now in the universe, as follows.

> (I) SOC : Let us divide all the things that now are in the universe into two, or rather, if you will, into three.
>
> PRO : With a view to what, might you say?
>
> SOC : Let's take up certain of our recent points.
>
> PRO : Which ones?
>
> SOC : We were saying, were we not, that the god had revealed that the things that are possess both limit and lack of limit?[12]
>
> PRO : Indeed.
>
> SOC : Then let us posit this pair as two of the forms, and as the third some one thing that is a mixture resulting from both these two. But I am, as it seems, a ridiculous sort of person, distinguishing according to forms and counting them up.
>
> PRO : What do you mean, my good chap?
>
> SOC : There seems to me need in addition of a fourth kind in turn.
>
> PRO : Say which.
>
> SOC : Consider the cause of the mixing together of these in relation to each other and posit this as my fourth in addition to those three. (23c4–d8)

It seems perverse not to take Socrates' back reference to signal that "*peras*" and "*apeiron*" are here intended for use in just the same way as they earlier featured in the ancients' characterization of reality, though much scholarly ink has been expended on whether and how this could be so.[13] With regard to the earlier passage, it is important to distinguish the *method* from the *characterization of reality* on which the method is based. Socrates' back reference is not to the *method*, but to the *characterization*. As such, it gives us little to go on, since, in truth, the terms were merely *mentioned* earlier. But, for this very reason, the implied continuity is not impugned.[14]

This is one point of continuity with the earlier passage. A second is methodological. I take passage (I) to give clear indications that Socrates is following the method earlier attributed to some Prometheus.[15] In generally describing that method, Socrates had indicated a process that begins with positing one, overarching form, then identifies two or some other number of subforms of that first form, continuing in this way with each posited subform until the precise number of subforms is identified and known (16d–e). Amongst the indications that, in embarking on his own classification, Socrates is enacting this earlier method is the fuss that he makes in passage (I) about the number of forms he is positing. A central feature of Socrates' earlier characterization of the method was stress on the importance of counting the forms posited.

It is true that Socrates' procedure does not well match his *general* description of the earlier method, for he does not begin by identifying one, overarching form. However, Socrates' procedure is nevertheless a version of that method, one comparable to a subsequent illustration of that method in discovery mode using the example of Theuth and literacy (18b–d). "Theuth" was said to be the name given in Egypt to the divine figure that first identified and articulated the phonetic elements of speech required to produce a phonetic alphabet for Greek and, in so doing, both discovered and baptized "*grammatikē*," the craft of literacy, a thorough command of which enables a person to read and write. Socrates described how Theuth went about this task, first identifying three forms of phoneme (vowels, semi-vowels, and mutes), next identifying the varieties of these forms of phoneme (subforms of vowel etc.), before finally identifying *stoicheion* (letter or phonetic element) as the overarching single form for the entire domain.[16] Like Socrates' four forms, the first results of Theuth's classificatory activity are intermediate forms.

This is a point of similarity with Theuth. There are several points of dissimilarity, but none need undermine the methodological parallel. Socrates and Protarchus' classification is certainly very much incomplete by comparison. In the discussion of the four forms of their classification, there is little explicit identification of sub-forms. Socrates does, however, make a point of identifying each of the dialogue's contestants – pleasure, intelligence, and the victorious mixed life – as apt for classification into one of the four forms; and, in the subsequent, lengthy examination of pleasure that occupies much of the remainder of the dialogue, several subforms of pleasure are also identified (most explicitly at 32b–c). Such integration of Socrates and Protarchus' admittedly incomplete classificatory moves into the dialogue's contest beyond their direct discussion of the four forms posited is grist to my mill.

The most striking indication of the incompleteness of Socrates and Protarchus' classification by comparison with that of Theuth is that there is no comparable identification of some single overarching form and no baptismal moment for some corresponding craft. Nevertheless, and with some qualifications I will articulate, my proposal is that, like Theuth, in embarking on their classification, Socrates and Protarchus undertake a process of discovery designed to establish the domain and intellectual program for a *technē*, a craft. What craft? Given the context, it should be pertinent to the dialogue's overall interest in the character of the best human life and the relative contributions of pleasure and intelligence to that character. It should, in brief, be a craft of human living. I defend this proposal further in what follows.

My proposal sets the framework for understanding Socrates' fourfold classification as a project tailored to the specifics of the dialogue's ethical project. But it is open to an obvious objection. Theuth was said to begin his classificatory work with project-specific voice (*phōnē*), available to him prior to alphabetization in the form of actual human speech (18b). Socrates, in contrast, takes as starting point *everything there is*: "all the things that now are in the universe" (23c4). Does not this general starting point suggest a different, broader project: the general classification of reality? So it is typically understood.

Socrates' general starting point *is* a point of disanalogy with Theuth. It can, however, be explained without compromising my proposal that Socrates' classification is no less tailored to the establishment of a *technē*, one pertinent to the dialogue's ethical project. First, that Socrates embarks on *a* classification of reality does not mean he takes them to arrive at *the* classification of reality, nor precludes his classification being tailored to some specific end.[17] Second, the generality of Socrates' starting point is arguably warranted by the specifics of their project and their contextual situation with respect to it. They have agreed, in the dialogue's first contest, that neither pleasure nor intelligence *is* the good, the best human life involving both of them. However, *what makes* such a mixed life good – in terms of the character or cause of its goodness – has not been identified. Taking the widest possible starting point is methodologically responsible inasmuch as it neither prejudges nor forecloses relevant avenues of exploration.

At the same time, Socrates' starting point is not *as general* as might appear. Socrates classifies "all the things that now are *in the universe*," using the Greek expression "*to pan*" for the natural world or cosmos, exactly as he will subsequently when he argues that the cosmos is well organized by wisdom (*sophia*) and intelligence (*nous*) (28c–30e).[18] This is the argument by which Socrates defends the classification of the family of contestants he advocates in the dialogue – intelligence (*nous*) – as belonging to the form or kind, cause. In arguing for this classification, he provides support for the possibility of regarding the natural cosmos as a macrocosmic model for the best human life and for regarding that life as an object of craftlike knowledgeable organization.[19]

Finally, the disanalogy of Socrates' (at least, somewhat) general starting point may reflect an actual disparity in starting position and argumentative object. Theuth began with voice in the form of actual human speech and, in articulating its phonetic elements, created the conditions for a craft, literacy, whose practical reality and achievement is evident to us with hindsight. He is not represented as having to argue for the appropriateness of a *technē* being envisaged for the project of literacy.[20] Socrates, by contrast, arguably has two distinct, but related tasks. His Theuth-like task is to identify the character and elements of the domain for understanding and enabling the best human life, as Theuth identified the character and elements of the domain for understanding and enabling reading and writing. But a prior task for Socrates is to secure the point that his domain is indeed an arena for craft.

This is the reason why the immediate result of Socrates' fourfold classification is articulation of the arena in which craft *in general* operates, a metaphysics of craft objects. The back reference we saw in (I) carries with it a constellation of connections to craft. The method that Socrates here deploys was earlier credited with all discoveries pertaining to craft (*technē*) (16c–17a) and, accordingly, fittingly ascribed to "some Prometheus" (16c6). In many versions of the Promethean Myth – including Plato's own in his *Protagoras* – the *technai* are counted gifts of Prometheus to human beings. That *method*, in turn, was premised on the *characterization of reality*, passed on by "the ancients," involving two of the four forms that Socrates first posits: *peras* (limit) and *apeiron* (lack of limit). In positing two forms central to the characterization of reality on which craft discovery is premised, Socrates embarks on a classification tailored to the conditions for craft expertise. I do not mean that he is focused on what makes a craft *expert*. Rather, he is focused on the general organization of pertinent aspects of reality, more specifically of the natural world, in which craft expertise finds an arena to operate. This serves the prior element of his twofold task.

Socrates' Theuth-like task will build upon the outcome of this prior element. By offering a *general* analysis of craft objects, broadly construed, Socrates has shown us what it would be for the best human life to be such an object. That it is so is something he will argue here at best indirectly and by analogy, though the implication is secured when he immediately classifies their victorious life as of the relevant kind (27d). Note that, while this outcome points to the existence of a craft of human living, it does not follow that this craft is something that Socrates and Protarchus exercise in pursuing the method to establish that this is so. This too finds a parallel in Theuth. How much of the expertise Theuth displays in identifying and articulating the phonetic elements whose representation and interconnection makes possible reading and writing is itself part of literacy? It seems to me as open a question how much of the philosophical dialectic the dialogue exhibits should be regarded as integral to the craft of living it projects.

III.   A READING OF THE CLASSIFICATION

I begin with an overview of how I understand each of Socrates' four forms: what is without limit (the *apeiron*), limit (*peras*), mixtures of these two (the *meikton*), and the cause of said mixtures (*aitia*). I will then defend this understanding in more detail.

I take *mixtures* to be all and only what is brought into being by craft, intelligently caused.[21] As such, they are always goods of some kind. Varieties of intelligent causation or craft exhaust the family of *cause*. The "ingredients" of what is brought into being by craft – *what is without limit* and the *limits* imposed thereon – are not components of mixtures, after the fashion of building materials, still to be found in the finished product. Nor are they like ingredients for a recipe, even though ingredients may be transformed beyond recognition by the cooking process. Rather, they are introduced to us stepwise as elements for an analysis of what craft accomplishes: to achieve a stable, valuable order in what it brings into being, craft must impose craft-determined *limits* that eliminate excess and deficiency. To be *without limit*, I will argue, is to be excessive or deficient from the perspective of the end product or target benefit of some craft.

Taking a cue from Socrates' own lead example of a mixture, *health*, scholars have not infrequently illustrated the ontology of Socrates' classification with objects of craft or at least deliberately constructed objects.[22] Nor has it escaped notice that Socrates' own focus on craft examples suits the ethical project of the dialogue. What is distinctive in the view I propose is to take craft objects not just as especially pertinent *examples* of Socrates' mixtures, but to *exhaust* the kind.[23]

How can a classification tailored exclusively to craft objects be a classification of "all the things that now are in the universe"? Part of the answer is that the class of craft objects turns out to be larger than might first appear, not least once Socrates argues that the cosmos and all the good things found within it are no less a product of craft intelligence than are the recognized objects of human crafts (28a–31a). But there is also a methodological point: Socrates' classification can be exhaustive for his purpose without every aspect of reality being accounted for. For comparison: Theuth's triple of vowels, semi-vowels, and mutes can exhaust the aspects of vocal sound pertinent to his project while leaving unclassified other aspects of sound (such as pitch).[24]

Support for treating the classification as exclusively oriented to craft is provided by Socrates' account of the fourth form, cause. Socrates assimilates cause to intelligent crafting, identifying the cause first as "what makes" (*to poioun*) and then as "what crafts" (*to dēmiourgoun*, 27b1), the latter a verb exclusively associated with craft production, including, of course, the divine crafting of the cosmos by the demiurge of Plato's *Timaeus*.

Socrates' fourth form, cause, is the only one of the four for which he provides a specific argument for its existence and its distinction from the three forms initially posited on ancient authority.

(II) SOC : ... Consider whether it seems to you necessary
that everything that comes to be comes to be as a result of some cause.

PRO : It seems so to me, certainly. How could anything come
to be absent this?

SOC : Then does the nature of what makes differ not at all from
the cause, except in name, and may what makes and the cause
be correctly said to be one?

PRO : They may.

SOC : And in turn we will find that what is made and what
comes to be differ not at all except in name, just as what
we recently said. Is that so?

PRO : Yes.

SOC : Then doesn't what makes always naturally lead,
whereas what is made follows it in coming to be?

PRO : Certainly.

SOC : Then too a cause and what is enslaved to the cause
with a view to coming to be are different and not the same.

PRO : What of it?

SOC : Then didn't the things coming to be and the things
from which they come to be furnish all three of our kinds?

PRO : Certainly.

SOC : But are we saying that what crafts all these is a fourth,
the cause, it having been adequately revealed as distinct
from those?

PRO : It is distinct. (26e2–27b3)

Socrates' argument has a subtle feature supporting the view
that the three other forms should also be seen through the lens of
intelligent crafting. When Socrates describes the cause as "what crafts
all these," context makes clear that this includes not only the resulting mixtures, but also the things from which they come to be, where
these are what is without limit and limits. Socrates has just described
these two as "enslaved to the cause."[25] I take this to mean their role in
intelligent crafting is to be understood as constitutive of these forms.

Before turning to the remaining three forms, I make one, more
general observation. In describing the fourth form in (II) as "what

crafts" or his third form in (I) as "some one thing that is a mixture resulting from both these two," Socrates' labels reveal a generally harmless, but potentially misleading slippage evident throughout the passage between characterizing the forms and characterizing the things in their extension. Limit or *peras* is on occasion characterized as "having limit" (e.g., 24e2). But this talk of "having limit" needs further clarification. For things in the extension of the form, limit, to *have* limit should not be understood as their *receiving* limit. What *receives* limit is what lacks it, the *apeiron*. Nor should it be understood as their being in *the condition of having received* limit, since it is mixtures that are in this condition. The sense in which things in the extension of the form, limit, *have* limit is that they are such as to *bring* limit to what lacks it. That is, they are themselves *limits*, the very limits to be found in the resulting mixture.[26]

Socrates offers three examples of mixtures: *health, music,* and *the seasons.* Of these, *health* is the lead example, inasmuch as we can trace its development as an example through all three forms, culminating – with some additional supplementation at this stage – in the characterization of "the nature of health as the correct combination of [limits]" (25e7–8), relevant ratios imposed upon *hotter* and *colder* – the lead examples of things without limit – and also *wetter* and *drier*.[27] (The list may also include: *more* and *fewer, quicker* and *slower,* and *greater* and *smaller* – Socrates' expanded list of things without limit at 25c5–11.)

Socrates' lead examples of things without limit (the *apeiron*) – *hotter* and *colder* – though not exclusive to *health* are evidently pertinent to *health.* Socrates does not clearly specify *examples* of limits (*peras*), as opposed to specifying *characteristics* of limits. But with *health* in mind, I will advance as candidate examples: ratios such as *equal temperature* (or *equal parts hot*) and *double in temperature* (or *two parts hot to one part cold*). Socrates' approach seems broadly consistent with contemporary approaches to health and disease.[28]

An understanding of *peras* and *apeiron* should make clear why Socrates gives examples of things without limit in comparative form: *hotter*, not *hot*. It should also determine whether the fact that they are repeatedly mentioned *as a pair – hotter* and *colder* – is of significance for their understanding.

Socrates makes four central claims about *hotter* and *colder* as examples of what is without limit:

1. More (*mallon*) and less (*hētton*) permanently reside within them (e.g., 24a9, b4–5).
2. The terms "exceedingly" ("*sphodra*") and "slightly" ("*ērema*") have the same force as "more" and "less" in their application to them (24b10–c2).
3. They preclude an end or completion (*telos*) (e.g., 24b7–8).
4. They preclude definite quantity (*poson*) and due measure (*metrion*) inasmuch as they "always advance and do not stand fast" (24d4) (24c3–d5).

Socrates then sums up his general characterization of what is without limit:

> (III) However many things[29] are evident to us as becoming both more and less and as admitting exceedingly and slightly and too much (*to lian*), it is necessary to place all these within the kind (*genos*) of what is without limit (*to apeiron*), as into a single thing, according to the previous statement we made regarding the necessity of gathering together so far as we can as many things as are scattered and split up and giving the seal of some single nature, if you recall. (24e7–25a4)

He follows this with the first of two brief remarks he makes over the course of the passage specifically about the second form, limit (*peras*). I quote both remarks in full.

> (IV) Surely then things that do not admit these [the above characteristics of what is without limit, more and less and so on],

but admit all the opposites of these, first, the equal or equality, after equal, the double and every case of number in relation to number or measure to measure, in reckoning all these together included in the limit (*to peras*), we would seem to do this well, don't you think? (25a6–b3)

(V) The [kind] of the equal and double and however many put a stop to the opposites differing/disagreeing (*diaphorōs echonta*) with one another, and by imposing number cause them to be commensurate (*summetra*) and harmonious (*sumphōna*). (25d11–e2)

In (IV), it is not clear whether "the equal," "the double," and so on are offered as sample limits or as characteristic features of limits – as more and less are characteristic features of what is without limit.[30] Either way, I take *equal temperature* and *double in temperature* to be contextually appropriate sample limits consistent with Socrates' point here. Either they count as pertinent examples of "equal" and "double" or they count as pertinent examples of what equal and double characterize.[31]

This is pretty much all the direct data we have from the dialogue about *peras* and *apeiron* as a pair: how should we interpret it? One common understanding of being without limit is as lack of determinacy.[32] Take (4): Things without limit preclude definite quantity; "they always advance and do not stand still." It would be implausible to think any hotter thing must always be *increasing* its temperature or that any temperature it has is not definite. But it seems correct that there is no *particular* determinate temperature such that it is true *of that temperature* that, in having it, one thing is hotter than another. It is in this sense that *hotter* may be understood to be indeterminate. Of course, so too may *hot*, so that this interpretation does not make clear why Socrates gives examples in comparative form. But the chief drawback of this common interpretation – fatal, if genuine – is that it does not evidently distinguish *peras* from *apeiron*. Take my candidate example of limit, *equal in temperature*. This too is indeterminate insofar as there is no specific temperature such that, in having that temperature, something (or some pair of things) counts as equal in temperature. We must try again.

"*Poson*" in (4), translated "definite quantity," corresponds to the answer to a question. How much? *So* much. In some contexts, the answer will be: just the right amount. And while "*poson*" does not itself have evaluative overtones of this sort, "*metrion*," translated "due measure" and mentioned alongside definite quantity in (4), does have such overtones. Indeed, this is a pattern in the evolution of Socrates' characterization of what is without limit. Evolve it does. He begins with quantitative terms that are not evaluative – "more," "less," "definite quantity" – and then he adds evaluative terms. A second example of this is his addition of "exceedingly" (*sphodra*) and "slightly" (*ērema*) in (2) alongside (1) "more" and "less." When something is *sphodron* it is vehement, violent, *excessive*. This progression is underlined by Socrates' addition of "too much" (*to lian*) in his summary in (III).

Socrates' point in (3), that things without limit do not admit an end or completion (a *telos*), is ambiguous between a quantitative and an evaluative reading. First introduced in the context of (1) – more and less permanently residing in *hotter* and *colder* – this might suggest lack of a *quantitative* end: the range of more and less extending to infinity. But a *telos* can also be a *goal*, setting standards for accomplishment, a target one might exceed or undershoot. So understood, we have a good explanation of Socrates' use of comparatives, *hotter* and *colder*. In Greek, the comparative form can be used to indicate excess and deficiency, pointing to what is *too hot, too cold*.[33] To be *in excess* or *deficient*, relative to some implicit target, is the understanding of being without limit that I propose we are to have arrived at by the time Socrates has completed his explanation.

A constraint on our interpretation is that our understandings of *peras* and of *apeiron* should complement each other, insofar as "*apeiron*" is a privative term formed to indicate lack of *peras*. This is why the failure of the *indeterminacy* reading to discriminate one from the other is fatal to that view if sound. How does my own proposal fare? *Equal temperature* does not have the connotations of excess or deficiency that Greek associates with the comparative *hotter*. But it is also not obvious how equality of temperature might *counteract* such excess or deficiency and, as (V) proposes, bring about commensurate harmony.

There is, however, one significant and pertinent contrast between Socrates' examples of limits and of things without limit, which emerges if we focus on his having repeatedly given us *pairs* as examples, and pairs, like *hotter* and *colder*, whose members are *opposed* to each other. Take a pair, <*a, b*> in which *a* is hotter than *b* and, correspondingly, *b* colder than *a*. *a* can change its temperature – across some range of temperatures – without ceasing to be hotter than *b*, as can *b* without ceasing to be colder than *a*. Contrast the pair <*c, d*> in which *c* and *d* are *equal in temperature*. Neither *c* nor *d* can change its temperature independently of the other and maintain its relation to the other. Putting this point somewhat figuratively, we might say that pairs such as <*c, d*> work as a team, whereas pairs such as <*a, b*> simply oppose one another.

This comes pretty close to what Socrates *does* say, in (V). Limits, he says, stop opposites "differing/disagreeing" with one another. My alternative translations reflect the fact that, like the verb "differ" in English, Greek "*diapherein*" can indicate *disagreement*, being at variance in a hostile sense. And surely it does here: It would be absurd to suggest that anything can prevent opposites simply being *different* from one another. The alternative translation allows for a way in which the teamwork I am suggesting is characteristic of limits can be associated with the good results that Socrates suggests in (V): producing commensurateness and harmony amongst elements in which, previously, there was simply strife.

Teamwork, of course, makes sense only in the context of some given project. This is one good reason why Socrates does not in fact give this general characterization of limits (V) until *after* he has begun to illustrate his third kind, mixtures. This is the last of the four I need to bring under the heading of my overall reading.

The bulk of Socrates' discussion of mixtures is taken up by elaborating examples. Three are detailed: *health, music,* and *the seasons* or good climatic conditions generally.

> (VI) SOC : In cases of sickness, did not the correct combination
> of these [limits] beget the nature of health?
>
> PRO : Absolutely.
>
> SOC : But in high and low and swift and slow, being without limit,
> did not these same things [limits] arising therein at once both
> produce limit and establish music in its entirety most
> perfectly?[34]
>
> PRO : Most beautifully indeed.
>
> SOC : And moreover, arising in cases of storms and heatwaves
> [these same things] do away with what is much in excess and
> unlimited (*to . . . polu lian kai apeiron*), whereas they effect what
> is both measured and commensurate.
>
> PRO : Indeed.
>
> SOC : Then it is surely out of these [limits] that we have come to
> have the seasons and all fine climatic conditions, when both
> unlimited things and things having limit have been mixed
> together?
>
> PRO : Of course. (25e7–26b4)

I restrict myself to a couple of observations. The first is that, though Socrates' specification of the domain in which *music* arises as "high and low and swift and slow" constitutes an exception to his use of comparatives, it need not challenge the view that the *apeiron* is a domain of excess and deficiency. Socrates uses this clause to *qualify* these features: These are features upon which limits are imposed when "being without limit," that is, on my reading, when excessive or deficient.[35]

The second is that Socrates' exposition confirms that we should not think of mixing *peras* and *apeiron* as a process of constructing a mixture for which these are ingredients that persist as is in the resulting mixture. *Health* is not a carefully balanced proportion *of sickness*. Rather, *health comes to be* from conditions of sickness, when limits are imposed that *eradicate* the relevant excesses and deficiencies.[36] In his example of climate, Socrates makes explicit that limits "*do away with* the much in excess and unlimited." Socrates' construction in Greek (here mimicked in English, using a single article) strongly suggests that being *much in excess* and being *unlimited* is a unit, in line with my view that being in excess is a way of being unlimited.

What Socrates' three examples of mixtures have in common, consistent with his understanding of causation as intelligent crafting, is that each is something good that is an object of craft. I am not suggesting that Socrates thinks that the analysis he offers here is itself reason to suppose each of these is something good. Rather, the goodness of these mixtures is assumed and the examples offered as evident goods. Socrates' third example – *the seasons* and good climatic conditions generally – looks least like an object of craft to us. There is no obviously existing craft of *human*, skillful production of good climate (alas!). But Socrates will shortly argue that the universe ("the all") and beneficial conditions of it, specifically including the seasons (30c6), are products of divine intelligence. The retrospective character of this argument is further indication that, consistent with its Theuth-like exploratory character, Socrates' classification offers a developing picture. I will now take stock of that picture and point to the argument from analogy it portends.

IV.   SOCRATES' ARGUMENT FROM ANALOGY

Socrates, I have argued, is faced with a double task: a Theuth-like task of identifying the character and elements of the domain for a craft of human living, and in such a way as to secure the prior point that this is indeed an arena for craft. While his response to this challenge is by no means finished once he has articulated his four forms, important framework moves have been made.

Socrates has offered a general metaphysical analysis applicable to a diverse range of crafts. Indeed, he is about to generalize on the basis of his three chosen examples. This is at most suggestive as a claim to provide an analysis that will indeed serve for every craft, not least given the breadth of the notion of craft in the dialogue that I have noted. Nor has Socrates done anything much to *argue* for the applicability of this analysis to the examples of mixtures he has offered us: *health*, his lead example, along with *music* and *the seasons*. He may here rely on suitably related, near contemporary analyses.[37] Nevertheless, in offering a *general* analysis of craft objects, if the analysis is plausible, Socrates has shown what *would* be involved if the best human life were an object of craft and provided a framework for arguing that this is so.

That *health* is Socrates' lead example is no accident. First, though it is the object of a familiar craft, medicine, medicine's status as a craft was something contemporaneous medical authors, such as the Hippocratic author of *On the Art of Medicine*, felt a need to defend. This is a direct, if implicit point of comparison with Socrates' situation with respect to a craft of human living. Second, *health* is the leverage for an argument by analogy that Socrates advances, if not explicitly, then at least very close to the surface of what he says.

Socrates signals the implied analogy when, after characterizing his three examples in (VI), he gestures to a list of examples he is not mentioning:

> (VII) SOC: There are also countless others I fail to mention: such as beauty and strength, alongside health, and in turn very many other very fine conditions occurring in souls. For the goddess herself, my fair Philebus, looking on *hubris* and the general wickedness of all, there being no limit at all to the pleasures and surfeits amongst them, instituted law and order, since they have limit. And whereas you say she spoiled them, I say that, on the contrary, she has preserved them. But how does it seem to you, Protarchus?
> PRO: That's very much in accord with my mind, Socrates.
> (26b5–c2)[38]

Like others, I take the goddess that Socrates obliquely mentions here to be Aphrodite, the name we were earlier told that Philebus gives to what Socrates instead chose, out of reverence, to call "pleasure" (*hēdonē*) (12b–c). Philebus is the unrepentant hedonist from whom Protarchus took over the role of the discussant at the very start of the dialogue; he plays little spoken role in the work. He makes a rare appearance by name in (VII) to signal that Socrates is in the process of remaking his conception of pleasure, since Phileban pleasure brooks no limit (27e). In doing so, Socrates draws on Hesiod's genealogy, according to which Aphrodite is mother of Harmonia.[39]

While Socrates does not mention the Greek term "*harmonia*" here, understood as some kind of psychological attunement, *harmonia* is a very natural understanding of what he has in view as the analogue, in soul, to bodily *health*, *strength*, and *beauty*.[40] Indeed, when, later, Protarchus is invited to recall the mixed form of which these unmentioned "fine conditions of soul" are examples, he recalls it as the one in which Socrates placed *health* "and, I think, also *harmonia*" (31c10–11). Protarchus' hesitant addition both nods to the fact that *harmonia* was not mentioned and shows that Protarchus got the point.

Socrates at most here suggests that these "fine conditions of soul" will include, or possibly combine to form, the as yet unidentified condition of soul responsible for human happiness in the life involving pleasure and knowledge. Socrates' proposed argument by analogy is not meant to *entail* that the good life whose character and understanding they seek is an object of craft, subject to the analysis articulated, still less to spell out the life's character and elements. Rather, we should think of Socrates as having put in place a heuristic through which to explore the life's character and elements on the motivated presumption that there is a craft of human living.

Socrates' proposed argument by analogy does not play any role in establishing that the condition of soul their contest has targeted *is* a good. That this is so, that there *is* such a good, is a presumption of their contest, as was the goodness of *health*. The work of Socrates' analogy is to set a framework in which, analogously to *health*, this good too is understood to be an object of craft and hence as something that this general analysis of craft objects can help us investigate.

I close this section with some pointers to ways in which this general analysis does subsequently help them that can be seen even absent the context of a reading of the remainder of the dialogue. After identifying and agreeing on the four proposed forms, they next classify their contestants. The good life involving both pleasure and intelligence is agreed to be a mixture (27d). Pleasure, along with pain, is identified as being without limit (27e–28a). Intelligence is placed in the fourth kind, cause (28a–31a). This classification of their contestants is confirmation of the intended salience of the fourfold classification to their contest.

Socrates' manner of classification of the contestants, however, immediately gives the lie to the apparent reason why Protarchus readily agrees that the life involving pleasure and intelligence is of the kind, mixture.

> (VIII) SOC : Come, then: We proposed that the mixed life of both pleasure and wisdom won first prize, did we not?
>
> PRO : We did.
>
> SOC : Then we see, I suppose, both what this life is and of which kind?
>
> PRO : Of course.
>
> SOC : And we shall declare it part of the third kind, I think. For that [the third kind] is not mixed of just two but of all things without limit that have been bound by limit, so that this victorious life would correctly turn out part of it.
>
> PRO : Most correctly. (27d1–11)[41]

Calling the life that includes both pleasure and intelligence "mixed" is misleading.[42] It cannot be simply in virtue of *including* both pleasure and intelligence that the life is *thereby* a mixture of the sort the classification intends, one in which every possible type of excess and deficiency has been eliminated by the imposition of limit. Protarchus' assent to Socrates' misdirection is nevertheless instructive. It points to the mistake it would be to try to map the position of pleasure and intelligence as *ingredients in the life* on to the role of *peras* and *apeiron* as constituents of an analysis of the goodness of the life.

This is most obvious for intelligence, which, though an ingredient in the life, is classified not as lacking limit nor as limit, but as *cause*. But the same caution holds for pleasure *as an ingredient in the life*. It is true that pleasure, alongside pain, is here agreed – notably, by *Philebus* – to *lack limit*.[43] But the role of the imposition of limit, in the analysis we were offered, was to *eradicate* such lack of limit, such excess and deficiency. Any pleasures to be included as ingredients in the good life must have limit imposed upon them, exactly the task of the law and order instituted by Aphrodite, as Socrates says in (VII).

Rather than mapping out the position of pleasure and intelligence as already agreed ingredients of the best human life, the agreed classification of pleasure and intelligence instead points to important aspects of the argument ahead, as Socrates and Protarchus pursue their second contest. Concerning pleasure, Socrates and Protarchus will distinguish a class of pleasures that are distinctive in being measured – in having the characteristics of mixtures – and it is these "pure pleasures," as they are called, that earn a place in the victorious life (52c–d, 66c).

Like pleasure, varieties of intelligence will later be ranked in terms of purity (55c–59d). But there is no indication of a corresponding need to *limit* intelligence. This suggests, strikingly, that, though it is possible to be deficient in intelligence, *intelligence as such* is not vulnerable to excess or deficiency.[44] Intelligence does, however, play an important role in *limiting* the excess or deficiency of pleasure. This too is substantiated by what comes later. But we should not conclude from this that intelligence's role *as ingredient in the life* is exhausted by its role as causal agent in the life. If the value of intelligence were exhausted by this role, its value could look correspondingly instrumental. But the classification of intelligence as cause does not preclude its having independent value *as an ingredient* in its own right. Arguably, identifying such independent value is a central task of the dialogue's later examination of forms of intelligence.[45]

This, then, is a quick sketch of some central ways in which the fourfold classification provides a lens though which Socrates and Protarchus go on to explore the character and ingredients of the best human life in the remainder of the dialogue.

V.   CONCLUDING BROADER MORALS

On the reading I have offered, Socrates' fourfold classification is well suited to the overall project of the dialogue in which it appears and plays an important role in shaping the dialogue's second and principal contest. Nevertheless, no "craft of living" is ever mentioned in the dialogue. This is an aspect of the comparative incompleteness of Socrates and Protarchus' Theuth-like exploration: no baptismal moment for the corresponding craft. But why does the absence of such mention not vitiate the reading proposed? Alternatively put, if the defense of the reading I have offered is successful, why does Plato write it this way?

The dialogue has overall what one might call a "designed incompleteness." I do not mean that the dialogue itself *is* in fact incomplete or unfinished. But part of its finished design is to represent itself as beginning in the middle of a conversation (11a) and for its final words to find Protarchus offering to remind Socrates of the "little" that he says "remains" (67b). This idea of work that is left to be done is consistent with the general and familiar point that Plato does not write in such a way as to serve his reader his philosophical views on a plate; there is work for the reader to do.

But the designed incompleteness is also, more specifically, consistent with the Theuth-like exploratory character of their second contest that is part and parcel of the reading I have proposed. Socrates' fourfold classification *evolves* and the position that it represents is fully clear, if at all, only in hindsight. Further, the exploratory classification that this fourfold classification initiates continues, more or less directly and explicitly, until the examination of all the contestants classified within it is complete, with only the final decision of their contest remaining to be stated by means of the fivefold ranking.[46]

Of course, it is consistent with the dialogue being written in such a way as to *represent* an exploration that its characters undertake that its *author*, Plato, have a clear idea of where that exploration is intended to go, and I do not mean to deny this. But the use of the fourfold classification as a heuristic by means of which to investigate the character and elements of the best human life allows that what Plato is offering the reader as food for reflection is not thought by him to be a *complete* argument to its conclusions, both stated and unstated, let alone a demonstrative one. Aptly, given the context, that argument is to some extent for the reader herself to organize and construct.

The reading I have offered gives importantly *restricted* understandings of the four forms of Socrates' fourfold classification, notwithstanding its apparently general framing as a classification of "all the things now in the universe." It is thus unclear how – and whether – the classification can be used in tackling more general questions about Plato's late ontology often asked of it. Examples include: In which, if any, of the four kinds should *forms* be placed, however such forms may best be understood? Which, if any, of the four is home to forms' particular, perishable counterparts? This is not to say the classification makes no general contribution to our understanding of Plato's ontology. Undoubtedly, it does, especially in ways comparable to the *Timaeus* in regarding the natural world and its organized features as products of superhuman craft. But the reading I offer cautions against looking beyond the immediate project of the classification for an answer to all the questions about Plato's ontology we might want to see answered.

This outcome, I propose, is a feature of the reading, not a bug. Any disappointment engendered, if such there be, should be tempered by having a reading of the classification that makes it non-accidentally well suited to the context of the dialogue in which it appears.

NOTES

1 "*Hēdonē*" is typically used to capture the pleasure family. "*Nous*" is one of two terms regularly used to capture the intelligence family, along with "*phronēsis*" ("wisdom").

2 On Socrates' "renaissance", see Frede 1997: Appendix I.

3 Some might object to my talk of "form" (*eidos*) here as implying disputable continuity with discussions of forms in works such as *Phaedo* or *Republic*. But the continuity of vocabulary is Plato's and should, I think, be taken as a starting point without deciding in advance to privilege some contexts over others in understanding his use of the term. For recent reflection on Plato's use of "*eidos*" and "*genos*" in other, presumptively later works, see Muniz and Rudebusch 2018.

4 On the Pythagorean connection, see Huffman 1999, while Mourelatos 2016 highlights a broader context in early Greek Philosophy. Striker 1970 is the classic study of the *Philebus'* use of the terms "*peras*" and "*apeiron*." See, for example, Sayre 1983 for focus on Plato's late ontology.

5 Frede (1997: 184–221) emphasizes the pertinence of the classification to their contest, although we differ as to how, and to what degree, this is so. Cooper (1973) makes the dialogue's contest central to his understanding of the classification; I am very sympathetic to the project of this paper, though we differ in how we pursue it.

6 Examples abound in works such as *Apology, Charmides, Protagoras*, and others. On the craft analogy for virtue, see Barney 2021.

7 Cf. *Chrm.* 156d–157c, *Grg.* 464b–465e, and *Rep.* 444b–e.

8 By "Socratic" I refer simply to the characterization of that figure in Plato. The view that there is a craft of living (a *technē tou biou*) is picked up by later, Greco-Roman philosophers, being, for example, a mainstay of Stoicism (on which see Striker 1986).

9 Socrates here uses "*nous*" ("intelligence") and "wisdom" ("*phronēsis*" or "*sophia*"), not "*technē*," explicitly comparing familiar crafts, "medicine and every variety of wisdom (*sophia*)" (30b3–4). As cause, such intelligence "crafts" (*dēmiourgein*) the orderly universe (27b1), inviting obvious comparison with the demiurge or craftsman of Plato's *Timaeus*.

10 See *Phil.* 57c9–d2 for mathematics, even its "philosophical" forms, as *technai*. Regarding dialectic, the evidence is less clear, but, at 57e6–59b9, Socrates seems prepared to use "*technē*" interchangeably with "*epistēmē*" ("knowledge") for dialectic too.

11 For discussion of the ways in which Plato's approach to knowledge sits ill with a familiar contrast between "practical" and "theoretical" knowledge, see discussion in Harte 2018 and Lane 2018.

12 With Delcomminette (2006: 215) I treat the genitive "*tōn ontōn*" as possessive, not partitive.

13 Striker (1970) and Frede (1997) dispute continuity of use; Delcomminette (2006) finds continuity.

14 Much confusion has been engendered by failing to recognize as a *distinct* question how the use of the *pair* of terms "*peras*" and "*apeiron*" in the *characterization of reality* relates to singleton uses of "*apeiron*" as part of the *method*. I do not address this question here.

15 Both Frede (1997: 212) and Delcomminette (2006: 202–12) find correspondence of some degree with the earlier method. Meinwald (1998: 168) advances an important – if in my view defeasible – objection to such claims to correspondence.

16 I agree with Menn (1998) in regarding *stoicheion* as the overarching single form for Theuth's classification.

17 For a more general defense of this approach to the method Socrates outlines at 16c–17a, see Harte (forthcoming).

18 See "*to pan*" at, e.g., 29b10, c2 and "*kosmos*" at 29e1.

19 Johansen (2004) offers a complementary reading of the *Timaeus*. Though the *Philebus* otherwise eschews cosmology, the parallel is recorded again linguistically, at 64b6–8, when Socrates describes the discussion up to this, close-to-final point as having provided "a sort of bodiless cosmos for the good governance of an ensouled body."

20 In Plato's *Phaedrus* Theuth is reportedly called upon to defend the beneficial character of his recent invention, writing, by a skeptical Thamus (274c–275b). Such a call to defend its benefit (*ōphelia*, 274d7) may be tantamount to a call to defend its status as a *technē*.

21 Though Socrates describes mixtures as generated beings (26b8–9), I do not take this to restrict his focus to perishable individuals. Contrast Silverman 2002: 230–40. While a given instance of individual crafting may produce something perishable (*may*, but need not do so – witness

the permanence of the Timaean crafted cosmos), the *object* of a given craft may include its epistemic focus, and this will include imperishable forms.

22 Examples include Irwin's tea (1995a: 324) or, in my own earlier work, a bath (Harte 2002: 186–8).

23 Frede (1997: 184–6) is an instructive contrast, who, despite her emphasis on the classification's pertinence to their contest, takes Socrates' starting point of "all the things that now are in the universe" to signify an extension beyond the domain of craft objects that was the focus of the earlier method.

24 Arguably, Socrates drew attention to this when he earlier offered two distinct examples involving classification of sound (17b–18d, cf. Harte, forthcoming). Thanks to Justin Vlasits for suggesting the Theuth comparison. For a (controversial) example of something Socrates' classification may leave out, consider diseases. These are not mixtures and, while they may be constituted by excess and deficiency, it is not clear that diseases as such are classified as things without limit.

25 Cf. Delcomminette 2006: 249. I am indebted to Udit Bery for discussion of this passage.

26 In a manner somewhat parallel to the Aristotelian relation between form and form–matter composite, it is thus rather hard to distinguish *limits* from *mixtures*, save conceptually.

27 There is an issue of translation regarding 25e7–8. Contrast Frede (1993, *ad loc.*) – for whom *health* is here identified as the "right combination of [*the opposites*]" – and cf. related discussion in Frede 1997: 31, 192–3. Nothing large hangs on the difference, since limits are limits upon Frede's opposites: *hotter* and *colder* and so on. My preferred translation allows that *health* (as is plausible) may involve some *complex* of limits imposed upon various opposites.

28 That relevant relations between hot, cold, wet, and dry – or the related elements of earth, air, fire, and water – played a central role in many contemporary medical theories of disease is clear from the characterization of his opponents by the author of *On Ancient Medicine* (Schiefsky [2005: 63–4] dates the work to the late fifth century BCE). Compare the central role accorded to the four elements in the account of

the origin of diseases in Plato's *Timaeus* (81e6–82b7), said to be "obvious to everyone" (81e6).

29 Socrates uses a neuter plural without specifying noun. I supply "things", but this should be read with wide scope so as to include things characterized, characteristics, and actions.

30 Cf. Frede 1997: 190–1. At issue is whether "all these" toward the end of (IV) refers to "the equal . . . " or only to "things that do not admit [characteristics of what is without limit] . . . but admit . . . the equal or equality."

31 It is not necessary to assume (with, e.g., Frede 1997: 190–1) that if *equal* and *double* are examples of limits, limits must be abstract ratios as opposed to pertinent instances thereof, such as two parts hot to one part cold. It is a familiar point that contemporary Greek talk of some number – e.g., "four" – can refer to some abstract entity, (a/the) "quartet," but also to some quartet of items, such as four dice (cf. *Tht.* 154c3).

32 Gosling (1975: 185–206) distinguishes and evaluates three possible understandings of the pair. This indeterminacy reading (defended in different versions by Irwin 1995a: 324–5, Frede 1997: 187–90, Cooper 1973 [1999]: 151–2, and Delcomminette 2006: 216–30) is common to those who do not assume Socrates here points to a *continuum* of temperature, another popular reading. It may be relevant that temperature *does* afford a continuum, but I do not think what is without limit is plausibly *identified* with this continuum.

33 Noted by Delcomminette (2006: 227–8), but understood to be merely *one example* of what is without limit.

34 Following Diès 1941, against Burnet 1901–1907, vol. 2, at 26a3.

35 This restrictive reading of the participle clause is permissible, though not required.

36 The reference to sickness as the condition *from which health* comes to be does not require that disease be *identified with*, as opposed to being constituted by, what is without limit. Cf. n. 24.

37 For *music*, there is a gesture to this earlier when it exemplifies the method (17c–e), but caution is needed insofar as this earlier passage describes the structure of expert musical knowledge rather than providing a metaphysical analysis of the object so known. Socrates will argue that *the seasons* are crafted mixtures brought into being by divine intelligence (28a–31a), but he does not further defend the analysis of this process in

terms of the imposition of relevant limits upon excesses and deficiencies pertinent to climate.

38 At 26b10, I follow Striker 1970: 60–1 and Frede 1997: 32n. against both Burnet 1901–1907 and Diès 1941 to read "*echontōn*" with MS B.

39 I follow Diès 1941 in seeing Hesiodic genealogy at work here.

40 At *Phaedo* 93b, while rejecting the view that *soul itself* is a *harmonia*, Socrates relies on the plausibility of viewing *virtues* of soul as *harmoniai*.

41 At 27d7, I follow Diès 1941 against Burnet 1901–1907 to read: οὐ γὰρ δυοῖν τινοῖν ἐστι μικτὸν ἐκεῖνο.

42 Talk of mixture was used sparingly earlier in connection with the life (first, at 22a1–2), but indicating only that *both* pleasure *and* intelligence are involved in the best life. Its repetition here seems deliberate misdirection.

43 Philebus' reasoning that the good of pleasure requires endless increase (27e) seems as specious as Protarchus' move from the fact of the life involving a *mixture* of pleasure and intelligence as ingredients to its being a *mixture* arising from the imposition of *peras* upon the *apeiron*.

44 Thanks to Richard Kraut for this observation.

45 See Harte 2018.

46 For related discussion of this ranking, see Harte 2019.

17 Law in Plato's Late Politics

Rachana Kamtekar and Rachel Singpurwalla

Throughout his political works, Plato takes the aim of politics to be the virtue and happiness of citizens and the unity of the city. But whereas the *Republic* claims that this requires rule by philosophers (471c–473e), the *Laws* takes it to be achievable by the rule of law. It is commonly thought that Plato turns to law in the late dialogues due to his increased pessimism about the possibility of philosophical rule.[1] In fact, however, even Plato's earliest dialogues conceive of law as aimed at cultivating virtue, and of virtue as expressed in obedience to the law.

In the *Gorgias*, Socrates divides political expertise, which aims at the good of the soul and has an account of the means by which it produces this good, into two departments, legislation and justice (463e–465a), with legislation being the superior of the two (520b). Socrates' explicit parallel between these two expertises and the expertises that aim at the good of the body – gymnastics and medicine – indicates that the aim of legislation is to put and maintain the soul in a good condition, while the aim of justice is to correct souls that have gone wrong.

The *Apology* and *Crito* indicate that Plato sees a close connection between being a just person and obeying the law. In the *Apology*, Socrates presents himself as both an advocate of justice and as someone who opposes the unjust and illegal dealings of the city. He refuses, for example, to participate in the illegal (*paranomōs*, 32b4, *para tous nomous*, 32b6) mass trial of the generals of the battle of Arginousae,

We would like to thank David Ebrey, Zena Hitz, Richard Kraut, André Laks, Jeremy Reid, and Clerk Shaw for comments on previous drafts, as well as audience members at the Chicago Consortium in Ancient Philosophy 2018, the Central New York Corridor Workshop on Plato and Platonism 2019, and the Law and Virtue in Ancient Philosophy conference at Renmin University 2019 for helpful discussion.

and he resists the illegitimate orders of the Thirty to arrest Leon of Salamis (32c–d).[2] In the *Crito*, Socrates argues that his commitment to justice requires that he abide by the city's laws, for he has made a just agreement to either follow the laws or persuade the city that its judgments are unjust (50c–53a).[3]

In light of Plato's longstanding interest in law and its relation to virtue, this chapter examines the roles played by law in the *Republic*, *Statesman*, and *Laws*, focusing on *how* law conduces to individual virtue and civic unity in each of these dialogues. Section I argues that in the *Republic*, laws regulate important institutions, such as education, property, and family, and thereby create a way of life that cultivates virtue and unity. Section II argues that in the *Statesman*, the political expert determines the mean between extremes and communicates it to citizens through laws that guide their judgment and conduct, so that they become virtuous themselves and the city is unified; this suggests how even non-expert legislation can contribute to virtue and unity. Section III argues that the *Laws* affirms and develops the idea that citizens should know and accept the laws to become virtuous themselves and to unify the city; this explains how the persuasive preludes and sanctions for violation attached to the laws contribute to citizen virtue and civic unity.

I   LAW IN THE REPUBLIC: STRUCTURING VIRTUE-CONDUCIVE INSTITUTIONS

The *Republic* is structured as a response to a challenge from three interlocutors: (1) Thrasymachus, who says that it is folly to be just or law-abiding, for the laws of each constitution aim at the advantage of its rulers (338e); (2) Glaucon, who claims that living a just and law-abiding life is a compromise between the goodness of outdoing others and the badness of being outdone by them (358e–359c); (3) Glaucon and Adeimantus, who argue that one would do better to appear just without being so in fact (362b–367e). In reply, Socrates presents an account of the just person that shows that it is rationally choiceworthy to be just. He develops his account by analogy with justice in the city. In the city, justice is the condition in which each class does the work for which it is best suited (433a–434c), with the result that all of the citizens are happy. Most importantly, philosophers, who possess wisdom about what is best for the city as a whole, rule; and spirited "auxiliaries," who have been educated to be courageous and moderate, help them to guard the city. By analogy, individual justice is the condition in which each part of the soul does the work for which it is best suited, with reason ruling on the basis of knowledge of what is good for each part and the whole, and spirit serving as its auxiliary in ruling over appetite (441d–442b). This condition is also the condition of psychological health, without which life is not worth living (445a–b); indeed, how happy or unhappy a person is depends on how just or unjust she is (580b–c).

Many readers come away from the *Republic*'s account of the just and happy city, which Socrates calls Kallipolis, with the impression that law plays little role in the virtue and happiness of the citizens, since it is philosophical rule that makes Kallipolis possible, and in Kallipolis citizens' virtue, and therefore happiness, is produced by their education. Against this, Annas (2012, 2017) argues for the significance of law in the *Republic*, observing that it mentions terms for law and lawgiving over forty times (2012: 168)[4] and that Socrates and his interlocutors characterize themselves as founders and legislators of Kallipolis (2017: 13–14, citing, e.g., *Republic* 380b–c, 403b, 458c–d, 497c–d). Similarly, Lane (2013) argues that the *Republic* "rehabilitates" law in the wake of Thrasymachus', Glaucon's, and Adeimantus' challenge, and concludes that law is "the ally of everyone in the city" (citing 590e).

Building on these observations about the presence of law in the *Republic*, we argue below that law's role in fostering virtue is *indirect*. Law regulates institutions (especially education, property, and family) that structure the citizens' way of life, and it is the way of life, in particular education, that directly conduces to virtue. To see this, consider three examples of Kallipolian legislation:

1) Laws and patterns (*nomōn te kai tupōn*, 380c8) regulate the stories about the gods told to the guardians during their musical education. Because the citizens admire the gods and so imitate their way of life (442a–b, 411e–412b), the content of stories about the gods requires regulation. But it is the stories, not the laws, that are in the citizens' consciousness, and so it is the stories rather than the laws that directly shape their values and conduct.

2) The founders lay down laws (*nomothetēsōmen*, 417b8) abolishing private property among the guardians, specifying that they are to live in communal housing, eat communal meals, and refrain from even touching gold and silver. This legislation blocks guardians from temptations to intemperance and competition with those they are supposed to guard (416a–417b). For this they *need not* be aware of the property laws; what is needed is that they not see wealth as something to strive for, so they are told they have no need of external gold or silver because they already have it "in their souls" (416e).

3) Legislation (*nomothetēteai*, 459e5) regulating marriage and childrearing (459d–e, 460c–461b) ensures that the guardians do not know about any biological relations, but regard their contemporaries as siblings, their elders as parents, and those younger as children. Socrates claims that these laws are in tune with the laws forbidding private property. They prevent the citizens from having strong desires favoring their own households, which would threaten their concern for the good of the city as a whole and thus the unity of the city (464b–d). Here the guardians *should not* know the laws, for they are to believe that their marriages are determined by a lottery rather than the rulers' attempts to ensure that the best men and women marry each other (459c–460a).

Let us call this kind of indirect legislation "institutional legis-lation," for in each case, the laws aim at the virtue of the citizens and the unity of the city by creating and maintaining institutions (an educational system, communal living, a non-biological family) which are themselves more directly virtue-conducive.

The concept of institutional legislation helps clarify a passage that some readers have, we think wrongly, taken to show the irrele-vance of law to virtue in the *Republic*. After laying down the property laws for the guardians of Kallipolis, Socrates describes them as minor (*phaula*) so long as the guardians safeguard the one great (*hen mega*) or sufficient (*hikanon*) thing, their education (423e). He continues,

> whenever children play in a good way right from the start and
> absorb lawfulness (*eunomia*) from musical training ... lawfulness
> follows them in everything and fosters their growth, correcting
> anything in the city that may have been neglected before ... And
> so such people rediscover the seemingly insignificant
> conventional views their predecessors had destroyed: ... the
> silence appropriate for younger people in the presence of their
> elders; the giving up of seats for them and standing in their
> presence; the care of parents; hairstyles; clothing; shoes; the
> general appearance of the body; and everything else of that sort ...
> To legislate about such things is naive, ... since verbal or written
> decrees will never make them come about or last ... [I]t looks as
> though the start of someone's education determines what
> follows ... And the final outcome of education ... is a single,
> complete, and fresh product that is either good or the opposite ...
> That is why I ... would not try to legislate about such things ...
> Then, by the gods, what about all that market business, the
> contracts people make with one another in the marketplace, for
> example, and contracts with handicraftsmen, and slanders,
> injuries, indictments, establishing juries, paying or collecting
> whatever dues are necessary in the marketplace and harbors, and,

in a word, the entire regulation of any marketplace, city, harbor, or what have you – should we venture to legislate about any of these?

[Adeimantus:] No, it would not be appropriate to dictate to men who are fine and good. For they will easily find out for themselves whatever needs to be legislated about such things.

[Socrates:] Yes, provided that a god grants that the laws we have already described are preserved. (425a–e, tr. Reeve slightly modified)

Socrates here contrasts education, which his last remark emphasizes is governed by (institutional) legislation, with laws that directly command citizens to perform certain actions, and concludes that institutional legislation is more effective for producing virtuous conduct than direct legislation. He goes on to compare direct legislation to medical treatment which, when prescribed to intemperate people who refuse to change their way of life, "achieves nothing" (425e–426a). Indeed, while direct legislation aims to stop people from cheating and other wrongdoing, it is just "cutting off a Hydra's head" (426e–427a), for if laws only prescribe or proscribe particular acts, vice will find an outlet. Thus it is better for laws to structure education so that citizens develop virtuous habits. In this way, citizens become lawful without having to think about the law as such. Of course, as Adeimantus says, the guardians will legislate where necessary, but the point of the passage is that the more consequential legislation is legislation regulating education.

It is striking, given all Socrates' talk of law in the *Republic* – and given the seriousness of his attitude toward the laws in the *Apology* and *Crito* – that he does not discuss Kallipolis' citizens' attitude toward the laws. He does say that the citizens are aware of and endorse a central feature of the *constitution*: that philosophers rule and non-philosophers are ruled (431e–432a), and that they call each other by names reflecting their appreciation of each other's contributions: "preserver," "auxiliary," "providers of upkeep," "co-guardian" (463b). But these are not attitudes toward the laws *per se*.

Two passages might seem to suggest that the citizens are to know the law and that appreciating it is somehow related to their virtue. In the first, Socrates defines civic courage as the ability to preserve the "law-inculcated true belief about what is and is not to be feared" and distinguishes it from beliefs about the same matters found in slaves and animals (430b). One might suppose he means that while slaves and animals obey the law out of fear of punishment, citizens are law-abiding because they think "the law aims at my good," or because they respect the law, and so accept its pronouncements about good and bad. But in this passage Socrates repeats *three times* that the laws inculcate the citizens' beliefs through education (429c3, c6, 430a1). Thus the beliefs are "law-inculcated" only indirectly, in the sense that laws regulate the education that forms citizens' beliefs.

In a second passage, Socrates says that it is better for everyone to be ruled by a divine and wise ruler, preferably one that is his own and within, but failing that, one imposed from the outside, so that all of the citizens can be as similar and friendly as possible; and he goes on to say that this is also the aim of the law, the ally of everyone in the city (590c–591a). Annas (2017: 16) reads this passage as evidence of citizens' consciousness of and motivation by law, for "law presents reason to the citizens in a directive way." But this passage compares the law's aim to what parents intend in raising their children: "by fostering their best part with the similar part of our own, we establish it as guardian and ruler instead of us," and "then we set them free" (590e2–591a3). Thus the law aims to nurture citizens' own reason and (psychic) justice. But it is education by which reason comes to rule and a soul comes to be just (442a), so this passage too points to the laws as structuring citizens' education.

Why does the *Republic* focus on institutional legislation to the neglect of citizens' awareness of their laws, even though the challenge to the rational choiceworthiness of justice was also a challenge to lawfulness? We propose two complementary explanations. First, the abovementioned parallel between institutional legislation and medical regimen (or gymnastics, in *Gorgias*) might suggest that institutional legislation can effect virtue without citizens' awareness of it. If what secures and maintains a patient's bodily health is his medical regimen (his diet, his exercises), then what secures and maintains a citizen's virtue would be the regimen of his actions and experiences. Neither the patient nor the citizen needs to know how his regimen effects bodily health or virtue for the regimen to do its work. As we will see in section III, the *Laws* revises this parallel.

Second, in the *Republic*, Thrasymachus and Glaucon challenge justice and law on the assumption that human nature is pleonectic, so that justice and law curb its pursuit of happiness. Socrates' account of the soul introduces a different picture of human nature, according to which pleonectic pursuits lead to psychic distress but rationally limited pursuits lead to harmony, so that law is not opposed to human nature but a means to its perfection. Given the fundamentality of Thrasymachus' and Glaucon's challenge, and of Socrates' defense, the question of Kallipolis' citizens' attitude toward law *per se* may be too fine-grained for the *Republic*. It is appropriate, then, that this question should be in the spotlight in Plato's more exclusively political works, the *Statesman* and *Laws*.

II LAW IN THE STATESMAN: WEAVING CITIZENS TOGETHER WITH THE BOND OF (TRUE) OPINION

The *Statesman* is structured as a dialectical exercise, led by an Eleatic Visitor, that aims to define political expertise or statesmanship.[5] The Visitor says that statesmanship is an expertise that controls and cares for everything in the city, including the other expertises that care for citizens (e.g., generalship, judgeship, and rhetoric, as well as legislation), by weaving everything together in order to unify the city (305d–e). As we will see, "everything" includes citizens of different natural temperaments (308e–311c). The Visitor draws special attention to the difference between the human statesman's care for humans, on the one hand, and God's care for humans or humans' care for other animals, on the other. Rather than caring for every aspect of his subjects' nurture by himself, the human statesman coordinates the many potentially subordinate and cooperative expertises concerned with the care of humans practiced by the subjects (274e–276d).

The *Statesman* advances a direct role for expertly formed laws in the inculcation of citizen virtue and civic unity: Citizens' awareness and acceptance of the law shape their beliefs about what is good, just, and fine. Understanding this role enables us to see, in the *Statesman*'s evaluation of non-ideal constitutions, how even non-expert laws contribute to the virtue of citizens and the unity of the city. Let us begin with the expertly formed laws.

To see how statesmanship uses law to cultivate virtue and unity, we need first to appreciate the challenges to virtue and unity faced by cities. According to the Visitor, civic conflict originates in the natural differences between two personality types: some people are quick, vigorous, sharp, and so by nature inclined to courage (call them "naturally courageous"), while others are gentle, slow, soft, and so by nature inclined to moderation ("naturally moderate"). These different inclinations, along with an affinity for what is similar to oneself and familiar, lead the two kinds to disagree in their praise and blame, and their disagreement leads them to feelings of enmity toward each other. A naturally courageous person, for example, might call swift and severe retaliation to a slight "courageous," while a moderate type might call the very same action "manic." Both, if unchecked in their natural tendencies, fall to extremes and ultimately destroy the city: naturally moderate people, wanting to live the quiet life and encouraging others to do the same, are eventually enslaved; and naturally courageous types are so interested in making war that they eventually destroy their land or are enslaved by their enemies (306e–308b). Thus, avoiding civil war and enslavement requires tempering and harmonizing citizens' natural tendencies.[6]

The statesman's laws resolve civic conflict in two ways. First, as in the *Republic*, laws govern citizens' birth and upbringing. The statesman will not put a city together out of good and bad human beings, and the educators and tutors, *who function according to law* (*tois kata nomon paideutais kai tropheusin*, 308e5), shape the citizens so that they acquire a disposition suitable for the acquisition of virtue. However, education is *preparation* (*paraskeuazousin*, 308d7) for the statesman's intertwining activity, which suggests that even when all of the citizens have been educated to care for virtue, they can still disagree about what sorts of actions and policies are praiseworthy and blameworthy; consequently, statesmanship is still needed to weave citizens together.

The Visitor describes statesmanship as binding the naturally courageous and naturally moderate "by fitting together that part of their soul that is eternal with a divine bond, in accordance with its kinship with the divine, and after the divine, in turn fitting together their mortal aspect with human bonds" (309c, tr. Rowe). To fit the citizens together with a divine bond, it ensures that all of the citizens have the same true opinion about what is fine or shameful, just or unjust, and good or bad; and to fit the citizens together with a human bond, it arranges that the naturally courageous and moderate types intermarry, instead of allowing each type to go with their natural feelings and marry those like them (309c–310e).

We suggest that the divine bond – the citizens' shared true opinion about what is good, just, and fine – is due, at least in part, to their awareness and acceptance of the law. This second way of resolving civic conflict by law is indicated not only by the Visitor's description of education as preparation for binding, but also by his claim that the citizens' true opinion "only takes root, through laws (*dia nomōn*), in those dispositions that were both born noble in the first place and have been nurtured in accordance with their nature" (310a, cf. 309d). So, while the *Republic* emphasizes that the citizens' true opinions about the just, fine, and good are formed by their education and way of life, the *Statesman* adds that the statesman's laws express the correct norms regarding what is just, good, and fine and the citizens' grasp of the laws informs their true opinions.

The Visitor claims that a naturally courageous soul that acquires true beliefs becomes tame and willing to share in what is just, and a moderate type becomes genuinely moderate and wise (309e). Considering how the Visitor's general claims about expertise apply to the expertise of the statesman-legislator (so-called at 294a, 305b) clarifies how this works. For every expertise there is a normative art of measurement that determines when things are excessive, deficient, or appropriate relative to a standard (metron) (284a–b). Since statesmanship uses legislation, the statesman's laws must express his determination of what is appropriate, given the end of the good of the city, which would be a mean between the extremes to which the naturally courageous and temperate tend. When naturally courageous and temperate people accept the statesman's determinations as just, good, and fine, so as to judge and act in accordance with them, their excesses are tempered, bringing them in line with genuine virtue; and their disagreements are reduced, unifying the city. For example, the statesman might lay down a law governing military deliberations: "if the city is attacked, the generals should deliberate for two days before deciding on a response." Such a law would temper both the naturally courageous inclination to retaliate immediately, and the naturally moderate reluctance to counter-attack. The deliberators' acceptance of this law would also give both a reason to praise the outcome of deliberation as just, good, and fine, thereby harmonizing them with each other and unifying the city.

Why does the *Statesman* advance this new role for law in inculcating virtue and unity? One reason may be the abovementioned account of statesmanship as directing and coordinating subordinate expertises. While the *Republic* lumps together the expertises of general, judge, and educator under "ruling" or "guarding," the *Statesman* distinguishes these expertises both from each other and from statesmanship, so that in the city they would be practiced by distinct office-holders.[7] If these office-holders have different natural tendencies, the laws regulating their offices would need to guide them toward the mean. Moreover, since these offices may be entrusted to a group of citizens including both naturally courageous and moderate types (310e–311b), the different types need to be able to deliberate productively and achieve consensus (rather than remain polarized), which requires them to have some shared standards of what is good, just, and fine for the city as a whole. The laws can provide these standards. Although the *Statesman* does not tell us how or why citizens come to accept the expert's laws, we will see this question addressed in the *Laws*.

The Contribution of Non-expert Legislation to Citizen Virtue and Civic Unity

So far, we have discussed how expertly formed law secures citizen virtue and civic unity. The Visitor also gives a ranking of constitutions that reveals his attitude toward inexpertly as well as expertly formed laws. The best constitution is the one in which the statesman rules, since he has the expertise required to secure the good of the citizens and the unity of the city (296e), using laws since he cannot be everywhere at once (295a–b). Since law is too general and inflexible, and human affairs are too dissimilar and variable, for law to prescribe what is best for every situation (294b–c), the statesman has the authority to change or disregard the laws he has instituted if he determines they do not prescribe the optimal action for a certain situation (295b–297b). The Visitor goes on to claim, however, that in the absence of the expert ruler, a constitution where laws have the highest authority imitates the statesman's constitution better than any other and is a second-best.

This claim is striking, because it allows that laws not formulated by experts can have ultimate authority. This is evident from the Visitor's description of the origins of the law-abiding constitution. He describes how, when people think their rulers have been abusing them, and so do not trust that they possess wisdom or act in the interests of the citizens (298a–b; 301c–d), they decide that all citizens, experts and non-experts alike, may give their opinions on civic matters, and they establish as written law and unwritten ancestral custom whatever the majority decides is best. The citizens accord these

laws the greatest authority, appointing officers in the city to ensure
that everything is done in accordance with the laws, and legislating
severe punishment for anyone who inquires into the laws and recommends anything other than what the law prescribes – "for there must
be nothing wiser than the laws" (299c). According to the Visitor,
although this way of proceeding destroys expertise, it is nonetheless
better than a situation in which officers who are tasked with oversee-
ing the law ignore or change it in ignorance and for the sake of
personal profit (298a–300b).

How is the law-abiding constitution so described an *imitation* of the ideal and a second-best? The Visitor indicates that the
laws of the second-best constitution imitate the statesman's laws
(300c, 301e), and are good laws (302e).[8] The challenge is to explain
why, given his critical account of the origins of the law-abiding
constitution, he should think this.[9] We suggest that the answer
lies in the legislative process of collective deliberation aimed at
generating shared standards that allow the citizens to live well
together. While the Visitor is initially dismissive of the legislative
process, he ultimately explains why the law should have the
highest authority by appeal to features of this process:

> for if, I imagine, contrary to laws that have been established on the
> basis of *much experiment (ek peiras pollēs)* with some *advisers or
> other having given advice on each subject in an attractive way
> (sumboulōn hekasta charientōs sumbouleusantōn)*, and *having
> persuaded the majority (peisantōn . . to plēthos)* to pass them – if
> someone were brazen enough to act contrary to these, he would be
> committing a mistake many times greater than the other [rigidly
> adhering to ordinary laws] and would overturn all expert activity
> *(pasan ... praxin)* to a still greater degree than the written rules.
> (300b, our emphasis)

Consensus achieved out of experience, consultation, and persuasion
across differences, we suggest, is the collective's counterpart to expert
knowledge about what is best for the whole.

Laws III gives a similar account of the process of legislation. The Athenian claims that legislation begins when several household dynasties, previously isolated from one another, come together. These households have different customs, originating in the temperamental differences in natural courage and moderation between their progenitors and educators. Within each household the authority of the eldest is unquestioned, and so the customs approved by the authority are also accepted without question. We may surmise that this unquestioning acceptance is due to the natural affection between the head of the household and his dependents, a natural affection which assures the dependents that the customs are not contrary to their interests. But when these households combine, they have to select which of their different customs they should all together live by (681b–d). The name "legislation" (nomothesia) refers to the intentional selection process by which such a diverse community determines its laws. In this process legislators are elected to examine and choose among the existing customs; they present their selection to the uncontested kings over each of the dynasties; when the kings ratify the selected customs, they become law. Because the legislators select laws acceptable to all from among a pool of customs aiming at the good of the whole, we have reason to expect that these laws reflect a concern for the common good, and because the legislators include customs from both the naturally courageous and moderate, that these laws express a mean between extremes.

Even if Plato thinks that a consensus-seeking and experience-based deliberative process generates decent laws, the Statesman's insistence that the second-best constitution is one in which the citizens never change the laws raises serious questions. Couldn't non-expert legislation result in some laws that are bad for the citizens and the city? If so, shouldn't a constitution that aims at the good of the whole allow some changes to the law in order to better secure its aim? Plato might acknowledge this consideration but still think the costs of changing the law are too high.[10] Laws can provide shared standards of what is good, fine, and just, so that even inexpertly formed laws generate civic unity and stability. But for the laws to play this role, citizens must see them as authoritative. Perhaps Plato thinks allowing that a law is bad threatens the authority not only of that law, but of the laws in general, opening the door to further changes to the law, which gives citizens opportunities to favor themselves and their friends by new legislation. Citizens might then come to doubt that their laws are a result of a legitimate process aimed at arriving at standards that are good for all and instead suspect that they serve special interests, which would lead to further conflict and instability. Finally, if law-abidingness is itself a virtue, then changing the laws and thereby undermining their authority also detracts from the citizens' virtue. These costs do not apply to the statesman's suspension, change, or disregard of laws if he finds they do not prescribe what is best on a certain occasion, because his laws are accompanied by the proviso: Unless I determine otherwise, these will have to do as best for the most part.[11]

III   LAW IN THE LAWS: CULTIVATING VIRTUE THROUGH PERSUASION AND COMPULSION

In the *Laws*, Plato's last dialogue, an unnamed Athenian discusses legislation with the Cretan Cleinias and the Spartan Megillus. While the first four books address theoretical questions about law, including the proper aim, origins, and form of law, as well as the question of what should have authority in a well-governed city, the remaining eight books have a more practical focus, and describe in detail the law-code for Magnesia, a new colony which Cleinias has been tasked with founding (702b–c).[12] Accordingly, as Annas (2017: 23–31) has argued, the *Laws* shows a greater concern with implementation than the *Republic*.

This concern with implementation explains two striking features of the *Laws'* treatment of law. First, on the grounds that unaccountable power is corrupting to any merely mortal nature (691c–d, 715d, 875a–d), the Athenian claims that in Magnesia's constitution, it is the laws (and not philosophers, as in the *Republic*, or the expert, as in the *Statesman*) that should have supreme authority. Second, in place of Kallipolis' political division of labor (philosophers ruling and others being ruled), Magnesian membership in the assembly and eligibility for office are co-extensive with citizenship. Since officials must rule in accordance with laws regulating their office (715d), they are first raised to be law-abiding and then tested for their law-abidingness before their election (751c–d). Thus, civic virtue requires that the citizens know and be committed to the laws.[13]

In the opening theoretical discussion, the Athenian claims that legislation aims at the good of the whole city (rather than, as cynics claim, serving the interests of the stronger, 714b–715b). This aim is achieved distributively, by making individual citizens as virtuous, and thereby as happy, as possible; and collectively, by making the city as a whole as unified and friendly as possible. The law should aim at not just one part of individual citizens' virtue (as do Sparta's and Crete's laws, which, because of their focus on victory in war, cultivate only courage), but complete virtue, including wisdom, moderation, and justice, for it is complete virtue that both makes the citizens happy and ensures that they are friends to one another (*Laws* I–II, especially 688a, 631b–32d).

Magnesian law cultivates virtue and unity both indirectly, by regulating institutions that are themselves virtue-conducive as in the *Republic*, and directly, insofar as the citizens' awareness of law forms their true beliefs about what is best, as in the *Statesman*. The Athenian defines complete (individual) virtue as wisdom or true judgment along with non-rational feelings (e.g., pleasures and desires, pains and aversion) in agreement with this (653a–c, 864a) and says that education channels non-rational feelings so that they are in accord with the true judgment (653a–c). Accordingly, he lays down laws for the institutions that structure the citizens' birth and upbringing – the latter in the broadest sense, including not only their schooling but their whole environment: the stories they hear and the music they listen to, the bodily movements they engage in, and family life. Since the *Laws*, in contrast with the *Republic*, allows for so-called private property and households, laws also manage wealth inequality (737b–747e) and prescribe communal meals (780e–781d) in order to foster friendship and a concern for the common good.

That law also plays a direct role in cultivating virtue is suggested by the Athenian's (1) claim that the name "law" is given to reasoning that has become the common opinion (*koinon dogma*) of the city (645a), (2) prescription that each citizen study the text of the *Laws* during their education (811c–e) – rather than being in the dark about the regulations that shape their lives, as they are about the selection of sexual partners in the *Republic* (459d–460c) – and (3) description of the good and virtuous person as a servant of the law, one who lives his life following the legislation, praise, and blame in the lawgiver's writings (822e).[14]

The *Laws* discusses issues concerning the direct role of law not addressed in the *Statesman*. First, how should the laws address the citizens so that their acceptance of the law conduces to virtue and unity? Second, what role does the citizens' awareness of the punishments associated with law play in cultivating virtue and unity? Below, we take up these questions by discussing, first, the preambles to the laws, and second, the normative underpinnings of the provisions for punishing wrongdoers.

Preambles

The *Laws*' signature innovation in legislation is to preface persuasive preambles (*prooimia*) to the law-code as a whole and the particular laws within it. At the start of his discussion of the preambles the Athenian states their goal: that citizens should be as obedient (or persuaded, *eupeithestatous*) as possible in relation to virtue (718c). For this reason, the legislator should not just state each law and the penalty for disobedience without offering any "word at all of encouragement or persuasion (*paramuthias de kai peithous*)" (720a), but should instead practice a "dual method" of lawgiving, combining persuasion and force (722b–c, 722e–723a). To explain, the Athenian compares legislation with the prescriptive practices of two kinds of doctor:

> You realize, don't you, that the people who fall sick in our cities may be slaves or free-born? And that it is the slave-doctors who for the most part treat the slaves? ... [N]one of these doctors gives any explanation of the particular disease of any particular slave – or listens to one; all they do is prescribe the treatment they see fit, on the basis of trial and error – but with all the arrogance of a tyrant, as if they had exact knowledge. Then they're up and off again, to the next suffering slave ... [By contrast] the free-born doctor spends most of his time treating and keeping an eye on the diseases of the free-born. He investigates the origin of the disease, in the light of his study of the natural order, taking the patient himself and his friends into partnership. This allows him both to learn from those who are sick, and at the same time to teach the invalid himself, to the best of his ability; and he prescribes no treatment without first getting the patient's consent. Only then, and all the time using his powers of persuasion to keep the patient cooperative, does he attempt to complete the task of bringing him back to health. (720b–e, tr. Griffith)

The free doctor, the model for the legislator, prescribes based on the study of nature; pays attention to the causes of the particular patient's disease; and persuades the patient to follow his regimen – indeed, teaches him, to the best of his ability (cf. 857d–e). The analogy between free doctor and legislator marks a new direction in the medical regimen–legislation parallel we have encountered in earlier dialogues. In the *Laws*, the free are to be made healthy or virtuous by a health- or virtue-conducive regimen *of which they approve*.[15]

While the Athenian is clear that the aim of the preludes is to persuade the citizens to accept the law willingly (723a), scholars disagree about whether the persuasion involved is rational or emotional. Some maintain that the preludes appeal to the citizens' reason by giving them good reasons to follow the law.[16] As evidence, they note that the analogy between the doctor and the legislator suggests that the legislator teaches and the citizens learn (cf. 857c–858a). In addition, they highlight the preludes that persuade through argument. The general prelude to the law-code, for example, argues that virtue, as a good of the soul, is the highest good and the aim of all the laws (726a–734e), and the preamble to the impiety law consists of philosophically sophisticated arguments that the gods exist, care for us, and cannot be bribed (890b–907c). Other scholars claim that despite the Athenian's programmatic remarks, most preludes engage in rhetorical persuasion, exhorting the citizens to follow the law by praising the actions they recommend and expressing disapproval of those they prohibit, thereby appealing to the citizens' sense of honor and shame.[17] The preamble to the hunting law, for example, simply praises certain forms of hunting as courageous and disparages others as lazy (823d–824b); and the preamble to the law prohibiting temple defilement does not argue that temple robbing is bad, but characterizes the desire to rob temples as evil and alien and follows up with instructions on how to manage the desire should it arise (854b–c).

One might worry that if many of the preludes engage in rhetorical persuasion, then their primary aim is simply to encourage the citizens to obey the law, without instilling any real understanding of the value of doing so. But this worry is misplaced. First, even if a rhetorical or emotional appeal only produces behavioral conformity with the law, behavioral conformity in turn offers agents opportunities to appreciate their own actions, and hence, eventually, to appreciate the law requiring these actions. Second, rhetorical persuasion *can* enable the citizens to grasp the reasons behind the law.[18] Annas argues that the preludes are diverse – engaging in rational argument, emotional appeal, and discussion – because they must respond to varied motivations and address citizens of varied intellectual abilities and educational achievements.[19] This diversity notwithstanding, she argues that all of the preludes present, in a range of ways, "the ethical ideals implicit in the way of life structured by the various laws" (2017: 93–8).

We agree that most preludes present the virtues and values achieved by following the laws as fine and praiseworthy. The general prelude to the law-code makes clear that the laws aim at the divine good of virtue; and many preludes to particular laws show that the law in question aims at a specific virtue, often a concern for the common good.[20] Thus, the preludes simultaneously give the citizens good, if not fully philosophically grounded, reasons to accept and abide by the laws, and engage their emotions by presenting the aim of the laws as worthy of aspiration. In this way, the preludes directly contribute to both the intellectual and emotional components of the citizens' virtue. Since the citizens' early education aims to foster a love of virtue, we can see the preludes and education as working together to bring out the connection between what the citizens have been trained to value in their education and the specific laws.

We propose that the preludes also contribute to citizens' virtue in the following way: Understanding the aims of the laws enables the citizens to act virtuously in situations where the law is silent. For while a legal command can only state which actions are obligatory and forbidden, the virtuous agent must choose which among the permissible actions is best. Because the preludes convey the aim of the specific laws, and so the virtues and values that citizens should aspire to in the relevant domains, they can guide citizens to go above and beyond the letter of the law, since they have internalized its spirit.[21] We see this when we consider two features of the law-code together. First, the Athenian argues against sanction-backed legislation regulating every detail of citizens' private lives on the grounds that since citizens can easily ignore such legislation and yet go undetected, it undermines law-abidingness and the stability of the written law-code (788b–c, 793a–d, 823b). Second, many of the Athenian's preludes recommend conduct that is more demanding

than is contained in the legal command. Let's consider some
examples.

1) The hunting law forbids night hunting and some forms of catching
   birds and fish. But while this permits hunting of all land animals,
   the prelude indicates that hunting can be done in more and less
   courageous ways, and describes particularly courageous forms of
   hunting, i.e., hunting four-footed land animals on foot using
   horses, dogs, and the citizens' own bodily effort (823b–824c).

2) The marriage laws require men to marry by the age of 35. But the
   preludes explain that the aim of marriage is having children and
   that one should choose a partner not with a view to what is best for
   oneself but rather what is best for the city. One prelude
   recommends, specifically, that rather than choosing mates who
   are like themselves, the more wealthy should marry the less
   wealthy, the more powerful the less powerful, and the naturally
   courageous the naturally moderate, in order to avoid polarization
   between these classes of people (772d–774c, 721b–d).

3) The agricultural laws specify that if someone encroaches on
   another's land, he must pay the injured party twice the damages.
   By explaining that the aim of these laws is to avoid bitterness and
   resentment between neighbors and instead promote friendly
   feeling, the lawgiver's writings encourage citizens to go further
   than correcting their own wrongs, by helping to rebuild what has
   been damaged (843b–d).

In all these and other cases, while the law states what is obligatory and
impermissible, the preludes indicate what virtue calls for, by making
clear the virtues and values expressed in actions, and by signaling the
lawgiver's praise and blame.

   It is for this reason that the Athenian says:

   Once our laws, and the social and political system as a whole, have
   been written down in the way we are suggesting, our approval of the
   citizen who is outstanding in terms of human excellence will not

confine itself to saying that whoever is the best servant of the laws, and the most obedient to them – that this is the one who is good. A fuller description would be: "whoever passes his whole life, consistently, in obedience to the writings of the lawgiver – both his laws and his (positive or negative) recommendations (*epainontous kai psegontos*)." This is the most accurate form of words when it comes to praising a citizen, and it puts a corresponding onus on the lawgiver to do more than merely write the laws; in addition to the laws he has to write down his views – say what he thinks is good, and what not good (*kala kai mē kala*) – blended in with the laws. The perfect citizen should treat these as immovable, no less than the ones which have the backing of the law and its penalties. (822e–823a)

If this is right, then in addition to giving citizens reasons to obey the law, the preambles enable citizens to behave virtuously in situations not explicitly addressed in the existing law. The familiar worry in Plato, and in virtue ethics, about the limitations of law for action-guidance, is in the *Laws* addressed by the persuasive preambles.

The action-guidance provided by understanding the law's aim extends to citizens' performance of their offices. This has the interesting consequence that the Guardians of the Law and other relevant office-holders and experts who are to supplement the existing law-code are enabled to do so by the preludes to the existing laws.[22] The Athenian compares citizen-legislators to painters. Just as a painter who wants his painting to remain beautiful forever must leave behind a successor who is able to repair damage and improve the painting over time, so a legislator must also leave behind successors to supplement the law-code (769b–770b). He imagines saying to these citizen-legislators:

Friends, protectors of laws, our position is this: in any particular branch of our legislation there are all kinds of things we shall be leaving out. That's unavoidable. Not that we won't do our best to include the important points and the general idea in a kind of outline sketch. Your job will be to fill in the outline. What your aim should be as you carry out a task of this nature, we are now going to tell you ... We want you to be in sympathy with us, to be our students, having those aims in view which we agree with one another should be the aims both of the guardian of the law and of the lawgiver. (770b–c)

Since virtue is the highest good, virtue is the aim they should keep in view as they amend the laws (770d–771e). Citizens will need to supplement the law-code with new legislation and regulations regarding, for example, songs and dances (772a), competitions at festivals (835a–b), judicial procedure (846b, 855d, 957a–b), and marketplace regulations (917e, 920b).[23] To do this well, it is not enough for the citizens to know the existing laws, for they are not deciding whether a certain action falls under the existing law. Rather, they are, as citizen-legislators, determining whether a proposed law promotes the relevant aims, for which they need to understand the aims of the law in general, and of the laws in a certain domain. Since this determination is always made by relevant office-holders and experts deliberating together, the citizen-legislators must give reasons for and against a proposed law with reference to the aims of the law-code. So, while the *Statesman* stresses that law provides shared standards and thereby facilitates successful deliberation and agreement, the *Laws* adds that citizens' knowing and agreeing about the aims of the laws is required for successful deliberation *about legislation*. Inculcating a grasp of and commitment to these aims is the job of the preludes.

Finally, insofar as the preludes secure this commitment to the spirit of the law, they enable the political participation of the citizens, and so contribute in a distinctive way to the friendship and unity of the city. The Athenian claims that the correct constitution must blend monarchical or authoritarian and democratic elements, which secures the freedom, friendship, and wisdom of the city (693d, 701d–e). He illustrates with the examples of Persia and Attica. Although Persia under Cyrus was a monarchy, the citizens enjoyed a share of freedom, including freedom of speech, and were on an equal footing, which encouraged friendship between the rulers and the ruled (694a–b). When Cyrus' successors took away the freedom of the common people, they destroyed the principle of friendship and cooperation in the state, and the rulers' policies no longer aimed at the common good (697c–d). Although Attica during the time of the Persian wars was a democracy, the citizens' participation was guided by their respect for the norms and laws of their society, which, along with their fear of the Persians, increased the friendship and solidarity between citizens. But when the Athenians started to question the authority of social norms, which ultimately led them to question the authority of the laws proper, the city degenerated into chaos (698a–701c).[24]

So, while the *Republic* claimed that philosopher-rulers and producers can be friends, despite the producers' lack of political participation and indeed despite the producer's being referred to as a slave (*doulos*) to the philosopher-rulers in this respect (590c–d), the *Laws* stresses that some degree of political equality and freedom is required for civic friendship, for "slaves and masters can never be friends" but "equality creates friendship" (757a). Granting some degree of political equality and freedom promotes friendship and trust between the rulers and the ruled, both by acknowledging the potential of citizens of different walks to contribute to the affairs of the city (cf. their competing claims to authority, 690a–c), and by ensuring that the policies of the city aim at the common good. At the same time, the citizens' participation must be constrained by an authoritarian element that ensures that it is guided by wisdom aimed at the common good.

Magnesia achieves the balance between the authoritarian and democratic elements as follows: The laws have the ultimate authority in the constitution and indeed office-holders must think of themselves as slaves to the law (715b–d), but all citizens are eligible to participate in the political life of the city in accordance with the wisdom expressed in the laws. More specifically, all citizens are members of the assembly;

all citizens are eligible to fill most political offices; all citizens select, by vote, the majority of office-holders; and all participate in the system of the courts. The preludes, by securing the citizens' appreciation of and commitment to the ideals of law, equip them to participate in the affairs of the city, thereby promoting the citizens' political freedom and the friendship between them.

Punishment

Magnesia's laws will be not only prefaced by the preambles we have been discussing, but also accompanied by specifications of the various penalties for violating the law. The Athenian explains that they must specify these penalties because they are legislating for humans, not gods or heroes, and some humans will fail to be "softened" by the laws; citizens that continue to have motivations contrary to the law will need the threat of punishment to deter them (853b–d). The most common penalties for citizens are fines and dishonors, and in the extreme, death and exile; penalties for slaves and foreigners add branding and whipping to this list. The schedule of penalties restricts judicial discretion considerably more than in contemporary Athens. For example, a man who remains unmarried after the age of 35 must pay an annual fine, the amount of which is determined by his property class (774a–b); the law concerning water use assigns a penalty of double the damage done to the party harmed by wrongful use of water resources (844d–e); the law concerning stealing requires the convicted thief to repay twice the value of the stolen article (857a).

How do such penalties fit with the law's overall aim of citizens' virtue and civic unity? Below, we argue that in the *Laws*, punishment is forward-looking, with compensation of the injured and reform ("cure") of wrongdoers and onlookers as *proximate* aims, which in turn serve the law's *ultimate* aims of individual virtue and civic unity.[25] After laying out the Athenian's vision of punishment, we address apparent tensions between these aims and the bases on which penalties are assessed.

In the course of laying out the penalties for such serious crimes as temple defilement and homicide, the Athenian identifies the aims of penalties by distinguishing between two aspects of an act, injury – whether someone was harmed – and injustice – whether the harm was a manifestation of psychic injustice, i.e., the tyranny of one's conception of the good by anger, appetite, and pleasure, or ignorance, in the soul (863e–864a).

> So there are in fact two things he [the lawgiver] has to look out for – injustice and harm – and any harm done he must use the laws, as best he can, to render harmless, restoring what has been lost, raising up again what has been cast down, making remedy for what has been killed or injured, and when he has achieved atonement, by means of compensation, in regard to those who did a particular injury and those who had it done to them, he should always then try to use the laws to bring friendship in place of disagreement. (*Laws* 862b–c, cf. 933e–934b)

The Athenian's distinction between harm and injustice (an injustice [*adikēma*] being an intentional violation of the law) allows him to distinguish between two functions a penalty may serve: compensating a victim and punishing a wrongdoer. Even if an injury is unintentional and not the expression of an unjust character, the victim needs to be compensated.[26] But, according to the Athenian, compensation's ultimate aim is not simply to make good the victim's material loss; it is to restore friendship in place of discord. The Athenian might think that if an injured citizen believes that the law of her city does not protect her and compensate her for the injuries she suffers in the course of her civic associations, then the law does not include her in the collective at whose good it aims, and at which she too is expected to aim. Losing self-interested reasons to obey the law is likely to erode her disposition to obey it and to promote the good of the city. If this is right, then compensating the injured party is necessary for civic unity, and, if obedience to the law conduces to individual virtue, it also preserves the injured party's and the injurer's individual virtue.

For cases in which an act of injustice has been committed, the Athenian adds:

> When we come to unjust injuries and benefits (if one person treats another unjustly, yet causes him some benefit), he is to treat these as diseases of the soul, curing them when they are curable ... if someone commits an act of injustice, great or small, the law will [A] instruct him and categorically compel him either never to have the effrontery to do such a thing again, if he can help it, or certainly to do it far less – not to mention the payment of damages. That's the aim; whether by means of actions or words, or with pleasures or pains, privileges or loss of them, financial penalties or even rewards – in fact any way at all you can make someone hate injustice and embrace (or not hate) the nature of true justice – that, and only that, is the function of the finest laws. [B] But those who, in the lawgiver's perception, are incurable in this respect – what sentence, and what law, will he put in place for them? He will be aware, I take it, that for anyone of this character, two considerations apply: for them, it is no longer better to remain alive; and for everyone else, there will be a double benefit if they take their leave of life – they will serve as an example to others not to act unjustly, and they will empty the city of evil men. (862c–863a)

Likening the condition of the wrongdoer to disease, in [A] the Athenian makes clear that the (proximate) aim of punishing the intentional wrongdoer, whose unjust act is evidence of an unjust character, is to disincentivize committing such acts again and to make him love, or at least not hate, justice.[27] But how does this work? After all, merely refraining from unjust actions does not make for a virtuous citizen. As Glaucon remarks in the *Republic*, even slaves and animals obey the law out of fear of punishment (430b).[28] Granted that neither punishment nor its prospect can make anyone virtuous, still, refraining from intentional violation of the law is a step a vicious person can take in the direction of virtue. The experience of inhibiting an action one is inclined to do teaches that it is not so difficult to restrain an impulse. Acting lawfully on one occasion makes doing it again easier, and eventually, easy enough to do even when the threat of punishment is absent, so that instead of calling to mind the nonmoral goods to be enjoyed by breaking the law, the agent eventually just does the lawful thing. The citizen is now in a position at least to see the value in acting according to the law – the sort of value that Magnesia's education inculcates and that the preludes point to – which is a step in the direction of coming to love justice. On this picture, the incentives provided by penalties promote virtue not directly, but by enabling the beginning of a process of habituation through action.

In [B], the Athenian adds that even when the wrongdoer cannot be cured or reformed by punishment, he may still be punished, by death, because (1) his life is no good (but presumably bad) for him, (2a) his example will disincentivize others from wrongdoing, and (2b) the city will be freed of a bad person. But even in these cases, the Athenian has virtue and unity in view. The point of seeing another person punished (2a) is to disincentivize wrongdoing, and the point of refraining from wrongdoing is to create the conditions for progress toward virtue.[29] Finally, the point of freeing the city of bad people (2b) is to reduce the injuries that hinder civic unity and, as a result, other citizens' virtue.

We have argued that the Athenian emphasizes that the penalties are forward-looking, intended to compensate the injured for the sake of civic unity, and to cure wrongdoers. Indeed, the thought that penalties must serve some good end is so central to the Athenian's outlook that he refuses the name "penalty" (dikē) to the worst consequence of vicious actions, namely that their agent acquires a vicious character, on the grounds that this is simply a bad outcome, but a penalty must be something fine (728b–c). Still, it has seemed to many readers (e.g., Mackenzie 1981, Adams 2019) that in practice his system of penalties must serve additional aims, including deterrence and perhaps even retribution, because (1) the penalties he outlines are assigned not on the basis of character but action; (2) the penalties are fixed in proportion to the wrong done; and sometimes (3) penalties are determined by the discretion of the victim. Let's address these in turn.

One reason for (1), punishing on the basis of actions rather than character even though the same act might issue from two different states of character, is epistemic. The legislator and the judge cannot peer into the souls of citizens, and so must rely on actions to indicate character. Similar considerations account for (2), proportionality. The Athenian says that larger violations are indicators of greater corruption of the soul (presumably it takes more chutzpah to steal something larger, given that it is likely better protected, and its loss likely to harm its owner more):

> Any theft of public property, be it substantial or indeed trivial, calls for the same penalty, because the person who steals something small has the same desire to steal – merely less power; and the one who makes off with something larger, not having deposited it there in the first place, is a wrongdoer through and through. Therefore, if the law decides on a lesser punishment for either of them, it is not on account of the scale of the theft, but rather because one offender might perhaps be curable, whereas another is incurable. (941c–942a)

The same reasoning can explain why an injury committed by violent means receives a bigger penalty than the same injury committed without violence, and one done in secret receives a bigger penalty than the same one done openly (864c, 908d–e); why a crime committed impulsively receives a smaller penalty than one committed with premeditation (866d–67c); and why a repeat offense is punished more heavily than a first-time one (868a). In each of these scenarios, the aggravating condition indicates that the overruling of the agent's conception of the good by some passion or appetite or ignorance is relatively hardened, so that disincentivizing wrongdoing requires a greater penalty.

A second reason to punish for actions rather than on the basis of character evaluation (1), even when the goal is reform, is that such penalties teach the wrongdoer that she should not do the type of action she has done or is contemplating doing. What would a wrongdoer learn from being penalized for her character? That she was bad, to be sure, but then what should she do to improve? After all, it is actions that shape our characters.

A further explanation for (2), proportionality, is that law is by nature fixed. When laws, rather than magistrates, rule and guide behavior, not only the prescriptions and proscriptions of the laws, but also the penalties must be fixed. But this does not detract from the penalty's aiming at reforming the wrongdoer.

Finally, the Athenian gives the victim or his family discretion in determining the punishment for homicide or wounding when the wrongdoer is a slave and the victim free, suggesting that victims are allowed to indulge in retributive feelings (868b–c; cf. 731d, which restricts such feelings to the punishment of incurables). But rather than indicate that the penal code has retribution as an aim this may be evidence of its concern with civic unity. Perhaps when no suitable compensation is available for those who have been harmed, the law must make a concession to their feelings and allow them some satisfaction – even if the legislator does not condone the feelings – on pain of risking their behaving unjustly as a response to harm. This would also explain why agents of unintentional homicides are exiled for a year, even though by definition their act is not an act of injustice or evidence of an unjust character.

One might worry, however, that purely forward-looking punishment (whether aiming at compensation, reform, or deterrence) licenses Magnesian legislators and judges to over-punish, e.g., to slap very costly penalties on minor wrongs or scapegoat an innocent for the example his punishment sets for others.

It is striking that the Athenian never makes or argues for such trade-offs. (He does privilege the good of the whole city or family over the good of any particular individual [923b], but this is not the same as choosing what is bad for an individual because the whole benefits.) Instead, he likens the role of legislator to that of a judge considering a family of good and bad sons, and asks which of three judges would be better:

> the judge who destroyed those of them who were bad, and told the better ones to be their own rulers, or the one who told the good ones to be rulers, but allowed the worse to live, having made them willing to be ruled? And presumably, with our eye on excellence, there is a third judge we should mention – supposing there could be such a judge – the one who would be able to take this single family which is at odds with itself and not destroy any of them, but reconcile them for the future, and give them laws to keep them on good terms with one another. (627d–628a)

Although the Athenian does not say why the third judge is the best, we suggest that it is because by reforming the bad brothers and achieving reconciliation, *all* of the brothers are benefited. The best judge aims to reform the bad brothers, for their status as family members entails that one try as hard as possible to reform them. But in addition, once reformed, the family can reconcile and each brother can contribute something to the family, making the whole family better off. Similarly, the Athenian emphasizes reforming the wrongdoer because as a citizen, his good is part of the overall good at which the city aims, and the city may not forsake this unless he is actually incurable. But in addition, as a good citizen he will be able to make a civic contribution that benefits the whole city. Even in his discussion of punishment, then, Plato holds the twin aims of the law – the virtue of the citizens and the unity of city – clearly in view.

NOTES

1 See, e.g., Klosko 2006.

2 The case of Leon of Salamis raises the issue of the legal status of decrees given by rulers established by coup – are they "laws," and if not, why not?

3 The classic account of the logic of the laws' speech is Kraut 1984.

4 In the *Republic* "law" can designate (1) specific pieces of legislation (e.g., the law requiring that women and men receive the same education [456c, 457b–c], and the law prohibiting the guardians from ravaging the country or burning the houses of Greeks in war [471c]), or (2) *whatever* civic institutions the interlocutors introduce as conducive to the happiness of the city. For example, when he replies to Adeimantus' criticism that depriving the guardians of private property makes them less happy than they might otherwise be, Socrates says, "in establishing our city, *we* aren't aiming to make any one group outstandingly happy but to make the whole city so, as far as possible" (420b); when he replies to Glaucon's complaint that requiring the philosophers to rule is making them live a worse life, he says, "You are forgetting again that it isn't the *law's* concern to make any one class in the city outstandingly happy but to contrive to spread happiness throughout the city" (519e). "The law" has replaced "we [sc. the legislators]." Again, after having described the character of the philosopher, Socrates calls rule by philosophers, first, "just those [sc. arrangements] that seem best to us" (*haper hēmin dokei*) and a couple of lines later, "this legislation" (*nomothesia*) (502c).

5 Lane (1998) and El Murr (2014) discuss the dialogue as a whole with special attention to how it "weaves together" the two themes of dialectic and politics. For detailed discussions of the parts of the *Statesman* see also Dimas, Lane and Meyer 2021.

6 This account of the obstacle to virtue and unity contrasts with the *Republic*'s, where civic conflict arises from pleonectic and privatizing desires (358e–369c, 462a–c).

7 Cooper (1997b) argues that the *Statesman*, in contrast with the *Republic*, allows for independent experts who are not rulers to contribute to the moral development of the other citizens.

8 Against this, Rowe (1995: 15–18 and 2000: 244–51), Lane (1998: 158–9), and Klosko (2006) deny that ordinary laws bear any resemblance to the statesman's laws. They argue that the law-abiding constitution imitates the best in a formal or structural way only. In the best constitution, after

the statesman legislates, the citizens do not change the laws; similarly, in the law-abiding constitution, after the citizens legislate, they do not change the laws. Lane argues that the second-best constitution's citizens do not change the law because they are aware of their lack of expertise.

9 Sorensen (2016: 91), citing 297d, 300c, argues that the expert uses ancestral law (i.e., the ordinary laws described here) as material when framing his own laws (94–5). According to Sorensen, the sense in which the law-abiding constitutions imitate the best is in *pretending* to rule by expertise (67–70), because subjects, having the wrong expectation of political expertise, overthrow expert rulers and institute democratic deliberation instead.

10 Plato's *Crito* offers an alternative in the speech of the laws of Athens, which allow the citizen who does not wish to obey the city's law to persuade the city that it (or its application) is unjust. Citizens of such a city might uphold their laws in part because they know that which laws remain in effect is revisable by them, if they have good arguments for revision. Here in the *Statesman* the Visitor brushes aside Young Socrates' alternative, that one who wishes to change the law might persuade the city that other laws are better (296a).

11 It is useful to compare the status of laws in the statesman-ruled vs. second-best good constitutions with rules under act- vs. rule-utilitarianism. Act utilitarianism can use rules of thumb when directly calculating the right (utility-maximizing) act is impossible or too costly. The rule is clearly a second-best, and direct calculation is more authoritative. This is the situation in the constitution ruled by expertise. In rule utilitarianism, however, even though rules are chosen because they maximize utility, they are authoritative even when an act contrary to the rule would, in that instance, secure greater utility. This is the situation in the second-best, law-abiding, constitution. Whereas utilitarians are concerned with the costs of rule violation or suspension to the stability of rules, Plato is also concerned about the bad effects on character.

12 For a fuller account of the structure of the *Laws*, see Laks (forthcoming), ch. 1.

13 The concern with implementation might also explain why the Athenian distinguishes between the two parts of a constitution: the arrangement of offices, or of who is going to rule over what, and laws or rules

governing the various offices (735a), which allows him to assess not only the aims of a given constitution but also the fit between constitutional aims and laws, a twofold assessment also used by Aristotle in *Politics* II.

14 For the historical significance of Plato's emphasis on written law, see Nightingale 1999.

15 Some commentators see a disanalogy between being persuaded to follow one's medical regimen and one's legal regimen in that the former is a precursor to, rather than part of, the production and maintenance of bodily health, whereas the latter does away with the need for law (see, e.g., Stalley 1983 and Laks 1990). Laks argues that the preambles are Plato's attempt to "reduce" law, i.e., to minimize its compulsive form of command and threat of sanction for disobedience. Schofield (2006) argues that the doctor analogy is not a model for the actual preludes to the laws, which are one-way instruments of social control to bring about compliance, with punishment as a back-up in case they fail. Instead, the doctor analogy models a hypothetical discussion between a legislator and his citizen critic, "encapsulating the voluntary outcomes that *would* be achieved by innumerable exercises in Socratic dialogue" (85). But justification via hypothetical consent is a device in liberal political philosophy where the standard for political legitimacy is acceptance by parties characterized as free, equal, and rational, because of rock-bottom disagreement over substantive conceptions of the good, whereas in Plato the standard for political legitimacy is a substantive conception of the good, viz., the virtue and happiness of the citizens and the unity of the city. These ends require citizens to be *actually* persuaded.

16 Bobonich (1991; 2002: 97–119) argues that the preludes engage in rational persuasion and discusses the implications of this for Plato's politics. See also Irwin 2010: 98–9.

17 Hitz 2009: 375–9; Morrow 1954 and 1960: 552 60; Stalley 1983: 42 4, and 1994; and Wilburn 2013: 88–97.

18 Note that the *Statesman* includes rhetoric as one of the subordinate expertises in the best constitution, which suggests a role for rhetoric in the citizens' acceptance of the law and so of their true and shared beliefs about what is good, fine, and just (304c–d).

19 Buccioni (2007), Fossheim (2013), and Baima (2016) also argue that the preludes are diverse, reflecting the Athenian's awareness of the intellectual and motivational diversity of the citizen body. See also

Meyer 2006: 385–97. Samaras (2002: 305–25) argues that the psychology of the *Laws* shows that there is no inconsistency in the preludes' using both rational and non-rational persuasion, and spells out the implications of this for Plato's attitudes to authority and democracy.

20 There are exceptions. The preludes to the murder laws, for example, claim that murderers will be subject to supernatural revenge (865d–e; 870d–e, 872a–873a). Perhaps the Athenian thinks that preambles addressing citizens with strong murderous desires must elicit strong contrary motives (i.e., fear) in order to encourage them to follow the law (Annas 2017: 95–6).

21 Silverthorne (1975) argues that the preambles overcome the two deficiencies in law mentioned in the *Statesman*, that (1) it is overly general, insofar as a law, which states what one ought to do in all circumstances, couldn't possibly state what is correct for every situation; and (2) it is inflexible, and "resembles a stubborn individual." He thinks this provides jurors with guidance on how to apply the law during trials. But in fact, Plato overcomes (1) by making the laws as specific as possible, thereby lessening the problems with (2).

22 There is some debate over the extent to which the guardians of the law can change (as opposed to supplement) the original laws. See Reid 2021 for a survey of the debate and an argument in favor of the view that changes to the law-code are minimal.

23 See Bobonich (2002: 573, n. 67) for a complete list of passages assigning the guardians of the law the task of completing the laws.

24 The Athenian's description of the excessive freedom which developed in Attica recalls Socrates' description of democracy in *Republic* VIII.

25 Mackenzie (1981: 195–204) argues that by contrast with the *Gorgias*, which considers punishment only from the perspective of the individual wrongdoer and hence focuses on punishment's reformative function, the *Laws* takes up a political perspective and considers the effects of wrongdoing and punishment not only on wrongdoers, but also on victims and observers, as a result adding prevention, deterrence, and restitution to the aims of punishment. We dispute these other aims below.

26 Must compensation always come from the injuring party, even when the injury is unintentional and involves no fault on the part of the injurer, or may it in that case come from the city's funds? In cases where the injury is

due to malice or negligence, as in the case of water-damage (844d–e), there remains some ambiguity about how much of what is paid to the injured party is compensation – for example is he compensated more than his material loss because of loss of use of his materials? – and how much penalty.

27 Stalley (1983: 143–50) raises difficulties for punishment's ability to effect this result and argues that in practice the penalties aim not only at cure but also deterrence.

28 Saunders (1991: 172–8) proposes that the pain of punishment can disrupt habitual psychic motions, preparing a wrongdoer for an opportunity to develop a new behavioral regimen. Note that citizens are typically punished by fines and dishonors rather than by painful corporal punishments (exceptions include beating for young people caught stealing fruit [845c], for officers who have left the barracks where they are supposed to remain [762c], and for citizens who assault their parents [881d]; and whipping for younger citizens who neglect their parents [932b–c]). The fact that it is typically slaves and foreigners who are given corporal punishment (e.g., slaves and foreigners are branded and whipped for temple robbery but citizens, who have been educated according to and by the law, are put to death [854d–e]; cf. the differential punishment for theft of public property [941d]) suggests that the Athenian takes psychic pain to be more curative and conducive to virtue than is bodily pain.

29 Adams (2019) argues that the penal code has two equally important aims: reforming the criminal *and* deterring others from committing a crime. This is supposed to explain why the Athenian's punishments are (allegedly) all painful even though in [A] the Athenian allows that pleasures too might reform a wrongdoer. A pleasant reformative treatment would not deter others, but a painful punishment both reforms and deters. But the Athenian's claim in [A] that even pleasures and rewards may be used to reform the wrongdoer emphasizes that the penalties are merely instrumental to the aim of reform and are justified to the extent that they promote reform. This does not imply that as a matter of psychological fact, some wrongdoers will be reformed by being rewarded. Adams adds that if the most effective means of reforming the criminal differs from the most effective means of deterring others, then the Athenian would favor deterrence, since this benefits the whole. But if reform and deterrence are really twin aims on a par, why restrict the exemplary use of the death

penalty to incurables? Couldn't administering the death penalty to some curables turn out to be a more effective deterrent overall? And surely there are punishments worse than death, such as torture or solitary confinement (e.g., being sent to the countryside prison "named after retribution" [908a], to which the unjust and dissembling among the impious are sent), that would deter even more than the death penalty.

Bibliography

Abrams, M. H. 1953. *The Mirror and the Lamp*. New York: Oxford University Press.

Acerbi, F. 2003. "On the Shoulders of Hipparchus: A Reappraisal of Ancient Greek Combinatorics," *Archive for History of Exact Sciences* 57: 465–502.

2008. "In What Proof Would a Geometer Use the Ποδίαια?" *Classical Quarterly* 58: 120–6.

Adam, J. 1902. *The* Republic *of Plato*, 2 vols.: Text and Commentary. Cambridge University Press.

Adams, M. 2019. "Plato's Theory of Punishment and Penal Code in the *Laws*," *Australasian Journal of Philosophy* 97 (1): 1–14.

Ademollo, F. 2011. *The* Cratylus *of Plato*. Cambridge University Press.

2018. "On Plato's Conception of Change," *Oxford Studies in Ancient Philosophy* 55: 35–83.

Adkins, A. W. H. 1960. *Merit and Responsibility*. Oxford University Press.

1970. "Clouds, Mysteries, Socrates and Plato," *Antichthon* 4: 13–24.

1978. "Problems in Greek Popular Morality," *Classical Philology* 73: 143–58.

Ahbel-Rappe, S. 2009. *Socrates: A Guide for the Perplexed*. London: Continuum.

2018. *Socratic Ignorance and Platonic Knowledge in the Dialogues of Plato*. Albany, NY: SUNY Press.

Allen, R. E. 1965. *Studies in Plato's Metaphysics*. London: Routledge & Kegan Paul.

Annas, J. 1975. "On the Intermediates," *Archiv für Geschichte der Philosophie* 57: 146–66.

1981. *An Introduction to Plato's Republic*. Oxford University Press.

1982. "Plato on the Triviality of Literature," in J. Moravcsik and P. Temko (eds.), *Plato on Beauty, Wisdom, and the Arts* (Totowa, NJ: Rowman & Littlefield), 1–28.

1986. "Classical Greek Philosophy," in J. Boardman, J. Griffin, and O. Murray (eds.), *The Oxford History of the Classical World* (Oxford University Press), 234–54.

2012. "Virtue and Law in the *Republic*," in R. Patterson, V. Karasmanis, and A. Hermann (eds.), *Presocratics and Plato: Festschrift at Delphi in Honor of Charles Kahn* (Las Vegas: Parmenides), 165–82.

559

2017. *Virtue and Law in Plato and Beyond*. Oxford University Press.

Anton, J. (ed.) 1980. *Science and the Sciences in Plato*. New York: Eidos.

Apolloni, D. 1996. "Plato's Affinity Argument for the Immortality of the Soul," *Journal of the History of Philosophy* 34(1): 5–32.

Archer-Hind, R. D. 1973. *The* Timaeus *of Plato*. New York: Arno Press.

Armstrong, J. 2004. "After the Ascent: Plato on Becoming Like God," *Oxford Studies In Ancient Philosophy* 26: 170–83.

Arnim, H. von 1912. "Sprachliche Forschungen zur Chronologie der platonischen Dialogue," *Sitzungsberichte der Kaiserlichen Akademie der Wissenschaften in Wien: Philos. Hist. Klasse* 169(1): 1–210.

Arruzza, C. 2019. *A Wolf in the City: Tyranny and the Tyrant in Plato's* Republic. Oxford University Press.

Arsen, H. 2012. "A Case for the Utility of the Mathematicals," *Philosophia Mathematica* 20: 200–23.

Asmis, E. 1986. "Psychagôgia in Plato's *Phaedrus*," *Illinois Studies in Classical Philology* 11: 153–72.

2015. "Art and Morality," in P. Destrée and P. Murray (eds.), *A Companion to Ancient Aesthetics* (Malden, MA: Wiley Blackwell), 486–504.

Austin, E. 2010. "Prudence and the Fear of Death in Plato's *Apology*," *Ancient Philosophy* 30: 39–55.

2013. "Corpses, Self-Defense, and Immortality: Callicles' Fear of Death in the *Gorgias*," *Ancient Philosophy* 33: 33–52.

Bailey, D. 2014. "Platonic Causes Revisited," *Journal of the History of Philosophy* 52: 15–32.

Baima, N. 2016. "Persuasion, Falsehood, and Motivating Reason in Plato's *Laws*," *History of Philosophy Quarterly* 33: 117–34.

Barnes, J. 1979. *The Presocratics*, Vol. 2. London: Routledge.

(ed.) 1984. *The Complete Works of Aristotle*. Princeton University Press.

Barney, R. 2006. "The Sophistic Movement," in M. L. Gill and P. Pellegrin (eds.), *A Companion to Ancient Philosophy* (Oxford: Blackwell), 77–97.

2021. "*Technē* as a Model for Virtue in Plato, " in T. K. Johansen (ed.), *Productive Knowledge in Ancient Philosophy: The Concept of Techne* (Cambridge University Press), 62–85.

Barney, R., Brennan, T., and Brittain, C. (eds.) 2012. *Plato and the Divided Self*. Cambridge University Press.

Baron, C. 1897. "Contributions à la chronologie des dialogues de Platon," *Revue des Etudes grecques* 10: 264–78.

Bartninkas, V. 2019. "Traditional Gods and Civic Religion in Plato's Later Dialogues." PhD dissertation. University of Cambridge.

Battin, M. P. 1977. "Plato on True and False Poetry," *Journal of Aesthetics and Art Criticism* 36: 163–74.

Belfiore, E. 1984. "A Theory of Imitation in Plato's *Republic*," *Transactions of the American Philological Association* 114: 121–46.

2012. *Socrates' Daimonic Art: Love for Wisdom in Four Platonic Dialogues.* Cambridge University Press.

Benson, H. H. (ed.) 1992. *Essays on the Philosophy of Socrates.* Oxford University Press.

2000. *Socratic Wisdom.* Oxford University Press.

2013a. "The Priority of Definition," in Bussanich and Smith 2013, 136–55.

2013b. "What Should Euthyphro Do?" *History of Philosophy Quarterly* 30: 115–46.

2015. *Clitophon's Challenge.* Oxford University Press.

Bernabé, A. 2007. "L'âme après la mort: modèles orphiques et transposition platonicienne," *Études Platoniciennes* 4: 25–44.

2011. *Platón y el orfismo: diálogos entre religión y filosofía.* Madrid: Abada Editores.

Bernabé, A. and Casadesús, F. 2008. *Orfeo y la tradición órfica: Un reencuentro.* Madrid: Akal.

Bernabé, A. and Jiménez San Cristóbal, A. I. 2008. *Instructions for the Netherworld: the Orphic Gold Tablets.* Brill: Leiden.

Betegh, G. 2009. "What Makes a Myth *eikôs*? Remarks inspired by Myles Burnyeat's EIKÔS MYTHOS," in Mohr and Sattler 2009, 213–24.

2013. "Socrate et Archélaos dans les *Nuées*," in A. Laks and R. Saetta Cottone (eds.), *Comédie et Philosophie* (Paris: Éditions Rue d'Ulm), 87–106.

2018. "Cosmic and Human Cognition in the *Timaeus*," in J. Sisko (ed.), *Philosophy of Mind in Antiquity* (Routledge: London), 120–40.

2020. "The Ingredients of the Soul in Plato's *Timaeus*," in F. Leigh (ed.), *Themes in Plato, Aristotle and Hellenistic Philosophy: Keeling Lectures 2011–18*, *BICS* Supplement 141 (London: Institute of Classical Studies), 83–104.

(unpublished) "Plato and the Origins of the Concept of Body."

Bett, R. 2006. "Socrates and Skepticism," in S. Ahbel-Rappe and R. Kamtekar (eds.), *A Companion to Socrates* (Oxford: Blackwell), 298–311.

Beversluis, J. 1974. "Socratic Definition," *American Philosophical Quarterly* 11: 331–6.

2000. *Cross-Examining Socrates.* Cambridge University Press.

Billig, L. 1920. "Clausulae and Platonic Chronology," *Journal of Philology* 35: 225–56.

Blank, D. L. 1993. "The Arousal of Emotion in Plato's Dialogues," *Classical Quarterly* 43: 428–39.

Blass, F. 1874. *Die attische Beredsamkeit*, Vol. 2. Leipzig.

Blondell, R. 2002. *The Play of Character in Plato's Dialogues*. Cambridge University Press.

Bobonich, C. 1991. "Persuasion, Compulsion and Freedom," *Classical Quarterly* 41: 365–88.

2002. *Plato's Utopia Recast: His Later Ethics and Politics*. Oxford University Press.

(ed.) 2010. *Plato's Laws: A Critical Guide*. Cambridge University Press.

2011. "Socrates and Eudaimonia," in Morrison 2011, 292–322.

Bond, G. W. (ed.) 1981. *Euripides:* Heracles. Oxford University Press.

Bordt, M. 2006. *Platons Theologie*. Freiburg: Verlag Karl Alber.

Bosanquet, B. 1892. *A History of Aesthetic*. London: Swan Sonnenschein.

Bostock, D. 1984. "Plato on 'Is not'," *Oxford Studies in Ancient Philosophy* 2: 89–119.

1986. *Plato's* Phaedo. Oxford: Clarendon Press.

1990. "Plato and Nominalism: Critical Notice of Terry Penner, *The Ascent from Nominalism*," *Oxford Studies in Ancient Philosophy* 8: 259–74.

Boter, G. 1989. *The Textual Tradition of Plato's* Republic. Supplement to *Mnemosyne*. Leiden: Brill.

Bowden, H. 2010. *Mystery Cults in the Ancient World*. London: Thames & Hudson.

Bowen, A. and Goldstein, B. 1988. "Meton of Athens and Astronomy in the Late Fifth Century, B.C.," in E. Leichty, M. Dej Ellis, and P. Gerardi (eds.), *Scientific Humanist: Studies in Memory of Abraham Sachs* (Philadelphia: University of Pennsylvania Museum), 39–81.

Boys-Stones, G. and Rowe, C. (ed. and trans.). 2013. *The Circle of Socrates*. Indianapolis, IN: Hackett.

Brandwood, L. 1990. *The Chronology of Plato's Dialogues*. Cambridge University Press.

Bremmer, J. N. 2014. *Initiation into the Mysteries of the Ancient World*. Berlin: De Gruyter.

Brickhouse, T. C. and Smith, N. D. 1989. *Socrates on Trial*. Princeton University Press.

1994. *Plato's Socrates*. Oxford University Press.

2000. *The Philosophy of Socrates*. Boulder, CO: Westview Press.

2010. *Socratic Moral Psychology*. Cambridge University Press.

Brisson, L. 1994. *Le Même et l'Autre dans la Structure Ontologique du Timée de Platon*. Sankt Augustin: Akademia Verlag.

1997. "Plato's Theory of Sense Perception in the *Timaeus*: How it Works and What it Means," *Proceedings of the Boston Area Colloquium in Ancient Philosophy* 13: 147–76.

2011. *Platon:* Parménide, 3rd ed. Paris: Flammarion.

Broadie, S. 2012. *Nature and Divinity in Plato's* Timaeus. Cambridge University Press.

Brock, R., 1990. "Plato and Comedy," in Craik 1990, 39–50.

Bronstein, D. 2010. "Meno's Paradox in *Posterior Analytics* 1.1," *Oxford Studies in Ancient Philosophy* 38: 115–41.

Bronstein, D. and Schwab, W. 2019. "Is Plato an Innatist in the *Meno?*," *Phronesis* 64(4): 392–430.

Brown, E. 2000a. "Justice and Compulsion for Plato's Philosopher-Rulers," *Ancient Philosophy* 20: 1–17.

2000b. "Socrates the Cosmopolitan," *Stanford Agora: An Online Journal of Legal Perspectives* 1: 74–87.

2009. "False Idles: The Politics of the 'Quiet Life'," in R. Balot (ed.), *A Companion to Greek and Roman Political Thought* (Oxford: Basil Blackwell), 485–500.

2017. "Plato's Ethics and Politics in *The Republic*," in E. N. Zalta (ed.), *The Stanford Encyclopedia of Philosophy* (Fall ed.), https://plato.stanford.edu/archives/Fall2017/entries/plato-ethics-politics/

Brown, L. 1994. "The Verb 'to be' in Greek Philosophy: Some Remarks," in S. Everson (ed.), *Companions to Ancient Thought: Language* (Cambridge University Press), 212–36.

1999. "Being in the *Sophist*," in G. Fine (ed.), *Plato 1: Metaphysics and Epistemology* (Oxford University Press), 455–78.

2008. Review of Scott 2006, *Philosophical Review* 117: 468–71.

Buccioni, E. 2007. "Revising the Controversial Nature of Persuasion in Plato's *Laws*," *Polis* 24: 262–83.

Burkert, W. 1960. "Platon oder Pythagoras? Zum Ursprung des Wortes 'Philosophie'," *Hermes* 88: 159–77.

1985. *Greek Religion.* Trans. J. Raffan. Cambridge, MA: Harvard University Press.

1987. *Ancient Mystery Cults.* Cambridge, MA: Harvard University Press.

Burnet, J. 1901–1907. *Platonis Opera*, Vols. 2–5. Oxford Classical Texts. Oxford University Press

1911. *Plato's* Phaedo *Edited with Introduction and Notes*. Oxford: Clarendon Press.

1924. *Plato:* Euthyphro, Apology of Socrates *and* Crito. Oxford: Clarendon Press.

Burnyeat, M. F. 1971. "Virtues in Action," in Vlastos 1971, 209–34.

1977a. "Examples in Epistemology," *Philosophy* 52: 381–98.

1977b. "Socratic Midwifery, Platonic Inspiration," *Bulletin of the Institute of Classical Studies* 24: 7–16. Reprinted in Benson 1992, 53–65.

1985. "Sphinx Without a Secret," *New York Review of Books* 32 (May 30): 30–6.

1987. "Platonism and Mathematics: A Prelude to a Discussion," in A. Graeser (ed.), *Mathematics and Metaphysics in Aristotle* (Bern: Haupt), 213–40.

ed. 1990. *Plato's* Theaetetus. Indianapolis, IN: Hackett.

1992. "Utopia and Fantasy: The Practicability of Plato's Ideally Just City," in J. Hopkins and A. Savile (eds.), *Psychoanalysis, Mind and Art* (Oxford: Blackwell), 175–87.

1997. "The Impiety of Socrates," *Ancient Philosophy* 17: 1–12.

2000. "Plato on Why Mathematics is Good for the Soul," *Proceedings of the British Academy* 103: 1–81.

2003. "Socrates, Money, and the Grammar of ΓΙΓΝΕΣΘΑΙ," *Journal of Hellenic Studies* 123: 1–25.

2005. "*Eikôs muthos*," *Rhizai* 2: 143–65. Reprinted in Partenie 2009.

2012. *Explorations in Ancient and Modern Philosophy*, Vol. 2. Cambridge University Press.

Burnyeat, M. F., and Frede, M. (eds.) 1997. *The Original Sceptics: A Controversy.* Indianapolis, IN: Hackett.

2015. *The Pseudo-Platonic Seventh Letter*, ed. D. Scott. Oxford University Press.

Bury, R. G. 1897. *The* Philebus *of Plato.* Cambridge University Press.

1932. *The* Symposium *of Plato.* Cambridge: Heffner and Sons.

Bussanich, J. and Smith, N. D. (eds.) 2013. *The Bloomsbury Companion to Socrates.* London: Bloomsbury.

Calcidius 2016. *On Plato's* Timaeus, ed. and trans. J. Magee. Cambridge, MA: Harvard University Press.

Callard, A. 2017. "Everyone Desires the Good: Socrates' Protreptic Theory of Desire," *Review of Metaphysics* 70(4): 617–44.

Calvo, T. and Brisson, L. (eds.) 1997. *Interpreting the* Timaeus-Critias (Proceedings of the IV Symposium Platonicum: Selected Papers). Sankt Anton: Academia Verlag.

Campbell, L. 1867. *The* Sophistes *and* Politicus *of Plato.* Oxford: Clarendon Press.

Carone, G. R. 2005a. *Plato's Cosmology and Its Ethical Dimensions.* Cambridge University Press.

2005b. "Mind and Body in Late Plato," *Archiv für Geschichte der Philosophie* 87: 227–70.

Carpenter, A. 2008. "Embodying Intelligence: Animals and Us in Plato's *Timaeus*," in J. Zovko and J. Dillon (eds.), *Platonism and Forms of Intelligence* (Berlin: Akademie Verlag), 39–58.

2010. "Embodied, Intelligent (?) Souls: Plants in Plato's *Timaeus*," *Phronesis* 55: 281–303.

Cartledge, P. A. 1993. *The Greeks: A Portrait of Self and Others*, 2nd ed. Oxford University Press.

1997. "Deep Plays: Theatre as Process in Greek Civic Life," in P. Easterling (ed.), *The Cambridge Companion to Greek Tragedy* (Cambridge University Press), 3–35.

Casadesús Bordoy, F. 2013. "On the Origin of the Orphic-Pythagorean Notion of the Immortality of the Soul," in G. Cornelli, R. D. McKirahan, and C. Macris (eds.), *On Pythagoreanism* (Berlin: De Gruyter), 153–76.

Castagnoli, L. 2018. Review of Fine 2014, *Philosophical Review* 127: 225–8.

Chance, T. H. 1992. *Plato's* Euthydemus*: Analysis of What Is and What Is Not Philosophy*. Berkeley and Los Angeles: University of California Press.

Charles, D. 2006. "Types of Definition in the *Meno*," in L. Judson and V. Karasmanis (eds.), *Remembering Socrates: Philosophical Essays* (Oxford: Clarendon Press), 110–28.

2010. "The Paradox in the *Meno* and Aristotle's Attempts to Solve It," in D. Charles (ed.), *Definition in Greek Philosophy* (Oxford University Press), 115–50.

Cherniss, H. 1932. "On Plato's *Republic* X 597B," *American Journal of Philology* 53: 233–42.

1933. Review of Field 1930. *American Journal of Philology* 54: 79–83. Reprinted in *Selected Papers* (Leiden: Brill, 1977).

1944. *Aristotle's Criticism of Plato and the Academy*, Vol. 1. Baltimore, MD: Johns Hopkins Press.

1945. *The Riddle of the Early Academy*. Berkeley: University of California Press.

1947. "Some War-Time Publications Concerning Plato. II," *American Journal of Philology* 68: 225–65.

1957. "The Relation of the *Timaeus* to Plato's Later Dialogues," *The American Journal of Philology* 78: 225–66.

Chomsky, N. 1965. *Aspects of the Theory of Syntax*. Cambridge, MA: MIT Press.

1980. *Rules and Representations*. New York: Columbia University Press.

1988. *Language and Problems of Knowledge: The Managua Lectures*. Cambridge, MA: MIT Press.

Clay, D. 1983. "The Tragic and Comic Poet of the *Symposium*," in J. P. Anton and A. Preus (eds.), *Essays in Ancient Greek Philosophy*, Vol. 2 (Albany, NY: SUNY Press), 186–202.

Clinton, K. 1992. *Myth and Cult: the Iconography of the Eleusinian Mysteries* (the Martin P. Nilsson lectures on Greek religion, delivered 19–21 November 1990 at the Swedish Institute at Athens). Stockholm: Svenska institutet i Athen.

2005. *Eleusis, the Inscriptions on Stone: Documents of the Sanctuary of the Two Goddesses and Public Documents of the Deme.* Athens: Archaeological Society at Athens.

Cohen, S. M. 1971. "The Logic of the Third Man," *Philosophical Review* 80: 448–75.

Collingwood, R. G. 1925. "Plato's Philosophy of Art," *Mind* 34, 154–72.

Cook Wilson, J. 1904. "On the Platonist Doctrine of the ἀσύμβλητοι ἀριθμοί," *Classical Review* 18: 247–60.

Cooper, J. M. 1973. "Plato's Theory of Human Good in the *Philebus*," *The Journal of Philosophy* 74: 327–49. Reprinted in *Reason and Emotion: Essays on Ancient Moral Psychology and Ethical Theory* (Princeton University Press, 1999), 150–64.

1977. "The Psychology of Justice in Plato," *American Philosophical Quarterly* 14: 151–7.

1984. "Plato's Theory of Human Motivation," *History of Philosophy Quarterly*: 3–21.

(ed.) 1997a. *Plato: Complete Works.* Indianapolis, IN: Hackett.

1997b. "Plato's *Statesman* and Politics," *Proceedings of the Boston Area Colloquium in Ancient Philosophy* 13: 71–103.

Cope, E. M. 1854. "The Sophists," *Journal of Philology* 1: 145–88.

Cornford, F. M. 1937. *Plato's Cosmology.* London: Routledge & Kegan Paul. Reprinted: Indianapolis, IN: Hackett, 1997.

1939. *Plato and Parmenides.* London: Kegan Paul.

1971. "The Doctrine of Eros in Plato's *Symposium*," in G. Vlastos (ed.), *Plato II: Ethics, Politics, and Philosophy of Art and Religion* (Garden City: Doubleday), 119–32.

Coulton, J. J. 1977. *Ancient Greek Architects at Work: Problems of Structure and Design.* Ithaca, NY: Cornell University Press.

Coventry, L. 1990. "The Role of the Interlocutor in Plato's Dialogues," in C. B. R. Pelling (ed.), *Characterization and Individuality in Greek Literature* (Oxford University Press), 174–96.

Craik, E. M. (ed.) 1990. *Owls to Athens.* Oxford University Press.

Creed, J. L. 1973. "Moral Values in the Age of Thucydides," *Classical Quarterly* 23: 213–31.

Crombie, I. M. 1963. *An Examination of Plato's Doctrines*, Vol. 2. London: Routledge.

Cross, R. C. and Woozley, A. D. 1964. *Plato's* Republic*: A Philosophical Commentary*. London: Macmillan.

Curd, P. 2007. *Anaxagoras of Clazomenae: Fragments and Testimonia*. University of Toronto Press.

Dancy, R. 2004. *Plato's Introduction of Forms*. Cambridge University Press.

Delcomminette, S. 2006. *Le* Philèbe *de Platon: Introduction à l'agathologie Platonicienne*. Leiden: Brill.

Demos, R. 1984. "A Fallacy in Plato's *Republic*?," *Philosophical Review* 73: 395–8.

Denyer, N. 2007. "The *Phaedo*'s Final Argument," in Dominic Scott (ed.), *Maieusis: Essays in ancient philosophy in honour of Myles Burnyeat* (Oxford University Press), 87–96.

   (ed.) 2019. *Plato and Xenophon: Apologies of Socrates*. Cambridge University Press.

Derrida, J. 1981. "Plato's Pharmacy," in *Dissemination*, tr. Barbara Johnson (University of Chicago Press), 61–171.

Des Places, E. 1964. "Platon et la Langue des Mystères," *Annales de la Faculté des Lettres et Sciences Humaines d'Aix* 38.1: 9–23.

Destrée, P. 2011. "The Speech of Alcibiades," in C. Horn (ed.), *Platon: Symposion* (Berlin: Akademie Verlag), 191–205.

Destrée, P. and Giannopoulou, Z. (eds.) 2017. *Plato's* Symposium*: A Critical Guide*. Cambridge University Press.

Destrée, P., and Smith, N. D. (eds.) 2005. *Socrates' Divine Sign: Religion, Practice and Value in Philosophy* (*Apeiron* 38,2).

Devereux, D. 1978. "Nature and Teaching in Plato's *Meno*," *Phronesis* 23: 118–26.

   1992. "The Unity of the Virtues in Plato's *Protagoras* and *Laches*," *Philosophical Review* 101: 765–89.

   1994. "Separation and Immanence in Plato's Theory of Forms," *Oxford Studies in Ancient Philosophy* 12: 63–90.

   1995. "Socrates' Kantian Conception of Virtue," *Journal of the History of Philosophy* 33: 318–408.

Díaz Tejera, A. 1961. "Ensayo de un metodo lingüístico para cronologia de Platón," *Emerita* 29: 241–86.

Diels, H. and Kranz, W. 1954. *Die Fragmente der Vorsokratiker*, 7th edn. Dublin and Zürich: Weidemann.

Diès, A. 1941. *Platon: Oeuvres Complètes:* Philèbe. Paris: Les Belles Lettres.

Dillon, J. 2003. *The Heirs of Plato: A Study of the Old Academy*. Oxford University Press.

Dimas, P. 2003. "Recollecting Forms in the *Phaedo*," *Phronesis* 48: 175–214.

   2014. "Knowing and Wanting in the *Hippias Minor*," *Philosophical Inquiry* 38: 106–18.

Dimas, P., Lane, M., and Meyer, S. (eds.) 2021. *Plato's* Statesman: *A Philosophical Discussion*. Oxford University Press.

Dinkelaar, B. M. 2020. "Plato and the Language of Mysteries," *Mnemosyne* 73: 36.

Dittenberger, W. 1881. "Sprachliche Kriterien fur die Chronologie der platonischen Dialoge," *Hermes* 16: 321–45.

Dixsaut, M. 1991. *Platon:* Phédon. Paris.

Dorion, L.-A. 2011. "The Rise and Fall of the Socratic Problem," in Morrison 2011, 1–23.

Dover, K. J. 1965. "The Date of Plato's *Symposium*," *Phronesis* 10: 2–20.

(ed.) 1968. *Aristophanes'* Clouds. Oxford: Clarendon Press.

1974. *Greek Popular Morality*. Oxford: Blackwell.

1978. *Greek Homosexuality*. Cambridge, MA: Harvard University Press.

(ed.) 1980. *Plato's* Symposium. Cambridge University Press.

(ed.) 1993. *Aristophanes:* Frogs. Oxford University Press.

Dowden, K. 1980. "Grades in the Eleusinian Mysteries," *Revue de l'histoire des religions* 197: 409–27.

Duke, E. A. et al. (eds.) 1995. *Platonis Opera*, Vol. 1: *Tetralogias I–II*. Oxford: Clarendon Press.

Ebert, T. 2004. Phaidon: *Übersetzung und Kommentar*. Göttingen: Vandenhoeck & Ruprecht.

Ebrey, D. 2014a. "Making Room for Matter: Material Causes in the *Phaedo* and the *Physics*," *Apeiron* 47.2: 245–65.

2014b. "Meno's Paradox in Context," *British Journal for the History of Philosophy* 22: 1–21.

2017a. "Plato's *Phaedo*," *Oxford Bibliographies in Classics*. DOI: 10.1093/obo/ 9780195389661-0272 .

2017b. "The Asceticism of the *Phaedo*: Pleasure, Purification, and the Soul's Proper Activity," *Archiv für Geschichte der Philosophie* 99: 1–30.

2017c. "Socrates on Why We Should Inquire," *Ancient Philosophy* 37: 1–17.

2023. *Plato's* Phaedo: *Forms, Death, and the Philosophical Life*. Cambridge University Press.

Echterling, T. 2018. "What Did Glaucon Draw?: a Diagrammatic Proof for Plato's Divided Line," *Journal for the History of Philosophy* 56: 1–15.

Edmonds, R. G. 2004. *Myths of the Underworld Journey: Plato, Aristophanes, and the "Orphic" Gold Tablets*. New York: Cambridge University Press.

2011. *The "Orphic" Gold Tablets and Greek Religion: Further Along the Path*. New York: Cambridge University Press.

2013. *Redefining Ancient Orphism: a Study in Greek Religion*. New York: Cambridge University Press.

2017. "Alcibiades the Profane: Images of the Mysteries," in Destrée and Giannopoulou 2017, 194–215.

El Murr, D. 2014. *Savoir et Gouverner: Essai sur la Science Politique Platonicienne*. Paris: Vrin.

Ferrari, G. R. F. 1989. "Plato and Poetry," in G. A. Kennedy (ed.), *The Cambridge History of Literary Criticism* (Cambridge University Press), 92–148.

1991. "Moral Fecundity: A Discussion of A.W. Price, *Love and Friendship in Plato and Aristotle*," *Oxford Studies in Ancient Philosophy* 9: 169–84.

1992. "Platonic Love," in Kraut 1992, 248–76.

(ed.) 2007. *Cambridge Companion to Plato's* Republic. (New York: Cambridge University Press).

Field, G. C. 1930. *Plato and his Contemporaries*. London: Methuen.

Fine, G. 1978. "Knowledge and Belief in *Republic* V," *Archiv für Geschichte der Philosophie* 60: 121–39.

1984. "Separation," *Oxford Studies in Ancient Philosophy* 2: 31–87.

1986. "Imminence," *Oxford Studies in Ancient Philosophy* 4: 71–97.

1988. "Plato on Perception," *Oxford Studies in Ancient Philosophy* supp. vol.: 15–28.

1990. "Knowledge and Belief in *Republic* V–VII," in S. Everson (ed.), *Companions to Ancient Thought I: Epistemology* (Cambridge University Press), 85–115.

1993. *On Ideas: Aristotle's Criticism of Plato's Theory of Forms*. Oxford: Clarendon Press.

(ed.) 1999a. *Plato 1: Metaphysics and Epistemology*. Oxford University Press.

(ed.) 1999b. *Plato 2: Ethics, Politics, Religion and the Soul*. Oxford University Press.

2004. "Knowledge and True Belief in the *Meno*," *Oxford Studies in Ancient Philosophy* 27: 41–81.

2007. "Enquiry and Discovery," *Oxford Studies in Ancient Philosophy* 32: 331–67.

2008. "Does Socrates Claim to Know that He Knows Nothing?," *Oxford Studies in Ancient Philosophy* 35: 49–88.

2014. *The Possibility of Inquiry: Meno's Paradox from Socrates to Sextus*. Oxford University Press.

(ed.) 2019. *Oxford Handbook of Plato*, 2nd ed. Oxford: Oxford University Press.

Fletcher, E. 2016. "*Aisthēsis*, Reason and Appetite in the *Timaeus*," *Phronesis* 61: 397–434.

Foley, R. 2008. "Plato's Undividable Line: Contradiction and Method in *Republic* VI," *Journal of the History of Philosophy* 46: 1–23.

Forster, M. N. 2006. "Socrates' Demand for Definitions," *Oxford Studies in Ancient Philosophy* 31: 1–47.

2007. "Socrates' Profession of Ignorance," *Oxford Studies in Ancient Philosophy* 32: 1–35.

Fossheim, H. 2013. "The *prooimia*, Types of Motivation, and Moral Psychology," in C. Horn (ed.), *Plato: Gezetze/Nomoi* (Munich: Akademie Verlag), 87–104.

Foster, M. B. 1937. "A Mistake of Plato's in the *Republic*," *Mind* 46: 386–93.

Fowler, D. 1999. *The Mathematics of Plato's Academy*, 2nd ed. Oxford University Press.

2000. "Eudoxus: *Parapegmata* and Proportionality," in Suppes et al. 2000, 33–48.

Frajese, A. 1963. "Platone e la matematica nel mondo antico," *Testi e Documenti* 4: 59–218.

Frances, B. 1996. "Plato's Response to the Third Man Argument in the Paradoxical Exercise of the *Parmenides*," *Ancient Philosophy* 16: 47–64.

Franklin, L. 2001. "The Structure of Dialectic in the *Meno*," *Phronesis* 26: 413–39.

2012. "Inventing Intermediates: Mathematical Discourse and Its Objects in *Republic* VII," *Journal of the History of Philosophy* 50: 483–506.

Frede, D. 1978. "The Final Proof of the Immortality of the Soul in Plato's *Phaedo* 102a–107a," *Phronesis* 23: 27–41.

1993. *Plato: Philebus.* Indianapolis, IN: Hackett.

1997. *Platon: Philebos.* Göttingen: Vandenhoeck & Ruprecht.

Frede, M. 1967. *Prädikation und Existenzaussage, Hypomnemata* 18. Göttingen: Vandenhoeck & Ruprecht.

1980. "The Original Notion of Cause", in M. Schofield et al. (eds.), *Doubt and Dogmatism* (Oxford University Press), 217–49.

Friberg, J. 2007. *Amazing Traces of a Babylonian Origin in Greek Mathematics.* Singapore: World Scientific Publishing.

Friedländer, P. 1964: *Plato: The Dialogues*, Vol. 2, trans. H. Meyerhoff. New York: Bollingen Series.

Fronterotta, F. 2007. "Carone on the Mind–Body Problem in Late Plato," *Archiv für Geschichte der Philosophie* 89: 231–6.

Furley, D. 1976. "Anaxagoras in Response to Parmenides," in R. Shiner and J. King-Farlow (eds.), *New Essays in Plato and the Presocratics* (*Canadian Journal of Philosophy* 2, suppl.), 61–85.

Furth, M. 1974. "Elements of Eleatic Ontology," in A. P. D. Mourelatos (ed.), *The Presocratics* (Garden City, NY: Doubleday), 241–70.

Gallop, D. 1975. *Plato: Phaedo.* Oxford: Clarendon Press.

Gazziero, L. 2014. "'ἐὰν ὡσαύτως τῇ ψυχῇ ἐπὶ πάντα ἴδῃς' (Platonis Parmenides, 132a1–132b2). Voir les Idées avec son âme et le 'Troisième homme' de Platon," *Revue de Philosophie Ancienne* 32.

Geach, P. T. 1956. "The Third Man Again," *Philosophical Review* 65: 72–82.

1966. "Plato's *Euthyphro*: An Analysis and Commentary," *Monist* 50: 369–82.

Gentzler, J. 1994. "Recollection and 'The Problem of the Socratic Elenchus'," *Proceedings of the Boston Area Colloquium in Ancient Philosophy* 10: 257–95.

Gerson, L. 2013. *From Plato to Platonism*. Ithaca, NY: Cornell University Press.

Gifford, E. H. (ed.) 1905. *Euthydemus*. Oxford University Press.

Gill, C. 2000. "The Body's Fault? Plato's *Timaeus* on Psychic Illness," in M. R. Wright (ed.), *Reason and Necessity: Essays on Plato's Timaeus* (London: Duckworth), 58–84.

2006. "The Platonic Dialogue," in M. L. Gill and P. Pellegrin (eds.), *A Companion to Ancient Philosophy* (Oxford: Blackwell), 136–50.

Gill, M. L. 2012. *Philosophos: Plato's Missing Dialogue*. Oxford University Press.

Gonzalez, F. 1996. "Propositions or Objects? A Critique of Gail Fine on Knowledge and Belief in *Republic* V," *Phronesis* 41: 245–75.

Gosling, J. C. B. 1975. *Plato:* Philebus. Oxford University Press.

Gosling, J. C. B. and Taylor, C. C. W. 1982. *The Greeks on Pleasure*. Oxford University Press.

Gould, J. 1955. *The Development of Plato's Ethics*. New York: Russell and Russell.

Graf, F. 2004. "Trick or Treat? On Collective Epiphanies in Antiquity," *Illinois Classical Studies* 29: 111–30.

2006. "Mysteries," in *Brill's New Pauly* (online).

Graf, F. and Johnston, S. I. 2013. *Ritual Texts for the Afterlife: Orpheus and the Bacchic Gold Tablets*. London: Routledge.

Graham D. W. 2010. *The Texts of Early Greek Philosophy*, 2 vols. Cambridge University Press.

Grams, L. 2009. "Medical Theory in Plato's *Timaeus*," *Rhizai* 6 (2): 161–92.

Greene, W. C. 1920. "The Spirit of Comedy in Plato," *Harvard Studies in Classical Philology* 31: 63–123.

Griffin, J. 1999. "Sophocles and the Democratic City," in J. Griffin (ed.), *Sophocles Revisited* (Oxford University Press), 73–94.

Grote, G. 1867. *Plato and the Other Companions of Socrates*, 2nd ed., 3 vols. London.

1888. *A History of Greece*, 6th ed., 10 vols. London.

Grube, G. M. A., 2002. *Plato: Five Dialogues*, rev. J. Cooper, 2nd ed. Indianapolis, IN: Hackett.

Grube, G. M. A. (trans.) and Reeve, C. D. C. (revised). 1992. *Plato's Republic*. Indianapolis, IN: Hackett.

Gulley, N. 1968. *The Philosophy of Socrates*. New York: St. Martin's Press.

Guthrie, W. K. C. 1956. *Plato:* Protagoras *and* Meno. Harmondsworth: Penguin.

1969. *History of Greek Philosophy*, Vols. 2–4. Cambridge University Press.

1978. *History of Greek Philosophy*, Vol. 5. Cambridge University Press.

Hackforth, R. 1936. "Plato's Theism," *Classical Quarterly* 30: 4–9. Reprinted in R. E. Allen (ed.), *Studies in Plato's Metaphysics* (London and New York: Routledge and Kegan Paul, 1965), 439–47.

1950. "Immortality in Plato's *Symposium*," *The Classical Review* 64: 43–5.

Hadot, P. 2002. *What is Ancient Philosophy?* Trans. Michael Chase. Cambridge, MA: Harvard University Press.

Hahn, R. 1983. "A Note on Plato's Divided Line," *Journal of the History of Philosophy* 21: 235–7.

Halperin, D. M. 1990. *One Hundred Years of Homosexuality and Other Essays on Greek Love*. London: Routledge.

Harte, V. 2002. *Plato on Parts and Wholes: The Metaphysics of Structure*. Oxford: Clarendon Press.

2018. "Some 'Value of Knowledge' Problems in Plato's *Philebus*," *Aristotelian Society Supplementary Volume* 92.1: 27–48.

2019. "The Dialogue's Finale: *Philebus* 64c–67b," in P. Dimas, R. Jones, and G. Lear (eds.), *Plato's* Philebus (Oxford University Press), 253–68.

forthcoming. "Plato's Butcher: Realism and Platonic Classification," in D. Bronstein, T. Johansen, and M. Peramatzis (eds.), *Aristotelian Metaphysics, Ancient and Modern: Essays in honour of David Charles* (Oxford University Press).

Haselberger, L. 1997. "Architectural Likenesses: Models and Plans of Architecture in Classical Antiquity," *Journal of Roman Archeology* 10: 77–94.

Havelock, E. 1963. *Preface to Plato*. Cambridge, MA: Harvard University Press.

Hawtrey, R. S. W. 1981. *Commentary on Plato's* Euthydemus. Philadelphia: American Philosophical Society.

Heiberg, I. L. 1904. "Mathematisches zu Aristoteles," *Abhandlungen zur Geschichte der Mathematischen Wissenschaften* 18: 1–49.

Heidel, W. A. (ed.) 1902. *Plato's* Euthyphro. New York: American Book Co.

Hitz, Z. 2009. "Plato on the Sovereignty of Law," in R. Balot (ed.), *A Companion to Greek and Roman Political Thought* (Oxford: Blackwell), 367–81.

Hoerber, R. G. 1962. "Plato's *Lesser Hippias*," *Phronesis* 7: 121–31.

Hornblower, S. 2011. *The Greek World 479–323 BC*, 4th ed. London: Routledge.

Howland, R. L. 1937. "The Attack on Isocrates in the *Phaedrus*," *Classical Quarterly* 31: 551–9.

Høyrup, J. 2002. *Lengths, Widths, Surfaces: a Portrait of Old Babylonian Algebra and Its Kin*. New York: Springer.

Huffman, C. 1999. "Limite et illimité chez les premiers philosophes grecs," in M. Dixsaut (ed.), *La fêlure du plaisir: études sur le* Philèbe *de platon 2: contextes* (Paris: Vrin), 11–31.

Hunter, R. 2004. *Plato's* Symposium. Oxford University Press.

Hussey, E. L. 1985. "Thucydidean History and Democritean Theory," in P. Cartledge and F. D. Harvey (eds.), *Crux: Essays Presented to G. E. M. de Ste Croix* (London: Duckworth), 118–38.

Imhausen, A. 2016. *Mathematics in Ancient Egypt: a Contextual History*. Princeton: Princeton University Press.

Ionescu, C. 2007. "The Transition from the Lower to the Higher Mysteries of Love in Plato's *Symposium*," *Dialogue* 46: 27–42.

Irwin, T. 1977. *Plato's Moral Theory*. Oxford: Clarendon Press.

1986. "Socrates the Epicurean?," *Illinois Classical Studies* 11: 85–112. Reprinted in Benson 1992, 198–219.

1989. *Classical Thought*. Oxford University Press.

1995a. *Plato's Ethics*. Oxford University Press.

1995b. "Plato's Objections to the Sophists," in A. Powell (ed.), *The Greek World* (London: Routledge), 568–90.

1999. "Plato's Theory of Forms," in Fine 1999a, 143–70.

2005. "Was Socrates Against Democracy?," in R. Kamtekar (ed.), *Plato's* Euthyphro, Apology, *and* Crito (Lanham, MD: Rowman and Littlefield), 127–49.

2009. "The Inside Story of the Seventh Platonic Letter: a Sceptical Introduction," *Rhizai* 6: 7–40.

2010. "Morality as Law and Morality in the *Laws*," in Bobonich 2010, 92–107.

2019. "The Platonic Corpus," in Fine 2019, 69–92.

Jackson, H. 1882. "On Plato's *Republic* VI 506D sqq.," *Journal of Philology* 10: 132–50.

Janell, G. 1901. "Quaestiones Platonicae," *Jahrbücher für classische Philologie*, Supp. 26: 263–336.

Jebb, R. C. 1893. *The Attic Orators*, Vol. 1. London: Macmillan.

Jenkins, M. 2016. "Plato's Godlike Philosopher," *Classical Philology* 111: 330–52.

Johansen, T. K. 2004. *Plato's Natural Philosophy: A Study of the* Timaeus-Critias. Cambridge University Press.

Jones, A. H. M. 1957. *Athenian Democracy*. Oxford: Blackwell.

Jones, R. E. 2016. "Socrates' Bleak View of the Human Condition," *Ancient Philosophy* 36: 97–105.

Jones, R. and Sharma, R. 2017. "The Wandering Hero of the *Hippias Minor*: Socrates on Virtue and Craft," *Classical Philology* 112: 113–37.

2020. "Xenophon's Socrates on Justice and Well-being: *Memorabilia* iv 2," *Ancient Philosophy* 40: 19–40.

Joseph, H. W. B. 1971. *Essays in Ancient and Modern Philosophy*. Freeport, NY: Books for Libraries Press.

Jowett, B. 1953. *The Dialogues of Plato*, Vol. 2, 4th ed. Oxford University Press.

Judson, L. 2019. "The *Meno*," in Fine 2019, 161–82.

Kahn, C. H. 1979. *The Art and Thought of Heraclitus*. Cambridge University Press.

1981. "Some Philosophical Uses of 'to be' in Plato," *Phronesis* 26: 105–34.

1987. "Plato's Theory of Desire," *Review of Metaphysics* 41: 77–103.

1996. *Plato and the Socratic Dialogue: The Philosophical Use of a Literary Form*. Cambridge University Press.

2001. *Pythagoras and the Pythagoreans*. Indianapolis, IN: Hackett.

2003. "On Platonic Chronology," in J. Annas and C. Rowe (eds.), *New Perspectives on Plato, Modern and Ancient* (Cambridge, MA: Harvard University Press), 93–128.

2004. "A Return to the Theory of the Verb Be and the Concept of Being," *Ancient Philosophy* 24: 381–405.

Kaluscha, W. 1904. "Zur Chronologie der platonischen Dialoge," *Weiner Studien* 26: 190–204.

Kamtekar, R. 2016. "The Soul's (After-)Life," *Ancient Philosophy* 36: 115–32.

2017. *Plato's Moral Psychology: Intellectualism, the Divided Soul, and the Desire for the Good*. Oxford University Press.

Kelsey, Sean. 2000. "Recollection in the *Phaedo*," *Proceedings of the Boston Area Colloquium in Ancient Philosophy* 16: 91–121.

Kerferd, G. B. 1981. *The Sophistic Movement*. Cambridge University Press.

Keyt, D. 1992. Review of John Malcolm, *Plato on the Self-Predication of Forms: Early and Middle Dialogues, Bryn Mawr Classical Review* 1992.01.08, http://bmcr .brynmawr.edu/1992/1992.01.08.html.

Kidd, I. G. 1990. "The Case of Homicide in Plato's *Euthyphro*," in Craik 1990, 213–21.

Kindt, J. 2012. *Rethinking Greek Religion*. Cambridge University Press.

Kirk, G. S. 1962. *Songs of Homer*. Cambridge University Press.

Kirk, G. S., Raven, J. E., and Schofield, M. 1983. *The Presocratic Philosophers*. Cambridge University Press.

Kirwan, C. A. 1965. "Glaucon's Challenge," *Phronesis* 10: 162–73.

Klosko, G. 2006. *The Development of Plato's Political Theory*, 2nd ed. Oxford University Press.

Knorr, W. R. 1975. *The Evolution of the Euclidean Elements: a Study of the Theory of Incommensurable Magnitudes and its Significance for Early Greek Geometry*. Dordrecht: Reidel.

1990. "Plato and Eudoxus on the Planetary Motions," *Journal for the History of Astronomy* 21: 313–29.

Kosman, L. A. 1976. "Platonic Love," in W. H. Werkmeister (ed.), *Facets of Plato's Philosophy* (Assen: Van Gorcum), 53–69.

Kraut, R. 1973a. "Egoism, Love and Political Office in Plato," *The Philosophical Review* 82: 330–44.

1973b. "Reason and Justice in Plato's *Republic*," in E. N. Lee, A. P. D. Mourelatos, and R. M. Rorty (eds.), *Exegesis and Argument* (Assen, The Netherlands: Van Gorcum and Co.), 207–24.

1984. *Socrates and the State*. Princeton University Press.

1990. Review of Reeve 1988, *Political Theory* 18: 492–6.

(ed.) 1992. *The Cambridge Companion to Plato*. Cambridge University Press.

1999. "Return to the Cave: *Republic* 519–521," in Fine 1999b, 235–54.

2008. "Plato on Love," in G. Fine (ed.), *The Oxford Handbook of Plato* (Oxford University Press), 286–310.

2017. "Eudaimonism and Platonic Eros," in Destrée and Giannopoulou 2017, 235–52.

Kripke, S. 1980. *Naming and Necessity*. Cambridge, MA: Harvard University Press.

LaBarge, S. 2005. "Socrates and Moral Expertise," in Lisa Rasmussen (ed.), *Ethics Expertise: History, Contemporary Perspectives, and Applications* (Dordrecht: Springer), 15–38.

Lacey, A. R. 1971. "Our Knowledge of Socrates," in Vlastos 1971, 22–49.

Laks, A. 1990. "Legislation and Demiurgy: On the Relationship Between Plato's *Republic* and *Laws*," *Classical Antiquity* 9: 209–29.

2000. "The *Laws*," in C. Rowe and M. Schofield (eds.), *The Cambridge History of Greek and Roman Political Thought* (Cambridge University Press: Cambridge), 258–92.

forthcoming. *Beyond the* Republic*: An Essay on Plato's* Laws. Princeton University Press.

Laks, A. and Most, G. W. 2016. *Early Greek Philosophy*, 9 vols. (Loeb Classical Library) Cambridge, MA: Harvard University Press.

Lane, M. 1998. *Method and Politics in Plato's "Statesman"*. Cambridge University Press.

2013. "Founding as Legislating: The Figure of the Lawgiver in Plato's *Republic*," in N. Nōtomi and L. Brisson (eds.), *Dialogues on Plato's Politeia (Republic): Selected papers from the ninth Symposium Platonicum* (Sankt Augustin: Academia) (= International Plato Studies vol. 31), 104–13.

2018. "Plato on the Value of Knowledge in Ruling", *Aristotelian Society Supplementary Volume* 92.1: 49–67.

Lang, M. and Crosby, M. 1964. *Weights, Measures and Tokens*. The Athenian Agora, vol. 10. Princeton, NJ: American School of Classical Studies at Athens.

Lasserre, F. 1987. *De Léodamas de Thaso à Philippe d'Oponte: Témoignage et fragments*. Naples: Bibliopolis.

Laum, B. 1928. *Das alexandrinische Akzentuationssystem*. Paderborn: Schöning.

Lautner, P. 2005. "The *Timaeus* on Sounds and Hearing and Some Implications for Plato's General Account of Sense Perception," *Rhizai* 2: 235–53.

2011. "Plato's Account of Diseases of the Soul in *Timaeus* 86b1–87b9," *Apeiron* 44: 22–39.

Lear, G. R. 2006. "Permanent Beauty and Becoming Happy in Plato's *Symposium*," in Lesher, Nails, and Sheffield 2006, 96–123.

2011. "Mimesis and Psychological Change in *Republic* III," in P. Destrée and F.-G. Herrmann (eds.), *Plato and the Poets* (Leiden: Brill), 195–216.

Ledger, G. R. 1989. *Re-counting Plato*. Oxford University Press.

Lee, D. 2008. *Plato:* Timaeus *and* Critias, with introduction and annotations by T. Johansen. London: Penguin Classics.

Lefka, E. 2013. *Tout est Plein de Dieux: Les Divinités Traditionnelles dans l'Oeuvre de Platon*. Paris: L'Harmattan.

Leibniz, G. 1981. *New Essays on Human Understanding*, tr. and ed. P. Remnant and J. Bennett. New York: Cambridge University Press.

1989. "Meditations on Knowledge, Truth, and Ideas," in *Philosophical Essays*, trans. R. Ariew and D. Garber (Indianapolis, IN: Hackett), 23–7.

Lesher, J. H. 1987. "Socrates' Disavowal of Knowledge," *Journal of the History of Philosophy* 25: 275–88.

Lesher, J. H., Nails, D. and Sheffield, F. C. C. (eds.) 2006. *Plato's* Symposium: *Issues in Interpretation and Reception*. Washington, DC: Center for Hellenic Studies.

Lewis, D. M. 1990. "The Political Background of Democritus," in Craik 1990, 151–4.

Linforth, I. M. 1946. *The Corybantic Rites in Plato*. Berkeley: University of California Press.

Lloyd, G. E. R. 1992. "The '*Meno*' and the Mysteries of Mathematics," *Phronesis* 37: 166–83.

Locke, J. 1975. *An Essay Concerning Human Understanding*, ed. P. Nidditch. Oxford: Clarendon Press.

Long, A. A. 1970. "Morals and Values in Homer," *Journal of Hellenic Studies* 90: 121–39.

Lorenz, H. 2006. *The Brute Within: Appetitive Desire in Plato and Aristotle*. Oxford University Press.

Lutoslawski, W. 1897. *The Origin and Growth of Plato's Logic*. London.

Mabbott, J. D. 1937. "Is Plato's *Republic* Utilitarian?," *Mind* 46: 468–74.

Mackenzie, M. M. 1981. *Plato on Punishment*. Berkeley/Los Angeles: University of California Press.

Madigan, A., S.J. 1999. *Aristotle:* Metaphysics *Books B and K 1–2*. Oxford University Press.

Mahoney, T. 2005. "Moral Virtue and Assimilation to God in Plato's *Timaeus*," *Oxford Studies in Ancient Philosophy* 28: 77–91.

Mann, W. 2000. *The Discovery of Things: Aristotle's* Categories *and their Context*. Princeton University Press.

Marianetti, M. C. 1993. "Socratic Mystery-Parody and the Issue of ἀσέβεια in Aristophanes' *Clouds*," *Symbolae Osloenses* 68: 5–31.

Mayhew, R. 2010. "The Theology of the *Laws*," in Bobonich 2010, 197–216.

McCabe, M. M. 2009. "Escaping One's Own Notice Knowing: Meno's Paradox Again," *Proceedings of the Aristotelian Society* 19: 233–56. Reprinted in *Platonic Conversations* (Oxford University Press, 2015), 190–207.

McCoy, M. 2008. *Plato on the Rhetoric of Philosophers and Sophists*. Cambridge University Press.

McCready-Flora, I. 2018. "Affect and Sensation: Plato's Embodied Cognition," *Phronesis* 63: 117–47.

McDowell, J. 1983. "Falsehood and Not-being in Plato's *Sophist*," in M. Schofield and M. Nussbaum (eds.), *Language and Logos* (Cambridge University Press), 115–34.

McNeill, D. N. 2010. *An Image of the Soul in Speech: Plato and the Problem of Socrates*. University Park, PA: Penn State University Press.

McPartland, K. 2013. "Socratic Ignorance and Types of Knowledge" in Bussanich and Smith (2013), 94–135.

McPherran, M. L. 1996. *The Religion of Socrates*. University Park, PA: Penn State University Press.

2006. "Medicine, Magic and Religion in Plato's *Symposium*," in Lesher, Nails, and Sheffield (2006), 71–95.

Meinwald, C. 1991. *Plato's Parmenides*. New York: Oxford University Press.

1998. "Prometheus's Bounds: *Peras* and *Apeiron* in Plato's *Philebus*," in J. Gentzler (ed.), *Method in Ancient Philosophy* (Oxford University Press), 165–80.

2005. "Literary Elements and Dialogue Form in Plato's *Parmenides*," in A. Havlicek and F. Karfik (eds.), *Plato's* Parmenides: *Proceedings of the Fourth Symposium Platonicum Pragense* (Prague), 9–20.

2014a. "How Does Plato's Exercise Work?," *Dialogue* 53: 465–94.

2014b. Review of M. L. Gill, *Philosophos*, *Journal of Hellenic Studies* 53: 288–9.

2016. *Plato*. London: Routledge.

Mendell, H. 1984. "Two Geometrical Examples from Aristotle's *Metaphysics*," *Classical Quarterly* 34: 359–72.

1998a. "Making Sense of Aristotelian Demonstration," *Oxford Studies in Ancient Philosophy* 16: 160–225.

1998b. "Reflections on Eudoxus, Callippus and their Curves: Hippopedes and Callippopedes," *Centaurus* 40: 177–275.

2000. "The Trouble with Eudoxus," in Suppes et al. 2000, 59–138.

2008. "Plato by the Numbers," in D. Føllesdal and J. Woods (eds.), *Logos and Language: Essays in Honour of Julius Moravcsik* (London: College Publications), 141–76.

2018. "Why did the Greeks Develop Proportion Theory: a Conjecture," in M. Sialaros (ed.), *Revolutions and Continuity in Greek Mathematics* (Berlin: De Gruyter), 189–233.

Menn, S. 1995. *Plato on Nous. Journal of the History of Philosophy* Monograph Series.

1998. "Collecting the Letters," *Phronesis* 43.4: 291–305.

Menza, V. 1972. *Poetry and the Technē Theory.* PhD dissertation. Johns Hopkins University.

Meyer, S. 2006. "Plato on the Law," in H. Benson (ed.), *A Companion to Plato* (Oxford: Blackwell), 373–87.

Mohr, R. and Sattler, B. (eds.) 2009. *One Book, The Whole Universe: Plato's Timaeus Today.* Las Vegas: Parmenides Publishing.

Moore, C. 2015. *Socrates and Self-Knowledge.* Cambridge University Press.

2020. *Calling Philosophers Names: On the Origin of a Discipline.* Princeton University Press.

Moravcsik, J. M. E. 1972. "Reason and Eros in the 'Ascent'-Passage of the *Symposium*," in J. P. Anton and G. L. Kustas (eds.), *Essays in Ancient Greek Philosophy* (Albany, NY: SUNY Press), 285–302.

1978. "Learning as Recollection," in G. Vlastos (ed.), *Plato 1: Metaphysics and Epistemology* (University of Notre Dame Press; orig. pub. Garden City, NY: Doubleday, 1971), 53–69.

1992. *Plato and Platonism: Plato's Conception of Appearance and Reality in Ontology, Epistemology, and Ethics, and its Modern Echoes.* Malden, MA: Blackwell.

2000. "Plato on Numbers and Mathematics," in Suppes et al. 2000, 177–96.

Morgan, M. L. 1990. *Platonic Piety.* New Haven, CT: Yale University Press.

Morrison, D. 2003. "Happiness, Rationality, and Egoism in Plato's Socrates," in Y. Yu and J. J. E. Gracia (eds.), *Rationality and Happiness: From the Ancients to the Medievals* (University of Rochester Press), 17–34.

(ed.) 2011. *The Cambridge Companion to Socrates.* Cambridge University Press.

Morrow, G. R. 1954. "The Demiurge in Politics," *Proceedings of the American Philosophical Association* 27: 5–23.

1960. *Plato's Cretan City: a Historical Interpretation of the* Laws. Princeton University Press. Reprinted 1993.

1962. *Plato's* Epistles, 2nd ed. Indianapolis, IN: Bobbs-Merrill.

Moss, J. 2007. "What is Imitative Poetry and Why Is It Bad?," in G. R. F. Ferrari (ed.), *The Cambridge Companion to Plato's Republic* (Cambridge University Press), 415–44.

2012. "Soul-leading: The Unity of the *Phaedrus*, Again," *Oxford Studies in Ancient Philosophy* 43: 1–23.

Mourelatos, A. 1980. "Plato's 'Real Astronomy'," in Anton 1980, 33–73.

2016. "'Limitless' and 'Limit' in Xenophanes' Cosmology and in His Doctrine of Epistemic 'Construction' (*dokos*)," *Logical Analysis and History of Philosophy* 19: 16–37.

Mueller, I. 1980. "Astronomy and Harmonics in *Republic* VII," in Anton 1980, 103–22.

1986. "On Some Academic Theories of Mathematical Objects," *Journal of Hellenic Studies* 106: 111–20.

Mulhern, J. J. 1968. "Tropos and polytropia in Plato's *Hippias Minor*," *Phoenix* 22: 283–8.

Muniz, F. and Rudebusch, G. 2018. "Dividing Plato's Kinds," *Phronesis* 63.4: 392–407.

Murdoch, I. 1977. *The Fire and the Sun*. Oxford: Clarendon Press.

Murphy, N. R. 1951. *The Interpretation of Plato's* Republic. Oxford: Clarendon Press.

Murray, O. 1993. *Early Greece*, 2nd ed. Cambridge, MA: Harvard University Press.

Murray, P. 1981. "Poetic Inspiration in Early Greece," *Journal of Hellenic Studies* 101: 87–100.

1992. "Inspiration and Mimēsis in Plato," *Apeiron* 25.4: 27–46.

(ed.) 1996. *Plato on Poetry*. Cambridge University Press.

Mylonas, G. E. 1961. *Eleusis and the Eleusinian Mysteries*. Princeton University Press.

Nagel, T. 1974. "Linguistics and Epistemology," in G. Harmon (ed.), *On Noam Chomsky: Critical Essays* (Garden City, NJ: Anchor Books), 219–28.

Nails, D. 1995. *Agora, Academy, and the Conduct of Philosophy*. Dordrecht: Kluwer.

2002. *The People of Plato: A Prosopography of Plato and Other Socratics*. Indianapolis, IN: Hackett.

Nehamas, A. 1975a. "Plato on the Imperfection of the Sensible World," *American Philosophical Quarterly* 12: 105–17.

1975b. "Confusing Universals and Particulars in Plato's Early Dialogues," *Review of Metaphysics* 29: 287–306.

1979. "Self-Predication and Plato's Theory of Forms," *American Philosophical Quarterly* 16: 93–103.

1982. "Plato on Imitation and Poetry in *Republic* 10," in J. Moravcsik and P. Temko (eds.), *Plato on Beauty, Wisdom, and the Arts* (Totowa, NJ: Rowman & Littlefield), 296–323.

1985. "Meno's Paradox and Socrates as a Teacher," *Oxford Studies in Ancient Philosophy* 3: 1–30.

1987. "Socratic Intellectualism," in J. J. Cleary (ed.), *Proceedings of the Boston Area Colloquium in Ancient Philosophy*, vol. 2 (Lanham, MD: University Press of America), 275–316.

1990. "Eristic, Antilogic, Sophistic, Dialectic: Plato's Demarcation of Philosophy from Sophistry," *History of Philosophy Quarterly* 7: 3–16.

1992. "What Did Socrates Teach and to Whom Did He Teach It?," *Review of Metaphysics* 46: 279–306.

2017. *Only a Promise of Happiness: The Place of Beauty in a World of Art.* Princeton University Press.

Nehamas, A. and Woodruff, P. 1989. *Plato:* Symposium. Indianapolis, IN: Hackett.

1995. *Plato: Phaedrus.* Indianapolis, IN: Hackett.

Nettleship, R. 1962. *Lectures on the Republic of Plato*, 2nd ed. London: Macmillan.

Netz, R. 1999. *The Shaping of Deduction in Greek Mathematics: a Study in Cognitive History.* Cambridge University Press.

2010. "What did Greek Mathematicians Find Beautiful?," *Classical Philology* 105: 426–44.

Neumann, H. 1965. "Diotima's Concept of Love," *The American Journal of Philology* 86.1: 33–59.

Nightingale, A. 1995. *Genres in Dialogue: Plato and the Construct of Philosophy.* Cambridge University Press.

1999. "Plato's Lawcode in Context: Rule by Written Law in Athens and Magnesia," *Classical Quarterly* 49: 100–22.

2004. *Spectacles of Truth in Classical Greek Philosophy: Theoria in its Cultural Context.* Cambridge University Press.

2005. "The Philosopher at the Festival: Plato's Transformation of Traditional *Theoria*," in J. Elsner and I. Rutherford (eds.), *Pilgrimage in Graeco-Roman and Early Christian Antiquity: Seeing the Gods* (Oxford University Press), 151–82.

2017. "The Mortal Soul and Immortal Happiness," in Destrée and Giannopoulou 2017, 142–59.

2018. "Divine Epiphany and Pious Discourse in Plato's *Phaedrus*," *Arion: A Journal of Humanities and the Classics* 26: 61–94.

2021. *Philosophy and Religion in Plato's Dialogues.* Cambridge: Cambridge University Press.

Nussbaum, M. C. 1986. *The Fragility of Goodness.* Cambridge University Press.

O'Brien, D. 1967. "The Last Argument of Plato's *Phaedo*. I," *Classical Quarterly* 17: 189–231.

1968. "The Last Argument of Plato's *Phaedo*. II," *Classical Quarterly* 18: 95–106.

1997. "Perception et intelligence dans le *Timée*," in Calvo and Brisson 1997, 291–305.

O'Brien, M. J. 1984. "Becoming Immortal in Plato's *Symposium*," in D. E. Gerber (ed.), *Greek Poetry and Philosophy* (Chico: Scholars Press), 185–205.

Obdrzalek, S. 2010. "Moral Transformation and the Love of Beauty in Plato's *Symposium*," *Journal of the History of Philosophy* 48.4: 415–44.

2013. "Socrates on Love," in Bussanich and Smith 2013, 210–32.

Ober, J. 1989. *Mass and Elite in Democratic Athens.* Princeton: Princeton University Press.

Owen, G. E. L. 1953. "The Place of the *Timaeus* in Plato's Dialogues," *Classical Quarterly* 47: 79–95.

1957. "A Proof in the *Peri Ideôn*," *Journal of Hellenic Studies* 77: 103–11.

1965. "Aristotle on the Snares of Ontology," in R. Bambrough (ed.), *New Essays on Plato and Aristotle* (London: Routledge and Keegan Paul), 69–95.

1970. "Plato on Not-Being," in G. Vlastos (ed.), *Plato 1* (Garden City, NY: Anchor), 223–67.

1986. *Logic, Science and Dialectic*, ed. Martha Nussbaum. London: Duckworth.

Parker, R. 1983. *Miasma.* Oxford University Press.

1995. "Early Orphism," in A. Powell (ed.), *The Greek World.* London: Routledge, 483–510.

1996. *Athenian Religion· A History.* Oxford: Clarendon Press.

2005. *Polytheism and Society at Athens.* Oxford University Press.

Parker, R. A. 1972. *Demotic Mathematical Papyri.* Brown Egyptological Studies VII. Providence, RI: Brown University Press.

Partenie, C. (ed.) 2009. *Plato's Myths.* Cambridge University Press.

Patterson, R. 1985. *Image and Reality in Plato's Metaphysics.* Indianapolis, IN: Hackett.

Peacock, H. 2017. "The Third Man and the Coherence of the *Parmenides*," *Oxford Studies in Ancient Philosophy* 52: 113–76.

Pelletier, J. and Zalta, E. 2000. "How to Say Goodbye to the Third Man," *Nous* 34: 165–202.

Pelling, C. B. R. 1997. "Conclusion," in C. B. R. Pelling (ed.), *Greek Tragedy and the Historian* (Oxford University Press), 213–36.

Penner, T. 1971. "Thought and Desire in Plato," in G. Vlastos (ed.), *Plato: A Collection of Critical Essays*, vol. 2 (Garden City, NY: Anchor Books), 96–118.

   1973a. "Socrates on Virtue and Motivation," in E. N. Lee, A. P. D. Mourelatos, and R. M. Rorty (eds.), *Exegesis and Argument* (Assen, The Netherlands: Van Gorcum and Co.), 133–51.

   1973b. "The Unity of Virtue," *Philosophical Review* 82: 35–68. Reprinted in Benson 1992, 162–84.

   1987. *The Ascent from Nominalism*. Dordrecht: Springer.

   2011. "Socratic Ethics and the Socratic Psychology of Action: A Philosophical Framework," in Morrison 2011, 260–92.

Penner, T. and Rowe, C. 2005. *Plato's Lysis*. Cambridge University Press.

Peterson, Sandra. 1973. "A Reasonable Self-Predication Premise for the Third Man Argument," *Philosophical Review* 82: 451–70.

   1996. "Plato's *Parmenides*: A Principle of Interpretation and Seven Arguments," *Journal of the History of Philosophy* 34: 167–92.

   2011. *Socrates and Philosophy in the Dialogues of Plato*. Cambridge University Press.

   2017. "Notes on *Lovers*," in A. Stavru and C. Moore (eds.), *Socrates and the Socratic Dialogue* (Leiden: Brill), 412–31.

   2019. "Plato's *Parmenides*: A Reconsideration of Forms," in Fine 2019, 231–62.

Petridou, G. 2013. "'Blessed is he, who has seen': The Power of Ritual Viewing and Ritual Framing in Eleusis," *Helios* 40: 309–41.

   2015. *Divine Epiphany in Greek Literature and Culture*. Oxford University Press.

Pitteloud, L. 2019. "Why is the World Soul Composed of Being, Sameness, and Difference?," in L. Pitteloud and E. Keeling (eds.), *Psychology and Ontology in Plato* (Philosophical Studies Series, Dordrecht: Springer), 85–108.

Platt, V. J. 2011. *Facing the Gods: Epiphany and Representation in Graeco-Roman Art, Literature and Religion*. Cambridge University Press.

Plutarch 1976. "*De Animae Procreatione in Timaeo*," in *Plutarch's Moralia*, vol. 13 pt. 1, trans. H. Cherniss (Cambridge, MA: Loeb Classical Library).

Prauscello, L. 2014. *Performing Citizenship in Plato's Laws*. Cambridge University Press.

Price, A. W. 1989. *Love and Friendship in Plato and Aristotle*. Oxford: Clarendon Press.

   2017. "Generating in Beauty for the Sake of Immortality: Personal Love and the Goals of the Lover," in Destrée and Giannopoulou 2017, 176–93.

Prince, B. D. 2014. "The Metaphysics of Bodily Health and Disease in Plato's *Timaeus*," *British Journal for the History of Philosophy* 22 (5): 908–28.

Prior, W. 1985. *Unity and Development in Plato's Metaphysics*. LaSalle, IL: Open Court Publishing.

2019. *Socrates*. Cambridge: Polity.

Pritchard, P. 1995. *Plato's Philosophy of Mathematics*. Sankt Augustin: Akademia Verlag.

Proclus 1987. *Commentary on Plato's* Parmenides, trans. G. R. Morrow and J. M. Dillon. Princeton University Press.

2007. *Commentary on Plato's* Timaeus, Vol. 1, ed. H. Tarrant. Cambridge University Press.

2008a. *Commentary on Plato's* Timaeus, Vol. 2, ed. D. Runia and M. Share. Cambridge University Press.

2008b. *Commentary on Plato's* Timaeus, Vol. 3, ed. D. Baltzly. Cambridge University Press.

2009. *Commentary on Plato's* Timaeus, Vol. 4, ed. D. Baltzly. Cambridge University Press.

2016. *Commentary on Plato's* Timaeus, Vol. 5, ed. D. Baltzly. Cambridge University Press.

2017. *Commentary on Plato's* Timaeus, Vol. 6, ed. H. Tarrant. Cambridge University Press.

Putnam, H. 1975. "The Meaning of 'Meaning'," in *Philosophical Papers*, Vol. 2 (Cambridge University Press), 215–71.

Rashed, M. 2009. "Aristophanes and the Socrates of the *Phaedo*," *Oxford Studies in Ancient Philosophy* 36: 107–36.

Rawls J. 1999. "Justice as Fairness: Political Not Metaphysical," in *Collected Papers*, ed. S. Freeman (Cambridge, MA: Harvard University Press), 388–414.

Reeve, C. D. C. 1988. *Philosopher-Kings: The Argument of Plato's* Republic. Princeton University Press.

1989. *Socrates in the* Apology: *An Essay on Plato's* Apology *of Socrates*. Indianapolis, IN: Hackett.

1992. "Telling the Truth about Love: Plato's *Symposium*," *Proceedings of the Boston Area Colloquium in Ancient Philosophy* 8: 89–114.

2006. "Plato on Eros and Friendship," in H. H. Benson, *A Companion to Plato* (Oxford: Blackwell), 294–307.

2013. *Blindness and Reorientation: Problems in Plato's* Republic. Oxford University Press.

Reid, J. 2021. "Changing the Laws of the *Laws*," *Ancient Philosophy* 41: 413–41.

Reshotko, N. 2006. *Socratic Virtue: Making the Best of the Neither-Good-Nor-Bad.* Cambridge University Press.

Rickless, S. 2007. *Plato's Forms in Transition.* Cambridge University Press.

Riedweg, C. 1987. *Mysterienterminologie bei Platon, Philon und Klemens von Alexandrien.* Berlin: W. de Gruyter.

Rijksbaron, A. (ed.) 2007. *Ion.* Leiden: Brill.

Ritter, C. 1888. *Untersuchungen über Platon.* Stuttgart.

1910. *Platon.* Munich.

1935. "Unterabteilungen innerhalb der zeitlich ersten Gruppe platonischer Schriften," *Hermes* 70: 1–30.

Roberts, J. 1988. "The Problem about Being in the *Sophist*," *History of Philosophy Quarterly* 3: 229–43.

Robinson, R. 1953. *Plato's Earlier Dialectic.* Oxford: Clarendon Press.

Robson, E. 2008. *Mathematics in Ancient Iraq: a Social History.* Princeton University Press.

Romilly, J. de. 1975. *Magic and Rhetoric in Ancient Greece.* Cambridge, MA: Harvard University Press.

Roochnik, D. 1996. *Of Art and Wisdom: Plato's Understanding of Techne.* University Park, PA: Penn State University Press.

Ross, W. D. 1955. *Aristotelis Fragmenta Selecta.* Oxford University Press.

Rowe, C. J. 1986. *Plato:* Phaedrus. Oxford: Aris and Phillips.

1993. *Plato:* Phaedo. Cambridge University Press.

1995. *Plato:* Statesman. Aris and Phillips.

1998a. *Plato:* Symposium. Warminster: Aris and Phillips.

1998b. "Socrates and Diotima: Eros, Immortality and Creativity," *Proceedings of the Boston Area Colloquium in Ancient Philosophy* 14: 239–59.

2000. "The *Politicus* and Other Dialogues," in C. Rowe and M. Schofield (eds.), *The Cambridge History of Greek and Roman Political Thought* (Cambridge University Press), 233–357.

Rowett, C. 2018. *Knowledge and Truth in Plato: Stepping Past the Shadow of Socrates.* New York: Oxford University Press.

Rudebusch, G. 2009. *Socrates.* Oxford: Wiley-Blackwell.

Rutherford, R. B. 1995. *The Art of Plato.* London: Duckworth.

Ryle, G. 1966. *Plato's Progress.* Cambridge University Press.

1976. "Many Things are Odd about our *Meno*," *Paideia* 5: 1–9.

Sachs, D. 1963. "A Fallacy in Plato's *Republic*," *Philosophical Review* 72: 141–58.

Samaras, T. 2002. *Plato on Democracy.* New York: Peter Lang.

Santas, G. X. 1979. *Socrates: Philosophy in Plato's Early Dialogues.* London: Routledge.

1983. "The Form of the Good in Plato's *Republic*," in, J. P. Anton and A. Preus (eds.), *Essays in Ancient Greek Philosophy*, Vol. 2 (Albany, NY: SUNY Press), 232–63.

1988. *Plato and Freud: Two Theories of Love*. Oxford: Blackwell.

1989. "Aristotle's Criticism of Plato's Form of the Good: Ethics without Metaphysics?," *Philosophical Papers* 18: 137–60.

2001. *Goodness and Justice*. Oxford: Blackwell.

Sattler, B. M. 2013. "The Eleusinian Mysteries in Pre-platonic Thought: Metaphor, Practise and Imagery for Plato's *Symposium*," in V. Adluri (ed.), *Philosophy and Salvation in Greek Religion* (Berlin: de Gruyter), 151–90.

Saunders, T. 1991. *Plato's Penal Code*. Oxford: Clarendon Press.

Sayre, K. M. 1983. *Plato's Late Ontology: A Riddle Resolved*. Princeton University Press.

1996. *Parmenides' Lesson*. University of Notre Dame Press.

Schaffer, J. 2016. "The Metaphysics of Causation," in E. N. Zalta (ed.), *The Stanford Encyclopedia of Philosophy* (Fall ed.).

Schanz, M. 1886. "Zur Entwicklung des platonischen Stils," *Hermes* 21: 439–59.

Schiefsky, M. J. 2005. *Hippocrates: On Ancient Medicine: Translated with Introduction and Commentary*. Leiden: Brill.

Schofield M. 2003. "The Presocratics," in D. Sedley (ed.), *The Cambridge Companion to Greek and Roman Philosophy* (Cambridge University Press), 42–72.

2006. *Plato: Political Philosophy*. Oxford University Press.

2019. "Plato in his Time and Place," in Fine 2019, 41–68.

Schwab, W. 2015, "Explanation in the Epistemology of the *Meno*," *Oxford Studies in Ancient Philosophy* 48: 1–36.

Scott, D. 1995. *Recollection and Experience*. Cambridge University Press.

2006. *Plato's* Meno. Cambridge University Press.

2011. "Plato, Poetry and Creativity," in P. Destrée and F.-G. Herrmann (eds.), *Plato and the Poets* (Leiden: Brill), 131–54.

2015. *Levels of Argument: A Comparative Study of Plato's* Republic *and Aristotle's* Nicomachean Ethics. Oxford University Press.

Scott, G. A. 2000. *Plato's Socrates as Educator*. Albany, NY: SUNY Press.

ed. 2002. *Does Socrates Have a Method? Rethinking the Elenchus in Plato's Dialogues and Beyond*. University Park, PA: Penn State University Press.

Sedley, D. 1998. "Platonic Causes," *Phronesis* 43: 114–32.

1999a. "The Ideal of Godlikeness," in Fine 1999b, 309–28.

1999b. "Parmenides and Melissus," in A. A. Long (ed.), *Cambridge Companion to Early Greek Philosophy* (Cambridge University Press), 113–33.

2003. *Plato:* Cratylus. Cambridge University Press.

2004. *The Midwife of Platonism: Text and Subtext in Plato's* Theaetetus. Oxford University Press.

2007a. *Creationism and its Critics in Antiquity.* Berkeley: University of California Press.

2007b. "Philosophy, the Forms, and the Art of Ruling," in G. R. F. Ferrari (ed.), *Cambridge Companion to Plato's Republic* (Cambridge University Press), 256–83.

2007c. "Equal Sticks and Stones," in D. Scott (ed.), *Maieusis: Essays in Ancient Philosophy in Honour of Myles Burnyeat* (Oxford University Press), 68–86.

2009. "Three Kinds of Platonic Immortality," in D. Frede and B. Reis (eds.), *Body and Soul in Ancient Philosophy* (Berlin: Walter de Gruyter), 147–61.

2016. "An Introduction to Plato's Theory of Forms," *Royal Institute of Philosophy Supplement* 78: 3–22.

2018. "The *Phaedo*'s Final Proof of Immortality," in G. Cornelli, T. Robinson, and F. Bravo (eds.), *Plato's* Phaedo*: Select Papers from the Eleventh Symposium Platonicum* (Baden Baden: Akademia Verlag), 210–20.

2019. "Plato's Theology," in Fine 2019, 627–44.

Sedley, D. and Long, A. 2010. *Plato:* Meno *and* Phaedo. Cambridge University Press.

Sellars, W. 1955. "Vlastos and the Third Man," *Philosophical Review* 64: 405–37.

Senn, S. J. 2013. "Ignorance or Irony in Plato's Socrates?: A Look Beyond Avowals and Disavowals of Knowledge," *Plato Journal* 13: 77–108.

Sharples, R. W. 1985. *Plato:* Meno. Warminster: Aris and Phillips.

Shaw, J. C. 2011. "Socrates and the True Political Craft," *Classical Philology* 106: 187–207.

2015. *Plato's Anti-hedonism and the Protagoras.* Cambridge University Press.

Sheffield, F. C. C. 2001. "Psychic Pregnancy and Platonic Epistemology," *Oxford Studies in Ancient Philosophy* 20: 1–33.

2006. *Plato's* Symposium*: the Ethics of Desire.* Oxford University Press.

2012. "The *Symposium* and Platonic Ethics: Plato, Vlastos, and a Misguided Debate," *Phronesis* 57.2: 117–41.

2017. "Eros and the Pursuit of Form," in Destrée and Giannopoulou 2017, 125–41.

Shorey, P. 1890. "Plato. *Republic* 532B," *Classical Review* 4: 480.

1895. "The Idea of the Good in Plato's Philosophy," *Studies in Classical Philology* 1: 188–239.

1903. *The Unity of Plato's Thought.* University of Chicago Press.

1927. "Ideas and Numbers Again." *Classical Philology* 22: 213–18.

1933. *What Plato Said.* University of Chicago Press.

Sidgwick, H. 1905. *Lectures on the Philosophy of Kant and Other Philosophical Lectures and Essays.* London: Macmillan.

Siebeck, H. 1888. *Untersuchungen zur Philosophie der Griechen.* Halle.

Silverman, A. 2002. *The Dialectic of Essence: A Study of Plato's Metaphysics.* Princeton University Press.

Silverthorne, M. J. 1975. "Laws, Preambles and the Legislator in Plato," *Humanities Association Review* 26: 10–20.

Singpurwalla, R. 2006. "Reasoning with the Irrational: Moral Psychology in the *Protagoras*," *Ancient Philosophy* 26: 243–58.

Slings, S. R. (ed.) 2003. *Platonis Rempublicam.* Oxford Classical Texts. Oxford University Press.

Smith, N. 1981. "The Objects of 'Dianoia' in Plato's Divided Line," *Apeiron* 15: 129–37.

2016. "Socrates on the Human Condition," *Ancient Philosophy* 36: 81–95.

2018. "Aristotle on Socrates," in A. Stavru and C. Moore (eds.), *Socrates and the Socratic Dialogue* (Leiden: Brill), 601–22.

Smith, N. D., and Woodruff, P. (eds.) 2000. *Reason and Religion in Socratic Philosophy.* Oxford University Press.

Solmsen, F. 1975. *Intellectual Experiments of the Greek Enlightenment.* Princeton.

Sorensen, A. D. 2016. *Plato on Democracy and Political Technē.* Leiden: Brill.

Sourvinou-Inwood, C. 1995. *"Reading" Greek Death: To the End of the Classical Period.* Oxford: Clarendon Press; New York: Oxford University Press.

2000. "What is Polis Religion?," in R. Buxton (ed.), *Oxford Readings in Greek Religion.* Oxford University Press, 13–37.

Southeast-European Association for Ancient Philosophy 2005. *Rhizai: Journal for Ancient Philosophy and Science*, Vol. 2, No. 2. Sofia, Bulgaria: East-West Publishers.

Sprague, R. K. 1962. *Plato's Use of Fallacy.* London: Routledge.

Stalley, R. F. 1983. *An Introduction to Plato's* Laws. Indianapolis, IN: Hackett.

1994. "Persuasion in Plato's *Laws*," *History of Political Thought* 15: 157–77.

Steiner, D. 1996. "For Love of a Statue: A Reading of Plato's *Symposium* 215A–B," *Ramus* 25: 89–111.

Stokes, M. 1992. "Socrates' Mission," in B. S. Gower and M. C. Stokes (eds.), *Socratic Questions: New Essays on the Philosophy of Socrates and its Significance* (London: Routledge), 26–81.

1997. *Plato:* Apology. Oxford: Aris & Phillips.

Strang, C. 1963. "The Physical Theory of Anaxagoras," *Archiv für Geschichte der Philosophie* 45: 101–18.

Strang, C. and Rees, D. A. 1963. "Plato and the Third Man," *Proceedings of the Aristotelian Society, Supplementary Volumes* 37: 147–76.

Strauss, L. 1952. *Persecution and the Art of Writing.* Glencoe, IL: Free Press.

Striker, G. 1970. *Peras und Apeiron: Das Problem der Formen in Platons* Philebos. Göttingen: Vandenhoeck & Ruprecht.

1986. "Antipater, or the Art of Living," in M. Schofield and G. Striker (eds.), *The Norms of Nature: Studies in Hellenistic Ethics* (Cambridge University Press), 185–204.

Strycker, E. de, and Slings, S. R. 1994. *Plato's* Apology *of Socrates: A Literary and Philosophical Study with a Running Commentary.* Leiden: Brill.

Suppes, P., Moravcsik, J., and Mendell, H. (eds.). 2000. *Ancient and Medieval Traditions in the Exact Sciences: Essays in Memory of Wilbur Knorr.* Stanford: CSLI Publications.

Tait, W. W. 1986. "Plato's Second Best Method," *Review of Metaphysics* 39: 455–82.

2002. "*Noēsis*: Plato on Exact Science," in D. Malament (ed.), *Reading Natural Philosophy: Essays in the History and Philosophy of Science and Mathematics* (Chicago, IL: Open Court), 11–31.

Tarán, L. 1981. *Speusippus of Athens: A Critical Study with a Collection of the Related Texts and Commentary.* Leiden: Brill.

1991. "Ideas, Numbers, and Magnitudes: Remarks on Plato, Speusippus, and Aristotle," *Revue de Philosophie Ancienne* 9: 199–231.

Taylor, A. E. 1911. *Varia Socratica.* Oxford: Blackwell.

1928. *A Commentary on Plato's* Timaeus. Oxford University Press.

1937. *Plato, the Man and His Work.* London: Methuen.

Taylor, C. C. W. 1967. "Pleasure, Knowledge, and Sensation in Democritus," *Phronesis* 12: 6–27.

1982. "The End of the *Euthyphro*," *Phronesis* 27: 109–18.

1990. "Popular Morality and Unpopular Philosophy," in Craik 1990, 233–43.

1998. *Socrates.* Oxford University Press.

1999. *The Atomists.* University of Toronto Press.

2019. "Plato's Epistemology," in Fine 2019, 429–54.

Thakkar, J. 2018. *Plato as Critical Theorist*. Cambridge, MA: Harvard University Press.

Thesleff, H. 1982. *Studies in Platonic Chronology*. Helsinki: Societas Scientiarum Fennica.

Thompson, E. S. 1901. *Plato's* Meno. London: Macmillan.

Thompson, W. H. (ed.) 1868. *Phaedrus*. London.

Tor, S. 2017. *Mortal and Divine in Early Greek Epistemology: a Study of Hesiod, Xenophanes, and Parmenides*. Cambridge University Press.

Tuozzo, T. M. 2011. *Plato's* Charmides: *Positive Elenchus in a "Socratic" Dialogue*. Cambridge University Press.

2018. "Appearing Equal at *Phaedo* 74b4–c6: an Epistemic Interpretation," *Oxford Studies in Ancient Philosophy* 54: 1–26.

Unguru, S. 2008. Review of Friberg 2007, *Isis* 99: 221–2.

Van Riel, G. 2013. *Plato's Gods*. Farnham: Ashgate.

Vasiliou, I. 2008. *Aiming at Virtue in Plato*. Cambridge University Press.

Verdenius, W. J. 1958. "Notes on Plato's '*Phaedo*'," *Mnemosyne* 11: 193–243.

Vlastos, G. 1954. "The Third Man Argument in the *Parmenides*," *Philosophical Review* 63: 319–49.

1956. *Plato:* Protagoras. New York: Bobbs-Merrill.

1965. "Anamnesis in the *Meno*," *Dialogue* 4: 143–67.

1969. "Reasons and Causes in the *Phaedo*," *Philosophical Review* 78: 291–325.

(ed.) 1971. *The Philosophy of Socrates: A Collection of Critical Essays*. New York: Anchor Books.

1975. *Plato's Universe*. Seattle: University of Washington Press.

1980. "Observation in Plato's Astronomy," in Anton 1980, 1–31.

1981. *Platonic Studies*, 2nd ed. Princeton University Press.

1983. "The Socratic Elenchus," *Oxford Studies in Ancient Philosophy* 1: 27–58. Revised and expanded in Vlastos 1994, 1–37.

1985. "Socrates' Disavowal of Knowledge," *Philosophical Quarterly* 35: 1–31. Revised in Vlastos 1994, 39–66.

1988. "Elenchus and Mathematics: A Turning-Point in Plato's Philosophical Development," *The American Journal of Philology* 109(3): 362–96.

1991. *Socrates: Ironist and Moral Philosopher*. Ithaca, NY: Cornell University Press.

1994. *Socratic Studies*, ed. M. F. Burnyeat. Cambridge University Press.

1995. *Studies in Greek Philosophy*, vol. 1, ed. D. W. Graham. Princeton University Press.

Walbank, F. W. 1985. "The Problem of Greek Nationality," in *Selected Papers* (Cambridge University Press), 1–19.

Wardy, R. 1986. *The Birth of Rhetoric: Gorgias, Plato and their Successors*. London: Routledge.

Wasmuth, E. 2015. "ΩΣΠΕΡ ΟΙ ΚΟΡΥΒΑΝΤΙΩΝΤΕΣ: The Corybantic Rites in Plato's Dialogues," *Classical Quarterly* 65: 69–84.

Waterfield, R. 2008. *Timaeus* and *Critias*, with introduction and notes by A. Gregory. Oxford University Press.

Waterfield, R. A. H. 1980. "The Place of the *Philebus* in Plato's Dialogues," *Phronesis* 25: 270–305.

Wedberg, A. 1955. *Plato's Philosophy of Mathematics*. Stockholm: Almqvist & Wiksell.

Weiss, R. 1981. "Ὁ Ἀγαθός as Ὁ Δυνατός in the *Hippias Minor*," *Classical Quarterly* 31: 287–304.

   2001. *Virtue in the Cave: Moral Inquiry in Plato's* Meno. New York: Oxford University Press.

   2006. *The Socratic Paradox and its Enemies*. University of Chicago Press.

Whewell, W. 1856. "Of the Intellectual Powers According to Plato," *Transactions of the Cambridge Philological Society*, 598–604.

White, F. C. 1989a. "Love and Beauty in Plato's *Symposium*," *The Journal of Hellenic Studies* 109: 149–57.

   2004. "Virtue in Plato's *Symposium*," *Classical Quarterly* 54: 366–78.

White, N. P. 1979. *A Companion to Plato's* Republic. Indianapolis, IN: Hackett.

   1984. "The Classification of Goods in Plato's *Republic*," *Journal of the History of Philosophy* 22: 393–421.

   1986. "The Ruler's Choice," *Archiv für Geschichte der Philosophie* 68: 34–41.

   1989b. "Happiness and External Contingencies in Plato's *Republic*," in W. C. Starr and R. C. Taylor (eds.), *Moral Philosophy* (Milwaukee: Marquette University Press), 1–21.

   1992. "Plato's Metaphysical Epistemology," in Kraut 1992, 277–310.

Whitehouse, Harvey. 2000. *Arguments and Icons: Divergent Modes of Religiosity*. Oxford University Press.

Wiggins, D. 1971. "Sentence Meaning, Negation, and Plato's Problem of Not-being," G. Vlastos (ed.), *Plato 1* (Garden City, NY: Anchor), 268–303.

Wilburn, J. 2013. "Moral Education and the Spirited Part of the Soul in Plato's *Laws*," *Oxford Studies in Ancient Philosophy* 45: 63–102.

Wishart, D. and Leach, S. V. 1970. "A Multivariate Analysis of Platonic Prose Rhythm," *Computer Studies in the Humanities and Verbal Behavior* 3: 90–9.

Wolfsdorf, D. 2004. "Socrates' Avowals of Knowledge," *Phronesis* 49: 75–142.

2008. *Trials of Reason: Plato and the Crafting of Philosophy*. Oxford University Press.

2013. "Socratic Philosophizing," in Bussanich and Smith 2013, 34–67.

Woodruff, P. 1982. "What Could Go Wrong with Inspiration? Why Plato's Poets Fail," in J. Moravcsik and P. Temko (eds.), *Plato on Beauty, Wisdom, and the Arts* (Totowa, NJ: Rowman & Littlefield), 137–50.

1990. "Plato's Early Theory of Knowledge," in S. Everson (ed.), *Companions to Ancient Thought 1: Epistemology* (Cambridge University Press), 60–84. Reprinted in Benson 1992, 86–106.

Wright, C. (ed.) 2000. *Reason and Necessity: Essays on Plato's* Timaeus. London: Duckworth.

Yunis, H. 2011. *Plato:* Phaedrus. Cambridge University Press.

Zeyl, D. 1982. "Socratic Virtue and Happiness," *Archiv für Geschichte der Philosophie* 64: 225–38.

2000. *Plato:* Timaeus. Indianapolis, IN: Hackett.

Ziff, P. 1960. *Semantic Analysis*. Ithaca, NY: Cornell University Press.

Zuntz, G. 1971. *Persephone: Three Essays on Religion and Thought in Magna Graecia*. Oxford: Clarendon Press.

Index Locorum

General Index

Baron, C., 93

beauty (*kalon*), 37, 204–27, 228, 230, 231, 268, 273, 289, 291, 304, 319, 336, 338, 352, 411, 412, 448, 467, 512

being: *see also ousia*
    identity, 144, 388, 429, 432, 438, 439, 445, 448, 461, 464
    non-existence, 71
    not being, 433–50, 462
    problem of, 436

belief (*doxa*), 47, 300, 385, 434, 531, 538

Billig, L., 101, 104, 106

Birds. See Aristophanes

birth in beauty, 212, 220, 231, 249, *See also* form, form of beauty

Blass, F., 93, 94, 98

body, as impediment to soul, 210, 254, 291, 478, 479

Bostock, D., 195, 438, 444, 461

Burnyeat, M., 35, 141, 402

Bury, R. G., 206, 494

Callicles, 54, 60

Campbell, L., 83, 84, 104, 108

cave, allegory of (*Republic*), 19, 20, 196, 226, 241, 244, 247, 305, 316, 325, 327, 355, 383–90, 395, 398

censorship, 18, 58

Chaerephon, 76, 119, 123, 125

chance (*tuchê*), 149, 161, 167, 171, 487

change, 45, 47, 70, 76, 276, 278, 281, 284, 285, 295, 386, 389, 408, 464, 508, *See also* flux

charioteer and horses (*Phaedrus*), 209, 221

Charmides, 10, 11, 14, 52, 65, 128, 143, 178, 247, 395, 517

Charmides (dialogue character), 12, 128

Charmides (historical individual), 52

Cherniss, H., 38, 356, 379, 380, 395, 396

Chomsky, N., 192, 200, 201

Cimon, 42

citizens, 10, 19, 27, 42, 54, 56, 61, 63, 122, 130, 133, 261, 262, 305, 351, 355, 361, 549–52

city of pigs, 339

civic courage, 528

civil conflict (*stasis*), 52, 56, 77, 531

class conflict, 56

Cleinias, 536

Cleisthenes, 41, 77

Clouds, 3, 54, 57, 66, 77, 78, 118, 237, 238, *See also* Aristophanes

Collingwood, R. G., 345

comedy, 66, 67, 80, 339, *See also* Aristophanes

community, political, 20, 23, 27, 53, 136, 234, 303, 312, 314, 316, 323, 535

companion (*hetaira*), 7, 11, 15, 225, 292, 346, 349, 353, 354

convention, legislation (*nomos*), 29, 45, 53, 262, 522–44, 553

Corcyra, 52

Corybantes, 234

cosmopolitanism, 136

cosmos (*kosmos*), 267, 326, 464–85, 486, 487, 488, 489, 491, 495, 499, 502, 518, 519

courage, 205, 530, 535

craft, 13, 120, 148, 156, 157, 158, 160, 162, 167, 334, 335, 357, 376, 392, 464–85, 486, 488, 494–517, 519 *See also* expertise (*technê*)

craft analogy, 148, 155, 156, 157, 158, 160, 171, 517

Cratylus, 13, 17, 21, 23, 26, 69, 70, 74, 81, 86, 97, 112, 284, 395

Cratylus (dialogue character), 17

Cratylus (Presocratic), 39, 46, 57, 68, 70

Creophylus, 346

Crete, 256

Critias, 24, 25, 82, 83, 89, 92, 97, 98, 99, 103, 109, 110, 494

Critias (dialogue character), 479

Critias (historical individual), 52

Crito, 10, 11, 15, 63, 80, 98–105, 159, 160, 165, 170, 263, 522, 527

Crito (dialogue character), 11, 160

Ctesippus, 452

cyclical argument (*Phaedo*), 258

Cynics, the, 537

daimon, 78, 144, 258

definition, 10, 12, 16, 24, 69, 126, 143, 157, 158, 174–93, 194, 195, 196, 207, 244, 245, 269–91, 293, 335, 343, 350, 363, 416, 430, 456, 551

Delphi, 125, 233, 238, 261, 267, 392

dēmēgoria, 334, 355

Demeter, 233, 242, 244, 249, 252

demiurge (*Timaeus*), 225, 248, 466–81, 486, 487, 488, 489, 490, 491, 502, 517

For EU product safety concerns, contact us at Calle de José Abascal, 56–1°,
28003 Madrid, Spain or eugpsr@cambridge.org.

www.ingramcontent.com/pod-product-compliance
Ingram Content Group UK Ltd.
Pitfield, Milton Keynes, MK11 3LW, UK
UKHW020346140625
459647UK00019B/2327